THE SOUTH AFRICAN HANDBOOK

OF AGENCY, FREEDOM AND JUSTICE

THE SOUTH AFRICAN HANDBOOK OF AGENCY, FREEDOM AND JUSTICE

Citizens in Conversation

VOLUME 1

Edited by
Muxe Nkondo and Reuel Khoza

UNIVERSITY OF KwaZulu-Natal PRESS

Published in 2024 by University of KwaZulu-Natal Press
Private Bag X01
Scottsville, 3201
Pietermaritzburg
South Africa
Email: books@ukzn.ac.za
Website: www.ukznpress.co.za

ISBN: 978 1 86914 559 0
eISBN: 978 1 86914 560 6

Managing editor: Sally Hines
Editor: Alison Lockhart
Typesetter: M Design
Proofreader: Catherine Munro
Cover designer: Marise Bauer, M Design

Printed by Novus Print

Contents

Foreword

Albie Sachs

I don't claim any special expertise in miracles, but I know one when I see one. Less than a year has passed since the editors of this book invited a wide range of scholars to send abstracts of chapters they would write, and now they have no less than 68 chapters across three volumes ready for publication! Getting authors to submit on time is always likened to herding cats. Yet 68 authors have come up with the goods in less than a year. If that is not a miracle, then I don't know what is. It is proof of both the editorial team's ingenuity, determination and organisational capacity, and of the eagerness of thinkers and scholars throughout South Africa to contribute their thoughts and wisdom to diagnosing and responding to the problems that are eating away at our country.

Some of the contributors took part directly in the struggle against apartheid; others have fought robustly to combat continuing and new forms of exclusion and marginalisation. They are politicians, thought leaders, academics and researchers from organisations and institutions throughout the length and breadth of the country, with diverse social and cultural backgrounds. They bring various kinds and levels of knowledge, skills and competencies critical for the task. Each one of them has worked in different disciplines and has different scholarly styles and modes of presentation. Some have vast experience working outside the country at various levels, and a number have had the benefit of successful practices elsewhere in the world. Between them, they combine years of experience on related aspects of South African politics. What is most important, each has their own voice. The result is a compendium of thought that is unafraid, engaged and diverse. Interestingly for me, despite their diversity, the authors by and large seem to share three fundamental points of departure:

- First, they are not Constitution-sceptics. They accept that in political terms, the new Constitution represented a major rupture with the past and established a strong vision for a better life for all people in South Africa.
- Second, they are of the view that a huge gap remains between the promise of the Constitution and the lives actually lived by a large portion of our people.
- And third, they search for ways of bridging this gap through linking agency, freedom and justice to enable the disadvantaged to have meaningful agency in bringing about equality and social justice.

The editorial team invited me to offer some opening reflections on how to achieve this link between agency, freedom and justice. At my request, they posed two questions for me to consider. I thank them for doing so. The first was short and sharp:

Question: How can you achieve a balance between competence and ethical leadership?

Answer: You can't. Competence and ethics are not to be balanced. The worst combination is a competent crook. No amount of competence can justify unethical behaviour. In the struggle days, I would often feel like weeping when I learnt of senior officials, sometimes the bravest of the brave and the smartest of the smart, who would use their positions for personal advantage. I would console myself by saying that the whole is better than the parts. And fortunately, the example set by most of the top leadership at that time was profoundly ethical.

Oliver Tambo (O.R.) himself set the most honourable example in everything he did. And he was not only the most ethical of the ethical, he was also the smartest of the smart, and effective, too, proving that nice guys can finish not last, but first. Moreover, he saw to it that the question of ethics would not be solely one of personal morality. Systems had to be put in place to guard against misconduct and the systems of accountability had to be fair themselves.

During a long legal life, I have worked on many legal documents of great significance, including constitutional texts and court judgments. But the most important document of all was the little-known Code of Conduct that O.R. asked me to draft at a very difficult time for the liberation movement. This was after he had received a damning report from the Stuart Commission of Inquiry into abuses in African National Congress (ANC) camps in Angola. Exhortations about what was called revolutionary morality were not enough. Torture had to be forbidden, unequivocally, in all circumstances. It wasn't a question of whether or not torture got results. Maybe it did. Yet, the use of torture brutalised not only those who were subjected to it, but all of us. It destroyed our coherence as freedom fighters. It introduced an element of ugly transactional cynicism right into the heart of what was a noble quest for liberation. As a Mozambican soldier poet put it: 'It's not enough that our cause be pure and just . . . / Purity and justice must exist inside ourselves.'

We worked hard to establish codified procedures for a fair trial. I was asked to present the Code to the delegates at the ANC Consultative Conference in Kabwe in 1985. It was enthusiastically endorsed. It was a high point in my life. Senior security personnel were removed from their positions. Members of the Constitutional Committee, which had been set up by Tambo to develop the ANC guidelines for a future democratic South Africa, played an active part in trials that followed. Ted Pekane sat as one of the judges and, over the protests of security officials, Penuell Maduna secured the acquittal of someone alleged to be a sleeper agent of the apartheid regime. The abuses came to an end. No further executions took place. And confidence in the movement soared. This was a stirring lesson for us all. Well-informed and principled leadership made a huge difference to our struggle at a vital time. Maintaining integrity and honour were placed above simply securing instrumental advantage. We rejected reliance on the statement that 'you can't make omelettes without breaking eggs'. And the result was not only a great boost to the morale of our members and the reputation of the organisation at large. It also meant that believing in and creating a form of a Bill of Rights for members of our organisation prepared us mentally and politically for having a Bill of Rights in a future democratic South Africa. In a vivid and effective way, the intersection of agency, freedom and justice was established, with enduring consequences.

Before responding to the second issue, let me state that my manifest admiration for Oliver Tambo should by no means be seem as indicating that only the ANC produced leaders of his character and calibre. When I was defence counsel in what was called the Philip Kgosana trial in Cape Town in 1960, I had the privilege of interviewing Robert Sobukwe in prison as a potential defence witness. Even in the short pants that black male prisoners had to wear, he conducted himself with quiet poise and admirable thoughtfulness and dignity. In the years that followed, he withstood concentrated repression with exquisite fortitude. And if he had done nothing else, during his banishment days in Kimberley, he persuaded a young woman from Galeshewe township to study law and, some years later, Yvonne Mokgoro became my esteemed and beloved colleague on the Constitutional Court. Similarly, the congruence between the life and thought of Steve Biko was remarkable. It was not only his liberatory ideas that inspired generations, but also his total integrity and lack of pomposity. The liberation struggle had many rich threads. I speak about the one with which I am familiar.

The second question was longer and more personal.

Question: In most of your writings, *The Soft Vengeance of a Freedom Fighter* and *The Strange Alchemy of Life and Law*, to mention only two, you remain determinedly optimistic and confident, but in what ways and to what extent has justice prevailed in South Africa and other post-colonies?

Answer: In elegant terms, this echoes a question I receive day in and day out, wherever I might be, in the country or abroad: 'Albie . . .' and, looking without looking at my right arm that was blown away by an apartheid bomb, my interlocutor asks, 'after all the sacrifices you have made, is this the country you were fighting for?' This is also the question that runs throughout this handbook. In responding to it, I will share with readers my own experiences. There are not many of us left; it is wonderful to have the opportunity of sharing my ideas with a new generation of critical authors and readers.

Let me stress right from the start that my response, which invariably comes as a surprise to my interlocutors, has nothing to do with any sacrifices I am said to have made. Forgoing the benefits that would have followed if I had pursued the ordinary career of a white South African lawyer was by no means a sacrifice. On the contrary, given my background, to have gone in for such a career would have been to sacrifice the most meaningful parts of myself that had been established from my infancy. My mother used to tell little me and my little brother Johnny: 'Tidy up, Uncle Moses is coming.' Uncle Moses wasn't Moses Kantor, but Moses Kotane, the secretary general of the Communist Party of South Africa. My mother, Ray, was his typist. He used to joke that Comrade Ray had taught him at night school to read and write, and now he was her boss. And my father, Solly, was the general secretary of the Garment Workers' Union, which contained militants such as Lilian Ngoyi, Bettie du Toit, Rosie Jardine and Helen Joseph. If I had set my heart on making money and becoming a significant figure in racist white society, it would have meant sacrificing my dignity and trashing my deepest values.

Similarly, it is worth mentioning that those from my generation who took a stand against apartheid didn't see ourselves as putting our lives on the line as self-appointed saviours of black people. We were fighting for our own dignity, for our own right to be free people in a free society. The only way we could achieve this was to make ourselves available to support the struggle of the oppressed black majority to bring down apartheid and create a society in which the dignity of all could be attained. And, although there were times of great pain and hardship, overwhelmingly, the journey we took turned out to be liberating and exhilarating. In the fires of our endeavours, the word 'comrade' came to have a beautiful meaning. It made us feel we were part of national and worldwide struggles against oppression. In addition, it introduced us to the richness of song, movement, speech, humour and human solidarity (today referred to as Ubuntu) that was so much part of African culture. By the same measure, I don't regard losing my arm in the struggle as a sacrifice. We were volunteers and knew the risks involved. When the regime came for me with the bomb, I was overjoyed that I had survived and only lost an arm. It wasn't a sacrifice, but simply a visible example of the kind of trauma that had been visited on millions of people fighting for their dignity over the decades.

I now respond to the issue of whether this is the country we were fighting for. Let me put my cards on the table. My answer is: yes, this is the country we were fighting for. What? Whoever is reading this must think I'm mad. At a time of massive load-shedding, following on rapacious diversion of resources during the Covid-19 pandemic, with a majority of municipalities dysfunctional, with everybody aware of the damning findings of state capture and corruption in the Zondo Commission Report, with grossly unacceptable levels of gender-based violence and other forms of crime, with massive unemployment, huge levels of poverty and inequalities, and a multitude of other ailments mentioned in this book, how can I possibly be saying that this is the country that we were fighting for? Let me rush to complete my sentence. Yes, this is the country we were fighting for but, no, this is not the society we were fighting for. And let me add that I remain optimistic that we can, in fact, use the country that we fought for to achieve the society our people are entitled to have.

The importance of the distinction between our country and our society was brought to me when I was campaigning in exile during the struggle days. Until we got a country with at least some degree of national cohesion, there was no way we could even begin to cure the ills of our society. People I encountered kept talking about the civil rights struggle in South Africa. I protested at this characterisation. I insisted that it was much, much more than a civil rights struggle. In essence, it was a struggle for self-determination by the oppressed majority. When, in 1910, the British brought four colonies together and granted independence to the Union of South Africa, they transferred sovereignty to the white population only. The black majority continued to be subject to a form of colonial despotism. The difference now was that the legal masters were in Pretoria and Cape Town, rather than in London.

This meant that self-determination for the black majority would not come about through cutting the links with Pretoria and Cape Town and creating an independent state. Rather, it meant that there had to be a national liberation struggle to overthrow the system of white supremacy within the borders of South Africa and its replacement by a united, non-racial democratic state that guaranteed dignity, equality and freedom for all. As I wrote at the time: 'In the process of destroying apartheid and reconstructing South Africa, sovereignty is the essence, national liberation the substance, democracy the form and human rights the goal.' The issue was not who could sit where in railway carriages, but who could decide who could sit where. What we needed was a country where the people as a whole, and not only a minority, could make such decisions. Accordingly, the first slogan I had learnt at the first public meeting I had attended, hadn't been Independence or Death! It was *Mayibuye iAfrika* (Come Back Afrika). It became (in the language of the time) One Man, One Vote! Later, it became *Amandla Ngawethu! Matla ke arona!* Power to the People! For their part, the Pan Africanist Congress had *Izwe Lethu* (Our Land).

This distinction between the struggle for national liberation and the struggle for civil rights had important strategic and practical consequences. A civil rights struggle presupposed that human rights could be achieved for all in the society through mobilisation within the existing political framework. Thus, the Civil Rights Movement in the United States used a combination of legal protests and non-violent challenges to existing racist laws and practices. In constitutional terms, the goal was to make the Union more perfect. In South Africa, it was the Constitution itself that was overtly and systematically oppressive. The Act of Union had been drafted by white men only and had expressly stated that only white men could be members of Parliament. Laws had soon been passed reserving 90 per cent of the surface area of South Africa for white ownership and subjecting the black majority to a system of control referred to as Native Administration. In addition to being landless and disenfranchised, the majority had been subjected to severe controls over their movement, as well as to all the forms of racial discrimination imposed on all persons of colour in South Africa. When non-violent forms of struggle had proved inadequate to bring about change, and all forms of protest against oppression had been closed down, the liberation movement embarked on the armed struggle and called for international sanctions to isolate racist South Africa.

During this period, I found myself travelling to countries in North America and South America, Western and Eastern Europe, Africa and Asia, calling for sanctions and the release of Nelson Mandela and all political prisoners. Wherever I went, when I said that the system of apartheid would be destroyed, there was applause. But when I added that we would go on and build a united, non-racial, democratic South Africa, there was disbelief and silence. It seemed that after 300 years of conquest, dispossession and overt racial domination, with untold hardships being imposed on the majority, the idea of all the people in South Africa living together as equals in one country was completely unsustainable. Driven by racist assumptions, Afro-pessimists were convinced that democracy was not for Africa. They pointed to failed states, countries under military rule and one-party states, where authoritarian presidents held power for decades. But even for sympathisers of our struggle, the idea of a united, non-racial, democratic South Africa seemed to be utterly unreal.

I explained as well as I could the three reasons why I felt that the democratic vision proclaimed in the Freedom Charter was in fact eminently achievable. Two were objective and one was subjective. The first objective reason was based on the relentless development of a capitalist economy that drove everyone in the country, black, brown, white, rich and poor, into a single interactive network. The society had become a common one, based on overt and officialised domination and subordination. The migrant labour system brought African peasants from all over the country and beyond to the diamond, gold and coal mines. There was hardly an enterprise in the country that did not have black and white people working together. Their relationships were grossly unfair, the exploitation intense. The people had become interdependent, whether they liked it or not. On the side of the oppressed, it was the very commonality of suffering that had led to the coming together of black leaders throughout southern Africa to create the ANC in 1912. We, in the liberation movement, knew that an extensive road, rail and communications network enabled us to engage in underground activities throughout the land. For their part, the police would capture and imprison us within hours, wherever we would be in the country.

Second, the institutions of democracy were strongly implanted in South Africa, for the whites. The whites had hotly contested elections. There were opposition parties. There were newspapers that slammed top government leaders. And there was a judiciary that gave a fair measure of justice to the whites, with some progressive-minded judges finding loopholes in the law to help black people. Nothing like this existed in virtually all of the rest of Africa. People who went to study in London, Paris or Brussels would encounter instruments of democracy in the metropole, but never do so on their home soil. The struggle in South Africa, then, was for the oppressed to seize the institutions of their subjugation and convert them from instruments of exclusion into instruments of inclusion. The system of apartheid that had lived by the vote (of the few) would die by the vote (of the many).

The third and subjective reason for my optimism was my belief in the liberation movement and its leadership for reasons I have mentioned above. I make these points not simply to record important aspects of our history. They are highly relevant to current debates. We were not fighting merely to get rid of racial discrimination, important though that was. The demand of our struggle then was to get rid of internal colonialism. Self-determination was at the very heart of our endeavours. And I believe that in political terms, at least, against all the odds, we were hugely successful in accomplishing the goal of politics of determination. Our understanding was that achieving this would open the way to securing economic, social and cultural self-determination. We weren't quite as confident as Kwame Nkrumah, who had said: 'Seek ye first the political kingdom and all other things shall be added unto you.' We also knew that the way we entered the political kingdom would be decisive in determining how the social and economic reconstruction could be achieved. And we knew from experience elsewhere on the continent that economic, social and cultural transformation rarely followed as a matter of course after independence was achieved. So, we focused on conceptualising legal and constitutional instruments that would both prevent the erection of constitutional barriers to change and promote proactive measures to better the lives of the majority. This approach would facilitate the achievement of the second phase of self-determination; namely, radical change in the economic, social and cultural spheres.

This book provides a kaleidoscope of materials illustrating how resistant deeply entrenched institutions and practices have been to self-determination of the majority in the economic, social and cultural spheres. The writers are to be congratulated for offering practical solutions that they believe will cumulatively accomplish the second stage of self-determination, popularly referred to as radical transformation. Fortunately, or unfortunately, since being appointed as a judge in 1994, I have been living in a judicial bubble. This has kept me out of political contestation in relation to the changes necessary to make our society fair and just. I have, however, been able to support processes of change in the judiciary itself. Along with many of my colleagues, I have actively challenged what is revealed in the book as patterns of path dependence in relation to the judiciary. We weren't aware of the term 'path dependence', which even now is new to me. Nor did we use the language of decolonisation. We just felt in our hearts and minds that the judiciary had to be different from what it had been, and in the way it had operated. Some of the most active persons in promoting change were progressive-minded colleagues who, sitting as judges in the apartheid era, had done what little they could to mitigate the cruelties imposed by the law and who had gone on to feel joyfully liberated by the new Constitution. Working as a team, we decided that we could no longer use the logo based on European heraldry, nor did we want to replace it with the imported blindfolded woman with the scales of justice in her hand. Instead, we commissioned a new design, which shows the diverse people of our country sheltered under and protected by a capacious tree. We also decided not to fill our walls with pictures only of dead white male judges. One day I will be a dead white male judge, so there's nothing wrong with that. But surrounding ourselves with symbols depicting white male hegemony would be out of keeping with the cardinal non-racial and non-sexist values of the Constitution. We changed the colours and patterns of our gowns, moved away from hierarchical seating in the court, and asked counsel please not to address us as 'my Lord' and 'my Lady'.

We chose the site of the Old Fort Prison as a place where a warm and friendly top court should be constructed. The jury to select the winning entry in an international competition for the new court building included three ex-prisoners and two architects from countries of the South. The building was designed on the principle of justice under a tree and filled with artworks, carpets, gates and chandeliers made by people from all over the country. Similarly, we recalibrated forms of judicial reasoning, cut out the use of Latin, made access to the court easier and cheaper, and generally placed the marginalised and dispossessed at the centre of the judicial gaze. These changes, we felt, were necessary to develop a judiciary that would, in its manner and form, be in line with the Constitution it was upholding. But, as I have said, we refrained from becoming involved in political contestation. A great number of the issues raised have ended up in court and more could do so in future. It would not be appropriate for me to comment on any of them. I can, however, share with readers experiences I have had over the years that might be helpful in creating an historical perspective in which to locate the issues.

One of the advantages of being of advanced years, is that, however bad things are, you can always remember a time when things were worse. But it's a shallow optimism that is based simply on the fact that things were worse before in our country, and are even worse today in other countries. There is a more positive foundation for optimism. It is to recall ways that we South Africans devised to break down seemingly insurmountable barriers and to create paths far more beneficial in outcome than those followed by other countries facing similar difficulties. Many activists have for decades been guided by Antonio Gramsci, the reflective Italian revolutionary imprisoned during the fascist Mussolini era, an opponent of Italian conquest in Africa, who famously declared that activists must function with pessimism of the intellect and optimism of the will. I would add to his mix a further ingredient, which I term hind-sightedness of experience. The word 'hindsight' is usually used in a mocking way to condemn people who glibly say that errors could easily have been avoided if only this, that or the other had been done. But there is no reason in principle why hindsight should not actively and effectively be deployed to record achievements actually accomplished.

During my decade as an activist lawyer exiled in Mozambique, I used to love hearing Samora Machel telling vast audiences: 'Kings come and Kings go, Presidents come and Presidents go, but the people never die (*O Povo nunca morre*).' These words echoed in my mind each time when, at crucial moments of our history, the people came to the party in the constitution-making process. In doing so, they gave us a Constitution that enables later generations to correct the defects in our society and enjoy their fundamental rights to human dignity, equality and freedom. The key element all the way through was the umbilical connection between constitutional concepts and lives and hopes of the majority of the people. The journey to recreate a new country through establishing a constitutional order for South Africa has been long and hard. What follows are a number of landmark moments on the journey that I personally lived and participated in.

I start with my participation as a seventeen-year-old, second-year law student in the Defiance Campaign against Unjust Laws of 1952, when I led a small group of three white students and one white worker to sit on benches in the General Post Office in Cape Town that were marked non-whites only. The Defiance Campaign had resulted from a decision of the ANC leadership, under pressure from the Youth League, to move away from speaking nicely to the white authorities and embarking on mass action to bring about change. All over the country, ordinary people of different backgrounds joined the leaders in non-violent resistance to racist laws. Volunteer No.1 was a certain young, black lawyer named Nelson

Mandela. I would have been Volunteer No. 8532, or something like that. The campaign was eventually crushed, but the principle was established that the mass of the people as a whole should be in the forefront of the national liberation struggle.

Then, when the Freedom Charter was adopted at Kliptown three years later, I experienced the extraordinary emotion of attending the Congress of the People. People who had travelled from Cape Town by road had been stopped, but I had managed to get there by train. More than 2 000 delegates from all over the country sat on the hard, cold, mid-winter ground as the preamble and the ten sections of the Freedom Charter were pronounced, discussed and adopted by acclamation. The text had not been created by lawyers sitting in back rooms. It had emerged by a collation in poetic language of the demands made by people on the ground in thousands of meetings throughout the country, expressing their vision of what life should be like in a free South Africa. When on the second day we were surrounded by police on horseback, while security forces armed with automatic weapons marched through our ranks to take control of the makeshift wooden platform, we stood up and sang beautiful freedom songs. One stone, and we would have been speaking of the Kliptown massacre (five years before Sharpeville). But, united by our longing for a future liberated country, we retained our discipline. The 156 leaders later put on trial for treason as a result of the adoption of the Freedom Charter came from all parts of the country and looked like our nation. Marching under the banner 'We Stand by our Leaders', people arrived at the court, while others afterwards brought food to the trialists in the Old Fort Prison (where the Constitutional Court now stands). The minute he arrived in prison, Oliver Tambo set up a choir, whose singing could be heard throughout Number 4. Fellow prisoner Albert Luthuli joined in the singing. Our leaders led from the front.

More than 30 years later, I was part of the Constitutional Committee of the ANC, working to transform the Freedom Charter into an operative constitutional document for a future free South Africa. It was March 1988, and I was one of more than 100 delegates at an in-house seminar organised by Tambo and the full ANC leadership at the University of Zambia. We were there to discuss and adopt Constitutional Guidelines for a Democratic South Africa. Zambian troops were on standby in case South African commandos were flown in to take us out.

The leadership had accepted a proposal by the Constitutional Committee that we not set out to craft a Constitution for South Africa while in exile. As a matter of principle, we felt that a Constitution could only be drafted by a democratically elected Constituent Assembly on South African soil. In the meantime, the ANC could set out guidelines for what it would propose to such a constitution-making body. Our leaders reminded the delegates who had come from ANC communities throughout the world that the organisation had first demanded a Bill of Rights for South Africa as far back as 1923 and repeated the demand in its African Claims Document in 1944. The Freedom Charter of 1955 had taken the process forward and provided the foundations of the Constitutional Guidelines.

I was asked to explain to the delegates the three reasons why we supported a Bill of Rights for a democratic South Africa. I was nervous. The first reason was easy. It made us look good – we were not blood-thirsty terrorists avid for power, but serious activists with a clear vision for a future South Africa. The second reason was a little more complicated. A Bill of Rights was the answer worked out by Pallo Jordan and Tambo to attempts by the regime and others to use group rights as the foundation of a new constitutional order in South Africa. Acceptance of group rights would have resulted in power-sharing by leaders of different racial groups, giving white people a veto over any future governmental action they regarded as undermining their rights as a minority. I pointed out that a Bill of Rights would protect everybody not because they were black, white or brown, or a minority or a majority, but because they were human beings. The delegates nodded their agreement. It was the third reason that was making my heart beat fast: I wasn't at all sure how happy the delegates would be at hearing it. I pointed out that the third reason why we needed a Bill of Rights was . . . against ourselves. I said that we knew of many examples of leaders who had fought bravely for freedom, but, when later in positions of power, had gone on to enrich themselves and disregard the rights of the majority. But instead of seeing looks of repudiation for bourgeois legal thinking, as I feared might happen, I noted delight in the eyes of the delegates. They had seen this process not only in other countries where they had been based, but also reflected in the behaviour of certain individuals in our own ranks. After several days of discussion, a number of amendments were made, and the Guidelines were distributed to the world. The accompanying note emphasised that they should not be seen as hard-and-fast prescripts, but rather as proposals for discussion that could be amended as a result of inputs made by members and others. Let me reiterate that the theme that ran through this whole process was the degree of popular involvement in the process of imagining and creating what became South Africa's new, united, non-racial and non-sexist democratic state.

The next occasion was deliberately quieter and solitary. But it showed how differently those of us in the struggle who were lawyers worked and thought, compared to other lawyers. Kader Asmal and I had day jobs, teaching law students – he in Dublin, I in Southampton and then Maputo. Now, we were being asked to draft a document, not as engaged scholars, but as members of a liberation movement for many years. It was to prepare a draft Bill of Rights for a Democratic South Africa. It was a wonderful pinch-me moment, intended, I suspect, as a get-well-card to me from Tambo and the Constitutional Committee. Four weeks after my presentation at the seminar in Zambia, I was blown up. After Mozambican doctors saved my life, I was flown to recover in a hospital in London. Not long after my discharge, I was asked by the Constitutional Committee to travel to Dublin to work with Kader Asmal on a draft Bill of Rights for a Democratic South Africa. I remember sitting at a table in the kitchen of the home of Kader and Louise with a pen and a blank piece of paper. No books, no texts. The themes of a Bill of Rights should spring from your innermost being. Kader and I had been immersed in the struggle for decades. We had heard what it was that the people were crying out for. We had ourselves in different ways been victimised by repressive and racist uses of power. We had noted and seen at first hand, positive and negative experiences both in Africa and on other continents. First, I jotted down the themes that came pouring out of me. Kader looked at mechanisms for implementation. Next, we swapped roles. Only then did we look at the classic texts. Everything was there in our draft, not because we were particularly erudite, but because we had been involved in a movement that was based on mass struggle.

In 1990, we were back on home soil. The chair of the Constitutional Committee, Zola Skweyiya, Kader and I were all based at the Community Law Centre at the University of the Western Cape (UWC). I had the interesting experience of speaking to law students about a future Bill of Rights at UWC on one day, and at the University of Cape Town (UCT) later in the week. It was striking for me to see that the overwhelmingly black students at UWC saw the Bill of Rights essentially as a progressive document that would open up completely new possibilities for their lives. Overwhelmingly, white students at UCT saw the Bill of Rights as a document they could welcome because the necessary changes would be brought about in a principled manner, without arbitrary harassment and marginalisation. It was an interesting lesson to me not to give one version of the Bill of Rights to one audience and a separate one to another audience, but rather to present both sides of the coin in identical fashion to both groups. I can see now how this experience prepared me to become a judge: yes, to radical disruption of the unjust status quo; no, to smash and grab. During that period, UCT made me an honorary professor and invited me to give an inaugural lecture. The lecture was titled 'Perfectibility and Corruptibility'. The basic theme was how in constitution-making to manage the tension between the need to aim for perfection while guarding against corruption. At the same time, in making my presentation, I drew heavily on positive and negative experiences from being inside the struggle and from living and working in African countries and abroad.

The most dramatic moments in our constitution-making process occurred during the Convention for a Democratic South Africa (CODESA) phase at Kempton Park starting in late 1991. This was a period of considerable violence in the country. It was also a time during which there was a head-on clash between the concepts of majority rule in a united South Africa coupled with a Bill of Rights, on the one hand, and power-sharing between leaders of political parties, on the other, each retaining a veto over matters of special concern for their respective group (effectively, it would have meant Mandela, F.W. de Klerk and Mangosuthu Buthelezi sharing the presidency, each in turn having six months at the helm and deciding issues by consensus). Although the breakdown in negotiations was triggered by the Boipatong massacre, the substantive underlying cause was the total incompatibility of these two constitutional visions. In the end, this clash of visions was not resolved through discussion at CODESA. The breakthrough came about as a result of the rolling mass action in the streets outside. Hundreds of thousands of well-organised and disciplined supporters of the liberation movement marched through the major cities of the country. The regime's negotiators eventually gave way and accepted five fundamental propositions. The first was that the Constitution would not be drafted at Kempton Park and put to a referendum, but, rather, it would be drafted by a Constitutional Assembly that would be elected by the people as a whole. The second was that the negotiators at Kempton Park would agree on principles that would be binding on the newly elected Parliament serving as the Constitutional Assembly. The third was that Parliament serving as a Constitutional Assembly would be chosen on a proportional representation basis. The fourth was that a two-thirds majority would be required. And the fifth was that the new and independent Constitutional Court would be established to certify that the text of the Constitution complied with the principles.

It can be seen that the key to the whole process would be South Africa's first democratic elections. The people as a whole would be choosing their representatives and giving them their mandates. In other countries, you had the situation of the country searching for a Constitution. In South Africa, it was the case of a Constitution searching for a country. The moment when South Africa became a country would be the moment when the people as a whole came together. Until then, South Africa had been a territory occupied by people without a common citizenship and allegiance. The law had been an instrument not of unity but of division, not of justice but of oppression. For the first time, the diverse people of South Africa would be acting together with common objectives in a common way. The importance of this moment was highlighted when Chris Hani was assassinated. The only thing that could save South Africa from a violent and chaotic reaction was the announcement of 27 April 1994 as the election date. I must mention that this was my last period as a political activist. Like many others, I was deeply involved in developing the two-stage process of construction-making and the interrelationship between struggles inside and outside of the negotiations chamber.

On 27 April 1994, I was one of twenty million people who voted as equals for the first time in South Africa's first democratic elections. This was the decisive moment in our constitution-making process. Black, white and brown stood in long lines to place our votes in the ballot boxes. This was the great moment of political decolonisation. It was the first part of a long-deferred dream come true. The image I will never forget is not that of Mandela or Desmond Tutu voting for the first time, but of an elderly, infirm black man in a rural area brought to the voting station in a wheelbarrow, determined to vote before he died. The combination of the process of popular involvement and the drafting of the Constitution came through the functioning of the democratically elected Parliament as a Constitutional Assembly. The bulk of the members came from families that had known great hardship and participated actively in the freedom struggle. Many had felt the effects of racist and oppressive laws and were determined to prevent any future government from conducting themselves in the way the colonial and apartheid authorities had done. There was very strong representation of the women's movement dedicated to ensuring, as they put it, that power would not be transferred from one group of men to another. The workers' movement also had powerful voices, insisting on issues such as the right to strike, fair labour practices and the right to collective bargaining. There were strong lobbies to ensure that social economic rights and the rights of the child would feature and would be well protected in the new Constitution. Idealism that had been invested in the freedom struggle was captured in a forceful, binding value system entrenched in the opening 39 sections of the Constitution. A unique feature is the creation of Chapter Nine to establish special institutions for the protection of democracy. These include the Independent Electoral Commission, the Judicial Services Commission (JSC), the public protector and the auditor-general. I was not a member of the Constitutional Assembly at the time of the 1994 elections. I had stepped down from the ANC in view of my decision to make myself available to the new Constitutional Court. After a robust interview by the JSC, my name was included in the list sent to Mandela, who appointed me to the Court. This led me to have the interesting experience of working with my colleagues on the Court to decide whether to certify that the text of the Constitution complied with the principles that the negotiators had agreed to in advance. An opportunity was provided for political organisations and members of the public to raise objections to the text. More than 70 objections were considered, most of which were rejected. Ultimately, we decided that although overwhelmingly the Constitution complied with the principles, in nine respects it failed to do so. In effect, we declared the Constitution to be unconstitutional! The matter went back to the Constitutional Assembly. Corrections were made and on 10 December 1996, before a large, jubilant crowd at Sharpeville, it was signed into law by Mandela.

In other parts of Africa, independence was granted, a Constitution was manufactured by the departing powers and sections of the elite to a greater or lesser extent. But the institutions were unfamiliar, armies took over, presidents stayed on for life. In most African states, the moment of independence came with the old flag coming down and the new flag being raised to the tune of a new national anthem. An invited number of dignitaries from the country concerned, as well from other countries, would be in attendance, together with a cheering local crowd. Others who might be interested would listen on the radio and watch the event on television. In effect, the people of the country concerned applauded the change but were not directly involved in crafting the country's new Constitution.

In at least two cases, where a revolutionary war of independence had been won, the victorious national leadership refused to negotiate the independence Constitution with the former colonial power. In Angola, after a bitter war in which hundreds of thousands of people had been killed or injured, the plan had been to have a Constituent Assembly draft a new Constitution for the country. The leadership of the FNLA (Frente Nacional de Libertação de Angola, National Front for the Liberation of Angola), however, promulgated a Constitution in which the FNLA was the only permitted party, and not long afterwards the army took over. At no stage in this process did the people have a say in how they were to be governed. In Mozambique, FRELIMO (Frente de Libertação de Moçambique, Liberation Front of Mozambique) refused to negotiate a constitution with Portugal, discussing only the terms of Portuguese withdrawal. Instead, the Central Committee of FRELIMO itself drafted the country's Constitution, which came into effect on Independence Day in 1975, creating a one-party state, in which FRELIMO was identified as the party driving unity and social transformation.

When I first arrived in Mozambique a year later, I felt and was inspired by the strength of what was called People's Power at the heart of the Mozambican Revolution. Since FRELIMO had organised the resistance to Portuguese colonialism and unified all progressive forces in the process, it seemed natural that it would itself draft and proclaim the new Constitution and continue to be in the driving seat of change. What I learnt, however, was that opposition did not go away in the one-party state. It went underground, got picked up by the West in the Cold War, and more particularly by the racist regimes of South Africa and in what was then Rhodesia, and then proceeded to embark on a brutal civil war. The result was hundreds of thousands of deaths, millions of refugees, child soldiers and thousands of civilians injured by landmines. A rough-edged peace was achieved only after a new Constitution allowed for a multiparty democracy that had been negotiated over a number of years. In my own case, this was the experience that convinced me beyond doubt of two things relevant to our struggle in South Africa. The first was to support the principle of having a multiparty democracy with a Bill of Rights. And the second was to have what we then called an elected Constituent Assembly on South African soil to draft our new Constitution. It would not be permissible for even the most honest, brave and enlightened leadership itself to draft the Constitution. The people themselves should be involved as fully as possible in the drafting of the Constitution that was to govern their lives and guarantee their freedom.

As far as I know, Namibia and South Africa are the only two countries on the African continent in which the elected representatives of the people themselves drafted their first post-colonial Constitution. In Namibia, the United Nations held the reins as the people of the country voted for their first democratically elected parliament. Parliament then went on to draft a Constitution in line with a number of broad principles that had been accepted in advance by the South West Africa People's Organisation and the racist regime of South Africa.

In South Africa, our Constitution was homegrown, developed by the Constitutional Assembly after the elections that mandated everybody to draft that Constitution. The Constitution then had a special meaning not simply as a new document to garland independence, but as a mechanism for achieving independence. The big achievement after the Constitution came into place, which is often ignored, is we hadn't been a country. We had Bantustans and separate parliaments and different educational establishments for the different races. We had Group Areas. And we abolished those and created a single country. We didn't eliminate spatial apartheid. We didn't eliminate the privileges that had gone with the systems, but we opened the doors to the practical elimination of the barriers that had been achieved and had been created in the apartheid era. Since then, when reactionary people had sarcastically predicted, 'One man, one vote, once', we've actually had six general elections. The elections are meaningful. Presidents step down. In fact, we haven't had a single president who has occupied the position for the full two-year terms, compared to other presidents who stay on for 30 or 40 years. We have a very lively press, and we have scholars who are guaranteed academic independence and the right to do research – it is in the Constitution.

Thirty years have passed since twenty million South Africans stood in long lines to inaugurate our new democracy. Although there have been setbacks and failures on many fronts and life is still exceptionally hard for more than half of our population, our democracy remains vibrant. We have had six general elections at national, provincial and local government levels, which have been free and fair. Far from having presidents for life, our first president stepped down voluntarily after one five-year term. Our second and third presidents stepped down voluntarily before completion of their second five-year terms, when it became clear that there would be a vote of no confidence in Parliament if they failed to do so. When the ANC lost elections in Johannesburg, Pretoria and Port Elizabeth (Gqeberha), it stepped down. It wasn't necessary for a million people to throng the public square to bring about a change of leadership, as in Egypt, or tanks to parade in the capital, as happened in Zimbabwe. Our elections are meaningful. Our democracy is not based simply on elections every five years. We have a lively civil society that speaks out openly and robustly. The trade union movement might not be as forceful as it once was, but millions of workers are organised with very vocal leadership. Business, too, speaks out through a number of organisations. Perhaps we are fortunate that we don't have one ethnic group that dominates the whole country. Millions of South Africans belong to faith communities that also don't hold back on expressing their views on questions of public interest. We don't have one hegemonic religious institution. The majority of our people are Christians, but they belong to different faith communities who see to it that no particular denomination is privileged over any other. So, there is no threat that one particular religious world view would be mobilised to provide a source of power domination. We have independent sporting bodies, professional organisations, educational institutions and cultural bodies that provide oxygen to public life. We have a very lively press, and we have scholars who are guaranteed academic independence and the right to do research – it is in the Constitution.

So, looking at South Africa today, we still live in one country, whether we like it or not. Our judiciary has been transformed and has strongly retained its independence. During my fifteen years on the Constitutional Court, I worked with extraordinary women and men from all parts of the country. When we swore our oath of office, five different languages were used. The judgments of the Court are cited with approval by courts throughout the world. It has been heartening for me to see how firmly and thoughtfully the judges have insisted that Parliament and the Executive fulfil their constitutional responsibilities. Another source of optimism for me is that we have an army that under the Constitution is subject to civilian control and is, fortunately, relatively weak. I'm proud of the peacekeeping work it does in various parts of the continent, as well as the support it has given to government at particular moments of stress in our country. We don't have the kind of laws that saw thousands of our people, me included, being detained without trial for long periods of time and subjected as a matter of state policy to torture and assassination. Change was brought about in our country not by tanks going into the streets or millions surging into the public square, but through elections, through debate, through discussion.

We may have achieved our freedom, but we are far from being an equal society. The disparities between rich and poor, largely on a racial basis, are intolerable and were intensified in heart-rending fashion by the recent Covid-19 pandemic. And we are far from being a safe society, where everyone can sleep peacefully at night and walk without fear in our streets at any time of the day. But we are a very open society. South Africans speak their minds. Our public media is lively. There is enormous expressivity through our social media. Our biggest growth industry is stand-up comedians. Through song, dance, film, photography, literature, poetry and visual arts, our artists comment with inimitable vibrancy on things beautiful and things ugly in our country, always exploring the different dimensions of what it means to be a South African. I am buoyed by the role that engaged and critical scholars are playing in our society. It is no accident that our Constitution expressly states in Section 16 that everyone has the right to freedom of expression, which includes freedom of artistic creativity, academic freedom and freedom of scientific research. During the apartheid years, many of us took part in struggles on university campuses to develop critical thinking in a free environment that would support liberation. Although academics had not played a leading role in developing the core ideas that lay at the heart of our constitutional transformation, their contributions at a technical level were enormously important in the proceedings of the Constitutional Assembly.

Finally, let me say that not too many years ago I was enthralled by the energy I felt at the height of the FeesMustFall movement, eloquently described by Barney Pityana as 'fallism' in Volume 2 of this handbook. I spoke to hundreds of students at the UCT Law School and commented to them that it might sound like the height of narcissism, but I felt that I was seeing hundreds of young Albie Sachs's in the room. I meet young people throughout the country who were as curious and full of questing energy as my generation was after the Second World War. This book is the product of the openness that our Constitution guarantees. Even if the Constitution does not provide the jobs, build the houses, and secure the equality and land redistribution that people want, it provides the mechanism for people to bring about the changes that we need. Our Constitution is one of the few in the world that expressly guarantees the right to academic freedom and the right to do research. And that is where this handbook comes in.

Scholars, thinkers and critics have a huge role to play in helping us find ways forward. Ideas have always mattered. They were particularly important in the decades when we were sent to jail, not for being bad but for being good, when books, plays and films were banned, not for telling lies or sowing hatred but for revealing the truth and promoting thoughtful and courageous brotherhood and sisterhood. Ideas kept us alive in prison and in exile. We argued and debated wherever we were. There is treasure in this handbook. May we all find it and contribute further sparkling gems of our own.

Preface

Agency, Freedom and Justice

Reuel Khoza

As this preface was being written, President Cyril Ramaphosa was contending with allegations that he seriously violated his oath of office and broke several laws (Leshilo 2022). Whatever the outcome, the reputations of both the man and the Office of the Presidency were tarnished, with the possibility that the country could face grey-listing for potential money laundering. This scandal was the latest in a long list of corruption cases that have exposed weaknesses of governance and impunity for state officials.[1]

Within the past three decades of South Africa's democratic era, the citizenry has experienced several identifiable dispensations: Nelson Mandela's iconic leadership; Thabo Mbeki's technocracy; Kgalema Motlanthe's transient caretaker government; Jacob Zuma's prebendalism, which rapidly morphed into kleptocracy, and Cyril Ramaphosa's dispensation, which is characterised by debilitating indecisiveness and a lack of implementation.

The argument made in this book is that the citizenry must take back agency in order to steer the country on a new course. Corruption takes place against a background of poverty, extreme economic inequality, joblessness and a rising sense of despair that nothing is being solved. Agency, freedom and justice are indissolubly linked. By definition, a democratic nation is one that has agency because the people are able to choose leaders and policies that deliver on the public good. Freedom and justice are lost when people feel powerless and at the mercy of forces they cannot control.

To call this a 'handbook' may be taken to mean that some form of point-by-point guidance is offered on how to tackle purely technical issues. The editors of this volume make no excuses for calling it a handbook, despite its apparently non-technical themes and broad sociopolitical intent. We live in times when solutions to humanity's self-created problems seem forever beyond reach because human nature is not amenable to fixes.

We are trapped in the confusions of a destiny that embraces both our failings and our great potential to do good. No nation illustrates that conflict better than South Africa. We have come through oppression only to find ourselves sliding backwards into the un-freedoms of a grossly skewed economic system, along with patriarchy, racism, corruption and crime. These factors cloud the face of one of the brightest dawns in human history: the ending of apartheid and its replacement by a constitutional democracy. But are we liberated? What does it mean to be free to starve? Today, the country is more free than almost any other on earth. We have a fine Constitution and wide-ranging protections under our Bill of Rights. Despite this, researchers report a pervasive sense of un-freedom. In 2011, an article in *Contemporary Politics* argued that there were four main reasons for the condition of collective un-freedom in South Africa: poverty, inequality, the electoral system and macroeconomic policy (Hamilton 2011).

Does this reflect reality – and is it fixable?

For people to take command of their lives is a matter of agency, which, on the face of it, cannot be reduced to the dos and don'ts of a mere handbook. If issues could be managed at the turn of a screw, we might all be better off as robotic citizens within an engineered social reality. Life is not manageable in such terms. We make our reality, but not according to formulae; instead what we shape also shapes us and we interact dynamically with one another in changing circumstances. We must tackle our problems in a systematic way.

Things have undoubtedly gone wrong in the grand project of the post-apartheid Reconstruction and Development Programme (RDP). That abbreviation was much bandied about for a few years, before being abandoned to pursue the Growth, Employment and Redistribution (GEAR) neo-liberal policy (Department of Planning, Monitoring and Evaluation 2014). Macroeconomic policies grew the economy, but failed to bring about a long-term broadening of the base of employment and production. Improvements in high-tech innovation failed to offset galloping deindustrialisation, with a concomitant blunting of our competitive edge in world markets. We have witnessed how sheer inattention to priorities has allowed the infrastructure of road, rail, air, ports, communications, electricity, water and waste removal to run down to critical lows (BusinessTech 2022). Less visibly, the neglect of standards of responsibility and accountability have caused the auditor-general, Tsakani Maluleke, to warn that the lack of consequence management threatens the entire institutional framework of governance, from local councils to national departments. Maluleke called for a culture of accountability to improve service delivery (Auditor-General South Africa 2022).

The chapters in this handbook argue that there is a collective responsibility for all South Africans to seize control and return agency to themselves. If those to whom we handed stewardship of the state have, by and large, failed us, we, as the ultimate owners of South Africa, now need to exercise our fiduciary and supervisory right to take command. We should do so through the instruments that the Constitution affords us: obviously, multiparty voting and parliamentary processes, but more directly and tellingly through the Chapter Nine institutions, which were specifically set up to prevent a negligent government from damaging the country through abuse of power or failure to act for the common good.

There are grounds for optimism if we accept the categorical imperative to take a direct hand in public affairs for the good of the nation. In short, to build a prosperous South Africa that realises its full human potential, we must get involved in civic and political action. We need to remind ourselves that if we leave piloting of public affairs and the state machinery entirely to politicians, we are trusting those who may not deserve it. The *Online Etymology Dictionary* notes that the word 'politician' has overtones meaning 'one concerned with public affairs for the sake of profit or of a clique'.[2]

However, we must acknowledge that the challenges faced by the first democratic government were monumental and some of them possibly even insurmountable. Global economic shifts and the 2008 Great Recession caused a contraction of formal employment. The digital era has put the country at a disadvantage due to its poor education system, which is judged among the worst in the world (The Economist 2017). We are not properly preparing our youth for the Fourth Industrial Revolution (much as we may claim to readying ourselves to keep up with the rest). If that were all – if we were merely the victims of structural deficits that have seen us stripped of agency in a world not of our making – it would still not be enough to explain why we have slipped so badly backwards. The picture drawn so far is not, sadly, the whole story.

We could repair infrastructure and restore competitiveness if the will and the vision were there. Less than a year into his presidency, President Mandela spoke boldly and decisively about corruption. In his closing address following the debate on his State of the Nation Address in February 1995, Mandela said:

> The threat that corrupt norms implanted by apartheid may survive and overwhelm us as we set about building on new values is one that alarms us. It is a threat that, as a government, we are determined to forestall. The Cabinet is finalising a Code of Conduct for its members, a code that shall be firmly applied. However, if the sanctions against corrupt practices are not carried out in every corner with equal fervour – government and civil service, political parties, private business and non-governmental organisations – this scourge will remain with us (Mandela 1995).

Tragically, sanctions were not carried out in every corner and the result is what we see today. We have become a normless society that expects nothing better.

Agency, freedom and justice are indissolubly connected. In the context of the rule of law, we cannot have one without the others. The constitutional state requires that people must be able, voluntarily, to exercise their rights and this means having the freedom to do so. Under apartheid, whites had freedoms denied to other races and in effect this allowed injustice to flourish as whites looked after themselves to the detriment of others. The courts condoned forced removals as being in line with the law. The law itself and legal processes were unjust. In the inquest into the murder of Black Consciousness leader Steve Biko in police cells, the magistrate found no one to blame, despite evidence of multiple brain traumas and other injuries (Steve Biko Foundation n.d.).

Today, South Africans experience injustice in a different way. Ours is not the plight of Russian, Iranian or Chinese protestors, who are beaten, imprisoned and sometimes disappear for daring to say 'No' to their oppressive regimes. There are such instances in South Africa, but we have left most of that paranoia behind. Our situation is more like the American model, where denial of freedom takes the form of economic deprivation and a racially structured and harsh capitalist environment that marginalises many who have no hope of a decent life. Police brutality continues to exist alongside freelance crime. In South Africa, the assassination of political opponents is now commonplace, as rivals seek to reap the fruits of positions in the state. This is a violent society, the injustices of which are masked by meritocracy and professions of care for the poor.

Our Bill of Rights needs to be enforced through the Chapter Nine institutions. The six state institutions that support constitutional democracy – known as the Chapter Nines after their place in the Constitution – consist of the public protector, the auditor-general, the Independent Electoral Commission, the South African Human Rights Commission, the Commission for Gender Equality and, lastly, the Commission for the Promotion and Protection of the Rights of Cultural, Religious and Linguistic Communities. To date, only the Office of the Public Protector has been constantly in the public eye, due to a saturation of media coverage, usually focusing on the politics of cases.

The range of concerns facing the Chapter Nines is wide. A study of these bodies found that their efforts were often unfocused (Konstant 2016). While they are intended as 'watchdogs', these institutions

> are not directly a branch of government . . . and they do not have the power to take disciplinary action against government officials. Their role is purely investigatory and administrative, providing a link between government and citizens . . . Media coverage of the Chapter Nines is often negative, suggesting that they are lurching from one crisis to another (Stander 2020).

Some achievements have been laudable, but if we 'do not want a democracy that exists only on paper, citizens must begin to play an active role in practicing democracy', concludes the report (Stander 2020).

Why are people apathetic? Partly, disengagement is due to what sociologist Émile Durkheim (1933) called anomie. Anomie is the condition of individuals in an atomised society, in which expectations are unclear and there are no longer common meanings that give purpose to life. Durkheim referred to expectations – or the lack of them – as lying at the root of a normless society. When people have no goals because their surroundings discourage them from striving for anything, anomie soon follows, with attendant deviant behaviours leading to violence, depression and suicide.

People who feel they have lost agency may react in several different ways. According to Robert Merton, a sociologist who developed Durkheim's initial concept of anomie within a framework of deviance, individuals and entire groups who are blocked from achieving the normal success goals of their society show five likely responses: retreat, ritualism or conformity (ways of accepting un-freedom); or innovation and rebellion (refusal to accept un-freedom). Crime is an innovation resulting from what Merton called a 'strain' between legitimate goals and lack of opportunities to achieve those goals (Thompson 2023). South Africans are all too familiar with that kind of strain.

The strains induced by poverty may cause crime and rebellion, but many people simply give up, disengage, accept their lot, follow populist preachers or beg for a living. They experience not just the normlessness of anomie, but also a deep estrangement from their own human nature: what Karl Marx called alienation. In terms of his class analysis, alienation is the condition of people who are forced to serve goals that are not their own in a system of labour value extraction. It puts them at odds with themselves, as it robs them of an authentic purpose in life.

Both anomie – which is felt subjectively – and alienation – an objective outcome of exploitation – are present in South Africa on a mass scale, as people confront what many see as a hopeless and heartless social milieu. Their expectations are reduced to what tomorrow will bring. There are great differences, of course, between the lived realities of different people and groups, but there is a pervasive sense that post-apartheid life is 'precarious' for the large number who are excluded from the benefits of liberation. They turn aside in dismay (Barchiesi 2011). To turn that on its head: we are a lively and outspoken nation, with great dynamism ready to be tapped – but who will take the lead to recharge our developmental mission?

Two deadly pandemics – Covid-19 and HIV and AIDS – have swept the world. South Africans felt some of their worst effects due to inequality, patriarchy, violence and the mismanagement of health resources. People stuck in their homes, with little money and ever-present hunger, turned on one another. Alcohol and drug abuse worsened the plight of family members suffering the physical and mental costs of diseases that hide in our immunity cells. Helplessness produces anomie on a large scale.

Black women and their children have suffered the most from gender-based violence at the hands of close male relatives. Being vulnerable, they are the biggest losers of personal agency in the vicious circle of service delivery breakdowns. A 2022 report found that nearly a quarter of women in South Africa are HIV-positive, indicating that the campaign to curb the disease is not succeeding (UNAIDS 2022). Schoolgirl pregnancies, widespread rape, gender-based abuse and failures of policing and prosecutions have pushed women into a corner, from which escape is virtually impossible without a major change in gender relations, ethics and law enforcement.

The Covid-19 lockdowns produced evidence of the same pathologies. Limited research has been done into the impact of hard lockdown restrictions on families, specifically how these restrictions impacted on women and children's experiences of domestic violence, including intimate partner violence and child abuse in South Africa. According to one recent report: 'The lockdown had unprecedented negative economic impacts on families and exacerbated some of the risk factors for violence against women and children in the home in South Africa' (Mahlangu et al. 2022).

If ever there were an indicator of national desperation, suicide is it. When one would rather depart the scene than continue to struggle against the odds, hope is lost and the victim blames the system or other people for this. It is men who show the highest rate of suicides in this country, perhaps because they experience the most desperation from their inability to perform as breadwinners. Peer pressure on men to match others is also a factor. Perhaps women are more resilient. While suicide rates worldwide are declining, South Africa has shown no improvement. Men are more than five times more likely to end their own lives than women, but figures for women increased sharply in recent decades before stabilising (Kootbodien et al. 2020).

Is disengagement curable? In one word: Yes. Let us invoke the concept of the categorical imperative – the necessity of acting morally – to insist that we do have agency, we are not captives of circumstance and we are able to change the downward trajectory of national expectations.

One does not use the term 'categorical imperative' lightly. It was coined by Immanuel Kant, a central philosopher in the European Enlightenment. As such, he may well be seen by Africans and other formerly colonised people as an agent of mental imperialism. Kant never left the small German city of Königsberg, where he created his world-aware moral philosophy. He forged concepts of reason and ethics that should persuade us, powerfully, to act in the best interests of all. That said, Kant was a racist. He did not see the increasingly massive industry of the transatlantic slave trade as the leading moral problem of his time, but rather regarded it as the upshot of certain dynamics in human history leading to racial dominance (Kleingeld 2007). To invoke Kant is to test the tolerance of readers, but let this be said: the categorical imperative provides a foundation for one of the keys to repair what is broken in our society.

Kant argued that any moral principle on which you act should be such that you could see it as a universal law. This is an absolute standard and not something we choose to apply because it would be to our advantage. The biblical commandment 'Thou shall not steal' is absolute. Adding 'because you may go to jail' turns it into an essentially amoral calculation of rewards and risks. We must learn the distinction or we will continue to wander in a desert of nihilism. Categorically and fearlessly, we have to adopt a standard of rightness to be the beacon that guides our actions going forward.

Since we are not Europeans, though much influenced by their example, we need our own beacon. It exists. It is the philosophy of Ubuntu, which must ultimately prevail over the collapse of values that plagues us. Ubuntu is ours. It makes us jointly and severally responsible to others and to the human community of which we are a part. The Nguni expression 'umuntu ngumuntu ngabantu' means 'I am because you are, you are because we are'. Extended to all of us, it implies a belief in a universal bond of sharing that connects all of humanity. As a nation, we profess to live by Ubuntu, as it was mentioned in the 1993 Interim Constitution as a guiding principle. Its principles were carried over into the 1996 final Constitution. What that document lacks is any suggestion as to how Ubuntu should be implemented, let alone culturally interpreted to include South Africans of all races and creeds.

Kant's view that a moral principle is valid only if one can see it as a universal law applies to Ubuntu. Undoubtedly, this African philosophy has the potential to become universal, although it is hardly known outside Africa (except as the name of a digital operating system). It is not what some have called an ethno-philosophy, born out of Africa and restricted to our shores. It is not like some native species that might perish in the wider world. It does not matter whether it is universally embraced or not: the point is that we can acknowledge that to live in and through community with others does qualify as a universal moral principle.

How does Ubuntu relate to the themes of agency, freedom and justice set out in this book? Above all, Ubuntu lays stress on justice for all. Starting from the principle that we all share our human mortality and are essentially cut from the same root, Ubuntu enjoins all of us to apply equity, dignity and inclusivity in our dealings with each other. The rediscovery of Africa's cultural roots does not exclude people of other cultures from sharing its values. What it does is to transform the idea of humanity from a Western, individualist perception to one of community being among fellow Africans and humanity at large. It is an extremely humane philosophy that accepts the identities of all within one family of humankind, and hence sees justice as the common right of all. This perspective is one that South Africans sorely need in our culturally and historically fragmented lives. To embrace Ubuntu as a living, constitutionally endorsed creed of citizenship would go a long way towards forming a wholesome sense of nationhood. That, in itself, would help overcome anomie and alienation, turning future expectations from negative to positive.

This handbook outlines the categorical imperatives of responsible nationhood. We owe it to ourselves to arrest the slide into anarchy. We must advance the values that will make us – once again, as we were in the era of liberation – self-confident, free agents of justice and progress.

Notes

1. https://www.statecapture.org.za/ (accessed 19 December 2023).
2. https://www.etymonline.com/search?q=politician (accessed 19 December 2023).

References

Auditor-General South Africa. 2022. 'Auditor-General Calls on Government to Entrench a Culture of Accountability to Improve Service Delivery'. Media release, 23 November. https://www.agsa.co.za/Portals/0/Reports/PFMA/202122/2022%20PFMA%20Media%20 Release%20FINAL%20(interactive).pdf?ver=2022-12-01-105048-470 (accessed 19 December 2023).

Barchiesi, F. 2011. *Precarious Liberation: Workers, the State, and Contested Social Citizenship in Postapartheid South Africa*. New York: SUNY Press.

BusinessTech. 2022. 'South Africa Is Slowly Collapsing'. *BusinessTech*, 14 November. https://businesstech.co.za/news/government/642791/south-africa-is-slowly-collapsing/ (accessed 19 December 2023).

Department of Planning, Monitoring and Evaluation. 2014. *Twenty Year Review: South Africa, 1994–2014.* Background paper: Economy and employment. https://www.dpme.gov.za/publications/20%20Years%20Review/20%20Year%20Review%20Documents/20YR%20Economy%20and%20Employment.pdf (accessed 19 December 2023).

Durkheim, E. 1933. *The Division of Labor in Society*. Translated by George Simpson. New York: Free Press.

The Economist. 2017. 'South Africa Has One of the World's Worst Education Systems'. *The Economist*, 7 January. https://www.economist.com/middle-east-and-africa/2017/01/07/south-africa-has-one-of-the-worlds-worst-education-systems (accessed 19 December 2023).

Hamilton, L. 2011. 'Collective Unfreedom in South Africa'. *Contemporary Politics* 17 (4): 355–72.

Kleingeld, P. 2007. 'Kant's Second Thoughts on Race'. *The Philosophical Quarterly* 57 (229): 573–92.

Konstant, A. 2016. *Assessing the Performance of South Africa's Constitution: Chapter 6 – The Performance of Chapter 9 Institutions.* Report for the International Institute for Democracy and Electoral Assistance by the South African Institute for Advanced Constitutional, Public, Human Rights and International Law, a centre of the University of Johannesburg. https://constitutionnet.org/sites/default/files/chapter_6._chapter_9_institutions.pdf (accessed 19 December 2023).

Kootbodien, T., N. Naicker, K.S. Wilson, R. Ramesar and L. London. 2020. 'Trends in Suicide Mortality in South Africa, 1997 to 2016'. *International Journal of Environmental Research and Public Health* 17 (6), article 1850.

Leshilo, T. 2022. 'South Africa's President Ramaphosa Could be Impeached – 3 Essential Reads on the Phala Phala Scandal'. *The Conversation*, 1 December. https://theconversation.com/south-africas-president-ramaphosa-could-be-impeached-3-essential-reads-on-the-phala-phala-scandal-195738 (accessed 19 December 2023).

Mahlangu, P., A. Gibbs, N. Shai, M. Machisa, N. Nunze and Y. Sikweyiya. 2022. 'Impact of COVID-19 Lockdown and Link to Women and Children's Experiences of Violence in the Home in South Africa'. *BMC Public Health* 22 (1), article 1029.

Mandela, N. 1995. 'Closing Address by President Nelson Mandela: Parliamentary Debate on the State of the Nation Address, 24 February 1995'. https://www.sahistory.org.za/archive/1995-president-mandela-state-nation-address-24-february-1995-after-national-elections (accessed 19 December 2023).

Stander, A. 2020. 'Chapter 6: Chapter 9 Institutions'. In: *Constitutional Law for Students*. Cape Town: UCT Libraries. https://openbooks.uct.ac.za/uct/catalog/view/25/38/1266 (accessed 19 December 2023).

Steve Biko Foundation. N.d. 'Steve Biko: The Inquest'. https://artsandculture.google.com/
    story/steve-biko-the-inquest-steve-biko-foundation/TAWBwqmVZxgA8A?hl=en
    (accessed 19 December 2023).

Thompson, K. 2023. 'Merton's Strain Theory of Deviance'. https://revisesociology.com/2016/
    04/16/mertons-strain-theory-deviance/#google_vignette (accessed 19 December 2023).

UNAIDS (Joint United Nations Programme on HIV/AIDS). 2022. 'With New Infections
    1 Million Higher than the 2020 Target, UNAIDS and Partners Convene Emergency
    Meeting on HIV Prevention'. Press release, 10 October. https://www.unaids.org/en/
    resources/presscentre/pressreleaseandstatementarchive/2022/october/20221010_stop-
    new-infections (accessed 19 December 2023).

Acknowledgements

Muxe Nkondo

This book, in three volumes, was written during a period of crises in South Africa. Tembeka Ngcebetsha-Mooij, the co-ordinator of all the operations, bore with each one of us throughout that period. Her tireless, vigilant feeling for detail made the undertaking easier to work through, and we are profoundly grateful. Informing her vigilance is a rigorous scholarly intelligence.

My dear friend and co-editor, Reuel Jethro Khoza, surely one of South Africa's iconic figures, with a blending of engaged scholarship and sustained business management on the ground, gave us much confidence and encouragement. To him, we are genuinely indebted, particularly for convincing big business that the discourse and deliberations in this publication were good for the economy. Certainly, here, there is nothing pro forma about the feelings of respect and trust.

Our deepest gratitude goes to Justice Albie Sachs, whose foreword – a veritable meditation on the dialectical relationship between lived experience, politics and law – gives this book awesome power and authority. His wisdom, integrity and hospitality to complexity elude explicit expression.

In a project as vast and complex as this, everything depends on everything else; everything is individual and collective. A profound sense of gratitude is owed to the University of KwaZulu-Natal Press for accepting the responsibility of publishing these three volumes.

We are deeply indebted to the following sponsors for providing the much-needed financial support to deliver this project: Discovery Bank, Standard Bank, Anglo American and Exxaro.

We wish to thank all the contributors to the volume for bringing to bear upon the complex dynamics of agency, freedom and justice the wisdom that comes with vast experience and research.

Finally, much gratitude to Felicity Dire and Mbonga Nkondo for their technical assistance and their attentiveness to operational precision.

Abbreviations

ANC	African National Congress
ASGISA	Accelerated and Shared Growth Initiative – South Africa
AU	African Union
BEE	black economic empowerment
BRICS	Brazil, Russia, India, China and South Africa
CEDAW	Convention on the Elimination of All Forms of Discrimination Against Women
COSATU	Congress of South African Trade Unions
DDM	District Development Model
ERRP	Economic Reconstruction and Recovery Plan
FIFA	International Federation of Association Football
FRELIMO	Frente de Libertação de Moçambique, Liberation Front of Mozambique
GDP	gross domestic product
GEAR	Growth, Employment and Redistribution
HDI	Human Development Index
IDP	integrated development plan
IMF	International Monetary Fund
NATO	North Atlantic Treaty Organization
NDP	National Development Plan
NGO	non-governmental organisation
OAU	Organisation of African Unity
OECD	Organisation for Economic Co-operation and Development

PAC	Pan Africanist Congress
RDP	Reconstruction and Development Programme
SACP	South African Communist Party
SADC	Southern African Development Community
SAMPI	South African Multidimensional Poverty Index
SARS	South African Revenue Service
SMME	small, medium and micro enterprise
SOE	state-owned enterprise
Stats SA	Statistics South Africa
TRC	Truth and Reconciliation Commission

Introduction

The Deliberative Framework

Muxe Nkondo

Many South Africans suffer from varieties of 'un-freedom', injustice and demolished agency. Systemic violence occurs in the lives of the majority of the people, denying them the basic conditions for happiness and well-being – and many spend their lives fighting preventable morbidities, often succumbing to premature death. Diminished agency, un-freedom and injustice have other dimensions, including food and health insecurity, subjecting them to physical and social pain. The agency of individuals is a basic building block and its impairment is a handicap at the very core of a human life. The reason for this normative focus is that agency, freedom and justice are not only the bases for the evaluation of democracy, but they are also principal determinants of a meaningful life. Since agency, freedom and justice are constitutive elements of happiness and well-being, their denial is an existential crisis.

History tells us that there are always choices to be made between alternative perspectives of what agency, freedom and justice are, and so competing positions should be subjected to rigorous analysis. The authors in this book use these concepts to construct theories and practices of agency, freedom and justice that can accommodate and manage complexity. The chapters examine historical, political, social economic forces in depth and are backed by a pragmatic insistence on lived experience and possibilities on the ground. The authors do political theory and practise great service: they attend to the causes and consequences of the fraying of agency, freedom and justice.

Because of the complex relationship between freedom, agency and justice, a strategy is more appropriate than a plan and includes a set of questions to frame analysis and deliberation. A plan, on the other hand, rolls out a set of predetermined actions that must function in circumstances that allow their completion (Morin 2008; Taylor 2003). But for fundamental change, particularly in the light of Covid-19 and a globalising knowledge economy (with their radical uncertainties), strategy is preferred. Strategy, unlike a plan or a problem, is determined by taking account of the tentative, experimental drive of experience on the ground. Everything that is planned suffers from rigidity in comparison with strategy. The deliberative, pragmatic approach challenges us to think more complexly, at the levels of both theory and practice, about the interplay, in real life, of lived experience, politics, economics, knowledge and ethics (Morin 2008).

The chapters here are valuable for their contributions to practical knowledge; they are focused on solving problems in real-life situations. Readers will develop a high level of discourse and this knowledge will provide the context in which readers apprehend what is really going on in South Africa today and its place in a very complex global order. Understanding the analyses will enable readers to come up with solutions that will enhance their capacity to solve problems and conduct their lives much better, drawing on scientific knowledge from several disciplines and knowledge systems.

The authors use hermeneutics, which have been shown to work, in their own experience and that of others. The discourse includes interpretations and narratives, such as statistics on the economy or the results of social and economic surveys. In the time of Covid-19, particularly, this involved finding not the best solution, but one that is good enough. And for survival, practical knowledge matters a lot, especially now in extreme conditions of deepening poverty, intergenerational unemployment, severe social and economic inequality and systemic violence against women.

The organisation of this book is extremely complex. Almost all the themes covered depend upon one another, with each theme linked to everything else through a bond that connects even the most distantly separated. In analysing the political context of agency, freedom and justice, it is virtually impossible to understand one theme without understanding the entire field of questions and perspectives. Reading one chapter, you find yourself in the midst of so many other chapters.

Because of the complexity of the issues involved in an era of radical uncertainty, we do not set out a sequence of predetermined actions that must function in circumstances that allow their completion. This book provides strategies that elaborate one or several scenarios. Throughout the book, strategy prepares itself for the new and unexpected. It takes account of random situations and adverse elements, and modifies itself depending on the information furnished. So each chapter is a fresh raid into the radically uncertain. The factor at play is that of perplexing complexity, but also of flexibility and heightened sensitivity to difference and shifting realities. Imposing a plan, a programme, a template of fixed ideas, is not advisable. Practice must be based on a deep understanding of the tentative, experimental drama of lived experience. The movement from positivism to post-positivism, structuralism to post-structuralism is informed by this understanding. So, the various chapters are organised around the ideas of complexity and radical uncertainty; this is what connects them.

We believe, therefore, that the model of a rigid programme of action with clearly marked targets is not only an abstract model, it is also a model indifferent to complexity. Closely related to this is an imposition of a rigid grammar and style on the discourse. Writing, at the core, is subjective even within the order of rules and codes. In the handbook format, the individual author is irreducible to 'standard' forms of writing. Although writing and reading are acts of mutual recognition, they are fundamentally subjective.

The deliberations on agency, freedom and justice, no matter how exhaustive, cannot be complete. In particular, the yoking together of questions addressed and those not addressed explicitly in the body of the chapter is not as simple as it might seem to some. At close range, the concepts they invoke begin to be discerned as related in one way or another, even if the relationship seems equivocal, as tracing many and interrelated contours in the discourse on agency, freedom and justice soon confirms. It is perhaps the case that in being brought together, they give us to think a certain chiasmus, with which we must engage all the more fully. There are no confines here, no clear boundaries.

We can mobilise the spaces and the links between the chapters as, at once, initiating a discourse on agency, freedom and justice, and perhaps also a different thinking of them (a discourse coming from different environments), while at the same time articulating the dialectics between as part of an intellectual and political act.

Deliberations between members of the editorial team generated a consensus that this book should aim to provide a wide-ranging, in-depth overview of major perspectives and key debates on the complex link between agency, freedom and justice in South Africa, within a range of fields of study. In addition, we wanted authoritative chapters that discuss important developments, with a focus on the links between the three themes. We wanted to encourage different perspectives, rather than orthodoxy, let alone prescribing a preferred form of writing. Hence, this book displays a mix of different forms of presentation and styles of writing. 'The best style' would be strongly resisted.

The Handbook consists of three volumes. We have grouped the chapters in the three volumes in twelve parts to make the journey through the sixty-eight chapters less arduous. Our intention is to move from one set of questions to another, attentive to the dialectical relationship that informs them. So, accordingly, we acknowledge the growing interdisciplinary and inter-epistemic approach to knowledge, which explores issues as apparently diverse as agency, freedom, justice, happiness and well-being. No constraints were imposed on the authors.

The subtitle of this volume is 'Citizens in Conversation'. Here is a place for sustained, co-operative intellectual work. The reader should endeavour to discipline her or his personal preferences – to which we are all subject – and compose his/her differences with the authors in the common pursuit of openly reasoned consensus. Since it is often the case that deliberative collaboration takes the form of disagreement, one should be grateful to the author whom one finds it worth disagreeing with.

This handbook originated in a consciously collaborative enterprise – an intense and sustained effort to promote co-operative intellectual labour. It is, in general, a sort of plea for critical deliberation on the history of the liberation struggle in South Africa, for consideration of approaches other than along ideological lines. The conversations are conducted in a number of ways. They are not conducted via any direct medium, such as a conference, actual or virtual, but are brought together by the common pursuit of what it will take to bring about fundamental change in South Africa. They engender complementary questions and responses not delimited by any prior agreement.

The handbook concerns deliberations on questions of agency, freedom and justice, and whether change in policy, law, economy, public engagement, education and so on can be effected through writing and reading attentive to differences. Thus each chapter effects a deliberative rhythm that allows the emergence of openly reasoned consensus, as indicated earlier. This format points to an expression of collaborative thinking engendering attentiveness to complementary differences and equivalences. It addresses a spacing of different perspectives and overlaps. This allows a reading of diversity and complexity, irreducible to the hermeneutics simplicity of either a final interpretation or an absolute template. If this is the case, how do we bring this to bear, not only on our interpretations, but also on the political process, in the face of diversity? This is a discursive process.

So the Handbook is not meant to hand down a fixed stock of knowledge, with the passing on of a collection of findings and with the transmission of data. Its task is the continuation of the passionate, flexible and scholarly exploration of the dynamics of fundamental change. Therefore, readers have to continue to think through the dynamics again and again. So one does not have to start from scratch. We have no chance of dealing with these complex dynamics if we do not realise that they pass through us and that we belong, each of us, in a different way, to different interpretations. There is something quite marvellous about different interpretations of historical evidence committed to fundamental change.

Whatever we say about the dynamics of fundamental change, we need to listen attentively to each other and, while we are doing so, leave the next word to the next person. We need a kind of thinking that connects complementary differences and recognises diversity as it recognises equivalences in a multidimensional and systemic discourse. South African history has not reached a stagnant end, nor is it triumphantly marching to a 'brave, new world'. It is being catapulted into a future without clear contours, without a clear and stable end point, without a *telos*.

The narrative of agency, freedom and justice brings together themes that recur throughout the handbook. The motivation for the deliberations (and conversations) emerges from personal and collective experience, most dramatically with the decline of public confidence. It is grounded not in attempts to create new ideological frameworks, nor to further the agendas of a new ideology, but in the need to establish a new premise for human relations that is pertinent to the imperatives of agency, freedom and justice.

The paradigm of conversation and openly reasoned consensus opens a space in the deliberations and chases out intolerance. Conversational space is receptive to new and different perspectives. There is no search for 'facts', 'truth' or 'reason'. There is diversity in the chapters. We can say of complexity in this case that it arises in part out of the subjectivity of interpretation – from radical uncertainty, from the inability to be certain about fundamental change. It arises from something elusive, from our inability to avoid uncertainty.

Finally, there is the impression that 'the practical' simplifies, because with practice we close the matter. Certainly, the practical is a decision, a choice, but also a wager (Morin 2008). It does not escape subjectivity and error. It requires vigilance and it does not exclude innovation. In a real sense, it is a challenge. So, as we frame policies, laws and strategies for fundamental change, we have to contend with uncertainty. We should not forget that the state of the nation is always changing, something new can always spring up, and we must remember the ravages that simplifying explanations have caused, not only in policies, but in our daily lives.

The volumes are structured in parts, as follows:

Volume 1: Policy and Law; Economy; Public Management and Politics; International Relations and Diplomacy
Volume 2: Education, Knowledge and Knowledge Systems; Technology, Communication and the Media; Ethics, Faith and Belief in a Secular State; Aesthetics: The Functions of the Arts
Volume 3: Health, Environment and People living with Disabilities; Environmental Health; The Family and Community Action; Gender Justice.

Below, we outline the various parts of Volume 1.

Part 1: Policy and Law

Focusing on changes since the democratic transition in 1994, the essays here examine the role of policy and law in making the constitutional order work. They shed light on the relationship between policy and law, and argue that policy frameworks and legal norms have had a structuring effect on democratic processes and practices. But, for reasons examined in the first five chapters, policy and law have failed to eliminate poverty, unemployment, socio-economic inequalities and gender-based violence. Alternative perspectives on these conditions in these chapters are invaluable for the discourse on fundamental change. The authors use an interdisciplinary approach to reveal patterns, possibilities and constraints, significant connections and nuanced interpretations about the legacies of apartheid law. Going forward, transformative policy frameworks and legal norms are critical in mobilising for fundamental change. Some scholars have drawn attention to the spectre of path dependence. To what extent has it inhibited egalitarian policies, law and practices?

The Constitution is widely acclaimed as the supreme achievement of the democratic transition to inclusive and deliberative democracy (Meierhenrich 2008; Sunstein 2001). The chapters here present the Constitution in its historical, social and political context, providing readers an invaluable resource through which to understand the emergence, development and continuing application of the supreme law, its role in building a new democratic dispensation, its interaction with apartheid legacies and the strains placed on the new democratic order by poverty, unemployment, severe socio-economic inequalities and gender-based violence. But to what extent has it turned political, social and economic inequalities, however deep, into a force for radical transformation? In what ways has it generated a political economy that is inclusive, participatory and deliberative? The authors draw on empirical, comparative and post-structuralist literature to deepen understanding of fundamental change and the challenges ahead.

We asked the authors to consider a series of questions. What constitutes the social good in South Africa today? In what ways were all possible alternatives worked out in the political settlement? What strategies were used to find solutions? In what ways were the various pieces fitted together to form a coherent policy and legal system? Has the Constitution created workable solutions? Was consensus broad enough to support a democratic social life? For example, how was the land question addressed? How inclusive was the policy process? What lessons were drawn? How were questions of feasibility and power addressed? In all these processes, what was at stake? What strides have been made in improving our policies and laws? Accepting that performance is variable and at times patchy, how can we learn from the last 30 years? Responding to these questions requires that we must evaluate government, policy and legal structures and processes quite closely, measuring effectiveness and efficiency, recognising that policy and legal analysis is inherently a normative exercise and that the values of democracy are in need of particular attention.

What strategies were used to reduce conflict and uncertainty? Which and whose interests have had a significant impact on policy and law? To what extent are the policies and laws distributive and redistributive? How inclusive were the decision processes? In what ways did legal norms and institutions serve as historical cause to our democracy? What is the link between law, policy and politics? What are the consequences of policy and law post-1994? Without a military coup, in what ways was law used to negotiate the political settlement? How credible is the law 30 years later? To what extent is apartheid law still present? How effectively has the law transformed social and economic relations? In what ways does this matter in explaining democratisation since 1996?

These questions are meant to deepen understanding of the origins and history of the law in post-apartheid South Africa. The concept of path dependence is relevant to this context. How has it affected the democratic project? To what extent did it limit the scope and pace of change? To respond to these questions, we have to recognise the impact of history on law, as well as on the building of our constitutional democracy. In a way, South African law now represents both the old and the new. It is laden with inherent contradictions and sources of both hope and cynicism. It provides a sense of institutional stability and a source of continuing tension as the new society inherited the distribution of accumulated rights and injustices. And so it represents the old and the new in the process of transformation. It is therefore important to understand the law as part of a broader historical, political, social and economic context.

How workable are the structures of deliberative democracy in the liberal capitalist system? In this context, what is the first and indispensable virtue of a well-designed constitution? To what extent has it reshaped our social and economic order? These questions have large implications for how we think about citizenship, freedom and justice. To what extent has the Constitution turned political differences into a constructive force? In what ways has it generated a politics that is deliberative rather than destructive? Which decision structures and processes has it created to ensure inclusive deliberation and reasoning?

The authors review central questions of legality and morality, and reflect upon those contentious issues that affect the design and operation of legal processes and institutions. Why is it that the method of passing judgement is in dispute and the interpretation of evidence is subject to dispute? In this book, no legal argument is pursued and enforced without further debate. The authors develop, succinctly and broadly, the concept that justice is in its nature an increase in freedom. By empirical evidence, historical examples and rigorous analysis, the authors show how justice, broadly conceived, cannot be antagonistic to freedom. These chapters are, among other things, about the way that legal institutions take decisions; more specifically, the way the courts tackle decision-making. They are about political and legal culture, the way we think about political and legal arguments and the principles that control political and legal arguments – in particular, the principles that control the way we conduct interpretation and judgement, since interpretation and judgement are at the heart of any political discussion and at the heart of any attempt to change things fundamentally.

The authors here try to get inside deliberative and decision processes by merging empirical data with more discursive material. The essence of the method is an attempt to sift out of the legal language of practice, the philosophical assumptions of which can be found shaping arguments, interpretations and judgments. In doing this, the authors do not force a 'system' or a 'logic' on to narrative and testimony; they assume simply that people often think coherently and that ideas that enter popular culture can survive. In the process, a sort of reconstruction of ideas of justice takes place, which is parallel to the intellectual construction of theories, paradigms and scenarios, and which may be used to uncover the conflicts between different sorts of assumptions and philosophies, as those conflicts are played out in the arena of practical politics and decision-making.

In what ways, since 1994, have policy and law been used to assert the will to agency, freedom and justice? Policy and law are an assertion of the will and attempt to shape and control social, economic and political relations. There was a distinctly transformative feel to the undertaking, back then: self-confidence, married to a bold vision and a sense of mission to build the South Africa we want. To what extent have policy and law provided a solid point of reference for social, economic and political relations? What was done to ensure that laypeople who are affected by policy and law understood the values and principles that inform them? Why is it that policy and law seem to have failed to substantially reduce, if not eliminate, poverty, unemployment, inequality and gender-based violence? Has there been a rupture, an elision in the constitutional order? How did we get here? What have been the motivations of public representatives and how have democratic struggles been the source of fundamental change? How effective have they been? What choices are available? Is there a basis for optimism? What opportunities exist for us to make a freer and more just society? Are there successful practices in the world we can learn from? How translatable are they?

Do we need to look at our policies and law in a fresh way? Should we, as some constitutional experts advise, look at our political ideas, the assumptions, the values and the ideals that cohere around the current conception of the relation between individuals, society and the state? Are there fundamental conflicts between the various parties in Parliament about the meaning of agency, freedom and justice? What differences do they have and are there no equivalences that we can use to enhance the capability of the state to bring about fundamental change. The norms that inform our policies and laws, where do they come from? What impact have they had on our social, economic and political relations? In a severely unequal society, whose interests do they serve? Contributors to this part of the handbook address these questions. There is no privileged set of analytical or deliberative tools, no absolute form of reference. Fortunately, in a democratic society sufficient consensus is achievable. Despite the forces of resistance to fundamental change, we can draw strength from our capacity to realise the ideas of agency, freedom and justice. The questions and perspectives covered here have a wide reference in jurisprudence, policy science, philosophy, hermeneutics, discourse analysis and ethics (Sunstein 2001; Taylor 2007).

Part 2: Economy

What are the criteria that we should use to fundamentally transform social, economic and political relations? In what ways can we measure the state of the economic order? The following traits recommend themselves: lifespan, security from violence (systemic and subjective), food and health security, clean water and sanitation, safe and comfortable accommodation, reliable and affordable public transport and free, quality education for the poor.

The chapters in this part investigate the key ways of measuring the performance of our meta-economic policy framework with respect to how well the majority of the people have fared in these basic needs and fundamental interests. They examine those factors that have the greatest influence on others; for example, people's political and economic participation, happiness and well-being. The Human Development Index, produced by the United Nations Development Programme is useful here. Why has the current economic policy failed to stabilise social relations? How does it plan to eliminate unemployment and socio-economic inequalities? Is there no alternative system that is just at its core? Why is it that the majority of the people tend to be losers in the current economic establishment? Any lessons from comparable economies? Why has the idea of equality of individuals not benefited the majority of the people? Why is it that in spite of the fact that each citizen enjoys basic rights and fundamental freedoms, an independent judiciary, free elections and a multi-party system – we have deepening poverty, intergenerational unemployment and enduring inequality? Is there an intrinsic limitation – a lack – at the core of our economic order (Kotz 2015; Piketty 2020; Standing 2006; Stiglitz 2003; Streeck 2014)?

Why is it that the bulk of the means of production are privately owned and why is it that the state seems to be unable to regulate market forces? After decades of democratic struggles, why are the liberal capitalist forces so resilient and adaptive? Experience has taught us to treat the flows of capital and desire as parts of the same economy. Behind every investment of interest and capital, an investment of desire and vice versa. This relates desire directly to the social field and to the market system based on profit. This is the political economy of desire in tension with values; it is a private and social affair. But this libidinal investment is not itself revolutionary; it causes desire to penetrate and distort social and political processes. But there can be no revolutionary action where the relations between people are relations of desire, ungoverned by a collective political process. The challenge is how to control and reorientate desire through forging a collective political intersubjectivity – a revolutionary collective subject. The problem is how to control desire such that it is used to call into question the capitalist order.

Desire clasps action in its powerful embrace and reproduces it in a way all the more intense because it has no sense of contradictions. The body thus becomes a problem to the mind. It does so because it is driven by a lack that produces a fantasy that is related to an extrinsic process of production and consumption. This is precisely the significance of desire or need as a search in a void (Deleuze and Guattari 1986).

Perhaps this is why some men and women fight for their exploitation and servitude as stubbornly as if it were their own liberation. This is how the 'sovereignty of the people' and 'revolutions' have been subverted (Reich 2019). It is very difficult to provide a satisfactory explanation for the aberration, this perversion of the desire of the oppressed, the coexistence of the social field and desire. Fortunately, desire is insatiable and in time capitalism finds its limit. There is no relationship between the revolutionary mind and desire, between values and appetite. Testimonies and representations before the Judge Zondo Commission on State Capture provide abundant evidence.

Fortunately, there is a vitality and creative energy in both the body and the mind that animate revolutionary struggles. There are certain things that money cannot buy (Sandel 2012). The last 27 years in South Africa have witnessed a resurgence of the democratic temper. This has to do with the incompatibility of capitalism with democracy. The predicament facing post-colonial governments is not a contingent or mechanical one, nor a question of institutional re-engineering. It is of a deeper nature: it relates back to the key factor in capitalism's crisis, the incompatibility of democratic and market systems.

Part 3: Public Management and Politics

All things in the governance of inclusive democracy depend on one another; all things are immediate and mediated, as each thing is linked to everything else through a decision-making bond that cannot mediate even the apparently most distantly separated things. A reading of the National Development Plan, and the various reports from government portfolios, at all levels, soon confirms this. This complexity is captured in regulations, protocols, producers and codes. In the context of the introspective and retrospective approach recommended to authors, this has a particular relevance. The complexity in question is evidently highly problematic, particularly so, given the complex social, economic and political context in which the discourse on agency, freedom and justice has to be conducted. The multi-vocal decision processes, covering the governance of democracy, specifically in relation to agency, freedom and justice, are evidence of this. Like other governments committed to change, our government is a dialogic of order and change – in the sense that it is a question of two mutually inclusive notions, granting relative roles to the two imperatives (Morin 2008).

Contributors here and in the other parts develop a complex form of thinking and doing capable of understanding the ecology of public service in South Africa. This principle demands more and more specialist interdisciplinary focus and reach. The Republic of South Africa has a life of its own, with its policies, laws, management, structures and ethics – which allows all the forces at play to become interconnected around the ideas of agency, freedom and justice. On a wider scale, the state is itself part of the African Union and the United Nations governance system, rooted in the dynamic of continuous change. There is no *telos*: agency, freedom and justice are always work in progress. Given the apparent decline in public trust and confidence, the chapters here engage with the political psychology of decision-making in public office and how emotions and interests function within public service areas. Authors provide new insights into the nature of decision bias, particularly with regard to allocation of public resources and delivery of services. Why is it, they ask, that in the allocation of public resources and delivery of services, social bonds tend to trump expertise and hierarchy?

What can be done, practically, to reduce the discrepancy, increasingly often, between desire and emotion, on the one hand, and the public good, on the other? What can be done to negotiate and mediate the disjuncture between the private and the public in public service? Are there instances in the world where the discrepancy has been managed? There are political psychologists who allege that there are few things left in South Africa that money cannot buy. What has led to the commodification or commercialisation of public service? By what means can this trend be reversed? Corruption studies warn us against 'the pursuit of absolute integrity'. Is the cynicism warranted? Can public integrity be taught? In our information and knowledge institutions – libraries, archives, museums, innovation hubs – are there answers to these questions?

Part 4: International Relations and Diplomacy

What have been the main analytical tools of international relations and diplomacy studies in South Africa since 1994? Which theories shape our policy? In what ways has our international relations policy been informed by current and political economic problems within the country, in the region and the world? To what extent has the discourse on international relations, in South

Africa, been influenced by methodological developments in the social sciences – post-structuralism and decolonisation in particular? Has there been a single theoretical approach that has clearly won the day? Has there been an assessment of the alternative approaches that are available in the discourse to deal with a very complicated historical and contemporary reality? How, for instance, are we dealing with the Fourth Industrial Revolution and globalisation? How are we dealing with Covid-19? Have there been events and episodes, since 1994, which stood out for special attention?

Have there been debates in Parliament that broadened our international relations policy? How do the major ideological orientations – liberal capitalism, nationalism, Pan-Africanism and socialism – wrestle with the complex problems of regional integration and global solidarity? In what ways has realism influenced our practice? To what extent have our own fundamental values – freedom and justice – shaped our decisions? How rational has our approach been? In what ways have our overarching development goals – social cohesion, inclusive democracy, regional integration, solidarity – influenced our diplomacy? In light of this, how have we dealt with conflict in the region, in particular? How have we negotiated the tension between conflict and co-operation? How have we addressed the question of human rights? How have we dealt with the political economy of international relations in our time? How were priorities determined; and why does it seem that liberal capitalism has won the day?

References

Deleuze, G. and F. Guattari. 1986. *Anti-Oedipus: Capitalism and Schizophrenia*. Minneapolis: University of Minnesota Press.

Kotz, D.M. 2015. *The Rise and Fall of Neoliberal Capitalism*. Cambridge, MA: Harvard University Press.

Meierhenrich, J. 2008. *The Legacies of Law: Long-Run Consequences of Legal Development in South Africa, 1652–2000*. Cambridge: Cambridge University Press.

Morin, E. 2008. *On Complexity: Advances in Systems Theory, Complexity, and the Human Sciences*. Cresskill, NJ: Hampton Press.

Piketty, T. 2020. *Capital and Ideology*. Cambridge, MA: Harvard University Press.

Reich, R.B. 2019. *The Common Good*. New York: Vintage Books.

Sandel, M.J. 2012. *What Money Can't Buy*. New York: Farrar, Straus and Giroux.

Standing, G. 2006. *The Corruption of Capitalism: Why Rentiers Thrive and Work Does Not Pay*. Hull: Biteback Publishing.

Stiglitz, J.E. 2003. *Globalization and Its Discontents*. New York: W.W. Norton and Co.

Streeck, W. 2014. *How Will Capitalism End?* London: Verso.

Sunstein, C.R. 2001. *Designing Democracy: What Constitutions Do*. Oxford: Oxford University Press.

Taylor, C. 2007. *A Secular Age*. Cambridge, MA: Harvard University Press.

Taylor, M. 2003. *The Moment of Complexity: Emerging Network Culture*. Chicago, IL: University of Chicago Press.

PART 1

POLICY AND LAW

CHAPTER 1

Is the Law Doing Enough?

Recent Legislative Reforms to Combat Gender-Based Violence

Leona Theron

South Africa is plagued by extremely high levels of gender-based violence (GBV). About one-quarter of adult women in South Africa have experienced GBV (Mahlangu et. al. 2022). In the country's most populous province, Gauteng, this figure is about half of women (Mahlangu et. al. 2022). Feminist critic and academic Jacqueline Rose writes: 'In South Africa, the slogan of the campaign against sexual violence is not #MeToo or #TimesUp but, far more chillingly, #AmINext" (2021: 38). This slogan, while registering activists' vehement objection to the injustice of GBV and its prevalence in South Africa, also reflects resignation to the ubiquity of sexual violence. The law must play its role in addressing GBV and the South African state is making attempts to build a more suitable statutory and institutional framework to combat GBV and its corollaries.

However, legal interventions alone will not stem the rising tide of GBV and legal reform must be seen as only one of the branches of a broader, integrated societal strategy. GBV is both impacted by and impacts upon the climbing levels of poverty and inequality in the country. As the Constitutional Court noted in *S. v. Tshabalala*: 'Joint efforts by the courts, society and law enforcement agencies are required to curb this pandemic.'[1] GBV will only be eradicated when it is targeted jointly by various institutions. including schools, families, churches and community centres, in tandem with education for police and other first responders. This chapter seeks to outline recent legal reforms in South Africa and discusses the role that these reforms, and the law in general, can play in the fight against GBV. It asks the question: Is the law doing enough?

The existing legal landscape

South Africa's first democratically elected parliament recognised that common law was an inadequate safeguard against GBV and that a specially crafted statutory framework was required. The new government signed on to the Convention on the Elimination of All Forms of Discrimination Against Women (CEDAW) and expedited the development and passing of the Domestic Violence Act 116 of 1998 in order to comply with the requirements of CEDAW (Usdin et. al. 2000: 56). As discussed later, the Domestic Violence Act was viewed as a progressive piece of legislation, particularly for its time. In its first iteration, the Domestic Violence Act included a broad definition of domestic violence, which included, among other things, emotional and economic abuse and stalking. The Domestic Violence Act does not criminalise domestic violence. Instead, it facilitates prosecution of existing crimes (for example, assault or rape) that occur in a domestic setting. In addition, various legislations have been passed to introduce minimum sentences for such crimes. These statutes include the Criminal Law Amendment Act 105 of 1997, the Criminal Procedure Second Amendment Act 85 of 1997 and the Criminal Law (Sexual Offences and Related Matters) Amendment Act 32 of 2007.

Common law on GBV has also been developed in line with constitutional imperatives. At South Africa's democratic turn, the women's movement actively mobilised for the inclusion of women's rights in the Constitution. Through the lobbying of the Women's National Coalition during the constitutional negotiations, a strong equality clause, envisioned to be interpreted substantively, rather than formalistically, was included in the Constitution (Hassim 2002: 718).[2] The courts have since recognised that GBV is a dehumanising phenomenon that restricts a number of constitutional rights, including the rights to equality, life, human dignity, freedom and security of the person and privacy. Emerging from these violations, the courts have recognised a constitutional duty on the state 'to provide effective remedies against domestic violence',[3] and a delictual duty on the state to protect the public in general and women in particular, against violent crime.[4] In South Africa, human rights jurisprudence relating to GBV has largely involved the interpretation of civil and political rights. Social and economic rights are both violated in the context of GBV and can be used strategically as a tool in the fight against GBV. This will be explored in greater detail later in this chapter.

At a rhetorical level, the superior courts and the Constitutional Court, in particular, have made important statements on the nature of GBV. In *S. v. Baloyi*, Judge Sachs noted that domestic violence is 'systemic, pervasive and overwhelmingly gender-specific' and 'reflects and reinforces patriarchal domination . . . in a particularly brutal form'.[5] In *Masiya v. Director of Public Prosecutions Pretoria*, Chief Justice Langa recognised the patriarchal roots of the criminalisation of rape as a means of protecting men's proprietary interest in women, and wrote: 'Today rape is recognised as being less about sex and more about the expression of power through degradation and the concurrent violation of the victim's dignity, bodily integrity and privacy.'[6] More recently, in *S. v. Tshabalala*, Judge Khampepe wrote: 'Rape, at its core, is an abuse of power expressed in a sexual way. It is characterised with power on one side and disempowerment and degradation on the other. Without more being said, we know which gender falls on which side.'[7]

However, the treatment of GBV cases in the lower courts is often not aligned with the progressive tone of the Constitutional Court and, moreover, is inconsistent and difficult to monitor. A public interest law centre focused on women's rights issues has reported that many of its clients are of the view that they have been 'failed by the magistrates' courts', including through orders that survivors may not speak with others about their experiences of GBV (Blouws and Madlala 2022).[8] Strong oversight measures by the Department of Justice and Correctional Services and the Office of the Chief Justice could go some way to prevent these patterns from continuing in the magistrates' courts and to ensure that complainants are not victimised again during the legal process. This might entail introducing reporting requirements for GBV cases and creating official channels through which complainants can register (anonymously) their experiences in the magistrates' courts. Recent legislative amendments go some way towards reducing secondary victimisation of complainants in GBV matters.

Recent legislative amendments

On 1 August 2018, women across South Africa launched a mass action protesting against GBV under the banner of #TotalShutdown. In November 2018, a Presidential Summit against Gender-Based Violence and Femicide was convened, emerging from the demands made at the #TotalShutdown protests. The summit produced a declaration, which committed to developing a national strategic plan on gender-based violence and femicide and fast-tracking the review of existing laws and policies on GBV to ensure that they are victim-centred and fit into an integrated legislative scheme that responds effectively to GBV.

Emerging from this process, in January 2022, the president assented to three pieces of legislation in response to the GBV epidemic:

1) the Criminal Law (Sexual Offences and Related Matters) Amendment Act, 2021;
2) the Criminal and Related Matters Amendment Act, 2021; and
3) the Domestic Violence Amendment Act, 2021.

These laws focus on the criminal justice system's response to GBV. Broadly, the amendments relate to the following crucial issues: the process of applying for a protection order, police not taking harassment claims seriously, and the lack of accountability and adequate punitive measures for offenders. All of these amendments have now come into effect.

Criminal Law (Sexual Offences and Related Matters) Amendment Act, 2021

The ambit of the National Register for Sex Offenders, which previously only recorded persons convicted of or alleged to have committed sexual offences against children and persons with mental disabilities, has been extended to record those convicted of or alleged to have committed any sexual offence. 'Sexual offence' has a broad statutory definition and includes, among other things, rape, sexual assault, sexual grooming and 'flashing'. In other words, the National Register now seeks to protect a broader category of vulnerable persons, including women under the age of 25 who are undergoing higher education or training, or who live in student residence; persons being sheltered at facilities for victims of crime; persons with a physical, intellectual or sensory disability who receive external care or reside in a care facility; and persons who are 60 years or older and receive external care or reside in a care facility. The purpose of the National Register is to protect members of society who are vulnerable to sexual violence from sexual offenders by prohibiting such offenders from working with vulnerable persons, obtaining licences or approvals required to operate a business that involves supervision or care of vulnerable persons, or becoming the foster parent, kinship caregiver, temporary safe caregiver or adoptive parent of a child, or the curator of a person with a mental disability. Furthermore, the periods that must lapse before various categories of offenders may apply to have their particulars removed from the Register has been doubled under the Amendment Act.

The crime of incest has also been expanded. Previously, only sexual penetration between persons who may not marry each other on account of consanguinity, affinity or an adoptive relationship (closely related persons), regardless of whether the parties consented, was criminalised. Under the amended definition, when one of the parties is a child, any 'sexual violation . . . of such a nature that it was reprehensible for the adult person to have acted in that manner under the circumstances' between closely related persons is a crime.

The Amendment Act also introduces a new offence: sexual intimidation. Sexual intimidation occurs when a person makes a threat that inspires a reasonable belief of imminent harm, a belief that a sexual offence will be committed against the complainant, a family member of the complainant, or any person in a close relationship with the complainant. On conviction, the punishment for sexual intimidation may be equal to the punishment for the threatened sexual offence.

The Amendment Act also criminalises failure to report knowledge, reasonable belief or suspicion that a sexual offence has been committed against a vulnerable person. A person convicted of this offence is liable to a fine, up to five years' imprisonment, or both.

Criminal and Related Matters Amendment Act, 2021

The Criminal and Related Matters Amendment Act, 2021 tailors rules of criminal and civil procedure to ensure that they are more victim-centred and to reduce secondary victimisation. The Magistrates' Courts Act, 1944 has been amended to provide for the appointment of an intermediary through whom witnesses who are minors, older persons, or those living with a physical, psychological or mental condition, can give evidence in civil matters. The Act has also been amended to allow witnesses in civil matters to give evidence by an audiovisual link. Among the factors to be considered by a court in determining whether to make an order allowing for evidence via audiovisual link is whether doing so would 'prevent the likelihood that any person might be prejudiced or harmed if he or she testifies or is present at such proceedings'.[9] The effect of these amendments is that victims of

GBV are able to give evidence through alternative means, which reduce exposure to secondary victimisation in proceedings other than criminal proceedings – for example, when applying for a protection order. In criminal proceedings, the categories of witnesses who may testify through an intermediary have been expanded to include older persons and persons who suffer from a physical, psychological, mental or emotional condition. Similar amendments have been made to the Superior Courts Act, 2013 to provide for the use of intermediaries and audiovisual measures to give evidence in civil proceedings.

The Criminal Procedure Act, 1977 has been amended to remove the possibility of police or prosecutor bail (release on bail without appearance before a magistrate) for alleged perpetrators of domestic violence. At the bail hearing, if the prosecutor does not oppose the bail application of an alleged perpetrator of GBV, they are required to place their reasons for not opposing the application on record.[10] Furthermore, the presiding officer at a bail hearing is required to consider the view of the alleged victim regarding his or her safety. If it is likely that the accused will endanger the safety of the alleged victim, bail may not be granted. These amendments are a progressive step towards increased reporting of GBV because many victims are discouraged from reporting their abusers out of fear that the abuser will simply be released on bail and the abuse will be exacerbated by the victim's decision to report. In the event that bail has already been granted, if a presiding officer is informed that the accused has contravened a protection order or has failed to inform the court that a protection order for the protection of the alleged victim had been issued, a warrant of arrest may be issued in respect of the accused.[11]

In cases of domestic violence, the complainant is now empowered to make representations to the parole board in respect of any considerations to place a sentenced offender on parole or under correctional supervision. This is an important way of ensuring that victims are protected from their abusers and given a sense of agency within the criminal justice system. Victims' perception of their own safety and their views on the remorse (or otherwise) of offenders, if offered, must be considered by decision-makers in the parole process. However, it is important to consider the degree to which the correctional system is currently capable of rehabilitating perpetrators of GBV, especially in light of complex sexual politics and patterns of sexual violence within prisons.

Murder resulting from physical abuse or sexual abuse, as contemplated in the Domestic Violence Act, 1998, is now a Schedule 2, Part 1 offence. The categories of rape and compelled rape falling under Schedule 2, Part 1 have been expanded to include instances where the accused has previously been convicted of the offence of rape and compelled rape where the victim is or was in a domestic relationship with the accused. The effect of these amendments is that the minimum sentence for the expanded definitions of murder, rape and compelled rape is life imprisonment. Assault with intent to do grievous bodily harm under Schedule 2, Part 3 bears a minimum sentence of 10 years for a first offender, 15 years for a second offender and 20 years for a subsequent offender. The situation in which these minimum sentences apply has been expanded to include instances where the victim of the assault is or was in a domestic relationship with the accused.

Domestic Violence Amendment Act, 2021

The Domestic Violence Amendment Act, 2021 has expanded the definition of domestic violence considerably to include sexual harassment, related person abuse (any member of the complainant's family or household or with whom the complainant has a close relationship), spiritual abuse, elder abuse, coercive behaviour, controlling behaviour (behaviour that makes the complainant subservient to the respondent), exposing a child to domestic violence, entering the complainant's workplace or place of study without consent, where the parties do not share a workplace or place of study, and any other intimidating, threatening, abusive, degrading or humiliating behaviour towards the complainant. The threshold for proving that conduct amounts to domestic violence has also been lowered. Previously, conduct constituted domestic violence if it caused harm or may have caused imminent harm to the complainant. The amended threshold requires that conduct causes harm or inspires reasonable belief that harm may be caused to the complainant.

The thresholds in the definitions of various categories of domestic violence have been lowered. For example, the requirement that acts of economic abuse must be 'unreasonable' has been removed. Emotional, verbal or psychological abuse has been broadened in scope, and the requirement that such conduct must be repeated before it constitutes domestic violence has been removed. Similarly, the definition of harassment has been amended to remove the requirement that such conduct must be repeated. Physical abuse has been expanded to include threats of physical violence.

The Domestic Violence Amendment Act imposes duties on designated functionaries and members of the public to report actual or suspected domestic violence. If a designated functionary, in the course of fulfilling their duties and exercising their functions, comes to suspect that a child, a person with a disability or an older person may be experiencing domestic violence, they are required to submit a report to a social worker or to the South African Police Service (SAPS). Specific processes regulating the conduct of functionaries in relation to domestic violence will be contained in directives issued by the departments of Health, Social Development, Basic Education, Higher Education and Training, and Communications and Digital Technologies. Although failure to report domestic violence has not been criminalised for functionaries, the directives must include 'adequate disciplinary steps' for non-compliance. Adults, other than functionaries, who know, believe or suspect that an act of domestic violence has been committed against a child, a person with a disability or an older person are required to report this to a social worker or the SAPS, and will be guilty of an offence if they fail to do so.

The imposition of a duty to report known or suspected domestic violence against vulnerable persons recognises the fact that communities must be involved in ending the scourge of GBV. However, this provision is only effective once violence has already occurred. Community-based education – in schools, religious institutions, youth groups and the like – is crucial for rooting out the patriarchal attitudes that result in GBV.

The Domestic Violence Amendment Act clarifies the process of applying for interim and final protection orders. Notably, the recent amendments make it easier for an application for a protection order to be considered outside ordinary court hours. Previously, a court would only consider an application out of hours if it was satisfied that the complainant may suffer undue hardship if the application was not considered immediately. This standard has been relaxed; the court now needs to be satisfied that a reasonable belief exists that the complainant is suffering or may suffer harm. Similarly, the standard for granting an interim protection order has been relaxed from requiring prima facie evidence that undue hardship may be suffered by the complainant to now requiring prima facie evidence that the complainant is suffering or may suffer harm. A potentially significant administrative reform is the introduction of an integrated electronic repository for domestic violence protection orders. Although the Act does not specify the terms on which information in the repository may be accessed, at least one potential use is that judicial officers will be able to consult the repository to determine whether there are any protection orders in force against parties in domestic violence and related matters (for example, divorce or maintenance).

Policing powers in relation to GBV have been expanded under the Domestic Violence Amendment Act. The SAPS have been empowered to enter private residences without a warrant if they receive a report that physical violence has been committed during an incident of domestic violence and the SAPS member reasonably suspects that a person who may have information regarding the alleged physical violence is on the premises.

A complainant may now apply for a 'domestic violence safety monitoring notice' together with a protection order, if the complainant and respondent share a joint residence. The effect of such a notice is that the court may order the SAPS to take certain steps to protect the complainant, including by contacting the complainant electronically to enquire about their well-being, visiting the joint residence to communicate with the complainant in private and, where necessary, overcoming resistance to entry to the joint residence where SAPS is prevented from seeing the complainant.

While the Domestic Violence Amendment Act has expanded policing powers, it also recognises that persons working in the security sector have access to power and resources that can be misused. It does so by providing that a court may order the seizure of a weapon, even if the respondent's employment requires them to possess such a weapon. The Constitutional Court recognised this dynamic in *K. v. Minister of Safety and Security* where it was held that there is a relationship of trust between the public and the police, stemming from their constitutional duty to protect the public and prevent crime, which was egregiously violated in this case when the applicant was raped by three police officers.[12]

The circumstances under which a prosecutor may refuse to institute a prosecution or withdraw a charge in matters related to domestic violence have been further limited – specific authorisation from a director of public prosecutions is required to withdraw charges or refuse to institute criminal prosecution in respect of an offence where a complainant or related person suffers grievous bodily harm or is threatened with a weapon. It is a known fact that GBV is severely under-reported and, of the cases that are reported, only a small proportion are prosecuted to completion. This amendment is a welcome response to this unfortunate pattern and holds out the possibility of increasing the proportion of reported cases heard in court.

The Domestic Violence Amendment Act introduces new provisions regarding evidence in proceedings under the Domestic Violence Act. For example, a procedure for the subpoena of witnesses has been introduced. Additionally, in an application for a protection order, where the respondent used electronic communication to commit an act of domestic violence, the court may direct an electronic communications service provider to provide the court with the information necessary to determine whether the alleged electronic communication was made by the respondent. If the court issues a protection order, it must order the electronic communications service provider to remove or disable access to the electronic communication used to commit an act of domestic violence. The costs due to an electronic communications service provider for providing these services are for the complainant's account. However, if the court finds from an inquiry into the complainant's financial means that it is appropriate for the state to bear these costs, it may make an order to that effect. This recognition that approaching the courts can be prohibitive to complainants seeking justice, is a progressive step. More generally, the Act empowers the minister of Justice and Correctional Services to make regulations regarding the provision of financial assistance by the state to complainants, respondents and witnesses who participate in any proceedings under the Domestic Violence Act.

The Domestic Violence Amendment Act has also introduced longer maximum sentences for second or subsequent offences under the Domestic Violence Act.

Social and economic context and the limits of law

Legal interventions aimed at GBV have thus far focused mainly on policing and the justice system. The series of legislative amendments discussed in this chapter are an extension of that approach. This retroactive intervention, while crucial for the delivery of justice to victims of GBV, fails to address its causes. The appropriate place for the law is not only in punishing GBV, but also in preventing its occurrence in the first place. Punitive measures, such as lengthy minimum sentences and the recently expanded National Register, appear unlikely to significantly reduce rates of GBV. In *S. v. Tshabalala*, the Constitutional Court acknowledged that legislated prescribed minimum sentences for rape have not had the effect of deterring sexual violence.

Although women across all racial and class backgrounds experience GBV, it is exacerbated by social and economic conditions. It is more difficult for unemployed or low-income women to escape intimate partner violence. Outside the home, the poor public transport infrastructure means that women commuters are at higher risk of experiencing sexual violence. Beth Goldblatt proposes the use of social and economic rights as a novel legal tool in the fight against GBV (2019: 171). She argues that when we focus on the economic causes of GBV, 'the attention moves from responses that may be overly concerned with the protection of women to more empowering solutions that recognise the barriers to women's agency and participation' (2019: 173).

Although there is a well-established jurisprudence on socio-economic rights, rarely have judgments in socio-economic rights cases recognised gendered experiences of poverty (Goldblatt 2019: 173). Many of the applicants in landmark socio-economic rights cases have been women. However, the link between socio-economic rights violations and gender discrimination, including in the form of GBV, has not been widely recognised. For example, in *Government of the Republic of South Africa v. Grootboom*,[13] a case concerning the state's duty to provide emergency housing, the court did not consider GBV a possible cause of homelessness (2019: 175).

Similarly, Elsje Bonthuys points out that the application and development of the law on domestic violence and related matters, such as divorce and maintenance, are siloed in the courts, with the effect that orders relating to the care of and contact with children are granted without regard to domestic violence issues (2014: 112). Judicial officers should pay attention to the ways in which GBV overlaps with other forms of discrimination and harm suffered by women (and the laws that regulate them). This will certainly enrich our jurisprudence. In *Mahlangu v. Minister of Labour*, the Constitutional Court adopted an intersectional framework in a matter related to compensation for workplace injuries for domestic workers. In that case, Acting Justice Victor noted: 'There is nothing foreign or alien about the concept of intersectional discrimination in our constitutional jurisprudence. It means nothing more than acknowledging that discrimination may impact on an individual in a multiplicity of ways based on their position in society and the structural dynamics at play.'[14] The courts should adopt this framework when adjudicating matters that directly or indirectly relate to GBV – the overlapping discriminations experienced by women are not separable in life, so nor should they be in law.

The Domestic Violence Act is a model of a multi-pronged approach to GBV and has been recognised by feminist scholars for its provisions on social and economic elements of GBV (Bonthuys 2014: 111). This Act provides that, when issuing a protection order, a court may order the respondent to pay emergency monetary relief for losses suffered by the complainant as a result of domestic violence, including loss of earnings, medical expenses, relocation and accommodation expenses, and household necessities. Recent amendments have expanded this list to include education expenses, transportation costs, costs related to psycho-social services and counselling and maintenance, pending the finalisation of maintenance proceedings. However, implementation of these 'non-criminal remedies' in the Domestic Violence Act has been poorest (2014: 111). For example, magistrates have shown reluctance to order emergency monetary relief or to prohibit respondents from entering the shared residence (Artz and Smythe 2005: 213–16).

Activists often emphasise the importance of a 'whole-systems' approach to combating GBV (Malaudzi 2022: 2). This entails co-ordination among state agencies (including the courts, police and policymakers) and civil society actors (including faith groups and activists). While the law is but one element of such an approach, there are a number of varied legal remedies that can be mobilised. In addition to reactive measures that relate directly to GBV, we must also prioritise proactive measures that indirectly prevent GBV and mitigate its consequences. To the extent possible, a 'whole-systems' approach *within law* should be adopted by practitioners and judicial officers in our efforts to counter GBV. Such an approach requires judges and legislators to consider the intersecting social, cultural and economic factors that render women vulnerable to GBV.

Conclusion

Legislators and judges are fully aware of the awful reality of GBV in South Africa. This is reflected in the range of laws that aim to protect women from violent crime. The courts assume a corrective and a preventative function in relation to GBV. Where there has been a complaint, the courts ensure justice between the parties and, where there has been an offence, impose a conviction and appropriate sentence. The courts also issue protection orders that aim to protect victims from further or potential harm. However, since the adoption of GBV legislation and the development of common law on issues relating to GBV in line with the Constitution, GBV has not abated. This reflects, on the one hand, the limits of the law's ability to address a complex social issue, with roots in South Africa's traumatic history, and, on the other hand, the need for lawmakers to critically reflect on patterns in legal reforms related to GBV and how these might be inadequate. A critical gap in the law on GBV is a lack of meaningful engagement with the social and economic causes and ramifications of GBV. Lawmakers have acknowledged and responded to the social and economic barriers that prevent survivors from approaching the justice system. There is a need for legislators, litigants and courts to consider more broadly the multifaceted nature of GBV and to respond appropriately with multifaceted solutions.

Notes

1. *S. v. Tshabalala* 2020 (5) SA 1 (CC).
2. The equality clause in the South African Constitution reads:
   1) Everyone is equal before the law and has the right to equal protection and benefit of the law.
   2) Equality includes the full and equal enjoyment of all rights and freedoms. To promote the achievement of equality, legislative and other measures designed to protect or advance persons, or categories of persons, disadvantaged by unfair discrimination may be taken.
   3) The state may not unfairly discriminate directly or indirectly against anyone on one or more grounds, including race, gender, sex, pregnancy, marital status, ethnic or social origin, colour, sexual orientation, age, disability, religion, conscience, belief, culture, language and birth.
   4) No person may unfairly discriminate directly or indirectly against anyone on one or more grounds in terms of subsection (3). National legislation must be enacted to prevent or prohibit unfair discrimination.
   5) Discrimination on one or more of the grounds listed in subsection (3) is unfair unless it is established that the discrimination is fair (see https://www.justice.gov.za/constitution/chp02.html, accessed on 18 September 2023).

The courts have endorsed a substantive reading of the constitutional right to equality (Albertyn 2018: 454). For example, in *Minister of Finance v. Van Heerden* 2004 (6) SA 121 (CC), Judge Moseneke (as he then was), wrote: 'What is clear is that our Constitution and in particular section 9 thereof, read as a whole, embraces for good reason a substantive conception of equality inclusive of measures to redress existing inequality.'

3. *S. v. Baloyi* 2000 (2) SA 425 (CC).
4. *Carmichele v. Minister of Safety and Security* 2001 (4) SA 938 (CC).
5. *S. v. Baloyi* 2000 (2) SA 425 (CC).
6. *Masiya v. Director of Public Prosecutions Pretoria* 2007 (5) SA 30 (CC).
7. *S. v. Tshabalala* 2020 (5) SA 1 (CC).
8. The Western Cape High Court recently ruled in *Segerman v. Petersen* 2022 ZAWCHC 42 that a magistrate erred in finding that an alleged rape victim was harassing her alleged rapist by talking about her experience privately on WhatsApp messenger and alluding to the alleged rape (without naming the perpetrator) on social media.
9. Criminal and Related Matters Amendment Act, section 51C (2) (a) (i) (dd).
10. It is sadly far from unprecedented for GBV offenders to commit further offences after being released on bail. For example, in *Carmichele v. Minister of Safety and Security* 2001 (4) SA 938 (CC), the offender, Mr Coetzee, was released after being charged with assault of a woman, despite having a previous rape conviction. After he was released, Mr Coetzee brutally assaulted another woman, Ms Carmichele, the applicant in the case.
11. Criminal and Related Matters Amendment Act, section 68 (1) (eA).
12. *K. v. Minister of Safety and Security* 2005 (6) SA 419 (CC).
13. *Government of the Republic of South Africa v. Grootboom* 2001 (1) SA 46 (CC).
14. *Mahlangu v. Minister of Labour* 2021 (1) BCLR 1 (CC).

References

Albertyn, C. 2018. 'Contested Substantive Equality in the South African Constitution: Beyond Social Inclusion towards Systemic Justice'. *South African Journal on Human Rights* 34 (3): 441–68.

Artz, L. and D. Smythe. 2005. 'Bridges and Barriers: Five Year Retrospective on the Domestic Violence Act'. *Acta Juridica* 2005 (1): 200–26.

Blouws, C. and S. Madlala. 2022. 'Magistrate's Courts Fail to Protect Womxn Who Survive Violence'. Women's Legal Centre. https://wlce.co.za/op-ed-magistrates-courts-fail-to-protect-womxn-who-survive-violence/ (accessed 20 July 2022).

Bonthuys, E. 2014. 'Domestic Violence and Gendered Socio-economic Rights: An Agenda for Research and Activism?' *South African Journal on Human Rights* 30 (1): 111–33.

Goldblatt, B. 2019. 'Social and Economic Rights to Challenge Violence against Women: Examining and Extending Strategies'. *South African Journal on Human Rights* 35 (2): 169–93.

Hassim, S. 2002. ' "A Conspiracy of Women": The Women's Movement in South Africa's Transition to Democracy'. *Social Research* 69 (3): 693–732.

Mahlangu, P., A. Gibbs, N. Shai, M. Machisa, N. Nunze and Y. Sikweyiya. 2022. 'Impact of Covid-19 Lockdown and Link to Women and Children's Experiences of Violence in the Home in South Africa'. *BMC Public Health* 22, article 1029.

Malaudzi, M. 2022. 'Fund, Respond, Protect, Collect: A Desktop Review of the Legal and Policy Frameworks that Address Gender-Based Violence in Africa'. Nelson Mandela School of Public Governance, University of Cape Town. https://issuu.com/buildingbridgesuct/docs/gbv_research_paper (accessed 20 July 2022).

Rose, J. 2021. *On Violence and On Violence against Women*. New York: Farrar, Straus and Giroux.

CHAPTER 2

Why Land Restitution Has Failed and What Can Be Done about It

Tembeka Ngcukaitobi

The return of the land. *Mayibuye*. Of all claims in the struggle against colonialism and apartheid, the idea of the return of the land is the most venerated. It asserts both affinity and entitlement to the land. To the soil. It is also a protest. The Dutch and British occupation of South Africa founded on might was illegitimate. *Mayibuye* protests this illegitimacy of conquest. The founding of the African National Congress (ANC) is based on this promise to return the land. And so is that of its primary liberation rival, the Pan Africanist Congress (PAC). Yet the claim is charged with ambiguities. Who should the land be returned to? And from whom? In April 1955, the Congress of the People rejected the dichotomy of the coloniser and the colonised, engaged in a struggle for dominance over one another. South Africa, the 'Freedom Charter' argued, 'belongs to all who live in it' (Congress Alliance 1955).

It is important to return to the legislative origins of land loss and the prime focus of the Natives Land Act 27 of 1913 was the imposition of racial restrictions on landownership by Africans. To consider land restitution meaningfully, some perspective on the Native Land Act is necessary.

What the Natives Land Act was about

The Union of South Africa came into being on 31 May 1910. Then, there were some 6 million Africans, 4 million of whom lived in 'South Africa' and another 2 million in the reserves – forerunners to the 'homelands' – out of a total population just in excess of 8 million people. The reserves were the result of the territorial conquest of the nineteenth century. Although during apartheid there was a tendency to deny African ownership of the land, even the first prime minister, Louis Botha, admitted in 1916 that 'the natives' were in South Africa when the Europeans arrived.

By the end of the nineteenth century, most African land was under the control of Europeans. Leonard Thompson's estimate is that Zulu people lost two-thirds of their land and the Tswana people even more because of Afrikaner and British conquest (Thompson 2001). The Xhosa people in the Cape and the Sotho people in the Free State lost more than 90 per cent of their land. As a result, they were forced to form new relationships to the land. Most Africans lived on land owned by Europeans, with no legal rights to the land, and were often referred to as 'squatters'. As Harvey Feinberg (2006) notes, there was a complex range of relationships between Africans and white landowners, with Africans living on the land as labourers or tenants, meeting their obligations in money, crops or labour; or as sharecroppers or squatters.

Yet there was also a new mode. Land had been commodified. It could be bought and sold in the market, although the market itself was created through racial lenses and reflected state policy, rather than unpredictable economic forces. Ownership of land was proved through the mechanism of title deed. There was an uneven dispensation here. In the Cape, Africans could purchase land, according to the individual tenure system, although there were vast restrictions on this arising from the Glen Grey Act, 1894, which stipulated that African purchases of land had to be approved by the colonial government. The result was that in practice very few Africans actually owned land in their own right. Mostly, land was held in communal tenure systems. In the Free State, there was an outright prohibition on the purchase of land by Africans. In the Transvaal, official policy was to prohibit African land acquisition, although no formal law existed to that effect. After the 1905 case of *Edward Tsewu v. Registrar of Deeds*, which confirmed that Africans had the right to acquire land, official policy changed. Now, Africans could buy land in their own name, but the common practice remained that land was bought through white intermediaries, such as native commissioners and Christian missionaries.

These land acquisitions were largely marginal and did not affect the actual land territory held by Africans, which remained largely representative of the land taken through conquest. Yet after the formation of the Union, white farmers, under the political influence of Barry Hertzog, then Minister for Native Affairs in the Botha administration, began to agitate for a uniform land policy, to guarantee the security of white control over the land. Hertzog, in some respects, can be viewed as the intellectual father to Hendrik Verwoerd, widely regarded as the 'architect of apartheid'. He opposed 'mingling of the races' and proposed that each race must 'develop along their own lines'. On land, he was unequivocal that Africans should not own land in the 'white man's territory' and no white should acquire land in 'native reserves'. The problem, however, was that there was no legal entity known as a 'white man's territory'.

Enter the Natives Land Act

In December 1911 the Union government proposed the Native Settlement and Squatters Registration Bill. It roughly concerned measures to restrict African land purchases and ownership and to regulate the rights of so-called squatters on white-owned land. Although the Bill did not become law, its essence was taken up with much energy by Hertzog in the months that followed. He conceived the idea of native land legislation that would divide the country in two – one section for Europeans and the other for the rest of South Africa's people. What he wanted to achieve was territorial segregation. However, as he drafted the legislation, he realised that this was not possible, so the draft legislation focused on legal rights, rather than physical occupation. Whites could own land in European areas. Africans could not own land, even in native reserves, without forms of trusteeship under the tutelage of the white administration. Squatting was made illegal and criminal sanctions were proposed. The native reserves were placed under the control of the state. In this way, segregation in politics could be translated to racism with regard to land.

When the Natives Land Bill made its way to Parliament, in May 1913, Hertzog had been fired from Cabinet. He had been replaced by the liberal minded J.W. Sauer, a one-time ally of John Tengo Jabavu, the founder and editor of *Imvo Zabantsundu*. However, Sauer could not prevent the passing of the Natives Land Act, with its obnoxious content as theorised by Hertzog. Black views were not solicited as the Bill was publicised for only five weeks before it was passed into law, between 5 May 1913 and 19 June 1913. Its central tenet was the creation of 'scheduled areas', which demarcated areas for African occupation. From the 1916 report of the Natives Land Commission, these areas are reflected as follows: for the Cape, 8.47 per cent; Natal, 22.83 per cent; Transvaal, 3.22 per cent; and the Free State, 0.48 per cent, which gave a national total of less than 8 per cent of all land available in the country (Union of South Africa 1916). Section 1 of the Act proclaimed that no 'Native' could buy land in European areas and no European could buy land in native reserves, without the permission of the government. There is evidence that the right to grant permission for Africans to acquire land in European areas was sometimes granted by the government. Land purchases by Africans during the period of the 1913 Natives Land Act is an understudied field. Harvey Feinberg and André Horn note:

> Africans bought farms and lots at an increasing rate between 1913 and 1936 in the Transvaal (and the country as a whole). [While] territorial segregation was the most important principle underlying the Act, the Natives Land Act did not stop Africans from buying land in the Union of South Africa. More land was approved for sale during the Hertzog era than during the Botha–Smuts era and more land was owned by Africans in 1936 than in 1913. Thousands of Africans in the rural Transvaal (and tens of thousands in South Africa) became the owners of farms and lots, ranging in size from a few morgen to several thousand morgen. African initiative played a major role in this phenomenon, as Africans took advantage of the exception clause in the Land Act and the changed attitude of government officials (after 1918) towards allowing Africans to buy land. In addition, Africans and whites lived on neighbouring farms in those areas where African-owned farms existed. Overall, the evenness in the spatial mix of African-owned and white-owned land units increased rather than decreased in the rural areas of the Transvaal. The failure of the Natives Land Act to stop African purchases meant that the legislative goals of the supporters of the Act went unfulfilled (2009: 51).

The situation improved somewhat in 1936 when new areas were added into the schedule to increase the land size available in native reserves to around 13 per cent. The ANC's 'Freedom Charter' aimed to abolish racial restrictions on land acquisitions, proclaiming 'restriction of land ownership on a racial basis shall be ended' (Congress Alliance 1955). The Charter's promise was not to end private landownership, but its racialisation. But who would get the land? The Charter's answer was 'those who work it'. There was no further elaboration about who works the land. Perhaps none was necessary. By 1955 South Africa was primarily an agricultural economy, with large scores of young African men driven to work as cheap labour on the farms. Alive to this reality, the Charter promised to end cattle robbery, abolish forced labour and farm prisons.

Abolish racialised private property

ANC policy historically favoured the abolition of the Natives Land Act, dividing up the land among those who work it, enabling all to own the land. Dr A.B. Xuma's 'African's Claims in South Africa' is a case in point. Point 8 of the Bill of Rights states:

> The right to own, buy, hire or lease and occupy land and all other forms of immovable as well as movable property, and the repeal of restrictions on this right in the Native Land Act, the Native Trust and Land Act, the Natives (Urban Areas) Act and the Natives Laws Amendment Act (Xuma 1943).

Yet it was not explained how the land would be acquired by the state to enable non-racial ownership. Z.K. Matthews, the president of the Cape wing of the ANC in 1953, was the first to point to 'expropriation' of land as the mode of land acquisition for distribution: 'I think the state would have to use wide powers of expropriation. Experience shows that depending on people's willingness to sell is not sufficient'. But who would be faced with expropriation? Matthews says: 'We would expropriate absentee landlords and give both white and black farmers an opportunity or having their own land' (in Ngcukaitobi 2022). Matthews was also clear that compensation would have to be paid, although he would not expatiate on the methodology for calculation. Expropriation of land for wider distribution accordingly seems to have been part of official policy since the days of the 'Freedom Charter'.

The 'Freedom Charter' did not envisage the end of private property as such. Its concern was to end racialised private property ownership, which remained ANC policy for decades, until the 1990s. In the early 1990s, an opportunity arose for a negotiated settlement in South Africa. The ANC produced its own draft Bill of Rights, titled 'A Bill of Rights for a Democratic South Africa'. The land provisions were much more extensive than they had ever been in the entire history of the ANC. It retained the right to acquire and own private property, regardless of race. The apartheid government of F.W. de Klerk passed the Abolition of Racially Based Land Measures Act 108 of 1991 to scrap the Natives Land Act and all other laws that restricted property ownership by reference to race. The ANC's Bill of Rights did not mention expropriation of land, but it intended to give the state generic powers to take steps to overcome the effects of discrimination on property ownership. Without compulsory acquisition of land, the steps to overcome the effects of racial property distribution would have been stillborn. Hence, the draft Bill of Rights considered 'just compensation', which would take into account the need to strike an equitable balance between the public interest and the needs of those affected. An independent tribunal, subject to an appeal in court was envisaged as the body to take decisions regarding compensation.

The Reconstruction and Development Programme and its malcontents

Despite the draft Bill of Rights, much confusion remained about how to undo the effects of land dispossession. How would the land be placed in the hands of the dispossessed? A document produced in the ANC's first year of power, the Reconstruction and Development Programme (RDP), contained the clearest and most comprehensive vision for the future. In the chapter dealing with land, it acknowledged the fundamental truth about the limits of the market and law in land redress: 'The abolition of the Land Acts cannot redress inequities in land distribution. Only a tiny minority of black people can afford land on the free market' (ANC 1994). For the first time in a policy announcement, the ANC recognised the constraint of the 'free market' on land distribution. The existence of the 'free market' was despite the almost complete absence of any meaningful participation by black people, except as unfree labour, in the economy. The clever trick of apartheid was to superimpose free market ideas over a fundamentally unjust land system. Apartheid had created a thriving land market. But most importantly, that market was part of the larger market economy of the country.

The ANC's recognition that land transactions had to be subjected to the larger market economy was also influenced by global developments.

By February 1989, the collapse of the Soviet Union, the only platform that provided an alternative economic system to Western-style capitalism, was imminent. Francis Fukuyama, an expert on the Soviet Union, argued that if history is understood as a 'single, coherent, evolutionary process' when one factors in all human experiences, the collapse of the Soviet Union marked its end (1989). The most remarkable development of the previous quarter of a century had been the exposure of the weaknesses of military dictatorships, whether communist-led or right-wing dictatorships. What remained in their place were 'stable, liberal democracies' spanning different regions and cultures across the globe. With the ideological contestation settled, liberal principles in economics, the 'free market', had gained universal acceptance across the globe, producing unprecedented levels of material prosperity. There was no realistic possibility of reversing this, Fukuyama argued. Only in the fringes of the politics of the world was dictatorship tolerated. Elsewhere, it was fought, with many struggles underpinned by liberal economics. Old regimes once sworn enemies of the capitalist world order had come to appreciate its inevitability. Thus, History had ended.

As Louis Menand commented in the *New Yorker*, Mikhail Gorbachev had announced, in a speech at the United Nations on 7 December 1988, that the Soviet Union would no longer intervene in the affairs of its Eastern European satellite states. Those nations could now become democratic. 'It was the beginning of the end of the Cold War' (Menand 2018). The end of the Cold War reverberated across the globe. One of the ANC's sources of funds in the struggle against apartheid was the Soviet Union. If it could not support its European allies, it definitely could not do so in relation to its African allies. A few years before the watershed Gorbachev announcement, Oliver Tambo had met with Fidel Castro, then leader of Cuba, a strong military supporter of the ANC in exile. Castro was keen to understand how the 'Freedom Charter' would be implemented should the ANC assume power. Economic clauses, such as the nationalisation of banks and mines, had proved impossible to apply in certain contexts in Cuba, he had warned. For instance, Cuba's communist government wanted to nationalise private industry, only to discover that a controlling shareholder was registered in Florida, not in Cuba (Callinicos 2004: 601). And any seizure of assets in Cuba would have a ripple effect in the United States. Tambo was learning the hard lessons of a globally connected economic order. The ANC could no longer make the same demands as it did when it was formed in 1912. Castro suggested coexistence with the enemy, compromise and a negotiated settlement. The dream of a revolutionary insurrection had vanished. Freedom would come, but as process, not an event. And the story of freedom would also define the story of the land: a compromise.

The lessons from Castro were still fresh when the ANC conceived its RDP document. No longer driven by the communist dogma of the Cold War era, the ANC faced the real task of meeting the aspirations of multitudes of Africans, originally excluded from landownership by conquest, and now by the structure of the market. Property rights could not be abolished. They were integral to the functioning of the market economy. Racial distinctions in property ownership could. Yet as the RDP pointed out, the market could not abolish racialised property ownership. Something else had to be done. The RDP sought to navigate this treacherous terrain. Appropriating the language of the market, it promised a 'fundamental land reform programme', which would be 'demand driven' (ANC 1994). It would supply residential and productive land to the poor and aspirant farmers. Land reform should 'raise incomes and productivity'. Land should be used productively, for agricultural and residential purposes. Two programmes were proposed, land restitution and land redistribution.

Still, the question remained: how was land to be acquired? Nationalisation of land having been dismissed, 'market and non-market' mechanisms would be used (ANC 1994). The redistribution programme was intended to benefit those who needed land, but could not afford it. The state would use 'land already on sale and land acquired by corrupt means from the apartheid state or mortgaged to state and parastatal bodies' (ANC 1994). Annual land sales at the time accounted only for 6 per cent of land, and no reliable figures could be produced for illegally acquired land or state-owned land. The fact was that the majority of agricultural and residential land was in private hands. The RDP outlined the use of expropriation with compensation to acquire the land. It was envisaged that substantial funding would be provided by the state as part of the land reform programme. Land restitution emerged as an adjunct to land redistribution. Its aims were far more modest than the redistribution programme: to redress the loss of land caused by forced removals, which could be traced back to the Natives Land Act of 1913.

Constitutional land clause: Its wax and wane

On 27 April 1994, Nelson Mandela won the election as the first president of the democratic South Africa. A new Interim Constitution came into effect on that day. Unlike the previous policy positions of the ANC, the property rights provisions of the Interim Constitution had legal force. It contained a general expropriation of private property for public purposes, provided that just and equitable compensation was paid, as may be agreed or decided by a court. But historical claims to land would be resolved through the actual return of the land to the dispossessed. This was known as the 'restitution programme'. Some of the legal concepts in this programme include:

- restoration of rights in land: the return of land rights or a portion of land dispossessed after 19 June 1913 as a result of past racially discriminatory laws or practices;
- a right in land: defined broadly to include registered and unregistered rights, and customary rights in land;
- restitution of land right: which includes restoration and payment of equitable redress;
- racially discriminatory practices: to mean racially discriminatory practices, acts or omissions, direct or indirect, by –
  (a) any department of state or administration in the national, provincial or local sphere of government;
  (b) any other functionary or institution which exercised a public power or performed a public function in terms of any legislation.

In summary, the scheme was this: Those who could prove that they were dispossessed of rights in land after 19 June 1913 had the right to claim for restitution of rights in land. The claims would not be made directly to the landowners, but to the state, which would first mediate between the claimant and the registered owner. If mediation failed, steps could be taken through a legal process to force the restitution, provided that just and equitable compensation was paid. Restitution was the ultimate victory in the struggle. For the first time since the 1913 Natives Land Act Africans could finally 'return home'.

The RDP set a target of 30 per cent for the redistribution (not restitution) of land in the first five years of the new democratic government. The target was based on annual sales of land, which at that stage were estimated at 6 per cent. To test the model, some figures are necessary. In 2013, the state conducted a land audit. The director general of the Department of Land Affairs, Mdu Shabane, reported that their results showed that 'some 14% is registered State land and 4% recently surveyed State land, while 79% is in private hands. Of this 79%, a significant percentage is owned by private individuals, companies and trusts. We are unable to identify foreign ownership because the system does not provide for that analysis' (Department of Rural Development and Land Reform 2013: 6). A later audit, conducted in 2017, showed that

> whites own 26 663 144 ha or 72% of the total 37 031 283 ha farms and agricultural holdings by individual landowners; followed by Coloured at 5 371 383 ha or 15%, Indians at 2 031 790 ha or 5%, Africans at 1 314 873 ha or 4%, other at 1 271 562 ha or 3%, and co-owners at 425 537 ha or 1% (Department of Rural Development and Land Reform 2017: 2).

The gender figures are equally depressing:

> Individual males own 26 202 689 ha or 72% of the total farms and agricultural holdings owned by individual owners; followed by females at 4 871 013 or 13%. Male-female own 3 970 315 ha or 11%, co-owners 655 242 ha or 2%, and other 1 379 029 ha or 3% (Department of Rural Development and Land Reform 2017: 2).

The outcomes of this audit were disputed by the Institute of Race Relations. Its main claim was that the methodology did not account for restituted land or land acquired through the redistribution programme. If that land was added, the Institute of Race Relations argued, a 'far more balanced picture' would emerge (Institute of Race Relations 2018). Yet, there are two problems with the Institute of Race Relations' argument. The overwhelming majority of restitution claims are not individual claims; they are claims involving large numbers of people. Adding those claims to the figures hardly changes the picture of individual claims. Furthermore, urban restitution claims have tended to be settled by financial compensation, rather than resettlement (Bohlin 2004). Accounting for these simply changes the 'entry' into the land balance sheet, but hardly places land in the hands of the claimants. The stubborn reality is that landownership patterns still reflect a bias in favour of white owners. What was envisaged by the Natives Land Act in 1913 remains the truth in 2024.

That the patterns of 1913 remain true to date is a big claim. Some context is therefore necessary. The core of apartheid was 'political',[1] primarily implemented by carving out certain parts of the country as Bantustans and self-governing territories and denying franchise to black people living in white South Africa (Seekings and Nattrass 2005: 18). Jeremy Seekings and Nicoli Nattrass note that Bantustanism was consolidated by 1976 when the Transkei was granted 'independence', with the consequence that those living in the Transkei lost their South African citizenship and any economic and social entitlements attached thereto (2005: 21). Coloured people, who had lost their place in the national voters' roll in the 1950s, were completely removed from municipal voters' rolls by the 1970s. The reservation of political activity for whites persisted until 1984 when an attempt was made to include Indians and coloured people in the Tricameral Parliament, an attempt that was met with popular rejection. Universal franchise was only restored in 1994. By that stage, apartheid had produced social and economic inequalities. The change in the political landscape did not change the social and economic circumstances of black people – it simply allowed the possibility of change.

The expectation, however, of a gradual move towards an egalitarian society promised by the Constitution has not materialised. Instead, the economic upper echelons have de-racialised at a remarkable pace, effectively creating a superclass, while poverty at the bottom half of the population has become entrenched. Sampie Terreblanche has explained that one of the most 'remarkable' developments in the first eight years of a democratic South Africa has been the enrichment of the top 20 per cent of African households and the simultaneous impoverishment of the bottom 40 per cent (2002: 132). While the income of the top 20 per cent of African households (about 6 million people) increased by more than 60 per cent, that of the bottom 40 per cent (about 18 million people) declined by almost 60 per cent. In certain quarters there is some cynicism about the development of the 'black elite'. Terreblanche, however, considers this 'a healthy phenomenon', without which a new South Africa would not have been possible. But this development underscores a broader claim that I make in this chapter – that the development of the black elite has coincided with the development of a black underclass. Current discourses on inequality tend to mask the truth about the superclass/underclass dynamic that is South Africa's reality.

While the evidence of a causal connection between these two phenomena is absent, they can both be seen as by-products of societal transformation. The upward mobility of the black elite is explained by the shift in political power from white minority rule to a representative government, which opened up the possibilities of social and economic advancement where they previously did not exist (Terreblanche 2002: 133). The explanation for the deterioration in the living standards of the black underclass, however, presents certain complexities. It can be explained by apartheid racism, governmental incompetence, a stagnant economy unable to produce sustainable employment opportunities and the indifference of the black elite towards the plight of the poor. These factors combined have entrenched the poverty of the black underclass. The rule of law then is constrained by changing patterns of inequality – while race maintains its significant role in our popular imagination, it no longer fully explains inequality in landownership. We should therefore find other explanations for the persisting crisis of inequality in landownership.

Official explanations for the failure

Why is this the case then? In 2019 the Constitutional Court decided a case about the slow pace in resolving labour tenant claims,[2] which reflected on land reform generally. Placing land reform at the centre of South Africa's future, the court lambasted the state for placing in jeopardy the 'constitutional security and future' of South Africa. Little had been achieved in the first 30 years of freedom to undo the legacies of centuries of conquest, the court noted. The reason given was the state's 'failure to practically manage and expedite land reform measures in accordance with constitutional and statutory promises'. The consequence was to 'profoundly [exacerbate] the intensity and bitterness of our national debate about land reform'. The Constitution, the courts and the laws were not to blame. At fault was the 'institutional incapacity of the Department to do what the statute and the Constitution require of it'.[3]

The court is not alone in placing the blame at the foot of the state. In November 2017 former president Kgalema Motlanthe delivered the *Report of the High-*

Level Panel on the Assessment of Key Legislation and Acceleration of Fundamental Change. On land, it was a devastating critique of the state's performance in the settlement of restitution claims. The Panel found that despite the cut-off date for land claims being 1998, there were more than 7 000 unsettled claims and over 19 000 yet-to-be-finalised 'old order' claims. As the Constitutional Court noted, the Panel

> exposes the extremely slow rate of restitution claims, concluding that it will take up to 35 years to finalise all old order claims, 143 years to settle new order claims and, if land claims are reopened, up to 709 years to complete Land Restitution. Institutional capacity is evidenced in lack of skills and capacity, overlapping and conflicting claims, and inconsistent monetary awards. A possible explanation for these shortcomings is the lack of sufficient resources. However, the budget for land restitution has been consistently underspent; this evidences how severe problems lie in implementation and the capacity of the system itself.[4]

There is yet another feature of the land story: chronic, systemic and endemic corruption. Claimants are corrupt. Landowners are corrupt. The state's officials are corrupt. In 2018, the Special Investigating Unit, one of our corruption-busting institutions, presented its findings and recommendations on fraud, corruption and maladministration in the land reform programme (Special Investigating Unit 2017). Its basic finding was that the entire system of land reform was rotten from the bottom up. The Unit examined 148 individual land reform projects between 2011 and 2017 and found that 1 in 4 was fraudulent. There were also bogus beneficiaries. In one of the more egregious claims, the Unit concluded that although:

> grant applicants represented to the Department that 49 individuals were to benefit from the grant concerned and/or be intimately involved in the farming project and/or obtain meaningful rights in the land concerned (and hence effect land reform), the only real intended applicant/beneficiary was and always were to be the initiator of the grant application and his family. Almost all the other applicants/beneficiaries constituted a 'rent-a-crowd'.

The abovementioned misrepresentation impacted materially on (inter alia) the value-for-money and feasibility of the project criteria concerned, which resulted in the Department, having been fraudulently induced to approve and pay the grant (Special Investigating Unit 2017: 13).

In another case, it was found that there were gross misrepresentations in the price of land acquired by the state for resettlement, with one having been overvalued by some 100 per cent. The state did not contest the findings of the Unit. Purporting to act in terms of the recommendations of the Unit, it announced that some 58 farms would be returned. No further actions were announced, nor was there any evidence presented that any farms were returned to the state. Corruption, it seemed had captured the land reform project.

What about the structure?

These are seductive explanations. Not only do they condemn the state, they also embed solutions. We may consider removing the current minister or the current director general, or even replace the entire Commission for the Restitution of Land Rights with a brand-new organisation. We may also prosecute all those guilty of corruption. A combination of these strategies would finally place the land in the hands of claimants. As tantalising as these explanations sound, they are only tentative. A fuller picture can only emerge upon a structural analysis of the land restitution programme. Only then can we know whether the criticism that focuses on the misconduct of the managers of the restitution programme is only a partial answer or provides a complete answer to the restitution quagmire.

Theunis Roux, formerly professor of property law at the Wits University law school, has urged that we should locate the land reform programme in the political economy of the transition (2008). This accords with the views of Sampie Terreblanche, former professor of economic history at Stellenbosch University, who has commented on the decisive influence of the mineral-energy complex in the politics of transition (2012: 63). Terreblanche notes that the declaration of the state of emergency by P.W. Botha, the state president in 1986, convinced the global capitalist class with financial interests in South Africa that the 'crisis of accumulation' was real. If they did not intervene, an implosion was a real possibility. The concern of European and American businesses, including Anglo

American, which had South African interests, was the 'socialist orientation of the ANC'. They began having secret meetings and discussions with selected leaders of the ANC and separately with Botha's government. When Nelson Mandela was released from prison in 1990, these business interests intensified their attempts to influence the policy direction of South Africa. Mandela himself was party to some of these discussions in his capacity as president of the ANC. These discussions would reach their climax in October 1993, when the National Party under F.W. de Klerk formally surrendered power. De Klerk promulgated the Transitional Executive Council Act 151 of 1993. It allowed the ANC to nominate an equal number of representatives, together with the government, to make all crucial political decisions until elections were held in April 1994. Terreblanche recalls that the Transitional Executive Council ran out of money. It asked the International Monetary Fund (IMF) for the cash. The IMF agreed, but as a condition, the Transitional Executive Council was required to sign an undertaking on South Africa's future economic policy. When the Transitional Executive Council agreed to sign the statement, it was in effect agreeing to a neo-liberal economic policy (Terreblanche 2002: 96).

Tito Mboweni, former governor of the South African Reserve Bank, confirms Terreblanche's account. In a speech given in 2004 to the Black Management Forum, Mboweni explained the 'crisis' faced by South Africa, which resulted in Derek Keys approaching the IMF for funding: 'One of the problems/constraints facing the economy at that time, was that the country only had foreign reserves to cover for plus/minus three weeks of imports' (Mboweni 2004). The end result, as Mboweni explains, was that the government approached the IMF for funding through the Compensatory and Contingency Financing Facility. He disputes that this funding came with conditions, although he agrees that the IMF asked the Transitional Executive Council to sign a statement on economic policy, which Terreblanche refers to (Terreblanche 2002: 96). From Mboweni's perspective, the ANC's assent to the IMF's request did not contradict ANC policy as enunciated in the Ready to Govern strategy document at the time (Mboweni 2004). The IMF document simply required the ANC to follow a 'prudent' macroeconomic strategy. Yet, the core of Terreblanche's argument is that ANC policy should be seen in the context of the global forces at play. And this need not be viewed as a bad thing, simply an explanation for the agreements reached in the transition.

The IMF statement on economic policy committed the ANC to 'neoliberalism and market fundamentalism' (Terreblanche 2018).

The adoption by the ANC of the Growth, Employment and Redistribution (GEAR) strategy of 1996 was seen as a triumph of neo-liberal economics. Terreblanche has referred to this as part of the 'elite compromise', which excluded the possibility of a comprehensive redistribution policy (Terreblanche 2002). Thus, from the outset, land reform's redistributive potential was constrained by an overarching economic policy.

Economic pressure during the transition was not the only constraining factor. There were political pressures too. Roux (2008) has referred to the Truth and Reconciliation Commission (TRC) as a political model designed for the transition. A unique attribute of the TRC was that it allowed victims to face the perpetrators of crimes. One of its advantages was that the truth about the violations of human rights could be ventilated. If financial reparations were paid, they could take place alongside a larger scheme of psychological reparation for the pain of the violations.

However, perpetrators of human rights violations in the form of dispossession were shielded from coming to terms with the continuing trauma of their past actions. In its legislative design, the process of restitution begins with a claim lodged with a state body, the Commission for the Restitution of Land Rights, which must conduct a preliminary investigation. If the claim can be settled, mediation is conducted under the auspices of the Commission. The state acts as guarantor for payments, either to the claimants or the landowner. Landowners can ask the state for 'market value' of their land, which, for the most part, is paid. If actual restitution is not feasible, the state guarantees a cash payment for the claimant. Not only do landowners never have to face the dispossessed, they also do not have to make any financial contribution to the resettlement. Where market value is paid, they may in fact make a handsome profit from the enterprise. The scheme, facilitated and funded by the state, hardly accounts for the grief, the trauma and the pain of dispossession. It is entirely transactional. The consequence is that there is no scope for truth about the circumstances of the dispossession to be unearthed. If any truth is told, it is often in the acrimonious circumstances of a court trial. Dumisa Ntsebeza, former commissioner of the TRC, has recalled that there were voices inside the TRC who tried to have land dispossession included in the terms of reference of the TRC. With hindsight, Ntsebeza now thinks the country missed an opportunity to subject beneficiaries of forced removals to the same scrutiny of the TRC.

The political decisions included deciding on a cut-off date for land claims. The year 1913 was chosen – for obvious reasons. This was the year of the Natives Land Act. Yet there were many other possible contenders. Why not 1910, the year of the formation of the Union of South Africa, or 1894, the year of the Glen Grey Act? The state published its *White Paper on South African Land Policy* in 1997 (Department of Land Affairs 1997). It contained several justifications why 1913 was chosen as a cut-off year. It began by noting that the state did not believe it was possible to

> address pre-1913 claims through a judicial process, such as that laid out in the *Restitution of Land Rights Act* or Aboriginal Title Arguments that have been used in countries such as Canada and Australia. In South Africa, ancestral land claims could create a number of problems and legal-political complexities that would be impossible to unravel (Department of Land Affairs 1997: 77–8).

The paper claimed that since 'most historical claims are justified on the basis of membership of a tribal kingdom or chiefdom', this 'would serve to awaken and/or prolong destructive ethnic and racial politics' (Department of Land Affairs 1997: 78). The paper warned of 'overlapping and competing claims where pieces of land have been occupied in succession by, for example, the San, Khoi, Xhosa, Mfengu, Trekkers and British' (1997: 78). The merit of these claims is highly dubious. Ancestral claims are just as complex as any other claim, based on membership of a community or family. What determines the validity of these claims is not the date of dispossession, but the quality of evidence available. It is not obvious that the more recent a claim, the easier it is to prove. Nor does it follow that older claims, or dated claims are not easy to prove. Stories of dispossession of the 1800s were carefully written down by the colonisers, inscribed in books and archived. Arguments about difficulties in the excavation of the evidence in support of ancestral claims are exaggerated and unpersuasive. Justifications based on competing and overlapping claims are equally unattractive. All claims, including the post-1913 claims, face the same risk.

Arguments advanced in favour of the 1913 cut-off are weak. The date makes sense only if seen as part of the compromises of the transition. The date was attractive to both parties at the negotiating table. Its disruptive effects would be minimal. White landowners could live with the date because by 1913, the wars of dispossession were over. In the Cape, the last frontier war – Ngcayechibi's War – was fought in 1877–9. In Zululand, the last war was in 1879. In the Transvaal, the greatest symbol of resistance, King Sekhukhune I, had died in 1884. The Orange Free State had fallen into the hands of the Boers long before 1913. Rights to the land had long been cemented by 1913. This, of course, is not to downplay the significance of 1913. The Natives Land Act formalised land conquest, giving it the imprimatur of law. At the same time, the ANC could accept the 1913 land bargain because its own struggle for freedom was tied up with the 1913 Natives Land Act. There was thus an element of symbolism in agreeing to a package that confined the date to 1913, not before. Land claims beyond the restitution process could be referred to the redistribution arm of land reform, it was hoped. Thus, at the outset, the potential of the land restitution project was limited by a predetermined date, which excluded the vast majority of the dispossessed from reclaiming land.

Constrained by economics, politics and legislation, land claimants could perhaps look to the courts for legitimate claims to the land. But the design of the land claim adjudication process places a state institution, the Commission on Restitution of Land Rights, at the centre, not the claimant. Land claimants often have to force the Commission to take their matters to court after numerous unexplained delays. One such claim was that of the Kusile community in KwaZulu-Natal. A restitution claim was lodged in 1998. The Commission did nothing until 2004, when it confirmed that the claim was valid. And it did nothing again until 2009 when it was forced by the claimants to take the matter to court. When the matter was heard in court, in 2010, the file was in a shambolic state, leading the court to remark:

> The Commission, as an organ of state, bears an obligation to ensure that the work of this court is not impeded by inadequate investigation and that time is not unnecessarily spent on claims which, in the form in which they were referred to the Court by the RLCC [Regional Land Claims Commission], can manifestly not succeed. The RLCC failed in this duty.[5]

If the economic, political and legal infrastructure of the restitution process is framed in a way that works against the interests of the dispossessed, it might legitimately be asked whether it should not be discarded in its entirety. Ben Cousins, an expert in land matters, has made an explicit case for the closure of the restitution process (2016). He suggests that the restitution programme was probably a mistake and proposes that the majority of restitution claims should be settled, not by resettlement but through cash compensation. This is because the process is 'complex, cumbersome, conflict-ridden, expensive, consumes scarce capacity and yields few sustainable benefits' (2016: 18). He also points out that since relatively few claimants desire to be producers on the land, it may be wise to seek closure by the payment of compensation through standard settlement offers, as for most urban land claims. Cousins suggests:

> In some instances, where it is clear that claimants genuinely want to farm, restoration of at least some of the land should be considered, and in some contexts joint ventures with private sector partners will make sense. The department needs to focus primarily on land redistribution and tenure reform, the most important thrusts of land reform (2016: 18).

Abandon land restitution?

Should the state abandon the restitution programme? We should remember why the restitution programme was started in the first place. Its alignment with 1913 was deliberate. It was intended to answer the problem of forced removals, arising from the Natives Land Act. Let us now consider the problem of forced removals, which the restitution programme was intended to resolve.

The Native Trust and Land Act was passed in 1936. It made provision for the establishment of the South African Native Trust, a state agency to administer trust land 'for the settlement, support, benefit, and material welfare of the natives of the Union'.[6] While disallowing individual landownership by black people, the Act introduced trust tenure. The South African Development Trust, a government body, was responsible for purchasing land in 'released areas' for black settlement. These laws were consolidated by the Group Areas Act of 1950, which established group areas and imposed restrictions over land purchases in certain areas. Three racial groups were recognised: whites, natives and coloureds. Each of these groups had to stay in a designated area, failing which they would be criminally prosecuted. In 1966, the Group Areas Act was re-enacted to consolidate the laws relating to the establishment of group areas and to regulate control over the acquisition of immovable property and the occupation of land and premises. Under this Act, 'natives' were referred to as 'Bantu'. Massive, forced removals followed. According to one set of figures, it resulted in the removal of 305 739 coloureds, 155 230 Asians and only 5 898 whites by 1976 (Freund 1984).

As for Africans, the figures for forced removals are staggering. The estimates for 1960 to 1983 exceed 3 million people, including approximately 1 200 000 people removed as a result of evictions from farms; 600 000 people removed as a result of 'black spot' removal and homeland consolidation; 700 000 people removed under the pass laws from major metropolitan areas; 130 000 people removed from urban informal settlements, owing also to laws curbing 'illegal squatting'; and 900 000 people removed as a result of the group areas legislation (Surplus People Project 1983).

Writing in 1970, Cosmas Desmond sought to 'illustrate what apartheid means in practice' in his book *The Discarded People* (1970: 21). Between May and September 1969, he travelled across South Africa to document apartheid's forced removals. His book, which describes the horrors of the policy, resulted in an international outcry as it laid bare the callous ingenuity of apartheid South Africa – discarding its unwanted people. It describes how several million Africans were removed from their homes on land that had been declared 'white'. They were categorised as 'superfluous' and 'unproductive'. They were not wanted in white cities, towns and farming areas. Declared aliens in the land of their birth, they were dumped in the homelands, which were often remote rural slums, areas for which the government took no responsibility. Whoever was not seen as useful to the 'European labour market' – the aged, the unfit, widows, women with dependent children and families, and even professionals such as doctors, attorneys, agents, traders and industrialists who were 'not essential for serving their compatriots in the European areas', whoever was in an area regarded as 'badly situated', was discarded (1970: 43). Desmond summed up the policy:

I have seen the bewilderment of simple rural people when they are told that they must leave their homes where they have lived for generations and go to a strange place. I have heard their cries of helplessness and resignation and their pleas for help. I have seen the sufferings of whole families living in a tent or a tiny tin hut. Of children sick with typhoid, or their bodies emaciated with malnutrition and even dying of plain starvation. The enormity of relocation only hits the traveller when driving through the bantustans . . . Dispossession and exclusion lie at the heart of apartheid (Desmond 1970: 23).

The restitution programme is the only land reform programme that speaks directly to the injustice of dispossession. It answers what the struggle was about. It provides a succour for injustice. Not any act of injustice, a specific act of injustice: a forced removal of a person by a particular person at a particular time. It makes visible, tangible, human, the concepts and notions of struggle. Restitution gives dispossession a human face. A hundred years after the initial act of forced removals, families still celebrate the return to the land. In this sense, restitution is more than the material benefits from the productive use of the land. It is about memory, the public affirmation that black people's pain matters and restoration of lost identities. This is why restitution of land remains the most contentious and the most important of the land reform programmes, and is likely to remain so for some time to come.

Notes

1. Although this idea is contested by Merle Lipton in *Capitalism and Apartheid* (1985).
2. *Mwelase and Others v. Director-General for the Department of Rural Development and Land Reform and Another* (CCT 232/18) [2019] ZACC 30; 2019 (11) BCLR 1358 (CC); 2019 (6) SA 597 (CC).
3. *Mwelase and Others v. Director-General for the Department of Rural Development and Land Reform and Another*, para. 41.
4. *Mwelase and Others v. Director-General for the Department of Rural Development and Land Reform and Another*, footnote 87.
5. *Midlands North Research Group and Others and Kusile Land Claims Committee v. the Regional Land Claims Commissioner, KwaZulu-Natal and Others* LCC21/2007, para. 38.
6. Section 4(1) of the Natives Trust and Land Act, No. 18 of 1936.

References

ANC (African National Congress). 1994. 'The Reconstruction and Development Programme (RDP): A Policy Framework'. https://omalley.nelsonmandela.org/index.php/site/q/03lv02 039/04lv02103/05lv02120/06lv02126.htm (accessed 18 September 2023).

Bohlin, A. 2004. 'A Price on the Past: Cash as Compensation in South African Land Restitution'. *Canadian Journal of African Studies* 38 (3): 672–87.

Callinicos, L. 2004. *Oliver Tambo: Beyond the Engeli Mountains*. Cape Town: David Philip.

Congress Alliance. 1955. 'The Freedom Charter'. https://www.anc1912.org.za/the-freedom-charter-2/ (accessed 18 September 2023).

Cousins, B. 2016. *Land Reform in South Africa Is Sinking: Can It Be Saved?* https://www.nelsonmandela.org/uploads/files/Land__law_and_leadership_-_paper_2.pdf (accessed 18 September 2023).

Department of Land Affairs. 1997. *White Paper on South African Land Policy*. https://www.gov.za/sites/default/files/gcis_document/201411/whitepaperlandreform.pdf (accessed 18 September 2023).

Department of Rural Development and Land Reform. 2013. *Land Audit*. https://static.pmg.org.za/140515state_land_audit.pdf (accessed 18 September 2023).

———. 2017. *Land Audit Report: Phase II: Private Land Ownership by Race, Gender and Nationality*. https://www.gov.za/sites/default/files/gcis_document/201802/landauditreport 13feb2018.pdf (accessed 18 September 2023).

Desmond, C. 1970. *The Discarded People: An Account of African Resettlement in South Africa*. Johannesburg: Christian Institute of South Africa.

Feinberg, H.M. 2006. 'Protest in South Africa: Prominent Black Leaders' Commentary on the Natives Land Act, 1913–1936'. *Historia* 51 (2): 119–44.

Feinberg, H. and A. Horn. 2009. 'South African Territorial Segregation: New Data on African Farm Purchases, 1913–1936'. *Journal of African History* 50 (1): 41–60.

Freund, B. 1984. 'Forced Resettlement and the Political Economy of South Africa'. *Review of African Political Economy* 11 (29): 49–63.

Fukuyama, F. 1989. 'The End of History?' *The National Interest*. https://pages.ucsd.edu/~bslantchev/courses/pdf/Fukuyama%20-%20End%20of%20History.pdf (accessed 18 September 2023).

High-Level Panel on the Assessment of Key Legislation and Acceleration of Fundamental Change. 2017. *Report of the High-Level Panel on the Assessment of Key Legislation and Acceleration of Fundamental Change*. https://www.parliament.gov.za/storage/app/media/Pages/2017/october/High_Level_Panel/HLP_Report/HLP_report.pdf (accessed 18 September 2023).

Institute of Race Relations. 2018. *Who Owns the Land: A Critique of the State Land Audit*. https://irr.org.za/reports/occasional-reports/files/who-owns-the-land-26-03-2018.pdf (accessed 18 September 2023).

Lipton, M. 1985. *Capitalism and Apartheid: South Africa, 1910–1984*. Totowa, NJ: Rowman and Allanheld.

Mboweni, T. 2004. 'The Foundation Has Been Laid'. Speech at the Black Management Forum Corporate Update Gala Dinner, Gallagher Estate, 18 June. https://www.resbank.co.za/content/dam/sarb/publications/speeches/speeches-by-governors/2004/171/18+June+2004.pdf (accessed 18 September 2023).

Menand, L. 2018. 'Francis Fukuyama Postpones the End of History'. *New Yorker*, 27 August. https://www.newyorker.com/magazine/2018/09/03/francis-fukuyama-postpones-the-end-of-history (accessed 18 September 2023).

Ngcukaitobi, T. 2022. 'The Freedom Charter and the Land Question'. *Politicsweb*, 12 July. https://www.politicsweb.co.za/opinion/the-freedom-charter-and-the-land-question (accessed 18 September 2023).

Roux, T. 2008. 'Land Restitution and Reconciliation in South Africa'. In: *Justice and Reconciliation in Post-apartheid South Africa*, edited by F. du Bois and A. du Bois-Pedain, 144–70. Cambridge: Cambridge University Press.

Seekings, J. and N. Nattrass. 2005. *Class, Race, and Inequality in South Africa*. Pietermaritzburg: University of KwaZulu-Natal Press.

Surplus People Project. 1983. *Forced Removals in South Africa: Volume 1*. Cape Town: Surplus People Project.

Terreblanche, S. 2002. *The History of Inequality in South Africa, 1652–2002*. Pietermaritzburg: University of Natal Press.

———. 2012. *Lost in Transformation: South Africa's Search for a New Future since 1986*. Johannesburg: KMM Review Publishing.

———. 2018. 'The Co-optation of the African National Congress: South Africa's Original "State Capture" '. *Pambazuka News*, 25 January. https://www.pambazuka.org/node/98467 (accessed 18 September 2023).

Thompson, L. 2001. *A History of South Africa*. New Haven: Yale University Press.

Special Investigating Unit. 2017. *2017 Interim Report*. https://www.siu.org.za/wp-content/uploads/2017/12/SIU-Interim-Report-2017.pdf (accessed 18 September 2023).

Union of South Africa. 1916. *Report of the Natives Land Commission: Volume 1*. Cape Town: Government Printers. chrome-extension://efaidnbmnnnibpcajpcglclefindmkaj/https://uir.unisa.ac.za/bitstream/handle/10500/9779/SC_NL_1_Part1.pdf?sequence=1&isAllowed=y (accessed 18 September 2023).

Xuma, A.B. 1943. 'African Claims in South Africa'. Presented at the Conference of the African National Congress. https://www.sahistory.org.za/archive/african-claims-south-africa-dr-xuma-anc-conference-1943 (accessed 18 September 2023).

CHAPTER 3

South Africa's Broken Policy Design

Quo Vadis?

Pali Lehohla

Four centuries at a glance

The period prior to the abolition of apartheid in South Africa consists of four distinct phases. First was three centuries of an initial colonial encroachment that started in 1652, second was an evolution of settler colonisation through the establishment of the Boer republics in the 1800s, third was the establishment of the Union in 1910 and five decades of an apartheid state that started from 1948 and entrenched itself in all public life through the establishment of a republic in 1961 and fourth came the dawn of democracy in 1994.

According to John Dugard (2008): 'In 1966, the [United Nations] General Assembly labelled apartheid as a crime against humanity (resolution 2202 A (XXI) of 16 December 1966) and in 1984 the Security Council endorsed this determination (resolution 556 (1984) of 23 October 1984)'. The dawn of democracy brought hope to a country where the apartheid state apparatus had lost control of both the politics and the economy. The country was burdened with debt and could no longer sustain friendly relationships with Western powers. The total collapse of the apartheid state was precipitated by the collapse of the Soviet Union whose threat to the hegemony of the West had, in part, been the limited oxygen for the fragile and waning diplomatic ties the West held with South Africa.

The South Africa of our dreams at the dawn of democracy embraced significant hope and this hope survived fifteen years. The beginnings can be seen in the miracle transition and a peaceful election in 1994, hosting the Rugby World Cup in 1995, hosting the Africa Cup of Nations in 1996, hosting the African Union

Constitutive Act in 2002, hosting the Summit on Sustainable Development in 2002, and hosting the International Federation of Association Football (FIFA) World Cup in 2010. In a number of television interviews, Archbishop Desmond Tutu referred to South Africa as the Rainbow Nation and Nelson Mandela often said that what South Africa had achieved was a 'miracle'. In his well-known 'I Am an African' speech, upon the adoption of South African Constitution in 1996, Deputy President Thabo Mbeki (1996) captured the spirit and letter of the Constitution.

The period until the FIFA World Cup in 2010 can be seen as the pharaonic years of abundance. The post-2010 period, while in part a result of the accumulation of weaknesses that emerged in the first sixteen years of abundance, generated its own massive inputs of destruction into the subsequent period. To date, South Africa has been subjected to thirteen years of visible disappointment across the economy, society and in political organisation. Features that expose policy design challenges are reflected in deplorable performance in key indicators. Behind each of these statistics are hearts and minds, families and communities, including their hope and despair. The quest for the promise of reconstruction and development beckons. It is thus just to ask what has happened to the spirit of the Reconstruction and Development Programme (RDP) after it was perverted and captured in the Growth, Employment and Redistribution (GEAR) strategy.

This chapter is an attempt to understand the role that the disjointed history of scenario-building in South Africa played and what important contributions and lessons these have in the theory of change in systems, as well as how an enjoined scenario-building culture can contribute significantly to building the capacity and reconstituting the state in ways that offer beneficial change. It explores the choices in economic policy design that South Africa made and what these policies achieved. More importantly, the chapter makes invaluable suggestions as to what remedy – if any – is possible to get South Africa on a path of sustained and sustainable growth and development. The chapter highlights the significance of scenarios as tools of foresight and what role scenario quantification plays. This brings more clarity to the path and choices the country opens itself to. It allows the space of policy deliberations and consensus anchored in economic laws of motion to open and how they provide a pragmatic path that South Africa could pursue out of its chronic economic crisis.

Scenarios and why they matter

Scenarios are tools of foresight and provide conditions for defining a future in which everyone has the possibility of participating and bonding around the required sacrifices to be made towards achieving that future. Koosum Kalyan says: 'Scenarios encourage disciplined, systematic thinking about the future. A critical role of scenarios is to present different possible pathways into the future to challenge conventional thinking and to encourage debate in a process of learning' (in Le Roux and Maphai 1993: 8).

Scenarios are undergirded by a body of observations and public impulses of what the future may look like, given actions by society at home and elsewhere abroad. More generally, given the circumstances at hand, scenarios usually project outcomes. Ideally, scenarios should be accompanied by a path to the said outcome. But once there is general agreement, there must be robust tools of quantification to ascertain the feasibility of the promise. This is especially so in matters relating to the economy. Once a path is interrogated, a variety of quantified policy permutations can be undertaken. For example, in November 2016, President Juan Manuel Santos of Colombia and Rodrigo Londoño, the leader of the Revolutionary Armed Forces of Colombia – People's Army, signed a ceasefire agreement in Havana after 50 years of war. Among the elements that made possible a very difficult settlement was a commitment to reducing multidimensional poverty in the stronghold areas of Revolutionary Armed Forces of Colombia – People's Army activists.

In 1991–2, a group of 22 academics, activists, politicians and businessmen, from across the ideological spectrum, met at Mont Fleur and came up with four scenarios about what might happen in South Africa in the next ten years. Facilitator Adam Kahane had this to say:

> Based on my experience in strategic planning, this is one of the most meaningful and exciting scenario planning exercises ever undertaken. The project has shown that a group of experts and leaders with very different perspectives and backgrounds can develop a common understanding of what is going on now in South Africa and might (and should) go into the future. This seems to me to be a very positive sign for the future of the country (in Le Roux and Maphai 1993: 7).

The four scenarios range across a spectrum from the best outcome through to the very worst outcome. Each outcome is based on a set of assumptions about the future, given the current reality and possible plausible future influences.

Why scenarios matter

Mithun Sridharan, Naishadh Nannaparaju and Nehaal Patankar write about why scenarios matter and point out:

> Scenario planning is identifying a specific set of uncertainties, different 'realities' of what might happen in the future of your business. It helps participants to consider the 'what-ifs' of tomorrow, whether those are desirable or undesirable states. The simple task of imagining a different future can help to challenge the status quo and encourage creative thinking, which can lead to the development of more thoughtful and resilient plans (Sridharan, Nannaparaju and Patankar 2021).

Scenarios are developed to enable participants to test out possible decisions, analyse their impacts given the conditions in each scenario, and come to an agreement on a preferred course of action. Determining a path is based on an explicit articulation of policies and also the quantification of such policies. This is particularly true in the field of economic policies. Economics observes laws of motion and quantification is about capturing these laws of motion. Unfortunately, in the case of South Africa, our experience of scenario-building in the past 29 years is chequered, to say the least. Not only are policies generally not the centre of scenarios, but they are also not quantified, and they thus fail to mimic the laws of motion of the economy. However, since 2018, South Africa has had the benefit of the Indlulamithi South Africa Scenarios 2030 Trust, which has incorporated the principles of the law of economic motion into its scenario-building.

The architects and architecture of South African scenarios

A number of scenarios have been constructed for South Africa. A key feature of most scenario-building in South Africa is that they tend to be constructed exclusively outside government or exclusively inside government. However, those constructed outside government have attempted to negotiate their scenarios with government, but there has never been an attempt by government to engage those it has generated internally for common consumption outside government. I am aware of several scenarios that have come to the fore, but this chapter concerns itself with only four, constructed between 1991 and 2018.

Of the four scenarios discussed here, two were crafted within government and the other two were outside government. The two by government are *Memories of the Future: South African Scenarios to 2014* (PCAS 2003a) and *South Africa Scenarios 2025: The Future We Chose?* (PCAS 2008). The two scenarios generated outside government are the Mont Fleur scenarios (Le Roux and Maphai 1993) and the three scenarios generated by the Indlulamithi South Africa Scenarios 2030 Trust (2018).

While they were generated outside government, the Mont Fleur scenarios had a profound impact on shaping and informing the path South Africa chose for its transitional settlement. They had the benefit and privilege of receiving attention from South Africa's negotiators on the eve of its democracy. The Indlulamithi scenarios were constructed at the height of state-capture rhetoric and have continued to evolve, but have not had the same impact on government policy. However, the Indlulamithi scenarios continue to interpret outcomes of government policy positions and it may well be they will shed light on the dynamics of the Overton Window of political possibilities where the impossible becomes the inevitable.[1]

It is important to note that instead of the two government-based scenarios of the second and third administrations, the government produced the *National Development Plan 2030* (NDP) (National Planning Commission 2012). Unfortunately, instead of offering a number of possible scenarios, the NDP presents itself as the only scenario and has no alternative possibilities. In some quarters, the NDP is viewed as the only scenario because it has the authority of the South African government behind it, but it has often been fiercely criticised for its lack of a practical plan to implement its aims and goals, despite the use of the word 'plan' in its title.

It is important to note the difference in the design, content and form of the four scenarios. Scenarios must have at least four essential attributes. First, scenarios are storylines about the future path the country might take. Second, they should interpret economic and social policy and bring in policy as a design feature. Third, they should quantify the policy options. And, fourth, they should design a road map towards the policy eventuation.

The Mont Fleur scenarios had a storyline and an economic policy structure, but lacked quantification and a road map. The two government scenarios were rich in storylines and *Memories of the Future* embedded a policy design and road map, through the *Accelerated and Shared Growth Initiative – South Africa (ASGISA)* (The Presidency 2006), but *South Africa Scenarios 2025* had neither a policy design nor a road map. What they both lacked was quantification of the policy options. The Indlulamithi scenarios are the only ones that developed a storyline and policies to accompany each outcome, as well as quantifying the inputs and outcomes of the policy permutations and drawing up a road map towards the attainment of each of the possible outcomes.

Mont Fleur scenarios

The team that compiled the Mont Fleur scenarios was led by Adam Kahane. Mont Fleur projected four scenarios for South Africa: Ostrich, Lame Duck, Icarus and Flight of the Flamingos. These scenarios are outlined below:

- *Ostrich*, in which a negotiated settlement to the crisis in South Africa is not achieved, and the country's government continues to be non-representative.
- *Lame Duck*, in which a settlement is achieved but the transition to a new dispensation is slow and indecisive.
- *Icarus*, in which transition is rapid but the new government unwisely pursues unsustainable, populist economic policies.
- *Flight of the Flamingos*, in which the government's policies are sustainable and the country takes a path of inclusive growth and democracy (Le Roux and Maphai 1993: 1).

Koosum Kalyan, who was involved in the Mont Fleur deliberations and in the initial presentation of the scenarios to President Nelson Mandela, revealed some intimate details of how, when they finished presenting the scenarios, Madiba said: 'Now I have a plan I can communicate to South Africa and the world.' He was so convinced by the Mont Fleur Scenarios that he said: 'Go communicate this in the townships of Soweto and our villages. Go to the world and tell them that South Africa now has a plan.'[2]

By the end of his term in office, Madiba could tick off which of the Mont Fleur scenarios were not applicable: South Africa was not the Ostrich – the government was representative. It was not the Lame Duck – it did not pander to the West but was never fearful of entering environments that were controversial to the West, such as affirming friendship with Cuba and a commitment to Palestine and Western Sahara. South Africa had a principled position of driving its statehood thesis based on the struggle of the oppressed. The successful political transition was rapid, spawned by Madiba becoming a de facto president in taking charge of the country after the assassination of Chris Hani.

The Icarus scenario touches on an important topic in this chapter and the main fulcrum of negotiation and settlement:

> *Icarus* warned of the dangers of a new government implementing populist economic policy. This message – coming from a team which included several of the left's most influential economists – was very challenging to the left, which had assumed that government money could be used to eradicate poverty quickly. The business community, which was worried about Icarus policies, found the team's articulation reassuring. The fiscal conservatism of the Government of National Unity (GNU) was one of the important surprises of the post-election period (Le Roux and Maphai 1993: 2–3).

Sampie Terreblanche's analysis is helpful in trying to assess what benefits emerged from avoiding the Icarus scenario. In fact, his view is not whether the Icarus scenario was to be avoided, but rather that Icarus was a neo-liberal framing that sugar-coated the implausible Flight of the Flamingos as an appropriate outcome capable of bringing economic justice to South Africa. Little wonder that even those who expected an uphill battle were pleasantly surprised by the fiscal conservatism of the GNU.

In 2013, in a memory of Terreblanche's life, titled 'Economist, Critic of Neoliberal Capitalism, and a Veteran in the Struggle for Justice', Drucilla Cornell (2013) had this to say about how he analysed the 1994 settlement and how this could relate to the United States: 'Terreblanche argues that the capitulation to neoliberal capitalism in the United States form was decided behind closed doors. Economics, in other words, was not subject to constitutional negotiations.' She also points out that Terreblanche observed that the African National Congress (ANC) government 'inherited a deep state within which it finds itself exercising politics of democratic capitalism to the interests of the capitalist class'.

While the Mont Fleur scenarios inspired Madiba and succinctly captured the questions to be asked about the possibility, nature and pace of the transition, the scenarios did not help the government to deliver on what the RDP envisaged in terms of building the economy.

Memories of the Future

There is no doubt that democracy as a process of electing who should lead you was inclusive and proceeded apace from 1994, but the envisaged benefits of the Flight of the Flamingos in the Mont Fleur scenarios were not achieved in the economic calculus for the majority. It was thus time not only for reaction to this outcome, but also for a correction to the course taken.

In this regard, the second administration began to ask questions about the real accrual of inclusive democracy and growth. The government commissioned *Towards a Ten Year Review* (PCAS 2003b) and *Memories of the Future* (PCAS 2003a), which captured the key areas of concern and also pointed to weaknesses in the government's economic policy design. The scenarios were captured and evolved through a period of intense contestation.

Responses to these initiatives were uneven. But the Congress of South African Trade Unions (COSATU) unleashed a scathing critique, saying: 'In sum, while the review repeatedly points to the need for vigorous government intervention to ensure job creation and equity, its proposals do not measure up to the task' (COSATU 2003: 40).

As a consequence of the scenario construction, the focus was on addressing the macro-organisation of the state. The key questions asked were: is the state well equipped and has it the appropriate capacity to deliver on the task ahead? The scenarios provided a design that would enable the government to interrogate these questions. The scenarios, as described in *Memories of the Future*, are outlined below:

- *S'gudi S'nais* is characterised by conflicts between those who have-a-lot versus those who have-a-little. Although the world has taken heed of 'the fire next time' warnings from the developing world, and multilateralism now prevails, South Africa loses its place in the jostle for investment and access to international trade. Growth is initially high but perversely so, surging to 6–8%, but later dropping to an average of less than 1% per annum by the decade's end as the impact of social fragmentation takes effect. This is a result in the main of a situation in which the rich elect to ignore social inequalities and concentrate on selfish and often unethical amassing of wealth, and the state is indecisive in containing this.

- *Dulisanang* describes a much more considerate and inclusive society. South Africa has responded to heightened global insecurity and endemic economic crisis by turning inwards to its own resources. Although growth is low, participation in the economy is high and compassionate values emerge strongly. And, despite limited resources, the state delivers on its social obligations but is unable to sustain such social delivery in the long-term due to low growth.

- *Skedonk* is characterised by deep social divisions. Unilateralism in global relations is the order of the day, and the globe is beset with conflicts. Growth in South Africa is confined to areas like tourism and is stubbornly low all decade. The poor get poorer, AIDS has had devastating effects on the population, and, by decade's end, there is high unemployment and general social dislocation within South Africa. In this instance, the political and economic leadership would have responded to the unfavourable global climate by 'waiting for Godot' – through inaction.

- *Shosholoza* envisages South Africa, by the end of the Second Decade of Freedom, as a diverse and tolerant society whose local economy is surging ahead like a sleek express train. The global economy is also booming, and multilateral institutions have brought stability to the world's most intractable political conflicts. High economic growth has brought millions of jobs and much greater participation in the robust economy. South Africa is well poised for a third decade of freedom, and opportunity and prosperity (PCAS 2003a: 2–3).

In his State of the Nation addresses, President Mbeki focused the nation on what the art of building on previous victories should consist of and achieve. In his 2005

State of the Nation address, he said: 'During each one of the years that make up our Second Decade of Liberation, including this one, we must achieve new and decisive advances' (Mbeki 2005).

The emergence of the *Memories of the Future* scenarios was accompanied by the implementation plan of ASGISA from 2005 onwards. It had two main objectives of policy interventions that would be realised through a high economic growth path. It was envisaged that this approach would have the positive impact of halving both poverty and unemployment in the decade from 2004 to 2014. This period was marked by the best economic growth rates, a rapid decline in the high levels of unemployment and the expansion of social services. The country was heading towards the 2010 FIFA World Cup and a Shosholoza scenario was unfolding out of the ashes of the Mont Fleur scenarios.

However, towards the beginning of 2007, it was clear that the political landscape had become toxic. An intra-party battle had begun, triggered by law enforcement. In his State of the Nation address of 2008, President Mbeki captured the emerging crisis in the land:

> I am aware of the fact that many in our society are troubled by a deep sense of unease about where our country will be tomorrow . . . Most obviously it would be irresponsible to ignore these and other concerns or dismiss them as mere jeremiads typical of the prophets of doom. The real challenge is to respond to them in a manner that conveys the definite message to everybody in our country and the millions in Africa and elsewhere in the world who watch our country with keen interest, that we remain firm in our resolve to continue building the kind of South Africa that has given hope not only to our people, but also to many others outside our borders (Mbeki 2008).

The *Memories of the Future* scenarios, like their predecessor, the Mont Fleur scenarios, were not quantified. While execution of these scenarios did take into account the required policies to drive the outcomes, as shown in ASGISA, they suffered the same limitation of quantification as the Mont Fleur scenarios. Thus, it became difficult to evaluate their success.

South Africa Scenarios 2025

The three scenarios were described as below:

- *Not Yet Uhuru*: A Government strongly committed to accelerating economic growth struggles in the face of deteriorating global conditions and severe ecological challenges . . . (PCAS 2008: 13).
- *Nkalakatha*: Determined to play a more central role in the economy, Government prioritises poverty reduction and skills enhancement by articulating a national vision and fostering partnerships . . . (PCAS 2008: 30).
- *Muvhango*: Despite an initial resurgence of the economy, and positive world conditions, the Government battles to govern well . . . (PCAS 2008: 49).

Of all the scenarios, the 2025 scenarios had the worst outcomes options. Unlike Mont Fleur, *Memories of the Future* and the Indlulamithi scenarios, which were graded from worst to best options, there was no gradation here. What was also critical was the precision with which the option we settled for would pan out. This was in terms of the content of the scenario and the timing of it.

Continuity of change for the better or a rapture for the worst

In a discussion document for its 51st National Congress, the ANC elaborated on the subject of 'continuity and change: continuity in the substance of policy and change in the detail as well as style, pace and effectiveness of implementation' (ANC 2002). The end of the first decade of freedom and the march into the second was a hope-filled historical moment. In terms of the scenarios, *Memories of the Future* had opened up the space for course correction and continuity of change. But a different set of circumstances began to rear their head in 2007. Most important in these developments was the ANC's Polokwane Elective Conference, which saw President Mbeki's term of office coming to an end and the expectation was that this would also herald the end of his term as the president of the party, but he decided to contest. The deputy president of the ANC, Jacob Zuma, had been fired as the country's deputy president, but he held the party position as a deputy president. He was acquitted on a charge of rape, and charges against him relating to corruption were dropped on the eve of the elections. That then paved the way for him to be inaugurated as the country's president. Another challenge that emerged was the economic meltdown of the global financial and economic system in 2008 and South Africa was not spared, although its financial systems did not plunge into the turmoil that plagued the United States.

ASGISA had shown some important signals of the art of the possible in economic growth and job creation on the back of a massive infrastructure build towards the 2010 FIFA World Cup, but the financial crisis caused South Africa to get back to a policy stance that pre-dated *Memories of the Future*. We were back in the Mont Fleur scenario of austerity, but this was exacerbated by the spillover from political infighting and emerging corruption. Key civil servants, especially in the Presidency, left the public service. Those who replaced them did not stay long.

In the fullness of the recent state-capture investigation, it has emerged that the country had started a journey towards a Muvhango scenario. Zuma focused on the NDP, which galvanized all political parties into agreeing to its importance. However, the NDP is not a plan. It remains a document that diagnosed the problems and never moved forward with what could be a plan. Ten years after its launch in August 2012, the NDP should be up for review, but it is difficult to conceive of what it will provide.

Chief Justice Zondo tabled his report on state capture a year ago. Before then, as the Zondo Commission continued its work, the president of the ANC addressed the party in unambiguous terms on the matter of state capture in August 2020:

> As the inheritors of the legacy of Luthuli, Tambo and Mandela, we must be honest with our people and ourselves. We must acknowledge that our movement, the African National Congress, has been and remains deeply implicated in South Africa's corruption problem . . . Today, the ANC and its leaders stand accused of corruption.
>
> The ANC may not stand alone in the dock, but it does stand as Accused No. 1. This is the stark reality that we must now confront . . . Those who see the ANC as a path to wealth, to power, to influence or status must know that they do not belong in our movement. They must change their ways or they must leave (Ramaphosa 2020).

It is now the end of 2023 and, six months ago, Chief Justice Zondo, realising the limited progress on the uptake of the Commission's report, hazarded that it may not be a surprise for South Africa to have another state capture and said on 22 June 2023: 'If there was another attempt at state capture, Parliament would fail to prevent it' (Gerber 2023). He was also emphatic that state capture had placed South Africa's democracy at risk. The gap between pronouncements and action has remained palpable.

This is an appropriate time to shift to the Indlulamithi scenarios and understand what these may imply in the context of continued executive inaction on corruption.

Indlulamithi scenarios

In 2016, at the height of so-called state capture, South Africans began to say that 'Zuma Must Fall' and campaigned for the donning of orange overalls for wrongdoers. The situation required South Africans to put on their thinking caps and the country found itself seeking to undertake a scenario exercise – outside of government for the first time since the Mont Fleur scenarios of 1991–2. Hosted by the Mapungubwe Institute for Strategic Reflection (MISTRA), the Indlulamithi scenarios were launched on 21 June 2018. MISTRA possessed clear knowledge on scenarios because many of its key employees were part of the history of building scenarios in South Africa and for the South African government. MISTRA thus became the perfect home for incubating the Indlulamithi scenarios. There are three scenarios, as described on Indlulamithi's website:

- *Gwara Gwara*: The ups and downs of a false dawn. In a nation torn between immobility and restless energy, Gwara Gwara embodies a demoralised land or disorder and decay.
- *iSbhujwa*: An enclave bourgeois nation. Epitomising a loose-limbed, jumpy nation with a frenetic edge, iSbhujwa is a South Africa torn by deepening social divides, daily protests and cynical self-interest.
- *Nayi le Walk*: A nation in step with itself. In a precise sequence of steps, Nayi le Walk choreographs a vision of South Africa where growing social cohesion, economic expansion and a renewed sense of constitutionalism get South Africa going. (Indlulamithi South Africa Scenarios 2030 Trust 2018).

The Indlulamithi scenarios possess what everyone would look for in modern tools of foresight. The scenarios have well-crafted storylines, with very a clear articulation of the outcome of what each storyline means. They are based on a solid foundation of data from Statistics South Africa (Stats SA), the South African Reserve Bank and the National Treasury. These data are updated at regular intervals as and when released by these institutions.

Applied Development Research Solutions (ADRS) has more than twenty years of building models, especially those that relate to South Africa. ADRS ensured that each of the Indlulamithi scenarios has a clear policy analysis that drives the outcome of each of these scenarios. The policies are modelled on the laws of motion of economics. Finally, on the basis of the design, the models are quantified to generate not only traceable inputs, but also what the outputs, outcomes and impact are likely to be over time and space. Here we have, at last, a clear path towards outcomes. For instance, in contrast to the deafening silence on a conglomerate of policies deriving a particular outcome in the scenarios referred to earlier, under the Indlulamithi scenario construct, each scenario has specific policies and policy stances, a road map or path and quantification of societal outcomes, presented through a range of measured indicators.

The process of generating the econometrically determined outcomes follows the laws of motion and logic of economics. The logic is driven and implemented through a set of relational equations. It is operated on web-based, high-speed computers. Results from the computation and what-if scenarios are available instantaneously for interrogation by policymakers. This capability allows for deliberating options on the basis of sophisticated and logical analysis of evidence. The quantification of both thought processes and inputs makes the Indlulamithi scenarios both sophisticated and exceedingly helpful.

The Indlulamithi scenarios have acquitted themselves not only in unravelling the complex and endemic challenges of unemployment, poverty and inequality, but also the economics, technology and econometric modelling undergirding the construction of the scenarios shows a rare capability of explicating shocks of seismic proportions arising from other factors. In this instance, a set of Covid-19 scenario outcomes was created on a gradation of three outcomes of severe, moderate or mild Covid-19 manifestation.

The assessment of Indlulamithi scenarios is that, as of 2023, South Africa has stepped deeper into a Gwara Gwara scenario, a nation 'torn between immobility and restless energy'. Gwara Gwara captures appropriately South Africa as a land of disorder and decay.

In the next section, we put together the economic and social performance of post-apartheid South Africa and bring together data that measures the country's socio-economic performance.

South Africa's performance

Scenarios came to an end as practice in government in 2009, but they are nonetheless useful indicators of the progress or decline of the South African state in terms of its avowed goals. The performance of the state over the last 28 years will be assessed by interrogating what the implication and response to each of the scenario outfits were.

Economic performance

According to Stats SA (2005: 25), real gross domestic product (GDP) growth in South Africa in the first eight years of post-apartheid South Africa averaged 2.6 per cent. After adopting the *Memories of the Future* scenarios in 2003 and implementing ASGISA, South Africa's growth rose above 4 per cent, as tracked through Stats SA's quarterly GDP series (Stats SA n.d). This represented four years of the highest and longest growth ever from 2004 to 2007. This was abruptly interrupted by the financial crisis of 2008, which slowed down growth and with it came the first negative growth in 2009. After 2009, growth did not rise to pre-financial-crisis years and declined into 2021 and is poised to notch lower than 2 per cent up to the year 2026. This is, in part, because of Covid-19.

It must also be noted that in the 23 years of tracking economic performance, real GDP growth was higher than long-term real interest rates in only 5 of the 23 years. This suggests that borrowing for economic expansion remains unattractive.

Employment outcomes

As far as labour market performance is concerned, unemployment has been the biggest challenge in South Africa. By and large, unemployment affects young black people and black females, in particular. The labour market performance by race (as tracked by Stats SA's *Quarterly Labour Force Survey*) from 1994 to 2021 reveals a trend that is very persistent (Stats SA n.d.). At the one end of the race-age spectrum, there is high upward mobility while, at the other end, the labour market remains stuck and regressive.

Skilled employment

The results from Stats SA's *October Household Survey* series from 1994 to 1999 and *Quarterly Labour Force Survey* series from 2000 to 2021 reveal that whites and Indians of all ages in particular have had the greatest expansion over the 27-year period from 1994 to 2021 (Stats SA n.d.). In fact, for the age cohorts of 15–24 and 25–34, youth employment for these race groups actually doubled. For those aged 15–24, the level of employment in the skilled category rose from 17 to 35 per cent and from 25 to 49 per cent for Indian and White youth, respectively. The corresponding figures for black and coloured people were 9 to 10 per cent and 7 to 11 per cent, respectively. A calamitous outcome is for the 25–34 cohort. For black and coloured individuals in this cohort, employment in the skilled category moved from 17 to 15 per cent and from 14 to 20 per cent, respectively.[3]

Unemployment outcomes

The period of rapid economic growth spurred by the ASGISA intervention saw unemployment in South Africa drop from 27.1 per cent in 2003 to 22.9 per cent by 2008, according to Stats SA (2008: 3). But the trend has since been reversed from the time of the financial crisis of 2009. According to Stats SA's 2012 *Quarterly Labour Force Survey*, however, unemployment had risen to 25.2 per cent and over a period of ten years and compounded by Covid-19, official unemployment has reached 31.9 per cent.

The expanded definition has always been higher by about ten percentage points above the official unemployment rate. Thus, while official unemployment in 2002 was 30.5 per cent, the expanded definition was of the magnitude of 40 per cent. And according to the Stats SA *Quarterly Labour Force Survey, Quarter 2* (2022: 39), the expanded definition of unemployment stood at 44.1 per cent by 2022.

Poverty outcomes

Stats SA measures poverty in two ways, the money metric and the multidimensional measure. However, to date, the only official measure of poverty is the money metric. Despite attempts to address it, poverty in South Africa has remained stubborn. Statistics South Africa (2015) determined in its report on poverty outcomes that the money metric measure was 55.5 per cent for the upper-bound poverty line. This meant that a ratio of slightly more than one in two South Africans was poor. By any measure, this poverty rate is very high. Since then, living conditions have continued to decline, precipitated by, among other things, the drought in 2016, which impacted on subsistence agriculture.

Around 2016, South Africa became restless because of what has proved to have been rampant corruption, which continues to this day. The Zondo Commission was established to interrogate the state of corruption in South Africa and the findings are compelling – and, because of corruption, society has certainly been the poorer in a number of ways, the most obvious of which is energy poverty, to which South Africa remains exposed.

By 2020, the situation across the world deteriorated in terms of both livelihoods and lives. In 2021 Stats SA determined new poverty measures, using upward inflation-adjusted levels. Given the deteriorating economic prospects from 2017 onwards, it is not inconceivable to come to the conclusion that poverty has deepened in South Africa under the yoke of Covid-19, the fires of July 2021 and the floods that followed.

Decline in transport volumes

The design of the South African apartheid state was for a small minority, which should have had a concentrated infrastructure in a relatively small geographic space. However, its spatial geography was influenced by spatial attributes of agriculture and mining, but also by national security concerns. In that regard, infrastructure had to spread across the entire republic. The apartheid state's approach to infrastructure development had the unintended consequence of those it discriminated against benefiting from the infrastructure. One such infrastructure was rail transport. According to Stats SA's Land Transport Survey series, by 2008, as many as 52 million passenger trips per month were undertaken (Stats SA n.d.). Save for a three-week strike in May 2010, the volume of passenger trips in South Africa continued to be high. But, after 2014, there was a decline in monthly volumes of rail transport. By the beginning of 2020, well before Covid-19, the number of trips had declined to just about 10 million. Covid-19 collapsed passenger trips in 2020 and, by 2022, passenger transport had completely collapsed. Only a million trips could be undertaken at that point. The wanton destruction of rail infrastructure is to blame for this deplorable state of affairs. Hardship and poverty are bound to ensue.

Economic prospects for South Africa

The 2022 Estimates of National Expenditure projected unemployment at 38.3 per cent by 2026 and debt is estimated at 83 per cent (National Treasury 2022). South Africa is not expected to perform on the export front and its growth will not exceed 3 per cent. The question that has to be posed is whether alternative routes have been explored in terms of policy design. To date, they have not. So the question that the people of South Africa and the South African state has to engage is: what lessons have emerged from this parlous state of affairs? In this regard, it may be good advice to go back to the scenarios and ask pertinent questions. This holds the prospect of opening up a new avenue for South Africa, as it explores a new and different future out of the doldrums, away from teetering towards becoming a failed state. The question is why South Africa has such a high propensity for choosing the worst-case scenario. Only in the case of the *Memories of the Future* did South Africa navigate towards a positive scenario of Shosholoza. Unfortunately, this was short-lived.

Reflections on scenarios and conclusions

Almost three decades since the demise of apartheid, the Indlulamithi Trust points out that the indications are that South Africa is poised to become a Gwara Gwara state.[4] According to the *Review of the 'National Development Plan 2030'*, for the period 2010–19, unemployment averaged 26 per cent, economic growth was 1.68 per cent and debt-to-GDP ratio came out at 47.8 per cent (National Planning Commission 2020). The economic performance for the period to 2026 holds no prospect for better. According to the budget speech of the finance minister, the average economic growth by 2026 will be 1.3 per cent, unemployment will be above 38 per cent and gross government debt will be 83 per cent (Godongwana

2022). These indicators suggest that South Africa is faced with almost a similar economic meltdown experienced during the dying years of apartheid, when economic growth was low at about 1.3 per cent.

The current situation threatens the foundational pillars of South Africa's democratic order. The twin collapse of apartheid and the Soviet Union had a lot to do with how the West calibrated – to its advantage – how the post-Cold War settlement would deliver a unipolar and neo-liberal polity. Into the path of the post-apartheid state was laid a royal carpet that would deflect the economic path of the RDP it had designed as an instrument of liberation. The Mont Fleur scenarios influenced South Africa to adopt a different sequence and path to its development. The similarities in terms of economic consequences in Russia and South Africa from the shock therapy of the International Monetary Fund (IMF), spawned by what can be considered as a direct result of entering a neo-liberal economic pact, tend to reveal a lot of what weakened the post-apartheid South African state.

In her book titled *How China Escaped Shock Therapy: The Market Reform Debate*, Isabella M. Weber (2021) draws important lessons in the comparison she makes between China and Russia, and these are very cogent for South Africa, especially as a member of the BRICS (Brazil, Russia, India, China and South Africa) bloc.[5] This is especially as the world recalibrates its options in the post-Covid-19 period and amid the uncertainty surrounding the outcome of the Russian war in Ukraine.

While under the Mont Fleur scenarios, South Africa managed to avoid the Ostrich, the Lame Duck and Icarus, the question asked by Weber in the comparison made between China and Russia, which remains unanswered and relevant for South Africa, is one on the Flight of the Flamingos. Why did the promise of the Flight of the Flamingos fail to eventuate? The answer can be found in the mantra that Milton Friedman successfully preached in Russia of free market fundamentalism accepted by Mikhail Gorbachev, but China's Deng Xiaoping rejected. Instead, he continued on an age-long Chinese market of an ever-normal granary. In the case of *Memories of the Future* (PCAS 2003a), South Africa was certainly on the right path. In fact, in part, the action by the government represented a critique of the Mont Fleur scenarios and *Memories of the Future* represented a path of correction (however limited) and demonstrated positive results. This attests to the beneficial use and application of scenarios.

When the financial crisis came in 2008, South Africa managed its way through exceedingly well. It was during the period leading to the financial crisis that South Africa grew through a sustained four-year period and this was above 4 per cent and even danced with 6 per cent. Stats SA's Labour Force Survey showed that unemployment dropped from 27.1 per cent in 2002 to 22.9 per cent by 2008 (n.d.).

Polokwane and its aftermath

After the ANC's upheaval at Polokwane occurred, followed by the 2008 financial crisis, South Africa lost the plot. It dumped the Shosholoza scenario and the interventions contained in *Memories of the Future*. It opted for the Muvhango scenario in *South Africa Scenarios 2025*. Over the next ten years, policy options and the conduct of politicians and the administration mutated from the Muvhango scenario to the Gwara Gwara option in the Indlulamithi scenarios.

While the Mont Fleur scenarios were fully embraced, a critique emerged and correction was undertaken, with clear results of a move towards Shosholoza. However, this was short-lived. Not only did South Africa in this way fail to stay the Shosholoza course, but for the first time, it abandoned scenarios as a basis for planning. In the place of scenarios was the adoption of the NDP, which by itself is not a bad thing. However, the NDP, with all the possible benefits it could have ushered in, was not a plan and there was no effort to translate it into a plan. It was out of public exasperation and anxiety that the Indlulamithi scenarios were discussed and born in 2018.

Scenario quantification

The Indlulamithi group insisted on quantifying scenarios. This process set these scenarios apart from any of the others. The Indlulamithi scenarios had access to seven critical assets and skills provided by ADRS:

- They access laws of motion of economics. The scenarios were undergirded by strong understanding and application of laws of motion of economics.
- The economic models were empirical models constructed substantively out of Stats SA data, as well as data from the National Treasury and the South African Reserve Bank.
- The models are driven by complex computing power and they mimic and approximate the laws of motion of economics.

- They are web-based and therefore constitute collaborative tools, which are necessary in policy design.
- The exercise also had the benefit of validation of application by officials. The Gauteng Province deployed its own officials to be trained on the models and they constructed Growing Gauteng Together and chose the Nayi le Walk scenario to achieve their goals (but could not because they needed national provincial collaboration in policy design, which did not take place).
- To demonstrate their robustness, the models were used to draw scenarios on Covid-19 and generated pathways and results that are not far from the reality of the consequences of South Africa's response to Covid-19.
- The team created a training programme under the Economic Modelling Academy (EMA) in June 2022 to train people in the use of these models. The training will empower public servants, the private sector and non-governmental organisations to engage in training on policy design. The EMA is located at the Gordon Institute of Business Science (GIBS):

For Professor Morris Mthombeni, the dean of GIBS, establishing the relationship and locating EMA at GIBS was a no-brainer because the programme provides invaluable operational tools that bring the public and private sector into a sensible conversation on economic policy foresight, policy design, implementation and evaluation. Professor Somadoda Fikeni, the chairperson of the Public Service Commission, and no stranger to tools of modelling deployed at EMA, pointed in his keynote address to how these tools were deployed in the identification and quantification of policy options that defined the three outcomes in the Indlulamithi scenarios. Professor Tinyiko Maluleke, the Deputy Chairperson of the National Planning Commission, saw in EMA an addition to the arsenal of economic models that would be available to the Commission, but more importantly that public service could be exposed to the training. This, he concluded, would be useful not only in the contestation that models and modellers always have, but by enabling the users to understand the underlying economic debates, the approaches and the rationale for specific choices. Ms Phelisa Nkomo, who approaches economics from a feminist perspective welcomed the intervention of EMA because it provides an integrated lens on both economic and social impacts.

This is especially so in modelling multidimensional poverty as a forward-looking planning tool (Lehohla 2023).

Indlulamithi Scenarios 2035: A crystal ball into 2024

Many speakers emphasised the importance of foresight upon the launch of the EMA at GIBS. It is important to heed the Indlulamithi Scenarios 2035, which provide a new lens on which way South Africa may go, following on their Scenario 2030 (Indlulamithi South Africa Scenarios 2030 Trust 2023). Indlulamithi concluded that South Africa had arrived in the worst-case scenario and even deepened the Gwara Gwara scenario, in which South Africa is now reeling as a land of disorder. With emergent local and global vicissitudes, the Indlulamithi Trust had to establish which direction South Africa would take. The three new scenarios consist of three paths that South Africa could choose to follow and the underlying attributes of each of those are provided. They seek to answer the following questions:

> What is South Africa like in 2035?
> How prosperous are its people?
> How cohesive is its society?
> How far has it come in the 40 years since the dawn of democracy?
> (Indlulamithi South Africa Scenarios 2030 Trust 2023)

To explicate the scenarios, Indlulamithi introduced a bird culture to capture the moment. This is in the form of the Hadeda, the Vulture and the Weaver bird. They relate appropriately on prospects and possibilities, both good and bad, that South Africa can choose or has already chosen. This might help South Africa to wake up from its ill-fated end.

Hadeda home
- As social trust broke down leading up to 2035, South Africans retreated, pulling those close to them closer.
- People cluster in enclaves to protect themselves or hire private armadas to shield them from harm.
- Economy sputters along: mining is more mechanised, agriculture battles the weather, manufacturing growth is stalled.

- An unjust transition to renewable energy is resisted. Clean water is scarce; acid rain, power outages and wild weather threaten food production.
- Women bear the brunt of poverty and violence; crime rates remain high.
- Unemployment is around 37%; youth unemployment is 55% (Indlulamithi South Africa Scenarios 2030 Trust 2023).

Vulture culture

- South Africans have rallied together, primarily in opposition to the government, displaying an unprecedented level of unity and shared concern.
- Authoritarian, populist coalitions hold significant power, implementing restrictive laws that curtail media freedom and tightly regulate civil society, leading to a notable erosion of democratic values.
- The economy has experienced a prolonged period of stagnation since 2029, with every economic measure indicating contraction. South Africa now faces an impending fiscal catastrophe, resorting to desperate borrowing to keep the country financially afloat.
- The labor market presents a dire situation, with over half of adults facing unemployment. Official figures reveal an alarming 43% unemployment rate, with youth unemployment soaring above 60%.
- One-third of South Africans experience food insecurity, going to bed hungry at least once a week, highlighting a pressing issue of inadequate access to basic sustenance.
- Organized crime has taken advantage of a weakened and disorganized state, seizing the initiative and further exacerbating the challenges facing South Africa (Indlulamithi South Africa Scenarios 2030 Trust 2023).

Weaver work

- In the mid-2020s, discontent over high unemployment and crime sparked widespread public protest against an indecisive government striving for stability amidst global challenges.
- Social movements, unions, interfaith alliances, and NGOs orchestrated marches and strikes, exerting substantial pressure on government and businesses in response to prevailing issues.

- During the unrest, artists played a vital role in nurturing protest culture, drawing inspiration from sports and cultural icons, further fueling the movement.
- Post-2029 elections, a broad coalition government focused on 'listening to the people', effectively addressing concerns and attracting unprecedented foreign direct investment.
- The fiercely contested 2034 election saw major coalition parties improve positions, solidifying their influence, reshaping the political landscape.
- A managed shift to a greener economy spurred sector expansion, resulting in consistent unemployment reduction since 2029. Current rates stand at 18%, with youth unemployment at 35%, marking a significant improvement (Indlulamithi South Africa Scenarios 2030 Trust 2023).

The options articulated under the three scenarios are possible, but increasingly with the noisy Hadeda scenario of even more parties, the way is paved for the Vulture culture. The platform for the Vulture culture is predicated on the deep Gwara Gwara state we have successfully created. All indicators point to South Africa that is poised for a failed state of a Vulture culture. There exists a cancel culture and this is captured by Madiba's place of last breath. His house in Houghton, a mere six kilometres from Mandela Square in Sandton, where his gigantic statue awes the world, has turned into a pigsty. Not the Mandela family, not the ANC, not the Nelson Mandela Foundation, not the municipality under which Houghton resides, not the Gauteng provincial government, nor the national government are moved by this state of affairs. This shows clearly that not only has the Gwara Gwara state long been upon us, but the Vulture culture has now fully taken over.

The current state of affairs is not about policies, but about winning the elections. It is a state of national madness, where the ruling party is fighting hope against hope for survival. At no point in the history of South Africa have statistics been so elevated, not for informing policy but as a pole against which the drunkard seeks to secure support. The '50 + 1' in the national election has gained meteoric mentions, much like the word 'idiot' on Google, which has become an outlier and risen above the average but asymptotically since the turn of the century. Every discussion is whether the ruling party will poll above 50. The current discussion has now focused on personal survival, rather than the implementation of anti-poverty, anti-crime, anti-inequality, pro-education and pro-development programmes.

South Africa, in order to reverse the deeply foul momentum of Vulture culture into which it is now deeply invested, has to take a break and consider postponing the 2024 general election. A serious thought of breaking away from a vicious cycle of what Zhang Weiwei referred to as the elect and then regret style of neo-liberal democracies is now upon South Africa (Al Jazeera 2012). It will certainly stay with the country when the politics of coalitions exchange stillborn and deformed programme foetuses. A condition clearly articulated in the Weaver scenario, which needs to be adopted now, is a convention that restores the dignity of what South Africa fought for during liberation. The government could choose to end its term early, so that such a conversation is given space to take place. The essence of the convention is to reset the virtues and values of South Africa. Restate the key dilemmas of poverty, unemployment and inequality. Craft a path forward as a people's manifesto upon which a willing and capable jockey can be put to the test through a process of selection and then an election. Our party-dependent lists have proved over the last 30 years that the formula for elect and regret is an outcome of our fatally flawed democracy that embeds a critically poisonous ingredient that can only yield ill-fated coalitions of the elected for their own survival. The Weaver scenario is South Africa's path out of the deepened Muvhango, Gwara Gwara and Vulture culture scenarios the country has lived in for the past fifteen years. But for the Weaver scenario to materialise, the forthcoming election has to be postponed, with a possibility of the ruling party ending its rule early for a convention of equals to be engaged setting the new rules of select, elect and account instead of the elect, do not account and regret that have successfully landed the beautiful South Africa where it is today. For that to happen, foresight is a non-negotiable condition.

More recently, the National Advisory Council on Innovation has been building a concrete strategy for innovation. In its exploration since 2019 on how the strategy could materialise, it sought counsel from Russian institutions that have reached distinction in mature levels of foresight. While this initiative has sown seeds in the case of South Africa, there is a long way to go, especially in the area of scenario quantification in terms of econometric principles and practices. The National Advisory Council for Innovation could play a critical role as a feeder to a rethinking convention of a South Africa different from what has been experienced in the last fifteen years. This is a social, political, economic and cultural imperative.

Notes

1. 'The Overton Window is a model for understanding how ideas in society change over time and influence politics. The core concept is that politicians are limited in what policy ideas they can support – they generally only pursue policies that are widely accepted throughout society as legitimate policy options. These policies lie inside the Overton Window. Other policy ideas exist, but politicians risk losing popular support if they champion these ideas. These policies lie outside the Overton Window.' https://www.mackinac.org/OvertonWindow (accessed 20 September 2023).
2. Koosum Kalyan at the farewell party of Andile Sanqu, who was the CEO of Indlulamithi Scenarios.
3. Skilled employment based on own calculations from the 1994 *October Household Survey* and the 2021 *Quarterly Labour Force Surveys*.
4. See https://indlu.storiesandscience.co.za/wp-content/uploads/2022/09/Indlulamithi-Barometer-2022_-digital-brochure-2022-07-288416.pdf (accessed 20 September 2023).
5. In August 2023, six countries (Argentina, Egypt, Ethiopia, Iran, Saudi Arabia and the United Arab Emirates) were invited to join the BRICS bloc. Full membership will take effect on 1 January 2024.

References

Al Jazeera. 2012. 'Zhang Weiwei: The China Wave'. *Al Jazeera*, 14 January. https://www.aljazeera.com/program/talk-to-al-jazeera/2012/1/14/zhang-weiwei-the-china-wave (accessed 20 September 2023).

ANC (African National Congress). 2002. 51st National Conference: The Balance of Forces. Discussion document. https://www.anc1912.org.za/51st-national-conference-the-balance-of-forces/ (accessed 20 September 2023).

Cornell, D. 2013. 'Economist, Critic of Neoliberal Capitalism, and a Veteran in the Struggle for Justice'. https://www.ekon.sun.ac.za/sampieterreblanche/index.php/economist-critic-of-neoliberal-capitalism-and-a-veteran-in-the-struggle-for-justice/ (accessed 20 September 2023).

COSATU (Congress of South African Trade Unions). 2003. 'There's No Ten out of Ten after Ten!' *South African Labour Bulletin* 27 (6): 35–40. https://www.southafricanlabourbulletin.org.za/wp-content/uploads/2021/11/Theres-no-ten-out-of-ten-after-ten_0.pdf (accessed 20 September 2023).

Dugard, J. 2008. 'Introductory Note' to the Convention on the Suppression and Punishment of the Crime of Apartheid, New York, 30 November 1973. https://legal.un.org/avl/ha/cspca/cspca.html#:~:text=In%201966%2C%20the%20General%20Assembly,)%20of%2023%20October%201984 (accessed 20 September 2023).

Gerber, J. 2023. 'Zondo Says Parliament Will Not Be Able to Prevent a State Capture Repeat, DA Agrees'. News 24, 23 June. https://www.news24.com/news24/politics/parliament/zondo-says-parliament-will-not-be-able-to-prevent-a-state-capture-repeat-da-agrees-20230623 (accessed 20 September 2023).

Godongwana, E. 2022. *Budget Speech*. https://www.parliament.gov.za/storage/app/media/Pages/2022/2-february/23-02-2022_budget_speech/speech.pdf (accessed 20 September 2023).

Indlulamithi South Africa Scenarios 2030 Trust. 2018. 'The Three Scenarios'. https://sascenarios2030.co.za/resources/indlulamithi-scenarios/ (accessed 20 September 2023).

——. 2023. 'The Three New Scenarios'. https://indlulamithi.org.za/resources/indlulamithi-scenarios-2035/ (accessed 20 September 2023).

Lehohla, P. 2023. 'GIBS and EMA Collaboration to Strengthen Economic Policy Foresight, Policy Design, Implementation and Evaluation'. *Business Report*, 6 November. https://www.persfin.co.za/business-report/economy/gibs-and-ema-collaboration-to-strengthen-economic-policy-foresight-policy-design-implementation-and-evaluation-694c141e-a710-427e-afe8-334bb81d7586 (accessed 20 September 2023).

Le Roux, P. and V. Maphai. 1993. 'The Mont Fleur Scenarios: What Will South Africa Be Like in the Year 2002?' *Deeper News* 7 (1). https://exed.annenberg.usc.edu/sites/default/files/Mont-Fleur.pdf (accessed 20 September 2023).

Mbeki, T. 1996. 'Statement of Deputy President Thabo Mbeki, on Behalf of the African National Congress, on the Occasion of the Adoption of the Constitutional Assembly of "The Republic of South Africa Constitution Bill 1996": Cape Town, May 8, 1996'. https://www.justice.gov.za/legislation/constitution/history/MEDIA/ANC.PDF (accessed 20 September 2023).

——. 2005. 'Address of the President of South Africa, Thabo Mbeki, at the Second Joint Sitting of the Third Democratic Parliament, Cape Town'. https://www.gov.za/address-president-south-africa-thabo-mbeki-second-joint-sitting-third-democratic-parliament-cape (accessed 20 September 2023).

——. 2008. 'State of the Nation Address of the President of South Africa, Thabo Mbeki: Joint Sitting of Parliament'. https://www.sahistory.org.za/archive/2008-president-mbeki-state-nation-address-8-february-2008 (accessed 20 September 2023).

National Planning Commission. 2012. *National Development Plan 2030: Our Future – Make It Work*. https://www.gov.za/sites/default/files/gcis_document/201409/ndp-2030-our-future-make-it-workr.pdf (accessed 20 September 2023).

——. 2020. *A Review of the 'National Development Plan 2030': Advancing Implementation towards a More Capable Nation*. https://www.nationalplanningcommission.org.za/assets/Documents/NDP%20REVIEW.pdf (accessed 20 September 2023).

National Treasury of Republic of South Africa. 2022. *Estimates of National Expenditure*. https://www.treasury.gov.za/documents/national%20budget/2022/ene/Foreward%20and%20Introduction.pdf. (accessed 20 September 2023).

PCAS (Policy Co-ordination and Advisory Services, the Presidency). 2003a. *Memories of the Future: South African Scenarios to 2014*. https://www.rscnetwork.co.za/wp-content/uploads/2015/01/9b-2014-Scenario-4.pdf (accessed 20 September 2023).

———. 2003b. *Towards a Ten Year Review*. https://www.gov.za/sites/default/files/10year.pdf (accessed 20 September 2023).

———. 2008. *South Africa Scenarios 2025: The Future We Chose?* https://www.gov.za/sites/default/files/gcis_document/201409/sascenarios20250.pdf (accessed 20 September 2023).

The Presidency. 2006. *Accelerated and Shared Growth Initiative – South Africa (ASGISA)*. https://www.sahistory.org.za/sites/default/files/asgisa.pdf (accessed 20 September 2023).

Ramaphosa, C. 2020. 'Letter to the ANC'. *Business Live*, 24 August. https://www.businesslive.co.za/fm/opinion/2020-08-24-read-in-full-president-cyril-ramaphosas-letter-to-anc-members-about-corruption/ (accessed 20 September 2023).

Sridharan, M., N. Nannaparaju and N. Patankar. 2021. 'Scenario Planning: How to Plan for Uncertainties?' *Think Insights*, 14 December. https://thinkinsights.net/strategy/scenario-planning/ (accessed 20 September 2023).

Stats SA (Statistics South Africa). N.d. 'Statistical Publications'. https://www.statssa.gov.za/?page_id=1859 (accessed 20 September 2023).

———. 2005. *Statistical Release P0441: Gross Domestic Product: Fourth Quarter 2004*. https://www.statssa.gov.za/publications/P0441/P04414thQuarter2004.pdf (accessed 20 September 2023).

———. 2008. *Labour Market Dynamics in South Africa*. https://www.statssa.gov.za/publications/Report-02-11-02/Report-02-11-022008.pdf (accessed 20 September 2023).

———. 2015. *Methodological Report on Rebasing of National Poverty Lines and Development of Pilot Provincial Poverty Lines*. http://beta2.statssa.gov.za/publications/Report-03-10-11/Report-03-10-11.pdf (accessed 20 September 2023).

———. 2023. *Statistical Release P0211: Quarterly Labour Force Survey: Quarter 2, 2022*. https://www.statssa.gov.za/publications/P0211/P02112ndQuarter2022.pdf (accessed 20 September 2023).

Weber, I. M. 2021. *How China Escaped Shock Therapy: The Market Reform Debate*. New York: Routledge.

CHAPTER 4

An Analysis of the Role of Law and Policy in Eradicating the Legacies of Colonialism and Apartheid

Olaotse John Kole and Tshepo Aubrey Manthwa

In a constantly changing world, a regular review of laws and policy is essential to address the challenges facing the South African economy. The country's laws and policy, which have been revised several times since 1996, need further revision to address the current needs of citizens and meet the demands of the Fourth Industrial Revolution in the global economy. The colonial and apartheid legacies of inequality, unemployment and poverty (IUP) still prevalent among black South Africans need to be revisited. Most of the democratic activities in South Africa since 1994, which were revised in the 1996 Constitution, have not been discontinued as such, but have become diluted. The question is why IUP are most noticeable among black South Africans. This answer is that many black South Africans lack access to resources when they are faced with issues of the law and policy. Something else we would like to emphasise is the colonialism present in the South African economy. The rights, thoughts and position of our people have been taken away. They are unable to show what they are capable of and express their wishes regarding their schools, churches and communities. This implies that apartheid rules, which once colonised their bodies and minds, still exist. Instead of being addressed amicably, differences often result in violence, which was the norm during the apartheid regime.

The post-apartheid Constitution since 1996 indicates that, in terms of law and policy, the new democracy was supposed to have dealt with the culture of violence that was adopted to deal with the challenges faced on a day-to-day basis by both the government and citizens. However, this culture of violence has not disappeared and, in fact, has caused more chaos and is even likely to damage the economy if it is not adequately handled now.

Contrary to early expectations, those in power have failed as corruption has crippled the South African economy in the past few decades. Erika Serfontein and Elda de Waal (2015: 12) argue that corruption is an evil act that threatens employment and the economy. While it is important that government responds to socio-economic challenges, factors such as corruption threaten existing jobs, which could plunge the country further into extreme levels of IUP. Serfontein and De Waal (2015) argue that although government, through its policies and laws, has managed to increase the number of employment opportunities, the level of inequality is still of great concern (see also Gumede 2021: 184). Inequality is a global phenomenon (2021: 184) and can be addressed by means of capacitation or vocational training. Vocational training is the best way to address IUP and turn citizens into independent business owners and trustworthy government officials. However, there are a number of reasons that citizens of this country may not be willing or may not be ready to be capacitated – such as lack of funding and inadequate educational background. The government should ensure that all citizens have access to resources such as formal education and funding.

A nation with vast skills, knowledge and expertise is likely to grow and adhere to laws and policies. But when no one adheres to laws and policies, inequality abounds. Vusi Gumede (2021: 184) notes that, sometimes, inequality is a necessity as it could stimulate competition as a result of adherence to laws and policies for economic transformation. Since 1994, the South African economy has been characterised by inequality. The time to tackle it is now; otherwise, inequality will only get worse. Since 1994, the labour market has experienced a high rate of inequality, which has meant that there has been little intergenerational social mobility, resulting in the perpetuation of inequalities (Gugushvili 2016: 403).

Provision for social security is made in section 27 of the Constitution, which obliges the government to capacitate people through social security agencies – hence the establishment of the South African Social Security Agency (Goldblatt 2014: 24). But the creation of opportunities beyond social security remains problematic. Moreover, social security cannot cater for everyone because the system is aimed at capacitating the disabled and vulnerable sections of South African society (Altman, Mokomane and Wright 2014: 349). Provision has also been made for citizens to have better lives through free primary health care; free education; old-age pensions; housing; and free basic services (water, electricity and sanitation) to poor households. Although these policies have resulted in some solutions to the identified challenges, many of these challenges persist and call for a rigorous approach to solve them and build a better South Africa.

This chapter starts by, first, analysing the government's response to not only these challenges, but also insurrection and corruption. This cannot be ignored because insurrection and corruption pose a threat to existing jobs. The chapter then discusses the role of law and policy in alleviating IUP. In the last analysis, vocational training, artisanship and entrepreneurship are proposed as a solution to IUP.

The role of law and policy in alleviating inequality, unemployment and poverty

The Constitution of South Africa is seen as a transformative document aimed at solving various socio-economic challenges, such as IUP. Yet, 29 years after the democratic transition, these challenges persist. It has been argued that the problem is not the document itself, but the fact that the judiciary has not been transformed, not in terms of gender and race, but in terms of interpreting it as a responsive document (Dugard 2008: 215). Justice in South Africa is often sought in court, but the poor do not have access to the courts because of the considerable cost of litigation (2008: 232). A pro-poor approach is needed, whereby courts serve as the institutional voice of the poor in issues such as land redistribution. Such an approach should dispense with the winner-takes-all approach of the adversarial legal system. The judiciary is an important mechanism for alleviating IUP and needs to transform society through transformative justice (2008: 238). Courts are supposed to promote equality, non-racism and the rule of law in terms of section 1 of the Constitution. Equally important is the reinterpretation of the provision of education. Education is important in alleviating IUP and can help to solve the country's challenges by meeting the demands of the labour market.

Although laws and policies are only a part of making a noticeable difference in people's lives, they are an important link in the chain of transformation. South African policy sectors and government departments can learn from one another to address IUP more consistently and effectively. The key to accelerating the alleviation of IUP is a combination of policies and laws that promote inclusive growth through better access to education and the creation of skilled jobs. However, many students are denied entry to tertiary institutions and technical vocational education and training (TVET) colleges because of stringent admission criteria and a lack of funding. Tertiary institutions should relax their admission policies to cater for most young people as part of transformation and change, so that they can be sent out into the work environment and the gap between the skills required and the skills available can be closed.

In the first quarter of 2021, the official unemployment rate was at a 32.6 per cent; 'this rate was 46,3% among young people aged 15–34 years, implying that almost one in every two young people in the labour force did not have a job in the first quarter of 2021' (Stats SA 2021). It is worrying that countless young people between the ages of 15 and 34 are unemployable. Because they lack even basic numeracy skills, they are likely to be swayed by a populist agenda and may even fall prey to illegal or fraudulent money-making schemes. A practical solution would be to focus on the best model of educational skills. There is also a gap between law and policy because some policies are not met with the implementation of laws whereby legal institutions can ensure that policies are implemented in a manner that creates equality.

Vocational training, artisanship and entrepreneurship as a solution

South Africa's economic growth is far too slow to absorb all its young people into the economy. High-school graduation is crucial for a start in the labour market, but many youngsters barely meet this requirement (Altman, Mokomane and Wright 2014: 348). There is a need to focus on vocational training for black South Africans as the majority population group. Their history is steeped in colonial and apartheid laws and policies that imposed inferior education on them and deprived them of opportunities (Mungazi 1991). The Bantu Education Act of 1953 made it impossible for black people to compete on an equal footing with whites in the labour market – and its ramifications are still being felt today.

Former National Party leader, Dr Hendrik Verwoerd, argued that 'blacks don't qualify to receive university education, which offered whites "the greener pastures of education" and civilisation' (Sehume 2018). He regarded blacks as 'hewers of wood and drawers of water', in other words, manual labourers in mines and on farms (Nkomo 2021). It was hoped that the 1994 dispensation would bring change. Black people flooded into universities to get better opportunities and education. However, the challenge came when the government merged 152 vocational training centres, also referred then to as further education and training (FET) colleges, into 50 institutions and universities started relying on government subsidies. The effect of this merger on the production of skilled and qualified people is still felt today. In hindsight, it was a mistake to merge FET colleges and subsidise universities. It is known that universities equip learners with theoretical knowledge while the labour market urgently requires welders, builders, fitters, carpenters, bricklayers, plumbers and boilermakers. It is for this reason that the present minister of Basic Education, Angie Motshekga, has strongly recommended a shift from university to technical training (Business Tech 2022). This is in recognition of the fact that the current global economy simply cannot offer permanent job opportunities for all university graduates. More products should be exported to grow the economy and a buoyant economy will create job opportunities. Currently, South Africa imports welders and carpenters from the Far East when it has more than 264 technical-training campuses. The law, as a tool, must respond to these challenges.

Universities train graduates in areas of expertise that are saturated, such as law and medicine, instead of heeding the needs of the labour market. Education must shift its focus to areas with a huge labour demand. An example of this is artisanship. Minister of Mineral Resources, Gwede Mantashe, indicated that he has never seen an unemployed artisan (Grootes 2010). Therefore, more government resources are needed to ensure that technical colleges have qualified teachers and lecturers. The *National Development Plan 2030* (NDP) regards the training of artisans as important (National Planning Commission 2012). Partnerships with private companies should ensure that the curricula offered at vocational training centres meet the need for skilled technicians. Government should promote vocational enrolment by means of law and policies. This is an approach that can curb IUP. Institutions of higher learning must provide a guaranteed return on investment. Legislation that prioritises vocational training should be implemented. A pro-poor strategy should empower poor families through vocational training.

Universities must implement new curricula. The law must ensure legal sanction if policies are not implemented – because it is one thing to have policies, but quite another if policies are not implemented.

Another approach is the creation of entrepreneurial opportunities and activities to create jobs and reduce poverty. Sorely needed entrepreneurial skills can be obtained through university education and training. Entrepreneurship has the potential to reduce IUP (Audretsch and Belitski 2017:1030). It will enable South Africa to implement the NDP for sustainable employment creation. The funding of entrepreneur education, training and support, as a measure to grow the economy and create jobs, must be encouraged. The government must support emerging entrepreneurs by means of policies and support structures (Malecki 2018: 97). This can be achieved through new labour legislation to encourage entrepreneurship and an overhaul of the education sector, so that its focus is more on entrepreneurship and less on basic education. This is necessary because the current education system produces employees instead of entrepreneurs (Serfontein and De Waal 2015: 1). The education sector, policymakers, lawmakers and the private sector ought to focus on entrepreneurial education to capacitate the youth because they are the worst affected by IUP. This is important because many businesses have proved to be unsustainable and had to close down.

The government's response to IUP

South Africa's development policy and law are powerful tools to reduce IUP (Khanam 2018: 26). South Africa subscribes to three overarching values that reverberate through the Constitution: agency, freedom and justice. They have been the goal of the country's democracy and constitutional dispensation since 1994 (Corder 2022). This is detailed in the Reconstruction and Development Programme (RDP) and the NDP. In 1994 the African National Congress (ANC) government drafted a policy framework to address IUP through the RDP. A White Paper was drafted as a business-friendly and fiscally responsible addition to the policy framework (Aliber 2003: 490). In 1996 the Department of Finance structurally and substantively changed RDP into the Growth, Employment and Redistribution (GEAR) framework. The new framework focused on supply and demand as a driving force behind economic growth and job creation. Regrettably, the GEAR framework did not achieve the required outcome. It was succeeded by the *Accelerated and Shared Growth Initiative – South Africa (ASGISA)* (The Presidency 2006), which also floundered (Pollin et al. 2007). The guiding objective of the NDP is: 'No political democracy can survive and flourish if the mass of our people remain in poverty, without land, without tangible prospects for a better life. Attacking poverty and deprivation must be the first priority of a democratic government' (National Planning Commission 2012: 24).

The goal of the NDP is to create and increase employment and achieve socio-economic equality. The government has the responsibility to transform society and improve the lives of the poor by developing policies that can bring change (Stiglitz 2021: 2). This is a vision that the government is committed to. It must use its fiscal policies to bring about change. Social grants have been part of the government's efforts. Since the advent of the constitutional dispensation, social grants have been regarded as a redistributive mechanism to improve the lives of poor South Africans (Zikhali 2021: 17854). This includes the provision of free health care, child support grants, water and sanitation, and free basic education. The social wage was extended at the beginning of Covid-19, which resulted in many businesses closing down and countless people losing their jobs (Ullah et al. 2022: 333).

Part of the problem is that our policies and laws are not geared towards growing the economy, but towards reducing poverty, unemployment and inequality. The Constitution provides for social rights to be realised progressively, but the government has neglected economic growth. Social grants, as a measure to overcome the IUP, are welcomed and have prevented excessively high levels of poverty. But there are concerns that they are not sustainable in the long run and create a culture of welfare dependency.

A missed opportunity has been an export-driven economy (Jansen van Rensburg et al. 2020: 340). South Africa continues to experience a decline in manufacturing and mining employment opportunities. The economy is becoming a service-orientated economy that requires us to export services to grow our gross domestic product (GDP). These services include finance and insurance, wholesale, trade and transport, catering, storage and communication (2020: 347). Policies such as GEAR and the NDP concentrate on exports to drive economic growth and create jobs. Skills that meet labour market needs are in short supply, especially in view of the Fourth Industrial Revolution. There is a need for social reform. Even though social grants for the unemployed reduce extreme poverty, the fiscal space is not conducive to expansion. Inclusive growth can be achieved by unlocking the labour markets through skills training to accelerate the alleviation of IUP. Although the government and policymakers' ambition is to transform society to alleviate IUP through policy and laws, there is little evidence of success (Chibba and Luiz 2011: 309).

Another measure is black economic empowerment (BEE), as in the Broad-Based Black Economic Empowerment Act 53 of 2003. Critics argue that BEE has enriched only a small black elite and has done little or nothing to fight IUP (Andreasson 2006: 3). The objective of BEE is to address past injustices, broaden the economic participation of the historically disadvantaged and promote socio-economic transformation by increasing the number of black people who own and manage companies. BEE requirements do not stimulate skills transfer and education to manage jobs. As a result, BEE has benefited only a few. BEE was supposed to improve the lives of black people and promote equality but, in reality, has benefited largely the elite. It manages the programme rather than the outcome. In as much as there is BEE, legislation regulates how BEE is implemented to ensure that everyone is afforded equal opportunities (Ponte, Roberts and Van Sittert 2007: 933).

Fighting IUP is important because of the knock-on effect it has on other challenges in South Africa, such as crime, prostitution and human trafficking (Naidoo 2020). One cannot ignore the fact that frustrated citizens have resorted to unrest. Although these may be dismissed as criminal tendencies, South Africa has inherited violence from the apartheid regime (Von Holdt 2013: 589). Today, one also sees South Africans accuse foreign nationals of taking jobs that were meant from them.

The government's response to insurrection and corruption

Another challenge is the government's response to insurrection, such as the July 2021 civil unrest, which left 2 million South Africans jobless (Erasmus 2022). Parts of KwaZulu-Natal and Gauteng were engulfed in looting, violence, death and destruction. Businesses were torched and the economy was plunged into a depression. Action has to be taken to prevent a recurrence. The unrest had far-reaching consequences for employees, as 40 000 businesses had to close (Layden 2021). It is therefore important that, while energy is focused on reducing IUP, events that could plunge the economy into a deeper crisis are avoided. According to the *Report of the Expert Panel into the July 2021 Civil Unrest*, the July 2021 civil unrest was caused by weak state institutions, youth unemployment above 70 per cent, poverty and inequality, and a lack of a clear plan to address them (The Presidency 2021). Clearly, the government needs to pay attention to IUP. While this is already a priority for the government, as detailed in the NDP, there is neither a clear solution to these problems nor any time limit (The Presidency 2021).

Because South African society is tired of corruption, civil unrest could easily flare up again. The government should pay close attention to poverty, underdevelopment and inequality. While we acknowledge that the government is aware of these issues, there seems to be no clear plan, budget or timetable to effectively address them. If one adds the general discontent over corruption within the ruling party, many commentators have warned that what happened in July 2021 could happen again if these issues are not addressed.

Violence has become an accepted and inherited culture in South Africa because of apartheid. Its consequences are the harshest for the unemployed and people living in deep inequality. Reducing IUP is important as a method to fight crime. It also does not help that opportunists take advantage of the government's failure to address IUP and target African foreign nationals as part of Operation Dudula (Nombembe 2022). Its architects claim that the operation is targeted at illegal immigration. It is, however, targeting all foreign nationals who do not possess a scarce skill in South Africa (Kasa and Nel 2022). It is arguable that the government's failure to address IUP has created an environment in which foreign nationals are too easily made the scapegoats. This cannot be condoned and highlights the urgency to address IUP. The energy expended on fighting xenophobia can be better spent on fighting corruption as a destroyer of jobs.

Corruption is a serious problem and threatens existing jobs. Due to widespread corruption in South Africa, millions of people have sunk into poverty (Corruption Watch 2020). The government needs to step up its fight against corruption because funds meant for creating jobs and improving the lives of people are ending up in the pockets of politicians (Adenike 2021: 133). From a legal perspective, the law needs to bite to get corruption under control. Law and policy play an important role in ensuring not only that IUP is alleviated, but also that issues threatening the growth of the South African economy, such as corruption, are addressed (Pellicer et al. 2011). Stricter oversight of government's use of funds allocated to alleviating IUP is required. There must be transparency in and accountability for how public funds are used. A special investigation unit on corruption should be appointed to address corruption in South Africa. The conduct of public officials must be under constant scrutiny and oversight institutions, such as Parliament, must play a central role in rooting out corruption (Karnani 2011: 86).

Conclusion

This chapter has established that law and policy are a panacea for the legacies of colonialism and apartheid in South Africa on condition that their implementation is placed in the hands of the appropriate personnel and that it is closely monitored. A new approach to capacitation through skills, knowledge and attitude transfer is required in formal institutions of higher learning to alleviate IUP. Such institutions should offer technical studies, so that their graduates can easily be accommodated in the labour market. Currently, the South African labour market is saturated and countless young graduates are unemployed. Youth unemployment cannot be attributed to a lack of policies alone, but the law must be used to enforce their implementation. The existing education system does not produce students with the skills required by employers. This means that there is a mismatch between the curricula and the requirements of the marketplace. Their lack of skills discourages many young people from applying for jobs. The youth are affected most severely by unemployment and poverty. This has a knock-on effect and causes civil unrest. More unrest in reaction to the extremely high levels of IUP in South Africa is expected. Unrest is inevitable because of a culture of violence inherited from apartheid – it has become the default setting for venting frustration with the slow pace of change. Equally important is to fight the threat to existing employment because if corruption is not stamped out many jobs will be lost.

References

Adenike, E.T. 2021. 'Poverty, Unemployment and Insecurity Challenges in Nigeria'. *Tanzanian Economic Review* 11 (1): 115–36.

Aliber, M. 2003. 'Chronic Poverty in South Africa: Incidence, Causes and Policies'. *World Development* 31 (3): 473–90.

Altman, M., Z. Mokomane and G. Wright. 2014. 'Social Security for Young People amidst High Poverty and Unemployment: Some Policy Options for South Africa'. *Development Southern Africa* 31 (2): 347–62.

Andreasson, S. 2006. 'Stand and Deliver: Private Property and the Politics of Global Dispossession'. *Political Studies* 54 (1): 1–10.

Audretsch, D.B. and M. Belitski. 2017. 'Entrepreneur Ecosystem in Cities: Establishing the Framework Conditions'. *Journal of Technology Transfer* 42 (5): 1030–51.

Business Tech. 2022. 'School Curriculum Changes to Boost Jobs in South Africa: Minister'. *Business Tech*, 22 March. https://businesstech.co.za/news/government/570100/school-curriculum-changes-to-boost-jobs-in-south-africa-minister/ (accessed 21 September 2023).

Chibba, M. and J. Luiz. 2011. 'Poverty, Inequality and Unemployment in South Africa: Context, Issues and the Way Forward'. *Economic Papers* 30 (3): 307–15.

Corder, H. 2022. 'South Africa's Constitutional Democracy Debate: Echoes of an Inglorious Past'. *The Conversation*, 18 April. https://theconversation.com/south-africas-constitutional-democracy-debate-echoes-of-an-inglorious-past-180802 (accessed 21 September 2023).

Corruption Watch. 2020. 'In South Africa Covid-19 Has Exposed Greed and Spurred Long-Needed Action against Corruption'. *Transparency International*, 4 September. https://www.transparency.org/en/blog/in-south-africa-covid-19-has-exposed-greed-and-spurred-long-needed-action-against-corruption (accessed 21 September 2023).

Dugard, J. 2008. 'Courts and the Poor in South Africa: A Critique of Systemic Judicial Failures to Advance Transformative Justice'. *South African Journal on Human Rights* 24 (2): 214–38.

Erasmus, D. 2022. 'Cyril Ramaphosa: "Attempted July Insurrection" Left Two Million Jobless and Wiped R50bn from the Economy'. *Daily Maverick*, 1 April. https://www.dailymaverick.co.za/article/2022-04-01-cyril-ramaphosa-attempted-july-insurrection-left-2-million-jobless-and-wiped-r50bn-from-the-economy/ (accessed 21 September 2023).

Goldblatt, B. 2014. 'Social Security in South Africa: A Gender and Human Rights Analysis'. *Verfassung und Recht in Übersee / Law and Politics in Africa, Asia and Latin America* 47 (1): 22–42.

Grootes, S. 2010. 'Analysis: Gwede Mantashe, a Serial Speech-Maker'. *Daily Maverick*, 24 November. https://www.dailymaverick.co.za/article/2010-11-24-analysis-gwede-mantashe-a-serial-speech-maker/ (accessed 21 September 2023).

Gugushvili, A. 2016. 'Intergenerational Social Mobility and Popular Explanations of Poverty: A Comparative Perspective'. *Social Justice Research* 29: 402–28.

Gumede, V. 2021. 'Revisiting Poverty, Human Development and Inequality in Democratic South Africa'. *Indian Journal of Human Development* 15 (2): 183–99.

Jansen van Rensburg, S.J., W. Viviers, A. Parry, M. Cameron and S. Grater. 2020. 'A Strategic Framework to Expand South Africa's Services Trade'. *South African Journal of International Affairs* 27 (3): 339–61.

Karnani, A. 2011. 'Reducing Poverty through Employment'. *Innovations* 6 (2): 73–97.

Kasa, S. and B. Nel. 2022. 'Operation Dudula Sets Sights on Parklands'. *IOL*, 15 May. https://www.iol.co.za/weekend-argus/news/operation-dudula-sets-sights-on-parklands-be97f547-4820-409f-ae8d-97cc11548909 (accessed 21 September 2023).

Khanam, T. 2018. 'Rule of Law Approach to Alleviation of Poverty: An Analysis on Human Rights Dimension of Governance'. *IIUC Studies* 15: 23–32.

Layden, C. 2021. 'Unrest, Inequality and Poverty in South Africa'. *Borgen Magazine*, 21 November. https://www.borgenmagazine.com/inequality-and-poverty-in-south-africa/ (accessed 21 September 2023).

Malecki, E.J. 2018. 'Technological Innovation and Paths to Regional Economic Growth'. In: *Growth Policy in the Age of High Technology*, 97–126. Abingdon-on-Thames: Routledge.

Mungazi, D.A. 1991. *Colonial Education for Africans: George Stark's Policy in Zimbabwe*. New York: Praeger.

Naidoo, S. 2020. 'So. Africa: Human Trafficking on the Rise due to Unemployment & Deepening Poverty under Covid-19'. Business and Human Rights Resource Centre, 30 September. https://www.business-humanrights.org/en/latest-news/so-africa-human-trafficking-on-the-rise-due-to-unemployment-deepening-poverty-under-covid-19/ (accessed 21 September 2023).

National Planning Commission. 2012. *National Development Plan 2030: Our Future – Make It Work*. https://www.gov.za/sites/default/files/gcis_document/201409/ndp-2030-our-future-make-it-workr.pdf (accessed 21 September 2023).

Nkomo, M. 2021. 'Hendrick Verwoerd's Dream of Black People as Hewers of Wood and Drawers of Water Has Become Our Nightmare'. *Daily Maverick*, 13 January. https://www.dailymaverick.co.za/opinionista/2021-01-13-hendrik-verwoerds-dream-of-black-people-as-hewers-of-wood-and-drawers-of-water-has-become-our-nightmare/ (accessed 21 September 2023).

Nombembe, P. 2022, 'Operation Dudula Now Targeting Both Legal and Illegal Immigrants'. *Times Live*, 15 May. https://www.timeslive.co.za/news/south-africa/2022-05-15-operation-dudula-now-targeting-both-legal-and-illegal-immigrants/ (accessed 21 September 2023).

Pellicer, M., V. Ranchod, M. Sarr and E. Wegner. 2011. 'Inequality Traps in South Africa: An Overview and Research Agenda'. Southern Africa Labour and Development Research Unit Working Paper No. 57, University of Cape Town. http://hdl.handle.net/11090/60 (accessed 21 September 2023).

Pollin, R., G.A. Epstein, J. Heintz and L. Ndikumana. 2007. *An Employment-Targeted Economic Programme for South Africa*. Amherst: Political Economy Research Institute. http://peri.umass.edu/fileadmin/pdf/UNDP_S.Africa.pdf (accessed 21 September 2023).

Ponte, S., S. Roberts and L. van Sittert. 2007. '"Black Economic Empowerment", Business and the State in South Africa'. *Development and Change* 38 (5): 933–55.

The Presidency. 2006. *Accelerated and Shared Growth Initiative – South Africa (ASGISA)*. https://www.sahistory.org.za/sites/default/files/asgisa.pdf (accessed 21 September 2023).

The Presidency. 2021. *Report of the Expert Panel into the July 2021 Civil Unrest*. https://www.thepresidency.gov.za/download/file/fid/2442 (accessed 21 September 2023).

Sehume, J. 2018. 'Solving Poverty, Unemployment and Inequality'. *IOL*, 24 June. https://www.iol.co.za/sundayindependent/dispatch/solving-poverty-unemployment-and-inequality-15658217 (accessed 21 September 2023).

Serfontein, E. and E. de Waal. 2015. 'The Corruption Bogey in South Africa: Is Public Education Safe?' *South African Journal of Education* 35 (1): 1–12.

Stats SA (Statistics South Africa). 2021. 'Youth Still Find It Difficult to Secure Jobs in South Africa'. https://www.statssa.gov.za/?p=14415 (accessed 21 September 2023).

Stiglitz, J.E. 2021. 'The Proper Role of Government in the Market Economy: The Case of the Post-COVID Recovery'. *Journal of Government and Economics* 1: 1–7.

Ullah, F., X. Ding Ding, M. Zeeshan and S.N. Khan. 2022. 'The Increasing Influence of Financial Incorporation: An Investigation into the Interplay of Earnings Inequity and GDP to Reduce Poverty in Emerging Economies'. *International Journal of Special Education* 37 (3): 332–61.

Von Holdt, K. 2013. 'South Africa: The Transition to Violent Democracy'. *Review of African Political Economy* 40 (138): 589–604.

Zikhali, P.T. 2021. 'Social Grants and Poverty Alleviation in South Africa: Addressing Dependency, Attitude and Behaviour'. *Gender and Behaviour* 19 (2): 17854–63.

CHAPTER 5

Towards a Post-colonial Feminist Perspective for Understanding Rural Women's Land Rights in South Africa in a Context of a Disjuncture between Policy and Practice

Tembeka Ngcebetsha-Mooij

About 31.67 per cent of the South African population live in rural areas,[1] where poverty and unemployment are highest (approximately 71 per cent and 52 per cent, respectively) (National Land Committee 2003).[2] The poverty levels are severe in the rural areas of the former homelands such as the Eastern Cape,[3] where women constitute about 50 per cent of the rural population, most of whom are household heads who rely on land to make a living. Although the overall proportion of rural households engaged in the agricultural production of food is fairly low, more than half of them (52.8 per cent) are women, who do it either as a main source or extra source of food for their households (Stats SA 2023). Yet rural women in South Africa do not enjoy the same legal rights to land (in terms of ownership and control) as men (Stats SA 2016, 2019; Walker 2002; Bob 2002).[4]

Even though the South African Constitution is non-discriminatory, rural women continue to be discriminated against within all land tenure systems – customary and statutory (Mann 2000; Cross and Hornby 2002).[5] This is mainly because of the persistent patriarchal perception that a woman's place is in the home, where they are expected to tend for the needs and welfare of their husbands and children. As discussed in this chapter, this perception was created by the colonial system, which used tradition or customary law to rob women of their strong rights to land and to marginalise them in land-related decision-making processes (Adams, Cousins and Manona 1999; Claassens 2005: 7–90). It created a situation where women only have use rights to land, which are unclear, dependent and unprotected by law, with virtually no right to make decisions about its use and management.

This chapter explores how rural women's land rights are understood in post-apartheid South Africa, in a context marred by a disjuncture between policy and practice. Supported by empirical evidence from fieldwork undertaken between 2007 and 2008 in the Tshezi communal area in Mqanduli in the Eastern Cape Province, the chapter examines rural women's experiences and the challenges they face in the process of acquiring rights to access land and in participating in land-related governance structures. Tshezi was selected as a case study because it shares important features with other rural communities in South Africa, where the institution of traditional leadership is strongly entrenched and where most of South Africa's challenges of poverty, illiteracy and unemployment are predominant. In the final analysis, I argue that a post-colonial African feminist perspective for understanding rural women's land rights in South Africa should be adopted.

Overview of women's land rights in communal areas

During the pre-colonial era in South Africa, communal land was owned by black African people under customary or indigenous group tenure, albeit with no records of either a person or title (Coleman 2014).[6] Land was held in custody by the chief on behalf of community members and administered by a nested hierarchy of traditional leadership (chiefs, headmen, male heads of households), who were responsible for the allocation of different resources, including land, to each household (2014).[7]

Land during this period was not regarded as private and personal property; it could not be sold to anyone. Land rights provided a bundle of use rights, including residence, ploughing, wood for fuel, building materials, water, *veldkos*,[8] medical plants and rights to the communal area and participation in communal forums. All members of the group had rights in the land by virtue of their membership of the group, and new members would also be absorbed into the group and allocated land for their use. Nelson Mandela, in a speech in 1962, stated: 'The land then was the main means of production, belonged to the whole tribe, and there was no individual ownership whatsoever' (National Land Committee 2003). The concept of 'ownership' was limited and more often embedded in social relationships, rather than an individual's exclusive claim over land as provate property. Entitlements to property were more in the form of obligations resulting from family relationships than a means to exclude people from the use of certain property (Du Plessis 2011). The operation of multiple and overlapping rights (nested rights) in the use of land and its different resources,[9] as well as the relative inclusivity of customary tenure systems were among the more 'positive' aspects of the pre-apartheid land tenure system (Walker 2002: 8).

During this period, the right to residential sites and arable fields usually implied that a member of the community had two plots – one for housing and one for farming. The holder of both these plots had exclusive rights over the land and was protected from trespass, but the rights were restricted to the extent that the use of the plots was limited to the cultivation of crops for domestic consumption. Members would also graze their stock on the commonage, where no individual would claim exclusive use of the land. Access was based on socially defined membership, reinforced and managed within the group, based on the reciprocal obligations of the members in the social hierarchy.

Women were the main cultivators of land, with full strong rights to the fields they cultivated, while men looked after the cattle and hunted to feed their families (Goheen 1996; Bundy 1988: 18). Just like any member of the community, they would be allocated land directly, not via their husbands. There are many accounts of unmarried women and widows who were also allocated land directly (Claassens 2005). A wife used to have strong rights to her 'house' property and the fields she cultivated and male family heads or traditional leaders could not interfere or make decisions that impacted on house property, without the consent of the wife of that house (Schapera 1943; Preston-Whyte 1974). Isaac Schapera (1943) describes fields as belonging to women, implying that there were no obstructions and no discrimination against women's rights to access land in their own right. John Henderson, an African missionary, writing in 1931 concurs: 'Each wife of a chief or of a commoner has a grant of land given her for the upkeep of her family. Once granted it can only be forfeited by misdemeanor on her part or it may lapse through the death of the holder' (in Soga 1931: 383).

The colonial system changed landownership rights of black African people. It introduced several pieces of legislation to regulate communal land tenure in accordance with a government policy of segregation. This began with the implementation of the Land Act No. 27 of 1913, which created so-called reserves as the only areas where Africans could legally occupy land, prohibiting them from purchasing land outside of these areas. Through conquest, forced removals and land dispossessions, the government introduced the Black Administration Act No. 38 of 1927, which immediately reduced land access for Africans to only 7 per cent of the total land area.[10] When the Pact government came to power in 1924, a uniform system of black administration throughout South Africa was created, which led to the introduction of the Native Trust and Land Act of 1936, which was to add more land for black settlement (Du Plessis and Pienaar 2010).

The effect of these laws was the elimination of independent access to land by Africans, which was replaced by introduction of the concept of landownership through a title deed. This further restricted black African people from either purchasing or owning land in their own right, and they were reduced to occupying it as employees of a white master. These restrictions formalised the separation of white and black people and opened the door for white ownership of 87 per cent of South African land area, expanding the total reserve area to approximately 13 per cent of the national land area (National Land Committee 2003).[11] The South African Native Trust was created to acquire and administer land in communal areas, as the registered owner of most reserve land. Although not much is written about the land rights of women during the colonial period, what is certain is that black ownership coud not be vested and women lost their rights to access land. The colonial legacy imposed patriarchal structures of land use and ownership and reinforced a gender division of labour, which empowered men and disempowered women (Mbilinyi and Shechambo 2009: 96).

Although it is well documented in history that women did not own land in their own right during this period, there is evidence of landownership by a woman in the nineteenth century. Princess Emma Sandile of amaRharhabe and great wife to Nkosi Stokwe ka-Ndlela, is recorded as the first black African woman in southern Africa to gain a formal education and to hold a title deed to land. Her land rights to a farm in the Eastern Cape were not accorded to her as an inheritance, but as a first-generation owner. When she died, she left the land to her four daughters and one son (Hodgson 2021).

The process of land dispossession in South Africa culminated in apartheid (1948–94), which introduced a 'labyrinth' of racially and gender discriminarory laws relating to land. Through the provisions of the Bantu Authorities Act of 1951 and other legislation, such as the Black Areas Land Regulations (Regulation R188 of 1969) and the Black Administration Act of 1938, the apartheid government formally demarcated Bantustans as homelands for occupation by black Africans. As soon as the apartheid government was in power, the unsurveyed land in communal areas continued to be legally owned by the state and men held 'derivative' or secondary rights to it, in the form of permission to occupy certificates (PTOs) (Adams, Cousins and Manona 1999; Cousins and Hornby 2009).

The Bantu Authorities Act of 1951 created Tribal Authorities in communal areas, which gradually introduced the PTOs as a new landholding system, managed by traditional leaders or chiefs. The Act retained certain rights for traditional leaders and took away others. It gave them the power to allocate, regulate, confiscate and/or expropriate land. Specifically, the Act gave them the authority to allocate land *only* to household heads (usually married men) on behalf of their families (Walker 2002, 2003; Claassens 2005; Boumans 2004). Power became centralised at the level of traditional councils and made no provision for localised decision-making and control over land at the level of the family, the user group, the village and the clan (Claassens and Cousins 2008). Consequently, women were given a secondary status in relation to land, which only granted them usufruct rights and limited their control of land.

What the Act took away was their right to have authority and control over the distribution and administration of land, and it placed such authority in the magistrates' office. In this regard, the Act swung the balance of power away from popular support for chiefs and towards bureaucratic control (Delius 2018: 232). This meant that the Tribal Authority would receive applications for sites through the headmen, who would certify the status of the applicant as a member of the community. The Department of Agriculture would demarcate the site and record it on 1:8 000 maps, after which the magistrates' office would issue the PTO certificate and record it on the land register (Coleman 2014). The PTO was a permit for occupation of unregistered state or trust communal land for specific purposes, either residential or arable allotment which was granted via the Department of Agriculture.[12] The PTOs were often deemed 'off-register' land as they are not registered in the Deeds Office (Mabasa and Mabasa 2021: 86–8).

Because formal registers of allotments were not always kept, a landholder (usually a man) would have to prove their right over land by showing evidence of effective ownership or possession over a period of time.

Because PTOs were issued only to married men, it implied that women could not legally acquire land in their own right, but could only do so through marriage (Ntsebeza 1999: 75; PLAAS/NLC 2003; Boumans 2004). Even so, the rights to land held by married women were limited, as they could lose such rights upon the death of their spouses, mainly because of the principle of male primogeniture (South African Law Reform Commission 2004), which usually excluded them from inheriting land rights when their husband died, in favour of the eldest son or the husband's brothers (Birgegard 1993; Goheen 1996; Meer 1997). In such cases, they would be allowed to remain on the matrimonial land and home until death or remarriage (Kameri-Mbote 2005).

Furthermore, since this system catered for married women only, it made the rights of single, divorced or widowed women particularly vulnerable, as they would not be allocated land unless they had support from a male relative (father, brother, uncle). In addition, the rules tended to favour women with children over those without (Mutangadura 2004). Landownership followed patrilineal descent within the family, handed down from generation to generation, according to rules of succession (Mabasa and Mabasa 2021: 93). The rules of access and inheritance were not only exclusive to men, but generally disqualified women from holding land independently of men, and from participating in land-related governance structures.

From 1994 onwards, the PTO system started to break down as a result of the removal of the land administration function from the magistrates' office, and the national land reform process has not yet replaced or repealed the existing land laws. This left a vacuum of land administration in communal areas, as evidenced by the neglect or loss of files and maps, which consequently led to a breakdown of the PTO landholding system between 1996 and 1999 (Adams, Cousins and Manona 1999: 15). Although PTO certificates are no longer issued by land administrators, the system remains the fundamental formally recognized land tenure in communal area, albeit with no formal authority and no clarity on its legal status (Mabasa and Mabasa 2021: 104). Where it continues to operate, it does so as part of living customary law, which regards land to have long been permanently allocated to families under already-settled chiefdoms (Bennet 2015; Mabasa and Mabasa 2021: 70). Because the PTO was constructed to discriminate against women, its continued recognition and administration within a democracy is in conflict with post-1994 legislation and creates a disjuncture between policy and practice.

Women's involvement in land-related governance structures

Throughout apartheid, land administration was the responsibility of Tribal Authorities. These structures were male dominated and marginalised women in decision-making processes. Those women who did participate assumed positions such as secretary. Since the breakdown of the PTO system, traditional leaders no longer allocate land; their role is only to approve transfer of land.

Although rural women were marginalised in land-governance structures, their marginalisation in land-related governance structures was not equally experienced by all women in all communal areas. In some areas, such as Xhalanga in the Eastern Cape Province, where women actively participated in non-governmental organisations (NGOs) and residents' associations during the 1980s and 1990s, women are reported to have successfully challenged the legitimacy of traditional authorities in issues of land administration (Hendricks and Ntsebeza 1999; Ntsebeza 2005). Among the issues addressed by these structures were land shortages, bribery and ensuring transparent and participatory processes of land allocation (Ntsebeza 2005: 245; Fay 2005). Because PTOs were no longer issued during this period, the NGOs and residents' associations allocated land to many women without any legal documents, leaving women with land rights that were unclear and insecure in law (Ntsebeza 2005).

In other communal areas, such as Tshezi and Pondoland, where NGOs and residents' associations did not exist, traditional leaders continued to discriminate against women and used customary law to justify why women would not be granted equal rights to access land. As discussed below, the rights of traditional leaders to allocate land were not necessarily legitimate, but they earned their powers and respect from community members by instilling fear (Ntsebeza 2005). It can be argued that under such circumstances, land administration was inconsistent with the national gender equality legislation, and discrimination against women continued as a result of the application of customary law and patriarchal relations, which accorded key positions to men, leaving women's rights to access land precarious (Ntsebeza 2005).

Post-1994 legislative developments to advance gender equity in South Africa

As many governments around the globe began to recognise the unfair treatment of women concerning land tenure in South Africa, together with the United Nations (UN) bodies and NGOs, they increased their efforts to combat all forms of gender discrimination, including discrimination against women with regard to access to land. In 1979, the UN General Assembly adopted the Convention on the Elimination of All Forms of Discrimination Against Women (CEDAW), which was monitored by the committee on the elimination of discrimination against women. Today, many countries, including South Africa, have gender equity firmly enshrined in their constitutions.

The Constitution of the Republic of South Africa accords international standards set by the UN on ensuring equal rights to property. Section 9 stipulates that everyone is equal before the law and has the right to equal protection and benefit of the law, including full and equal enjoyment of all rights and freedoms. It also outlaws unfair discrimination on the basis of race, gender, sex, marital status, ethnic or social origin and culture. Section 25, which deals with property rights, entitles all South African citizens to equal access to land and to tenure that is legally secure. Section 25 (5) says that the government 'must take reasonable legislative and other measures, within its available resources, to foster conditions which enable citizens to gain access to land on an equitable basis'.[13] In addition, the *White Paper on South African Land Policy* endorses the principle of gender equity and targets women as a specific category of beneficiaries (Department of Land Affairs 1997). In this regard, women's land rights in South Africa are viewed in the context of property rights, which are protected under the Constitution.

Since 1998, South Africa has been a signatory to the CEDAW, which advances the idea of gender equality in acquiring land and categorically states that women should enjoy equal treatment in the context of acquiring land and agrarian reform.[14] By signing the CEDAW, South Africa agreed to incorporate the principles of equality between men and women in its legal system, to abolish all discriminatory laws and to adopt appropriate new laws prohibiting discrimination against women. In 2000, the government passed the Promotion of Equality and Prevention of Unfair Discrimination Act to prevent, prohibit and eliminate unfair discrimination and to promote equality. Section 8 of the Act states:

> Subject to section 6, no person may unfairly discriminate against any person on the ground of gender, including . . . (c) the system of preventing women from inheriting family property . . . [and] (e) any policy or conduct that unfairly limits access of women to land rights, finance, and other resources.[15]

The above post-1994 policies and legislation show that the government, led by the African National Congress (ANC), has attempted to promote equality between men and women in all spheres of life, including equal access to resources such as land. In 2003, the government passed the Traditional Leadership and Governance Framework Act (TLGFA) and, in 2004, the Communal Land Rights Act (CLARA), which both aimed at according women legal rights to access land in their own right and granting them legal right to participate in land-related governance structures. Regrettably, CLARA received much criticism from a variety of sources, including civil society organisations and gender and land rights activists, for giving unelected traditional leaders substantial and unprecedented powers over land, which some feared would deny many South Africans security of tenure. The Act was later invalidated by the Constitutional Court for being unconstitutional, in that it did not guarantee the rights laid down in Section 25 (6) of the Constitution.[16] In 2017, a new Bill was circulated for comment, but it has not yet been reintroduced to Parliament (Mabasa and Mabasa 2021: 94).

Traditional leaders and their perceptions of gender equality

Although the birth of democracy in South Africa envisaged the development of an equality-driven society, where the political ideals and rights of all citizens have a legitimate voice and are guaranteed by the Constitution, not all traditional leaders have supported gender equality in land-acquisition processes (Meer and Campbell 2007). Since the discussions that led to the adoption of the Interim Constitution, traditional leaders have shown intransigence when it comes to gender equality. They were strongly opposed to subjecting customary law to the equality clause in the Constitution, which resulted in the unclear articulation of the relationship between the clauses on custom and equality (Albertyn and Hassim 2003:146).

However, in recent years, there is some evidence that traditional leaders have started to change their stance towards granting land rights to women and including them in land-governance structures.[17] On the issue of granting land rights to women, the former president of the Congress of Traditional Leaders of South Africa (CONTRALESA) and current Member of Parliament, iNkosi Phathekile Holomisa, has indicated on a number of occasions that the institution of traditional leadership supports gender equality and women's rights to access land in their own right, based on their acknowledgement that women have always been users of land in the past.[18] What is confusing is the land tenure policy that followed in 2014, which gave traditional leaders the status of being beneficiaries of communal land tenure reform. This policy is likely to create the same insecurity of tenure for current landholders, especially women, as its predecessor, CLARA. In support of the Ingonyama Trust in KwaZulu-Natal, the former chairperson of the Eastern Cape Provincial House of Traditional Leaders, Chief Mwelo Nonkonyana, believes that traditional leaders should own and control land in rural areas (Mabasa and Mabasa 2021: 114). Likewise, iNkosi Phathekile Holomisa, supports the registration of communal land in the name of traditional authorities.[19]

This half-hearted acceptance of gender equality by traditional leaders, and their continued reluctance to grant equal land rights to women while, at the same time, aspiring to retain authority over land, has left the implementation of constitutional rights for rural women in limbo. The lack of clarity on the position of traditional leaders, who are deemed by many people under their jurisdictions as custodians of both customary law and land, and who also play significant roles in land allocation, is highly problematic. It leaves much to be desired in practice, especially because the policy and related legislation have no provision for households to hold traditional leaders accountable (Ntsebeza 2005). This raises questions as to how post-apartheid democratic laws are implemented and what instruments are used by the government to monitor land-administration processes in rural areas to ensure that there is no discrimination against women in the process of land allocation.

Given the apparent disjuncture between policy and practice, how can land rights of women in communal areas be understood? In answering this question, the next section will first provide feminism as a theoretical framework to understanding the current rights held by rural women and their participation in land-related governance structures. This is followed by a critique by African feminist scholars, who point out that a Western feminist perspective does not adequately describe rural women's land rights in South Africa.

A feminist perspective on women's land rights

Feminism is a worldwide movement that seeks to raise women's political, economic and social status and fight for gender equality in all aspects of life in all societies (Tong 2009). It aims to realise the liberation of women from all types of oppression and to provide solidarity among women of all countries. A feminist perspective is therefore, by its very nature, primarily concerned with the politics of power (Parry 2020: 2). Feminist scholars and theorists put the unequal power relationship between men and women at the centre of their struggle against all forms of injustice against women (Bayu 2019). They endeavour 'to reveal realities of power inequalities and provide evidence that can be deployed in working towards addressing engrained inequalities' (Mabasa and Mabasa 2021: 414). Feminism has different approaches, perspectives and frameworks for explaining women's oppression and proposed solutions for its elimination (Tong 2009) and how best to increase and protect women's rights. The most remarkable difference among them is the growing gap between the Global North and the Global South. Women from the North (for example, Western feminism) are harvesting the fruits of capitalism and the global economy, whereas women from the South (for example, Third World feminism) are all too often confronted with poverty and terrible labour conditions. Whereas Western feminists make equality between men and women the centre of their struggles, Third World feminism considers gender discrimination as neither the sole nor the primary focus of the oppression of Third World women, but believe that other types of oppression such as racism and economic exploitation must also defeated.

Western feminists explain women's experiences from the historical perception of patriarchy in Africa, which, they argue, was constructed as a product of colonialism to benefit men, disadvantage women and strengthen male control over female labour (Palmer 2002: 1; Mutangadura 2004). They insist on living free of patriarchal oppression, discrimination and violence (Mama 2001; Sirleaf 2009). In general, feminists believe that gender roles have been constructed by a male-dominated society at the expense of the women, whom the society exploits. Thus, in explaining the women's land right in communal areas, they argue that the lack of women's land rights, is a product of the colonial and apartheid legacy, which created a system whereby custom was used to rob rural women (in particular, single, divorced and widowed women) of the same land rights as men.

African feminism, on the other hand, is a movement started by African scholars around the 1970s to dispel misrepresentations of African women in Western feminism (Mekgwe, P 2006:13; Du Toit 2009), as well as to critique other variations of feminism. Their main point of critique of Western feminism is the tendency to overemphasise the role of patriarchy and women's subordination in explaining women's experiences, without taking into consideration the context in which women live – that is, their cultures, norms and standards. They posit that African women have unique experiences rooted in Africa. Although African feminism is not against all the things that other feminists struggle for – respect, dignity and equality – they do not agree that patriarchal systems and social relations are all embedded in oppressive and exploitative structures for women. With regard to rural women's land rights, they argue that Western feminism fails to explain how women who live under the jurisdiction of traditional leaders manage their aspirations to access land in practice. Western feminists fail to recognise the traditional role of clan leaders that existed before the coming of European coloniser and how rural women cope with cultural practices such as polygamy and inheritance rights. Instead, they portray African women as oppressed subjects, which asserts their incompatibility with being African and women's liberation (Oyěwùmí 2003). Their resentment of Western feminism led African women to develop African feminism, a perspective that seriously considers the context, needs and experiences of African women (Coetzee 2017; Mikell 1997; Mama 2001; Sirleaf 2009). Marren Akatsa-Bukachi describes an African feminist as follows:

> She is not just fighting for political space or social space; she is fighting
> for justice that goes right to the core of male egocentrism, the fallacy of
> male superiority and female subordination. She is fighting to eliminate the

root cause of women's oppression. The African Feminist must be ready to endure criticism, humiliation even pain, in order to overcome (2005: 12).

There are many variations of the African feminist perspective, but I will only touch on two schools of thought: those who insist that feminism is foreign to the African environment, on the one hand, and those who argue that feminism is indigenous to Africa, on the other hand. Those who insist that feminism is foreign to Africa argue that inequalities between men and women are not indigenous to African values (Salami 2017; Coetzee 2017; Mama 2001). They maintain that during the pre-colonial era, the concept of gender inequality did not exist, and therefore this concept is un-African. For them, gender relations during the pre-colonial era were based on an African form of democracy, a system in which African women historically performed different roles to men, in accordance to their different biological make-up and traditional role expectations.

In explaining the rights to access land, they support the view that land during the pre-colonial era belonged to the community, usually acquired by birth and, wherever it was abundant, every group member had access to it, irrespective of gender (Letsoalo 1987; Muela 1998). As discussed earlier, women played a central role in agricultural production, with equal rights to land as men. African feminism criticises Western feminism for trying to destroy these traditional gender roles and for ignoring the fact that everyone benefited from recognising the natural differences between men and women (Jayawardena 1986). However, despite women's central role in agricultural production, their right to access land changed during colonial era, to only usufruct rights acquired through their husbands or fathers, who would pass on title to land through the male line. Thus, African feminists contend that it was hereditary customary law, and the general global order, which was patriarchal and caused discrimination against women.

In explaining gender roles, African feminists criticise Western feminism for overemphasising patriarchy by focusing on male privilege and the subordination of women (Oyěwùmí 2005: 99). They assume that in Africa, men and women enter social relations as per their biological differences – constituted as powerful (men) or powerless (female) subjects (Bayu 2019). African feminists condemn this anti-male standpoint and argue that this biological rather than sociological conception creates a false unity of African women. African feminists contend that men are similarly oppressed under patriarchy and that gender equality means oppression of neither gender. For them, African women – and men – suffer not only from the patriarchal social structure, but also from other types of oppressions, as victims of racism, economic exploitation, neo-colonialism, cultural imperialism, religion, socio-economic mechanisms of operation, dictatorial and/or corrupt systems, which must be defeated (Bayu 2019).

Not only does this group of African feminists consider inequality to be un-African, they perceive imperialism as the main enemy of African women. They consider all its associations with other oppressive imperialist-driven motives that include the inhumane treatment of women and girls from human trafficking, gender-based violence, and so on, to be un-African. They argue that feminism does not provide a solution for these problems. Instead, they argue that feminism exists in Africa as a way to deepen contradictions that were brought by colonialism and to shift the focus away from the struggle of dismantling capitalism and colonial oppression, and seeking validation from the oppressor.

On the other hand, African feminist scholars who argue that feminism is indigenous to Africa dispute the view that the struggle for women's empowerment comes from the West (Ogundipe-Leslie 1994: 207–43; McClintock 1995: 384; Du Toit 2009: 421; Mama 2001: 60). They contend that since colonial times in Africa, there have been indigenous manifestations of the ideals of equity and resistance to all forms of domination, which have propelled African women's social action for centuries. African women's roles in activism stem from a long tradition of their integration in collective structures, which shaped their resistance to Western hegemony and its legacy, as well as their concerns with many 'bread and butter culture and power issues' (Mikell 1997: 4). Therefore, 'denouncing all feminism as imperialist . . . erases from memory the long histories of women's resistance to local and imperialist patriarchies . . . Many women's mutinies around the world predated Western Feminism' (McClintock 1995: 384).

African feminists blame Western feminists for their relentless efforts to assert their own ideology on Africans and for using their basic tenets and conclusions as a universal discourse applicable to all women's experiences, globally. They argue that this approach, which is drawn from their entanglement with the history and practices of European and North American imperialism and the European colonisation of Africa and Asia, presents a limited, singular and homogeneous perspective for understanding women, without taking into account particular African issues, their cultures, norms and standards (Oyěwùmí 2003; Mikell 1997; Daniels 2016; Walker 2017). They posit that women are not one group of people with the same backgrounds. They have diverse experiences and perspectives and therefore, their oppression is differently experienced from one woman to another, depending on cultural variations, religion, class, race, marital status, age, economic status, educational status, sexuality, position in the family and the nature of household as a domestic unit (Mikell 1997; Oyěwùmí 2003; Walker 2017: 34).

In addition to these shared sources of oppressions, they argue that African women's experiences and needs are based on the entire societies in which they live. But Western feminism ignores the fulfilment of these primary needs, but instead focuses on women's secondary needs, such as the burden of domestic work. By ignoring the effects of culture and portraying African women as victims of culture, Western feminism deprives African women of their capacity for social cultural production and historical agency. Hence, African feminists do not want to accept or adopt Western feminist theories and values, claiming that they are an imposition of Western ideologies that could destroy their African identities (Bayu 2019).

What African feminism has in common with Western feminism, however, is the view that men's access to and control over resources such as land and rewards within the private and public spheres derive their legitimacy from the ideology of male dominance (African Feminist Forum. 2007).[20] They argue that singling out women without a corresponding attention to men is a strategy used in Western feminist discourse to create an impression that Third World societies are male-dominated and anti-women. They strongly believe that in order to make their feminism movement gendered, men should not be detached from the struggle of women. In dealing with this, African feminism is suffused with the language of compromise, collaboration and negotiation, an approach that invites men to be partners in social change, and that knows when, where and how to detonate or to go around patriarchal landmines (Nnaemeka 2003: 377–8). This approach has received wide acceptance among men towards the establishment of a just society. Thus, African feminism opts for principles that demand a transformative agenda that places human rights at the centre 'to address the structural factors that perpetuate inequality, with the potential to respond to the real needs and interests of all people, including the needs of marginalised women' (Musindarwezo 2018: 26).

This approach has led to the representation of diverse and unique lived experiences across gendered and cultural divides, in addressing long histories of inequality, gender-based violence, systemic discrimination of marginalised groups, denying people their rights and equal opportunities with impacts that extend across generations and the distributive nature of agency. Through intersectionality, a concept coined by Kimberlé Crenshaw in 1989,[21] African feminism examines the ways in which African women suffer most of the various forms of oppression mentioned above, and how these intersect in constructing and (re)producing 'gender', race and class, including the consequences of colonialism and its aftermath, as well as the new patriarchal order imposed by global capitalism (Spencer-Wood 2016). The feminist intersectional prism advocates for the viewpoints and voices of African women, in order to understand the depths of the inequalities and the relationships among them (Bulbeck 1998: 14). Fighting for equality means not only turning the tables on gender injustices, but also rooting out all forms of oppression.

This understanding helps us to understand that patriarchy is not static, but to see it as a fluid phenomenon that varies in space and time, and is interrelated with and informs relationships of class, race, ethnic, religious and global imperial relationships (Akatsa-Bukachi 2005: 5). By building bridges across these divides, patriarchal structures, which have for a long time been used to keep women oppressed and separated, can be dismantled (Mouzinho and Sizaltina 2017).

This approach is strongly supported in this chapter, as it offers an understanding of gendered relations related to land access in communal areas. Granting women rights to access land in their own right (or the titling system) in communal area confirms the perception that women are 'performing traditional roles . . . without traditional resources . . . while at the same time undertaking modern activities . . . but being denied access to modern support systems' (Akatsi-Bukachi 2005: 6–7).

Although this assertion seems to resonate more with African women in urban areas, who are now entering the traditionally 'male world', it does not seem to account for the majority of poor women in rural areas. However, because of the urban influence and a rise in more educated women in rural areas, custom has evolved and rural women must be located in between the traditional and the modern world. This implies that for progress to occur, certain aspects of traditional tenure systems and culture may have to be reconciled with certain aspects of the modern systems within a framework that recognises and accepts the existence of traditional 'nested' systems of land rights, with special protection of women's land rights. This perspective suggests that in a democracy, some aspects of the customary law should be identified, rejuvenated and integrated with the 'modern' to suit the changing social conditions and needs of women in communal areas.

Community views on women's land rights in Tshezi

To understand rural women's rights to access land and participate in land-related governance, qualitative research methods through in-depth interviews and focus group discussions were undertaken. This was complemented by observations in the community and at the meetings of the Traditional Council, which were held at the Tshezi Tribal Authority (the Great Place). I only attended meetings where land allocations were part of the agenda. These mixed research methods were used to recognise multiple ways of understanding women's experiences and to make sense of their lived realities as they access land. This required continuous involvement with community members, to uncover how gender operates in a manner that is 'reflexive, alert to power differences, and recognizes diversity among and between men and women' (Aune 2009: 311).

Throughout my fieldwork, women were particularly encouraged to speak out about their experiences, challenges and/or the constraints they face in actualising their land rights. The purpose was to uncover non-salient aspects of gender oppression that are often not talked about, but continue to constrain women's rights to access land in their own right and to participate in land-related decision-making processes in communal areas. Questions were directed at exposing and unsettling evident inequitable power dynamics, elements of gender oppression and unconscious patriarchal biases, which are deeply embedded in the mindsets and lived experiences of participants. I respectfully and ethically engaged with all participants and valued all their contributions.

Evidence from the field provided a detailed descriptive and interpretive understanding of women's experiences as they access land in Tshezi, in which the following challenges/constraints were identified: the land allocation process, traditional leaders' demands, insecurity of tenure, lack of or little participation of women in final decision-making processes, and the continued application of patriarchy and customary law.

The Tshezi Traditional Council

Since the promulgation of the TLGFA and the Eastern Cape Traditional Leadership and Governance Framework Act of 2017, the Traditional Authorities in most communal areas of the Eastern Cape have been transformed into Traditional Councils. The purpose of establishing Traditional Councils was to align traditional rule more strongly with the principles of democracy and to hopefully remove some of the negative sentiments associated with traditional rule (Meer and Campbell 2007). The Act stipulates that 60 per cent of its members must be hereditary traditional leaders, 40 per cent must be democratically elected counsellors, and at least a third (33 per cent) of the members must be women. The problem with the constitution of the Traditional Councils is that the structure is still dominated by unelected hereditary chiefs, who have historically been unaccountable, undemocratic and despotic (Ntsebeza 2005) and have marginalised women in land-acquisition processes.

My observations of the Tshezi Traditional Council indicated that the structure had all the characteristics of a democratically constituted forum. It was chaired by the chief, had a secretary who was recording all proceedings and comprised both men and women (almost a third). The constitution of the Traditional Council seemed to comply with the requirements of the TLGFA. In terms of the TLGFA, one of the functions of the Traditional Council, which they have uneasily shared with government-appointed ward councillors, is the responsibility of land administration, which includes land allocation.

According to the agenda, individual community members who were present, including women, were allowed to present their cases to the Traditional Council. The issues addressed included settling community disputes and applications for land for home building, agriculture, pastoral purposes and for grazing stock on communal pastures. This observation suggests that the idea that individuals have little or no say or agency in the context of customary land tenure (Mabasa and Mabasa 2021) is incorrect. On the contrary, I observed that even women had a right to engage with issues and to make individual requests for plots of land. What customary law did not allow, however, was for women to publicly talk in turn with men; they are expected to respectfully ask clarity from their husbands.

To my surprise, after all the items on the agenda were discussed, I observed a demonstration of patriarchal tendencies at play. All the men quietly left the room, one by one, and gathered in the kraal. I was confused because there was no formal announcement of this move or adjournment of the meeting. When I asked where they were going, my informant told me that they were going to the kraal to make final decisions on some important issues that were discussed. As dictated by custom, this meant that at that point, women were free to go home and would hear about the decisions from their husbands at their homes. This indicated that even though women were allowed to participate in discussions, they were excluded from final decision-making processes, even on issues that concerned them directly because of the deeply entrenched patriarchal values, which dictate that men must be the last to speak.

Traditional leaders and their role in land allocation

At the meetings of the Traditional Council, I noticed that many applicants for land were unmarried women with children, who were older than eighteen. At one of the meetings, three young women stood up to request for 'site papers' or 'levy papers', which they referred to as 'incwadi zemizi'. After being asked to introduce themselves, stating their clan names, they were allowed to state their case to the chief. By that time, I had already established that all women, irrespective of marital status, were allowed to speak for themselves at the Great Place. Since the young women were not accompanied by a male relative, it was very interesting for me to observe how this would be handled in practice. Noting that they had no accomplice, the chairperson told them that in order for their request to be heard, they needed to go back and bring their male relatives and sub-headman or headman (father, husband or brother who would stand as witness or to give support to their application). The fact that they also had to bring a headman indicates that land rights are only granted to those who are associated with a ward head or by way of affinity of consanguinity (Mabasa and Mabasa 2021: 1). That is why agreement with family and the headman in the application process was considered important before land could be allocated.

It seemed that these young women had already built their own houses on their family fields, and they understood that they needed to have papers to increase their security of tenure against family members and community members who might want to interfere with their rights. This supports the view that most of the time, those who apply for land are seeking transfer of a piece of land within family fields because land in communal areas has already been allocated to families for decades. It was clear that allocating land to unmarried young girls with children in Tshezi was not a problem, but a democratic right, which was mostly driven by the quest of applicants to sustain their families. For many rural families, it is not enough for women to produce food (as in cultivating crops in their gardens), it is a cultural expectation that they would also prepare and put food on the table for all family members, including extended family members, whether they are employed or not, and whether there is a man or not.

This showed that even though women were legally allowed to negotiate their rights to access land in their own right, those who applied for land still could not be granted land without a male relative. The procedure was so strict that, should the chief recognize that no proper or sufficient consent was made, or no proper agreement was reached between the parties, no land would be allocated. However, the fact that family and land disputes in the traditional council meetings are generally adjudicated by men only fuels the perception that men are favoured over women, and that consequently, women may not receive appropriate assistance in land disputes. This also demonstrated that although the impact of patriarchy was very strong, it has become selective on shaping the type and nature of land rights women may enjoy.

Traditional leaders and their relationship to land

Land in Tshezi is more complex than it appears. There are seven categories of land tenure, one of which is communal land tenure (Coleman 2014). Communal land is unregistered state land that neither belongs to the Traditional Authority nor the Tshezi Development Trust. When community members were asked who owns the land, they were divided. Those who regarded the land as belonging to the entire community (the Tshezis) also understood that the chiefs are custodians who have authority to allocate land on behalf of the community. Because of the role traditional leaders have played in land allocation, some participants regarded the land as belonging to the senior chief. The chiefs also understood that their power and control over land was subject to the will of the people (Delius 2018).

On the question of whether traditional leaders should continue to allocate land, participants were divided. There were those who thought that land allocation should be the sole responsibility of traditional leaders. They attribute this to the fact that it has always been that way, as part of custom, which regards traditional leaders as custodians of land and customary law. On the other hand, there were others who did not trust traditional leaders anymore, who felt that land should remain with government, or should be administered by elected ward councillors. Their reason was that traditional leaders had historically displayed corrupt tendencies in allocating land and had sold some portions of community land for personal gain, rather than on behalf of the community and can therefore not be trusted. In some communal areas such as Tshezi, their conduct has not always respected the will of the people. Some have even submitted claims for land benefits in their own names as though they were the rightful owners of communal land from which communities were removed (Mabasa and Mabasa 2021: 116). A notable tendency has been for some chiefs to regard themselves as having unlimited authority over land and/or even as its owners, which would in turn, make them abuse the system and undermine the rights of community members, especially the rights of women. As discussed above, in some instances, this practice has been challenged by communities and individuals, who have asserted their rights on land (Bennet, Ainslie and Davis 2013; Mabasa and Mabasa 2021). The reality is that, at present, there is little certainty as to who has rights to land in communal areas, whether the rights are held by family heads, families, local communities or chiefs and traditional leaders (Mabasa and Mabasa 2021: 90, 92–3).

They were also concerned that the process of land allocation by traditional leaders or land administrators was not fair and equitable, mainly because of the commodification of land or demand for a 'levy' before any land allocation could occur. They said that this practice has opened traditional leaders to corruption in some instances, where they have demanded large cash payments for sites. Because of this, they thought that the land-acquisition process had little or no consideration of the different socio-economic backgrounds of applicants. They saw it as oppressive and insensitive to vulnerable members of community, especially widows and very poor women with children, who have nothing to offer by way of 'levies' for land. Instead, it created competition for land, benefiting those who are well-off more than the poor. Despite their ill-feeling about this practice, many participants considered this practice to be customary law and were proud to give 'gifts of appreciation' to their traditional leaders. However, they thought that the chiefs and the government should change the procedures followed for land allocation – as one participant said, 'People should only apply for land and get it, without any financial obligations or conditions, as the standards of living have now changed.'

Insecurity of tenure

The above field findings indicate that traditional leaders in Tshezi still play a significant role in land administration. Although their legitimacy in land allocation was often questioned by the people during my fieldwork, it was acknowledged that land already allocated to families was permanent and secure. But the security of tenure was experienced differently by women who had recently been allocated land in their own right. Many women interviewed reported that they did not feel that they had full ownership or full control of land they had recently acquired, but felt that men and traditional leaders were still in full control. Because of this, they continued to experience land tenure insecurity and some kind of vulnerability to male control and domination.

Their insecurity of tenure was exacerbated by the fact that the PTO certificates, which previously made them feel secure, were no longer being issued and, instead, they were given receipts in respect of land allocated to them. They considered the receipt to be meaningless in terms of granting them secure tenure, as it only provided them temporal rights, which undermines their political agency to defend their land rights. It also increases their vulnerability by creating an environment that is conducive for external parties, including men and/or traditional leaders, to exploit them, a situation that might even lead to abuse or gender-based violence should they resist. One of the women said that these informal rights are not fair and they need to be revised: 'The receipt does not guarantee anything. For instance, I have no confidence that this land belongs to me. I think the PTO is the only document that can protect our rights.' What was found to be unpleasant for many married women who had already acquired land in their own right was that they would experience loss of such rights upon death of their husbands, divorce or when they marry (if they are single).

Still others, specifically female landholders who had moved and leased their land to developers along the coast in Tshezi for various development initiatives, including the Hole in the Wall Hotel, said they had succumbed to customary law and male domination. In this regard, they spoke of the abuse of authority displayed by traditional leaders. In the past, negotiations for large tracts of land were entered only with the ward councillor and the chief, without consultation with the community (Coleman 2014). Because the land is registered as state land, the law does not provide for local communities to receive direct financial income from land transactions (Adams, Cousins and Manona 1999). It was expected that the chiefs would assert their control over such development initiatives on behalf of the community and would also collect and share dues from developers with the community. But many participants reported that traditional leaders have failed to share with community the proceeds derived from benefits on land belonging to the community (Buiten and Ntsebeza 1998). This display of authoritarian rule and lack of concern for the people has no place in a democracy. To this day, this issue remains unresolved. It has created tension and a wedge of distrust between the Tshezi people and the traditional leaders, since the people's interests and consent have been overridden by those in authority, making the land rights of community members, including the rights of women who are household heads, unclear, insecure, unprotected and disempowering.

The limited rights for rural women to access to land has been further compounded by pandemics that include HIV and AIDS and, more recently, Covid-19, which have affected women and men differently (Mutangadura 2004; Albertyn and Hassim 2003). Widows and children, whose parents succumbed to such pandemics, or young women who are living with sick parents, often do not have the right to inherit their late husband's or father's agricultural land and are thus condemned to poverty and dependency (Mutangadura 2004). Without land rights and very few job opportunities in rural areas, women who are household heads could be confronted with poverty, which stems from the burden of caring for and feeding their families.

Access and ownership of land is fundamental to the basic livelihood sustenance of rural women, and the continued discrimination from accessing or owning this basic resource is a violation of human rights. It is also contrary to article 16 of CEDAW, which requires that marriage and inheritance laws regarding land rights should be based on equality (Mutangadura 2004). This means that land tenure reform must ensure the protection of women's land rights during marriage, at divorce and in the event of the husband's death.

Because many women felt insecurity of tenure, it became clear that the disjuncture between policy and practice was creating confusion. In many instances, land rights were misunderstood, and in some instances, total ignorance of land rights was noted. Those who were most vulnerable were not aware of how legislation can protect their rights. Specifically, they were not aware of many post-1994 laws, including:

- The Upgrading of Land Tenure Rights Act (ULTRA) of 1991 provides for upgrading and conversion into ownership of certain rights granted in respect of land. It refers to the upgrading of informal land rights such as PTOs into full ownership for, among others, vulnerable groups such as rural women, female-headed households, persons living in rural areas, low-income groups, racial groups disadvantaged by past discrimination laws, and so on. Because PTOs were issued mostly to men in the past, ULTRA could make it difficult for women to realise their rights if the land is registered in the name of an individual (Mabasa and Mabasa 2021: 100).

- Interim Protection of Informal Land Rights Act (IPILRA) of 1996 provides for temporary protection of certain rights and interests in land that are not otherwise protected by law. The aim is to protect the position of people with untitled land rights under informal customary law, to ensure that they may not be deprived of their rights without their consent (Mabasa and Mabasa 2021: 25) The provisions of IPILRA applied up to December 2022.

- The Customary Marriages Act of 1998, which came into effect on 15 November 2000, provides that a wife in a customary marriage has, on the basis of equality with her husband and subject to the matrimonial property system governing the marriage, full status and capacity, including the capacity to acquire assets and to dispose of them, to enter into contracts and to litigate, in addition to any rights and powers that she might have under customary law (Mann 2000). It introduced elements such as rescission, variation or suspension of orders, and an accrual system, which were previously 'foreign' under customary law (Ozoemena and Hasungule 2009). Thus, a woman entering into customary marriage subsequent to the enactment of this legislation has property rights upon dissolution of the marriage.

General community perceptions about patriarchy and customary law

When asked about the general perceptions about patriarchy and customary law versus democratic principles, many participants were divided. Those who strongly held patriarchal attitudes (both men and women) were of the view that patriarchy is part of customary law, which should be respected at all times. They firmly believed that it is customary that men, as heads of families, should show leadership at all times and women should not speak and debate issues in front of men. Even though they appreciated the right for women to speak at the Traditional Council meetings, they thought that they should not speak out of turn with men.

When asked if granting women rights to access land in their own right would change their traditional perceptions about patriarchy and customary law, they were also divided. On the one hand, there were men who thought that allocating land to women should be discouraged because it would change men's perceptions about them. These men felt strongly that giving democratic rights to women gives them more power, which contradicts customary law, claiming that it, in turn, tends to undermine their dignity as men. The few men who held this view thought that seeing women with power was not only irritating, but improper. According to them, what they found irritating was the fact that women in power tend to boast about it, which causes men to change their attitudes towards them and refuse to accept them. They thought that because women are prioritised by government in development projects, they as men feel useless and powerless. Thus, with no prospect for opportunities, they get frustrated and develop hatred or jealousy towards women, perceiving them as threatening their positions accorded by customary law as heads of households and community leaders. In some instances, this would lead to gender-based violence, to assert their masculinity against women. When a man's breadwinner status is threatened by a wife who supplements income by working outside the home, poverty would lead them to engage in gender-based violence (Atanga 2013).

A few of those who claimed to have accepted democracy felt strongly that the government and women themselves are attempting to change their culture. Even those who strongly supported the view that women have equal rights to men, including some headmen interviewed, thought that 'the rights are only theoretical, and not realisable in practice'.

On the other hand, many men who argued that women in power would not change perceptions believed that men are natural heads and women are not supposed to lead at all. They backed this with a biblical scripture of creation, stating that God created men first to lead women, which they understood to mean that women are biologically and naturally weak. So, according to one of these men, 'women have no right to own land, especially married women who must respect their husbands'. As pointed out by one woman: 'It is very funny to see women leading men and men do not appreciate it.'

With regard to female authority, an example that was often given by almost all participants was the authority of the late Regent (Headwoman) Nowinase, who was killed in 2007. Her authority was heavily contested by the community, especially by men and traditional leaders who could not accept being ruled by a woman. Almost all participants carefully narrated this story with fear of reprisal for expressing their true sentiments on the issue, which was most of the time, in defence of the authority given to the former headwoman, exposing the tension between culture and democracy.

Conclusion

Land provides a sense of identity for people living in communal areas, but insecurity of land tenure among rural women, who are the main users of land, diminishes their sense of identity and chances to improve their livelihoods (Mabasa and Mabasa 2021: 110). If citizenship is about participation, rights and obligations, rural women's continued lack of land rights may suggest that they are lesser citizens with fewer rights than men. Similarly, their lack of rights and non-participation in land-related decision-making processes may result in policies that have negative effects on their livelihoods.

Even though the birth of democracy in South Africa in 1994 allowed for the development of an equality-driven society where all citizens have a legitimate voice and their rights are guaranteed by the Constitution, failure to provide security of tenure for people living in communal areas implies that land reform in South Africa has failed to fulfil the dreams of many South Africans (Mabasa and Mabasa 2021: 113). If women are the main cultivators of land in communal areas, their continued discrimination from accessing or owning this basic resource is a violation of human rights. Without rights to land, rural women's economic and physical security is compromised (Mutangadura 2004).

The above reflections from the field prove that post-apartheid land legislation has not fully encompassed the specific values that are held and practised by the majority of people in communal areas, nor have they respected the needs of rural women. Most of the time, post-1994 land reform policies apply a blanket approach to gender transformation, which underestimates the prevalence of gender differences and intersectional inequalities among rural women in rural land-access patterns (2021: 161).

Abundant evidence shows that the patriarchal practices of customary law still apply in Tshezi and the continued existence of these social constructs is a major constraint to granting women's clear and protected rights to access land in their own right as well as on their equitable participation in land-related governance structures. This is because of a disjuncture between protecting existing land rights' holders (usually men and/or traditional leaders), while attempting to bring about equity and justice in the process of granting land rights to rural women.

This disjuncture is demonstrated by several contradictions and shortcomings in existing land policy frameworks, which proves that various pieces of post-1994 legislation have been slow to provide transformation in communal areas. A clear example is the continued recognition of customary law and the empowerment of traditional leaders in the land-allocation processes, which tend to create conditions that counter some of the non-discriminatory provisions in the Constitution and other land-related policies. As observed in the Traditional Council meetings discussed above, failure by the Traditional Council to involve women in final decision-making processes indicates that the influence of gender equity legislation has not yet filtered down to the level of decision-making processes.

It also implies that its influence has been less effective in changing the attitudes of men and traditional leaders, which could negatively affect their willingness to resolve issues specific to women, including their mandate to allocate land rights to women. If not challenged, the implementation of gender equity legislation in communal areas may remain theoretical and the rights of women may remain a pipedream.

An important observation was the fact that even though legally, rural women can now access land in their own right, and/or can participate in the Traditional Council, they have not derived any significant benefits from these developments insofar as actualising independent and protected land rights. Single, widowed and divorced women continue to be vulnerable to male control and domination. Although some forms of discriminatory behaviour by traditional leaders were still noted, the women's awareness of gender equity legislation seemed to have shaped their attitudes and aspirations to access land in their own right.

This has resulted in two developments: women's assertiveness to independently negotiate their rights to access land, irrespective of patriarchy, and agency among women to challenge the system in defence of their land rights. What I found interesting was that despite these aspirations, women still wanted to show respect to their custom. They were not totally against patriarchy, which placed men in leadership roles, but did not want to be totally excluded from decision-making processes.

With regard to the role of women in agriculture, the current policies pay scant attention to the involvement of women in informal food production, their reproductive labour and the gendered nature of food security (Mabasa and Mabasa 2021: 161). This lack of focus coincides with the Marxist and socialist feminist analysis that current land reform does not benefit women, but advances the interests of a small elite in the commercial sector (usually white men) at the expense of the land and citizenship rights of about 18 million South Africans living in communal areas. This limited notion of agrarian transformation has led to the preservation of gendered socio-economic inequalities in communal areas (Walker 2002).

In many post-colonial African national constitutions, gender justice is a right and value. Because the current policies have not been effective enough to alter discriminative and oppressive behaviour associated with customary law, it is clear that constitutions and international human rights instruments have not achieved gender justice. It is possible that failure to reform societal relations in diverse traditional African communities is because the application of these instruments within African traditional societies is inappropriate (Ozoemena and Hansungule 2009). In this regard, such legislation might be seen as tools that hamper the development of indigenous or customary law.

From a post-colonial African feminist perspective, this chapter has demonstrated gender-differentiated aspects of rural women's land rights, which allows for an understanding and untangling of the broader social dimensions of inequalities between men and women in accessing land and the underlying lack of power of women in land-related decision-making processes. Through understanding women's lived experiences, the analysis in this chapter has elucidated socially constructed stereotypes and unearthed subjugated experiences, which can be used as a framework to interface the coexistence of the indigenous ways of allocating land to women based on African values, cultures and lifestyles, with their quest for the application of democratic rights in the process of actualising their rights to land.

It can thus be concluded that the application of gender equity legislation, in a context that is largely shaped by patriarchy and customary law, tends to generate tension that continues to (re)entrench a colonial mindset of patriarchy in both traditional leaders and community members (especially men), which has, in turn, continued the marginalisation of women in land-access processes and their subsequent exclusion in land-related decision-making processes. This tension was demonstrated by women's despondence in complying with the demands of patriarchy and their apparent rejection of the continued role played by traditional leaders in land administration. Interestingly for Tshezi, while constraints on women's rights to access land seemed to be strongly related to the application of patriarchy and customary law, reflections from the field indicated that not all women (as a group) submit to patriarchy, but individual women, irrespective of background, devise strategies to independently negotiate access to land. The success of their negotiation, however, is largely dependent on whether or not they are able to persuade the traditional leaders of their need.

However, despite the assertiveness of women in negotiating their rights to access land, and the apparent dwindling of patriarchal attitudes and practices held by community members and traditional leaders mentioned above, patriarchy (a colonial construct) and customary law (a traditional construct) produce tension that continues to render rural women vulnerable to male control and domination.

It would seem that the following new developments have emerged in the process of allocating land to women communal areas, which are also enforced by law:

1) Patriarchy and customary law are fluid concepts that can coexist and can be used as analytic tools for understanding rural women's land rights and their participation in land-related governance structures.

2) Rural women are straddling two processes in actualising their land rights – neo-liberalisation and neo-traditionalism – and these constructs have a strong impact on understanding the existing gender and power relations in the process of land acquisition.

3) Rather than shoving customary land tenure aside in communal areas, it should be rejuvenated by recognising and retaining important aspects more consistent with pre-colonial land rights, which recognised strong rights held by women to arable land and to 'house' property (Claassens 2005; Mbasa and Mbasa 2021: 93).

Recommendations

The issue of substantive gender equality in relation to land cannot be separated from women's struggles for other socio-economic rights. Policy options should pay more attention to reducing land disparities between women and men, with propositions that appreciate the depth of the land question and its multiple dimensions (Mabasa and Mabasa 2021: 16, 179). To reduce the growing poverty among rural women, more focus should be on recognising intersectional inequalities among them, understanding their diverse interests and needs, as well as their relationship with land. This will require the removal of colonial distortions that have bred inequalities in land-access rights and political will to encourage advocacy for inclusive decision-making (Mabasa and Mabasa 2021: 25; Walker 2017).

Except for the Communal Land Tenure Bill of 2017 and the National Land Reform Framework Bill of 2017, there is currently no law in South Africa that provides for rural women's independent access to land in communal areas, and therefore, no guarantee that the land rights of rural women are protected. The government should revise the land laws, regulations and policies applicable to communal areas to strengthen and protect the existing land rights of women under customary tenure, including the security of tenure of single, married, divorced or widowed women, as well as the rights of orphans who have lost their parents due to pandemics.

The law must have clauses that give a clear and direct provision that ensures that rural women's rights to land will be protected and will not be discriminated against in land acquisition processes – whether in house property, informal food production or in small-scale farming. In this regard, all personal, family and customary law related to land access that discriminates against women should be repealed. This refers to any harmful traditional practices that are constraining rural women's rights to land, including provisions on inheritance, security of tenure, or any other legislation that could prevent them from owning land in their own right. There should also be instruments or strategies to monitor land-allocation processes, with a provision to hold traditional leaders who allocate land accountable.

To increase security of tenure for married women, and ensure that they are equal partners in marriage, there should be a provision for joint registration of customary and/or statutory household land rights for spouses. To correct this, legislative measures to remove legal and economic inequality between partners in marriage must be taken. The provisions of the Recognition of the Customary Law Marriages Act 120 of 1998 should be integrated to communally based norms, which consider the married woman to be part of a family group and clan, entitled to farm lands for growing cash crops and agricultural trees. In the case of divorce, neither spouse has a claim to the other's property which was acquired during the marriage.

Because most people in rural areas are poor women who play a crucial role in food security, the land reform legislation should recognise that women need to be effectively empowered with education, knowledge and skills not only to access resources such as land, but also, to fully participate, as equal citizens, in the economic and political development of their communities, including participation in the implementation of macroeconomic policies, national development plans and poverty-alleviation strategies.

Women should be provided with opportunities to develop collective responses to resist negative aspects of agrarian transformation. In this regard, the national land reform must support women-led collective agency and encourage active civil society action around their land rights and agrarian transformation (Mabasa and Mabasa 2021: 16, 161).

Communal areas must be integrated into the mainstream of land reform and agrarian policy, so that women's land rights in these areas can be expanded beyond the ghetto of 'custom' and 'tradition' (Walker 2017). It is obvious that the current

PTO system is no longer relevant for people in communal areas and preference should be for rightful ownership vested in all land users who qualify, including women. This implies that the status of informal rights should be legally confirmed and the legitimate cultural practices related to it in the eyes of the rights holders, whether male or female, should be recognised.

Alternatively, the government should be open to alternative policy options with regard to communal land-holding systems, which ensure that those with weaker rights (such as women) are not dispossessed, but instead should be given alternative land (Adams, Cousins and Manona 1999: 25). I concur with an alternative suggested by the Advisory Panel on Land Reform and Agriculture (2019: 36–7), a landholding system that builds on African traditional systems, where community control over land access and development is restored. Moreover, the findings in a study on the effect of titling on tenure security in two communities in the Eastern Cape, showed that in cases where rights or tenure are titled, people still evaluate their rights and security in tenure in the social context, rather than relying on the title deed owner (Kingwill 2008).

Another suggestion is a land records system that is parallel to the Deeds Registry, which records existing informal rights on communal land and makes them upgradable to title if the family agrees (Piennar 2010; Mabasa and Mabasa 2021). But the problem is that the South African registration system does not allow for the registration of African indigenous land rights, but rather classifies rights in terms of the common law notion of 'ownership' (Du Plessis 2011). If implemented, this may gradually move towards a single system that would guarantee secure tenure for all landholders, including women.

Lastly, in a country where women currently make up about 50 per cent of the rural population, the government could benefit from reversing the colonial and apartheid-era policies that still deny women formal rights to land and discriminate against women in land administration. In practice, this means removing all colonial legislative biases to communal land tenure and integrating a gender-sensitive approach that ensures equal representation of men and women in municipal councils, tribal authorities and all decision-making structures related to land into rural governance.

This should be complemented by national guidelines and training of legal personnel, government officials, NGOs, traditional leaders, land allocation committees and development community workers in rural areas. In addition, programmes, activities and education campaigns must be rolled out to decolonise the perception of patriarchy and customary law, which continue to be deeply entrenched in the mindsets of rural communties.

There should be more emphasis on how to implement gender equity in line with Article 14 of CEDAW and Goal 3 of the Millenium Development Goals, which specifically addresses women and calls for the eradication of gender inequality in rural areas. This may call for the decolonisation of the deeply entrenched patriarchal attitudes in relation to customary law that govern landownership in communal areas. Its success may require rethinking, rearticulation and/or redefinition of the concepts of patriarchy and customary law, from a post-colonial African perspective, an approach that places African standards, cultures and traditions at the centre.

Notes

1. https://www.theglobaleconomy.com/South-Africa/rural_population_percent/#:~:text=Rural%20 population%2C%20percent%20of%20total%20population&text=The%20latest%20value%20 from%202022,196%20countries%20is%2038.97%20percent (accessed 22 September 2023).
2. https://tradingeconomics.com/south-africa/rural-population-percent-of-total-population-wb-data.html (accessed 22 September 2023).
3. In this chapter, the term 'rural areas' is used interchangeably with 'communal areas' of South Africa. These areas include former homelands and South African Development Trust land, where land is either allocated by the chiefs or headmen and, more recently, by the Department of Agriculture.
4. In this chapter, 'rural women' refers to black African women living in communal areas of South Africa, as explained in note 3.
5. This chapter is from work in progress, which was initiated as part of my doctoral studies at the University of Cape Town.
6. Communal land is held in trust by the Minister of Rural Development and Land Reform, regarded as state land, but also co-owned by the local community. It is considered by the government as unregistered land, legally belonging to the state.
7. The concepts of chief, headman, headwoman or traditional leader are used interchangeably in this chapter to refer to persons that wield traditional authority.
8. *Veldkos*: 'Food gathered from the countryside, particularly bulbs and tubers, but also other plant foods, insects, grubs, and small game'. https://dsae.co.za/entry/veldkos/e07613 (accessed 22 September 2023).
9. 'Nested rights' focus on the status of women's land rights within the family, village or clan. It considers the rights of villagers or user groups to specific portions of land within the broader community or 'tribe'.
10. https://www.gov.za/1913-natives-land-act-centenary (accessed 22 September 2023).

11. https://www.gov.za/1913-natives-land-act-centenary (accessed 22 September 2023).

12. The rules governing the PTOs provided for residential and arable purposes and that they be granted by native commissioners, after consulting with the Tribal Authority, chief or headman. However, commissioners often vetoed headmen's allocations to women, thereby changing the practice of women being allocated land in their own right (Wilson and Mills 1952; Simons 1968).

13. https://www.justice.gov.za/constitution/chp02.html (accessed 22 September 2023).

14. Article 14 (2) (h) of the Convention on the Elimination of all Forms of Discrimination against Women.

15. https://www.justice.gov.za/legislation/acts/2000-004.pdf (accessed 22 September 2023).

16. Section 25 (6) reads: 'A person or community whose tenure of land is legally insecure as a result of past discriminatory laws or practices is entitled, to the extent provided by the Act of Parliament, either to tenure which is legally secure or to comparable redress.' https://www.justice.gov.za/constitution/chp02.html (accessed 22 September 2023).

17. Deliberations by traditional leaders at the Imbumba Yamakhosikazi Akomkhulu (IYA) conference, which was held at the Great Place in the Eastern Cape. IYA is a formation for wives of traditional leaders that is focused on the development of rural women and girls.

18. Cited in *Business Day*, 24 June 2002 and reiterated at the National Heritage Council's *imbizo* for the drafting of the Heritage Transformation Charter in December 2007.

19. 'Communal Land Is Private Property', *Daily Dispatch*, June 2018.

20. The *Charter of Feminist Principles for African Feminists* was formulated by the African Feminist Forum during a 2006 gathering of African women feminists from around the world in Accra, Ghana, to create baseline principles that address definitions of African feminism and patriarchy.

21. https://www.unwomen.org/en/news/stories/2020/6/explainer-intersectional-feminism-what-it-means-and-why-it-matters (accessed 22 September 2023).

References

Adams, M., B. Cousins and S. Manona. 1999. 'Land Tenure and Economic Development in Rural South Africa: Constraints and Opportunities'. Paper presented at the National Conference on Land and Agrarian Reform in South Africa, Pretoria.

Advisory Panel on Land Reform and Agriculture. 2019. *Final Report of the Presidential Advisory Panel on Land Reform and Agriculture*. https://www.gov.za/sites/default/files/gcis_document/201907/panelreportlandreform_1.pdf (accessed 22 September 2023).

African Feminist Forum. 2007. *Charter of Feminist Principles for African Feminists*. https://africlub.net/awdf/wp-content/uploads/AFF-Feminist-Charter-Digital-â%C2%80%C2%93-English.pdf (accessed 22 September 2023).

Akatsa-Bukachi, M. 2005. 'African Feminism: Does It Exist?' Presentation made at the Tanzania Gender Networking Programme, Gender Festival, 6–9 September.

Albertyn, C. and S. Hassim. 2003. 'The Boundaries of Democracy: Gender, HIV and Culture'. In: *The Real State of the Nation: South Africa after 1990*, edited by D. Everatt and V. Maphai, 137–63. Johannesburg: Interfund.

Atanga, L.L. 'African Feminism?' In: *Gender and Language in Sub-Saharan Africa: Tradition, Struggle and Change*, edited by L.L. Atanga, S.E. Ellece, L. Litosseliti and J. Sunderland, 301–14. Amsterdam: John Benjamins Publishing Company.

Aune, K. 2009. 'Feminist Ethnography'. In: *Encyclopaedia of Gender and Society, Vol. 1*, edited by J. O'Brien, 308–11. Thousand Oaks: Sage Publications.

Bayu, E.K. 2019. 'A Comparative Analysis on the Perspectives of African Feminism vs Western Feminism: Philosophical Debate with Their Criticism and Its Implication for Women's Rights in Ethiopia Context'. *International Journal of Sociology and Anthropology* 11 (4): 54–8.

Bennet, I., A. Ainslie and J. Davis. 2013. 'Contested Institutions? Traditional Leaders and Land Access and Control in Communal Areas of Eastern Cape Province, South Africa'. *Land Use Policy* 32: 27–38.

Bennet T.W. 2015 *Customary Law in South Africa*. Cape Town: Juta.

Birgegard, L.E. 1993. *Natural Resource Tenure: A Review of Issues and Experiences with Emphasis on Sub-Saharan Africa*. Uppsala: Swedish University of Agricultural Sciences, International Rural Development Centre.

Bob, U. 2002. 'Rural African Women, Food (In)security and Agricultural Production in the Ekuthuleni Land Redistribution Project, KwaZulu-Natal'. *Agenda* 51: 16–32.

Boumans, D. 2004. 'Land Reform and Empowerment: A Match Made by Law, an Illusion Ruined by Reality? The Case of Uganda'. Master's thesis, Centre for International Development Issues, University of Nijmegen.

Buiten, E. and L. Ntsebeza. 1998. *Resolution of Land Ownership and Governance Issues in the Tshezi Communal Area, Mqanduli, Coffee Bay Cluster*. Wild Coast Spatial Development Initiative, report submitted to Department of Land Affairs.

Bulbeck, C. 1998. *Reorienting Western Feminisms: Women's Diversity in a Post-colonial World*. Cambridge: Cambridge University Press.

Bundy, C. 1988. *The Rise and Fall of the South African Peasantry*. Claremont: David Philip.

Claassens, A. 2005. 'The Communal Land Rights Act and Women: Does the Act Remedy or Entrench Discrimination and the Distortion of the Customary?' Occasional paper, Land Reform and Agrarian Change in Southern Africa, Programme for Land and Agrarian Studies, and Legal Resources Centre, University of Western Cape, Cape Town. http://hdl.handle.net/10566/4398 (accessed 22 September 2023).

Claassens, A. and B. Cousins (eds). 2008. *Land, Power and Custom: Controversies Generated by South Africa's Communal Land Rights Act*. Cape Town: University of Cape Town Press; Athens: Ohio University Press.

Coetzee, A.A. 2017. 'African Feminism as Decolonising Force: A Philosophical Exploration of the work of Oyèrónké Oyěwùmí'. PhD diss., Stellenbosch University.

Coleman, C. 2014. 'Tshezi Land Tenure'. Draft. https://www.academia.edu/24018983/TSHEZI_LAND_TENURE (accessed 22 September 2023).

Cousins, B. and D. Hornby. 2009. '*Imithetho yomhlaba yaseMsinga*: The Land Laws of Msinga and Potential Impacts of the Communal Land Rights Act'. Church Agricultural Projects (CAP) and the Learning and Action Project (LEAP).

Cross, C. and D. Hornby. 2002. *Opportunities and Obstacles to Women's Land Access in South Africa*. Research report for the National Land Committee of South Africa and South Africa's Department of Land Affairs.

Daniels, A. 2016. 'South Africa: Women – A Focus on Land'. *Land News Portal.* https://landportal.org/node/28207 (accessed 22 September 2023).

Delius, P. 2018. *Mistaking Form over Substance: Reflection on the Key Dynamics of Precolonial Polities and Their Implications for the Role of Chiefs in Contemporary South Africa*. MISTRA Working Paper. https://mistra.org.za/wp-content/uploads/2019/10/Delius-Working-Paper_-201802.pdf (accessed 22 September 2023).

Department of Land Affairs. 1997. *White Paper on South African Land Policy*. https://www.gov.za/sites/default/files/gcis_document/201411/whitepaperlandreform.pdf (accessed 22 September 2023).

Du Plessis, W.J. 2011. 'African Indigenous Land Rights in a Private Ownership Paradigm'. *Potchefstroom Electronic Law Journal.* http://www.scielo.org.za/scielo.php?script=sci_arttext&pid=S1727-37812011000700003 (accessed 22 September 2023).

Du Plessis, W. and J. Pienaar. 2010. 'The More Things Change, the More They Stay the Same: The Story of Communal Land Tenure in South Africa'. *Fundamina* 16 (1): 73–89.

Du Toit, H.L. 2009. *A Philosophical Investigation of Rape: The Making and Unmaking of the Feminine Self*. New York: Routledge.

Fay, D. 2005. 'Kinship and Access to Land in the Eastern Cape: Implications for Land Tenure Reform'. *Social Dynamics* 31 (1): 182–207.

Goheen, M. 1996. *Men Own the Fields, Women Own the Crops: Gender and Power in the Cameroon Grassfields*. Madison: University of Wisconsin Press.

Hendricks, F. and L. Ntsebeza. 1999. 'Chiefs and Rural Local Government in Post-apartheid South Africa'. *African e-Journals Project* 4 (1): 99–126.

Hodgson, J. 2021. *Black Womanism in South Africa: Princess Emma Sandile*. Cape Town: Best Red, an imprint of HSRC Press.

Jayawardena, K. 1986. *Feminism and Nationalism in the Third World*. New York: Verso.

Kameri-Mbote, P. 2005. *The Land Has Its Owners! Gender Issues in Land Tenure under Customary Law in Kenya*. https://dlc.dlib.indiana.edu/dlc/bitstream/handle/10535/191/Gender_customary.pdf (accessed 22 September 2023).

Kingwill, R. 2008. 'Custom-Building Freehold Title: The Impact of Family Values on Historical Ownership in the Eastern Cape'. In: *Land, Power and Custom: Controversies Generated by South Africa's Communal Land Rights Act*, edited by A. Claassens and B. Cousins, 184–208. Cape Town: UCT Press.

Letsoalo M. 1987. *Land Reform in South Africa, A Black Perspective*. Johannesburg: Akotaville Publishers.

Mabasa, K. and B. Mabasa (eds). 2021. *Land in South Africa: Contested Meanings and Nation Formation*. Johannesburg: MISTRA.

Mama, A. 2001. 'Talking about Feminism in Africa'. *Agenda* 50: 58–63.

Mann, M. 2000. *Women's Access to Land in the Former Bantustans: Constitutional Conflict, Customary Law, Democratisation and the Role of the State*. Programme for Land and Agrarian Studies Occasional Paper No. 15, University of the Western Cape. http://hdl.handle.net/10566/4364 (accessed 22 September 2023).

Mbilinyi, M. and G. Shechambo. 2009. 'Struggles over Land Reform in Tanzania: Experiences of Tanzania Gender Networking Programme and Feminist Activist Coalition. *Feminist Africa* 12: 94–104.

McClintock, A. 1995. *Imperial Leather: Race, Gender and Sexuality in the Colonial Contest*. New York: Routledge.

Meer, S. (ed.). 1997. *Women, Land and Authority: Perspetives from South Africa*. Cape Town: David Philip.

Meer, T. and C. Campbell. 2007. *Traditional Leadership in Democratic South Africa*. Cape Town: Democracy Development Programme.

Mekgwe, P. 2006. 'Theorising African Feminism(s): The "Colonial" Question'. *Quest: An African Journal of Philosophy* 20 (1): 11–22.

Mikell, G. 1997. *African Feminism: The Politics of Survival in Sub-Saharan Africa*. Philadelphia: University of Pennsylvania Press.

Mouzinho, A. and C. Sizaltina. 2017. 'Reflections on Feminist Organising in Angola'. *Feminist Africa* 22: 33–51.

Muela, N.K. 1998. 'The Situation of Eritrean Female Immigrants in Uppsala: Practical Application of Participatory Rural Appraisal Methods'. Uppsala: Swedish University of Agricultural Sciences, International Rural Development Centre.

Musindarwezo, D. 2018. 'The 2030 Agenda from a Feminist Perspective: No Meaningful Gains without Greater Accountability for African Women'. *Agenda* 32: 25–35.

Mutangadura, G. 2004. 'Women and Land Tenure Rights in Southern Africa: A Human Rights Based Approach'. Paper prepared for Session Two: Gender, Land Rights and Inheritance, Church House, Westminister, London, United Kingdom, 8–9 November.

National Land Committee. 2003. *Land Tenure Reforms in South Africa*.

Nnaemeka, O. 2003. 'Nego-Feminism: Theorising, Practicing and Pruning Africa's Way'. *Signs* 29 (2): 357–86.

Ntsebeza, L. 1999. *Land Tenure Reform, Traditional Authorities and Rural Local Government in Post-apartheid South Africa: Case Studies from the Eastern Cape*. Programme for Land and Agrarian Studies Research Report No. 3. Cape Town: University of the Western Cape. https://repository.uwc.ac.za/bitstream/handle/10566/4370/op_22_decentralisation_natural_resource_management_south_africa_problems_prospects_2002.pdf?sequence=1&isAllowed=y (accessed 22 September 2023).

——. 2005. *Democracy Compromised: Chiefs and the Politics of Land in South Africa*. Leiden: Brill.

Ogundipe-Leslie, O. 1994. *Recreating Ourselves: African Women and Critical Transformations*. Trenton: Africa World Press.

Oyěwùmí, O. 2003. *African Women and Feminism: Reflecting on the Politics of Sisterhood*. Trenton: Africa World Press.

——. 2005. *African Gender Studies: A Reader*. New York: Palgrave Macmillan.

Ozoemena, R. and M. Hansungule. 2009. *Re-envisioning Gender Justice in African Customary Law through Traditional Institutions*. Johannesburg: Centre for Policy Studies.

Palmer, R. 2002. *Gendered Land Rights: Process, Struggle, or Lost C(l)ause*. https://mokoro. co.uk/wp-content/uploads/gendered_land_rights.pdf (accessed 22 September 2023).

Parry, B. 2020. 'Feminist Research Principles and Practices'. In: *Online Reading in Research Methods*, edited by S. Kramer, S. Laher, A. Fynn and H.H. Janse van Vuuren, 1–28. Johannesburg: Psychological Society of South Africa.

Pienaar, G. 2010. 'Land Information as a Tool for Effective Land Administration and Development'. Unpublished paper delivered at the Colloquium on Development, Pluralism and Access to Resources at the University of Cape Town, 26–27 November.

PLAAS/NLC (Programme for Land and Agrarian Studies/National Land Committee) Community Consultation Project. 2003. *Submission on the Communal Land Rights Bill*. Cape Town: Land and Agriculture Portfolio Committee.

Preston-Whyte, E. 1974. 'Kinship and Marriage'. In: *The Bantu-Speaking Peoples of Southern Africa*, edited by W.D. Hammond-Tooke, 177–210. London: Routledge.

Salami, M. 2017. 'The Question: Is African Feminism Un-African?' *The Africa Report*, 23 May. https://www.theafricareport.com/815/is-feminism-african/ (accessed 22 September 2023).

Schapera, I. 1943. *Native Land Tenure in the Bechuanaland Protectorate*. Alice: Lovedale Press.

Simons, J. 1968. *African Women: Their Legal Status in South Africa*. London: Hurst

Sirleaf, E.J. 2009. 'African Feminism Leads Way, Western Feminists Yet to Yield'. *Liberal Observer*, 30 December. http://www.liberianobserver.com/node/37 (accessed 22 September 2023).

Soga, J.H. 1931. *The Ama-Xhosa: Life and Customs*. Alice: Lovedale Press.

South African Law Reform Commission. 2004. *Report on the Customary Law of Succession*. https://www.justice.gov.za/salrc/reports/r_prj90_customarylawsuccession2004.pdf (accessed 22 September 2023).

Spencer-Wood, S.M. 2016. 'Feminist Theorizing of Patriarchal Colonialism, Power Dynamics, and Social Agency Materialized in Colonial Institutions'. *International Journal of Historical Archaelogy* 20 (3): 477–91.

Stats SA (Statistics South Africa). 2016. *Community Survey 2: Agricultural Households*. https://www.statssa.gov.za/publications/03-01-05/Presentation_CS2016_Agricultural_Households.pdf (accessed 22 September 2023).

————. 2019. *Towards Measuring the Extent of Food Security in South Africa: An Examination of Hunger and Food Inadequacy*. Report 03-00-14. https://www.statssa.gov.za/publications/ 03-00-14/03-00-142017.pdf (accessed 22 September 2023).

————. 2023. 'Focus on Food Inadequacy and Hunger in South Africa in 2021'. https:// www.statssa.gov.za/?p=16235#:~:text=One%20in%20five%20female%2Dheaded, agricultural%20activities%20to%20produce%20food (accessed 22 September 2023).

Tong, R. 2009. *Feminist Thought: A More Comprehensive Introduction*. New York: Routledge.

Walker, C. 2002. *Land Reform in Southern and Eastern Africa: Key Issues for Strengthening Women's Access to Land Rights in Land*. Paper prepared for the Food and Agriculture Organisation. Rome: FAO. https://www.jurisafrica.org/wp-content/uploads/2021/10/ Walker-on-Womens-access-to-Land.doc-min.pdf (accessed 22 September 2023).

————. 2003. 'Piety in the Sky? Gender Policy and Land Reform in South Africa'. *Journal of Agrarian Change* 3: 113–48.

————. 2017. 'Women's Land Rights, Agrarian Change and Gender Transformation in Post-apartheid South Africa'. In: *Du grain à moudre: Genre, développement rural et alimentation*, edited by C. Verschuur, 247–67. Open Edition Books (online).

Wilson, M. and M.E.E. Mills. 1952. *Land Tenure: The Keiskammahoek Rural Survey, Vol. IV*. Pietermaritzburg: Shuter & Shooter.

PART 2

ECONOMY

Examining the South African Social and Economic Landscape through a Statistical Lens

Risenga Maluleke, Solly Molayi and Faizel Mohammed

Background

In this chapter, we examine South African society from a statistical perspective, which reflects the experiences and viewpoints of its citizens. This includes having confidence in the Constitution. Recent data from the *Governance, Public Safety and Justice Survey* (GPSJS) (Stats SA 2022b) show widespread knowledge of the Constitution and that most people (70.7 per cent) believe it protects their rights. Approximately 66 per cent of people aged sixteen years or older believe that democracy gives them some influence over what the government does. These beliefs display consensus and harmony among the people in the country. Peace and fairness for all citizens are a requirement for growth in any society because they foster an environment that fosters social advancement.

The *National Development Plan 2030* (NDP) (National Planning Commission 2012) and the Constitution define South Africa as a developing state that is accountable, prioritises its citizens' needs and continuously provides high-quality services through collaborative governance and democratic participation (Stats SA 2020c). Additionally, the Constitution enshrines a number of basic human rights that should be realised immediately or gradually over time. To confront the triple challenge of poverty, unemployment and inequality, the government has developed and implemented several policies and policy frameworks since 1994. The *Revised Medium Term Strategic Framework (MTSF) 2019–2024* (Department of Planning, Monitoring and Evaluation 2019a) and the NDP are two frameworks South Africa has created at the national level to guide implementation and monitor growth.

On the global front, the United Nations' Sustainable Development Goals (SDGs) are a rallying call to the world aimed at eradicating poverty, protecting the environment and ensuring peace and prosperity for all by 2030. Achieving the SDGs in Africa requires the creation of inclusive, peaceful societies where everyone has access to justice. By collaborating and working together, governments, communities and civil society can guarantee opportunities for all and create a world where peace is not just a dream, but a reality. In 2013, the African Union adopted *Agenda 2063: The Africa We Want*, the continent's new long-term vision policy framework to maximise the use of Africa's resources for the benefit of its people to achieve prosperity (AU 2013; Stats SA 2020c).

To address the triple challenges of poverty, inequality and unemployment in the nation, the South African government launched the *Economic Reconstruction and Recovery Plan* (ERRP) in 2020, which economically empowers women, youth and persons with disabilities (South African Government 2020). More recently, the government introduced the District Development Model (DDM), which promotes integrated government co-ordination in addressing economic, environmental and social challenges over an extended period and goes beyond municipal, provincial and national election cycles, with a focus on empowering the marginalised sectors of the population (Department of Cooperative Governance and Traditional Affairs 2022).

It has been widely acknowledged through various frameworks that there is an urgent need for the collection and analysis of data and statistics to address the complex and interconnected challenges of poverty, inequality and unemployment. Additionally, there are other pressing issues, such as the Covid-19 pandemic and climate change, which require a strong emphasis on data and evidence-based decision-making. Data has grown to be a significant resource on a worldwide scale, providing a huge opportunity for citizens, companies and governments to make better-informed decisions. In today's culture, there is a critical need for official statistics, and stakeholders want new and improved statistics to characterise emerging phenomena (Stats SA 2020c). The highest scientific standards are used to inform all significant sectors of the economy, society and environment. Additionally, such data and statistics are a part of public discourse, the foundation for policy choices, a necessity for business use, a source of information for scientific research and a tool for monitoring and evaluating progress (Stats SA 2020c).

The United Nations Statistical Commission's *Fundamental Principles of Official Statistics* (1994) highlights the significance of national statistical offices (NSOs), particularly in the first principle, 'Relevance, impartiality and equal access'. The term 'official statistics' is typically synonymous with and understood to refer to those produced by NSOs: 'Official statistics provide an indispensable element in the information system of a democratic society, serving the government, the economy and the public with data about the economic, demographic, social and environmental situation' (United Nations Statistical Commission 1994: 1).

For public officials and the general public, official statistics are an indispensable element of a democratic society (Yung 2021). The Statistics Act of 1999, which declares that official statistics aim to aid governmental bodies, corporations, other organisations and the general public in planning, making decisions and monitoring or evaluating policies, echoes this (Stats SA 1999). This chapter uses statistical analysis to look at the social and economic landscape of South Africa. It offers a chance to examine three of the most important problems/challenges facing the country: intergenerational unemployment, extreme socio-economic disparity and growing poverty.

Demographic profile of South Africa

South Africa is currently experiencing several challenges, which require careful consideration and attention. One is the provision of education and skills to all citizens; another is the effective management of the HIV and AIDS epidemic and other non-communicable diseases – as we are starting to see an epidemiological shift in the cause of death, from communicable to non-communicable diseases (Stats SA 2011). In addition, ensuring that everyone in the working-age population has employment is also a pressing concern.

The National Planning Commission has provided a detailed report through the NDP, which highlights some of the key issues facing the country. These include spatial challenges that continue to marginalise the poor, corruption that undermines state legitimacy and service delivery, and a divided society. Moreover, the National Planning Commission points out that South Africa's growth path is highly resource-intensive, making it unsustainable. Lastly, the performance of the public service is uneven, necessitating the need for improvement (National Planning Commission 2012). By addressing these challenges, South Africa has the potential to create a stronger and more equitable economy, while achieving its developmental goals.

Demographic data can be used to fully understand the population's many characteristics, including sex, age, population group and marital status. The demographic profile's additional information can aid in quantifying the indirect effects of social institutions on gender equality, including the improvement of women's autonomy and access to high-quality education and basic amenities like health, water and sanitation. Every year, Statistics South Africa (Stats SA) releases the mid-year population estimates, which contain crucial indices and projections for the country's births, deaths and migratory movements by age, sex and geographic data to aid in population planning (Stats SA 2022e).

According to Stats SA's mid-year population estimates 2022 series, about 60.6 million people live in South Africa (Stats SA 2022e). From 2002 until 2022, South Africa's population grew every year. A positive growth rate indicates that the population is increasing despite the terrible impacts of Covid-19 abroad and within South Africa's borders. Figure 6.1 shows the effects of migration, births and deaths on the population, with births constituting the majority of population growth in South Africa.

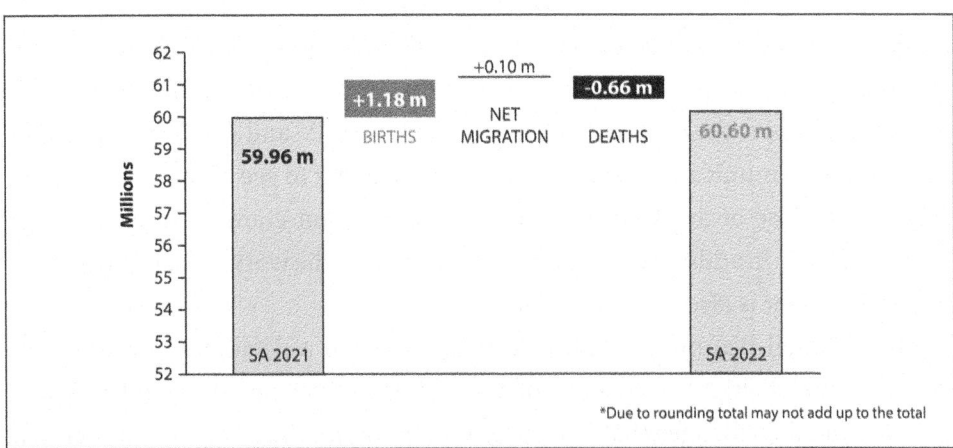

Figure 6.1 Major drivers of population movements

Source: Stats SA (2022e)

In 2022, just over 1 million births were officially reported in South Africa. It is clear from this that fertility still drives population movements. The 2022 mid-year population estimates show that for males, average life expectancy at birth decreased from 62.3 in 2020 to 59.2 in 2021 (a 3.1 year decline), while for females, it decreased from 68.4 in 2020 to 64.2 (4.2 year decline) (Stats SA 2022e). By 2022, measures of mortality indicate an improvement in life expectancy in South Africa for both males and females at birth, moving from 61.7 years in 2021 to 62.8 years in 2022 against the Medium Term Strategic Framework (MTSF) target of at least 70 years by 2030 (Stats SA 2022e). It is important to note that the life expectancy at birth indicator is a crucial health indicator. However, it should not be used to predict an individual's lifespan, but rather to illuminate the overall impact of a catastrophe like Covid-19 in comparison to current trends.

In terms of population growth on the African continent, South Africa ranks in the top ten nations, along with Nigeria, Ethiopia, the Democratic Republic of the Congo, Egypt, the United Republic of Tanzania, Kenya, Uganda, Sudan and Algeria (UNECA 2016). Furthermore, the 2022 mid-year population estimates indicate that there are roughly 31.0 million females, with males making up 48.9 per cent of the population (or about 29.6 million). However, despite having a numerical advantage, women in South Africa are still under-represented in numerous fields, including politics. Additionally, figures show that from 2017 to 2022, the female population remained stable, declining by a minimal 0.1 per cent. In a country with a history of exclusion, we must understand population group dynamics and we are still seeing high levels of inequality between population groups, as well as within the black African population, which makes up the majority (about 81 per cent or 49.1 million) of the population of South Africa. Estimates place the population of white people at 4.6 million, coloured people at 5.3 million, and Indian/Asian at 1.5 million (Stats SA 2022e).

As previously noted, issues about our youth now dominate the national conversation, whether they are about the high unemployment rates or how their skills do not fit the needs of the market. The youth population in South Africa has grown over the past twenty years and represents a sizeable portion of the country's overall population. There will be 4 million more young people (ages 15 to 34) between 2002 and 2022. Those under the age of fifteen make up 28.07 per cent of the population, or 17.01 million people, while 9.2 per cent, or 5.59 million people, are 60 years of age or older. All demographic age categories, with the exception of youth (those between the ages of 15 and 34), exhibited a decline in growth rate between 2020 and 2021, according to the data. There is a substantial youth bulge in South Africa's population. The median age of children and youth in South Africa is 28, as shown in Figure 6.2. It is imperative that this issue be given due consideration in the planning of future health, economic, and welfare strategies and policies (Stats SA 2022e).

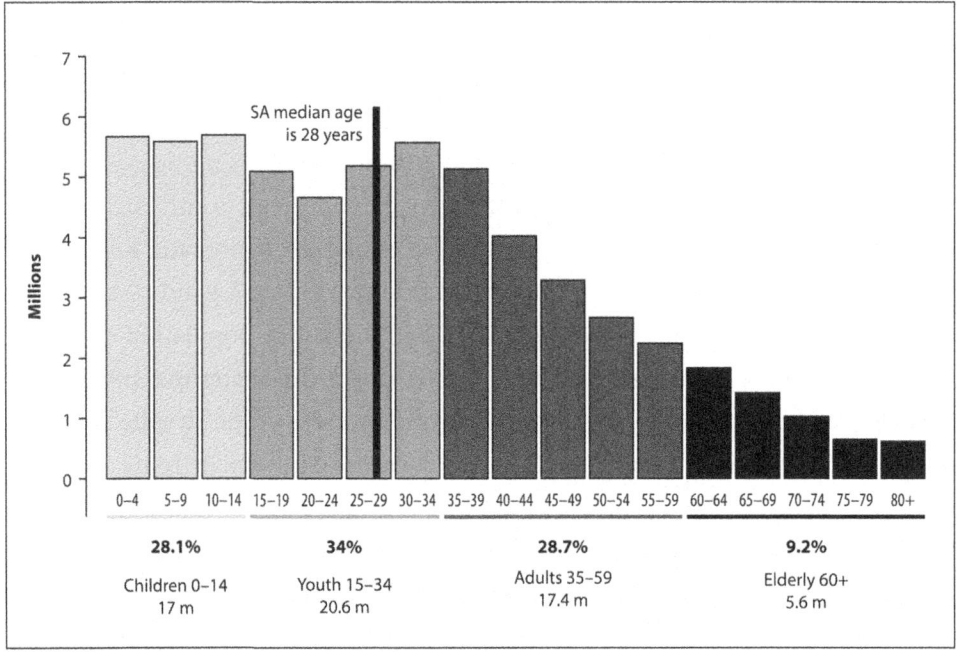

Figure 6.2 Population age structure, five-year age groups
Source: Stats SA (2022e)

Extensive research has been conducted on the connection between migration and the development of the communities of origin. Researchers have discovered that this connection can have both a positive effect (such as financial gain for the sending community) or a negative effect (such as brain drain) (Antobam 2015). The NDP, which predicted that migration, both within and outside of South Africa, will continue to be a major concern in the years to come, echoed similar ideas. Additionally, it asserts that migration will undoubtedly increase due to labour movement, urbanisation and geographic changes, particularly from developing countries (Stats SA 2021; National Planning Commission 2012). According to the 2022 mid-year population estimates, net foreign migration was predicted to decline to 600 000 between 2021 and 2026, as illustrated in Figure 6.3. This is true even though international migration has recovered since Covid-19. In the same time frame, African immigrants (595 000) will dominate domestic migration (Stats SA 2022e).

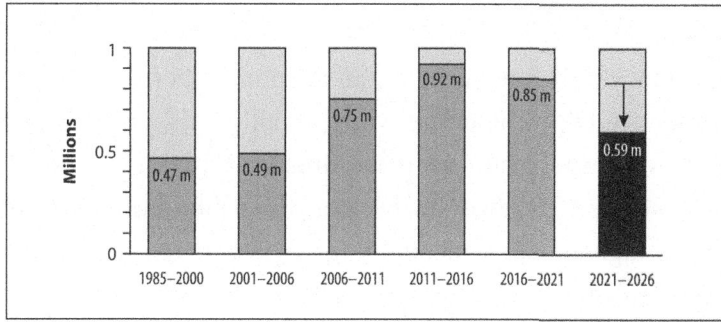

Figure 6.3
Net international migration,
1985–2026
Source: Stats SA (2022e)

Regarding migration, South Africa has the region's largest and most diverse economy from a continental viewpoint. On the other hand, internal migration follows a circular pattern, as people move back and forth between their rural homes and urban employment locations. As a result, it is not surprising that most migrants would settle in Gauteng, a province that continues to lure people from inside and outside of South Africa, including a large portion of South Africans from other more rural provinces. The circular nature of these movements, with young, productive ages migrating to potential work or educational places, is something else we need to comprehend. We have observed, however, that as people get older, migration back to remote communities begins to occur. Figure 6.4 shows that five provinces predict positive net migration between 2021 and 2026, with Gauteng

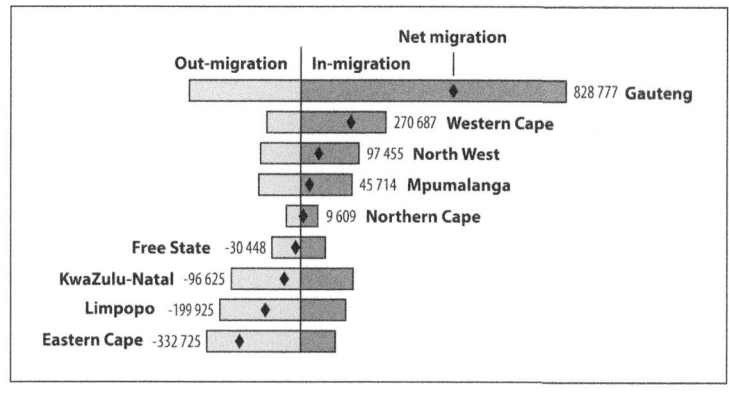

Figure 6.4
Net migration,
2021–6,
by province
Source: Stats SA (2022e)

attracting the most migrants. The data indicate that Gauteng will have the largest inflow of migrants, with an estimated total of 1 443 978 immigrants. At the same time, the Western Cape is estimated to experience the second-highest inflow of migrants from 2021 to 2026, which is about 460 489 (Stats SA 2021).

Economy: Gross domestic product and inflation

One of the most important metrics for gauging an economy's performance is its gross domestic product (GDP). The entire worth of all goods and services produced inside a country's borders within a given time frame, typically a year or a quarter, can be termed the GDP. Strong GDP growth enables businesses to recruit more staff and pay higher wages, encouraging consumers to spend more on products and services. In contrast, the opposite is true when GDP growth is extremely low or the economy enters a recession (workers may be laid off and/or paid less, and businesses may cut costs).

As can be seen in Figure 6.5, South Africa's economic growth is still sluggish and insufficient to combat the nation's high unemployment and poverty rates. The change in the economy's structure has implications for a society where we have large numbers of youth not progressing to higher levels of post-school education or obtaining the skills needed for an increasingly skills-intensive economy. The annual real GDP rose by 4.9 per cent in 2021, following a decline of 6.4 per cent in 2020 (Stats SA 2022d).

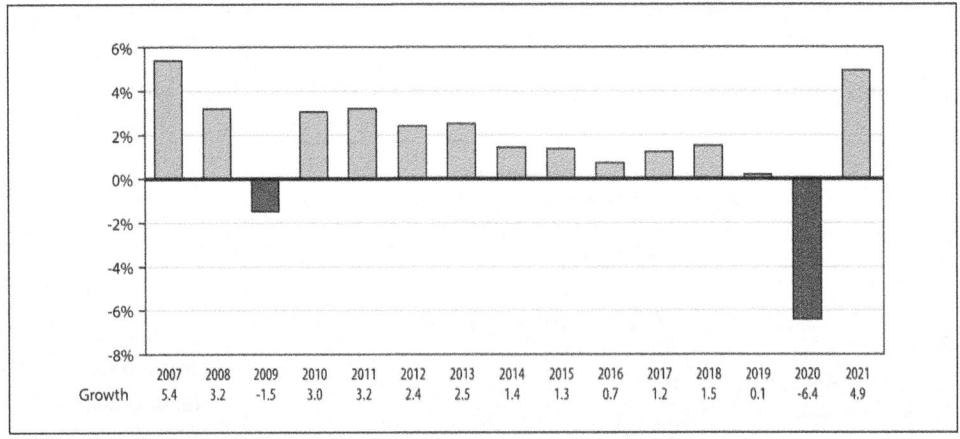

Figure 6.5 Annual GDP growth rates (constant 2015 prices)

Source: Stats SA (2022c)

The South African economy has moved from one driven by manufacturing to one where finance is now the largest contributor to GDP. Seven industries saw negative growth between the first and second quarters 2022, as shown in Figure 6.6. Manufacturing experienced a 5.9 per cent decline and lost 0.7 of a percentage point in GDP growth. Agriculture experienced a 7.7 per cent decline and lost 0.2 of a percentage point to GDP growth. The mining and quarrying sector experienced a 3.5 per cent decline and a 0.2 percentage point decline in GDP growth. The trading, catering and accommodation sector shrank by 1.5 per cent and reduced GDP growth by 0.2 percentage points (National Treasury 2022; Stats SA 2022d).

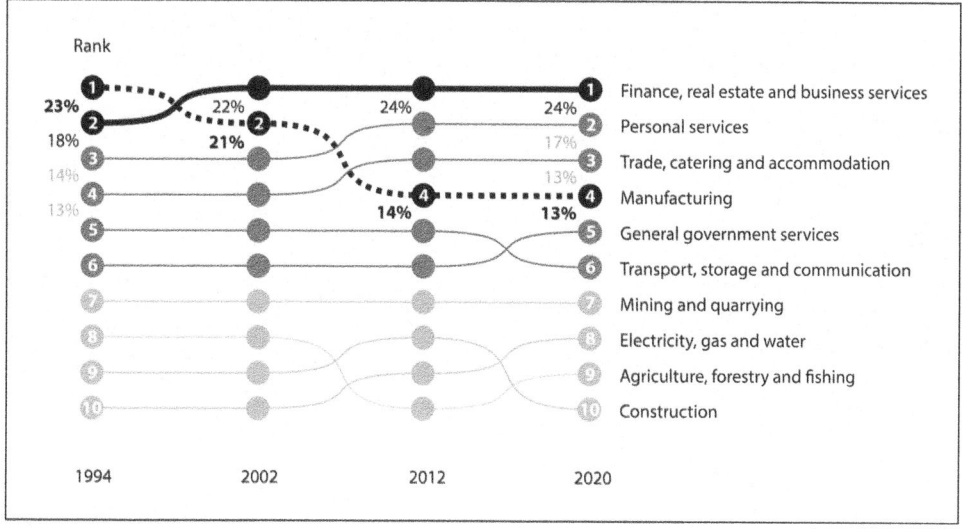

Figure 6.6 Contribution by industry to the GDP, ranked by selected period
Source: Stats SA (2022d)

The International Monetary Fund (IMF) cut its prediction for global growth in 2022 from 5.9 per cent to 4.4 per cent after the Covid-19 outbreak returned around the end of 2021 (IMF 2022). It is plausible to claim that the structure of global recovery has worsened disparities between nations and industries. Developed nations' output levels will have reached pre-pandemic levels by 2022, while many underdeveloped countries will not entirely recover. Employment recovery often proceeds more slowly than GDP. According to the National Treasury, real GDP growth will reach 2.01 per cent in 2022 and an average of 1.8 per cent during the following three years (National Treasury 2022).

The economy took over two years to recover from the effects of Covid-19, according to the GDP estimates for the second quarter of 2022, with real GDP returning to pre-pandemic levels in the first quarter of 2022. The recovery was only temporary, as, in the second quarter of 2022, GDP fell by 0.7 per cent to R1 148 billion, equivalent to the fourth quarter pre-pandemic level (Figure 6.7). Load-shedding, the domestic unrest and looting in July 2021, and the severe rains in KwaZulu-Natal all contributed to the decline, undermining the already weak national economy that had only just returned to pre-pandemic levels.

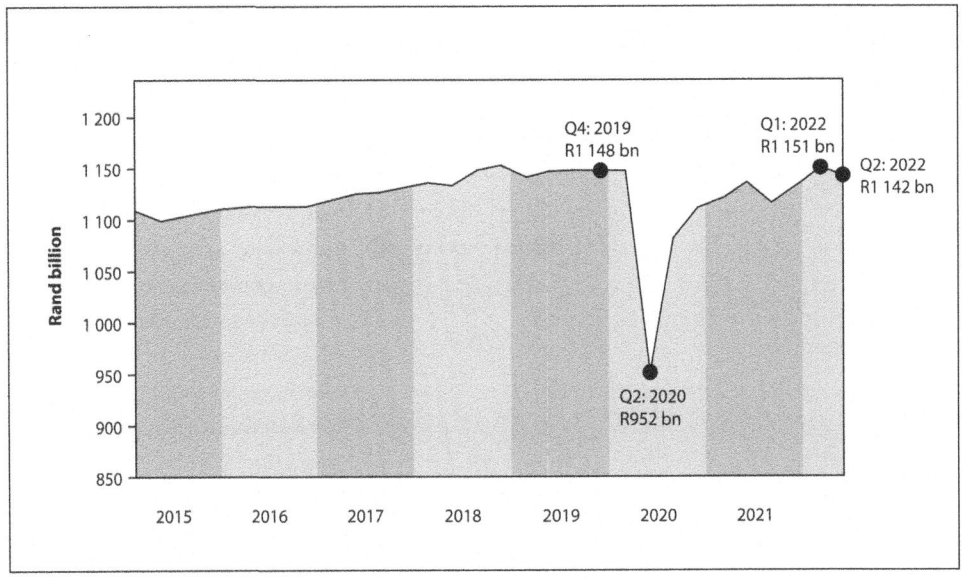

Figure 6.7 Real GDP (constant 2015 prices, seasonally adjusted)
Source: Stats SA (2022d)

Figure 6.8 demonstrates that the industries with the highest employment shares in relation to their GDP shares are construction, trade and agriculture. However, the community and social services industry generates the most jobs and makes up the largest proportion of nominal GDP. According to the results of the *Quarterly Labour Force Survey* for the second quarter of 2022 (Stats SA 2022g), community and social services (276 000), trade (169 000), finance (128 000) and construction (104 000) saw the largest job gains. In fact, one could argue that widespread structural unemployment is South Africa's biggest issue. It hinders growth and serves as a foundation for inequality and poverty. The manufacturing sector's subpar performance has played a significant role in this. Significant employment losses were in the manufacturing (73 000) and transportation sectors (54 000). In the second quarter of 2022, there were 15.6 million people employed overall (Stats SA 2022g).

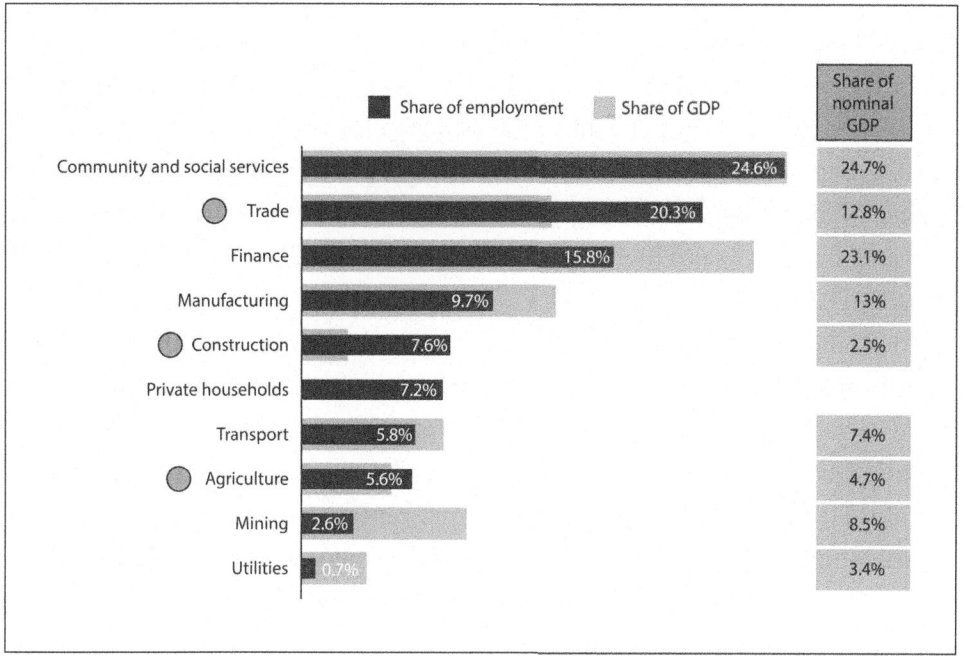

Figure 6.8 Share of employment and GDP share per industry (percentage)
Source: Stats SA (2022d, 2022g)

In addition, data indicates that only four industries were producing at or above pre-pandemic levels by the second quarter of 2022. The banking, real estate and business services sectors took two quarters to bounce back to the same level as the fourth quarter of 2019, following a decline in the second quarter of 2020, whereas personal services took three quarters to do the same. Agriculture, forestry, fisheries and the government appear to have fared rather well throughout the pandemic in terms of this metric (actual value added). Six industries, including construction, which is now in the poorest condition, have not yet recovered. The construction sector has decreased by 24 per cent since the outbreak of the Covid-19 pandemic. In the second quarter of 2021, mining recovered briefly, but it has since remained below what it was in the fourth quarter of 2019.

Consumer Price Index

The Consumer Price Index (CPI) is one of South Africa's two primary measures of inflation, together with the Producer Price Index. The inflation goal metric, the headline CPI, is the foundation for the South African Reserve Bank's interest rates. The Reserve Bank's target range of 3–6 per cent was exceeded by annual consumer price inflation in September 2022, which decreased from 7.6 per cent in August 2022. The CPI increased by 0.1 per cent month-on-month in September 2022. Headline inflation of 6.7 per cent was anticipated for 2022, falling to 5.1 per cent in 2023, according to the medium-term budget policy statement presented by Finance Minister Enoch Godongwana. The main drivers of inflationary pressure are rising fuel prices and high domestic food inflation (Stats SA 2022h; National Treasury 2022).

Food and non-alcoholic drinks, housing and utilities, transportation and other products and services were the major causes of the 7.5 per cent annual inflation rate, according to CPI data for September 2022 (Stats SA 2002h). As can be seen in Figure 6.9, the total CPI annual rate was 7.5 per cent, and food and non-alcoholic drinks climbed by 11.9 per cent year-on-year, or 2 percentage points. Utility and housing costs rose by 4.2 per cent year-on-year, adding 1 per cent to the overall increase. Transportation added 2.5 percentage points, which climbed by 17.9 per cent year-on-year. Services and other products increased by 4 per cent year-on-year and made up 0.6 per cent of the total. The annual

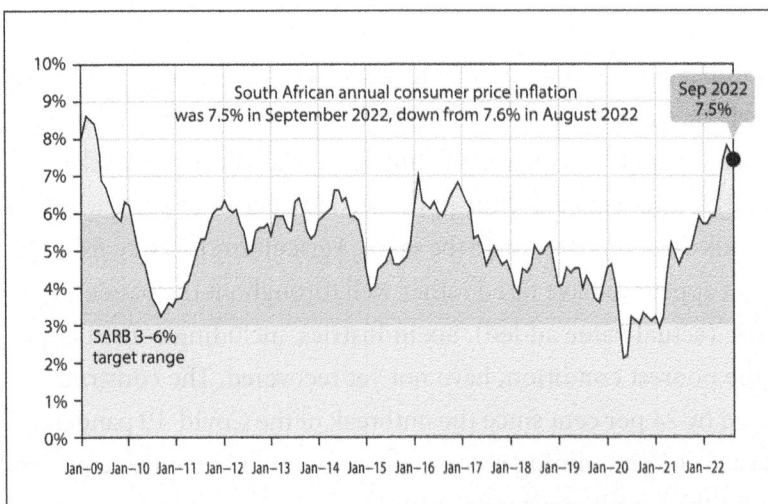

Figure 6.9
Consumer Price Index annual consumer inflation rate over time

Source:
Stats SA (2022h)

inflation rate for goods was 10.7 per cent in September, down from 10.9 per cent in August, and for services, it was 4.3 per cent, staying the same in August (Stats SA 2022h).

In 2022, the World Bank warned that the recent surge in inflation, debt and income inequality poses a threat to the global poverty reduction efforts made over the past two decades. The ongoing pandemic and the war in Ukraine have further worsened the situation, leading to an increase in global inequality and unprecedented inflation levels (World Bank 2022). As a result, the skyrocketing food prices are expected to push at least 5 per cent of the world's population into poverty (Buheji 2022). Furthermore, a report published in 2022 by the Food and Agriculture Organization (FAO), International Fund for Agricultural Development (IFAD), United Nations Children's Fund (UNICEF), World Food Programme (WFP), and World Health Organization (WHO) estimated that around 2.3 billion people, equivalent to 29.3 per cent of the global population, were moderately or severely food insecure in 2021, meaning they did not have access to sufficient food (FAO et al. 2022).

Salgado Baptista et al. (2022) argue that food scarcity and inflation disproportionately impact on the poor, creating a vicious cycle of poverty and inequality. According to their report, households in sub-Saharan Africa spend 40 per cent of household spending on food, which rises to 60 per cent in some cases. This means that when food prices rise due to inflation or shortages, low-income families are hit the hardest. Unfortunately, half of sub-Saharan Africa's population already lives below the poverty line and these crises only deepen their hardship. Mohamed Buheji (2022) predicts that the poorest people will suffer the most after Covid-19. He highlights how sensitive the poor are to inflation because they do not have the means to preserve their purchasing power. They cannot use credit to limit their expenditure since they have little access to the financial markets. Alternatively, if they do have access, they must borrow money to pay for their basic needs, usually from unregulated markets. Thus, we must consider the connections between economic indicators and their consequences on the general populace.

In South Africa, the country's high inflation rates and poverty levels have adversely affected a significant portion of the population. The poorest households allocate 50 per cent of their yearly budgets towards food and non-alcoholic beverages, while for those with higher spending power, these items contribute to only 11 per cent of their expenses. As a result, households with lower incomes are more susceptible to the impact of food price hikes (Stats SA 2023). As can be seen in Figure 6.10, the cost of necessities like bread and sunflower oil has increased noticeably.

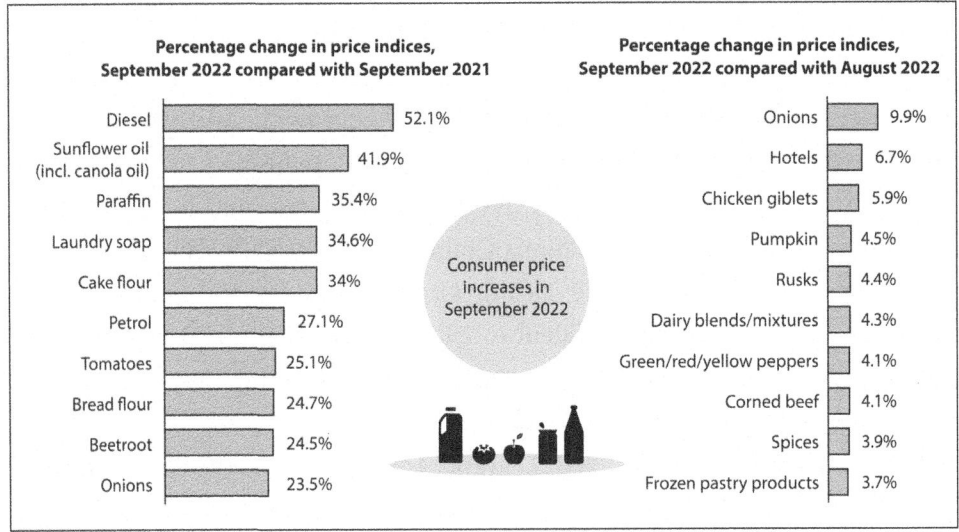

Figure 6.10 Change in price indices, September 2022 compared with September 2021, and September 2022 compared with August 2022

Source: Stats SA (2022h)

Education and youth

Many developing nations experience issues in the areas of youth employment and education, as well as in guaranteeing that all residents have access to high-quality education to find suitable and fruitful jobs. The NDP makes it very clear that investing significantly in high-quality education and skills development is necessary to eradicate poverty (National Planning Commission 2012). The *Bi-annual 2019–2024 MTSF Synthesis Report for the Period Ending March 2021* confirms that addressing the triple problem of unemployment, inequality and poverty requires government investments and opportunities to strengthen South Africans' social capital. Education and skills development initiatives are the cornerstones of an inclusive economy (Department of Planning, Monitoring and Evaluation 2020).

Figure 6.11 shows the number of people who attended educational institutions between the ages of 5 and 24 by single age. Despite almost ubiquitous attendance at educational institutions during the mandatory phase, the statistics show that many learners need more time to move to secondary or higher education (until age 15). The graph shows that more students attend high school between the ages of 7 and 14 years, after which there is a sharp decline in school attendance. At the age of 24, only one in ten (10 per cent) learners were still enrolled in some educational institution. Additionally, the graph clearly shows primary and secondary school scholars older than the recommended graduation age. The results also show that most pupils make the transition from primary to secondary school (Stats SA 2022a).

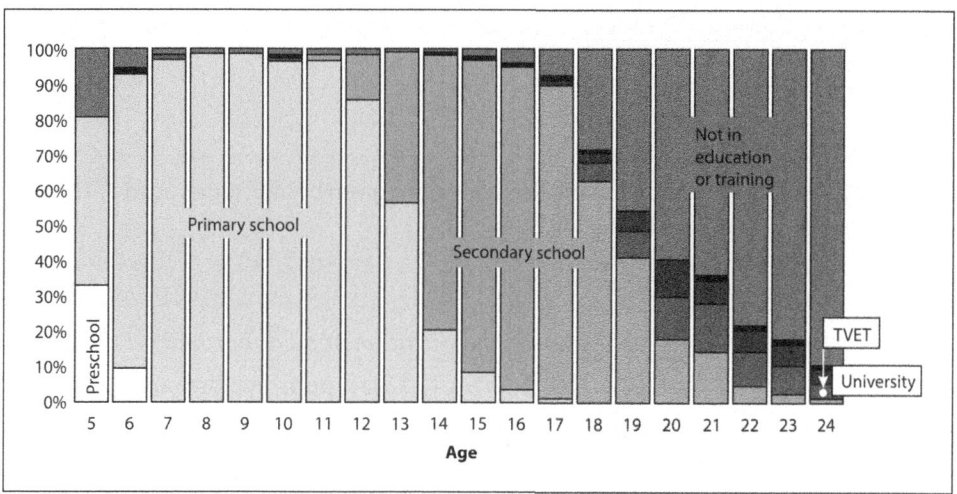

Figure 6.11 Types of educational institution attended by individuals aged 5–24 years, 2021
Source: Stats SA (2022a)

Figure 6.12 shows the main justifications for the relatively small proportion of males and females aged 7 to 18 years for not attending educational institutions. The three most prevalent reasons given by students for not attending an educational institution were poor academic performance (21.2 per cent), illness and disability (22.7 per cent) and a lack of funding for tuition (19.5 per cent). The girl child deserves a special mention here: 7.8 per cent of people discontinued their studies due to family obligations (such as getting married, caring for children and pregnancy) and, notably, females (13.4 per cent) were far more likely than men (0.5 per cent) to cite these reasons. Our young women are still under a lot of pressure from society to care for ailing family members and, in some circumstances, their own children. A little more than 2.3 per cent of respondents said that education was useless. Men were more likely than women to voice this opinion (Stats SA 2022a).

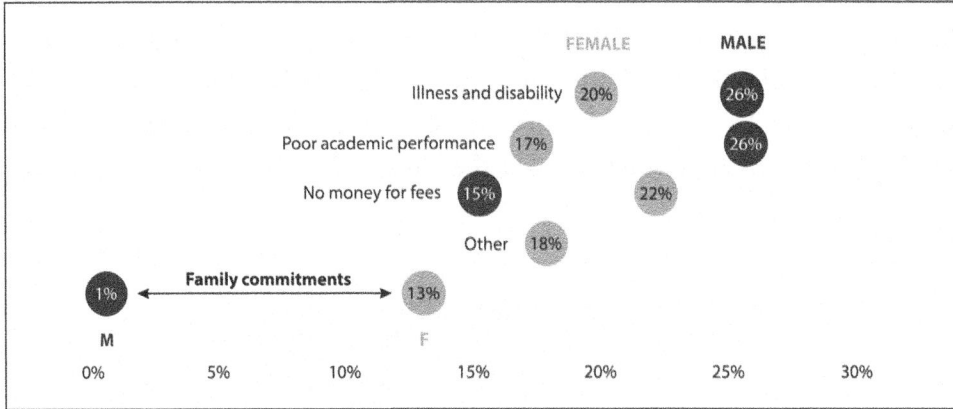

Figure 6.12 Percentage distribution of selected reasons given by individuals aged 7–18 for not attending an educational institution by sex, 2021

Source: Stats SA (2022a)

According to *Education Series Volume VI: Education and Labour Market Outcomes in South Africa, 2018*, published by Stats SA (2020a), poor performance was cited as a reason for absence by male students more frequently (19.2 per cent) than female students (13.6 per cent). Compared to Generation X (born between 1960 and 1979) and Millennial males, this rationale was also more prevalent among Born-Free Millennial males. Additionally, there are significant distinctions among the population groups in reasons for non-attendance. Only 14.5 per cent of white youth, compared to 35.6 per cent of black Africans aged 19 to 24, claimed financial constraints as the reason they could not be in a school.

The proportion of adults aged 20 and older who have finished at least Grade 12 has been increasing gradually since 2002, rising from 30.5 per cent in 2002 to 50.5 per cent in 2021 (Stats SA 2022a). During this time, the percentage of people with post-secondary education increased from 9.2 per cent to 14.6 per cent. In 2021, there were 3.2 per cent of people without a formal education, down from 11.4 per cent in 2002.

Figure 6.13 shows a big difference in post-secondary education attainment between provinces. Although there are still significant disparities in post-school qualification levels among the provinces, most provinces now reach National Senior Certificate levels closer to the national average. In terms of post-secondary education, Gauteng and the Western Cape are close to 20 per cent, whereas the national average is 14.6 per cent (Stats SA 2022a). The education dividend is clearly apparent in a range of statistics produced by Stats SA in domains such as employment, asset ownership and poverty figures.

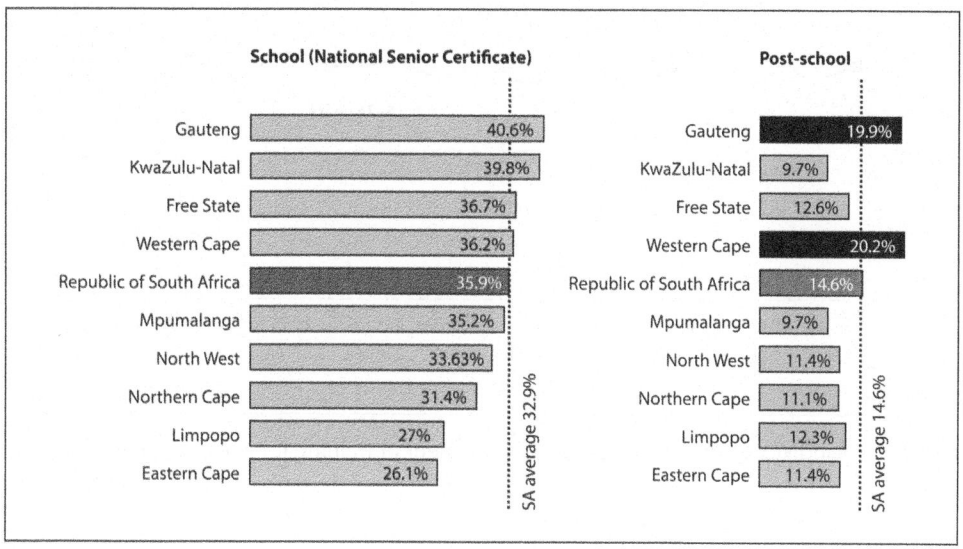

Figure 6.13 Percentage distribution of education attainment for persons aged 20 years and older, by province, 2021

Source: Stats SA (2022a)

Education Series Volume VI: Education and Labour Market Outcomes in South Africa, 2018, published by Stats SA (2020a), also demonstrates the slower transition from secondary to post-secondary education or employment. Every generation should do better than their parents, it is usually said. Significant generational shifts in South Africa have been influenced by important political developments that altered the options open to Generation Xers and Millennials regarding their educational and labour market engagement. The overall percentage of Born-Free Millennials who were not in education, employment or training was 46.1 per cent; the age group with the highest number of those not in education, employment or training was 23-year-olds (53.2 per cent). Furthermore, 7.6 per cent more Born-Free Millennial women were not in education, employment or training than men of the same group. When compared to those who had completed secondary school, 40.8 per cent of Born-Free Millennials not in education, employment or training had not completed their secondary education (see Figure 6.14).

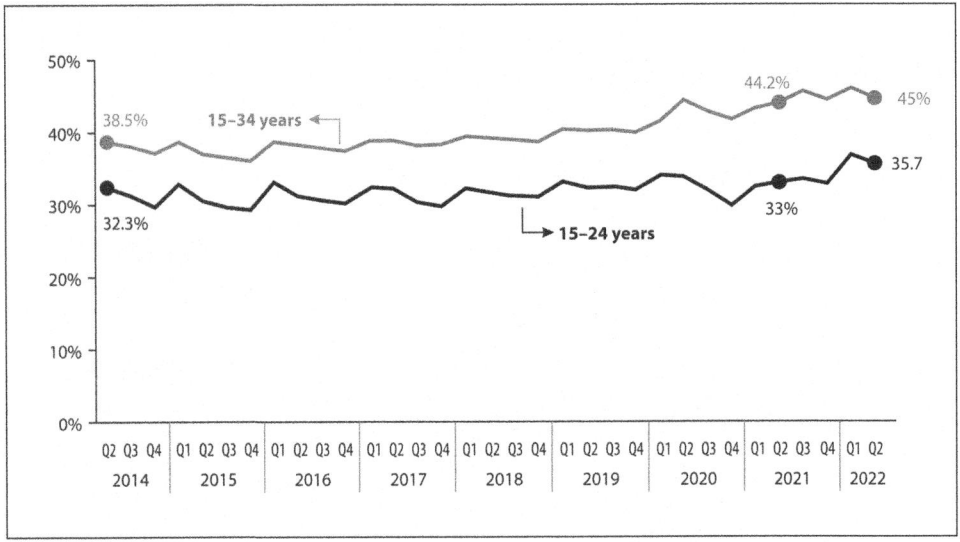

Figure 6.14 Individuals not in education, employment or training for ages 15–24 and 15–34, 2014–22

Source: Stats SA 2020a

In 2022 South Africa celebrated National Youth Day and Youth Month under the banner of 'Promoting sustainable livelihoods and resilience of young people for a better tomorrow'. The call to action for youth is to cultivate resilience and create opportunities for them to develop a sustainable livelihood, both now and in the future. The Fourth Industrial Revolution, which is sweeping South Africa and the rest of the world, is the backdrop for Department of Planning, Monitoring and Evaluation's *Towards a 25-Year Review, 1994–2019* (Department of Planning, Monitoring and Evaluation 2019b), which notes that youth unemployment and poverty, in particular, have been on the rise.

South Africa has over 10 million young people between the ages of 15 and 24. Yet, only 2.5 million were actively participating in the labour force through employment or unemployment. Of this group, 7.7 million, or 75.1 per cent, do not participate in the labour force. The main cause of this inactivity is discouragement or having given up on finding a job that matches their skills or is accessible where they reside. About 37 per cent of this group had stopped looking for work in South Africa. Many of these young people not in education, employment or training (NEET) are not motivated. A higher proportion of both males and females are NEET. However, each year, the gap between the NEET rate for both males and females has significantly shrunk (Stats SA 2022g). What context do these young people find themselves in to express their aspirations? If the engine of a developing country cannot find work in an economy that is not producing enough job opportunities for its citizens, the demographic dividend is unlikely to be realised.

The informal sector, also known as the employer of last resort, is a large part of employment in Africa and was the focus of the *Survey of Employers and the Self-employed 2017* in South Africa (Stats SA 2019). The most vulnerable people can rely on the informal sector for a living, including the urban poor, women who are the heads of homes, people with disabilities and families who reside in rural areas. When formal sector jobs are scarce, and social security institutions are insufficient, participation in the informal sector helps the marginalised endure economic downturns. South African youth, in particular, do not like the informal sector, with only 0.8 per cent of those aged 15 to 24 operating an informal business, compared to 7.3 per cent of those aged 34 to 44 (Stats SA 2019).

Poverty and unemployment

Poverty lines are essential tools for planning, observing and evaluating initiatives and policies intended to reduce it and for statistical reporting of poverty levels and patterns. The NDP predicts that by 2030, those living below the lower-bound poverty line should decline from 39 per cent of the population to 0 per cent. In 2007, the government formally entrusted Stats SA with developing a cut-off point that might be used to harmonise the country's money-metric definition of poverty (Stats SA 2022f). Figure 6.15 demonstrates that a significant portion of our population falls below the lower-bound and food poverty lines. In 2015, more than 25 per cent of people were considered to be food insecure. This marks the point of absolute deprivation, which is the amount of money required to purchase the minimum required daily energy intake.

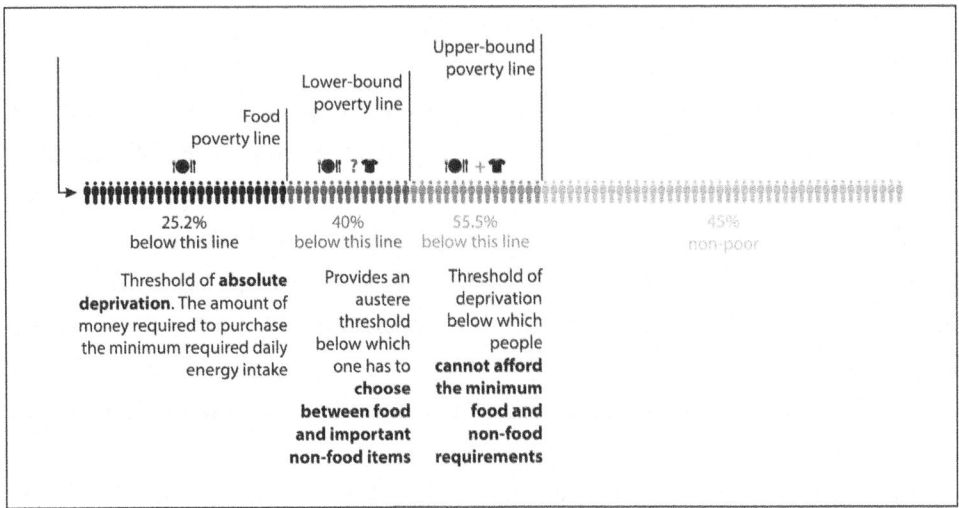

Figure 6.15 Money-metric poverty headcounts, 2015

Source: Stats SA (2017)

From a peak of 16.7 million in 2009, around 13.8 million South Africans lived below the food poverty line in 2015. The three poorest provinces in the nation have historically been KwaZulu-Natal, Eastern Cape and Limpopo. Regarding headcount, gap and severity indicators, females continue to be more disadvantaged than males, although the gap between the sexes is closing. (National Planning Commission 2012). Undoubtedly, recent global challenges like the Covid-19 pandemic and energy and supply shocks will also impact the poverty levels in our country.

To maintain their integrity and ongoing relevance, Stats SA updated national poverty lines in 2022 to reflect changes in the cost of living (price increases for goods and services). The national poverty lines are typically adjusted annually by Stats SA using the CPI series. Using prices of April 2022, the food poverty line is R663 per person per month, the lower-bound poverty line is R945 per person per month, and the upper-bound poverty line is R1 417 per person per month. These lines include food and non-food components of household consumption expenditure (Stats SA 2022f).

Because poverty is a multifaceted phenomenon, many ways exist to analyse it and find answers. The South African Multidimensional Poverty Index (SAMPI), which considers factors including living standards, health, education and economic activity, offers a more comprehensive perspective on poverty. Poverty, as measured by the national population, declined from 17.9 per cent in 2001 to 8 per cent in 2011 and 7 per cent in 2016. In 2016, KwaZulu-Natal had the highest SAMPI score (7.7 per cent). Between 2011 and 2016, the initial significant decrease in multidimensional poverty reached a plateau (Stats SA 2014, 2022f).

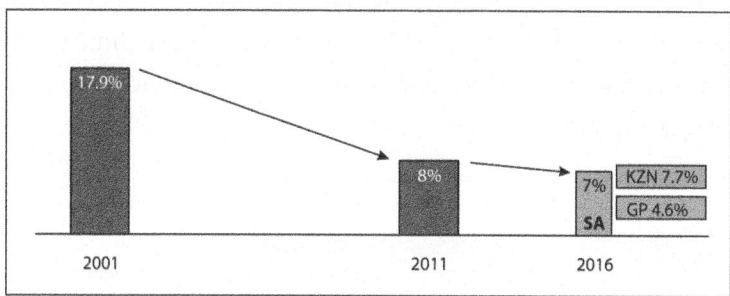

Figure 6.16
Multidimensional poverty headcount by geographic region 2001–16

Source: Stats SA (2001, 2011, 2016)

Although the number of people living in poverty has greatly decreased, it should be highlighted that between 2011 and 2016, there were still some areas where poverty intensity had increased. We cannot overlook that 2.7 per cent of people in our country reported suffering discrimination in the past twelve months, making poverty the second-most important reason, after race, why people believe they are subjected to it, as shown in Figure 6.17.

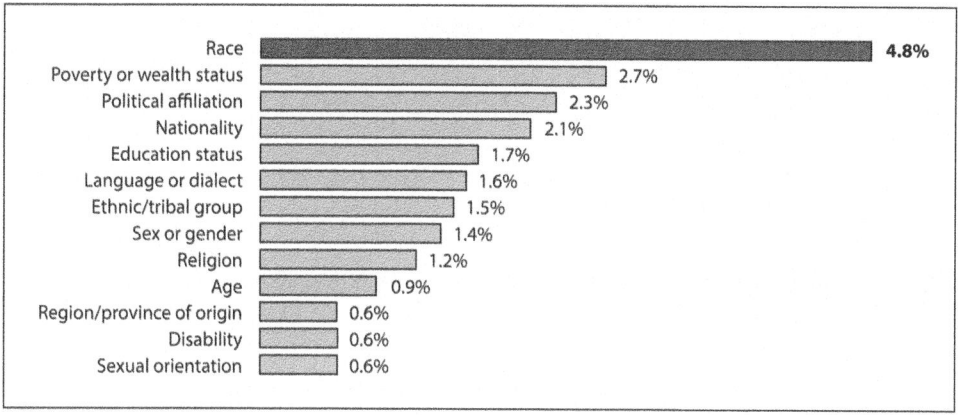

Figure 6.17 Percentage of individuals who experienced specified types of discrimination in the past twelve months, 2021–22

Source: Stats SA (2022b)

A vital question to consider, especially in South Africa, is what is driving the poverty situation. Figure 6.18 indicates that unemployment and a lack of education are the two main long-term drivers of poverty (number of years of schooling). The figure also shows the difference between three points in time. In 2001, unemployment accounted for 33 per cent of the SAMPI, while education made up 16 per cent of the index. By 2016, the proportion of the unemployment component had increased to 52 per cent, while the role of education had declined to 11 per cent. The increased contribution of the economic activity dimension underlines the nation's rising unemployment issues and its implications for poverty (Stats SA 2001, 2011, 2016).

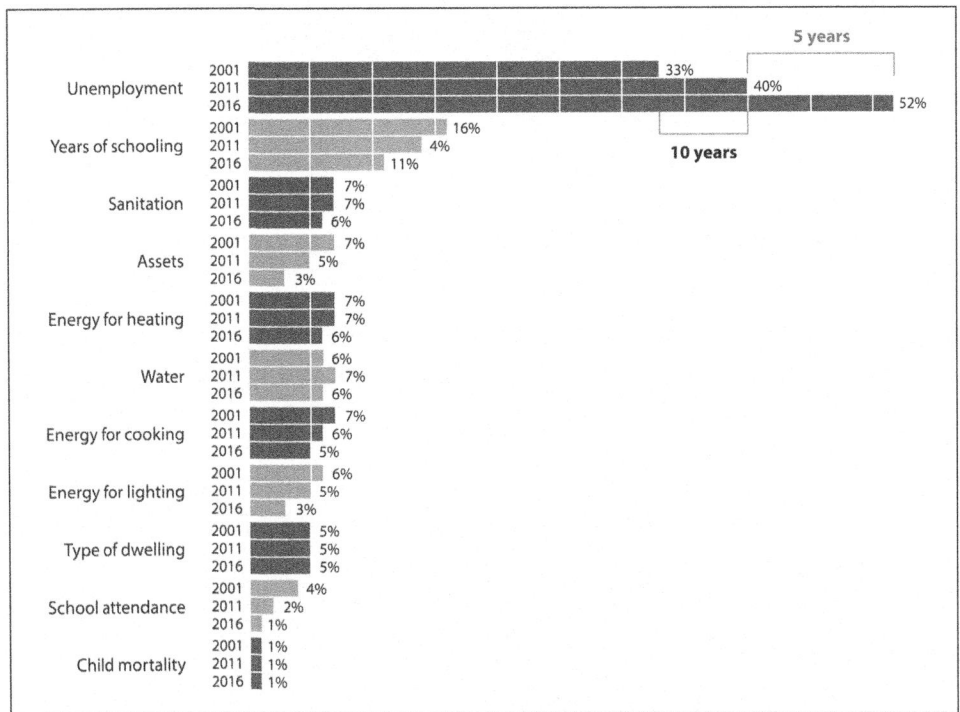

Figure 6.18 Multidimensional drivers of poverty in South Africa, 2001, 2011, 2016

Source: Stats SA (2001, 2011, 2016)

According to the *Bi-annual 2019–2024 MTSF Synthesis Report for the Period Ending March 2021*, the percentage of the population expected to be below the upper-middle-income national poverty line by 2020 will show the worsening of poverty and reach 60 per cent. Children in South Africa were 60 per cent more likely to live in poverty in 2018 if their parents were in the bottom quintile of the income distribution. The report also confirms little upward mobility and intergenerational poverty (Department of Planning, Monitoring and Evaluation 2020).

Figure 6.19 shows that the percentage of people who received social grants climbed gradually from 12.8 per cent in 2003 to roughly 31 per cent between 2017 and 2019, before rising dramatically to 35.7 per cent in 2021. The growth of households that received at least one social grant, which increased from 30.8 per cent in 2003 to 45.5 per cent in 2019 and 50.6 per cent in 2021, closely followed this growth. Grant recipients were most prevalent in the Eastern Cape (47.8 per cent) and Limpopo (46.5 per cent), while Gauteng (23.6 per cent) and the Western Cape (26.2 per cent) had the lowest proportion (Stats SA 2022a).

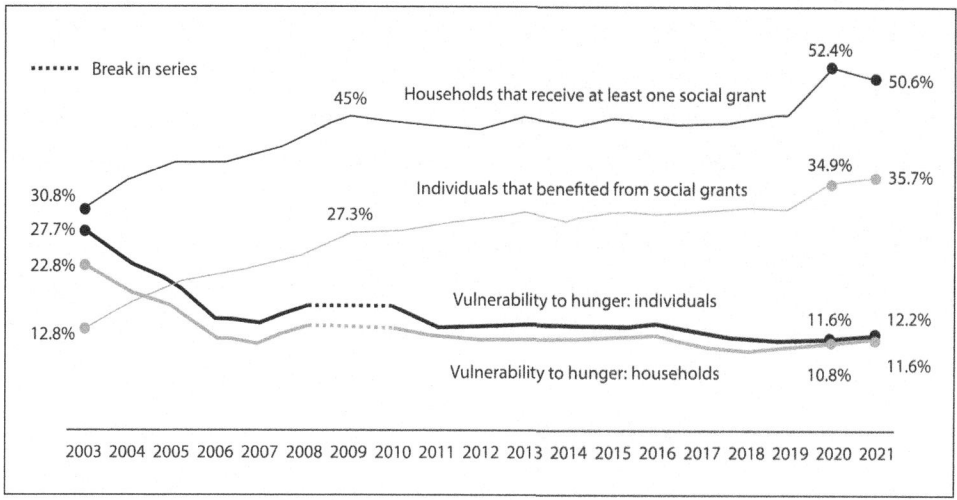

Figure 6.19 Access to grants versus estimated percentage of households and persons vulnerable to hunger in South Africa, 2002–21

Source: Stats SA (2022a)

Social grants continue to be an important safety net, especially in the poorest provinces. To safeguard people and households from the loss of income at this time, the special Covid-19 Social Relief of Distress grant roll-out in 2020 was crucial. This special grant was extended for one additional year, according to a statement from the minister of Finance on the medium-term budget policy for 2022 (National Treasury 2022). Most likely, this will result in more people receiving social grants.

The number of households with inadequate access to food increased to 20.9 per cent in 2021, after falling from 23.6 per cent in 2010 to 17.8 per cent in 2019. The proportion of people with less access to food decreased from 25.2 per cent in 2011 to 19.5 per cent in 2019 before rising again to 23.8 per cent in 2021. The results show that, until 2019, individual and household vulnerability to hunger decreased as access to grants increased. Over 50 per cent of households have received at least one social subsidy, while hunger vulnerability has increased marginally since 2020.

It is believed that diversifying livelihood methods is crucial to reducing poverty and enhancing household livelihoods. Numerous variables may encourage households to diversify their numerous sources of income. These might, among other things, include the necessity to produce enough money to guarantee a sufficient standard of living and minimise the risk involved with relying just on one source of income. Compared to social grants (24 per cent), salaries and earnings were the primary sources of income for 52.4 per cent of households nationally.

However, as can be seen in Figure 6.20, the percentage of households in the Eastern Cape that had grants as their primary source of income outnumbered those with salaries and wages (42 per cent versus 37.3 per cent). In quintile 5 (77.3 per cent), salaries and wages were more prevalent as primary sources of income than in quintile 1 (14.8 per cent), although social grants and social remittances were the opposite. Pensions were only received by 0.2 per cent of quintile 1 households as opposed to 8.4 per cent of quintile 5 households (Stats SA 2022a).

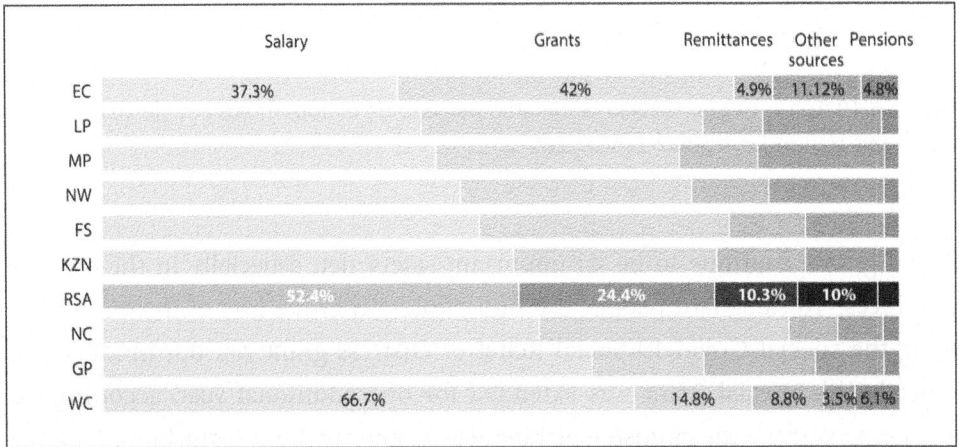

Figure 6.20 Percentage distribution of main sources of household income by province, 2021

Source: Stats SA (2022a)

Although the number of working people has nearly doubled over the past 25 years, the economy has not produced enough jobs to accommodate the army of unemployed people and new workers (Department of Planning, Monitoring and Evaluation 2019b). The *Quarterly Labour Force Survey* (Stats SA 2022g) confirms this for quarter 2 of 2022, with a significant portion of working-age people actively seeking jobs. In the second quarter of 2022, the labour force participation rate rose by 1.7 percentage points, from 56.9 per cent in the first quarter to 58.6 per cent. In contrast, women's labour force participation rates in quarter 2 of 2022 were 53 per cent and men's 64.4 per cent, a difference of 11.4 percentage points.

The absorption rate represents the share of the working-age population that is actually used by the economy (see Figure 6.21). Compared to the first quarter of 2022, the absorption rate rose by 1.4 percentage points to 38.7 per cent in the second quarter. Women's absorption rates are the lowest, coming in at 34.2 per cent in quarter 2 of 2022 compared to 43.4 per cent for men. From 2012 through 2022, the absorption rates of men and women are clearly different (Stats SA 2022g).

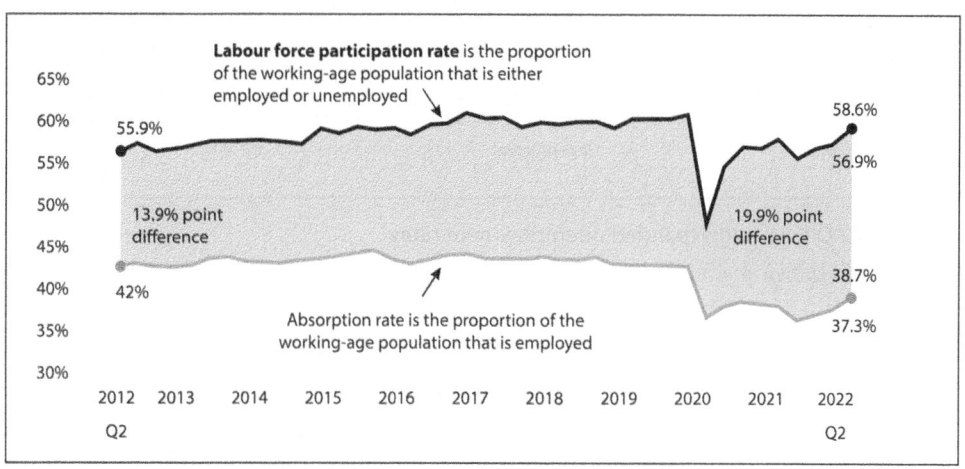

Figure 6.21 Labour force participation and absorption rates, second quarter of 2012 to second quarter of 2022

Source: Stats SA (2022g)

By 2020 and 2030, the unemployment rate should have decreased from 24.9 per cent in June 2012 to 14 and 6 per cent, respectively. Currently, the unemployment rate in South Africa dropped from 34.5 per cent in quarter 1 of 2022 to 33.9 per cent in quarter 2 of 2022 (see Figure 6.22). In in the second quarter of 2022, 132 000 more people were unemployed than in the previous quarter, a decline of 60 000. Since the Covid-19 national lockdown, unemployment has increased sixfold. In quarter 2 of 2022, compared to quarter 1 of 2022, the expanded unemployment rate fell by 1.4 percentage points to 44.1 per cent. The official unemployment rate for 2022 is 19.9 per cent, higher than the 14 per cent anticipated by the NDP. The expanded unemployment rate, however, is 30 per cent higher than the NDP's aim (Stats SA 2022g).

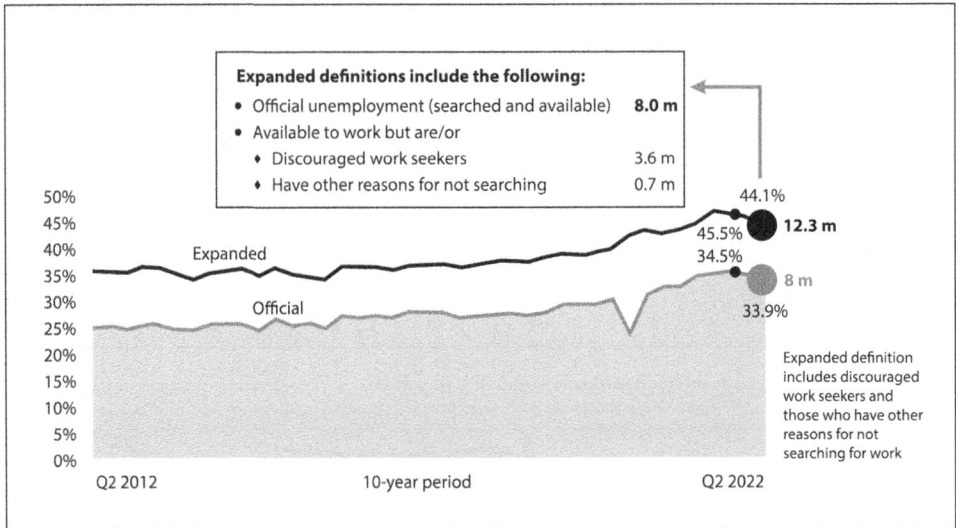

Figure 6.22 Official and expanded unemployment rates

Source: Stats SA (2022g)

The highest expanded unemployment rate in the second quarter of 2022 was 51.8 per cent in the Eastern Cape, followed by 49.4 per cent in KwaZulu-Natal and 49.2 per cent in the North West. The official national unemployment rate is 23.7 percentage points higher than the graduate unemployment rate (10.2 per cent). In the second quarter of 2022, there were 3.6 million discouraged job seekers, a reduction of 183 000 (4.9 per cent). The costs of looking for or failing to locate a market that needs talents that have already been acquired are the main cause of the rise in discouragement. *Labour Market Dynamics in South Africa, 2020* (Stats SA 2020b) makes it abundantly clear that not finding work after a prolonged period of unemployment may be due to being discouraged due to the lack of jobs in the area, the inability to find work requiring the skills held by individuals, or the hopelessness of finding work. As opposed to 11.9 per cent of individuals who were looking and available to work, just about 5.9 per cent of those who were discouraged in the third quarter of 2020 were able to find a job the following quarter (Stats SA 2020b).

The unemployment rate for black Africans (37.8 per cent) is still higher than the national average and that of other demographics (Figure 6.23). Compared to other population groups, white men and women had the lowest unemployment rate, the highest absorption rate and the highest rate of labour force participation.

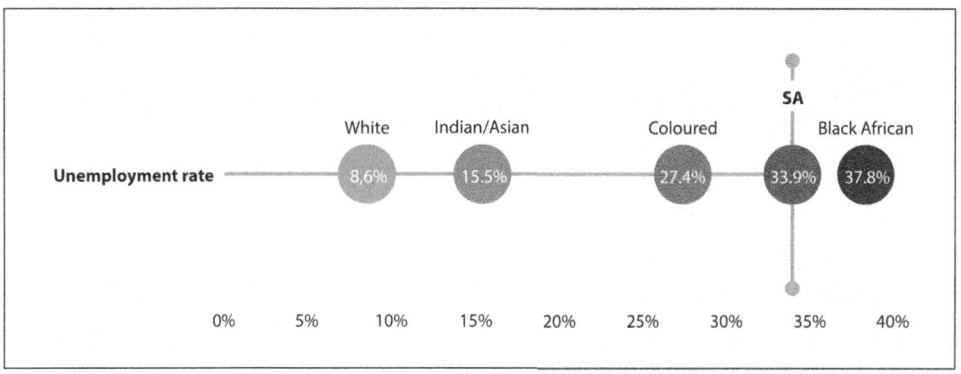

Figure 6.23 Official unemployment rates by population group, second quarter of 2012 to second quarter of 2022

Source: Stats SA (2022g)

The labour market still favours men and doesn't appear to be changing the opportunities for women much. Regardless of population categories, there is still a gender gap in the labour market. Compared to men, women had higher rates of unemployment, lower absorption rates and lower employment rates. The unemployment rate for women remained higher than the national average from 2012 to 2022 (Stats SA 2022g). Women's unemployment rates were 3.7 percentage points higher than men's in 2012, but by 2022, there was only a 2.9 percentage point difference. Women currently have a 35.5 per cent jobless rate compared to a rate of 32.6 per cent for men. In South Africa, women's labour force participation rates in the second quarter of 2022 were 53 per cent and men's were 64.4 per cent, a difference of 11.4 percentage points. The proportion of the working-age population that is actually utilised by the economy is measured by the absorption rate. Women's absorption rates are the lowest, coming in at 34.2 per cent in the second quarter of 2022 compared to 43.4 per cent for men. Between 2012 and 2022, a pronounced difference between men's and women's absorption rates can be seen. The Stats SA (2022g) survey results unequivocally show that the presence of children can indirectly contribute to unemployment, particularly among women. This might be explained by the financial resources needed for childcare and cultural expectations that women will raise their children until they reach a certain age.

As already noted, the youth now makes up a sizeable portion of the population in South Africa and has done so for the past twenty years. However, South Africa's youth suffer disproportionately from unemployment. With an unemployment rate above the national average, youth in South Africa continue to face disadvantages in the job market. Figure 6.24 shows that youth between the ages of 15 and 24, and 25 and 34, had the highest unemployment rates, at 61.4 per cent and 41.2 per cent, respectively, in the second quarter of 2022. These unemployment rates are higher than the 33.9 per cent national unemployment rate. In a similar vein, youth between the ages of 25 and 34 have poor labour absorption rates (42.4 per cent), and those between the ages of 15 and 24 have the lowest rates (10.3 per cent).

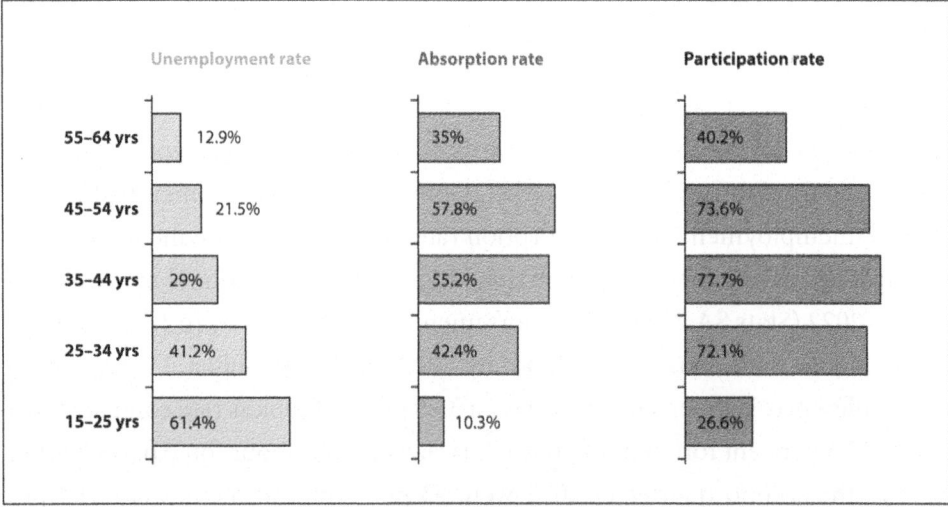

Figure 6.24 Labour rates by age group, second quarter of 2022

Source: Stats SA (2022g)

Conclusion

Through a statistical analysis, it is evident that South Africa has observed a notable rise in its young population over the past twenty years, which currently comprises a considerable sector of the country's overall population. Between 2002 and 2022, there were 4 million more young people (ages 15 to 34); 17.01 million people, or 28.07 per cent of the population, under the age of 15, while 5.59 million people, or 9.2 per cent of the population, were 60 years of age or older (Stats SA 2022e). Furthermore, by 2022, measures of mortality indicate an improvement in life expectancy for both males and females at birth, moving from 61.7 years in 2021 to 62.8 years in 2022 against the MTSF target of at least 70 years by 2030. The gap in reaching 2030 NDP target is thus 7.2 years. Such significant population shifts can have an impact on the economy, housing, health care and education.

It is important for policymakers to consider the unique needs of the youth, women and other marginalised groups in their decision-making processes. This requires a comprehensive understanding of the challenges faced by these groups and measures to address them effectively. Additionally, it is crucial to establish specific and measurable indicators to evaluate progress towards achieving the desired outcomes. By establishing and monitoring these indicators, policymakers can ensure that their policies are effective and that they are making tangible progress towards their goals. Ultimately, prioritising the needs of youth, women and other marginalised groups and creating clear, quantifiable benchmarks for success will help to promote greater equity and inclusivity in society. Perhaps the most important question to be addressed in our development discourse is: what are the implications of these demographic changes for our provincial or continental ecosystems?

Since the Covid-19 national lockdown, unemployment has increased six times. In the second quarter 2 of 2022, compared to the first quarter of 2022, the expanded unemployment rate fell by 1.4 percentage points to 44.1 per cent. The official unemployment rate for 2022 is 19.9 per cent, higher than the 14 per cent reported by the NDP. The expanded unemployment rate, however, is 30 per cent higher than the NDP's aim.

The economy took over two years to recover from the effects of Covid-19, according to the GDP estimates for the second quarter of 2022 (Stats SA 2022d), with real GDP returning to pre-pandemic levels in the first quarter of 2022. The recovery was only temporary, as, in the second quarter of 2022, GDP fell by 0.7. per cent to R1 148 billion, the pre-pandemic fourth quarter level. Load-shedding, the domestic unrest and looting in July 2021 and the severe rains in KwaZulu-Natal all played a role in the decrease, undermining the already weak national economy that had only just returned to pre-pandemic levels.

One could argue that widespread structural unemployment is South Africa's biggest challenge. It hinders growth and serves as a foundation for inequality and poverty. The manufacturing sector's subpar performance has played a significant role in this. Significant employment losses were recorded in the manufacturing (73 000) and transportation sectors (54 000). In the second quarter of 2022, there were 15.6 million people employed overall.

Persistently high unemployment rates and challenges with unequal educational outcomes, among other things, as well as the recent unrest and its subsequent knock-on effects, as reported by the GDP figures, highlight the issues of unemployment, societal frustration and youth who are not fully engaged in education or training in South Africa. By addressing these challenges, we have the opportunity to create a stronger and more equitable economy, while achieving South Africa's developmental goals.

As a national statistics office, Stats SA is mandated to be a provider of evidence as seen on the ground. As official statisticians, we hold on to the independence granted by our position and as legislated in the Statistics Act No. 6 of 1999. However, just as we measure the changing landscape of our nation, we also live among its people and observe the success and challenges that emerge. We advocate for using these numbers to drive policy agendas by using firm evidence. Stats SA continues to provide data to inform and allow those who manage state and private sector resources to have a sound basis for planning. As we release these statistical reports monthly, quarterly and annually, it is encouraging that more stakeholders are interested in using official statistics to advance evidence-based policymaking.

As we continue to examine the South African social and economic landscape through a statistical lens, we aim to share critical insights to achieve the goal of building a data ecosystem that supports evidence-based policy. Stats SA has released census data from the fourth population census in a democratic dispensation conducted in 2022. Information collected from the census is crucial for proper planning in the country. Furthermore, Stats SA is preparing to disseminate comprehensive household income and expenditure data by visiting over 31 000 dwelling units across the country during the income and expenditure survey. The data collected from the survey is essential in providing evidence-based information for monitoring the main NDP targets of reducing the Gini coefficient to 0.6 and the population living below the lower-bound poverty line to 0 per cent by 2030.

As South Africa works to tackle inequality and poverty via various legislative frameworks and initiatives, Stats SA aims to create high-quality statistics and give stakeholders reliable information. The following strategic questions are becoming more and more crucial to decision-makers: Can marginalised groups coexist in a society and economy with significant disparities that continue to widen? How can we address the apparent gender, urban–rural and population divides? How do we accommodate unskilled workers in an economy currently dominated by the financial services industry? Can the youth envision alternatives to not being employed, educated, or trained? What real opportunities might there be for women and young people in the country in terms of skills, job opportunities and education? How do we solve triple challenges of poverty, inequality and unemployment as well as other real challenges affecting women, the youth and other marginalised groups? How can we stop marginalised communities from experiencing impoverishment due to a series of shocks, including the domestic riots and looting in July 2021, pandemic spillovers and escalating power outages? Is the current social grant system sustainable? If not, are there any sustainable alternatives that could replace it? Although official statistics do not allow us to address these questions directly, they allow us to see the necessary interventions more clearly.

For over two decades, millions of South Africans have taken part in choosing their preferred government every five years through democratic elections. By using accurate and official statistics to highlight inconsistencies between policy intent, its delivery system and policy outcomes, we can identify inefficiencies in the government system and the performance of various sectors. Although creating a master plan is different from implementing it, statistics can help us improve governance and promote systemic effectiveness and efficiency. We should aim to leverage the power of data-driven insights to enhance the standard of living in South Africa through the development of robust data ecosystems.

References

AU (African Union). 2013. *Agenda 2063: The Africa We Want*. https://au.int/sites/default/files/documents/33126-doc-framework_document_book.pdf (accessed 9 January 2024).

Antobam, S.K. 2015. 'Migration, Urbanisation, and Development in South Africa'. In: *Social Demography of South Africa: Advances and Emerging Issues*, edited by C.O. Odimegwu and J. Kekovole, 136–64. New York: Routledge.

Baptista, D.M.S., M. Farid, D. Fayad, L. Kemoe, L.S. Lanci, P. Mitra, T.S. Muehlschlegel, C. Okou, J.A. Spray, K. Tuitoek and F.D. Unsal. 2022. *Climate Change and Chronic Food Insecurity in Sub-Saharan Africa*. International Monetary Fund Departmental Paper, 15 September. https://www.imf.org/en/Publications/Departmental-Papers-Policy-Papers/Issues/2022/09/13/Climate-Change-and-Chronic-Food-Insecurity-in-Sub-Saharan-Africa-522211 (accessed 9 January 2024).

Buheji, M. 2022. 'Impact of Post-pandemic Inflation on Global Poverty: A Holistic Perspective'. *International Journal of Management* 13 (5): 11–23.

Department of Cooperative Governance and Traditional Affairs. 2022. *The District Development Model*. https://www.cogta.gov.za/cgta_2016/wp-content/uploads/2023/05/District-Development-Model-DDM-Booklet_230524_110720.pdf (accessed 9 January 2024).

Department of Planning, Monitoring and Evaluation. 2019a. *Revised Medium Term Strategic Framework (MTSF) 2019–2024*. https://www.dpme.gov.za/keyfocusareas/Provincial%20Performance%20Publication/Documents/Revised%20MTSF%20100321A.pdf (accessed 9 January 2024).

———. 2019b. *Towards a 25-Year Review, 1994–2019*. https://www.dpme.gov.za/news/SiteAssets/Pages/25-Year-Review-Launch/Towards%20A%2025%20Year%20Review.pdf (accessed 9 January 2024).

———. 2020. *Bi-annual 2019–2024 MTSF Synthesis Report for the Period Ending March 2021*. https://www.dpme.gov.za/keyfocusareas/outcomesSite/MTSF_2019_2024/Bi-Annual%202019-2024%20MTSF%20Synthesis%20Report%20for%20the%20period%20ending%20March%202021.pdf (accessed 9 January 2024).

FAO (Food and Agriculture Organization), IFAD (International Fund for Agricultural Development), UNICEF (United Nations Children's Fund), WFP (World Food Programme) and WHO (World Health Organization). 2022. *The State of Food Security and Nutrition in the World 2022. Repurposing Food and Agricultural Policies to Make Healthy Diets More Affordable*. https://www.fao.org/3/cc0639en/cc0639en.pdf (accessed 9 January 2024).

IMF (International Monetary Fund). 2022. *World Economic Outlook: Rising Caseloads, a Disrupted Recovery, and Higher Inflation*. https://www.imf.org/en/Publications/WEO/Issues/2022/01/25/world-economic-outlook-update-january-2022 (accessed 9 January 2024).

National Planning Commission. 2012. *National Development Plan 2030: Our Future – Make It Work*. https://www.gov.za/sites/default/files/gcis_document/201409/ndp-2030-our-future-make-it-workr.pdf (accessed 9 January 2023).

National Treasury. 2022. *Medium Term Budget Policy Statement.* https://www.treasury.gov.za/ (accessed 9 January 24).

South African Government. 2020. *The South African Economic Reconstruction and Recovery Plan.* https://www.gov.za/sites/default/files/gcis_document/202010/south-african-economic-reconstruction-and-recovery-plan.pdf (accessed 9 January 2024).

Stats SA (Statistics South Africa). 1999. *The Statistics Act 6 of 1999.* https://www.gov.za/documents/acts/statistics-act-6-1999-21-apr-1999 (accessed 9 January 2024).

———. 2001. *Census in Brief.* Report, 3 February. https://www.statssa.gov.za/census/census _2001/census_in_brief/CIB2001.pdf (accessed 9 January 2024).

———. 2011. *Mortality and Causes of Death in South Africa: Findings from Death Notification.* https://www.statssa.gov.za/publications/P03093/P030932011.pdf (accessed 9 January 2024).

———. 2014. *The South African MPI: Creating a Multidimensional Poverty Index Using Census Data.* https://www.statssa.gov.za/publications/Report-03-10-08/Report-03-10-082014.pdf (accessed 9 January 2024).

———. 2016. *Community Survey 2016.* Statistical release P0301. https://cs2016.statssa.gov. za/wp-content/uploads/2016/07/NT-30-06-2016-RELEASE-for-CS-2016-_Statistical-releas_1-July-2016.pdf (accessed 9 January 2024).

———. 2017. *Poverty Trends in South Africa: An Examination of Absolute Poverty between 2006 and 2015.* https://www.statssa.gov.za/publications/Report-03-10-06/Report-03-10-062015. pdf (accessed 9 January 2024).

———. 2019. *Survey of Employers and the Self-employed, 2017.* http://www.statssa.gov.za/publications/P0276/P02762017.pdf (accessed 9 January 2024).

———. 2020a. *Education Series Volume VI: Education and Labour Market Outcomes in South Africa, 2018.* http://www.statssa.gov.za/publications/92-01-06/92-01-062018.pdf (accessed 9 January 2024).

———. 2020b. *Labour Market Dynamics in South Africa, 2020.* http://www.statssa.gov.za/publications/Report-02-11-02/Report-02-11-022020.pdf (accessed 9 January 2024).

———. 2020c. *Strategic Plan 2022/21–2024/25.* https://www.statssa.gov.za/strategy_plan/Stats%20SA%20Strategic%20Plan.pdf (accessed 9 January 2024).

———. 2021. *Alternative Sources of Demographic Data.* http://www.statssa.gov.za/publications/03-00-17/03-00-172021.pdf (accessed 9 January 2024).

———. 2022a. *General Household Survey, 2021.* https://www.statssa.gov.za/publications/P0318/P03182021.pdf (accessed 9 January 2024).

———. 2022b. *Governance, Public Safety and Justice Survey 2021/22.* https://www.statssa.gov.za/publications/P0341/P03412022.pdf (accessed 9 January 2024).

———. 2022c. *Gross Domestic Product: GDP Time series 2023Q2.* https://www.statssa.gov.za/publications/P0441/GDP%20P0441%20-%20GDP%20Time%20series%202022Q2.xlsx (accessed 9 January 24).

———. 2022d. *Gross Domestic Product, Second Quarter 2022.* https://www.statssa.gov.za/publications/P0441/P04412ndQuarter2022.pdf (accessed 9 January 24).

———. 2022e. *Mid-year Population Estimates, 2022.* https://www.statssa.gov.za/publications/
P0302/P03022022.pdf (accessed 9 January 24).

———. 2022f. *National Poverty Lines, 2022.* https://www.statssa.gov.za/publications/P03101/
P031012022.pdf (accessed 9 January 2024).

———. 2022g. *Quarterly Labour Force Survey, Quarter 2: 2022. P0211.* https://www.statssa.gov.
za/publications/P0211/Presentation%20QLFS%20Q2%202022.pdf (accessed 9 January
2024).

———. 2002h. 'Softer Fuel Prices Take the Edge off Inflation in August'. https://www.statssa.
gov.za/?p=15754 (accessed 9 January 2024).

———. 2023. Inflation: The Most Vulnerable Are at Risk. https://www.statssa.gov.za/?p=16357
(accessed 9 January 2024).

United Nations Statistical Commission. 1994. *Fundamental Principles of Official Statistics.*
https://unstats.un.org/unsd/dnss/gp/fp-english.pdf (accessed 9 January 2024).

UNECA (United Nations Economic Commission for Africa). 2016. 'The Demographic Profile
of African Countries'. https://repository.uneca.org/ds2/stream/?#/documents/b51a7ff9-
188b-590e-809b-ba27495a251a/page/1 (accessed 9 January 2024).

World Bank. 2022. 'Global Growth to Slow through 2023, Adding to Risk of "Hard Landing" in
Developing Economies'. https://www.worldbank.org/en/news/press-release/2022/01/11/
global-recovery-economics-debt-commodity-inequality#:~:text=Global%20growth%20
is%20expected%20to,is%20unwound%20across%20the%20world (accessed 9 January 2024).

Yung, W. 2021. 'The Evolution of Official Statistics in a Changing World'. *Harvard Data
Science Review* 3 (4). https://hdsr.mitpress.mit.edu/pub/w8l955ol/release/3 (accessed 9
January 2024).

CHAPTER 7

To Fix South Africa, Fix Its Framing

Declinism as a Behavioural Bias and Failed Strategy for Solving Systemic Challenges

Adrian Gore

South Africa is a country worth fighting for. It is uniquely beautiful, with diverse people, and it has considerable potential to ignite the development of the African continent. It also has unacceptable levels of poverty, inequality and unemployment, with the youth most disadvantaged. While reforms are needed to address these, this chapter is not about such reforms, but about the sentiment in the environment that moderates the success of their implementation. In this chapter, I argue that an impediment to addressing these challenges is how the country is framed: South Africa's narrative is worse than the reality and this perception gap is corrosive and causal – creating a sense of inevitable decline and 'nothing left to lose' when, in fact, there is a considerable amount at stake. Among other things, this leads to a loss of skills (the so-called brain drain) and deters the investment and collaboration required to help drive inclusive growth. This chapter challenges the dogma that progress on fundamentals is what changes attitudes and proposes the inverse – a shift in attitude is necessary to drive development. It thus advocates for a leadership approach from the government, business and civil society, which would trigger a positive, self-fulfilling dynamic – modifying the national narrative to one that is more balanced and providing a vision of the future that inspires hope, action and, critically, change.

Behavioural economics explains that perception and judgement are often not accurate. Individuals have deeply ingrained biases, a coping mechanism for our overtaxed brains that are required to process a deluge of information (Hollingworth and Barker n.d.). Reality and truth are therefore elusive. Evolutionary biology is at the heart of many of these biases, including the processing affinity for negative signals. Humans evolved on the savannahs over millions of years, in conditions that were extremely challenging – reality was short and brutal. Critically, threats were physical. Successful strategies for survival centred on the ability to scan for these dangers because those who lacked this ability met with untimely death. Humans are therefore the descendants of those who were intrinsically wired to seek out negative signals in the environment around them.

The risks inherent to the present-day environment, however, are not physical (for example, being eaten by a lion), but rather systemic (for example, the sustainability of public utilities, education, and so on) – and the human brain has not kept pace with the acceleration of its social and physical order (Mark 2019). This is because while humans spent millions of years on the savannahs, the revolutions that followed (agricultural, cognitive, scientific, and so on) happened only during the last 15 000 to 20 000 years (Hancock 2022). There is thus a cognitive mismatch.

This mismatch is problematic because to solve systemic challenges and threats, seeking out solely negative signals is fundamentally the wrong approach. Yuval Harari (2014: 21–6) explains why this is problematic in his book *Sapiens: A Brief History of Humankind*: human ancestors used to live in small clans of approximately 30 people, where everyone knew one another, including who could be trusted and who could not. Compare this to how people live and work today: in cities of tens of millions of people; in companies of thousands of employees. To get a system to work requires motivating strangers, who are dispersed across time and space, to foster trust and co-operation. For this, positive frameworks and feedback loops are needed, not negative ones.

This mismatch sets us up for failure and manifests in the present-day bias of declinism, the belief that the world, a country, an organisation, is on an irreversible downhill trajectory. When compounded with confirmation bias (the inclination to seek out facts that affirm entrenched beliefs) and negativity bias (unpleasant news and experiences occupy more attention than pleasant ones), the result is a persistent and pervasive public pessimism. Take the World Economic Forum's *Global Risks Report* (2022), sourced from its extensive network of academic, business, government and civil society organisations: 84 per cent of global respondents were either concerned or worried about the outlook for the world (Figure 7.1).

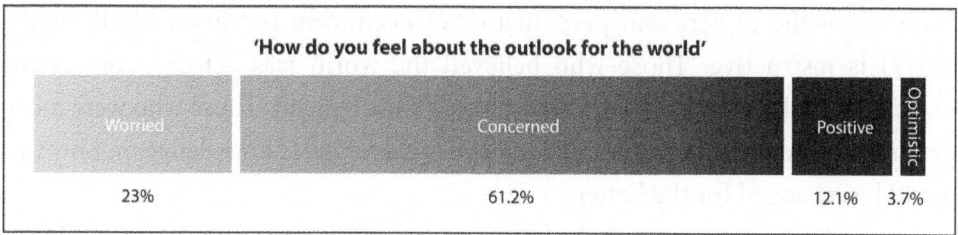

Figure 7.1 Perceptions of participants in the 'Global Risks Report 2022'
Source: World Economic Forum (2022)

While this may be understandable, given the fractious state of the world at the time of survey, the results are climate agnostic – that is, similar irrespective of the year and the state of the world at the time of survey. An expansive survey conducted by the global research organisation Ipsos MORI (2017) revealed that 62 per cent of respondents globally believed the world was getting worse and in a global survey run by YouGov, 71 per cent of respondents said they thought the world was getting worse, and only 5 per cent said it was getting better (Etchells 2015).

To illustrate the point further, consider the following graphs (Figure 7.2) from the European Union's Eurobarometer surveys. From the end of 1995 to the middle of 2015, the majority of people expected the economic situation in their home country to get worse or stay the same (Roser and Ritchie 2018).

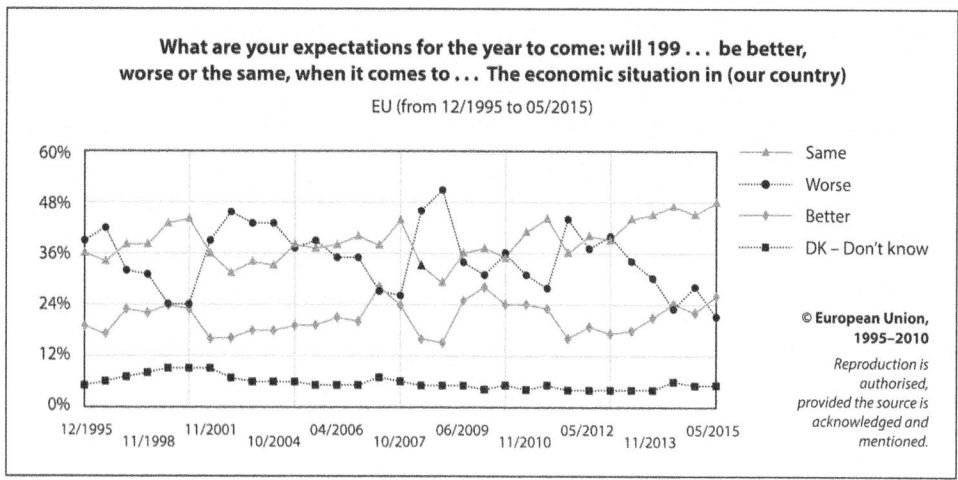

Figure 7.2 Declinism is pervasive and country agnostic
Source: Roser and Ritchie (2018)

In terms of the drivers and perpetuators of declinism, the Ipsos MORI study (2017) is instructive. Those who believed the world was getting worse were inaccurate in their readings of how the world had changed. Those who were most pessimistic about the future tended to have the least basic knowledge on how the world has changed for the better.

South Africans suffer acutely from this cognitive bias. In the Ipsos MORI survey (2017), not only were South Africans gloomy about how the world had changed and what the future held, on a broad range of issues, South African survey respondents gave the least accurate answers to questions relating to global and national development. Furthermore, South Africans were not just impervious to the facts on progress; the study revealed they were confident in their erroneous perceptions (Figure 7.3).

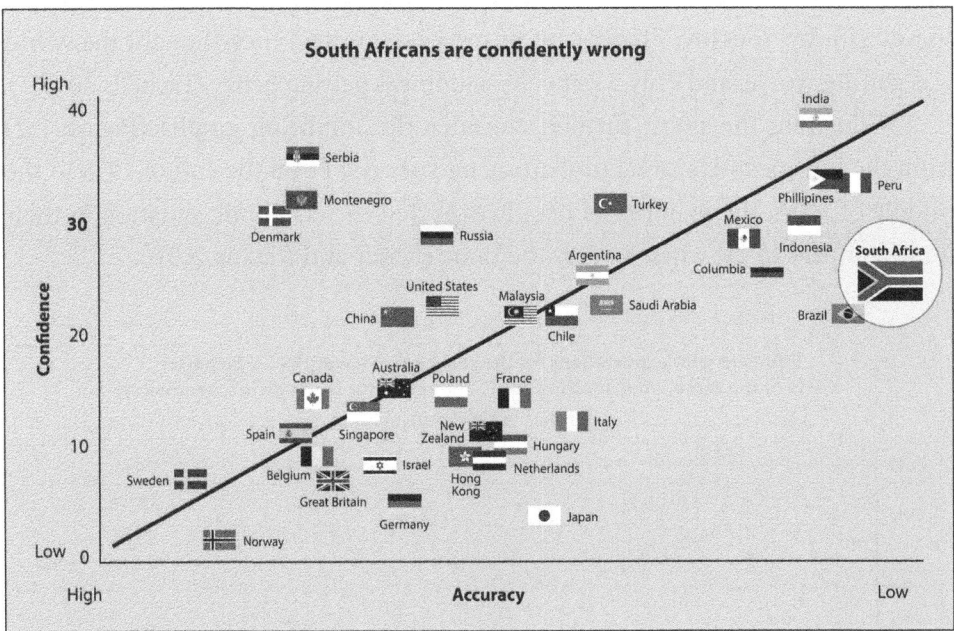

Figure 7.3 The gap between perception and reality

Source: Ipsos MORI (2017)

Being negative is, therefore, the perceptual default, the evolutionary instinct and the path of least cognitive resistance – the consequence of which is declinism. While being critical and cynical may appear to be sophisticated, under the illusion that scanning for risk is both prudent and realistic, it is not necessarily the most accurate perception. What was once a successful strategy for survival in an environment of physical risk is a failed one in an environment of systemic risk. In the South African context, where the challenges that require solving are complex and tragic – like the youth unemployment burden (Stats SA 2022b) – it pollutes the environment with despair and disengagement, so that tolerance for failure prevails and much-needed reforms become difficult to implement successfully.

Manifestations of declinism and the gap between narrative and reality

The centrality of poverty, inequality and unemployment is factual: the data is unequivocal and the lived experience of millions of people, especially the country's youth, unacceptable (BusinessTech 2021a). However, there are central, deeply held beliefs that the data shows to be inaccurate, with the perception gap resulting in profoundly damaging consequences.

The South African economy is perceived as uniquely risky and fragile when it is not

A central measure of economic risk is the volatility in the rate of gross domestic product (GDP): the historical standard deviation of the rate of growth in GDP (Cariolle 2012). If the country were in fact risky, it would experience high levels of GDP growth volatility – in some years GDP would grow rapidly and in others it would plunge. The data below shows clearly that while South Africa's growth rate is too slow, it is not volatile or risky.

Consider the period from the beginning of democracy to the start of the Covid-19 pandemic (1994–2019): South Africa's growth volatility is similar to developed countries like the United States, the United Kingdom and Japan, and far from the instability experienced by others, including some of its BRICS (Brazil, Russia, India, China and South Africa) counterparts (World Bank 2022a).[1] Then consider the GDP growth volatility of economies of similar size (South Africa's GDP is +/- US$150 billion), as can be seen in Figure 7.4. Adjusted for GDP size, South Africa exhibits one of the most stable performances, with variance in GDP growth rate comparable to the economies of Denmark and Norway (OECD 2022).

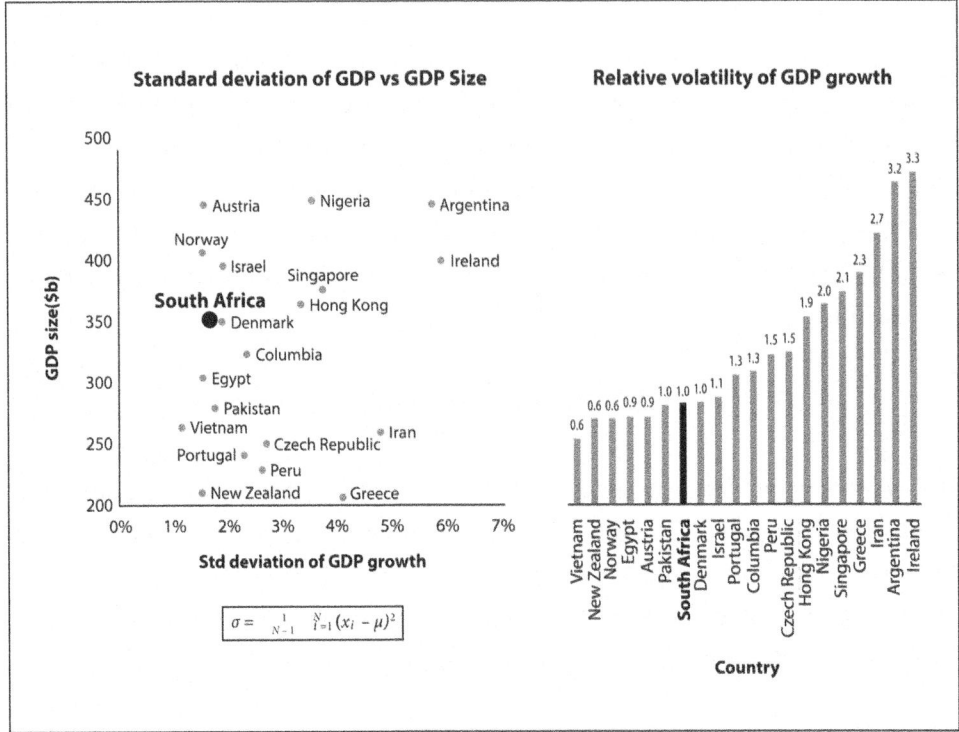

Figure 7.4 GDP growth volatility, 2022

Sources: OECD (2022); World Bank (2022a)

While the data on volatility is clear, the fundamental issue is one of perception – how do people judge the economy, fundamentals aside? Does perception differ from what facts portray? Consider: if the country is regarded as the 'company', GDP can be used as a proxy for the 'revenue' of the country and the volatility of its growth rate the extent of real risk. However, a country's exchange rate is akin to its 'share price' – its volatility is a measure of perception. By considering the two, the perception of risk versus reality can be assessed: the higher the ratio between the currency and GDP volatility, the more disproportionately the country is perceived as risky.

When one examines the ratio between currency and GDP volatility, the asymmetry between perceived and actual risk is pronounced (Figure 7.5). Herein lies the tragedy. It infers that the country's flawed framing leads investors to misprice risk and thus to miss opportunities.

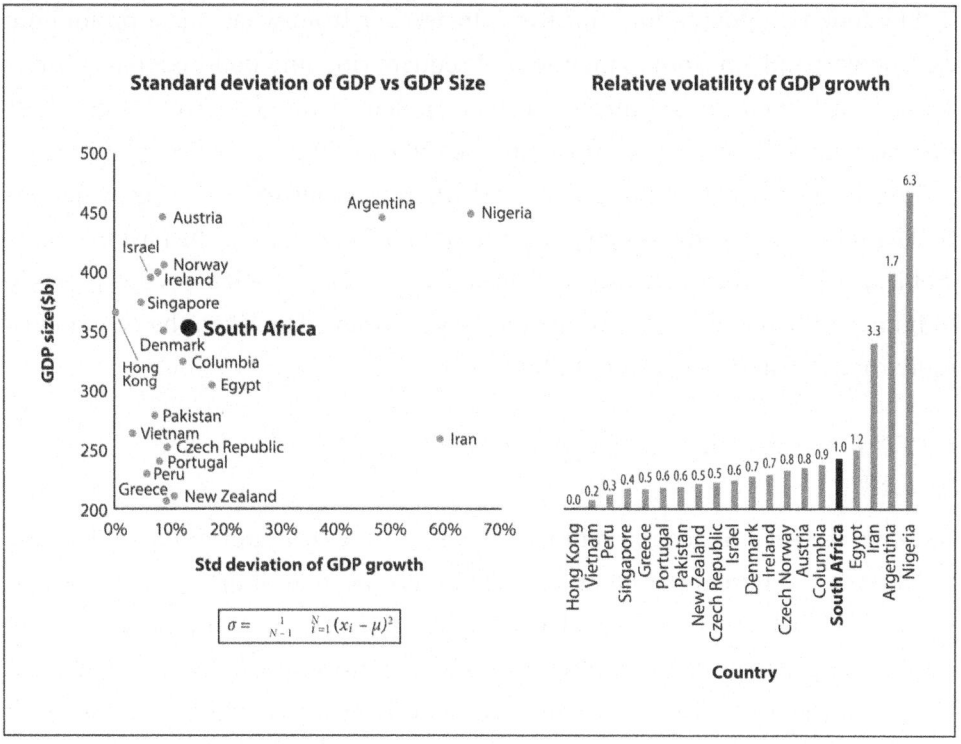

Figure 7.5 Current volatility equals perceived risk

Sources: OECD (2022); World Bank (2022a)

The analysis above considered the period from democracy to Covid-19, with lockdowns being a considerable distortion for the latter. However, consider perception versus reality through the pandemic and the gap continues. The prevailing narrative was that the country was condemned to economic doom. Headlines such as 'Covid-19 Has Throttled South Africa's Economy' in *The Economist* of 18 July 2020 and 'Lockdown Meltdown: SA Economy Contracted 51% in Q2' (Stoddard 2020) prevailed, with reputable business media citing estimates that the country's economy would likely only get back to pre-Covid-19 levels by 2025 (Vanek and Maseko 2020). Fast-forward to the end of the first quarter of 2022 and the economy was at the same level in terms of GDP as it was in the first quarter of 2020 when lockdown began (OECD 2022). The median of thirteen economists' estimates in a Bloomberg survey was for growth of 1.2 per cent; in fact, the economy grew 3 per cent from a year earlier (BusinessTech 2022).

It thus took two years – and not five – to recover from what was a profoundly destructive pandemic, not to mention subsequent riots and flooding in KwaZulu-Natal, which incurred significant costs, as noted in the *SA News* article 'Cost Recovery for KZN Floods Estimated in the Billions' *SA News* of 26 April 2022.

This is not to say that the economy is where it needs to be. It is growing too slowly, with real growth averaging a pedestrian 0.5 per cent for the past five years and 1 per cent for the last decade (BusinessTech 2022). Growth is needed urgently to improve the quality of life of the country's citizens. However, the economy is more robust than it is given credit for.

South Africa is perceived as small and unsophisticated, when it is not

Not only is South Africa relevant globally, it is an African powerhouse. The war in Ukraine is a humanitarian crisis and has also been an illuminating lesson in Ukraine's global relevance, as evidenced by the impact of the war on international trade. Now consider that South Africa's GDP is almost double Ukraine's, in 2020 US$ terms. In fact, Gauteng's economy alone is nearly as big as the Ukraine's (World Bank 2022a).

Additional data points provide a sense of the country's size and significance. South Africa:

- has a R5.52 trillion economy (US$335.4 billion), 33rd largest in the world and represents about 14 per cent of the African continent's overall GDP (IDC 2022);
- has the nineteenth-largest stock exchange in the world with a market cap of US$1.36 trillion (70 per cent that of Africa's);[2]
- had the 18th most traded currency in the world before Covid-19 ('Rand Trading' 2020);
- comprises 75 per cent of the pension fund assets in Africa (Bright Africa 2020);
- generates over 28 per cent of all electricity consumed in Africa, more than Switzerland, Ireland, Ethiopia, Israel and New Zealand combined (BP 2021);
- had the 11th busiest airline route (Cape Town to Johannesburg) in the world in 2019, before Covid-19 (Rosen 2019);

- has a market that enables substantial companies to be built, so that Discovery's revenue footprint is roughly the same as the GDP of Mauritius (World Bank 2022a);
- has a progressive Constitution and independent judiciary: its mature, accessible legal system provides certainty and respect for rule of law, and it has a sound regulatory framework adhering to international standards (IDC 2022);
- has an advanced financial services and banking sector: Standard Bank is bigger than the top five Nigerian banks combined on a Tier 1 capital basis, with FirstRand at 98 per cent thereof (BusinessTech 2021b); and
- has globally recognised universities that lead the way on many frontiers of global innovation, including the continent's scientific response to Covid-19, as manifested in vaccine development and delivery during the first year of the pandemic. In fact, 6 of South Africa's 26 tertiary institutions are ranked among the top 500 in the world in the US News and World Report's best global universities rankings (2022). However, getting more graduates through university, particularly in science, technology, engineering and mathematics, remains a challenge.

This chapter does not argue that South Africa is sophisticated across the board. It does, however, call for acknowledgement of the country's due significance, as a basis off which to improve global relevance and generate more positive sentiment and economic growth.

South Africa is perceived as deteriorating since the Zuma years, but there has been progress

South Africa, like the world as a whole, has become fundamentally better as time goes on. GDP (in 2015 prices) in 2021 was 1.88 times what it was in 1994 (Stats SA 2022a). Over a similar period, the black middle class increased in size by 173 per cent (Zwane 2019); household access to electricity increased by 58 per cent (Stats SA 2021) and new HIV infections and the murder rate both reduced dramatically (UNAIDS 2022; SAPS 2021; World Bank 2022b).

Even when accounting for the policy missteps and the mismanagement of public resources between 2009 and 2017 – the stagnant Zuma years – South Africa still made progress over most measures, albeit stodgy and marginal in places (Figure 7.6). This is in spite of what the Bureau for Economic Research quantified at a now-modest R500 billion cost to the economy and opportunity cost of 2.5 million additional jobs for the period (BusinessTech 2018). The murder rate is an exception and needs to be addressed urgently to give investors and citizens confidence.

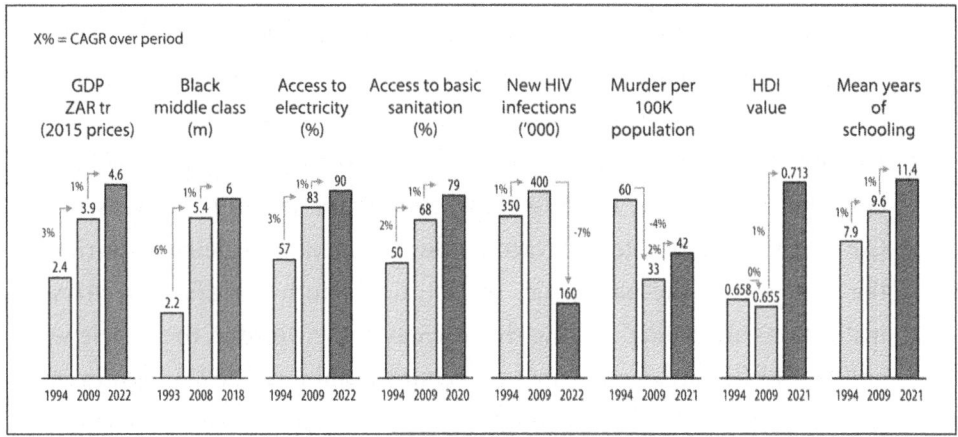

Figure 7.6 Data showing South Africa is a better place

Sources: Stats SA (2022a); St. Louis Fed (2023); UNAIDS (2022); Zwane (2019); UNDP (2022); World Bank (2022a); WHO (2022); Department of Water Affairs and Forestry (2004); Möller (1995)

In addition, many are unaware of the directional progress made by the government. Consider Operation Vulindlela, a unit in the Presidency and National Treasury set up specifically to accelerate the implementation of structural reforms. The team supports implementation, monitors progress and helps address challenges. Business has provided support and expertise to Operation Vulindlela to help progress the priority interventions (Bulbulia 2022).

Declinism shapes the narrative with a focus on what has not been achieved, as opposed to what has. Of the 26 reforms listed in Operation Vulindlela, approximately half have been or are on track to be completed and implemented in the first quarter of 2022 (The Presidency 2022). These include a number of initiatives related to:

- Energy: raising the licensing threshold for embedded generation to 100 megawatts; procuring new generation capacity in terms of the Renewable

Energy Independent Power Producer Procurement Programme 2019 bid windows 5 and 6, which contribute additional renewable energy supply to the national grid (Department of Mineral Resources and Energy 2022); enabling municipalities to procure power from independent power providers; and restructuring Eskom (once the red tape challenges bedevilling these interventions are removed, these reforms will result in many more megawatts added to the grid);

- Telecoms: the spectrum auction has been completed;
- Water: the blue drop, green drop water quality certification systems have been revived; an independent economic regulator for water is being established; the revised raw water pricing strategy finalised; and a national water resource infrastructure agency is being established;
- Transport: a transport economic regulator is being established and the White Paper on National Rail Policy has been published; and
- Investment and ease of doing business: a revised critical skills list has been published; the policy framework and processes for work visas are being reviewed; and an e-visa system implemented in fourteen countries.

In addition, in an unpublished document in 2022, Business Unity South Africa prioritised a limited set of interventions to focus on in the immediate term to address economic and social challenges. These included energy/just transition; transport (roads, rail and ports); water and sanitation; infrastructure (new builds and public–private partnerships); and security and law and order (including the fight against corruption).

This chapter does not argue that progress since democracy has been inclusive. Clearly, distributing gains more equitably is fundamental to the country's financial and social cohesion, and its future. It also does not argue that all current reforms have progressed at a satisfactory pace. Improving the energy availability factor; improving the efficiency of the ports; implementing new visa systems and critical skills categories; and greater use of municipal infrastructure budgets are examples of where greater speed and excellence in execution are required. This chapter does, however, argue that where progress has been achieved, it remains vastly understated and unrecognised.

South Africa is perceived as having intractable problems that cannot be solved when they can

Henry Kissinger, the American politician, diplomat and geopolitical consultant once shared a fascinating insight at a private breakfast I attended in 2011 – that economies of the West see problems as aberrations, whereas those of the East see problems as the normal run of order.

Most South Africans share the Western perception, where challenges are viewed as painful and stubborn deviations from the norm. Yet the country's problems are not insoluble. If anything, South Africans have an amazing capacity to generate creative solutions, unique to a country having to simultaneously address high levels of inequality while nurturing pockets of sophistication.

Take, for example, the HIV pandemic, which exploded in the 1990s, leading to South Africa having one of the world's heaviest burdens of HIV-related morbidity and mortality (Allinder and Fleischman 2019). Today, South Africa has the world's largest and arguably most effective anti-retroviral therapy programme (Be in the Know 2020). Similarly, state capture allegations monopolised media attention from 2016 onwards, yet the strength of the country's democracy and the independence of its judiciary is evidenced by the corruption charges former president Jacob Zuma is facing. Insofar as Covid-19 goes, while the country was hard-hit infection wise, its well-established scientific capability was a key contributor to some of the most important Covid-19 vaccine trials (Wits University 2020) and its genomic sequencing capabilities have enabled its identification of new variants (Adepoju 2021).

The argument in this chapter is not centred on minimising the country's problems; they need to be solved. It also does not propose that the problems that have been addressed have been done so neatly. In many cases, South Africans gain traction on issues, but could do so more efficiently. This chapter also does not claim that all problems have been resolved. At the time of writing, load-shedding is one such justifiable pain point, with urgent progress needed by Eskom and the government on the generation, transmission and distribution of electricity. The argument in this chapter is that problems of the day are sought out and obsessed over as evidence of doom and yet they are not, implying a cognitive shortcoming: when progress is made, the nation's sentiments and psyche are not revised to take progress into account. Citizens simply move onto the next all-consuming crisis in a cycle of perpetual cynicism and angst (Figure 7.7).

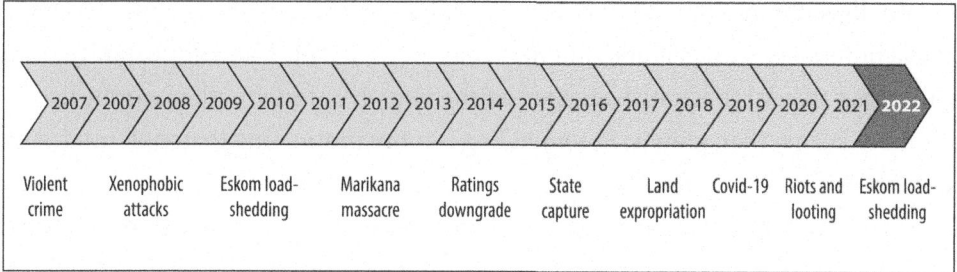

Figure 7.7 New topical crisis every 18–24 months, 2006–22

The pernicious impact of the perception-reality gap: Despair and a 'nothing-to-lose' mentality

The impact of the misperceptions discussed above is disastrous, given they are self-fulfilling: a corrosive narrative leaves citizens feeling despairing and that they have nothing to lose. This profoundly jeopardises progress because behavioural economics teaches that perceiving something to be at stake is a fundamental motivator. The concept is called loss aversion – individuals are doubly motivated by loss than they are by a gain of equal magnitude.

Nobel Prize winners Daniel Kahneman and Amos Tversky's work on Prospect Theory (1979) explored this phenomenon. They looked at what is known as utility theory, the value people derive from things, both positive and negative.

The assumption is that utility is a linear relationship – the more of something positive people get, the greater their enjoyment or satisfaction. Annual leave is a good example: the more employees get, the happier they are. But what Kahneman and Tversky found was, firstly, that the curve is an S-shape, not a straight line (Figure 7.8). So, in other words, when individuals get more of something, their enjoyment of it starts declining,

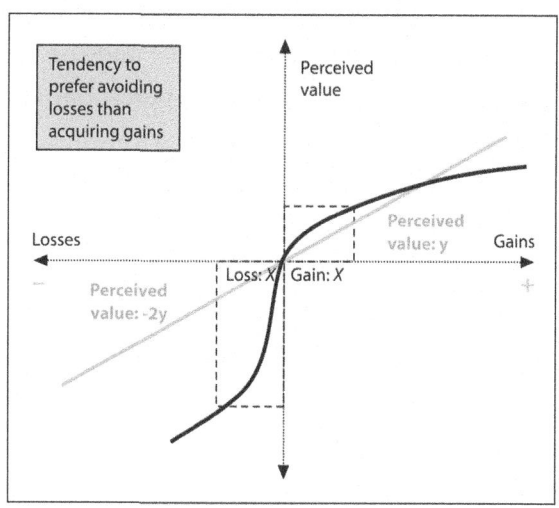

Figure 7.8 Loss aversion

Source: Kahneman and Tversky (1979)

eventually flattening out. So that next day of annual leave counts slightly less and, after a number of weeks, it does not matter as much. Second, and importantly, they found that the curve is much steeper on the negative side. In other words, loss is felt more keenly than gain is. Potential loss is more motivating than potential gain and that is a crucial issue.

The point is that declinism and its manifestations perpetuate a narrative that is worse than reality. They propagate a no-future scenario. There is nothing to lose. The consequences are causal and catastrophic. For one thing, investors start perceiving the country and its economy as risky and avoid investing. Ironically, the opposite should be the case. On top of this, innovation and activism around the country's challenges is stifled. If the future is already forgone and a bleak place, why bother being constructive? Motivation is diluted: leaders and citizens give up on trying to improve the country's prospects. Disillusionment follows and a vicious cycle of social unrest is created, given citizens become vulnerable to radical populism. Perception becomes reality. Deteriorating sentiment informs deteriorating fundamentals.

Remedy: A call for a new model of leadership

The remedy proposed is fundamentally one of leadership. This chapter proposes that leaders across sectors need to create a positive framework that triggers a dynamic of accountability, social cohesion and collaboration. Central to this is appreciating progress, strengths and the potential to effect a more balanced national narrative and create the perception that the future is worth fighting for.

A stronger form of the above is setting meaningful goals with realistic glide paths – creating an acute sense of something to lose and thereby triggering loss aversion. When faced with externally imposed goals, the country has risen to the challenge.

A good example is the 2010 International Federation of Association Football (FIFA) World Cup. When built, Johannesburg's Gautrain airport service route was similar in time and price per trip to the Heathrow Express, but took 45 months to build versus 65 months (Railway Technology 2000, 2020) and handled over three times the passengers per day (Le Blond 1999; Venter 2013). The country's largest stadium in Johannesburg had more seating capacity than Wembley Stadium – but was built for close to half of the price in a year less (StadiumDB 2022; Stadium Guide 2022).

The country's vaccination roll-out is further proof. While South Africa was slow to procure vaccine supply initially, during the full throes of the country's mass vaccination programme, its maximum daily capacity of 418 000 doses in August 2021, according to an unpublished analysis by Business for South Africa, compared to what the United Kingdom was administering daily over its seven-day average peak (Mathieu et al. 2020) – that is, 0.7 per cent of its population. While vaccine hesitancy led to poor vaccination uptake, the capability was established. A unique example of private and public sector collaboration globally and a brilliant model off which to build.

The leadership imperative is clearly to set these goals proactively

The above examples are powerful, given the science of hope, a topic of increasing discussion within health-care literature. According to Charles Snyder's cognitive model of hope (2002), hope is a function of the perceived ability to set goals, to define pathways towards realising those goals and the sense of agency one has in pursuing the goals. Snyder makes it clear that higher hope is consistently related to better outcomes in academics, athletics, physical health, psychological adjustment and psychotherapy. In the health-care context, this makes intuitive sense. Positioning a patient as powerless to external forces is not constructive to their perspective or well-being: it removes their sense of control over their lives, disconnects them from others offering support and extinguishes their sense of purpose and opportunity. A bruised and wounded outlook is profoundly disabling to a patient's sense of self and consequent engagement in life. Goals, pathways and self-determination are central to navigating through a health issue. The same can be said of South Africans and a country that is on a bumpy journey to realising its potential. Providing citizens with hope is essential. When individuals have a compelling view of the future, with bold goals and a realistic glide path, such as 'end load-shedding within two years', a sense of agency with regard to the issue at hand and a binding solidarity with others in its pursuit – meaning and motivation blossom.

Conclusion

South Africa is far from perfect and its real and profound challenges demand urgent action, such as economic reforms and rooting out corruption. This chapter is not about reforms, but rather how to create an environment conducive to reforms being effectively implemented. Central here is leadership. South Africa's challenges make it fashionable to be negative, with optimism viewed as naive and not sufficiently cognisant of the issues facing the country. Yet, talking down the country is both morally and strategically destructive: supporting this narrative creates the climate for it to take hold further and multiply. This entrenches challenges and hurts the prospects of the nation's children. Ironically, without optimism, the capacity to address challenges diminishes. By framing a more balanced narrative, one that recognises progress and strengths, alongside challenges – and setting a compelling vision and goals – leaders can help build confidence and trigger the higher rates of economic growth and job creation that the country's future depends on. A different frame of the country is proposed: not 'a country in exorable decline', but 'a resilient country, underperforming but with potential'.

Leaders can either perpetuate declinism or provide an antidote. The latter is how change happens. Attitude drives fundamentals, not the other way around.

Notes

1. In August 2023, six countries (Argentina, Egypt, Ethiopia, Iran, Saudi Arabia and the United Arab Emirates) were invited to join BRICS. Full membership will take effect on 1 January 2024.
2. See https://www.tradinghours.com/markets (accessed 1 June 2022).

References

Adepoju, P. 2021. 'Why South Africa Keeps Detecting COVID-19 Variants Like Omicron'. *Devex*, 6 December. https://www.devex.com/news/why-south-africa-keeps-detecting-covid-19-variants-like-omicron-102212 (accessed 27 September 2023).

Allinder, S.M. and J. Fleischman. 2019. 'The World's Largest HIV Epidemic in Crisis: HIV in South Africa'. *Center for Strategic and International Studies*, 2 April. https://www.csis.org/analysis/worlds-largest-hiv-epidemic-crisis-hiv-south-africa (accessed 27 September 2023).

Be in the Know. 2020. 'At a Glance: HIV in South Africa'. https://www.beintheknow.org/understanding-hiv-epidemic/data/glance-hiv-south-africa (accessed 27 September 2023).

BP. 2021. *Statistical Review of World Energy 2021*. https://www.bp.com/content/dam/bp/business-sites/en/global/corporate/pdfs/energy-economics/statistical-review/bp-stats-review-2021-full-report.pdf (accessed 27 September 2023).

Bright Africa. 2020. *Bright Africa 2020 Pension Industry*. https://brightafrica.riscura.com/wp-content/uploads/2021/05/Bright_Africa_Pensions_2020_Download.pdf (accessed 27 September 2023).

Bulbulia, T. 2022. 'Busa Welcomes Operation Vulindlela Progress, but Calls for Further Advances'. *Creamer Media's Engineering News*, 11 May. https://www.engineeringnews.co.za/article/busa-welcomes-operation-vulindlela-progress-but-calls-for-further-progress-2022-05-11 (accessed 27 September 2023).

BusinessTech. 2018. 'How the Stagnant Zuma Years "Cost" South Africa R500 Billion'. *BusinessTech*, 10 October. https://businesstech.co.za/news/finance/276599/how-the-stagnant-zuma-years-cost-south-africa-r500-billion/ (accessed 27 September 2023).

———. 2021a. 'South Africans Have Become Poorer over the Last 6 Years: Government'. *BusinessTech*, 5 July. https://businesstech.co.za/news/finance/503297/south-africans-have-become-poorer-over-the-last-6-years-government/ (accessed 27 September 2023).

———. 2021b. 'These Are South Africa's Biggest Banks in 2021'. *BusinessTech*, 1 July. https://businesstech.co.za/news/banking/502541/these-are-south-africas-biggest-banks-in-2021/ (accessed 27 September 2023).

———. 2022. 'South Africa's Economy Is back to Where It Was before Covid – but Citizens Are Becoming Poorer'. *BusinessTech*, 8 June. https://businesstech.co.za/news/finance/594782/south-africas-economy-is-back-to-where-it-was-before-covid-but-citizens-are-becoming-poorer/ (accessed 27 September 2023).

Cariolle, J. 2012. *Measuring Macroeconomic Volatility: Applications to Export Revenue Data, 1970–2005*. FERDI Working Paper No. I14. https://ferdi.fr/dl/df-ffDuTsM2SZQq6ftuTVVBGV5C/ferdi-i14-measuring-macroeconomic-volatility.pdf (accessed 27 September 2023).

'Cost Recovery for KZN Floods Estimated in the Billions'. *SA News*, 26 April 2022. https://www.sanews.gov.za/south-africa/cost-recovery-kzn-floods-estimated-billions (accessed 27 September 2023).

'Covid-19 Has Throttled South Africa's Economy'. *The Economist*, 18 July 2020. https://www.economist.com/middle-east-and-africa/2020/07/18/covid-19-has-throttled-south-africas-economy#:~:text=About%20half%20of%20the%20erstwhile,is%20set%20to%20rise%20further (accessed 27 September 2023).

Department of Mineral Resources and Energy. 2022. 'Minister Gwede Mantashe Announces 5th Bid Window of Renewable Energy IPP Procurement Programme (REIPPPP Bid Window 5)'. https://www.gov.za/speeches/minister-gwede-mantashe-announces-5th-bid-window-renewable-energy-ipp-procurement-programme (accessed 2 November 2023).

Department of Water Affairs and Forestry. 2004. 'A History of the First Decade of Water Service Delivery in South Africa 1994 to 2004'. https://www.gov.za/sites/default/files/gcis_document/201409/dwafirstdecade070720060.pdf (accessed 3 November 2023).

Etchells, P. 2015. 'Declinism: Is the World Actually Getting Worse?' *The Guardian*, 16 January. https://www.theguardian.com/science/head-quarters/2015/jan/16/declinism-is-the-world-actually-getting-worse (accessed 27 September 2023).

Hancock, J. 2022. 'Dynamics of the Neolithic Revolution'. *World History Encyclopedia*, 7 February. https://www.worldhistory.org/article/1937/dynamics-of-the-neolithic-revolution/ (accessed 27 September 2023).

Harari, Y.N. 2014. *Sapiens: A Brief History of Humankind*. New York: Random House Harper.

Hollingworth, C. and L. Barker. N.d. 'Debunking Myths and Re-establishing Truths: New Frontiers in Behavioural Science Series – Article 5'. *The Marketing* Society. https://www.marketingsociety.com/think-piece/system-1-and-system-2-thinking (accessed 27 September 2023).

IDC (Industrial Development Corporation). 2022. *South Africa: Replete with Opportunities for a Better World*. https://v9x2w3s4.stackpathcdn.com/wp-content/uploads/2021/11/South-Africa-Replete-with-Opportunities-IDC-and-InvestSA-publication-FINAL-8-November-2021-1.pdf (accessed 27 September 2023).

Ipsos MORI. 2017. *The Perils of Perception 2017*. https://www.ipsos.com/sites/default/files/ct/news/documents/2018-02/ipsos-perils-of-perception-2017-charts_0.pdf (accessed 27 September 2023).

Kahneman, D. and A. Tversky. 1979. 'Prospect Theory: An Analysis of Decision under Risk'. *Econometrica* 47 (2): 263–92.

Le Blond, P. 1999. 'Heathrow Express'. *Japan Railways and Transport Review* 19: 20–4.

Mark, C. 2019. 'You're Afraid of the Wrong Things: What Evolution Made You Scared of versus What Actually Might Kill You'. *CBC*, 5 April. https://www.cbc.ca/life/culture/you-re-afraid-of-the-wrong-things-what-evolution-made-you-scared-of-versus-what-actually-might-kill-you-1.5086576 (accessed 27 September 2023).

Mathieu, E., H. Ritchie, L. Rodés-Guirao, C. Appel, D. Gavrilov, C. Giattino, J. Hasell, B. Macdonald, S. Dattani, D. Beltekian, E. Ortiz-Ospina and M. Roser. 2020. 'Coronavirus Pandemic (COVID-19)'. *Our World in Data*. https://ourworldindata.org/coronavirus (accessed 27 September 2023).

Möller, V. 1995. 'Indicators for Africa: The October Household Survey'. *Indicator South Africa* 12 (3): 86–90.

OECD (Organisation for Economic Co-operation and Development). 2022. 'Quarterly GDP'. https://data.oecd.org/gdp/quarterly-gdp.htm (accessed 27 September 2023).

The Presidency. 2022. *Operation Vulindlela Progress Update Q1 2022*. Available at: https://www.thepresidency.gov.za/download/file/fid/2498 (accessed 27 September 2023).

Railway Technology. 2000. 'Heathrow Express'. *Railway Technology*, 2 May. https://www.railway-technology.com/projects/heathrow-express/ (accessed 27 September 2023).

———. 2020. 'Gautrain Rapid Rail Link'. *Railway Technology*, 24 July. https://www.railway-technology.com/projects/gautrain/ (accessed 27 September 2023).

'Rand Trading Has Increased by 182% – Most of It Is outside South Africa'. *Business Insider*, January 2020. https://www.businessinsider.co.za/rand-trading-has-increased-by-182most-of-it-is-outside-south-africa-2020-1 (accessed 1 June 2022).

Rosen, E. 2019. 'The 2019 List of Busiest Airline Routes in the World'. *Forbes*, 2 April. https://www.forbes.com/sites/ericrosen/2019/04/02/the-2019-list-of-busiest-airline-routes-in-the-world/?sh=47dcd4411d48 (accessed 27 September 2023).

Roser, M. and H. Ritchie. 2018. 'Optimism and Pessimism'. *Our World in Data*, 27 July. https://ourworldindata.org/optimism-and-pessimism (accessed 27 September 2023).

SAPS (South African Police Service). 2021. 'Crime Report'. SAPS. https://www.saps.gov.za/services/crimestats.php (accessed 27 September 2023).

Snyder, C.R. 2002. 'Hope Theory: Rainbows in the Mind'. *Psychological Inquiry* 13 (4): 249–75.

StadiumDB. 2022. 'FNB Stadium (Soccer City)'. http://stadiumdb.com/stadiums/rsa/soccer_city (accessed 27 September 2023).

The Stadium Guide. 2022. 'Wembley Stadium'. https://www.stadiumguide.com/wembleynew/ (accessed 27 September 2023).

Stats SA (Statistics South Africa). 2021. *General Household Survey*. https://www.statssa.gov.za/publications/P0318/P03182020.pdf (accessed 27 September 2023).

——. 2022a. *Gross Domestic Product*. https://www.statssa.gov.za/publications/P0441/P04414thQuarter2022.pdf (accessed 27 September 2023).

——. 2022b. 'South Africa's Youth Continues to Bear the Burden of Unemployment'. *Stats SA*, 1 June. https://www.statssa.gov.za/?p=15407 (accessed 27 September 2023).

St. Louis Fed. 2023. 'GDP Implicit Price Deflator in South Africa'. https://fred.stlouisfed.org/series/ZAFGDPDEFQISMEI (accessed 3 November 2023).

Stoddard, E. 2020. 'Lockdown Meltdown: SA Economy Contracted 51% in Q2'. *Daily Maverick*, 8 September. https://www.dailymaverick.co.za/article/2020-09-08-lockdown-meltdown-sa-economy-contracted-51-in-q2/ (accessed 27 September 2023).

UNAIDS (Joint United Nations Programme on HIV and AIDS). 2022. 'South Africa Factsheet'. https://www.unaids.org/en/regionscountries/countries/southafrica (accessed 27 September 2023).

UNDP (United Nations Development Programme). 2022. 'Human Development Index'. https://hdr.undp.org/data-center/specific-country-data#/countries/ZAF (accessed 3 November 2023).

US News and World Report. 2022. '2022–2023 Best Global Universities Rankings'. https://www.usnews.com/education/best-global-universities/rankings (accessed 27 September 2023).

Vanek, M. and L. Maseko. 2020. 'S. Africa GDP Far from Pre-Covid Levels even as Recession Ends'. *Bloomberg*, 8 December. https://www.bloomberg.com/news/articles/2020-12-08/south-africa-exits-longest-recession-since-1992-with-gdp-bounce (accessed 1 June 2022).

Venter, I. 2013. 'Longer Than Planned Gautrain Trips Limit Passenger Growth'. *Creamer Media's Engineering News*, 21 January. https://www.engineeringnews.co.za/print-version/longer-than-planned-gautrain-trips-limit-passenger-growth-2013-01-21 (accessed 27 September 2023).

WHO (World Health Organization). 2022. 'JMP Data'. https://washdata.org/data/household#!/table?geo0=country&geo1=ZAF (accessed 3 November 2023).

Wits University. 2020. 'The First Covid-19 Vaccine Trial in South Africa Begins'. *University of the Witwatersrand Research News*, 23 June. https://www.wits.ac.za/news/latest-news/research-news/2020/2020-06/the-first-covid-19-vaccine-trial-in-south-africa-begins.html#:~:text=The%20first%20clinical%20trial%20in,Witwatersrand%2C%20Johannesburg%20(Wits) (accessed 27 September 2023).

The World Bank. 2022a. 'GDP (Current US$)'. https://data.worldbank.org/indicator/NY.GDP.MKTP.CD (accessed 27 September 2023).

———. 2022b. 'Intentional Homicides (per 100,000) – South Africa'. https://data.worldbank.org/indicator/VC.IHR.PSRC.P5?locations=ZA (accessed 27 September 2023).

World Economic Forum. 2022. 'The Global Risks Report 2022'. https://www.weforum.org/reports/global-risks-report-2022/ (accessed 27 September 2023).

Zwane, T. 2019. 'Black Middle Class More Than Doubled but the Struggle Continues'. *City Press*, 29 April. https://www.news24.com/citypress/business/black-middle-class-more-than-doubled-but-the-struggle-continues-20190429 (accessed 27 September 2023).

CHAPTER 8

Social Justice and the City

Invisible Boundaries and the Hidden Hand of Social Dispossession in the Post-apartheid Transition

Malcolm Ray

> *There is a politics of space because space is political.*
> — HENRI LEFEBVRE, *THE PRODUCTION OF SPACE*

The city, wrote the urban sociologist Robert Park, is:

> man's [*sic*] most consistent . . . attempt to remake the world he lives in more
> after his heart's desire. But, if the city is the world man created, it is the
> world in which he is henceforth condemned to live. Thus, indirectly, and
> without any clear sense of the nature of his task, in making the city man has
> remade himself (Park 1967: 3).

Folded into Park's assertion is the geographer David Harvey's imprimatur that
the kind of city we want 'cannot be divorced from the question of what kinds of
social relations we seek, what relations to nature we cherish, what . . . livelihoods
we desire . . . what aesthetic values we hold' (Harvey 2008: 23). As the spatial and
social articulation of contemporary political economy, the city is, thus, far more
than an abstract right to resources that urban space theoretically embodies: it is,
Harvey insists, both an ideologically contested terrain and a systemic challenge,
since remaking the political economy of urban livelihoods inevitably presupposes
recontouring and harmonising the social and spatial limits of growth with
inclusive processes of urbanisation.

In extending this argument to South Africa, I want to suggest that the freedom to make – and remake – ourselves and our cities is one of the most existentially barren, legally porous and politically spurious of our human rights since the end of apartheid, mirroring Henri Lefebvre's prescient observation in the 1960s that 'the clear distinction which once existed between the urban and the rural is gradually fading into a set of porous spaces of uneven geographical development under the hegemonic command of capital and the state' (in Harvey 2008: 36).

In the African National Congress (ANC) government's attempt to grapple with the problem, dominant discourses that underpin neo-liberal agendas in South Africa typically invoke a dichotomised race-class lens. Framed in terms of an unresolved 'national question' (National Planning Commission 2012), the most widely held theoretical perspective holds that the proliferation of squatter settlements flows directly from a structural legacy of apartheid social engineering in black townships. While this may hold true on one level, it is in itself an inadequate explanation precisely because it abstracts from sharply divergent post-apartheid trajectories of local government formation and a new poverty in informal settlements.

Instead, this chapter represents a bolder theoretical re-engagement than official policy discourses on race and class. My central argument is that in the government's attempt to decompress and corral historical race and class differences around a series of hegemonic neo-liberal adjustments and into a narrative of progress and deliverance, a subaltern class, disincorporated from the official economy and apparatuses of the state, is emerging as a collateral cost.

Drawing on an adaptation of Harvey's concept of 'accumulation by dispossession' as the vehicle through which I try to convey more concrete insights and meanings on the post-apartheid dynamics of urbanisation, my research illuminates a new *social dispossession* – as historically and politically distinct from racialised dispossession – in what appears to be an endemic feature of urbanisation. Grounded in interviews with residents of a recent slum situated on a buffer strip demarcating the Johannesburg township of Alexandra from the official economy, I demonstrate how the spatial configuration of accumulation and racial dispossession that had been entrenched in peri-urban labour reserves during apartheid is being rearticulated, recontoured and harmonised behind invisible boundaries of urban ghettos beyond apartheid. In this indifferent setting, we see an urban landscape emptied off the original meaning of 'city', which in its original sense is 'citizenship' and so, literally, 'the body of citizens, the community' (Mahmud 2010: 72). In its place, we encounter an informal ghetto economy as a liminal space, where the social costs of growth are decanted into a socio-temporal zone of extra-legality and illegality – an invisible yet indivisible boundary where, in Tayyab Mahmud's poignant portrayal of life in India's slums, the official economy 'finds its *spatial* limits' (2010: 4).

What appears to be emerging from informal squatter settlements like the one in Alexandra, then, serves not only as an important caveat of the social and spatial embeddedness of market triumphalism in post-apartheid South Africa, but also as an emerging paradox: the articulation of slum-dwellers as political subjects while othering them as socially dispossessed citizens. In the face of escalating material inequality and poverty, I contend that this belies a hidden dynamic of the post-apartheid growth trajectory, where an emerging subaltern class of what the Algerian pan-Africanist Frantz Fanon, in his withering indictment of ghettoised poverty in post-colonial African cities, describes as non-citizen citizens (Fanon 2004: 129), nominally live in cities as political subjects but ambivalently *belong* in them as social citizens.

Theorising informal space: Accumulation by dispossession and hegemony

In recent years, an expanding literature derived from the political economy of growth (Baran 1957), dependency theory (Frank 1969), world systems theory (Wallerstein 1974), accumulation on a world scale (Amin 1974) and articulation of modes of production (Wolpe 1982) has been used to explore the emerging phenomenon of urban dispossession in South Africa. In sharp contrast to transition studies on racialised dispossession in black townships that have come to dominate official policy discourses over the past two-plus decades, it is useful to trace a brief genealogy of the concept of urban dispossession – and its salience in emerging heterodox Marxist critiques – that foreshadows how I will bring them together in the analytical framing in this chapter.

In his seminal treatise *The Production of Space* (1991), first published in 1974, in the aftermath of the 1968 student-worker uprising in Paris, Lefebvre poured the foundations for new understandings of urban poverty that challenged dominant

Western theorisations on urban space as an abstract topology (Hart 2002: 33). Most crucially, and inextricably bound up with the core of his analysis, was his attempt to ground social meaning in space, suggesting that the social production of space 'serves as a tool of thought and of action; that in addition to being a means of production it is also a means of control, and hence of power relations' (Lefebvre 1991: 26). In other words, rather than an 'indivisible emptiness', in Gillian Hart's Gramscian rendition of Lefebvre, urban space is socially and, therefore, *actively* constructed, 'both as a product and medium of capitalist domination' (Hart 2002: 34). The key innovation in Lefebvre, as Hart has pointed out in her brilliant exposition of his ideas, is to see the social and spatial as 'mutually constitutive practices . . . mediated through power relations' (2002: 35).

Complementing this relational dynamic, a still-expanding scholarship on the left has, since the early 1990s, advanced the idea of 'socio-spatial temporality' as the mutually constitutive process by which informal spaces emerge as transient warehouses of either privatization or liberalisation and the state's deployment of extra-economic and economic coercion (Mahmud 2010: 25), or 'the expansion of new non-market spheres of accumulation that the state and capital seek to capture' (Samson 2015: 815). Particularly noteworthy, for example, are Doreen Massey (1994) and David Harvey (2004), who both draw on Lefebvre to claim a more rigorous relational understanding of the temporal dimensions of socio-spatial configurations in which informal settlements are presumed to be inured.

Fashioned from Karl Marx's concept of primitive accumulation, it was Harvey (2004) who first drew attention to a key lacuna in Marx's opus, *Capital* (1990), first published in 1867. In contrast to Adam Smith's account of the accumulation of landed property as a function of the thrift and virtue of the bourgeoisie, Marx devoted several chapters in *Capital* to an exhaustive exposition of the dynamics of dispossession of direct producers from land as a pre-capitalist condition for industrialisation. Central to Harvey's analysis was a reinterpretation of the nature of primitive accumulation as a deeply embedded, distinctly non-Western characteristic of contemporary capitalism (Hart 2002; Samson 2015; Mahmud 2010). Thus, by extending the actively constitutive character of informal settlements to a critical engagement with more nuanced, heterodox Marxist understandings, primitive accumulation springs to life, in Jim Glassman's (2006) perspective, not as a nineteenth-century historical precondition, but as 'a basic ontological condition for contemporary capitalist production' (Mahmud 2013: 218). In this way, a distinctly non-market realm of the market enters the circuits of capital accumulation as an *ongoing process* (Harvey 2004: 74). The uneven form of labour reproduction under conditions of contemporary capitalist production, in other words, is deeply infused with new social and spatial spheres of capital accumulation in non-market enclosures.

Conceptually, Harvey saw this ongoing dynamic as 'accumulation by dispossession' (Harvey 2004: 73). As accumulation, the extraction of surplus-value is mediated by extra-legal means as a site for the construction of hegemony linked to specific 'spatio-temporal fixes' of capital (2004: 64). As a form of dispossession, the hegemonic project describes the quiet but ruthless devastation of traditional entitlements, the – often violent – conversion of various forms of property rights (common, collective, state) into exclusive private property rights, and the endemic dislocation of direct producers from their means of labour (2004: 176). Suspended between a shrinking subsistence economy and formal markets in a kind of demi-existence is an extra-legal realm of the market that Mahmud (2010), in his eloquent lyricism, has described as 'an imaginary waiting room of surplus humanity':

> They tend to their subsistence needs as best as they can by exchanging needs and capacities in networks of barter, petty trade, and casual employment under the radar of the law. The result is the emergence of a 'need economy' – a zone outside the formal legal frames of contract and regulation, signifying '[i]nformalization within the accumulation economy'. This temporal zone is the informal economy (Mahmud 2010: 19).

Viewed from this broad theoretical perspective – one that goes well beyond reductionist race-class discourses on urban poverty – the analyses offered by Lefebvre and Harvey resonate with conditions in post-apartheid South Africa. The current neo-liberal context – marked by a deep and multifaceted crisis of capital accumulation and labour reproduction – is precisely one in which accumulation by dispossession has come into conjuncture as the dominant form of hegemony. In this setting, the post-apartheid state has not only constructed and replenished its hegemony through social dispossession linked to specific socio-spatial configurations in cities; it has accomplished this task, as Lefebvre (1991) puts it, by 'articulating "the people" into a political subject . . . with – not against – the power bloc' (in Hart 2002: 32) through the false abstraction of social justice. Symptomatic of this is the increasing reliance on an expanded social protection system as a palliative for dispossession and the shift over the past decade from the state as a disciplining whip to the courts in mediating the rights of capital over and above access of the homeless to cities.

As many of the dispossessed have turned to the informal economy for their livelihoods, this understanding opens new vistas for reimagining and theorising the relationship between local state formation, informal enclosure and dispossession. Building on Harvey's adaptation of Lefebvre, my theoretical lens also incorporates conceptions of hegemony, derived from Antonio Gramsci (1971). In his prison notebooks, Gramsci's relational approach to hegemony focused on meta-theoretical and strategic spatial configurations of the state and civil society, which fuse various class fractions and social groups in 'historic blocs' on which hegemony and social order are constructed and replenished (Kipfer 2002: 126). In this Gramscian sense of hegemony, we come to see social order based on an 'economic core', which frames the limits of the politically possible for labour reproduction and capital accumulation (Kipfer 2002: 128).

In Lefebvre's relational conception of urbanisation, hegemony is mediated by the social construction of urban space in daily life. In this relational logic, urban socio-spatial dynamics fuse with hegemony to produce accumulation by dispossession. These insights not only extend Lefebvre's thought about the actively constitutive character of local state and class formation in informal enclosures; they also allow us to see how, through urbanisation, the Gramscian concept of hegemony reappears in lived spaces as the fusion of informal settlements and neo-liberal social order. The lineage between Gramsci and Lefebvre, then, forms the crux of how I put Harvey's concept of accumulation by dispossession to use in post-apartheid South Africa.

Divergent trajectories: The social ontology of Gomorrah

The main road to Alexandra traces the recent history of an urban landscape that has been reordered around the post-apartheid growth trajectory and, consequently, disincorporated from formal legality. Situated on a buffer strip of industrial land on the outskirts of London Road, where predatory entrepreneurs once operated unfettered by law or public scrutiny, the area, covering roughly a square kilometre, has emerged as a liminal zone of a regulatory vacuum.

At dawn, there is a stench from the heavily polluted Jukskei River nearby and sulphur and dioxide from paraffin-fired stoves. Along the embankment on one side, a wall of squat mobile toilets offers inhabitants a semblance of personal dignity. There are burst water pipes everywhere; a confusion of illegal electricity cables crowds the sky; rubble and green ponds of raw sewage fill the streets – rundown monuments to formal and informal economies that remain entangled, with cruel disappointment for the latter born of the growth of the former.

A few hundred metres down London Road, tiny tin shacks (colloquially called *imikhukhu*) appear to 'invade' the physical landscape as far as the eye can see before disappearing on the horizon. Its inhabitants refer to the place by a name that comes straight out of the Old Testament. They call it Gomorrah. Although nominally a part of Alexandra, in practice Gomorrah exemplifies quite different trajectories to the township. Unlike the well-heeled business districts and suburbs, 'township' in South Africa is a designated imprimatur for black peri-urban areas built during apartheid as cheap labour reserves. Despite its growth since I last visited the place in 2001, Alexandra has never grown into official 'suburban' status.

In their splendid history of Alexandra, Phil Bonner and Noor Nieftagodien (2008) call attention to the evolution of industrial, labour and township politics in mapping the contours of twentieth-century segregation and apartheid. They retrace early township life to 1905, when Henry Mbanjwa, the cook of a white Midrand farmer, built a mud hut on the farm Zandfontein around present-day Alexandra as a donkey refreshment station for carts carrying milk from Midrand to Johannesburg. Over the years, black rural dwellers, lured by the prospect of jobs in the burgeoning mines of Johannesburg, squatted near the Mbanjwas.

As capital poured into Johannesburg during the 1960s and 1970s, much of the black population on 'white' farms was forcibly exiled – by mass dispossession from land and 'black spot' removals – to dormitory townships, where they were compelled, silently, to construct apartheid's new facade of 'economic growth' (Wolpe 1972). By the early 1980s, the official jargon of 'redundant' and 'surplus' communities was dropped and relocation townships like Alexandra became showcases of cheap labour. Bonner and Nieftagodien record the township having grown from a few thousand residents with 'transient' status into permanent residential status granted by the apartheid government. Over time, more than a million people disappeared behind the squalor of a burgeoning informal economy and everything continued to deteriorate.

Thus it was, on the day I visited the township in March 2021, that I came to see Gomorrah not as a child of apartheid, but rather as the poor stepchild of post-apartheid planners. Unlike official residents of Alexandra, the poverty of Gomorrah's inhabitants is enclosed and internalised in ghettos of resource scarcity, joblessness and ecological ruin. For many years, the area was a red line between the township and the 'official' economy. Since the early 1980s, a handful of white-owned businesses began settling there because property values were low and the supply of cheap, casual labour from the township was plentiful.

The story, related to me by a Ghanaian South African who has made the township his home since 2010, is that every day men and women would gather outside the construction and motor-repair plants on one side of the road. Most were seeking work; others were informal street vendors and hustlers who brought their desperation and hopes directly to the front gates of the factories. I was regaled with stories of how many would gesture with signs and jocular placards trying to explain why they needed to get in; on the other side of the gates, stood security guards doing 24-hour shifts, keeping them out.

These divergent trajectories allow us to see why the closure of factories on London Road during the hard Covid-19 lockdown, between March and June 2020, led to the occupation of the buildings by destitute families. In recalling their version of events to me, the factory owners on London road were quick to provide contrasting narratives of 'chaos' and 'anarchy', portraying the occupation as an 'invasion' of their businesses and the surrounding industrial and residential suburbs that lie directly in the path of the expansion of Gomorrah. Their stories, told in dour and baleful terms, typically revolved around 'criminals' and 'unruly people', whose insularity and short-sightedness threatened businesses as 'guarantors of their livelihoods' and a 'well-ordered economy'.

Yet the term 'invasion' by itself is arid and limited; it abstracts from historically and spatially dynamic processes through which urban ghettos have come to be formed. Despite government policy declarations about 'revitalising' and 'humanising' township economies, we see people stepping outside the law because they are not allowed inside. Thus, when the term 'invasion' is contemplated, the question arises whether a strong element of dispossession, rather than illegality, is not hidden in this brooding frontier.

Frontiers of dispossession: The false abstraction of invasion

On the border of Gomorrah and the industrial district of Wynberg there is a verge of grass on Louis Botha Avenue where township residents and inhabitants of Gomorrah gather every morning in the vain hope of a few hours' work. Many of the motor-repair plants, clothing and textile factories and retail warehouses in Wynberg began closing in 2018, pushing unemployment in the area to a record 70 per cent high. Among the casualties was Alfred Msinga, who guided me around the area where some factories still stand empty. Equally distressing was his dismal account of how the few remaining firms followed a pattern of forcing down wages and casualising labour.

Contrary to some residents of Alexandra, who claimed that the occupation was an orchestrated invasion by 'African immigrants', Msinga traces Gomorrah's origins to job losses in the Wynberg area. Once factory owners in London Road vacated their premises during the Covid-19 lockdowns in 2020, many destitute residents of Alexandra were the first in line to move in. Among them was Boniswa Tomi, who left her home because she could not afford the rent and settled in Gomorrah to look for domestic work in neighbouring suburbs. In this way, she declared to me, 'Gomorrah becomes a place to find employment for residents of Alexandra. People here call it survival.'

In other words, the 'chaos' and 'anarchy', which factory owners and managers I spoke to described as an 'invasion', was a false verdict. The misrecognition is particularly ironic, since part of what led to the occupation, at least during the initial wave, seems to have been underwritten by shifts in capital's accumulation capacities and operational strategies. There is, in fact, a double irony, since it was just the opposite of invasion – namely, the collateral consequences of retrenchments – that, at least in part, laid the foundation for the occupation.

More generally, what official narratives conceal behind the false abstraction of 'invasion' are sharply divergent trajectories of what the term actually means in lived spaces. To understand the evolution of urban ghettos like Gomorrah is to see the situational power dynamics of the word 'invasion' with mixed perplexity: to avoid official policy tropes and false binaries – of formal/informal and legal/ illegal that have tended to skew interpretations of dynamic processes of change – and see the shifting capital accumulation trajectories and their social impact on historically specific spatial and power configurations behind the conceptually slippery term.

In the novelist Annie Proulx's (1997) textured portrayal of America's economic backwaters, the lived experience of the poor and marginalised is not a scripted, one-dimensional narrative. Their actions, she argues, are more often than not contradictory, overcrowded and chaotic intersections of multilayered and evolving cultural, social and political frontiers, moulded by economic conditions. As Hart, drawing on Lefebvre's *The Production of Space*, has noted: 'Places are always formed through relations with wider arenas; boundaries are always socially constructed and contested; and the specificity of a place – however defined – arises from the particularity of interactions with what lies beyond it that intersect or come into conjuncture in particular ways' (2002: 35).

The situational dynamics traced out on the road to Gomorrah speak directly to informal settlements as socially constructed spaces, both as products and agents of neo-liberal hegemony. What has bound people in Gomorrah, in other words, is the accumulation capacity of capital and its consequences – the social devastation and desolation of unemployment and poverty. To 'invade', in this sense, is an act of dispossession: it is the evolution of an extra-legal terrain, or the so-called informal economy, which has had a long frontier with the legal world, a place where inhabitants of Gomorrah have taken refuge because the costs of obeying the rules of the game outweigh the benefits.

Most significantly, for my purposes in this chapter, I am suggesting that a new hegemonic market logic, characterised by adjustments to a deep and multifaceted economic crisis, underscores new trajectories of capital accumulation by dispossession that have come into conjuncture in recent years. My contribution in the analysis that follows is, therefore, attendant upon a conjunctural interpretation of multilayered intersections between local state formation under conditions of neo-liberal adjustments and the rapid accretion of a new social dispossession in urban informal enclosures flowing directly from the deployment of hegemonic trajectories in capital accumulation.

Neo-liberal reordering: The spatial contours of social dispossession

Just as black urban townships like Alexandra bear the political hallmarks of apartheid spatial engineering, the necklaces of informal squatter settlements now girding cities are the social imprints of dispossession in its post-apartheid, neo-liberal incarnation. From the perspective of current policy concerns about escalating urban poverty, these divergent trajectories mark important continuities with apartheid, but they also signify radical departures: they bring into conjuncture how the social fault lines of post-apartheid urbanisation run far deeper than historically racialised geographies.

A central theme in the race-class discourse on urban renewal beyond apartheid derives from conceptions of black townships as dormitory enclosures during apartheid, which posits that, at least until the late apartheid era between the mid-1970s and early 1990s, capital harnessed reserve armies of cheap black labour to its accumulation strategy. Whereas the 'functionalist' inflection in this perspective has reflected the post-apartheid policy imperative of confronting historically and geographically specific articulations of townships as spatial configurations of racialised dispossession, an alternative reading may describe the hegemonic accumulation trajectory of dispossession as 'an enduring ontological feature' of post-apartheid capitalism (Sampson 2015: 813; Glassman 2006: 615).

Depicting the South African transition as a 'neoliberal reordering' of society, Hein Marais (2011: 399) has written that a new dispossession was unleashed by 'a masonry of reforms from above since 1996 . . . grounded in a new social compact which set the limits of the possible'. In its formative stage, those limits marked the spatial and social contours of capital expansion in townships through casualisation and outsourcing that were subsequently remapped onto new geographies of dispossession.

The first phase of neo-liberal adjustments under the Growth, Employment and Redistribution (GEAR) strategy, which Alan Hirsch (2005) bookmarks between 1996 and early 1999, witnessed 'a retreat of the state from its social provisioning and regulatory duties in favour of the "invisible hand" of the market' (Marais 2011: 338). In Hirsch's telling, GEAR enabled South Africa's largest corporations to restructure, consolidate and globalise their operations 'as a momentary tonic of adjustment' (Hirsch 2005: 4).

From this macro-level, state power was devolved, through the late 1990s and early 2000s, to sub-national scales of governance on a groundswell of local institutional realignments, economic restructuring, market reforms and accelerated capital flows. The neo-liberal impulses driving this process were starkly evident in Johannesburg where the iGoli 2002 programme became the designated road map for a 'world-class city'. More concretely, the restructuring of local government unleashed an assortment of social and political tensions around a massive remapping of boundaries, through which areas previously designated as 'white' and 'black' under the Group Areas Act became institutionally incorporated into single administrative entities. The subsequent introduction of the city's annual integrated development plans (IDPs) in 2003 proposed to radically transform the city's racially skewed economy, merge financial revenues drawn from municipal taxes, and achieve greater equity between wealthy localities and township economies.

The second phase of neo-liberal reordering coincided with President Thabo Mbeki's 'class corporate' agenda from 1999 onwards, a conceptual distinction Gramsci drew as 'a series of purely class solidarities, led by the state and a fraction of capital' that eventually form the material and ideological basis for the hegemony of capital (Hall 1996: 423). In his attempt to recast the terrain and neuter social instability and political rupture in townships, Mbeki embroidered inclusive gestures to patriotic values with earlier popular entreaties to a 'patriotic bourgeoisie'. Key to these feats, as Marais argues, 'was his deployment of policies geared to service the needs of corporate capital', along with an emergent stratum of new junior black capitalists and mid-scale entrepreneurs, into a narrative of progress and broad cross-class ideological alliances as a 'hegemonic work-in-progress' (Marais 2011: 397; Satgar 2008: 42).

Yet the neo-liberal reordering of society, as Hart (2002: 47) has written more generally of early local economic adjustments, 'meant that local governments were assigned the task of not only attracting capital, but also securing the conditions for capital accumulation' – including privatisation and flexible labour – in the face of global competition. For short periods since 1999, the attempts at corralling an assortment of social and spatial tensions into the reordering process appeared to vacillate between the class corporate stage and hegemony. In its touting of decentralised service delivery, local entrepreneurship and public–private partnerships, official policy narratives – couched in the official jargon of 'developmental' local government – veered between stern neo-liberal nostrums of 'efficiency' and 'fiscal discipline', on the one hand, and invocations of local participation, democracy and social justice, on the other (Marais 2011: 400). 'The entrenched dominance of capital in the local economy,' Marais argues, 'helped fuel the turbocharged surge of the financial sector, wedged open the economy for speculative international capital and unleashed a wave of cost-cutting, outsourcing and casualisation of labour' (2011: 360).

What has emerged as a collateral consequence of this corporate class-driven trajectory is a dichotomous logic in which embattled township economies have come to coexist with what Mahmud (2010: 4) calls 'a legal no-man's land' of informal enclosure. In explaining the social consequences, informal traders I spoke to in Alexandra and Gomorrah seemed to invoke the hidden hand of market forces in underwriting the extra-legal realm of capital accumulation. I met Tisa Mothae, a recent arrival in Gomorrah, in the gloom of an airless fifth-floor room of a rundown building in Commissioner Street, Johannesburg, shortly after my visit to Alexandra in early 2021. Some of those in the room were homeless squatters; most of the others were informal seamsters. The seamsters and squatters share a kinship: the latter get casual work for a pittance; the former are cheap labour.

I first encountered Mothae in 2006 in a bustling part of Bree Street on the east end of the city, where squatters and informal traders had taken refuge. He started a small informal clothing business, after losing his job in a clothing factory in the aftermath of the 1998 Asian market crash, subcontracting to his former employer below factory gate prices. Then, in 2012, he and others were evicted from the building they occupied and relocated by city authorities to a part of Alexandra that is completely without any shade, barren in the dry season and muddy in the wet. The pressures of entering the economy were insidious, he told me: 'We were blamed for everything. We brought crime and disease and squatters and foreigners. To add insult to injury, we were barred from trading as unregistered small businesses.'

Narratives such as Mothae's, I want to suggest, underscore a local corporate class strategy that has disincorporated a growing number of township residents from the state and official economy and shunted them to populous informal settlements. Despite claims by one IDP policy official I interviewed, that 'the city faces an explosion of informal settlements and has no choice but to remove them' and that 'it is in the metropolitan centre that the greatest pressure for land reform lies', attempts at recasting the terrain and managing the crisis reveal an IDP strategy starkly at odds with the socio-spatial imperatives of developmental local state formation.

There is certainly a strong body of evidence to suggest that whereas township economies on the margins of the city are declining, deregulated markets are pushing up land and property values in well-heeled suburbs and industrial areas, creating new barriers to social inclusion. Theoretically, recent academic work on the new economic geography demonstrates that firms (both formal and informal) tend to locate in places that bring them higher productivity and thus returns to capital (Venables 2008). These benefits are called local scale externalities, or 'agglomeration economies'. Consistent with this theory, a 2008 IDP spatial development survey found that employment opportunities in well-off areas north of the city outweighed residents by a ratio of 22 000 jobs to 14 000 residents (City of Johannesburg 2009). In black townships south of the city, however, the ratio was inverted.

In extending these relational insights to a theorisation of the link between accumulation by dispossession and informal settlements more generally, I want to insist on the salience of ongoing processes of dispossession to grasping what appears to be an evolving post-apartheid social and spatial pattern: the migration of the most vulnerable from townships to places where the prospects of finding a house may be slim but squatting is cheap and the proximity to prospective casual employment is convenient. The lasting effect of deregulated housing markets in the Johannesburg metropolitan area has been a rent and price structure that precludes lower-income households from access to accommodation anywhere near economic opportunities. If spatiality is conceived in these terms, the pattern of informal settlement comes into conjuncture as a direct result of neo-liberal market logics. The bitter irony of this urban dynamic, which nearly always has a class dimension, was presciently captured by Frederick Engels in 1872: 'In reality, capital . . . solves the housing question after its fashion . . . in such a way that the solution continually reproduces the question anew' (Engels 1995).

These insights not only illuminate how the trajectory of neo-liberal reordering has come to define the social and spatial contours now shaping local state formation. They also show how multilayered limits and constraints of post-apartheid adjustments, as well as ongoing hegemonic market logics through which such limits are disciplined and reinforced, have forged a new dispossession.

Neo-liberal paradoxes: Dispossession and social justice

A growing body of literature argues that because the neo-liberal reordering of post-apartheid capitalism and its key modality, accumulation by dispossession, has displaced urban poverty behind invisible boundaries of ghettos, it has dispossessed the poor of any right to the city and reduced the pursuit of social justice to a false abstraction (Harvey 2008; Mahmud 2010; Marais 2011). As I argue below, what is potentially enabling about the conceptions of spatiality and hegemony derived from Lefebvre and Gramsci, respectively, is that they enable us to move beyond simple understandings of social justice as an emancipatory endeavour. Instead, the focus shifts to social justice as disciplinary duty in the process of mediating the socio-spatial contradictions of local state formation.

Policy officials and city planners I interviewed for this chapter prefer the official smokescreen of growth and employment data. Under these rules, 'informal' is simply a measure of those who have no prospect of ever finding work. Officially, they are 'demotivated' and forced into a welfare culture. With the informal economy left out of the narrative, typical ghetto narratives seem apocryphal – faintly survivalist tales devoid of official data and other complicating factors.

With the informal economy in the narrative, it is a picture of dispossession every bit as egregious as apartheid. Under the post-apartheid dispensation, much has changed. For one thing, black people can move freely. Above the surface and just below, though, such liberties have, in great part, been restrained for the burgeoning slums. With the homeless now crowding the slums of the city, the government has effectively criminalised more than 3 million people in the informal economy. With the privileges of the capital overseen by the government, complaints about 'crime' and 'grime' are unrelenting – crime being code for the encroachment of slums across the old dividing line between rich and poor, white and black.

In Gramsci's exposition, such regimes of criminalising and reordering rely on replenishing consent within the 'bulwarks' and 'trenches' of civil society by drawing civil society into the disciplining apparatuses of the state (Marais 2011:

400). The issue is, in fact, even more profound: if slum-dwellers are othered from the apparatuses of the state, cities like Johannesburg have become local states with rules that combine the injustices of racialised dispossession with policies designed to criminalise urban informal communities like Gomorrah. These spatial configurations signal that markets, to some extent, rely on non-market forces, particularly legal orders and extra-legality, to discipline the permissible boundaries of dispossession. Within this milieu, Marais draws on Gramsci to argue that the performance of disciplinary duty falls on 'shoehorning the assortment of contradictions into a narrative of social justice broadly centred on social provisioning' (2011: 400).

The issue, as the perceptions of business owners in London Road remind us, is quite convenient to those who control the economy, for it reminds the government of where its priorities lie. Indeed, one of the government's celebrated achievements has been its acclamation of growth as a basis for its hegemonic project. However, in the passage from apartheid to post-apartheid capitalism, government policymakers may display a studied courtesy to the poor, invoking palliative concepts such as 'inclusive growth' and 'social justice', but the underside of growth is social exclusion.

Increasingly, we see the right to the city falling into the hands of private or quasi-private interests. In Johannesburg, spatial planning is recontouring the city along lines favourable to large property developers promoting well-heeled suburbs and business districts as optimal locations for agglomeration economies. They are, in effect, turning these enclaves into gated communities for capital.

The right to the city, as it is now constituted, is too narrowly confined, restricted in most cases to elites in a position to shape the city in terms of their own desires. One of the most abiding myths to emerge in official policy discourse has been the failure of official economies to grow at rates that benefit the poor. Yet, as a growing literature on 'degrowth' (Pilling 2018; Fioramonti 2007) demonstrates, the fate of the formal and informal economies has remained entangled, with cruel disappointment for the latter born of the prosperity of the former.

If the Johannesburg city official I spoke to is right in worrying that 'it is in the city that the greatest pressure for land reform lies', Lefebvre was right to insist that the solution has to be urban, in the broadest sense of that term – just not along the current neo-liberal growth trajectory.

Conclusion

In considering the salience of the concept of urban dispossession, articulated by Harvey, to the reconfiguration of post-apartheid settlement patterns in Johannesburg, this chapter has argued that the relationship between social justice and democracy is being complicated by the phenomenon of a new dispossession. Central to an understanding of the City of Johannesburg's embrace of an IDP is that the trajectory has constituted and inaugurated not a rupture with the apartheid urban spatial and economic form, but a highly contradictory pattern of spatial reconfigurations, which are recontouring the city along elite enclaves and urban ghettos.

Although the chapter analyses the dynamics of dispossession that led directly to the occupation and birth of Gomorrah, it develops theoretical insights relevant to rethinking the relationship between informal occupations, local state formation, accumulation by dispossession and social justice more generally. Rather than a simple race-class dichotomy rooted in a legacy of racialised dispossession in townships, accumulation by dispossession conveys deeper meanings of the relational conception of formal-informal as a mutually constitutive dynamic of local state and subaltern class formation. Dispossession beyond apartheid, therefore, emerges as a multilayered social and spatial modality of the neo-liberal reordering of the local state. Paradoxically, the reordering of the local state has entailed the injustice of displacing and othering the most vulnerable as 'disorderly criminals'. Focusing on informal settlements as products of local state formation, rather than racial dispossession, allows us to develop more nuanced understandings of the forms that accumulation by dispossession takes and how alternatives can be imagined and created.

What is needed, in other words, is a research strategy that recognises multiple arenas, beyond traditional race–class dichotomies, of urban dispossession and socio-economic change; which challenges theoretical rights to the city and their contradictions to open up new understandings of social justice and which searches for new relationships between formal and informal economies in urban settings and their policy implications for a more inclusive and sustainable growth path.

References

Amin, S. 1974. *Accumulation on a World Scale: A Critique of the Theory of Underdevelopment*. New York: Monthly Review Press.

Baran, P. 1957. *The Political Economy of Growth*. New York: Monthly Review Press.

Bonner, P. and N. Nieftagodien. 2008. *Alexandra: A History*. Johannesburg: Wits University Press.

City of Johannesburg. 2009. *Integrated Development Plan 2008/9*. https://joburg.org.za/documents_/Pages/Key%20Documents/Intergrated%20Development%20Plan/IDP%20PORTIA/LINKS/2010%20IDP/Links/IDP-200809.aspx (accessed 29 September 2023).

Engels, F. (1872) 1995. *The Housing Question*. https://www.marxists.org/archive/marx/works/download/pdf/Housing_Question.pdf (accessed 29 September 2023).

Fanon, F. (1961) 2004. *The Wretched of the Earth*. New York: Grove Press.

Fioramonti, L. 2007. *Wellbeing Economy: Success in a World without Growth*. Johannesburg: Pan Macmillan.

Frank, A.G. 1969. *Latin America: Underdevelopment or Revolution – Essays on the Development of Underdevelopment and the Immediate Enemy*. New York: Monthly Review Press.

Glassman, J. 2006. 'Primitive Accumulation, Accumulation by Dispossession, and Accumulation by "Extra-Economic" Means'. *Progress in Human Geography* 30 (5): 608–25.

Gramsci, A. 1971. *Selections from the Prison Notebooks*. Edited by Q. Hoare and G.N. Smith. New York: New York University Press.

Hall, S. 1996. 'Gramsci's Relevance for the Study of Race and Ethnicity'. In: *Stuart Hall: Critical Dialogues in Cultural Studies*, edited by D. Morley and K-H. Chen. London: Routledge.

Hart, G. 2002. *Disabling Globalization: Places of Power in Post-apartheid South Africa*. Pietermaritzburg: University of Natal Press.

Harvey, D. 2004. 'The "New" Imperialism: Accumulation by Dispossession'. *Socialist Register* 40: 63–87.

———. 2008. 'The Right to the City'. *New Left Review* 53: 23–40.

Hirsch, A. 2005. *Season of Hope: Economic Reform under Mandela and Mbeki*. Pietermaritzburg: University of KwaZulu-Natal Press.

Kipfer, S. 2002. 'Urbanization, Everyday Life and the Survival of Capitalism: Lefebvre, Gramsci and the Problematic of Hegemony'. *Capitalism Nature Socialism* 13 (2): 117–49.

Lefebvre, H. (1974) 1991. *The Production of Space*. Oxford: Blackwell.

Mahmud, T. 2010. ' "Surplus Humanity" and the Margins of Legality: Slums, Slumdogs, and Accumulation by Dispossession'. *Chapman Law Review* 14 (1): 1–73.

———. 2013. 'Cheaper Than a Slave: Indentured Labor, Colonialism and Capitalism'. *Whittier L. Rev.* 215: 215–43.

Marais, H. 2011. *South Africa Pushed to the Limit: The Political Economy of Change*. Cape Town: UCT Press.

Marx, K. (1867) 1990. *Capital: A Critique of Political Economy, Vol. 1*. London: Penguin.

Massey, D. 1994. *Space, Place, and Gender*. Minneapolis: University of Minnesota Press.

National Planning Commission. 2012. *National Development Plan 2030: Our Future – Make It Work*. https://www.gov.za/sites/default/files/gcis_document/201409/ndp-2030-our-future-make-it-workr.pdf (accessed 29 September 2023).

Park, R.E. 1967. *On Social Control and Collective Behavior*. Chicago: Chicago University Press.

Pilling, D. 2018. *The Growth Delusion: Wealth, Poverty, and the Wellbeing of Nations*. New York: Tim Duggan Books.

Proulx, A. 1997. 'Brokeback Mountain'. *The New Yorker*, 6 October. https://www.newyorker.com/magazine/1997/10/13/brokeback-mountain (accessed 29 September 2023).

Samson, M. 2015. 'Accumulation by Dispossession and the Informal Economy: Struggles over Knowledge, Being and Waste at a Soweto Garbage Dump'. *Society and Space* 33 (5): 813–30.

Satgar, V. 2008. 'Neoliberalized South Africa: Labour and the Roots of Passive Revolution'. *Labour, Capital & Society* 41 (2): 39–69.

Venables, A.J. 2008. 'New Economic Geography'. In: *The New Palgrave Dictionary of Economics*. London: Palgrave Macmillan. https://doi.org/10.1057/978-1-349-95121-5_2329-1.

Wallerstein, I. 1974. *The Modern World-System: Capitalist Agriculture and the Origins of the European World-Economy in the Sixteenth Century*. New York: Academic.

Wolpe, H. 1972. 'Capitalism and Cheap Labour Power in South Africa: From Segregation to Apartheid'. *Economy and Society* 1 (4): 425–56.

———. (ed.) 1982. *The Articulation of Modes of Production*. London: Routledge & Kegan Paul.

CHAPTER 9

Shaking off the Burden of the Past

Rethinking Poverty and Inequality

Steven Friedman

If the millions of South Africans who live in poverty are to enjoy a brighter future, policy debate will need to think in the present, not the past. When South Africans debate policy, the argument is often passionate and polarised. Supporters of state intervention, of unfettered markets and much in between join pitched battle: racial dynamics are never far from the surface. But the participants have more in common than they think: they are all usually trapped in a way of thinking that reflects the country's past and so has little to offer its future.

Government policy and law are only part of the problem. In the main, policy is simply another reflection of the thinking of those who shape the policy debate. And government attitudes at times show a cleaner break with the past than those of the other voices in the debate (although the intention to chart a new course is often diluted in the details of policy). One of the great ironies of the South African debate is that, for all its heat, those who are shouting at each other often share assumptions that are grounded in the past (Friedman 2021a).

The 'Great Jobs Debate' illustrates the point. This is the contest of ideas on how to create formal-sector jobs for the millions of South Africans who lack them. All participants insist that their chosen remedy will create millions of jobs. But the jobs are never created – and not because, as a common cliché insists, the policies are appropriate but the capacity to implement them is absent. The problem is the policies themselves. All promise that their favoured remedy will create the formal jobs that are being snuffed out throughout the world. There is no reason to believe that jobs that are not being created anywhere else will miraculously emerge here.

Since this is well known to anyone who monitors labour markets, why do well-informed people continue to insist that the impossible is possible? The answer lies at the heart of the South African policy debate's failure to get to grips with the country's problems: it is a relic of a time that has passed.

The root of the problem

In a recently published book (Friedman 2021b), I argue that the problem of post-1994 South Africa is not that too much has changed, but too little. This does not mean, as some claim, that most South Africans are no better off than they were under apartheid. There has been significant change since 1994, as opportunities have opened to people who were denied them simply because they were black. People now enjoy rights that they can use to press for the changes they want. But core patterns of the pre-1994 past still shape social, economic and political life.

Under apartheid, South African society was divided into insiders and outsiders by racial laws and policies – whites were insiders, blacks outsiders. Today, some of the insiders – anyone who earns a regular income from the formal economy – are black. But the outsiders, just about all of whom remain black, are still on the outside. Public debate on politics and policy is an insider monopoly – it is shaped by what the roughly one-third who benefit in some way from a formal income think the majority, whose voice they ignore, needs. So, its assumptions about the life of most South Africans are often based more on abstract reasoning than on concrete knowledge.

Among the one-third, thinking is mired in the past in one important way. The assumption at the core of much of what had been done since 1994 is that what whites enjoyed under apartheid is the standard to which a democratic and prosperous South Africa should aspire. While the need for change is widely agreed, it is defined not as the creation of new ways of performing society's tasks, but as the inclusion of black people in the organisations and procedures that white privilege created. This way of thinking is shared by both elites across the racial divide.

This places the jobs debate in its proper context. At the height of apartheid, any white person who was physically able worked in a factory, shop or office. The policy debate assumes that the only 'proper' way of earning a livelihood is to do the same. People who earn a living on the streets or in the backyard of shacks are assumed to be lacking, even if they create wealth as they provide for their needs.

Policy is thus devoted to creating 'decent' jobs (Duarte 2018) – those created by the formal sector, rather than those people create for themselves.

The thinking is flawed since, as noted earlier, the jobs that are meant to be created are being extinguished across the planet: at a time when driverless cars could mean the end of taxi driving as a job (Fleischman 2022), plans and proposals ignore this and similar realities in the search to revive for all what a minority enjoyed by using laws and force to dominate everyone else. Thinking that is in touch with current realities would recognise that a formal job is only one way to earn a living and it is under pressure everywhere. And acknowledging this would offer support to the many who earn their living informally – protection from crime, the infrastructure and the access to markets they need to grow. But this is not possible now – not because it is unworkable but because the way in which the policy debate looks at the problem makes this discussion impossible. The jobs example is not isolated – it reflects policy thinking more generally.

Whose power?

South Africa's efforts to deracialise an economy that is still largely white controlled (Fin24 2018) seem at first glance to propose radical change – movement from an economy in which race determines privilege to one in which only aptitude and qualifications matter. But its starting point is that what existed in the past is to be preserved.

There is a strong emphasis in much thinking on black economic empowerment (BEE) on incorporating black people into what the strain of liberation politics led by the African National Congress (ANC) called 'the commanding heights of the economy' (Munck 1994) – the large corporations that dominate the market place. Since they were created by the ruling white minority before apartheid ended, the goal is integration into the corporations created by minority rule.

Policy and law are not the chief reason for this approach. BEE policy uses public procurement as an instrument and this could – and sometimes does – create opportunities for black business people to build their own companies, rather than slotting onto those created in the past. It has, since 2015, included a black industrialists' programme and has, President Cyril Ramaphosa says, 'injected R55bn into black enterprises over the last eleven years' (Gumede 2022). But much of South Africa's strategy, outside as well as inside government, centres on enhanced black participation in historically white companies. One of the earliest BEE proposals, the '3-4-5-6' programme suggested by the National African Chambers of Commerce (NAFCOC) in the early 1990s, was solely focused on companies listed on the Johannesburg Stock Exchange and set out minimum percentages for black directors, shareholders, managers and suppliers to be achieved in ten years (Acemoglu, Gelb and Robinson 2007: 7). Only the reference to suppliers gave priority to black-owned companies – which is striking when we consider that NAFCOC is a traders' organisation. Its thinking has remained the dominant approach to deracialising the economy.

Until 2000, BEE was largely an initiative not of the government, but of corporations (Acemoglu, Gelb and Robinson 2007: 5, 6) who wanted to ward off government action – this has prompted claims that BEE was a corporate initiative designed to prevent deeper changes (Smith 2021). While this is, at best, partly true – corporates did what they did because there were demands for racial change in the economy– it does reflect the degree to which integration into existing corporations has been a cornerstone of thinking on racial equality in the marketplace.

Criticising this appears to miss an obvious point – that the corporations wield power in the economy. If they remain white controlled, it could be argued, black people will remain trapped in second-class economic citizenship. A policy that supports black street traders, while leaving the largest companies in minority hands, would perpetuate racial minority control. But the problem is not black participation in major corporations – it is the manner in which it has been pursued. Black people have been absorbed into these corporations as board members and senior managers. But no fundamental shift in power has occurred and it is therefore inaccurate to describe this as 'empowerment'.

It would be easy to conclude from this a need to achieve a transfer of power by nationalising the corporations and transferring them to black owners. This is what an important strain of thinking within the ANC believed would be necessary during its fight against apartheid. The often-misunderstood term 'national democratic revolution' was not, as right-wing ANC critics suggest (Hoffman 2022), a euphemism for a socialist uprising. It was meant to de-racialise the market economy. Its advocates argued that white economic power was so entrenched that the only way this could be done was through the aggressive state intervention that socialist states used (Hudson 1990). But there are ways of addressing this problem that do not require an assault in property rights, which would alienate investors.

The issue is not whether black people should seize these corporations from their white owners. It is how economic power can be no longer restricted to those who have held it for a century. The approaches adopted over the past three decades do not address this issue. While legislation has been introduced to address 'fronting', the crude process in which black ownership is simulated by whites (Staff Reporter 2013), little or no attention has been given to ensure black economic decision-making, whether in existing companies or newer ones. The standard measures of racial change concentrate on numbers in positions, not on whether decisions are being taken by black board members and managers. Measuring this is difficult, introducing policies that change power balances even more so. But we do not know what is possible since real change has not been tried. As long as this is so, racial equality in the economy will remain obstructed because the major organisations will be controlled by people much like those who ran them before 1994.

The consequence, as the sociologist Karl von Holdt shows, is that democracy has not triggered the same economic consequences as changes of power in the period of white rule (Von Holdt 2019). When the British colonisers governed, this opened up opportunities for British business, in particular the Randlords, who presided over the mining industry. For a few decades, white, English-speaking business dominated the economy. When Afrikaner nationalism took over in 1948, white, Afrikaans-speaking business was boosted.

But majority rule has not produced the same result for black business – an important reason for corruption is, Von Holdt argues, 'class formation', by which he means the emergence of a class of black people who want to become owners, who wield power in the economy (2019). An ill often blamed on racial change is, therefore, embedded in South Africa's past. Change has not been deep enough to change the racial power balance in the formal economy.

Whose initiative?

Another symptom of thinking that wants to extend the past to all, rather than think a different future, is the way in which productive economic activity is viewed. It was noted earlier that 'decent jobs' are assumed to be those in formal offices, factories or shops. This assumes that 'decent' economic activity can only occur in these venues. It is illustrated by the curious nature of the country's mainstream understanding of entrepreneurship. It is common to claim that one of the economy's problems is a lack of entrepreneurship among South Africans (Soni et al. 2016). Although the claim is usually made without a racial label, more often than not it is implied that black South Africans are those who lack this quality.

This flies in the face of observed reality. It also lacks logic. Since everyone in the debate knows that millions of people do not occupy formal jobs and the support available to the jobless is limited – a point to which I shall return – it is not clear how the South Africans who are said to lack entrepreneurship are able to survive. The answer is surely that they do this by finding ways to generate wealth (albeit not a huge amount) – in other words, through entrepreneurship. To put the issue bluntly, if people in the areas where poverty is a reality were not entrepreneurial, they would not be alive.

In this light, the policy priority to find roles in the formal sector for people who have shown their ability to create wealth outside it is futile. It should, rather, be programmes to assist those who have shown this capacity to maximise their potential. Part of this would be focused on providing an environment in which they can operate more effectively, part would require provision of the kinds of support mentioned earlier. It would also entail linking these entrepreneurs to formal-sector companies and opportunities.

The discussion on the measures that would be required to do this has, however, not even begun because the mainstream policy debate labels these entrepreneurs as a problem. While there is some evidence that the need to begin treating them as assets is well understood by key public servants, political decision-makers seem still wedded to the idea that only businesses that operate within rules framed before 1994 are legitimate contributors to the economy. The costs should be obvious. South Africa does not need to find a way to boost entrepreneurship – it needs policy thinking that values and promotes the entrepreneurs it already has.

Suburban fantasies

Housing policy in the post-1994 period also conforms to the pattern. The die was probably cast in the early 1990s when the National Housing Forum was convened to discuss post-apartheid policy. It brought together a wide range of interests, political parties and activist groups and its discussions formed the basis of post-1994 housing policy. A theme of its discussions, a focus of much hard bargaining, was how to get mortgage finance to people living in townships. This sounds admirable, but research at the time showed that the people earmarked to become beneficiaries wanted nothing to do with mortgages (Tomlinson 1996). After the right to own property in the cities was extended to black people in 1985, home-loan companies, whose excitement at a new market far outweighed their knowledge of the segregated areas in which they were lending, sold mortgages to people who could not afford them – or at least not when they lost their jobs, which many did. And so, while the forum participants associated mortgages with a pleasant suburban lifestyle, township residents associated them with repossessions.

This example has been used elsewhere to illustrate the gap between the parties that negotiate policies and most citizens affected by their policies (Friedman, Hlela and Thulare 2005). But it could equally well underline the argument made here. The 'ideal' householder that mortgages were meant to produce was the comfortable suburban citizen – in other words, most whites when apartheid reigned. Solutions that would have provided much-improved housing but in environments that white suburbia would find strange and unappealing were rejected because all participants assumed that suburbia was the state of being to which everyone should aspire.

The problem was illustrated in Alexandra township, north of Johannesburg, in the late-apartheid years. After a protracted battle, a residents' committee, headed by a respected clergyman, managed to thwart the apartheid government's plan to turn Alexandra, one of the country's very few areas where black people could own property outside the apartheid-created Bantustans, into a vast single-sex barracks – the committee also won approval for developing the area. It insisted that it wanted to turn Alexandra into a 'garden suburb' like neighbouring Sandton, despite warnings from the town planners it consulted that this would mean displacing thousands of people. The result was, as the planners predicted, wholesale displacement and violence, which persisted for many years (Webster 2019) because a garden suburb was simply not a realistic possibility for most of its residents.

Alexandra's committee was explicit about its desire to replicate suburbia – it pointed out that the (white) planners who warned against its wishes lived in garden suburbs themselves, but did not feel it appropriate for black people to do so. The argument is hard to fault – until we recognise that the circumstances in which the planners lived were as much a problem as those in which the people of Alexandra lived. The township residents had too little, but the suburban residents had too much because laws restricting the vast bulk of national resources to a small white minority at the expense of everyone else gave it to them. Admittedly, under apartheid the committee would not have achieved much by proposing that suburbia's unsustainable lifestyle be changed. But thinking did not change after 1994, when it would have been possible to see suburbia as no less a problem than the townships and shack settlements.

The assumption that white conditions were the required standard have influenced housing policy since 1994. The researchers who played a significant role in shaping policy in the early years of democracy insisted that a core goal was not simply to provide people with shelter – being a homeowner, they expected, would also enable hitherto homeless people to become citizens (Tomlinson 1995). On the surface, this was odd since they had become citizens in 1994. But 'citizen' did not, in their understanding, mean a person with rights. It meant a suburban resident who paid for services and valued property – people who would turn the areas in which they lived from wild places, in which middle-class people might fear to tread, to replicas of the places in which the researchers lived.

Then and since, the new homeowners have repeatedly disappointed these expectations by not behaving as the 'citizenship' theories wanted. Their decisions on whether to pay for services did not change. Some angered policymakers by selling the houses they were given, not only because they needed the money, but also because their shacks had been nearer to schools, shops and transport hubs – and were often larger too (Tomlinson 2002). They refused to be remade into something that did not fit their experience and the challenges they faced.

While housing policy has undergone shifts since 1994, thinking of this sort has remained influential. Concessions have been made to recognising that, in the circumstances in which they find themselves, the choices of housing beneficiaries are reasonable and that policy should respect them – for example, by upgrading existing sites, rather than expecting people to move to places that remove them even further from amenities and opportunities. But policy has not clearly rejected the view that only suburban housing is 'decent' (as only formal work is 'decent').

It has been left to the courts to defend the housing choices of people in poverty –
often against official attempts to remove them (Wilson 2011).

A recurring theme since 1994, which persists, is the repeated resort to
evictions to enforce housing policy. In essence, people who are poor and black are
repeatedly assumed not to belong in the accommodation they choose – because
permission has not been obtained or their dwellings are considered 'unsightly' by
middle-class people. Again, protection is offered by the courts, not by politicians
responding to citizens' needs. And, because the logic of the apartheid city has
not changed in a quarter century of democracy, black people living in poverty
are still expected to dwell far from the hubs of economic activity – many cannot
earn a living by selling basics in the more affluent areas of cities because they
cannot afford the travel costs. Ensuring that people who are not suburbanites
can live close to economic opportunities has been a stated official intention for
years, expressed in, among other documents, the National Development Plan
(National Planning Commission 2012: 69) and at least one local programme has
been implemented – in Johannesburg (Harrison et al. 2019) – but the promised
national change is still only a promise.

Government policy and law do, of course, need to take into account property
rights, which are guaranteed by the Constitution, and the need to ensure that
people's housing choices do not expose them or others to harm. But it is possible
to pursue a housing policy that recognises these imperatives, but does not assume
that they can be respected only by a futile attempt to turn people with housing
needs into carbon copies of the suburban residents who were the backbone of
white life under apartheid.

Restraints on trade

The prejudices that underpin housing policy are even more apparent in responses
to informal traders. As traders' organisations repeatedly point out (Thulare 2004),
people who do business on the pavements of the major cities are considered a
problem, not an asset. They are routinely subjected to police action, which seeks
to remove them from their trading sites (Mafata 2021). At times, cities have
claimed to improve traders' prospects by removing them from the sites they
have chosen to trading precincts, which are cleaner than the city streets and have
more facilities (Thulare 2004). Traders who are moved to such sites have access to

everything they may need – except customers. The inevitable consequence is that, sooner or later, they decide that they would rather have clientele than amenities and return to the sites they originally occupied – only to be harassed by police again.

The parallels with housing policy are clear. Special interests play a role in the constant attempt to keep traders off the streets – those of formal businesses who complain about the informal trade on their doorstep (Motala 2002). But, beyond that, much the same prejudices that persuade officials that shack-dwellers' lives improve if they are removed a distance away from amenities are responsible for the thinking that assumes traders are better off in a neat precinct far removed from customers.

The attitude of major cities towards traders is the most obvious illustration of the point made earlier – that business activity is considered 'decent' only if it occurs in the formal environments whites created under apartheid. As in the housing case, there is an obvious need for health standards and measures to ensure that street trading does not threaten the safety of clients or passers-by. But that could be achieved by improving and regulating the sites where people want to trade, not by assuming that the public good can be served only if they do business in environments that seek to mimic those that served white needs during apartheid.

Taken for granted

Prejudices against the government's social grants programme, common among commentators and some policymakers, are yet another product of the assumption that white society under apartheid is the norm to which the society should aspire.

Grants have been routinely denounced in the national debate as sources of 'dependence'. The government is derided for handing out grants, rather than creating jobs (Ngidi and Howson 2022) and the grants programme is depicted as a source of shame, an admission that the country cannot meet the needs of citizens. But grants are, in fact, the fuel that powers the growth of local economies (Nnaeme 2022). They are often used not to enable alcohol or drug addiction, as is sometimes claimed, but to meet important local needs (Seloane 2008). They have been identified as the government's most effective anti-poverty programme since 1994 (Van der Berg, Siebrits and Lekezwa 2010). They are, therefore, an important resource, not only for the beneficiaries, but for the economy. Unlike many social programmes, they are highly valued by recipients and are often the main reason why people who receive them vote for the governing party (Patel et al. 2014). This reality fuels another prejudice – the claim that the ANC has remained in power only by using grants to 'buy' support (Smith 2021). Implementing programmes that meet the needs of voters is precisely what governments are meant to do: the complaint makes as little sense as blaming a government for 'buying' voter support by adopting policies that improve their living standards.

While the grants programme is official government policy, it is not universally admired in government – the view of Minister of Finance Enoch Godongwana, that the government should find an alternative to grants (Phakati 2022), is shared by many official decision-makers. Opposition is usually based on the claim that grants are unsustainable because a minority is paying the taxes used to sustain the majority, or the already-mentioned insistence that there is something demeaning about receiving a grant.

The first point ignores the fact that programmes are sustainable indefinitely if their cost is affordable to taxpayers, regardless of how many people are paying and how many receive the benefit. The second is deaf both to the already-mentioned economic contribution that grants make and to the reality that the government also offers subsidies and other sources of support to companies and middle-class people. It is not clear why a subsidy enabling a company to enhance its contribution to the economy is not demeaning, but a grant that stimulates local economies by placing resources in the hands of people who use it productively is – or why transport subsidies benefiting the middle class (Gedye 2020) are acceptable, but those extended to people living in poverty are not. But this logic does not alter the fact that grants are treated with disdain by many in government. The programme survives only because government politicians know that grants are popular among voters and possibly also because they know, as an important study (Scott 1976) has shown, that people are far more likely to rebel if something they value is taken away than if they know that others have a great deal more than they do.

Prejudices against grants are not purely South African. They are common in societies where grants are used to address poverty – recipients are caricatured as parasites who are living off the hard-working efforts of people in employment, even where it is clear that they receive grants because there are no jobs available for them (Gilliam 1999). But in South Africa they are reinforced by the view discussed here. Grant beneficiaries are stigmatised and the programme maligned because it acknowledges, in effect, that the shop, office or factory is not the only place where people can earn income – that a job is only one way of earning a livelihood and that grants are a building block that enable people to create wealth on street corners or in backyard shacks.

The grants programme is not only popular and necessary. It is, given the reality that many South Africans will not gain access to a job for many years, essential. It is also consistent with thinking in other parts of the world that sees cash transfers as the key to sustaining economies in a world in which traditional jobs are diminishing (Stanford n.d.). It is stigmatised only because it is a very visible sign that the formal activity that sustained whites before 1994 is not the only route to an income and a contribution to the economy.

Escaping the past

The examples discussed in this chapter illustrate the concrete ways in which policy discussions are trapped in thinking that sees the world that one-tenth of the population inhabited when the law protected them as the country's goal.

A common theme in all the examples given here is that breaking with the past is rejected by the assumption that doing so would force black people, excluded from opportunities by apartheid, to once again settle for second or third best. Why should black people be denied leadership positions in corporations, formal jobs or suburban houses when whites still enjoy them because they were advantaged by apartheid? Was the Alexandra committee not justified in pointing out that the planners who argued against a garden suburb lived in these suburbs themselves?

The purpose of new thinking is not to preserve the divisions of the past – it is to erode or end them. As my discussion of housing policy points out, thinking rooted in the present does not suggest that the lives of a mainly white elite would remain unchanged. A core flaw of the assumptions that remain trapped in the past is that they offer no criticism of the way whites lived under apartheid and assume that this can be extended to all in a democracy. Squeezing as many black people as possible into existing corporations excludes many because the economy remains highly concentrated – some twenty companies are reported to own 80 per cent of the asserts on the Johannesburg Stock Exchange (Makgetla 2018). Nor is the existing model for incorporating black people into the major corporations the only possible one – while at present black entrants are meant to change to fit the logic of large companies, an alternative would see the companies changing to accommodate new black entrants.

Similar arguments apply to the other examples discussed in this chapter. People trading on street corners or finding accommodation in empty areas of the suburbs are realities to which middle-class people need to adjust. They might need also to accept rules that, at the very least, make it far more costly to own houses that take up large tracts of land when the need for shelter is severe. And, as noted earlier, they will need to accept settlements of lower-income black people in their midst, rather than on the outer edges of their cities. They might also need to pay more to ensure not only a grants programme that offers more money to more recipients, but also to fund support programmes that would enhance the likelihood that grants will generate productive activity.

None of this will, of course, be welcomed by the one-third of citizens who benefit from current arrangements. Since it is in this group that the capital needed to build growth is found, simply imposing these changes would severely damage the country's already fragile economic prospects. But the costs of remaining trapped in the past is continued low growth, the inevitable cost of ignoring the talents and energies of two-thirds of the population. And so, the path out of this dead end is negotiation. Just as formal democracy was achieved by a bargain between those with a stake in what existed and those who needed urgent change, so a new negotiation is needed on how our society and economy can become appropriate to a majority-ruled country on the tip of Africa. Bargaining is likely to be noisy and tense as sections of the society try to maximise their power to secure their interests. But that is true of any negotiation process that yields real and lasting change.

Negotiation will, however, remain impossible until those with the power to end the fixation with the past recognise the need for change. And so, it will not begin unless those who see the need to move into the present and the future convince those mired in the past of the value of a shift. This analysis has been a very modest attempt to begin that conversation.

References

Acemoglu, D., S. Gelb and J.A. Robinson. 2007. *Black Economic Empowerment and Economic Performance in South Africa*. https://www.treasury.gov.za/publications/other/growth/06-procurement%20and%20bee/02-black%20economic%20empowerment%20and%20economic%20performance%20in%20so.pdf (accessed 30 September 2023).

Duarte, J. 2018. 'Jobs and Decent Work in Line with Nasrec Remains the ANC's Top Priority'. *Daily Maverick*, 9 November. https://www.dailymaverick.co.za/opinionista/2018-11-09-jobs-and-decent-work-in-line-with-nasrec-remains-the-ancs-top-priority/ (accessed 30 September 2023).

Fin24. 2018. 'Black Ownership Dropped in JSE-Listed Companies – Report'. *Fin24*, 3 August. https://www.fin24.com/Economy/black-ownership-dropped-in-jse-listed-companies-report-20180803 (accessed 30 September 2023).

Fleischman, T. 2022. 'Technology Helps Self-driving Cars Learn from Their Own Memories'. *Cornell Chronicle*, 21 June. https://news.cornell.edu/stories/2022/06/technology-helps-self-driving-cars-learn-own-memories (accessed 30 September 2023).

Friedman, S. 2021a. *One Virus, Two Countries: What Covid-19 Tells Us about South Africa*. Johannesburg: Wits University Press.

———. 2021b. *Prisoners of the Past: South African Democracy and the Legacy of Minority Rule*. Johannesburg: Wits University Press.

Friedman, S., K. Hlela and P. Thulare. 2005. 'A Question of Voice: Informality and Pro-poor Policy in Johannesburg, South Africa'. In: *Urban Futures: Economic Growth and Poverty Reduction*, edited by N. Hamdi, 51–68. Rugby: ITDG.

Gedye, L. 2020. 'Public Transport Inequality'. *Mail & Guardian*, 25 February. https://mg.co.za/article/2020-02-25-public-transport-inequality/ (accessed 30 September 2023).

Gilliam, F.D 1999. 'The "Welfare Queen" Experiment: How Viewers React to Images of African-American Mothers on Welfare'. *UCLA: Center for Communications and Community*. https://escholarship.org/uc/item/17m7r1rq (accessed 30 September 2023).

Gumede, M. 2022. 'Ramaphosa Calls on Corporates to Ramp up Support for Black Industrialists'. *Business Live*, 20 July. https://www.businesslive.co.za/bd/national/2022-07-20-ramaphosa-calls-for-private-sector-to-back-black-industrialists/ (accessed 30 September 2023).

Harrison, P., M. Rubin, A. Appelbaum and R. Dittgen. 2019. 'Corridors of Freedom: Analyzing Johannesburg's Ambitious Inclusionary Transit-Oriented Development'. *Journal of Planning Education and Research* 39 (3): 1–13.

Hoffman, P. 2022. 'The National Democratic Revolution Is Deeply and Darkly Inconsistent with the Constitution'. *Daily Maverick*, 8 February. https://www.dailymaverick.co.za/opinionista/2022-02-08-the-national-democratic-revolution-is-deeply-and-darkly-inconsistent-with-the-constitution/ (accessed 30 September 2023).

Hudson, P. 1990. 'The Concept of Class and the Class Content of National Liberation in South Africa: Empiricism and Essentialism in the Theory of the South African Revolution'. In: *Views on the South African State*, edited by M. Swilling, 209–22. Pretoria: HSRC Press.

Mafata, M. 2021. 'Joburg's Informal Traders Call for Police to Stop Confiscating Their Goods'. *GroundUp*, 20 August. https://www.groundup.org.za/article/i-come-here-every-day-knowing-that-at-some-point-i-will-have-to-grab-my-things-and-run-from-jmpd/ (accessed 30 September 2023).

Makgetla, N. 2018. 'Big Business's Hold on Economic Power Spawns Pervasive Inequality'. *Business Day*, 23 October. https://www.businesslive.co.za/bd/opinion/columnists/2018-10-23-neva-makgetla-big-businesss-hold-on-economic-power-spawns-pervasive-inequality/ (accessed 30 September 2023).

Motala, S. 2002. *Organizing in the Informal Economy: A Case Study of Street Trading in South Africa*. SEED Working Paper No. 36. https://www.ilo.org/wcmsp5/groups/public/@ed_emp/@emp_ent/@ifp_seed/documents/publication/wcms_117700.pdf (accessed 30 September 2023).

Munck, R. 1994. 'South Africa: The Great Economic Debate'. *Third World Quarterly* 15 (2): 205–17.

National Planning Commission. 2012. *National Development Plan 2030: Our Future – Make It Work*. https://www.gov.za/sites/default/files/gcis_document/201409/ndp-2030-our-future-make-it-workr.pdf (accessed 30 September 2023).

Ngidi, B. and K. Howson. 2022. 'Debunking the "Culture of Dependency" Argument against Social Grants'. *Daily Maverick*, 22 February. https://www.dailymaverick.co.za/article/2022-02-22-debunking-the-culture-of-dependency-argument-against-social-grants/ (accessed 30 September 2023).

Nnaeme, C.C. 2022. ' "The Community Comes to Life": How Social Grants Enable Participation in the Local Economy and Possible Effect on Post-COVID-19 Economic Recovery in Soweto, South Africa'. *Forum for Development Studies* 49 (3): 493–510.

Patel, L., Y. Sadie, V. Graham, A. Delaney and K. Baldry. 2014. *Voting Behaviour and the Influence of Social Protection: A Study of Voting Behaviour in Three Poor Areas of South Africa*. Johannesburg: Centre for Social Development in Africa and Department of Politics, University of Johannesburg. https://www.uj.ac.za/wp-content/uploads/2021/10/csda-voting-behaviour-research-report-_-nov-2014-_-print.pdf (accessed 30 September 2023).

Phakati, B. 2022. 'All Social Grants Will Be Reviewed, Says Enoch Godongwana'. *Business Day*, 23 February. https://www.businesslive.co.za/bd/national/2022-02-23-all-social-grants-will-be-reviewed-says-enoch-godongwana/ (accessed 30 September 2023).

Scott, J.C. 1976. *The Moral Economy of the Peasant: Rebellion and Subsistence in Southeast Asia*. New Haven: Yale University Press.

Seloane, M. 2008. 'Resource Flows in Poor Communities: A Reflection on Four Case Studies'. In: *Giving and Solidarity: Resource Flows for Poverty Alleviation and Development in South Africa*, edited by A. Habib and B. Maharaj, 121–58. Cape Town: HSRC Press.

Smith, C. 2021. 'Moeletsi Mbeki: BEE and Affirmative Action Are Biggest Drivers of Corruption in SA'. *Fin24*, 9 March. https://www.news24.com/fin24/Economy/moeletsi-mbeki-bee-and-affirmative-action-are-biggest-drivers-of-corruption-in-sa-20210309 (accessed 30 September 2023).

Soni, P., A. Shaikh, A. Karodia and Z. Hamid. 2016. 'Psst! The World's Trumpeting Entrepreneurship but South Africa Is Not Listening and Responding'. https://regent.ac.za/wp-content/uploads/2016/03/Psst-The-worlds-trumpeting-Entrepreneurship-but-South-Africa-is-not-listening-and-responding.pdf (accessed 30 September 2023).

Staff Reporter. 2013. 'Law to Stop "Black Empowerment" Fronting Approved'. *Mail & Guardian*, 21 June. https://mg.co.za/article/2013-06-21-00-law-to-stop-black-empowermentfronting approved/ (accessed 30 September 2023).

Stanford Basic Income Lab. N.d. 'What Is Basic Income?' https://basicincome.stanford.edu/about/what-is-ubi/ (accessed 30 September 2023).

Thulare, P. 2004. *Trading Democracy? Johannesburg Informal Traders and Citizenship* https://archive.ids.ac.uk/gdr/cfs/drc-pubs/summaries/summary%2011-Thulare-Trading Democracy.pdf (accessed 30 September 2023).

Tomlinson, M. 1995. *The First Million Is the Hardest: Will the Consensus on Housing Endure?* Johannesburg: Centre for Policy Studies.

———. 1996. *From Rejection to Resignation: Beneficiaries' Views on the South African Government's Housing Subsidy Scheme*. Johannesburg: Centre for Policy Studies.

———. 2002. 'Efforts and Errors: South Africa's Search to Extend Housing Finance to Low-Income Households'. *Housing Finance International* 17 (2): 8–14.

Van der Berg, S., K. Siebrits and B. Lekezwa. 2010. *Efficiency and Equity Effects of Social Grants in South Africa*. Working Papers 15/2010, Department of Economics, Stellenbosch University. https://ideas.repec.org/p/sza/wpaper/wpapers115.html (accessed 30 September 2023).

Von Holdt, K. 2019. *The Political Economy of Corruption: Elite-Formation, Factions and Violence*. Society, Politics and Work Institute Working Paper No. 10. https://docs.wixstatic.com/ugd/de7bea_0590611beee14069a0e98f83dd26e9ae.pdf (accessed 30 September 2023).

Webster, D. 2019. 'Alex Shutdown Reopens Old Divisions and Old Wounds'. *New Frame*, 4 April. https://www.newframe.com/alex-shutdown-reopens-old-divisions-and-old-wounds/ (accessed 30 September 2023).

Wilson, S. 2011 'Litigating Housing Rights in Johannesburg's Inner City: 2004–2008'. *South African Journal on Human Rights* 27 (1): 127–51.

CHAPTER 10

The Role of Companies in Solving Deep-Rooted Societal Problems

Michael Katz

The need for resourceful solutions

The societal problems in South Africa are manifold and growing. Noteworthy among these are poor service delivery, deficiencies in housing and human settlements, inadequate health care for a large portion of the population and deficiencies in education. In addition, South Africa is experiencing a massive deterioration in basic infrastructure. A solution to these problems, and the many others, does not appear to be readily visible. It is clear that the government alone will not be able, at least in the short term, to solve these problems. In many cases, the state does not have the financial resources and, even where it does, there appears to be a lack of capacity in certain instances. In this latter regard, departments with huge budget allocations are not making an effective contribution, as the budget allocation does not seem to reach the target. This gives rise to a self-fulfilling, downward spiral. Resourceful solutions are clearly needed.

Fortunately, South Africa has historically demonstrated that it has a resourceful, talented and responsive private sector. Now more than ever is the resourceful response of the private sector required. As will be demonstrated in this chapter, the growing consensus internationally on the purpose of companies in society enables new thinking on the important role that companies in the private sector can play in resolving many of South Africa's seemingly intractable problems. As Danielle Allen remarks: 'Taxes and the State are not the only answer. We also need innovation so that our market incentives can do a better job of helping private actors function in ways that support public goods' (2021: 101). This chapter demonstrates, based on international experience, that there is no tension between profits and laudable purpose. In approaching this topic, the fundamental submission argued in this chapter is analysed on an incremental basis, drawing attention to the involvement of relevant role-players and topics.

The role of government

Currently, there is much discussion on the competent state. It is frequently said that to win the war against poverty and inequality, we must strengthen the policies, culture and institutions that underpin the competent state. There is a powerful correlation between a competent state and good economic and social outcomes (McKinsey & Company 2015). Clearly, the government has a major role to play in the enhancement of a healthy, inclusive and equal society. The suggestions in this chapter about the role that the private sector can play must not be understood as an argument that it should substitute for an effective government. The private sector must operate in parallel with the government.

Evolution of the purpose of companies

The role of companies and their purpose has evolved in recent times beyond the conventional wisdom of the Chicago School in the 1970s. Milton Friedman, in expounding the doctrine of the Chicago School that the firm's only duty is to maximise shareholder value, states: 'There is one and only one social responsibility of business – to use its resources and engage in activities designed to increase its profits' (1970). An illustration of the radical change in conventional wisdom is the statement released in August 2019 by the Business Roundtable – an organisation composed of the chief executive officers of many of the largest and most powerful American corporations. The statement included the following, redefining the purpose of the corporation: 'To promote an economy that serves all Americans for the benefit of all stakeholders: customers, employee, suppliers, communities and shareholders' (Business Roundtable 2019).

Another powerful illustration of contemporary thinking on the purpose of the company is the letter sent in January 2018 by Larry Fink, the chief executive officer of BlackRock, the world's largest financial asset manager. The letter, which was sent to the chief executive officers of all the firms in his portfolio, contained the following passage:

Society is demanding that companies, both public and private, serve a social purpose. To prosper over time, every company must not only deliver financial performance, but must also show how it makes a positive contribution to society. Companies must benefit all of their stakeholders, including shareholders, employees, customers, and the communities in which they operate (Fink 2018).

Illustrative international literature

Reimagining Capitalism: How Business Can Save the World
– REBECCA HENDERSON (2020)

In her groundbreaking book, Rebecca Henderson, John and Natty McArthur Professor at Harvard University, dispels the widely held view that there is a tension between profits and purpose. Her analysis of the phenomenal work done by Norsk Gjenvinning (NG), the largest waste-handling company in Norway, indicates that any assertion of a tension between profits and purpose misses the point. As the back of the dust cover of Henderson's book points out, 'the approach that business has a positive duty to society is not only a moral imperative but also an extraordinary opportunity to drive growth and innovation in an increasingly competitive world'. She suggests that this approach to the purpose of business has the 'potential to balance the power of the market with the power of democratic, accountable government and strong civil society – the only long-term solution to the problems that we face'.

Net Positive: How Courageous Companies Thrive by Giving More Than They Take
– PAUL POLMAN AND ANDREW WINSTON (2021)

Paul Polman works to accelerate action by business to achieve the United Nations' Sustainable Development Goals. He was the chief executive officer of Unilever from 2009 to 2019. Andrew Winston is one of the world's leading thinkers on sustainable business. In their book, they draw attention to the devastation caused by runaway climate change and rampant inequality and other challenges such as pandemics, resource pressures and shrinking biodiversity. They demonstrate how Unilever and other companies around the world can make profit by fixing the world's problems, instead of creating or contributing to them. Similar thinking as to how business, by pursuing a constructive societal purpose, can make profits is expressed by a number of leading experts (Edmans 2020; Mayer 2018; Bower, Leonard and Paine 2011).

Shareholder activism

How are shareholders thinking about these issues? The answer to this question is unequivocal in an article in the *Economist*, dated 23 April 2022 and titled 'Annual Meetings Are the New Frontline in the Battle over Corporate Purpose':

> Companies have always had to answer to their investors. But these days shareholders have new questions – lots of them. On April 28th shareholders in three big drug companies, Johnson & Johnson (J&J), Moderna and Pfizer, are set to vote on resolutions filed by Oxfam, a charity, that seeks to widen access to Covid-19 vaccines. In May Amazon's shareholders are due to vote on a proposal from New York State's pension fund, asking for an audit of the e-commerce giant's policies on racial equality. Carl Icahn, a notoriously fierce corporate inquisitor, has broadened his attention from profits to pigs. He has filed proposals at McDonald's and Kroger, a grocer, in a quest to end the confinement of pregnant sows ... This barrage points to the next phase of America's fight over corporate purpose. Executives who have endorsed 'stakeholder value', a much broader measure of corporate worth than profits and cashflow, are now seeing their declarations put to the test.

A similar pattern of shareholder resolutions at annual general meetings seems to be gaining favour in South Africa. Banks, in particular, are facing requests from activist shareholders to place resolutions before annual general meetings dealing with issues related to environmental, social and corporate governance, funding of fossil fuel producers and so forth. So too are big emitters of carbon.

International case studies

As mentioned above, one of the interesting case studies referred to by Henderson (2020) relates to NG, the largest waste-handling company in Norway. When Eric Osmundsen became the chief executive officer of NG, the waste business was an unfashionable corner of the economy. But, as pointed out by Henderson, Orsmundson believed it was on the edge of significant transformation. Historically, the business had been largely a matter of hauling garbage to local landfills. Orsmundson saw that the future of the industry was in recycling, which had the potential to be a high-tech business selling into a global market, with significant economies of scale. He also believed that the waste business held the key to addressing two of the world's greatest global challenges: 'climate change and the increasing shortage of raw materials' (in Henderson 2020: 32). Osmundsen succeeded in ensuring that NG began to industrialise the waste industry's value chain by embracing increasingly high-tech recycling. Henderson reveals:

> As NG stepped up its production of great quality metals, it was able to diversify its customer base, significantly increasing the prices it received. In combination, these moves created significant economies of scale, driving down costs, increasing margins and allowing NG to out compete its rivals, further increasing volumes. By 2018 NG was one of the largest and most profitable waste companies in Scandinavia (Henderson 2020: 35).

Potential for reconciliation of profits and purpose in South Africa

In an article in the *Daily Maverick*, Tony Carnie discusses the ' "mammoth effort" and R8-billion needed to clean up SA's stinking sewage and wastewater crisis' (2022). He draws attention to *Green Drop 2022*, which indicates that the cost of restoring South Africa's sewage and wastewater facilities to basic functionality will be R8 141 644 365 (Department of Public Works 2022). The Green Drop scheme rates the treatment of polluted water after passing through municipal and private facilities and then being released into rivers, wetlands or the sea. This is entirely separate from the Blue Drop system, which rates the quality of drinking water flowing from municipal taps.

One wonders whether the example of the NG in Scandinavia could prompt private enterprise in South Africa to tackle the sewage and wastewater problems in a manner that benefits society and is also profitable. This is but one example of a potential challenge that combines profits with social purpose.

It is interesting to note the spectacular success of the Solidarity Fund. This was a private-sector initiative, in response to a plea from President Cyril Ramaphosa to establish an agile plan to meet the challenges of the Covid-19 pandemic. In a short time, the Solidarity Fund raised approximately R3.4 billion, almost all from the private sector, which was used to fund personal protective equipment, humanitarian aid to the victims of the pandemic and their families, and mount an educative programme across the population, urging the wearing of masks, social distancing and hand sanitising. This is a wonderful recent example of private-sector activism to confront societal problems.

There are notable examples of South African companies combining profits with good purpose in solving some of society's needs. These include Discovery in the provision of medical aid, Netcare, Life Health and MediClinic in the provision of health care and Curro in the provision of education.

The law

As a matter of company law, it is fair to say that South Africa adopts the enlightened share value doctrine. This is pursuant to a development of the common law and essentially means that while directors primarily owe their duties to shareholders, they are entitled and obliged in discharging that duty to take into account the interests of other stakeholders, including employees, customers, suppliers, the local community and the environment. It also implies, in discharging their duties, they must take into account both the short-term and long-term consequences of their actions. Thus, taking into account the environment makes for more sustainable companies in the longer term. A suggestion has been made to make this doctrine of enlightened shareholder value more explicit by adopting an approach as set out in section 172 (5) of the English Companies Act of 2006, which embodies explicitly the aforegoing principles, as set out above, which are part of South African common law.

It is also noteworthy that in terms of the listings requirements of the Johannesburg Stock Exchange, there are a number of mandatory disclosures relating to the environmental, social and corporate governance policies of companies. In addition, the King code of best practice (Institute of Directors Southern Africa 2016) also deals with duties of directors to promote good corporate citizenship. The purpose of a corporation, which would be consistent with principles of South African company law, has been admirably well expressed as a matter of law in the United States as follows:

The purpose of a corporation is to conduct a lawful, ethical, profitable and sustainable business in order to ensure its success and grow its value over the long term. This requires consideration of all the stakeholders that are critical to its success (shareholders, employees, customers, suppliers and communities), as determined by the corporation and its board of directors using their business judgement and with regular engagement with shareholders, who are essential partners in supporting the corporation's pursuit of its purpose. Fulfilling purpose in such manner is fully consistent with the fiduciary duties of the board of directors and the stewardship obligations of shareholders (Wachtell, Lipton, Rosen & Katz 2020).

Promotion of environmental, social and corporate governance

Universally, it is becoming a growing expection that directors, in managing the affairs of their companies, will take into account the importance of environmental, social and governance (ESG) issues. Various stakeholders are demanding that ESG compliance will be a requirement for investment by asset managers in the shares of companies. Against such expectations of ESG compliance, there is a growing consensus that there is a need for proper corporate reporting that enables the measuring of purpose:

This will be helpful to a number of stakeholders including executives of companies who formulate strategies, allocate resources and incentivise people in their organisations on the back of measures of performance.

The second is middle management who make investment decisions, implement projects and deliver performance within the organisations.

Third, institutional investors who make portfolio allocations, monitor investments and steward the companies in which they invest.

Fourth, is policy makers who seek to align corporate behaviour with public interest (Barby et al. 2021).

South Africa has a number of requirements dealing with environmental, social and corporate governance disclosures and reporting obligations. For example, the Institute of Directors Southern Africa's *King IV Report on Corporate Governance for South Africa 2016* contains a guidance document for companies to report annually in an integrated manner and promote good governance, transparency and leadership. There is also a guidance document relating specifically to climate change (Institute of Directors Southern Africa 2016).

As another example, the Johannesburg Stock Exchange (2022) has published *Leading the Way for a Better Tomorrow: JSE Sustainability Disclosure Guidance*, which includes guidance from the Global Reporting Initiative's sustainability reporting standards, the Taskforce on Climate-Related Financial Disclosures, the International Financial Reporting Standards Foundation's International Sustainability Standards Board's prototypes.

Environmental-related reporting requirements are also contained in specific legislation that seeks to deal with environmental impact, including the National Environmental Management Act 107 of 1998, the National Environmental Management: Air Quality Act 29 of 2004 and the National Greenhouse Gas Emission Reporting Regulations of 2017, among others.

Impact of corruption

The pervasive corruption, in both the public and private sector, has exhausted a significant portion of South Africa's resources and decapacitated a number of significant state institutions. While it is certainly the function of state law-enforcement institutions to prosecute unlawful conduct, the private sector has an important role to play in the prevention of corrupt and unlawful activity. A successful prevention or mitigation of corrupt activity would go a long way to saving significant state resources, which would then be available to provide for societal needs. Organised business has a mandate to encourage businesses to adopt measures, including codes of best practice and the pursuit of a culture of ethics to achieve a reduction in this vast waste of resources. So, too, should universities and business schools promote these objectives.

It has also been established there is a correlation between good governance and an ethical culture, on the one hand, and superior financial performance, on the other. Lynn Sharp Paine argues on the back of the dust cover of her 2002 book *Value Shift*: 'Instead of adding more new programs, today's corporate leaders need to go back to basics and adopt a different kind of management.' She continues: 'They will find an approach that is suited to the corporation's contemporary role in society – an approach aimed at melding high ethical standards with outstanding financial results.'

Conclusion

Much more can be achieved in meeting the numerous challenges facing South Africa by companies in the private sector following policies that combine profits with good purpose. There is no tension between the achievement of profits and the pursuit of beneficial purpose. In this context, numerous projects could be undertaken by companies in the private sector in pursuing their business purpose. Such projects could include the provision of education, health care, housing, security, energy, water management, waste reclamation and infrastructure, to name but a few.

References

Allen, D. 2021. *Democracy in the Time of Coronavirus*. Chicago: University of Chicago Press.

'Annual Meetings Are the New Frontline in the Battle over Corporate Purpose'. *The Economist*, 23 April 2022. https://www.economist.com/business/annual-meetings-are-the-new-frontline-in-the-battle-over-corporate-purpose/21808834 (accessed 30 September 2023).

Barby, C., R. Barker, R. Cohen, R.G. Eccles, C. Heller, C. Mayer, B. Roche, G. Serafeim, J.C. Stroehle, R. Younger and T. Zochowski. 2021. *Measuring Purpose: An Integrated Framework*. https://papers.ssrn.com/sol3/papers.cfm?abstract_id=3771892 (accessed 30 September 2023).

Bower, J.L., H.B. Leonard and L.S. Paine. 2011. *Capitalism at Risk: Rethinking the Role of Business*. Boston: Harvard Business Review Press.

Business Roundtable. 2019. 'Business Roundtable Redefines the Purpose of a Corporation to Promote "An Economy That Serves All Americans"'. *Business Roundtable*, 19 August. https://www.businessroundtable.org/business-roundtable-redefines-the-purpose-of-a-corporation-to-promote-an-economy-that-serves-all-americans (accessed 30 September 2023).

Carnie, T. 2022. '"Mammoth Effort" and R8-billion Needed to Clean Up SA's Stinking Sewage and Wastewater Crisis'. *Daily Maverick*, 7 April. https://www.dailymaverick.co.za/article/2022-04-07-mammoth-effort-and-r8-billion-needed-to-clean-up-sas-stinking-sewage-and-wastewater-crisis/ (accessed 30 September 2023).

Department of Public Works. 2022. *Green Drop 2022*. https://ws.dws.gov.za/iris/releases/Report_DPW_Rev02_29Mar22_MN%20web.pdf (accessed 30 September 2022).

Edmans, A. 2020. *Grow the Pie: How Great Companies Deliver Both Purpose and Profit*. Cambridge: Cambridge University Press.

Fink, L. 2018. 'A Sense of Purpose'. *Harvard Law School Forum on Corporate Governance*, 17 January. https://corpgov.law.harvard.edu/2018/01/17/a-sense-of-purpose/ (accessed 30 September 2023).

Friedman, M. 1970. 'A Friedman Doctrine: The Social Responsibility of Business Is to Increase Its Profits'. *New York Times*, 13 September. https://www.nytimes.com/1970/09/13/archives/a-friedman-doctrine-the-social-responsibility-of-business-is-to.html (accessed 30 September 2023).

Henderson, R. 2020. *Reimagining Capitalism: How Business Can Save the World*. London: Penguin.

Institute of Directors Southern Africa. 2016. *King IV Report on Corporate Governance for South Africa 2016*. https://www.adams.africa/wp-content/uploads/2016/11/King-IV-Report.pdf (accessed 30 September 2023).

Johannesburg Stock Exchange. 2022. *Leading the Way for a Better Tomorrow: JSE Sustainability Disclosure Guidance*. https://www.jse.co.za/sites/default/files/media/documents/JSE%20Sustainability%20Disclosure%20Guidance%20June%202022.pdf (accessed 30 September 2023).

Mayer, C. 2018. *Prosperity: Better Business Makes the Greater Good*. Oxford: Oxford University Press.

McKinsey & Company (ed.). 2015. *Reimagining South Africa: 20 Reflections by Leaders from South Africa and Beyond*. Johannesburg: McKinsey & Company.

Polman, P. and A. Winston. 2021. *Net Positive: How Courageous Companies Thrive by Giving More Than They Take*. Boston: Harvard Business Review Press.

Sharp Paine, L. 2002. *Value Shift: Why Companies Must Merge Social and Financial Imperatives to Achieve Superior Performance*. New York: McGraw-Hill.

Wachtell, Lipton, Rosen & Katz. 2020. *Enacting Purpose within the Modern Corporation*. https://www.wlrk.com/webdocs/wlrknew/ClientMemos/WLRK/WLRK.27064.20.pdf (accessed 30 September 2023).

Chapter 11

Towards a South African Economy that 'Belongs to All Who Live in It'

Sim Tshabalala

There are many reasons to be deeply dissatisfied with the performance of the South African economy – including, among others, real income per head has stagnated for more than a decade; South Africa is the world's most unequal major economy; the unemployment rate is chronically and catastrophically high; and opportunities, incomes and assets are distributed in ways that reflect past and current patterns of privilege far more than talent, effort or social utility. The South African economy, in other words, is both deeply inefficient and deeply unjust.

There thus is a strong – and completely understandable – tendency to propose radical solutions. From the ideological right, for instance, one hears calls for the complete dismantling of the black economic empowerment framework (SAIRR 2021). From the left, it is argued that a larger proportion of the South African economy should fall under direct state control, usually by way of expropriation, nationalisation or the creation of new state-owned enterprises (EFF 2022). By contrast, this chapter will argue, perhaps counter-intuitively, that no radicalism is required. Both the performance and the fairness of the South African economy can be greatly improved by diligent execution of existing policies. In order to make this argument, this chapter addresses five questions on the economy posed by the editors of this book.

What criteria to use to fundamentally transform social, economic and political relations?

It is tempting to suppose that fundamental transformation will require fundamentally new decision criteria. In the South African context, the creation of new decision criteria would amount to amending the Constitution, which is the founding text of modern South Africa and the ultimate source of decision criteria for this state and its citizens. The question is whether revised criteria (that is, Constitutional changes) are needed from legal, public policy and cultural angles.

To begin with a legal perspective: consider the founding text of modern South Africa – the Constitution. The Constitution commits the people and the government of South Africa to recognise the inalienable dignity of every human being, to uphold the human and civil rights of everyone in South Africa, to take active steps, including affirmative action, to correct the injustices of the colonial and apartheid eras – certainly including redistribution of income, assets and opportunities – and to the 'progressive realisation' of the rights to housing, food, health care, social security and education.

What could one justly and reasonably subtract from this set of rights? It has, of course, been prominently argued, for instance during the Parliamentary hearings in 2021 on the proposed amendment of section 25 of the Constitution, that the protection of property rights granted by this section of the Constitution has posed a barrier to the achievement of redress and equity (Parliament of South Africa 2021). This argument has shown itself to have considerable emotional and political resonance, but the text of the Constitution makes it clear that 'fair and equitable' compensation for the expropriation of property could very easily be of such a low monetary value as to pose no practical barrier to redistribution. To the credit of South Africa's politicians and civil society, deprivations of other constitutional rights on grounds, for example, of nationality or race, have not hitherto been proposed.

It is easier to imagine that South Africa's citizens, their civil society organisations and political leaders might wish to clarify or expand the existing constitutional rights or to add new ones. Again, and despite the surrounding political messaging, this was precisely what the proposed constitutional amendment of 2021 on property rights was intended to do. Changing social mores and economic expectations may in future lead competent majorities of South Africans to add constitutional rights to, say, the recognition of changing or multiple gender identities or to goods and services not contemplated by the framers of the Constitution in the twentieth century – including, conceivably, a right of access to the digital realm. No valid legal objections to such constitutional developments come easily to mind – except to make the obvious points that the creation of such rights would need to be compatible with existing rights and that a legal right does not lead directly to its practical realisation. This last is an obvious point, no doubt – but an important one and one to which this chapter returns more than once.

Turning from the relatively firm ground of the law to the unavoidably more speculative realm of public policy considerations. As it currently stands, the South African Constitution is widely recognised as one of the best-constructed and most progressive in the world (see, for example, Young 2020). This global recognition is not a decisive argument for retaining the Constitution as our central set of decision criteria, but it surely counts in favour of our doing so, not least because the high regard in which the Constitution is held is a national economic asset, in that it makes it easier to attract and retain investment.

The public policy argument against subtracting rights from the Constitution is often made by adducing various dramatic examples, including, for instance, the economic outcomes experienced in Venezuela or Zimbabwe following radical curtailments of property rights in those countries. These negative outcomes should certainly give one pause – but it is always possible to argue that these outcomes were the result of other factors, or to point to cases where sweeping changes to property rights were followed by rapid economic growth, as in Japan after the Second World War. More confidence in the economic value of secure rights can be created by considering 'natural experiments', rather than individual cases. Consider, for example, the very different economic trajectories of twin states such as East and West Germany or North and South Korea. Both pairs of twins were 'born' with almost identical endowments of human and physical capital. Human, civil and property rights were severely limited in East Germany and remain so in North Korea, whereas both West Germany and South Korea provided their citizens with basic human and civil rights from the start, steadily expanding into the broad range of rights typical of economically advanced social democracies. East Germany experienced very slow economic growth; West Germany underwent its famous 'economic miracle'. North Korea remains one of the world's poorest countries; South Korea's rise to being a highly advanced high-income economy was even more rapid than West Germany's.

Just to anticipate some obvious objections, by no stretch of the imagination could West Germany or South Korea be hailed as 'free market' by those on the economic right or derided as neo-liberal by the left. Both were characterised by strong states, strong labour unions – and strong firms (Müller-Armack 1978; Wade 2003; Kohli 2004). It is also appropriate to point out that the deprivation of the constitutional right to redress by way of affirmative action and black economic empowerment would be just as ill-advised as the proposed elimination of any other rights: closing down routes to advancement without constructing better alternatives is a recipe for political and economic dislocation (Hirschman 1973).

The public policy arguments for adding new rights to the Constitution are, this chapter argues, almost wholly benign, except to the extent that they could create unrealistic expectations. However, when citizens are able to create and give effect to new rights that fit within the broader constitutional framework, both economic logic and the historical evidence suggest that this is all to the good. A good example of this is the expansion of civil rights to women in much of the world in the first half of the twentieth century. This led, for instance to higher workforce participation by women and higher investment in girls' and women's education and training, raising both the quantity and quality of human resources available to society, leading to higher economic output per head and to more inclusive human development (World Bank 2012).

The last part of this section briefly considers whether the cultural heritages of South Africans provide warrants for changes to South Africa's existing social decision criteria. To state this question in the same terms as those who have made this argument for change: is the Constitution in some important sense an illegitimate quasi-colonial imposition or relic that is incompatible with African aspirations and culture (Mpofu-Walsh 2021)? Putting aside for the moment – merely to shorten the debate, rather than to agree with the claim – the fact that there is no single, dominant African culture from which it is possible to read off what society's decision criteria should be like, what does that 'African culture' require? To the extent that it is legitimate to generalise, it seems fair to propose that African culture is characterised by themes such as a sense of mutual connectedness and inter-reliance, a preference for consensus and – perhaps most of all – a deep commitment to defending individual and collective human dignity, even at the expense of socially or economically efficient outcomes. If African culture can – very roughly – be characterised in this way, it does not seem to provide warrants for the arbitrary deprivation of rights in the interests either of 'justice', as the far left might see it, or 'efficiency', as the far right could argue.

Thus, this section reaches what could well be perceived as a disappointingly conservative conclusion: in its Constitution and the legislation that flows from it – including affirmative action and the black economic empowerment framework – South Africa already has the decision criteria we need to build a better society.

Why has the idea of equality not benefited the majority of the people?

There are powerful and legitimate reasons to be disappointed with the apparently conservative conclusion of the previous section. As mentioned at the start of this chapter, the South African economy has performed poorly for more than a decade and our society remains the most unequal in the world.

In response to the kind of disappointment expressed in this question, this section argues that the commitments to greater equity contained in the Constitution, and in the policies pursued by South Africa's series of democratic governments since 1994, have in fact had some highly positive outcomes. Make no mistake, more could and should have been done. More should be done in future. But it is simply inaccurate to suggest that the aspiration towards greater equality has not been pursued, or that it has had no positive results.

The mostly widely accepted aggregate measure of the quality of life is the United Nations' Human Development Index (HDI) (UNDP 2022a). The HDI combines income per head, educational achievement and life expectancy. Between 1990 and 2021, South Africa's HDI increased from 0.627 to 0.713, an increase of 13.7 per cent. Income per head increased by 19.1 per cent over this period and average years of schooling increased by 4.9 years. Life expectancy increased only slightly over the whole period, but this outcome actually reflects a dramatic recovery from the HIV and AIDS pandemic, which began in 2005 (UNDP 2022b).

Some of the reasons for improvements are found by looking at South Africa's own more detailed statistics. For instance, in 1994, 62.2 per cent of South Africans had access to mains electricity, rising to 86 per cent in 2015. In 1994, 83.4 per cent of South Africans had access to clean drinking water. By 2015, this had risen to 93.2 per cent (Stats SA 2018: xxi). Immediately after 1994, South Africa's social grant system was de-racialised and it has been steadily expanded since and reached 30 per cent of all South Africans in 2019, rising to 41.3 per cent of the population following the introduction of the Social Relief of Distress grant in response to the Covid-19 pandemic. As it currently stands, the grant system reduces extreme poverty (poverty measured at the food poverty line) from 38.4 per cent to 36.3 per cent (Bhorat and Kohler 2021). To be clear, it is appalling and unacceptable that more than a third of South Africans are regularly at risk of hunger. But it is simply not the case that the South African authorities have made no progress in improving the living conditions of the majority of the country's citizens.

Some proponents of the idea that there has been no progress since 1994 are prone to suggest that there has been very little or no progress in transforming the economy. In one very important sense, this is absolutely correct. The economy worked well for only a small minority of the population in 1994 and continues to work well only for a minority – albeit a much larger minority, and with a significantly different and more equitable race and gender composition. However, the argument that there has been no progress in transformation is often made in a narrower sense, to suggest that there has been no significant change in management control of large private-sector firms. This narrower claim is only partially supported by the evidence. For instance, 86.8 per cent of junior managers, 67 per cent of middle managers, 42.6 per cent of top managers and 40 per cent of board directors of South Africa's private-sector banks were black in 2020 (Banking Association 2022). Again, it is essential to be clear: the composition of the private-sector managerial workforce will be neither truly equitable nor sustainable until it closely resembles the population of South Africa as a whole – 42.6 per cent of top managers and 40 per cent of board directors is not nearly enough. However, it is also not zero progress.

Looking back over the democratic era, then, it is certainly plausible to argue that successive South African governments have consistently placed a great deal of emphasis on expanding the social safety net and on promoting transformation in the private sector. The data suggests that these consistent policy efforts have met with considerable – but very far from complete – success.

It remains possible to argue, of course, that the South African economy would have performed better had the idea of equality been even more vigorously pursued. There is certainly some merit in this idea. Other things being equal, if South Africa's income had been more evenly distributed, it is very likely that aggregate demand would have been higher, the composition of this demand would have been more favourable for domestic production, and political uncertainty would have been reduced, which could have improved investor confidence. It would follow, therefore, that growth and job creation would have tended to be faster if income, assets and opportunities had been less unevenly distributed.

This consideration leads to the question of whether the South African economy should be moved away from its current social democratic Constitution and policy settings and towards socialism. This thought, in turn, leads to the next three questions posed by the editors of this volume.

Why is it that the bulk of the means of production is privately owned; why is it that the state seems unable to regulate market forces?

Taken together, these two questions, elegantly express the classical Marxist view of a market economy. Within this very important and distinguished intellectual tradition, the answer to the first of these questions is, of course, that private ownership of the means of production arose from the stage of the dialectic in which the bourgeoisie replaced the landed aristocracy as the ruling class, ushering in the period of capitalism. The answer to the second question follows immediately. Under capitalism, the classical Marxist argues, the state is in effect controlled by the bourgeoisie and therefore lacks both the will and the capacity to seek to mitigate the inherently exploitative outcomes of capitalism in general and of market exchange in particular.

No well-informed South African could deny the enormous contribution that the left made – and continues to make – to the liberation and human development of our country. Equally, no serious student of history or economics could deny that the socialist challenge to unfettered capitalism has led to very positive outcomes in many countries. Indeed, this chapter would argue, it is precisely the dialectic between liberal capitalism and classical socialism that has led to social democratic synthesis expressed in our Constitution and statistically associated with the highest levels of human development, in the Scandinavian countries and other mature social democracies.

Having acknowledged this, another set of facts should also be acknowledged. First, that classical Marxism is a nineteenth-century theory of political economy that has long since been overtaken by events and superseded by more accurate theories of the relationships between political power and economic outcomes (see, for example, Stedman Jones 2016).

Second, with the exception of large-scale network industries (such as roads, railways and electricity transmission), state ownership is, at best, less efficient that private ownership within a competitive market. Far more often, state ownership is not merely relatively inefficient, but actually severely dysfunctional. Global economic history is replete with evidence for this. China's transition away from state ownership of the means of production, accompanied by deep poverty, towards a mixed economy containing a great deal of private enterprise, accompanied by an extraordinarily rapid rise to prosperity, is only one example of a pattern so widespread that it approximates a universal law. Competitive and well-regulated markets just work better than either state ownership or a free market.

It is important to emphasise 'well-regulated' here. This chapter argues that Marxist thought is entirely correct to warn us against ineffective regulation and particularly against regulation in the interests of a narrow group, rather than of the society as a whole – precisely what South Africans would now refer to as 'state capture.' A compelling description of the social and economic damage done by these worst forms of regulation has recently been provided by the Zondo Commission (Judicial Commission 2022).

The case in favour of high-quality regulation is even more compelling. There is a clear statistical relationship between regulatory quality and economic development, with many studies demonstrating a strong link between transparent, consistent and efficiency regulation and faster growth (Parker and Kirkpatrick 2012). This statistical finding is supported and explained by the qualitative literature on economic development, which finds that both the early European and later Asian cases of sustained and rapid growth were accompanied by improvements in the capacity of the state to manage markets fairly, reliably and in the national interest (see, for example, two classic studies: North and Weingast 1989; Evans 1995).

South Africa's industrial structure also provides compelling evidence that the best economic outcomes arise from well-regulated markets containing robust competition between private firms. South Africa's most internationally competitive industries include finance, mining, automotive construction, tourism, business process outsourcing and private health care. The leading firms in each of these sectors are 'national champions' and among the most successful firms in their respective sectors in the world. Each of these sectors has benefited from equally world-class regulation by the South African state, either at crucial times during the formation of the sector, or to the present day, or both. The symbiosis between the private financial sector and its regulators has been particularly strong and consistent, and it is no coincidence that the South African Reserve Bank is widely recognised as one of the best-quality regulators in its area in the world.

To be specific, as a result of the symbiosis between the banking sector and its regulators, the sector's banks are frequently rated as among the most proficient and competitive in the world. To take one recent example, the South African banking industry is ranked second in the world, after Singapore, in terms of the digital services offered to customers (Calvey et al. 2021). The sector employs more than 155 000 people – and given the three-times employment multiplier of the sector – sustains a total of 620 000 jobs. The banks pay 30 per cent of all the corporate tax raised in South Africa (R63 billion in 2021); they lend and otherwise finance black-owned small and medium enterprises to the value of R34.5 billion; they extend home loans to the value of R1.7 trillion; and they spend around R600 million a year on corporate social investment (Banking Association 2022).

Observations such as these, incidentally, also tend to refute the premise underlying the question in this section. There is, unfortunately, no doubt that many elements of the South African state are weak and that some markets are woefully under-regulated. But other elements of the state continue to show that they are entirely capable of channelling the energies of the market towards sustainable and inclusive economic development.

What is the role of the private sector in job creation?

Answers to this question vary between 'no role whatsoever in a fully socialised economy' and 'some role on the fringes of the commanding heights of the economy, such heights being controlled by the working class through its vanguard party'. This chapter has argued that South Africa would be well advised not to become a socialist command economy, but should rather continue on its current path of being a social democratic mixed economy. On that assumption, the private sector should be – directly or indirectly – the primary source of job creation, as indeed it is at present. The public sector employs roughly 1.3 million people and has done so for more than a decade (National Treasury 2021: 64). The private sector employs roughly 14 times more people – 13.7 million people (Stats SA 2022: 2). Of course, this is not nearly enough – a topic to which this chapter will now turn, by way of conclusion.

Why is there deepening poverty, intergenerational unemployment and enduring inequality in spite of the rights and freedoms guaranteed in the Constitution?

As this chapter has shown, South Africa does not in fact continue to experience deepening poverty. However, it is correct that the country has been the most unequal major economy for at least a century and that aggregate inequality has shown no sign of improvement in the democratic era – although its racial and gender character has certainly changed. It is also, tragically, true that many young and middle-aged South Africans have never been able to find a formal-sector job, and that this has been the experience of their parents too. It is also, of course, true that South Africans do indeed enjoy the human and civil rights guaranteed by the Constitution.

A Marxist response can better explain why these challenges are experienced, in spite of the fact that each citizen enjoys basic rights and fundamental freedoms, an independent judiciary, free elections and a multiparty system. The 'bourgeois freedoms' enumerated are a smokescreen behind which the immiseration of the working class and colonialism of a special type continue. However, this chapter rejects such an analysis and offers a simple alternative. These freedoms are indeed necessary for inclusive and sustainable growth and human development in South Africa, but they are far from sufficient to secure it. What, then, would be sufficient?

Given the scale of South Africa's challenges, there is no single magic bullet or even a single list of imperatives to be followed. As global experience has shown, the task of development takes generations and requires the capacity to adapt over time. (For example, China has successfully escaped poverty following a carbon-intensive and export-oriented growth path. But its transition to sustainable high-income status is requiring significant changes to its policies.)

The best we can aim for, therefore, is a set of policies for the time being. These should include:

- Robust responses to the global trends of 'deglobalisation' and, possibly, a 'new cold war'. If poorly handled by the authorities, these could significantly slow South Africa's development. Conversely, a more regionalised world economy could create valuable opportunities to increase South Africa's industrial production, services output and trade.

- Making maximum use of South Africa's endowments of sunlight, wind and the platinum group of metals and rare earths needed to generate sustainable energy, which should be used to the maximum both in the domestic economy and for export.
- More – and more focused – investment in increasing South Africa's resilience to climate change. These investments should also aim to maximise labour absorption.
- Much lower tolerance for rent-seeking and rent-taking across society. This would include continued anti-corruption prosecutions and a competition policy focused more rigorously on lowering barriers to entry.
- Lower barriers to entry and more competition in the policy arena. We should, for instance, encourage more policy and delivery experimentation by municipalities and provinces.
- Continued policy reform to stimulate more private investment in hard infrastructure, particularly in energy and transport.
- Administrative and legal reform to improve socially and economically valuable institutions (soft infrastructure), such as property and company registration, the administration of trusts and estates and licensing systems.
- More support, within the existing black economic empowerment framework, for black industrialists and exporters, with a sharp focus on black-owned and -managed firms that directly produce physical goods for the local and international markets.
- A much greater focus on improving scientific and technical education and training.
- More interventions to improve the human capital of South Africa's post-school young people by way of training and job experience.

The National Treasury estimates that reforms of this kind would nearly double South Africa's annual growth from around 2 per cent on average to around 3.7 per cent per year, creating about 3.6 million jobs over the next decade (Republic of South Africa 2020: 37). This would be a great improvement but not, unfortunately, a dramatic or radical one.

The anti-colonial freedom fighter Amilcar Cabral famously wrote: 'Hide nothing from the masses of our people. Tell no lies. Expose lies whenever they are told. Mask no difficulties, mistakes, failures. Claim no easy victories' (Cabral 1969). No easy victories are possible for South Africa. Nevertheless, if we choose to remain guided by the values of the Constitution, and if we undertake the kinds of reforms listed above, we will be able to move slowly – but steadily and surely – towards more rapid growth and greater inclusion and, ultimately, to being a great African social democracy.

References

Banking Association of South Africa. 2022. *Transformation Report 2022*. https://www.banking.org.za/wp-content/uploads/2022/07/BASA-Transformation-Report-2022.pdf (accessed 2 October 2023).

Bhorat, H. and T. Kohler. 2021. 'Casting the Net Wider: How South Africa's COVID-19 Grant Has Reached the Once Forgotten'. *Econ3x3*, 25 August. https://www.econ3x3.org/sites/default/files/articles/Bhorat%2C%20H_SA%20COVID%20grant_Aug21%5B1%5D_0.pdf (accessed 2 October 2023).

Cabral, A. 1969. 'Extract from *Revolution in Guinea*'. https://www.marxists.org/subject/africa/cabral/1965/tnlcnev.htm (accessed 2 November 2023).

Calvey, P., P. Romagny, J. Stacey, K. Spangenberg and B. Plantier. 2021. 'Digitalization in Financial Services in South Africa: Is the Juice Worth the Squeeze?' *Oliver Wyman*, October. https://www.oliverwyman.com/za/our-expertise/insights/2021/oct/digitalization-in-financial-services-in-south-africa.html (accessed 2 October 2023).

EFF (Economic Freedom Fighters). 2022. 'About Us'. https://effonline.org/about-us/ (accessed 2 October 2023).

Evans, P. 1995. *Embedded Autonomy: States and Industrial Transformation*. Princeton: Princeton University Press.

Hirschman, A. 1973. 'The Changing Tolerance for Income Inequality in the Course of Economic Development: With a Mathematical Appendix'. *Quarterly Journal of Economics* 87 (4): 544–66.

Judicial Commission of Inquiry into State Capture. 2022. *Final Reports*. https://www.statecapture.org.za/site/information/reports (accessed 2 October 2023).

Kohli, A. 2004. *State-Directed Development: Political Power and Industrialization in the Global Periphery*. Cambridge: Cambridge University Press.

Mpofu-Walsh, S. 2021. *The New Apartheid*. Cape Town: Tafelberg.

Müller-Armack, A. 1978. 'The Social Market Economy as an Economic and Social Order'. *Review of Social Economy* 36 (3): 325–31.

National Treasury. 2021. *Medium Term Budget Policy Statement, Annexure B: Compensation Data*. https://www.treasury.gov.za/documents/mtbps/2021/mtbps/Annexure%20B.pdf (accessed 2 October 2023).

North, D.C. and B.R. Weingast. 1989. 'Constitutions and Commitment: The Evolution of Institutions Governing Public Choice in Seventeenth-Century England'. *Journal of Economic History* 49 (4): 803–32.

Parker, D. and C. Kirkpatrick. 2012. *Measuring Regulatory Performance: The Economic Impact of Regulatory Policy: A Literature Review of Quantitative Evidence*. OECD Expert Paper No. 3. https://www.oecd.org/gov/regulatory-policy/3_Kirkpatrick%20Parker%20web.pdf (accessed 2 October 2023).

Parliament of South Africa. 2021. *Report on Public Participation on the Eighteenth Constitution Amemdment Bill, Ad Hoc Committee to Initiate and Introduce Legislation Amending Section 25 of the Constitution*. https://www.parliament.gov.za/storage/app/media/1_Stock/Events_Institutional/2020/Constitution_18th_Amendment_Bill/Docs/ATC_57_2021_05_07_ENG.pdf (accessed 2 November 2023).

Republic of South Africa. 2020. *The South African Economic Reconstruction and Recovery Plan*. https://www.gov.za/sites/default/files/gcis_document/202010/south-african-economic-reconstruction-and-recovery-plan.pdf (accessed 2 October 2023).

SAIRR (South African Institute of Race Relations). 2021. 'Scrap BEE, Says New Initiative'. https://irr.org.za/media/scrap-bee-says-new-initiative (accessed 2 October 2023).

Stats SA (Statistics South Africa). 2018. *Overcoming Poverty and Inequality in South Africa: An Assessment of Drivers, Constraints and Opportunities*. https://www.statssa.gov.za/wp-content/themes/umkhanyakude/documents/South_Africa_Poverty_and_Inequality_Assessment_Report_2018.pdf (accessed 2 October 2023).

——. 2022. *Quarterly Employment Statistics March 2022*. https://www.statssa.gov.za/publications/P0277/P0277March2022.pdf (accessed 2 October 2023).

Stedman Jones, G. 2016. *Karl Marx: Greatness and Illusion*. Cambridge, MA: Harvard University Press.

UNDP (United Nations Development Programme). 2022a. *Human Development Report 2021–22: Uncertain Times, Unsettled Lives: Shaping Our Future in a Transforming World*. https://hdr.undp.org/content/human-development-report-2021-22 (accessed 2 November 2023).

——. 2022b. 'South Africa Briefing Note 2022'. https://hdr.undp.org/data-center/specific-country-data#/countries/ZAF-(accessed 2 November 2023).

Wade, R. 2003. *Governing the Market: Economic Theory and the Role of Government in East Asian Industrialization*. Princeton: Princeton University Press.

World Bank. 2012. *World Development Report 2012: Gender Equality and Development.* https://openknowledge.worldbank.org/entities/publication/51c285f6-0200-590c-97d3-95b937be3271 (accessed 2 October 2023).

Young, N. 2020. 'Why Ruth Bader Ginsburg was a fan of South Africa's Constitution.' *Quartz,* 3 September. https://qz.com/africa/1907952/why-ruth-bader-ginsburg-was-a-fan-of-south-africas-constitution (accessed 2 October 2023).

CHAPTER 12

The Case for Alternative Economic Approaches to Development and Human Well-Being in South Africa

Lebohang Liepollo Pheko

Background and key concepts

Although the idea of well-being is multifarious, there is literature that suggests three simultaneous perspectives of its conceptualisation: material (up to a certain point), subjective (life satisfaction and 'feeling good') and relational (culture, social relations and status, and sense of respect) (Mayson 2021).[1] Gross domestic product (GDP) growth has gained prominence as the dominant economic policy trajectory across most countries and this coincided with the consolidation of neo-liberalism during the 1980s (D'Alisa, Demaria and Kallis 2015). Simon Kuznets is often cited as the originator of GDP (particularly because of his attempts to estimate the national income of the United States in 1932 to gain better insights on the Great Depression). However, the popular definition of GDP was fostered by John Maynard Keynes during the Second World War. Kuznets critiqued its utility as the only form of economic accounting and as a commensurate indicator with progress (Coscieme et al. 2019; Hoekstra 2019; Pheko and Verma 2022). The concept of GDP gained further traction following the 1944 Bretton Woods conference, despite Kuznet's warnings against using GDP as a catch-all policymaking tool (Schmelzer 2015). Having been diffused globally over the last 25 years of inescapable globalisation in international economies, it has come to dominate other crucial policy imperatives such as social equality, mortality rates and healthy communities (D'Alisa, Demaria and Kallis 2015). Since the 1970s, average per capita incomes have dramatically expanded in the Global North and yet there is little evidence that there has been a corresponding rise in societal well-being – on the contrary, growing inequalities have given rise to deleterious impacts on well-being, as manifested in a across contexts and income groups (Kesebir 2016.)

Several studies extensively examine the effects of income disparity on growth. However, empirical evidence yields divergent conclusions. While several individuals propose that inequality has a detrimental effect on economic progress, others contend that it actually fosters and promotes growth. A recent study indicates a substantial correlation between inequality and GDP (Dabla-Norris et al. 2015). Based on an analysis of cross-country data from 159 advanced and emerging economies, the study reveals that a one percentage point increase in the Gini index is associated with a 0.07 percentage point decrease in the growth rate of GDP (Kakwani and Son 2015).

Although these rankings are often considered arbitrary, South Africa has been ranked as a middle-income country and has a per capita income equivalent to Thailand or Brazil, lower than that of Turkey or Mexico. Although, among middle-income countries, South Africa is deemed to be an outlier by some analysts, there are other factors that can be further examined.

The complex idea of South Africa as a liberated democracy is often discussed in conjunction with a strongly drafted Constitution, often called the 'best constitution in the world', and a robust framework of institutional checks and balances. Following the 1994 dispensation, both the quality of its judicial institutions and the efficacy of government functions have been evaluated as higher than those of its middle-income country peers.

While sourcing quality data can be a challenge, of the countries with credible statistics, South Africa is regularly cited as the most unequal country in the world (a slightly complex and problematic claim). The inequality index measures the broad distribution of wealth and income and in the racialised composition of that distribution.

The democratic transition propelled a political party with a political base and social programme utterly opposite to its white-settler-minority antecedent. Ostensibly, with a historical commitment to radically building a more socio-economically egalitarian society, the African National Congress (ANC) government has faced constant accusations of 'left talk, right walk' through many iterations of market-friendly economic policy frameworks. The South African scenario is indeed salient beyond middle-income countries and holds some insights for higher-income countries, particularly because even Global North institutions that are considered strongly stable have been undermined by political polarisation, social inequality and dissatisfaction among the polity. This was exemplified by the tumultuous events following United States election results in 2021.

South Africa's post-1994 political settlement aimed to transform the nature of engagement within the elite and presented a pathway to inclusivity for the dispossessed African underclass. Implicit in the negotiated agreement were promises to recalibrate political relations and the distribution of economic benefits between the elites (emerging and entrenched). This entailed negotiating the delicate landmines of political rivalries among emerging elites, particularly those ensconced within the ANC's broad church. Furthermore, it required building a consistent platform of economic and political stability, by formulating avenues for the upward mobility of the broader society beyond the 'usual suspects'. An integral part of the democracy compact was an undertaking to substantively address South Africa's legacy of intergenerational poverty, as encapsulated by the hackneyed refrain of 'a better life for all'.

South Africa's negotiated settlement was buttressed by a blend of ideation and institution building, the central tenet being a tacit agreement among key role-players to believe in the benefits of co-operation. It was hoped that this would enable South Africa to grow beyond competitive politicking in favour of win-win outcomes. Among the pillars of the settlement were the informal and formal institutions, which seemed to endow these aspirations for co-operation with credibility. Instead, what in fact became apparent was that the formidable challenge of addressing South Africa's extremely complex, racially skewed political economy deeply hindered its leaders from maintaining the worthy aspirations of socio-economic transformation, African-centred growth and confident inclusion. Indeed, failure to deliver on the redistributive and restorative liberation agenda – albeit diminished by negotiated compromises – also increased pressure on the country's institutions, diminishing economic performance and an ideational shift away from co-operation. This seems to suggest that pursuing a well-being economy, as opposed to a neo-liberal one, could offer South Africa greater shared dividends.

Despite all the challenges that South Africa has faced in translating its economic ambitions into implementable actions, there are possibly useful lessons to glean from this experience. The tumultuous period leading up to the 1994 elections was a visceral illustration of Africans' determination to resist ongoing colonial domination and, while the liberation project is not complete, the resistance to dehumanisation continues to manifest itself through various civic activities and protests. While it is arguable that the election of Cyril Ramaphosa as ANC president in December 2017, and subsequently as president of the Republic in February 2018, following Jacob Zuma's resignation, suggested that the broader population continues to focus on developing an intergenerational endowment of a transformational socio-economy, to date, the Ramaphosa presidency has been characterised by hyperbolic promises of growth, jobs and 'the new dawn'. While South Africa remains a key geopolitical player, the country's nearly 30 years of democracy have been marked by deep social fissures and unconsolidated promises while in pursuit of the market orthodoxy that GDP measures prescribe.

A test case called South Africa

It is useful to set out some heterodox, mainly post-Keynesian, macroeconomic policy ideas for further debate and research in the context of severe macroeconomic challenges in post-1994 South Africa. These have been characterised, for most of the last quarter of a century, by low growth, rising unemployment and increasing inequality, which have combined to dilute the stability of the post-1994 democratic project (Lephakga 2017). Unless South Africa creates a supportive and progressive macroeconomic framework, many other economic and social policy interventions for addressing growth, employment and inequality will likely fail to gain much traction for budgetary and related reasons (for more details, see Pheko and Verma 2022).

Lebohang Pheko and Ritu Verma note that despite economic growth being a strong pillar of the government's *National Development Plan 2030* (National Planning Commission 2012), real GDP per capita has declined and there have been several recessionary periods since adoption of the NDP (Pheko and Verma 2022). Even periods of higher growth have not propelled the achievement of the core goals of poverty reduction and employment within what the NDP refers to as the 'Cycle of Development' (National Planning Commission 2012: 16). For example, at the time of writing, youth unemployment is the highest in the world at 56 per cent and rising (Africa Check 2020). Inequalities also continue to rise, with South Africa having the highest income inequality in the world (Feketha 2018; Pheko and Verma 2022). In light of the findings on inequality and well-being mentioned above (Kesebir 2016), between 2017 and 2020, despite its relative affluence as a middle-income country, South Africa dropped 7 places to 108 of the 153 countries measured in the *World Happiness Report 2020* (SDSN 2020). Inequalities result in increased violence and fear, and reduced life expectancy (Pheko and Verma 2022).

The state's attempt to anchor the South African economy is captured by Vishnu Padayachee:

> The neo-liberal economic policies that the African National Congress–led government surprisingly adopted in 1996 in order to assuage global markets sceptical of its historical support for statist economic policy, have simply not worked. Appropriate progressive macroeconomic interventions are urgently needed to head off the looming prospect of a hollowed state. What happens in Africa's southern tip should still matter for progressives all around the world (2019: 3).

Ubuntu was part of the founding ideas of South Africa's Constitution (Tshoose 2009). Though often cited as an alternative philosophy or pathway out of neo-liberal constructions of economies and community well-being, it is not an index. Mogobe Ramose (2006), in interpreting Ubuntu, describes it as a community-based standpoint. He further argues that human individuality is a prerequisite for being a person, yet it is not adequate on its own. Unless an individual becomes a part of a specific community, they are seen as entities and do not completely meet the criteria of a 'person'. Personhood is a state that is an act of constant becoming. Therefore, Ramose contends that personhood is not bestowed upon someone by virtue of being born from human reproductive cells. Rather, the community plays a crucial function as a catalyst and in establishing standards during the extensive process of personal development.

While this is a worthy aspiration, in line with indigenous, emancipatory values, the reality is that many South Africans do not live out the precepts of the literal meaning of Ubuntu and, indeed, Ubuntu has been cynically appropriated by a variety of enterprises, whose mission sharply departs from any emancipatory vision (Dladla 2017).

The South African sociopolitical milieu

South Africa joined the BRICS group of countries (Brazil, Russia, India, China, and South Africa) in December 2010 as a result of the country's important role as a gateway to the remainder of the African continent, which holds significant economic value (Pheko and Verma 2022).[2] The establishment of BRICS is deeply rooted in a problematic, colonial, Western perspective, having been named and conceptualised by Jim O'Neill, a prominent economist at Goldman Sachs. However, it also embodies a burgeoning type of economic and international relations multilateralism in a world that is becoming more multi-polar, with numerous centres of power. Notably, this involves the establishment of the New Development Bank as a possible competitor to the dominance of the World Bank and International Monetary Fund (Suchodolski and Demeulemeester 2018). South Africa is a member of the Southern African Development Community (SADC), encompassing sixteen countries across southern Africa. Several of these nations have a compelling shared history as frontline states, which coalesced to resist settler apartheid colonialism in South Africa. However, some of the current political and economic stances of SADC frequently contradict its radical origins (Nathan 2012).

Twelve strategic priorities

In the post-1994 era, South Africa has actively embraced various economic ideas while maintaining a strong dedication to neo-liberal globalisation. The economic research institution Trade & Industrial Policy Strategies (TIPS), which provides extensive support to the government's efforts in industrial policy, inequality studies and sustainable growth, carried out the Beyond GDP project in 2012. The main focus was to determine if GDP and alternative metrics, such as real wealth or adjusted net savings, could serve as more effective indicators of the South African government's twelve strategic priorities:

1) enhanced primary education;
2) universal access to quality healthcare for all South Africans;

3) ensuring safety and security for all individuals in South Africa;

4) attaining satisfactory employment opportunities through a process of inclusive economic expansion;

5) a proficient and competent labour force to facilitate an all-encompassing trajectory of economic development;

6) an effective, competitive, and agile economic infrastructure network;

7) thriving, fair, and environmentally sustainable rural communities ensuring universal access to food;

8) establishing enduring human habitats and enhancing the standard of living inside households;

9) a municipal government system that is prompt, responsible, productive, and streamlined;

10) consistently safeguarded and improved environmental assets and natural resources;

11) foster the development of a more prosperous South Africa and actively contribute to the improvement and security of Africa and the world; and

12) an optimal and productive development-oriented public service that is in harmony with an empowered, equitable, and all-encompassing citizenship (Department of Planning, Monitoring and Evaluation 2010: 13; Pheko and Verma 2022).

Several of these priorities are clumsily formulated, but they do indicate the government's consistent policy goals of promoting social harmony and improving the equitable allocation of resources and wealth (Khambule and Siswana 2017). The TIPS project evaluated the South African government's performance in sustainable development, while also providing substantiating evidence for policies. The twelve strategic priorities were additional provisions to the *Medium Term Strategic Framework (MTSF) 2014–2019* (Republic of South Africa 2014). Despite the recent publication of a revised and overhauled system of national accounts by Statistics South Africa (Stats SA), there appears to be a lack of follow-up research of similar magnitude. This revised system incorporates modifications to the inputs of economic activity, specifically alterations to the composition of the supply and demand sides of economic activity. Stats SA maintains steadfast in upholding GDP indices as the primary measure of economic growth, despite the shortcomings exposed by the Covid-19 pandemic and recently recalibrated the GDP as the principal indicator of economic expansion.

Meanwhile the *Revised Medium Term Strategic Framework (MTSF) 2019–2024* has reframed the strategic priorities to include:

1) building a capable, ethical developmental state [including improving financial management capability];

2) economic transformation and job creation [including creating 275 000 jobs per year and 200 000 small business by 2024];

3) education skills, education and health [including improving childhood disease for under-fives, increased teacher recruitment and training, HIV health and anti-retroviral roll-out management];

4) consolidating the social wage through reliable and quality basic services [such as community-based personal assistance, food and nutrition security];

5) spatial integration, human settlements and local government [including increased land cultivation in rural areas, implementation of green gas reduction measures];

6) social cohesion and safe communities [promote constitutional values, reduction in violence against women and children, promotion of access to community facilities]; and

7) a better Africa and world [measured by increased foreign direct investment, regional integration and trade and increased international travel into South Africa] (Department of Planning, Monitoring and Evaluation 2019: 24–40).

Stats SA has implemented a technique to improve the evaluation of poverty in South Africa and to align with the growing global trend of assessing poverty beyond the traditional monetary-based approach (Stats SA 2014). The measure was designed to supplement the current monetary indicators in the country, including the food poverty line, the lower-bound poverty line and the upper-bound poverty line (Pheko and Verma 2022).

Stats SA published the South African Multidimensional Poverty Index (SAMPI) in early 2014. It incorporates a fourth dimension – economic activity – alongside the three dimensions of education, living standards and health, as measured by the Global Multidimensional Poverty Index. Unemployment is used as the indicator for economic activity (OPHI and UNDP HDRO 2021). The multidimensional approach includes poverty measures made up of several components that capture indigent people's experiences of deprivation. These factors include education, housing, energy, safety, unemployment, health and access to credit (Finn, Leibbrandt and Woolard 2013; Finn, Leibbrandt and Oosthuizen 2014). The Alkire-Foster technique was utilised, with modifications to account for the specific circumstances of youth unemployment in South Africa. The purpose of SAMPI is to enhance the current monetary indicators used in South Africa. The government has consistently demonstrated a commitment to the 'social wage', maintaining public service expenditure even during times of crisis, such as the aftermath of the 2008 economic crisis and the ongoing Covid-19 pandemic (OPHI and UNDP HDRO 2021). The South African government allocated 10 per cent of the nation's GDP to combat the consequences of the epidemic and to fulfil its current and potential future obligations. Although these are laudable efforts deserving of some commendation, it is important to acknowledge that Covid-19 presents new and additional challenges. This should further strengthen our determination to uphold the government's pledge to a national social wage (OPHI and UNDP HDRO 2021; Pheko and Verma 2022).

What exactly is the 'economy'?

By using the concept of diverse economies as a starting point, it becomes evident that economies are not merely an intangible entity dominated by market-oriented neo-liberalism. Essentially, alternative and well-being economics questions the idea that development and efficiency always lead to positive social results, as well as the dominance of economic rationality over other social domains and goals. Well-being economics advocates not only for reducing material consumption, but also for a deliberate and democratic restructuring of the economy. Economies are complex structures that encompass and are shaped by various social relationships at different levels (Zademach and Hillebrand 2013: 13). The Community Economies Collective is an example of a formation grounded in the economic geography method, which distils multiple economies at local scales that are globally interrelated. The economy is described as including all the aspects that enable us to sustain ourselves and take care of one another and the environment (Pheko and Verma 2022).

Democratic restructuring of the economy would entail changing the fundamental principles and priorities that guide economic relations, such as emphasising care, solidarity, justice and conviviality (Akbulut 2021). The goal is to create a completely new and qualitatively different world, which would emerge through a process of challenging and confronting the current system. The well-being economics community has made attempts to interact with other perspectives that challenge the concept of growth. This involves placing degrowth within a broader framework of ideologies that share the notion of sustainable living within ecological limits.

Limitations of GDP growth over government policy

Globalisation is arguably a camouflage for 'part of a discourse of neo-imperialism that serves to obscure the continuing exploitation of much of the world by a few superpowers and giant transnational corporations, thus cloaking some of the more barbaric and destructive aspects of contemporary development' (D'Alisa, Demaria and Kallis 2015: 25). A central plank by which this domination has been buttressed includes the GDP-aligned, market-driven policies that are routinely imposed on the Global South by the Northern-dominated International Monetary Fund (IMF), the World Bank and other international financial institutions. The glaring disparity of power, voice and influence sustained by globalisation has resulted in social dislocation across many African countries, including South Africa, as well as other nations in the Global South, and has further diminished the economic conditions of the most economically precarious, including women. While several African countries formally introduced structural adjustment programmes in 1986, many had already subscribed to capitalist or neo-liberal economic policies. These national development plans, and the previous frameworks that were antecedents to structural adjustment programmes, prioritised market and private initiatives. These policy choices were often made at the cost of much-needed social infrastructure developments (Pheko and Verma 2022).

By the time the structural adjustment programme was introduced, many African economies were ailing and neo-liberal economists sold structural adjustment programmes as 'national economic stabilisation and recovery through the simultaneous liberalisation of the market and the retrenchment of the state' (Olukoshi and Laakso 1996: 80). South Africa's ill-advised entry into the architecture of globalised economic relations is instructive, particularly given the history and experience of several other African countries.

Through the 1980s and into the pre-election 1990s in South Africa, the Economic Trends Group, the Macro-Economic Research Group (MERG), the World Bank and the IMF were already converging around the macroeconomic policies that would govern post-1994 South Africa. Underlying the MERG was the notion of a 'post-Keynesian' economic policy, which was concerned with building state infrastructure and, eventually, evolved into examining private investments to enable sustainable economic growth (Peet 2002: 70). Inexplicably, the original MERG document submitted to the ANC in 1993, pertaining to South Africa's transitional and democratic economic policies, was not implemented by the ANC. Sagie Narsiah (2002) argues that this signified the first defeat of a valiant effort of the faction within the ANC that advocated growth through redistribution. The seismic shift from leftist, socially inclusive Marxist policies to market orthodoxy illustrates the considerable impact that the global neo-liberal mandarins had on South Africa's early transition. The pursuit of often-elusive GDP growth policies has largely failed to attend to the deeply seated socio-economic inequality in South Africa. Indeed, many of these approaches are seemingly exacerbating existing economic dispossession across contemporary South African society.

The challenges of GDP, the natural environment and growth

Increasingly, various literature lays responsibility on the GDP for the diminishing natural environment globally and gaping local and global inequalities (Escobar 2015; Fioramonti 2020). A country like South Africa is experiencing multiple layers of social dispossession, racially skewed access to land and wealth and manifest forms of inequality. An increasingly chronic manifestation of these inequalities is the flooding across South Africa and extending to Zimbabwe and Mozambique. Between 11 and 12 April 2022, approximately one year's worth of rain descended on the eastern coast of South Africa, resulting in one of the most devastating natural disasters to hit the country in the twenty-first century so far. The rain caused more than US$1.57 billion in infrastructural wreckage.

There is a persuasive view that it is impossible to delink economic growth from environmental damage, particularly as technology is viewed as intrinsic to this toxic growth model. Economic history suggests a different view on this

(Fletcher and Rammelt 2017; Jackson 2016). The often-cited claims of decoupling normally omit the resource exploitation and emissions that are 'embedded' in imports, in extractive enterprises and in largely Northern-driven purveyors of the extraction. Indeed, the substantial transfer of the Global North's toxic ecological impact to the Global South in recent decades is producing a dangerously false impression of 'shared climate culpability' (D'Alisa, Demaria and Kallis 2015; Jackson 2016). Characterising the climate 'bursts' that are the consequence of centuries of crude extractivism and are accelerated by many states' disinvestment in affordable public transport is problematic. Foreign direct 'investment', which often has little regard for environmentally ethical protocols and the huge industry in transporting goods and services in this globalised world is part of creating this deep inequity and to ignore this is deeply disingenuous.

Many emerging proposals have that have suggested that 'green growth' has not been successful at decoupling. Proponents of this view argue that this is the result of increased efficiency arising from technological change that does not result in a reduced rate of consumption (D'Alisa, Demaria and Kallis 2015). The logic does not hold very well, given the correlation between climate degradation, extractive capitalism and the deep violation of ecological and social boundaries by Northern multinationals in countries like South Africa. Long before the inception of neo-liberalism as an entrenched ideology, capitalist economies disseminated the notion that people who were violently and inequitably impacted by structural impacts of an exploitative system, including unemployment, ill-health, truncated life outcomes, endemic poverty – in other words, a lack of well-being – were somehow personally deficient and responsible for their situation.

While Kuznets cautioned that GDP should not be utilised as a measure of social welfare, the presumed correlation between income and 'progress' or well-being still wields considerable influence over economic policy across nations (Fioramonti 2020). However, Tim Jackson (2016) posits that more than half a century of research has debunked this idea. Leading economic thinkers such as Amartya Sen and Joseph Stiglitz have asserted that enhanced quality of life is not inherent to GDP growth (Stiglitz, Sen and Fitoussi 2009). South Africa's failed trickle-down policy, advocated by ex-President Thabo Mbeki, is one example of this (Smith 2017).

Globally, many Global South countries like Cuba, Ethiopia and Costa Rica have shown far better 'objective' quality of life indices and life expectancy, where the 'developed' United States is not as successful. A twenty-year longitudinal study carried out by the International Journal of Health Equity illustrates that in the period between 1997 and 2018, the life expectancy for Ethiopia and Brazil increased by three years and two years respectively. In the same period, the life expectancy in the United States decreased by 2.9 years, even though the GDP per capita in Ethiopia was US$2 153 and US14 941 in Brazil, compared to US$62 840 in the United States (Freeman et al. 2020).

Pheko and Verma's 2022 paper argues how the 'Easterlin Paradox' illustrates that subjective indicators like life satisfaction do not translate to economic growth, particularly for nations in the Global North (Cummins, Lau and Davern 2012). Although real income per capita in the United States has tripled since the 1970s, various indices indicate a significant decrease in well-being during the same period (Jackson 2016; Van den Bergh 2011). Countries in the Global South have exhibited comparable paradoxes. A research study conducted on eighteen Latin American countries and published in the *Harvard Business Review* revealed a negative association between economic growth and subjective well-being (Kesebir 2016; Pheko and Verma 2022). The tenuous association between well-being and financial wealth can be succinctly expressed as the aphorism 'money doesn't buy happiness' (Pheko and Verma 2022). Or, perhaps more realistically, money may indeed purchase happiness, but the amount it can buy is often so insignificant that it becomes inconsequential (Boyce et al. 2017). Research on well-being has shown that at the microeconomic level, people's well-being increases in proportion to their financial resources, but this improvement is only temporary (Diener, Lucas and Scollon 2006). This phenomenon is partially responsible for the concept known as the 'hedonic treadmill' (Barrington-Leigh 2016), which refers to the tendency of individuals to revert back to a baseline level of happiness that surpasses the influence of material possessions. As a result, people are driven to continuously strive for higher and often unattainable levels of material 'success' (Pheko and Verma 2022).

Linking well-being with inequality

Even within the group of strongest neo-liberal economists, there is concern about increasing wealth disparities globally (Avent 2020). The Covid-19 pandemic has only aggravated this, rescinding important advances made in the last twenty years.

In 2022, the richest ten individuals on the planet had a twofold increase in their fortune, while 99 per cent of the global population has suffered material, financial or bodily depletion due to the impact of Covid-19 (Pheko and Verma 2022). The epidemic had a disproportionate impact on Black women and individuals in the Global South, exacerbating existing structural inequalities. There is a general consensus that inequality has a detrimental impact on well-being, as evidenced by several indices (Kakwani and Son 2015).

Scandinavian countries like Norway and Denmark, recognised for comparatively low levels of income inequality, consistently attain top positions in the World Happiness Report (SDSN 2020). Conversely, the United Kingdom and the United States, characterised by more pronounced discrepancies in socio-economic parity, exhibit lower outcomes and significant discrepancies in the well-being of their various demographics, influenced by variables such as race, income and gender (SDSN 2020). The disparity in quality of life between Sandton and Alexandra in Gauteng is often cited as a template of deep structural inequality, despite their geographic proximity. This illustrates the considerable variations that can exist within a single metropolis. There exists a correlation between wealth discrepancy and unequal access to adequate health care, food and material comforts (Pheko and Verma 2022).

Popular literature categorises inequality into three main forms: vital inequality, which encompasses health and death; existential inequality, which applies to freedom of choice and action; and material inequality, which relates to the distribution of resources (Pheko and Verma 2022). The definition of poverty is subjective and cannot be standardised due to its diverse indicators. The issue encompasses more than just money and limited purchasing power, and also involves ideological and political consequences, which are partly shaped by people's viewpoints. Hence, apart from this overarching assertion, poverty can be examined by several lenses, such as geographical, urban/rural and marginalised groups and minorities (Pheko 2010). According to Richard Wilkinson and Kate Pickett (2009), inequality is a multifaceted societal problem that entails various adverse outcomes, such as anxiety, bullying, violent crime and restricted career prospects. Nevertheless, it is crucial to acknowledge that these viewpoints primarily represent the encounters of industrialised nations, rather than taking into account the worldwide situation. The notions of justice, equality and fairness within liberal frameworks are inherently intertwined with the historical contexts of imperial power, economic and distributive systems shaped by colonialism, racism and gender-based discrimination in those interactions, and other related aspects (Pheko and Verma 2022).

Stratification economics posits that heightened income disparity leads to amplified perceptions of status discrepancies. This indicates that acts of violence, such as crimes, are frequently motivated by the desire to get social status and society recognition. This is particularly true for younger individuals who are often unable to achieve status in other ways. When studying the underlying causes of differences between different groups, economists who specialise in stratification analyse both the environmental and structural variables that contribute to these disparities. They also investigate how these factors negatively impact on the outcomes for marginalised and disadvantaged groups. Stratification economics does not directly evaluate the disparities based on a community's dysfunctional group and the relatively unfavourable results. Stratification economists do not provide explanations for group-related variables in life outcomes that imply genetic, regional or cultural distinctions between groups. Evaluating disparities in race, gender and income across several aspects such as health, family connections, wealth, education and social resources is highly challenging when relying on limited or region-specific definitions of well-being (Pheko 2021).

Sen (1998) argues that the fundamental physiological requirements for optimal physical health are universally consistent across regions and nations. However, there may be disparities in the economic status of individuals within a given context. In order to attain a life free from shame and characterised by dignity, and to sustain robust relationships with friends and family, it is imperative to allocate funds towards material things. A compelling illustration implies that it is comparable to the scenario when every person in a crowd is standing on their tiptoes, yet no one is able to gain a more favourable vantage point. Certain individuals can only attain improved perspective when standing on their tiptoes, whereas others do the same just to maintain their current position (Jackson, Jager and Stagl 2004).

Are there alternatives to learn from?

Situating South Africa within the construct of social stratification and linking this to well-being economics is a more useful measure of this country's complex and skewed economic realities. The pool of South Africans that could be considered as an established middle or upper class is still small and when accounting for African families, it is even smaller. The pool is significantly smaller than the 30–55 per cent range suggested by some research (Burger et al. 2015; Visagie and Posel 2013). Additionally, forms of poverty prevalent in South Africa suggest enormous and genuine dependence on state support. Indeed, the forms and experiences of South African poverty, even when considered apart from other household features and resources, strongly indicate continued, intergenerational deprivation. Precarious and casual work do not mitigate poverty risks and when the key breadwinner has a higher level of education and access to more steady labour, these play an essential role in attaining economic stability in South Africa. Finally, the temporarily indigent and the constantly precarious are characterised by relatively high instability and a constant movement in and out of poverty. While these two strata are relatively similar, they are also distinct from both the chronically indigent and the established or stable middle class. This is manifest not only in their household attributes, but also profoundly shapes their specific policy requirements.

To many, the well-being economy praxis is more descriptive of what social policy framing should be (Lakoff 2010). In South Africa's case, it could potentially invite a deeper engagement with the structural foundations that uphold the assumptions that financial profits should be the primary drivers of economics. Furthermore, this presents a range of social actors with the opportunity to explore alternatives, rather than those mandated by government policy and the tax system, for example. South Africa is a country where the majority do not have access to basic needs or the financial resources to utilise them.

Can we un-grow to grow forward?

Degrowth as an idea was named by radical French eco-socialists in the early 2000s as a reaction to unfettered market economic policies under the influence of Reaganomics (deep cuts in social expenditure, tax reductions) and Thatcherism (free market and withdrawal of state intervention), both of which were factors in globalisation. Another central anchor of globalisation is the well-documented Washington Consensus framework, which encompasses trade and financial liberalisation, privatisation, deregulation, property rights, foreign direct investment, tax reforms, competitive exchange rates, positive real interest rates, public expenditure reprioritisation and fiscal discipline. These economic policies have impacted on countries in both the Global North and South. While it is arguable that the Washington Consensus has withered away, its inscription is visible across global economics and national policies, with the same uneven power play tangibly manifested, through shrinking public investment, while accelerating globalisation further consigns millions to precarity.

Prevailing economic orthodoxy uncritically insists that ongoing growth is feasible, sustainable and advantageous, without assessing the cost and character of that growth. Well-being and degrowth suggest that a shift in economic orientation is required. As far back as the 1970s, Richard Easterlin (1974) suggested that growing societal wealth did not necessarily translate into greater well-being for the broader populace and that GDP did not necessarily grow concurrently with societal health. Serge Latouche (2014), a leading degrowth advocate, similarly suggests that degrowth needs to shift away from the hollow GDP growth numbers game to a more encompassing view of physical and social health, environmental health and societal happiness. Latouche infers that degrowth is a new way of life and social relationality beyond economics. In relation to the South African context, as we assess the efficacy of pursuing the growth model that so far seems to elude us, perhaps this is an ideal opportunity to rethink the utility of growth and consider how to grow a healthier, more socially coherent society.

However, while degrowth may be available and attractive to elites both locally and globally, the idea itself is arguably ahistorical and does not account for the differentiated levels of growth across the world. While rightly positing that the overindulgences of globalised capitalism have become unsustainable, very little is said about the toxic and extractive origins of Western capitalism and its ongoing impact on the Global South, particularly across African, Asian, Caribbean and Latin American countries. It is not a choice available to those impoverished by the same system. There has been conscious overproduction of commodities, systemic and destructive extraction of natural resources and the 'fierce accumulation by dispossession which are symptoms of a system that is desperate to stave off the declining rate of profit. It doesn't make sense then to treat only the symptoms (degrowth) without addressing the underlying causes (capital accumulation)' (Manji 2015: 2).

Conversations on degrowth have gained immense traction as observers debate the failed Washington Consensus policies and the resulting global impact. These include non-trickle-down economics that have produced a glut of billionaires, who now hold more wealth than 4.6 billion people (Coffey et al. 2020). This is against the backdrop of massive parts of the global population who are in structural poverty or precarity and communities that are frequently situated within or adjacent to disintegrating ecosystems. Not surprisingly, thought leaders have also started calling for degrowth in South Africa and have been attracted to it, with its more explicit 'beyond GDP' critique. It is not surprising that there is some interest in exploring alternative economics in South Africa, including degrowth.

It is arguable that the real issue is neither growth nor degrowth, but rather the form of growth. The GDP matrices measure or mismeasure the things that are important and that add value to society in ways that may not immediately be quantifiable. Indeed, some posit that GDP growth is an indication of the enrichment of a minority while enlarging the destitution and impoverishment of the majority.

For most of the last 28 years in South Africa, we have seen structural inequality and intergenerational unemployment, which have contributed to elongating the socio-economic deficits of the post-1994 ideation (Lephakga 2017). South Africa has developed an architecture of progressive macroeconomic frameworks to deal with the socio-economic fissures, but has not succeeded in addressing these issues.

Buen Vivir and gross national happiness

Various African intellectuals and analysts, including some from South Africa, have suggested that reducing carbon emissions, improving cost-effective and functional educational infrastructure, optimising green spaces for enhanced and equitable community health, and enhancing the design of public health and hospital facilities would significantly improve the quality of life for South Africans. This is especially important in a country where the majority of the African population lacks access to public services and live with little human dignity.

Ritu Verma and Karma Ura (2022) argue that GDP alternatives from the Global South vary in their explicit conceptual location in decolonial or anti-racist theory.

Gross national happiness (GNH) promulgated by His Majesty Jigme Singye Wangchuck, the Fourth King of Bhutan, in the early 1970s, includes innovative indicators such as time use, psychological well-being, community vitality and culture, along with more conventional indicators such as education, health, living standards, governance and environment, which allow for the engagement and analysis of gender in development domains.

Verma and Ura (2022) further contend that Buen Vivir emerged from decolonial movements and foundations and, as described by Juan Francisco Salazar (2015), it derives from the Spanish term for 'good living' or 'living well'. Western concepts of welfare and well-being are fundamentally different and cannot be seen as similar. Buen Vivir focuses on the holistic well-being of individuals, considering their social context within the community and their specific environmental circumstances (Balch 2013).

Both GNH and Buen Vivir have a fundamental characteristic: they are indigenous moral principles that have been derived from ancient indigenous histories and transmitted orally over generations. In some scholarship, these concepts are clearly decolonial as they originated from social movements. Buen Vivir emerged from indigenous rights social movements in the 2000s, while Ubuntu represents a marginalised knowledge system embedded in the realities of African people. In addition, Wim van Binsbergen argues that while Ubuntu adopts a globalised form in academic contexts, it primarily originates from the experiences of suffering, exclusion, justified rage, and the fight to restore dignity and identity in response to the domination and oppression by Northern powers (2001: 79). Bhutan's pioneering GNH concept was innovated from a society that was historically secluded from global influences and largely devoid of the colonial legacies that burdened other nations (Verma and Ura 2022).

Alternative frameworks to measure economic activity, other than GDP, should be considered, especially in nations with a colonial history that has influenced their economic development. A notable instance has been recorded from Aotearoa, New Zealand: Ngā Tūtohu Aotearoa, which skillfully incorporates Maori cultural concepts.[3] Although these alternative indexes do not expressly oppose racism, they do have components that can be utilised by anti-racist movements. The decolonial aspects present in their ideology can also be utilised to combat racial discrimination (Pheko and Verma 2022).

Bhutan's GNH index exemplifies the recognition of well-being as a complex concept, considering various dimensions beyond just GDP. It emphasises the importance of factors like social cohesion, life satisfaction and optimism for the future (Metz, Hirata and Verma 2015). Certain indices communicate the concept of 'sufficiency' or 'adequacy' (Ura, Alkire and Zangmo 2012; Engels 2022). One of the most important components of this measurement is that it does not allow anybody to exceed the limits of 'sufficient' in relation to broader material attainment, especially if this does not contribute to the enhancement of GNH. One of the benefits of this system is that it allows state funds to be distributed and disbursed at the local level through highly collaborative formations and savings organisations. The objective is to mitigate economic disruptions and foster self-sufficiency among economically marginalised groups. This is based on the notion that well-being is an integral part of forming relationships and communities, which is a fundamental aspect of African knowledge systems and ways of life. This deeply resembles community economics, which is a practical application of diverse economies (Pheko and Verma 2022).

Centring diverse and feminist economics

Extensive literature on diverse economies has improved the concept of an 'alternative' economy by proposing that the portrayal and implementation of economic diversity should not circulate around capitalism. This means that economic diversity should not be judged or considered eccentric or unconventional in relation to the dominant economic system (Gibson-Graham 2016). Essential to this is the need to prioritise feminist economics and imaginations in the development of alternative and inclusive well-being economies. This necessitates a reconsideration of how to redefine alternative realities and various methods to undermine dominant institutions.

The convergence of a well-being economy and a feminist economy should be established based on the principles of human well-being and equitable distribution of resources and opportunities. The fields of well-being economics and feminist economics converge with social economics, as they all prioritise both the action being performed and the individual carrying out the action. The concept of global common good is underpinned by the interconnectedness and relationality among families, communities, regions and nation states, which are fostered by social cohesion and solidarity. This social relationality serves as the foundation to coalesce feminist and well-being economics.

Sen's influential work has demonstrated that 100 million women are completely obscured and unacknowledged for their labour contributions. This crucial insight emerged after Sen's revaluation of the criteria and concepts surrounding activities, labour and remunerative labour (Croll 2001).

Although women's involvement and presence in politics should prompt us to consider alternate possibilities, policy discussions in the West tend to concentrate on development issues. Both well-being and feminist economies are characterised by their descriptive nature, rather than strict definitions. For instance, they prioritise discussing poverty as a deficiency in human connection, rather than simply defining it as living on an income below a specific monetary threshold, which is highly influenced by contextual factors, including regionalism and one's social, economic and geographic circumstances (Kachingwe 2018). By adopting this approach, we can articulate the connection between poverty and emotions, such as the sensation of humiliation resulting from the lack of access to resources like the market or land, or the feeling of being constrained by restricted options or job prospects, ultimately leading to a sense of being stuck in our current circumstances.

Similarly, abundance or well-being can be characterised by factors such as having a family, being part of a faith group, having a robust social network, or possessing a sense of purpose or clarity. A feminist approach to the economy aims to overhaul power dynamics that perpetuate oppression, including those related to gender, ecology, race and ability. Feminist economics prioritise the care of all living forms and critically examine the gendered and colonial underpinnings of the current economic system. Their aim is to bring about systemic change by altering material conditions, as well as power dynamics and social structures (Kachingwe 2018).

Observations on market orthodoxy and well-being in South African policymaking

There are several observations that this chapter makes on various forms of economics. The one is that there are fundamental proposals about how we might reframe economics and move it towards a clearer focus on human well-being. This view further suggests that state intervention can be utilised only where there is insufficient social distribution, even if these are not Keynesian policies. The approach suggests that trickle-down economics – the neo-liberal economics that deify markets – are not a viable option for a country that is already dealing with ongoing manifestations of visceral, race-based economic violence. The vagaries of market allocation are not the appropriate instruments to address ongoing structural inequalities, particularly because these were initiated and institutionalised with intent and require similar intent to dismantle their impact.

The level of accumulation and economics in South Africa is profoundly influenced by intensive agricultural processes and fossil fuels. The agricultural sector is still deeply dependent on pesticides, chemical fertilisers (rather than natural forms of compost) and water-based irrigation (in a water-scarce country). A shortcoming of trickle-down and accumulation logic is that wealth is largely siphoned to a rarefied, still largely racialised minority and a small African elite, leaving structural and intergenerational poverty largely unchallenged. The extent to which the economic status quo is challenged is illustrated by the wealth retention of the three richest billionaires in Africa. An Oxfam report (Lawson et al. 2019) places the collective of the wealth of Africa's three wealthiest people (Aliko Dangote, US14.1 billion; Nicky Oppenheimer, US$7.7 billion; and Johann Rupert, US$7) at a staggering US$28.8 billion. Two of those magnates are South African, the beneficiaries of intergenerational settler capitalist wealth (Seery, Okanda and Lawson 2019).

Furthermore, there are calls for more effective distribution of the commons, including electricity, parks and public recreational utilities, water and state transport. A central component of this distribution is community management of these resources and more integrated cities and spaces. In South Africa, it is estimated that 60 per cent of people are living in urban areas, drawn largely by economic opportunities. While well-managed cities can potentially increase social integration, integrative lifestyles and economic expansion, in a country like South Africa, they often reproduce apartheid-style race and class exclusion, social binaries, economic precarity and unsafe spaces for commuters and residents. Ideally, well-integrated work, home, educational and recreational spaces should result in more family time and leisure and far less time and expense on commuting. A 2020 survey shows that average travel time in Gauteng increased by 17 per cent from 46 minutes in 2014 to 57 minutes in 2019/20. Average travel time between

2002 and 2020 almost doubled (Gauteng Department for Roads and Transport and CSIR 2020: 86).

The government's integrated spatial planning framework should concentrate efforts on land reform, including the fast-tracked transfer of plots to a much greater number of recipients. Substantive and productive landownership and the economic citizenship of the most indigent and of the working poor is essential, particularly in the countryside where there are very limited or even desirable job opportunities. In a country where inflation targeting has had no tangible impact on wage distribution, and the repo rate has no direct correlation to household savings, there is evidence that the interest rate approach redistributes wealth in ways that favour the wealthiest decile, rather than supporting the most indigent and dispossessed.

Conclusion

There are several arguments that market orthodox economics could be instigated to retract state intervention by utilising free market methods to redistribute wealth and integrate society (Williamson 2017). Other suggestions say that neo-liberal policies inhibit or combat racism through greater market competition that potentially results in social and economic progress and limited state intervention (Williamson 2017). This view of structural racism and the toxic violence of white supremacy and coloniality is dangerously naive and denialist. This view also suggests that post-1994 South Africa can exercise the forms of neo-liberalism that constrain state capacity and restrict social movements and state-sponsored interest groups.

Covid-19 has exposed many limitations of capitalism and presents the opportunity to re-examine language and assumptions about how power, privilege and distribution work. This includes the assets and distribution between the Global North and the Global South, a deeply racialised economic distribution, which results in raindrops of wealth (as in the trickle-down theory). The profound coloniality in trade and economic structures, including the notion of primitive accumulation, has presented deep dilemmas for South Africa. This is an important opportunity to rethink global economic architecture, to rethink well-being economics and pluriversal schools of thought. This might require a post-colonial perspective on how economies like South Africa ought to be oriented towards a black African feminist construction.

One of the primary assertions of this chapter is not that we need more indicators. GDP is formulaic and also ignores the political nature of resources and how those are shared within and between nations and communities. Profoundly extractive economies, exemplified by South Africa, have experienced history in particular ways. GDP indices do not take into account the social cost of social reproduction or where they are situated in the context of social sustainability. These treat black women's labour, in particular, as an endless gift to orthodox, extractive economic forms. A fundamental shortcoming of GDP is the narrow focus on people's financial and material wealth. Qualitative indicators, such as loss of culture, a sense of despair, a dread of going to work, the decimation of animal and plant species, a loss of time and creativity, lacking a feeling of joy or satisfaction, or a sense of feeling rested, all deplete the oxygen of our existence. None of these are measured by GDP.

This all suggests that each person in South Africa must be afforded the opportunity of redistributive economics in order to build and anchor themselves in self-determined lives that move towards a posterity of well-being well beyond GDP and its insufficiencies.

Notes

1. This chapter was developed from my doctoral work in Politics at the University of Johannesburg (SARChI Chair: African Diplomacy and Foreign Policy). It also partly draws from extensive research conducted by Dr Ritu Verma and myself across six countries. The original research is as yet unpublished. South Africa is one of the six countries we investigated.
2. In August 2023, six countries (Argentina, Egypt, Ethiopia, Iran, Saudi Arabia and the United Arab Emirates) were invited to join BRICS. Full membership will take effect on 1 January 2024.
3. https://statisticsnz.shinyapps.io/wellbeingindicators/ (accessed 5 December 2023).

References

Africa Check. 2020. "Fact Check: Does SA Have the World's "Worst Levels" of Youth Unemployment?' *Eyewitness News*, 12 November. https://ewn.co.za/2020/11/12/fact-check-does-south-africa-have-the-world-s-worst-levels-of-youth-unemployment (accessed 5 December 2023).

Akbulut, B. 2021. 'Degrowth'. *Rethinking Marxism*, 33 (1): 98–110.

Avent, R. 2020. 'Covid-19 Leaves a Legacy of Increased Inequality'. *The Economist*, 17 November. https://www.economist.com/the-world-ahead/2020/11/17/covid-19-leaves-a-legacy-of-increased-inequality (accessed 5 December 2023).

Balch, O. 2013. 'Buen Vivir: The Social Philosophy Inspiring Movements in South America'. *The Guardian*, 4 February. https://www.theguardian.com/sustainable-business/blog/buen-vivir-philosophy-south-america-eduardo-gudynas (accessed 5 December 2023).

Barrington-Leigh, C. 2016. 'Sustainability and Well-being: A Happy Synergy'. *Development* 59 (3–4): 292–8.

Boyce, C.J., M. Daly, H.O. Hounkpatin and A.M. Wood. 2017. 'Money May Buy Happiness, but Often So Little that It Doesn't Matter'. *Psychological Science* 28 (4): 544–6.

Burger, R., C.L. Steenekamp, S. van der Berg and A. Zoch. 2015. 'The Emergent Middle Class in Contemporary South Africa: Examining and Comparing Rival Approaches'. *Development Southern Africa* 32 (1): 25–40.

Coffey, C., P. Espinoza Revollo, R. Harvey, M. Lawson, A. Parvez Butt, K. Piaget, D. Sarosi and J. Thekkudan. 2020. *Time to Care: Unpaid and Underpaid Care Work and the Global Inequality Crisis*. Oxfam Briefing Paper. https://oxfamilibrary.openrepository.com/bitstream/handle/10546/620928/bp-time-to-care-inequality-200120-en.pdf (accessed 5 December 2023).

Coscieme, L., P. Sutton, L.F. Mortensen, I. Kubiszewski, R. Costanza, K. Trebeck, F.M. Pulselli, B.F. Giannetti and L. Fioramonti. 2019. 'Overcoming the Myths of Mainstream Economics to Enable a New Wellbeing Economy'. *Sustainability* 11 (16), article 4374.

Croll, E.J. 2001. 'Amartya Sen's 100 Million Missing Women'. *Oxford Development Studies* 29 (3): 225–44.

Cummins, R., A. Lau and M. Davern. 2012. 'Subjective Wellbeing Homeostasis'. In: *Handbook of Social Indicators and Quality of Life Research*, edited by K. Land, A. Michalos and M. Sirgy, 79–98. Cham: Springer.

Dabla-Norris, E., K. Kochhar, N. Suphaphiphat, F. Ricka and E. Tsounta. 2015. *Causes and Consequences of Income Inequality: A Global Perspective*. International Monetary Fund Staff Discussion Notes No. 2015/013. https://www.imf.org/en/Publications/Staff-Discussion-Notes/Issues/2016/12/31/Causes-and-Consequences-of-Income-Inequality-A-Global-Perspective-42986 (accessed 5 December 2023).

D'Alisa, G., F. Demaria and G. Kallis (eds). 2015. *Degrowth: A Vocabulary for a New Era*. Abingdon-on-Thames: Routledge.

Department of Planning, Monitoring and Evaluation. 2010. *Guide to the Outcomes Approach*. https://www.dpme.gov.za/publications/Guides%20Manuals%20and%20Templates/Guideline%20to%20outcome%20approach.pdf (accessed 5 December 2023).

———. 2019. *Revised Medium Term Strategic Framework (MTSF) 2019–2024*. https://www.dpme.gov.za/keyfocusareas/Provincial%20Performance%20Publication/Documents/Revised%20MTSF%20100321A.pdf (accessed 5 December 2023).

Diener, E., R.E. Lucas and C.N. Scollon. 2006. 'Beyond the Hedonic Treadmill: Revising the Adaptation Theory of Well-Being'. *American Psychologist* 61 (4): 305–14.

Dladla, N. 2017. 'Towards an African Critical Philosophy of Race: Ubuntu as a Philo-Praxis of Liberation'. *Filosofia Theoretica* 6 (1): 39–68.

Easterlin, R.A. 1974. 'Does Economic Growth Improve the Human Lot? Some Empirical Evidence'. In: *Nations and Households in Economic Growth: Essays in Honor of Moses Abramovitz*, edited by P.A. David and M.W. Reder, 89–125. Cambridge, MA: Academic Press.

Engels, M. 2022. 'From Growth to Wellbeing: Rethinking Development for a Digital, Green, and Just Transformation'. Unpublished Conference Paper, GIZ Futures Forum.

Escobar, A. 2015. 'Degrowth, Postdevelopment, and Transitions: A Preliminary Conversation'. *Sustainability Science* 10 (3): 451–62.

Feketha, S. 2018. 'South Africa World's Most Unequal Society – Report'. *The Star*, 28 March. https://www.iol.co.za/news/south-africa/south-africa-worlds-most-unequal-society-report-14125145 (accessed 5 December 2023).

Finn, A., M. Leibbrandt and M. Oosthuizen. 2014. *Poverty, Inequality, and Prices in Post-apartheid South Africa*. WIDER Working Paper No. 2014/127. https://www.wider.unu.edu/sites/default/files/wp2014-127.pdf (accessed 5 December 2023).

Finn, A., M. Leibbrandt and I. Woolard. 2013. *What Happened to Multidimensional Poverty in South Africa between 1993 and 2010?* SALDRU Research Brief. https://www.opensaldru.uct.ac.za/handle/11090/615 (accessed 5 December 2023).

Fioramonti, L. 2020. 'Well-Being Economy: A Scenario for a Post-growth Horizontal Governance System'. In: *The New Systems Reader: Alternatives to a Failed Economy*, edited by J.G. Speth and K. Courrier, 145–56. Abingdon-on-Thames: Routledge.

Fletcher, R. and C. Rammelt. 2017. 'Decoupling: A Key Fantasy of the Post-2015 Sustainable Development Agenda'. *Globalizations* 14 (3): 450–67.

Freeman, T., H.A. Gesesew, C. Bambra, E.R.J. Giugliani, J. Popay, D. Sanders, J. Macinko, C. Musolino and F. Baum. 2020. 'Why Do Some Countries Do Better or Worse in Life Expectancy Relative to Income? An Analysis of Brazil, Ethiopia, and the United States of America'. *International Journal for Equity in Health* 19 (1): 1–19.

Gauteng Department for Roads and Transport and the Council for Scientific and Industrial Research (CSIR). 2020. *Gauteng Province Household Travel Survey Report 2019/20*. https://www.csir.co.za/sites/default/files/Documents/GHTS%20201920%20FINAL_LOW%20RES%20%281%29.pdf (accessed 5 December 2023).

Gibson-Graham, J.K. 2016. 'Building Community Economies: Women and the Politics of Place'. In: *The Palgrave Handbook of Gender and Development: Critical Engagements in Feminist Theory and Practice*, edited by W. Harcourt, 287–311. London: Palgrave Macmillan.

Hoekstra, R. 2019. *Replacing GDP by 2030: Towards a Common Language for the Well-Being and Sustainability Community*. Cambridge: Cambridge University Press.

Jackson, T. 2016. *Prosperity without Growth: Foundations for the Economy of Tomorrow*. 2nd edition. Abingdon-on-Thames: Routledge.

Jackson, T., W. Jager and S. Stagl. 2004. 'Beyond Insatiability: Needs Theory, Consumption and Sustainability'. In: *The Ecological Economics of Consumption*, edited by L.A. Reisch and I. Røpke.

Elgar online. https://china.elgaronline.com/configurable/content/9781843765127.00013.
xml?t:ac=9781843765127.00013.xml (accessed 5 December 2023).

Kachingwe, N. 2018. *Fearing Our Silence and Silencing Our Fears*. Opening Address
at the 8th Convening of the Uganda Feminist Forum, Jinja, Uganda. https://www.
akinamamawaafrika.org/wp-content/uploads/2019/08/Opening-Address-Uganda-
Feminist-Forum-2019.pdf (accessed 5 December 2023).

Kakwani, N. and H.H. Son. 2015. *Income Inequality and Social Well-being*. Society for the
Study of Economic Inequality Working Paper Series No. 380. http://www.ecineq.org/
milano/WP/ECINEQ2015-380.pdf (accessed 5 December 2023).

Kesebir, S. 2016. 'When Economic Growth Doesn't Make Countries Happier'. *Harvard Business
Review*, 25 April. https://hbr.org/2016/04/when-economic-growth-doesnt-make-countries-
happier (accessed 5 October 2023).

Khambule, I. and B. Siswana. 2017. 'How Inequalities Undermine Social Cohesion: A Case
Study of South Africa'. G20-Insights Policy Brief, May. https://repository.hsrc.ac.za/
handle/20.500.11910/11044 (accessed 5 December 2023).

Lakoff, G. 2010. 'Why It Matters How We Frame the Environment'. *Environmental
Communication* 4 (1): 70–81.

Latouche, S. 2014. *Essays on Frugal Abundance: Degrowth: Misinterpretations and Controversies,
Part 1*. https://simplicityinstitute.org/wp-content/uploads/2011/04/FrugalAbundance1
SimplicityInstitute.pdf (accessed 5 December 2023).

Lawson, M., M-K. Chan, F. Rhodes, A. Parvez Butt, A. Marriott, E. Ehmke, D. Jacobs, J. Seghers,
J. Atienza and R. Gowland. 2019. *Public Good or Private Wealth?* Oxfam Briefing Paper.
https://oxfamilibrary.openrepository.com/bitstream/handle/10546/620599/bp-public-
good-or-private-wealth-210119-en.pdf (accessed 5 December 2023).

Lephakga, T. 2017. 'Colonial Institutionalisation of Poverty among Blacks in South Africa'.
Studia Historiae Ecclesiasticae 43 (2): 1–15.

Manji, F. 2015. 'The Relevance of Rodney's HEUA to the Struggle for Emancipation in the 21st
Century'. *South* 1 (1).

Mayson, S.S. 2021. 'Enabling a Wellbeing Economy in the Eastern Neighbourhoods of Inner
City Johannesburg'. PhD diss., University of the Witwatersrand.

Metz, T., J. Hirata and R. Verma. 2015. 'Good Governance: How Can Politics Promote
Wellbeing?' *Druk Journal* 1 (2): 90–9.

Narsiah, S. 2002. 'Neoliberalism and Privatisation in South Africa'. *GeoJournal* 57 (1): 3–13.

Nathan, L. 2012. *Community of Insecurity: SADC's Struggle for Peace and Security in Southern
Africa*. Farnham: Ashgate Publishing.

National Planning Commission. 2012. *National Development Plan 2030: Our Future – Make It
Work*. https://www.gov.za/sites/default/files/gcis_document/201409/ndp-2030-our-future-
make-it-workr.pdf (accessed 5 December 2023).

Olukoshi, A.O. and L. Laakso (eds). 1996. *Challenges to the Nation-State in Africa*. Nordiska Afrikainstitutet, Uppsala, and Institute of Development Studies, University of Helsinki. http://liu.diva-portal.org/smash/get/diva2:277324/FULLTEXT01.pdf (accessed 5 December 2023).

OPHI (Oxford Poverty and Human Development Initiative) and UNDP HDRO (United Nations Development Programme Human Development Report Office). 2021. *Global Multidimensional Poverty Index 2021: Unmasking Disparities by Ethnicity, Caste and Gender*. https://ophi.org.uk/global-mpi-2021-archive-page/ (accessed 5 December 2023).

Padayachee, V. 2019. 'Can Progressive Macroeconomic Policy Address Growth and Employment while Reducing Inequality in South Africa?' *Economic and Labour Relations Review* 30 (1): 3–21.

Peet, R., 2002. 'Ideology, Discourse, and the Geography of Hegemony: From Socialist to Neoliberal Development in Postapartheid South Africa'. *Antipode* 34 (1): 54–84.

Pheko, L.L. 2010. 'Gender, Economic Globalization, Movement and Citizenship'. *Development* 53 (3): 402–6.

———. 2021. 'Dismantling and Deconstructing "Care" Work as a Critique on Extractive Capitalism'. Paper presented at webinar, Coady Institute.

Pheko, L.L. and R. Verma. 2022. 'Scoping Research on Alternative Measurements to GDP'. Unpublished internal Oxfam report.

Ramose, M.B. 2006. 'Philosophy and Africa's Struggle for Economic Independence'. *Politeia* 25 (1): 3–17.

Republic of South Africa. 2014. *Medium Term Strategic Framework (MTSF) 2014–2019*. https://www.gov.za/sites/default/files/gcis_document/201409/mtsf2014-2019.pdf (accessed 5 December 2023).

Salazar, J.F. 2015. 'Buen Vivir: South America's Rethinking of the Future We Want'. *The Conversation*, 24 July. https://theconversation.com/buen-vivir-south-americas-rethinking-of-the-future-we-want-44507 (accessed 5 December 2023).

Schmelzer, M. 2015. 'The Growth Paradigm: History, Hegemony, and the Contested Making of Economic Growthmanship'. *Ecological Economics* 118: 262–71.

SDSN (Sustainable Development Solutions Network). 2020. *World Happiness Report 2020*. https://worldhappiness.report/ed/2020/ (accessed 5 December 2023).

Sen, A. 1998. 'Mortality as an Indicator of Economic Success and Failure'. *Economic Journal* 108 (446): 1–25.

Seery, E., J. Okanda and M. Lawson. 2019. *A tale of Two Continents: Fighting Inequality in Africa*. Oxfam Briefing Paper. https://www-cdn.oxfam.org/s3fs-public/file_attachments/bp-tale-of-two-continents-fighting-inequality-africa-030919-en.pdf (accessed 5 December 2023).

Smith, M. 2017. 'How Inequality Is Wrecking SA's Economy, and What We Can Do about It'. *Business Day*, 16 October. https://www.businesslive.co.za/bd/opinion/2017-10-16-alarming-statistics--how--sas-economy-suffers-from-inequality/ (accessed 5 December 2023).

Stats SA (Statistics South Africa). 2014. *The South African MPI: Creating a Multidimensional Poverty Index Using Census Data*. https://www.statssa.gov.za/publications/Report-03-10-08/Report-03-10-082014.pdf (accessed 5 December 2023).

Stiglitz, J., A. Sen and J-P. Fitoussi. 2009. *Report by the Commission on the Measurement of Economic Performance and Social Progress*. https://ec.europa.eu/eurostat/documents/8131721/8131772/Stiglitz-Sen-Fitoussi-Commission-report.pdf (accessed 5 December 2023).

Suchodolski, S.G. and J.M. Demeulemeester. 2018. 'The BRICS Coming of Age and the New Development Bank'. *Global Policy* 9 (4): 578–85.

Tshoose, C.I. 2009. 'The Emerging Role of the Constitutional Value of Ubuntu for Informal Social Security in South Africa'. *African Journal of Legal Studies* 3 (1): 12–20.

Ura, K., S. Alkire and T. Zangmo. 2012. *GNH and GNH Index*. Centre for Bhutan Studies. https://ophi.org.uk/wp-content/uploads/GNH_and_GNH_index_2012.pdf (accessed 5 December 2023).

Van Binsbergen, W.M.J. 2001. 'Ubuntu and the Globalisation of Southern African Thought and Society'. *Quest* 15 (1–2): 53–89.

Van den Bergh, J.C. 2011. 'Environment versus Growth: A Criticism of "Degrowth" and a Plea for "A-growth"'. *Ecological Economics* 70 (5): 881–90.

Verma, R. and K. Ura. 2022. 'Gender Differences in Gross National Happiness: Analysis of the First Nationwide Wellbeing Survey in Bhutan'. *World Development* 150, article 105714.

Visagie, J. and D. Posel. 2013. A Reconsideration of What and Who Is Middle Class in South Africa'. *Development Southern Africa* 30 (2): 149–67.

Wilkinson, R. and K. Pickett. 2009. *The Spirit Level: Why More Equal Societies Almost Always Do Better*. London: Allen Lane.

Williamson, S.H. 2017. 'Globalization as a Racial Project: Implications for Human Trafficking'. *Journal of International Women's Studies* 18 (2): 74–88.

Zademach, H-M. and S. Hillebrand (eds). 2013. *Alternative Economies and Spaces: New Perspectives for a Sustainable Economy*. https://library.oapen.org/bitstream/handle/20.500.12657/31476/627770.pdf?sequence=1 (accessed 5 December 2023).

CHAPTER 13

South Africa and the Developmental State Model

Lessons from the Asian Historical Experience

Dan Motaung

What experience and history teach is this – that peoples and governments never have learned anything from history, or acted on principles deduced from it.
— G.W.F. HEGEL

The economic developmental paradigm that came to be known as the developmental state (DS) is 'shorthand for the seamless web of political, bureaucratic, and moneyed influences that structures economic life in capitalist Northeast Asia' (Woo-Cumings 1990: 1). From the viewpoint of modernisation, it is a singular economic event since European industrialisation and may, therefore, if properly scrutinised for the key lessons it epitomises, offer some critical strategic insights, not least for the developing Global South. Remarkably, 'in less than 40 years, the Asian Newly Industrialised Countries (NICs) have industrialised rapidly, gained phenomenal rates of growth, and captured ever larger shares of export markets, while at the same time eliminating unemployment and achieving a relatively egalitarian income distribution' (Weiss and Hobson 1995: 138).

Not to be outdone, the South African government has grabbed onto the DS concept with both hands, declared itself one (Williams 2014), without so much as a discursive delineation of exactly the model of DS it imagined itself to be. This lack of a clear theoretical grounding of the DS is all the more surprising given that the concept is found in the government's key macroeconomic policy documents. The nearest South Africa came to officially articulating this concept was when it set out its development vision in the the *New Growth Path: The Framework* (South African Government 2010) and the *National Development Plan 2030* (NDP) (National Planning Commission 2012).

Even then, the documents couch this notion in the vaguest of terms. This chapter aims to correct this conceptually impoverished grounding by not only offering a historicised understanding, theorisation and generic definition of the concept, but also suggesting and critiquing possible pathways in terms of which South Africa can successfully adopt the notion of the DS.

I hope this chapter makes it clear that the specificity of the historical conditions under which this concept evolved are not necessarily repeatable and I therefore agree with Michelle Williams that 'the concept of the DS has to be critically re-examined in order to revitalise debate on the role of the state in social and economic transformation in the twenty-first century' (2014: xiii). Given the reality of the changed historical circumstances, this chapter also cautions that implementing the DS model today is a far more intricate enterprise, for which political imagination is imperative. At the same time, it maintains that without familiarity with the defining conceptual features embedded in the historical trajectory of the DS the concept may fall between two stools, becoming neither fish nor fowl.

This is all the more critical given the social inequalities, poverty, unemployment and political fractiousness driven by often-toxic social identities, as well as the polarisation between capital and labour, which haunt the South African political imaginary. Therefore, this chapter argues for the adaptive adoption of the model of the DS, sensitive to South Africa's historical particularity, so that it accords with the distinctive characteristics that define the historical and human landscape of the country.

Origins of the developmental state

It is helpful to outline the historical origins of the idea of a DS, since the definition is retrospectively applied to impose conceptual meaning on the evolution of unique historical processes whose patterns congeal into something akin to this particular governance model. The DS originated in North East Asia, more specifically, in Japan (Weiss and Hobson 1995; Evans, Rueschemeyer and Skocpol 1985). As described by Chalmers Johnson in his landmark book *MITI and the*

Japanese Miracle: The Growth of Industrial Policy, 1925–1975 (1982), this model of governance stirred to life on the heels of the Second World War, as Japan scrambled for recovery and reconstruction.

Following its humiliation by the West, the Japanese state 'followed the policy known as *Fukoku Kyohei* (rich country, strong army)' (Weiss and Hobson 1995: 84). An ambitious industrialisation programme followed. To this end, the Japanese state set about 'the familiar pattern of creating an industrial infrastructure through the development of naval shipyards, munitions factories, railways, steelworks, and engineering yards' (Weiss and Hobson 1995: 84–5). In this sense, Japanese industrialisation was a function of force of circumstances, following its geopolitical predicament.

The peculiar history of North East Asia explains the emergence and evolution of what came to be known as the DS. This region, comprising Japan, South Korea and Taiwan, had come under the colonial dominion of Japan before the war (Woo-Cumings 1999). Both South Korea and Taiwan 'learnt lessons, absorbed advanced technologies and capital from Japan, and embarked on a similar trajectory of light-industrial exporting under multi-year plans, guided by strong state ministries' (1999: xii). This meant that the two former colonised nations would be locked in the Japanese conception of development, sharing essentially defining features with the latter. Two of these features, as Woo-Cummings points out, were a strong neo-mercantilism and nationalist orientation.

Johnson argues that 'credit for the post-war Japanese economic "miracle" should go primarily to conscious and consistent government policies dating from at least the 1920s' (in Woo-Cumings 1999: 37). He also insists that what a state depends on is what it prioritises. In the case of the Japanese state, a good 50 years have been devoted to the goal of economic development.

The essence of a DS also consists of managing foreign trade in such a way as to not only protect local industry, but also to ensure that it benefits from its own growth. Japan promulgated laws in this regard. It enacted the Foreign Capital Law (1950), as well as the Foreign Exchange and Foreign Trade Control Law of 1949 (Woo-Cumings 1999), among others. Through these laws, the Japanese government was empowered to 'control import through the use of foreign exchange budget' (Woo-Cumings 1999: 38). One common strategy used by all the East Asian nations was the curbing on imports, except for foreign technology, which naturally had enormous benefits for domestic industrial development. In the case of Japan, the Ministry of International Trade and Industry suppressed all finished products that threatened to compete with local products (Woo-Cumings 1999). The Japanese government was more concerned with separating 'the technology from its foreign ownership, patents rights, know-how agreement, proposals for joint ventures, capital participation, voting rights, and foreign managers on board of directors' (1999: 38). Ultimately, the Foreign Capital Law was meant to address this challenge, which it did by requiring all foreign investors who wanted to participate in any of the above areas get a licence from this committee.

During its imperial reign over both Taiwan (1895–1945) and Korea (1910–45), Japan's colonisation model bequeathed its colonised entities with the foundational template for a DS, which set these societies on a predefined path dependence in their post-colonial iterations after the Second World War, following Japan's defeat (Evans, Rueschemeyer and Skocpol 1985). Unlike the violent Western colonial modernisation of Africa, the Japanese model of colonisation sought to bring its colonies to its level of development, motivated by the ambition to integrate them into the emerging Japanese Empire. Both Taiwan and Korea therefore experienced a 'positive' form of colonisation, which catalysed their modernisation, rather than subjecting them to structural underdevelopment, which would have wilted their potential, as was the case on the African continent.

What is the developmental state?

Broadly speaking, the DS is a form of governance characterised by state-led development philosophy or what is called state activism (Weiss 1998; Evans 1995). It pivots on state-defined strategic capitalism, which is in turn shaped by a shared national political vision (Weiss and Hobson 1995). Richard Stubbs argues that DS is 'a generic term to describe governments that try to actively "intervene" in economic processes and direct the course of development rather than relying only on market forces' (2009: 5).

According to the *Little Book of Economics*: 'The environment from which the Asia Tigers emerged was shaped by government intervention and dense links between the state and the economy' (Ip 2012: 162). What set the newly industrialised countries (NICs) apart in this period was the activist role of the state, which, in the case of North East Asia, drove industrialisation processes while channelling investment towards strategic areas of development. These states prioritised investment in education, as well as the promotion of domestic technological development. As a result, 'industrial enterprises soon began to export their products, becoming the motors for sustained, trade-driven growth' (2012: 162).

The goals of the development state are about 'economic growth through industrial policy and necessary characteristics (Weberian bureaucracy, embedded autonomy, capacity to discipline capital)' (Williams 2014: xiv). These are the universal, generic features constitutive of the very idea of the DS. Of course, how a particular country recasts them into its particularised iteration is the result of conscious decisions of policymakers.

Johnson delineates the defining features of what came to constitute the model of state he calls 'developmental'. These features are as follows:

- the existence of a small, inexpensive but elite state bureaucracy staffed by the best managerial talent available in the system;
- the duties of this bureaucracy would be first to identify and choose the industries to be developed (industrial structure policy);
- to identify and choose the best means to rapidly develop the chosen industries (industrial rationalisation policy); and
- third, to supervise competition in the designated strategic sectors in order to guarantee their economic health and effectiveness (in Woo-Cumings 1999: 38).

Linda Weiss and John M. Hobson (1995) highlight the impact that political institutions have on the performance of national economies, within the context of the historical emergence of the DS. Based on their study of NICs, they argue that linkages between states and economic actors are indispensable for shaping developmental outcomes of nations. They define development as 'the study of long-term, large-scale socio-economic and political change irrespective of epoch or region in which it occurs' (1995: 1). They ascribe successful national economic development and effective industrial transformation in modern history to the existence of strong states, while acknowledging that the definition of 'strong states' is historically contingent. They maintain that 'strong economies require strong states' (1995: 2). Their study of the NICs leads them to conclude that it is the strength of states that imbue them with the ability to mobilise national resources with a view to bringing about the realisation of national economic development.

While Weiss and Hobson agree with the contention that 'a central coordinating intelligence, whether in the form of political and/or financial institutions, is at most important for "late" industrialisation in the earlier states of national development' (1995: 2), they go further to submit that the idea of an activist state needs not fade away once a comparable level of national economic development has been reached.

Furthermore, because external global historical conditions differ, state strengths are by nature fluid and therefore always changing (Weiss and Hobson 1995). For instance, unlike the strength of older despotic states, the strength of modern states is defined by 'infrastructural power' (Weiss 1998), or 'the penetrative capacity'(Weiss and Hobson 1995: 3), by virtue of which states embed themselves in society at large with the aim of being able to have legitimate access for the extraction of resources required for national development projects (Weiss and Hobson 1995). Only when states have embedded themselves in society, forging durable and meaningful co-operation and collaborations, or what in South Africa is called a social compact or partnerships, can they be in a position to leverage such a strategic positioning to provide leadership for developmental ambitions.

Another important feature of state strength is the capability of states to command 'co-ordinating capacity': the ability to bring all important social and economic – in other words, power actors – together behind a clearly defined vision of national development, riding on collaboration spearheaded by the state (Weiss and Hobson 1995). This concept ties in with the concept of 'a central co-ordinating intelligence' mentioned earlier. The key concept that Weiss and Hobson employ for the function of co-ordinating, or that equates to a centrally co-ordinating intelligence, is what they term 'governed interdependence' (1995: 148). Further affirming the historical impact of the state's co-ordinating role as central within the DS, Weiss and Hobson (1995) also point to contributions of other scholars who have conceptualised this political leadership of the state. Among others are terms such as the 'disciplined market' by Alice Amsden (1989), the 'guided market' by Robert Wade (1990), and 'embedded autonomy' according to Peter Evans (1995), all of which resonate with the concept of 'governed interdependence'.

Referring to the history of Japan, South Korea and Taiwan, Weiss and Hobson hold that governed interdependence,

> entails the ability to mobilise and co-ordinate society's resources in such a way as to augment the overall investible surplus (and ultimately raise living standards). Such efforts, most visible in the recent rise of Japan and the Asia NICs, have focused largely on expansion of value addition manufacturers and of export market shares (1995: 4).

They further state that there is no single best manner of governing markets, a point emphasised above about the need to read DS in terms of country specificity. They also take issue with the zero-sum game view of a strong state and insist, based on the history of the NICs, that 'strong states wield infrastructural power . . . and that the greater infrastructural power, the more effective is the promoting of strategic industrial state' (Weiss and Hobson 1995: 5). Therefore, a structured collaboration between the state and key economic players in pursuit of industrial transformation entails competition and collaboration, as exemplified by the cases of the late industrialisers of North East Asia. Eventually, 'the combination of market orientation and active state involvement is central to the story of' the success of Japan, Taiwan and South Korea (1995: 12). Developing closer and mutually beneficial, structured relationships with civil society and the private sector enhances the powers of both the state and other national players, a prospect that is invariably rewarding for national interests. To this extent, it is completely incorrect to see the strength of the state as possible only at the expense of the private sector.

Ultimately, infrastructural power is constituted of the combination of penetrative, extractive and negotiatory capacities, all of which are interrelated and are the indispensable ingredients for governed interdependence, where state is able to guide the markets towards the vision of national development.

One of the foremost scholars of the DS, Evans locates the nature of a DS in the notion of 'embedded autonomy', by which he means a state characterised by a 'contradictory combination of corporate coherence and connectedness' (1995: 12). He further argues that 'only when embeddedness and autonomy are joined together can a state be called developmental'. One of the key aspects of the DS is a labour selection process, which is uncompromisingly biased in favour of high qualifications, skills and experience and careers based on long service, leading to organisational coherence and dedication (Evans 1995). Evans maintains that corporate coherence generates a form of 'autonomy', where the bureaucracy is embedded in a concrete set of social ties that binds the state to society and provides institutionalised channels for the continual negotiation and renegotiation of goals and policies (1995: 12).

Research converges on the fact that to be successful a DS has no option but to implement a form of protectionism through trade policy and provision of strategic resources (Evans 1995; Chibber 2014; Weiss 1998). Furthermore, as has been the case with the East Asian nations, the state moves in to create conducive conditions through shaping the macroeconomic environment, as well as facilitating capital accumulation through affordable loans, among other things (Chibber 2014). This dispensation calls for a need for 'partnership between political elites, and state managers on the one side and local industrialists on the other. Each needs the other – the state cannot industrialise on its own, since it does not directly control the investments process, industrialists cannot hope to succeed in world markets without the state's assistance' (Williams 2014: 31).

The other important instrument at the disposal of the DS is the state's power to direct investment in certain designated areas for their strategic value for the country's industrialisation process. This form of state interventionism is of paramount importance as, other than its high-impact value, it also reflects the state capacity to direct the economic processes within the framework of the national collaboration. This dispensation thus cements the role of the state as the first among equals, a partner with the power to dictate terms in the collective interests of all.

South Africa and the developmental state

Despite its self-characterisation of itself as a DS, South Africa does not fit the classical definition of the DS, as defined in the literature (Weiss 1998; Weiss and Hobson 1995; Evans 1995; Turok 2008). A DS is not about half-measures, where some of its features are inserted into an overall policy framework that departs from its generic structure in its essentials. It is a full-strength socio-economic model of governance, which drives a clearly delineated vision. This explains the view that in most NICs the DS was powered by a strong patriotic sentiment (Weiss 1998).

Most importantly, a DS is a national vision. This means that in South Africa, the government, labour and business would have engaged in a national process of legitimation of the vision being espoused. The absence of a clear national compact explains the fact that despite this concept being articulated in all these seminal national development documents neither it nor the thrust of these documents approach anything akin to a DS.

It is therefore recommended that government reframes all its key development documents into one text, grounded on the idea of a DS, which will further receive inputs from all relevant power actors in the country. It is further recommended that the process that would culminate in the adoption of the policy of DS in South Africa be modelled on the process that formulated the Reconstruction and Development Programme (RDP). The RDP base document was a product of national consensus (Turok 2008) and we could draw some valuable lessons from its drafting process. For instance, Ben Turok argues that during the formulation of the RDP,

> the ANC [African National Congress], COSATU [Congress of South African Trade Unions], the SACP [South African Communist Party], and SANCO [South African National Civic Organisation], with many participants from civil society formations, held a series of meetings where the proposed RDP went through six drafts and contentious issues were hammered out (2008: 88).

Turok's account of the process leading up to the adoption of the RDP as a national vision shows strong affinities with the history of DS in East Asia. It also bears traces of what Weiss (1998) calls the infrastructural power of the state, marked by a penetrative, extractive and negotiatory capacities. Penetrative capacity and infrastructural power are key elements, which equip the state with the strength it needs to drive development through the mobilisation of internal national resources. According to Weiss and Hobson: 'Infrastructural capacity has thus been identified with the increasing ability to penetrate and extract resources from society and allocate them to desired ends' (1995: 4).

Unlike Japan or South Korea, South Africa was a heavily internally fragmented society along race, ethnicity, class and geographic spaces when the RDP was brought into being. In addition, some sections of business, including mining, which had relied on the exploitation of cheap labour, did not necessarily show enthusiasm for the RDP, nor was the state in a position to impose its will on private capital to fall into line, as was the case in South East Asia (Turok 2008; Evans 1995). This does not mean that business opposed the RDP outright. Since business in South Africa is historically differentiated, 'many business sectors gave their tentative support to the programme, as it could lead to an expansion of the economy' (Turok 2008: 88).

The 1994 democratic moment opened up new economic policy direction under the ANC government. As Turok explains, 'The ANC government of 1994 chose to implement an austerity economic policy which has been successful in introducing macro-economic stability and, until recently, low inflation, a balanced budget and a sound economic framework' (2008: 11). The making of the RDP is a repeatable historical process and offers some valuable lessons for modern South Africa. Not only was it an all-inclusive process, but it also elaborated a superordinate national vision based on national interests, to which a cross-section of society could gravitate. In fact, given the economic reversals it has suffered, as well as the blight of stagnation in some areas, South Africa still shows the same socio-economic features that prompted COSATU to suggest a 'Reconstruction Accord' (Turok 2008). South Africa is reeling under structural inequality, unemployment and social inequality. Ironically, the country is endowed with plenty of mineral resources which, if properly managed, could ignite a flourishing society.

There is a need for South Africa to rethink, critically, the notion of the DS according to modern imperatives and in the light of country-specific experience from elsewhere. The twenty-first century is a historical period with unique socio-economic and geopolitical characteristics, which warrant a re-examination of the concept of the DS as it is adopted by and adapted to the conditions of countries such as South Africa. Given the changing historical conditions in which states are existing today, the DS faces a complex set of challenges unknown to its twentieth-century predecessor (Williams 2014).

Necessary as all the above goals are, for a country such as South Africa to fully realise the goals of a DS within the context of its historical conditions, 'the local politics and global economy in which states are embedded are also vital parts of the story' (Williams 2014: xiv). State power, political will and domestic politics should necessarily predicate the very thought of building a DS in South Africa.

Country-specific conditions in which the notion of the DS evolves mean that South Africa's vision of the DS has to be shaped by its unique socio-political configuration. It has already been pointed out above that domestic state power, political will and domestic politics are key requirements to facilitate sustainability of a DS. In a late-developing country riven by a fractious history, such as South Africa, this is all the more important in view of the defining role of state, labour and capital in the construction of the DS.

South African 'black business' and the imperative for social compact

One area where South Africa's business and the state relationship bears similar historical conditions to East Asia is in the domain of state–business relations, with regard to emerging black business. Relations between the state and traditional white capital have blown hot and cold, but quite often white business has failed in its national duty to make commensurate contributions to national developmental goals (Terreblanche 2002). What instantiates this indifference is the culture of investment strike, which has been a consistent example of this lacklustre attitude by the traditionally white capital towards the stated developmental goals (Turok 2008). Continued engagement with traditional white capital is still necessary, for there is equally a great deal of goodwill that this faction of capital has shown to the country.

A key lesson the South African government could learn from the history of East Asia is the nurturing of domestic business, with which the state can enter into a specific strategic partnership, which will see support from the former in return for performance standards from business. The South African government has cultivated positive relations with black business through the black economic empowerment framework. East Asia's strategic relationship with infant industry through policy instruments, which translated to carrot and stick incentives, offers valuable lessons for South Africa (Kohli 1999). Arguing for social compacts as one of the key instruments for a successful DS for African states, Thandika Mkandawire defines them thus:

Social compacts refer to the institutionalisation of consultation and cooperation on economic policy involving representation from the State,

Capital, Labour, and other organisations of civil society. Social compacts
have been used to address distributive and growth objectives of society at
the micro-level; to improve labour management at the firm level and, as in
the current usage of 'social pacts' in Europe, to manage the distributional
issues of macroeconomic policies (2012: 9).

Social compacts aligned to national development goals with business
representation biased in favour of both domestic and black capital means that the
state can, through the instrumentalist approach of intergovernmentality, begin
to direct capital investment towards strategic economic areas. Jenn-Hwan Wang
contends:

In order to rapidly catch up with the developed economies, the states in
the late industrialisation countries have to facilitate industrialisation by
either nurturing a small number of domestic firms to compete in the world
market or by attracting huge numbers of foreign firms into the domestic
market to diffuse technologies to local firms (in Williams 2014: 84).

Throughout its history in East Asia, the DS clearly shows coherence of national
politics, or at least some form of consensus among the political society, which
enabled these countries to see through their ambitious industrialisation projects
successfully. This is what Weiss (1998) calls governed interdependence, which
she has defined as a situation 'where both state and social groups are "strong",
i.e., the state is insulated and industry is highly organised in a robust negotiating
relationship, but where domestic linkages for industrial transformation are
relatively narrowly yet tightly constituted' (1998: 37). Governed interdependence
had a strong presence in the NICs, which enabled the political class to implement
their national economic development strategies unimpeded.

Like the Kuomintang in Taiwan, the ANC government in South Africa
commands enough political power to drive the transformation process within the
bounds of possibility. It is in charge of the state. As Turok says: 'The ANC insists
that it remains the national liberation movement. This characterisation means that
there is still a huge transformation agenda in store' (2008: 16). While historical
conditions differ, the socio-economic level of development that confronts South

Africa under the ANC government today does not differ much from those that beset North East Asian societies in the early twentieth century.

As a political agency, the ANC, like the Kuomintang, has the political power to articulate economic policies and to drive government performance in implementing those policies. Currently, under the ANC government the party 'leadership makes all the top appointments and drives policy, while government acknowledges its obligation to be accountable to the ANC' (Turok 2008: 16). This means that the ANC government commands both the intellectual and political means to articulate the imperatives for the DS clearly and coherently and to begin with implementation.

Scrutinised against the background of the history of the NICs, both the RDP process and the RDP base document reveal the typical conditions in which the DS was incubated in East Asia. With the exception of white capital, the RDP base document was a product of a mass-based exercise, which included civil society and the ANC-aligned political formations. At this point, the ANC showed a high commitment to a participatory form of democracy, which legitimated, a priori, all processes.

A closer look reveals that the spirit and intellectual grounds for the argument for RDP for South Africa typifies the frameworks in which the East Asian societies conceived of the DS through the mobilisation of the primary socio-economic actors in the country. This national consensus, legitimated by the participation of a cross-section of power actors, becomes the driving national vision, which enables the state to guide the markets through the framework of a broad national collaboration. Such a national collaboration does not in any way dilute the powers of the state to exercise its legitimate authority where private capital is seen to be violating any of the basic tenets of the vision.

Each and every country has its own unique historical conditions, which shape its path dependence in terms of which it is locked into specific templates determining its future. Japan faced a ruling class revolution, which toppled the conservative, change-averse Tokugawa Shogunate dynasty while also sensitive to its geopolitical vulnerability (Bendix 1964; Toynbee 1973; Weiss and Hobson 1995). When they embarked on their developmental state-defined pathways, Taiwan and South Korea had been shaped by the brutal but development-oriented Japanese colonialism.

When it first proclaimed itself a 'developmental state' in 2014, South Africa was still a country shaped by the peculiarities of its history of racial capitalism (Terreblanche 2002). The democratic state came into power in the context of vested corporate interests of white capital, both domestic and international. Within the global ascendancy of neo-liberal dogma, it therefore had to temper its economic policies to prevent offending the sensibility of capital while not compromising on the electoral mandate to effect structural transformation. Turok explains that the ANC government 'faced a highly organised and powerful white economic power bloc and an international environment that demanded free-market liberalisation and would obstruct any contrary major reforms. This is a situation that required caution and compromise in pursuing economic change, especially with respect to industry and mining' (2008: 111).

Turok (2008) advocates for the DS as an option for South Africa, seeing that private capital has demonstrated an unwillingness to invest in the new industrial capacity. His view is that South Africa needs 'a developmental state strategy which will tackle dualism and under-development in the urban townships and former homelands' (Turok 2008: 246). The ANC government seems keen to run with the hare and hunt with the hounds. It maintains that it is a developmental state (though it has still failed to set down in finer detail the nature of this state) while embedded in neo-liberal economic policies, which, by definition, militate against developmentalist, state-driven transformation programmes such as the DS.

For instance, the government has dispensed with many trade policy instruments that are known to be stock-in-trade for effectively implementing the DS. Among the steps it took to liberalise, in keeping with the policy prescript of the Western orthodoxy, was the reduction of the tariffs, dismantling its trade barriers to 4 per cent, despite the fact that the Organisation for Economic Co-operation and Development (OECD) average is 32 per cent (Turok 2008). As it turns out, the intended objective of this has not yielded results, as export performance is reported to have remained stagnant (Turok 2008).

Turok (2008) laments the fact that the ANC government shows a huge discrepancy between intention and performance. The governing party has adopted many progressive policies that have not seen the light of day in government. He ascribes this inability to implement policies to lack of skills in the civil service, a critical requirement for the building of the developmental state.

State, business and labour relations

The South African state is defined by a system of constitutional democracy, which valorises national consensus as opposed to authoritarian politics. In consequence, the successful implementation of the DS in South Africa necessarily mandates the practice of engagement among the key players, including business and labour, based on which there is a need to develop a political framework on the basis of which a DS could be put in motion. This is all the more advisable given that in all the successful DS countries not only was there an authoritarian form of politics, but the NICs also exercised labour control, which would not pass constitutional master in a country such as South Africa, where progressive labour laws are enshrined in the Constitution. Trade unions and employers' organisations may apply to form bargaining councils, which 'deal with collective agreements, solve labour disputes, establish various schemes and comment on labour policies and laws'.[1]

Based on this democratic system of laws, South Africa already has a conducive environment to consolidate a social compact in the area of labour unions and business relations. Taiwan and South Korea enforced tough labour repression laws with regard to organised labour, as well as outright restraints on trade union activity. Weiss and Hobson (1995) attribute the suppression of labour not so much to curbing wage increases as to minimising social unrest in the Cold War context. This means geopolitical considerations impinged, at least in part, on national politics of the NIC region, which impacted on the shape of the developmental state.

However, the other reason governments intervened in the labour market was 'to control the share of national income allocated to wages, as well as to maintain employment levels' (Weiss and Hobson 1995: 147). Such interventions were designed to protect labour from unfair labour practices, including dismissals. Therefore, although the East Asian developmental state is known for labour repression, it did build into this suppressive system mitigating elements, such as a social wage, which cushioned labour from the worst-case scenarios. For example, the state helps keep labour costs low through subordinating 'trade unions, minimal state spending and informal wages policy' (1995: 152). In turn, the private sector was expected to train their workforce and not carry out lay-offs of employees during recessionary periods.

Skills capacity and the South African developmental state

In its formulations about the DS, the South African state never fails to emphasise the imperative for a capable, developmental state. Yet if one looks at the track record of the implementation of national policy in South Africa, the lack of skills capacity is the national Achilles' heel. It is widely acknowledged that the South African state is hobbled by this dearth of skills in its developmental ambitions. Possession of technical, managerial and administrative skills is indispensable to the vision of a DS. Johnson states that the DS 'recruits a highly talented, cohesive, and disciplined economic bureaucracy on the basis of merit' (in Weiss and Hobson 1995: 149). This was the experience of the North East Asian development.

Nowhere does the lack of skills and a disciplined cadre of state bureaucrats steeped in patriotic consciousness show more than in the failure to achieve the targets of the NDP. This much has been admitted by Minister Mmamoloko Kubayi, the head of the ANC's economic transformation subcommittee (Makinana 2022). However, Kubayi ascribes the lethargic performance in this vital economic development project to low economic growth as a result of the outbreak of the global Covid-19 pandemic. In view of the centrality of the notion of state-led developmentalism at the core of the DS, attention has to be centred on state capacity in its broadest sense (managerial, administrative, technical) within the context of its role of leading this project. Creating human capital is a prerequisite for driving sustainable growth. South Africa has to promote human capital immediately. No successful DS has ever occurred without a highly skilled, knowledgeable bureaucracy, which is a function of an effective national education system.

The specificity of the developmental state

Given South Africa's history of racialised capitalism, the post-apartheid government's relations with traditional white capital have been complementary, but also contradictory (Turok 2008). Building a DS would need to take full account of this historical context. The history of the NICs points to the intrinsic tensions between state and capital due to the need for the former to direct the developmental trajectory of the country (Weiss and Hobson 1995; Williams 2014; Weiss 1998) into certain pathways. Such unavoidable tensions, which are, however, manageable within the established political framework, are triggered by the fact that the 'developmental state does not only try to create conditions favourable to more rapid capital accumulation but also tries to affect the direction and the quality of investment' (Chibber 2014: 32). Part of the problem is that owners of capital do not willingly co-operate with what they see as 'interference' in how they manage their businesses.

Put differently, the relationship between capital and the state in this specific case reflects the structural opposites or the antithetical locations of the main players in the national economy. Vivek Chibber reasons that 'in a capitalist setting the control of productive assets resides, by definition, in private hands. This means that final decisions over investment are also at the discretion of nonstate actors' (2014: 32). Managing these tensions puts the state's strength to the test. A state that commands enough strength to square the circle of directing investments appropriately, in key strategic areas, without ownership of the said capital, is one capable of disciplining capital. To this end, the state needs administrative capacity and institutional mechanisms to carry out planning, preferably in consultation with the owners of capital, for the management of the flow of capital.

According to Chibber (2014), one of the fruitful ways of managing the flow of capital while minimising the potential tensions is for the state to issue directives that prescribe where investment should be. In the event that investors balk at being given direction, the state could incentivise such a move through subsidies. The package could include 'cheap loans, price supports, market protections' (2014: 33), which would attract business to invest along desirable lines. Most scholars warn against extending 'gifts' to businesses (Weiss and Hobson 1995; Weiss 1998; Evans 1995). In other words, the subsidy should carry performance standards and a form of reciprocity (Weiss and Hobson 1995) to ensure that businesses do not ignore their side of the bargain by diverting the money elsewhere. As Chibber (2014) points out, in the East Asian experience, if business did not comply with the conditions of the subsidies, appropriate sanctions followed, invariably in the form of discontinuation of the assistance.

However, private capital is South Africa is defined by the history of racial capitalism to which South Africa has been subjected since the onset of mineral revolution (Terreblanche 2002; Mbeki 2009). Historically, South Africa's capital has been divided into domestic and international, both of which are white-owned. The post-apartheid moment has seen the emergence of black capitalists, nurtured through state policy and largely dependent on white capital (Mbeki 2009; Terreblanche 2002). In relation to black business, there is a view that 'the state has had limited success in comprehending and aligning these varied interests to strategic national socioeconomic objectives' (Mabasa 2014; 126). This view suggests that we need to rethink the possible strategic relations between the state and black business, which the former can build with an eye to harnessing black business to the project of national economic development.

The strategic partnership the state could enter into with black business would also mean that the latter would be expected to focus and perform in designated economically vital spheres. The state would provide low-interest loans and apply other supportive measures, so that these black-run industries can develop and enter international markets on their own. One of the defining characteristics of a DS is the protection of infant domestic industries against cut-throat international competition (Evans 1995; Chibber 2014; Weiss 1998; Weis and Hobson 1995). This practice was evidenced by the industrialisation policies of the three NICs, which instrumentalised it to ensure that industries in targeted, strategic areas were nurtured into full strength to stand on their own. Invariably, they mobilised a range of measures in their trade policy to this effect, especially trade barriers such as tariffs, but also subsidies. Going by this practice, South Africa jumped the gun when it did away with trade barriers in the early 1990s, exposing our domestic economy to the overwhelming force of multinational companies. Most of the competitors in the South African export business had advantages of 'first movers – knowledge of consumer taste, links with sales outlets, familiarity with commercial networks, ties with financial intermediaries' (Chibber 2014: 30).

Conclusion

The DS is a proven blueprint for national industrial development, but has historically depended on country specificities (Kozul-Wright and Rayment 2007). This chapter has tried to sketch the history of this unique model. For reasons of space, unfortunately much was left out of my analysis that could have been of value. For instance, there was no systematic reflection on the politics of the country vis-à-vis the issue of the developmental-oriented elite. In addition, justice could not be done to thematic areas such as relative state autonomy and bureaucratic embedded autonomy, bureaucratic power, legitimacy and performance. Also, the South African education system is woefully inadequate to provide the skills required for the exacting managerial, administrative and technical standards of the DS, given its poor performance and quality. Land and agrarian reforms were critical to the DS, especially in Taiwan, as they are to South Africa. Neither could the chapter look at the conditions understood to be conducive to a viable DS, including the presence of visionary, nationalistic and development-oriented leaders; a meritocratic bureaucracy that is powerful and relatively autonomous; trade liberalisation or privatisation and performance-based legitimacy. These issues may prove fruitful areas for future researchers.

Despite these omissions, the substance of what constitutes the DS was captured in this chapter, as were its implications for South Africa. At attempt was made to analyse the South African scenario within the context of the theoretical delineation of the DS as it unfolded in East Asia. The purpose of this chapter was to give credence to the fact that the DS is a viable development vision for South Africa, but that exercise has to be predicated by a thorough understanding of the historical odyssey of this governance model, as well as a transcendent national vision, which enjoins society to move towards this model.

Notes

1. See https://www.gov.za/services/trade-unions/register-bargaining-council (accessed 6 October 2023).

References

Amsden, A.H. 1989. *Asia's Next Giant: South Korea and Late Industrialisation*. New York: Oxford University Press.

Bendix, R. 1964. *Nation-Building and Citizenship: Studies of Our Changing Social Order*. Berkeley: University of California Press.

Chibber, V. 2014. 'The Developmental State in Retrospect and Prospect: Lessons from India and Korea'. In: *The End of the Developmental State?*, edited by M. Williams, 30–54. Pietermaritzburg: University of KwaZulu-Natal Press.

Evans, P. 1995. *Embedded Autonomy: States and Industrial Transformation*. Princeton: Princeton University Press.

Evans, P.B., D. Rueschemeyer and T. Skocpol. 1985. *Bringing the State back in*. Cambridge: Cambridge University Press.

Hegel, G.W.F. 1900. *The Philosophy of History*. Kitchener: Batoche Books. https://www.marxists.org/reference/archive/hegel/works/hi/lectures.htm (accessed 6 October 2023).

Ip, G. 2012. *The Little Book of Economics*. London: Dorling Kindersley.

Johnson, C. 1982. *MITI and the Japanese Miracle: The Growth of Industrial Policy, 1925–1975*. Stanford: Stanford University Press.

Kohli, A. 1999. 'Where Do High-Growth Political Economies Come From? The Japanese Lineage of Korea's "Developmental State"'. In: *The Developmental State*, edited by M. Woo-Cumings, 61–92. Ithaca, NY: Cornell University Press

Kozul-Wright, R. and P. Rayment. 2007. *The Resistible Rise of the Market Fundamentalism: Rethinking Development Policy in an Unbalanced World*. London: Zed Books.

Mabasa, K. 2014. *Building a Bureaucracy for the South African Developmental State: An Institutional-Policy Analysis of the Post-apartheid Political Economy*. Pretoria: UNISA Press.

Makinana, A. 2022. 'SA Will Not Meet NDP Goals by 2030, Says ANC'. *Business Day*, 30 May. https://www.businesslive.co.za/bd/national/2022-05-30-sa-will-not-meet-ndp-goals-by-2030-says-anc/ (accessed 6 October 2023).

Mbeki, M. 2009. *Architects of Poverty: Why African Capitalism Needs Changing*. Johannesburg: Picador Books.

Mkandawire, T. 2012. *Building the African State in the Age of Globalisation: The Role of Social Compacts and Lessons for South Africa*. Johannesburg: Real Africa Publications.

National Planning Commission. 2012. *National Development Plan 2030: Our Future – Make It Work*. https://www.gov.za/sites/default/files/gcis_document/201409/ndp-2030-our-future-make-it-workr.pdf (accessed 6 October 2023).

South African Government. 2010. *The New Growth Path: The Framework*. https://www.gov.za/sites/default/files/NGP%20Framework%20for%20public%20release%20FINAL_1.pdf (accessed 6 October 2023).

Stubbs, R. 2009. 'What Ever Happened to the East Asian Developmental State? The Unfolding Debate'. *Pacific Review* 22 (1): 1–22.

Terreblanche, S. 2002. *A History of Inequality in South Africa, 1652–2022*. Pietermaritzburg: University of Natal Press.

Toynbee, A. 1973. *A Study of History*. Oxford: Oxford University Press.

Turok, B. 2008. *From The Freedom Charter to Polokwane. The Evolution of ANC Economic Policy*. Cape Town: Picasso Headline.

Wade, R. 1990. *Governing the Market: Economic Theory and the Role of Government in East Asian Industrialisation*. Princeton: Princeton University Press.

Weiss, L. 1998. *The Myth of the Powerless State*. Ithaca, NY: Cornell University Press.

Weiss, L. and J.M. Hobson. 1995. *States and Economic Development: A Comparative Historical Analysis*. Cambridge: Polity Press.

Williams, M. (ed.). 2014. *The End of the Developmental State?* Pietermaritzburg: University of KwaZulu-Natal Press.

Woo-Cumings, M. (ed.). 1999. *The Developmental State*. Ithaca, NY: Cornell University Press.

CHAPTER 14

Breaking the Vicious Circle of the Divide-Rule-Extract Strategy

Yolisa Pakela-Jezile

Before attempting to break the vicious circle of the divide-rule-extract strategy that has gripped South Africa for 370 years, there is a need to first acknowledge and understand both historical and current events that led to and perpetuated the cycle. It then becomes easier to be deliberate and mindful in coming up with alternative strategies that benefit all of society.

This chapter is divided into five parts. The first part briefly examines the divide-and-rule strategy used to colonise South Africa. The second part is an appreciation of the strategy's efficiency in devastating the country while also highlighting some major events that led to the current state of affairs. Part three looks at the post-colonial state of affairs and the continued use of the divide-rule-extract strategy. This part ponders the question 'Is democracy just a distraction?'. Based on personal experiences, part four offers alternative solutions and attempts to provide strategies to establish a parallel economy (not second economy), designed and implemented by the people for the people.

Acknowledging the greatest strategy of all time

The divide-and-rule strategy has been used as far back as biblical times, as in the story of the Tower of Babel:

> 1. Now the whole earth had one language and the same words. 2. And as they migrated from the east, they came upon a plain in the land of Shinar and settled there. 3. And they said to one another, 'Come, let us make

bricks and fire them thoroughly.' And they had brick for stone and bitumen for mortar. 4. Then they said, 'Come, let us build ourselves a city and a tower with its top in the heavens, and let us make a name for ourselves; otherwise we shall be scattered abroad upon the face of the whole earth.' 5. The Lord came down to see the city and the tower, which mortals had built. 6. And the Lord said, 'Look, they are one people, and they have all one language, and this is only the beginning of what they will do; nothing that they propose to do will now be impossible for them. 7. Come, let us go down and confuse their language there, so that they will not understand one another's speech.' 8. So the Lord scattered them abroad from there over the face of all the earth, and they left off building the city. 9. Therefore, it was called Babel, because there the Lord confused the language of all the earth, and from there the Lord scattered them abroad over the face of all the earth (Genesis 11:1–9).

The meaning in this Bible passage is clear: when the people are united, 'nothing that they propose to do will be impossible for them'. Once the strategy of dividing the nation through different languages has been implemented, they can no longer communicate with each other.

Throughout history, the divide-and-rule strategy (sometimes referred to as divide-and-conquer) is almost like a cult, often applied in the arenas of politics, sociology, psychology and economics and just about everywhere else where absolute power is sought. In its simplest definition, divide-and-rule refers to strategies of maintaining control over one's subordinates or opponents by deliberately breeding dissent among them, thereby preventing them from uniting in opposition. In this strategy, one power breaks another power into smaller, more manageable pieces and then takes control of those pieces one by one. It generally takes a very strong power to implement such a strategy. In order to successfully break up another power or government, the conqueror must have access to strong political, military, economic machines and resources (Goettel 2023). In addition, the ruling power/conqueror must have extreme Machiavellian tendencies and be sly, cunning, unscrupulous and ruthless.

According to Matthew A. McIntosh (2019), the elements of divide-and-rule technique involve:

a) creating or encouraging divisions among the subjects to prevent alliances that could challenge the sovereign power;

b) aiding and promoting those who are willing to cooperate with the sovereign;

c) fostering distrust and enmity between local rulers; and

d) encouraging meaningless expenditures that reduce the capability for political and military spending.

In 1885, European leaders met at the infamous Berlin Conference to divide Africa and arbitrarily draw up borders that exist to this day.

'The Berlin Conference was Africa's undoing in more ways than one,' wrote Jan Nijman, Peter Muller and Harm de Blij in their book, *Geography: Realms, Regions, and Concepts*. 'The colonial powers superimposed their domains on the African continent. By the time independence returned to Africa . . . the realm had acquired a legacy of political fragmentation that could neither be eliminated nor made to operate satisfactorily' (Gathara 2019).

At the time of the conference, 80 per cent of Africa remained under traditional and local control. What ultimately resulted was a hodgepodge of geometric boundaries that divided Africa into 50 irregular countries. This new map of the continent was superimposed over 1 000 indigenous cultures and regions of Africa. The new countries lacked rhyme or reason and divided coherent groups of people and merged together disparate groups who really did not get along (Rosenberg 2021).

In South Africa, the National Party government introduced apartheid law in 1948. Apartheid, from the Afrikaans word meaning 'apartness', called for the separate development of the different racial groups in South Africa. Apartheid-made laws forced the different racial groups to live separately and develop separately, and grossly unequally, too. It tried to stop all intermarriage and social integration between racial groups. During apartheid, to have a friendship with someone of a different race generally brought suspicion upon you, or worse. More than this, apartheid was a social system that severely disadvantaged the majority of the population (black), simply because they did not share the skin colour of the rulers. Many were kept just above destitution because they were 'non-white'.

So, what happens when the nations, principalities, communities and people are ultimately divided and the ruler has absolute power? According to Henk Wesseling (1996), the colonisation of Africa did not create anything essentially new, but merely occasioned the acceleration of a social and economic modernisation process that had already begun. He further states that the partitioning was an important event for African people, bur was of marginal importance to Europe. This is a sad truth for Africans to contend with. However, to be able to understand and devise strategies to deal with the aftermath of colonisation, one needs to know their history. Europe's period of exploration and colonisation was fuelled largely by necessity. Their Silk Road to Asia was under threat due to the rise in power of the Ottoman Turks and decline of the Mongol Empire. At the same time, there were a number of improvements in shipbuilding and navigation, making it possible to travel further and for longer periods of time. European countries expanded their empires by aggressively establishing colonies in Africa, so that they could exploit and export Africa's resources for their own industrial ambition; to use Africans as labour to fuel industrialisation and to fight their wars, especially after the plague of 1894; to ensure protection of their trade routes; to benefit from the discovery of diamonds and gold; and for political power/exploitation. During the process of implementing the divide-and-rule strategy, the power extracts whatever resource they need and want from the people and the land. In Africa, Britain and Europe discovered reservoirs of unimaginable of wealth that continue to give, time after time.

The colonisation of South Africa is somewhat unique and slightly different from the rest of Africa. The two rulers – the Netherlands (1652–1795) and Great Britain (1795–1961) occupied South Africa under different circumstances. During these periods, the discovery of gold and diamonds spurred wealth and immigration and intensified conflicts between the Dutch and the British, and at the same time intensified the subjugation of indigenous inhabitants. Consequently, the successive colonial administration systematically deprived black communities of their land and livelihoods. The loss of this crucial resource was arguably the most important factor leading to the impoverishment and marginalisation of African communities.

Appreciating the extent and sophistication of extraction

Extraction, in this context, refers to extractive capitalism, generally described as the political-economic system that extracts wealth from the earth, from workers and from communities without fair payment or regard for the problems that ensue (Byrnes and Collins 2017). There are three areas where one can fully appreciate the thought that went into designing and implementing the extortion machination during and after apartheid: land, minerals and people.

From the onset of colonisation in South Africa, conquest and land seizure were achieved through warfare, complemented by dubious 'treaties', which colonists claimed were signed by leaders of communities of those times. African communities fought to defend and regain their lost land, but the superior weaponry and collaboration by other local communities enabled the colonists to prevail. Many discriminatory laws were passed against black people, but the most severe, the 1913 Natives Land Act codified those injustices by preserving some 87 per cent of the Union's land for the exclusive use of the white minority and a paltry 13 per cent for use by African farmers and some 80 per cent of the population. The Natives Land Act forced many black farmers to work as wage labourers on land they had previously owned.

The explosion of the mineral revolution with the discovery of diamonds and gold gave more impetus to the colonial government to consolidate and entrench its rule. United, the white British and Afrikaner landowners and industrialists set in motion a process that would consolidate their wealth, while excluding black people through legislative means.

International banks and private lenders increased cash and credit available to local farmers, miners and prospectors and they, in turn, placed growing demands for land and labour on the local African populations. The cycle of economic growth was stimulated by the continual expansion of the mining industry and with new-found wealth, consumer demand fuelled higher levels of trade. The mining boom and industrialisation gave birth to migrant workers. Migrant labour provided abundant cheap African labour for white-owned mines and farms (and later factories) and, at the same time, enforced racial segregation of land. Male migrants employed by white-owned businesses were prohibited from living permanently in cities and towns designated for whites only. Hundreds of thousands of African men lived in crowded single-sex hostels near their jobs and were not allowed to live with their wives and children, who were described as 'superfluous appendages' (Vosloo 2020).

The mining industry was locked into the migrant labour system, which gave it control over the labour force so that there was no question of strikes, which were illegal, and management was completely dominant over labour. Apartheid was not only embedded physically in the landscape of South Africa, but in the very souls of all the individuals and future generations.

A report by Hennie van Vuuren (2006), titled 'Apartheid Grand Corruption: Assessing the Scale of Crimes of Profit from 1976 to 1994', presents the extent of extraction over a 30-year period. The report acknowledges that the apartheid system ensured that white settlers – and, later, white South Africans – were at the helm of a racial oligarchy that was built on the subjugation of black South Africans. It was a corrupt system of governance. A near-monopoly on money, power and influence was in the hands of a minority and they used this to either violently suppress the majority or, at best, transfer resources in order to stave off the inevitable revolution.

Subsequent investigations on the extraction (corruption and looting) during and after apartheid is an ongoing process by the public protector and various reports have been presented to the general public via media or during various judicial commissions. One such report is where government reportedly contracted CIEX in 1997 to investigate the theft of R26 billion of state money during apartheid, and as the findings were never acted on, the public protector's office was asked to probe the matter (Business Tech 2017).

It is important to note that 'by the time of the advent of the new South Africa, about 17 000 statutory measures had been issued to segregate and control land division, with 14 different land control systems in South Africa' (Du Plessis 2011: 45). This demonstrates the importance of land dispossession in creating a racially and spatially divided South Africa. These thousands of statutory measures ensured a sophisticated system was developed for the apartheid order to function.

The Broederbond (an exclusively Afrikaner Calvinist and male secret society in South Africa dedicated to the advancement of the Afrikaner people, which operated between 1920 and 1994), in their effort to dismantle apartheid to save their own skins and develop a new Constitution for South Africa that would continue to serve their interests, state: 'The abolition of statutory discriminatory measures must not be seen as concessions but as a prerequisite for survival'. Furthermore, 'the head of government does not necessarily have to be white', but the presidency should be defined and its prerogatives restricted 'in such a way that the power that this post entails will not be applied in such a way that one group dominates the others' (Wren 1990). This statement shows clearly the attempt of the previous regime to ensure that freedom and equality was still going to be policed and benefit the white minority.

While the Constitution of the Republic of South Africa is considered the supreme law of the land and no other law or government action can supersede its provisions, it does not completely unravel all the 17 000 separatist statutory measures that were crafted and implemented during apartheid. This means the policy implementation in South Africa has yet to live up to the value of the Constitution, such as human dignity; the achievement of equality; the promotion of human rights and freedoms; non-racialism and non-sexism and the rule of law. This failure undermines the core of the democracy, which makes one wonder: is democracy simply a distraction, a smokescreen to blind the masses while divide-rule-extract continues?

Is democracy a distraction?

In post-colonial African politics many rulers have also relied on divide-and-rule politics to survive in office. A well-known example of this kind of rule is Mobutu Sese Seko, the leader of the Democratic Republic of the Congo from 1965 to 1997. By frequently rotating government officials, Mobutu established a system of uncertainty and vulnerability, where public officials were totally dependent on him (Acemoglu, Verdier and Robinson 2004; Leslie 1993).

Cabinet reshuffles happen in parliamentary systems for a variety of reasons – to replace ministers who have resigned, retired or died; to 'refresh' the government, often in the face of poor poll numbers; to remove poor performers; and reward supporters and punish others. In South Africa, there have been endless Cabinet reshuffles for a wide range of reasons, some not related to performance, but to allegations of crimes and corruptions. Since South Africa's 1994 political transition, a major feature of the country's new politics has been the centrality of issues of corruption in public controversy. From the embezzling of paltry pension payments by civil service clerks to allegations of Cabinet members' involvement in shady practices surrounding the procurement of multimillion rand arms deal, charges and counter-charges concerning the extent of dishonesty in public administration have flown thick and fast (Hyslop 2005).

Corruption erodes the trust in the public sector to act in the best interests of its citizens. It wastes taxes or rates that have been earmarked for important development initiatives. This means citizens have to put up with poor-quality services, degeneration of infrastructure or even miss out altogether on the benefits of democracy. At organisational levels, the impact of corruption is financial loss; damage to employee morale; damage to the organisation's reputation; organisational focus and resources diverted away from delivering core business and services to the community; and increased scrutiny, oversight and regulation. At an individual level, the impact is disciplinary action (sometimes unlawful); termination of employment; criminal charges; and damage to relationships with family, friends and colleagues. And, at community level, the impact of corruption is wasted taxpayer funds; loss of goods and services; lower community confidence in public authorities; and disadvantage to honest businesses that miss out on government contracts.

In a nutshell, corruption increases inequality, decreases popular accountability and political responsiveness, and thus produces rising frustration and hardship among citizens, who are then more likely to accept (or even demand) heavy-handed and illiberal tactics. Corruption therefore undermines the Constitution and destabilises democracy.

Parallel economies

Having dissected the problem and acknowledged the cause of divide-rule-extract and without wasting time pointing fingers, how do we formulate strategies for the destruction of this vicious circle? Most important is a deliberate and conscious change in mindset – the decolonisation of the mind – followed by an awareness of how a 'fair' world could work, taking relevant successes and modifying them for our situation. Once that mindset and empowerment is achieved, the specific question is how to turn extractive institutions into inclusive economic hives, paving the way for prosperity.

My personal and simple answer is to establish parallel economies. There is really no point trying to compete or keep up with the First Economy and its extractive tendencies from the past, but rather to develop what works with the little one has. This may sound defeatist, but the battle is being lost fast in trying to compete, whereas we could gain ground by focusing on building from what we have currently. Parallel economies refer to the deliberate and mindful building of social and economic hubs within communities and keeping money within communities. Parallel economies will allow a lot of people to participate in economic activities, with minimal (corrupt) government interference. Most important in such a system is an understanding of what is being done and deliberately, cohesively (inclusively) pursuing the goal by the people for the rest of the people.

In South Africa, pertinent issues remain: infrastructure requisite for economic growth, private property rights, contract rights for all, education, roads, electricity, housing and affordable credit. Enterprise uses and requires inclusive institutions. Education is critical for innovation to advance the technological world. Education needs to be adequately financed. The state needs to be inclusive for economic growth to occur. At this present moment, one can only dream of such strong inclusive institutions, a capable state, social cohesion and a conducive policy environment and, even more so, the collaborative implementation of policies.

However, in the meantime, responsible citizens can consider implementing the following strategies, some based on lessons from the past or other countries.

Decolonising the mind

Steve Biko puts this eloquently in his book *I Write What I Like*:

> This is the first truth, bitter as it may seem, that we have to acknowledge before we can start on any programme designed to change the status quo . . . The first step, therefore, is to make the black man come to himself; to pump back life into his empty shell; to infuse him with pride and dignity, to remind him of his complicity in the crime of allowing himself to be misused and letting evil reign supreme in the country of his birth (1996: 29).

This cleansing of the mind and soul of the evils of apartheid is a must for every man, woman, child and future generations that have been affected by apartheid. The cleansing must be immediately followed by constantly infusing an attitude of pride and dignity.

Deliberate reversal of separatist and extractive statutes

Some of the 17 000 separatist measures are still in force today, making it difficult for most black people to own property, access capital, access good education and so on. It is important to be a responsible citizen and participate in policy development and provide the required evidence to inform that policy. Some good policies were implemented during the apartheid era, even though they were extractive and destructive to the masses. Even worse policies are being implemented now because people do not question or lobby to amend these based on new or overlooked evidence.

Implement programmes that build rural economies

Where there is an opportunity to do so by government officials or non-governmental organisations or any other entity, we need to deliberately implement programmes and projects where there will be economic gains for the participants. When these programmes succeed, they are often implemented by collaborative partners, such as academics, researchers, the private sector, policymakers and social structures of a particular community.

Empowered social movements/networks

There is no lack of examples of social networks in South Africa – organised efforts that endeavour to bring about or impede social, political, economic or cultural change. Normally, social movements often work outside the system by engaging in various kinds of protest, including demonstrations, picket lines, sit-ins and sometimes outright violence. All of this is good, but that can always be elevated to deal with issues in a more constructive manner, rather than destructive (of own infrastructure), which usually results in both the message and the cause being lost.

Examples of some successful social movements are found in Brazil, where a grassroots movement of empowered people, rather than politicians, overthrew the country's military dictatorship in 1985. Social movements led by these people paved the way for a coalition that resisted any future dictatorships. Ever since Brazil broke that cycle, it has seen a huge rise in prosperity. In fact, between the years 2000 and 2012, it was one of the world's fastest-growing economies (Acemoglu and Robinson 2012). This serves as proof that it is never too late to shatter the chains of poverty.

Build, protect and own institutions and infrastructure

Institutions are at the centre of rebuilding the nation. In the stereotypical Western view of previously colonised people, there is a tendency to assume wildness of the mind and behaviour, lacking class and organisation. This is simply not true of any humans. A strong physical infrastructure and solid institutions already exist, which were inherited from previous governments. Our biggest problem is failure to understand that these belong to *all* who live in the republic. There is a tendency to destroy and disown everything in the path as retaliation for lack of access to or simply lack of knowledge about the importance of a particular structure or infrastructure. Much has been written about the destruction of efforts to rebuild families, to restore rule of law, to change curricula to build a good education system. This destruction is so rife that infrastructure destruction has brought the country to its knees at different times, such as during the unrest and subsequent looting and destruction of property in Gauteng and KwaZulu-Natal in July 2021.

Conclusion

The divide-and-rule strategy is a double-edged sword; with both negative and positive effects, depending on the context. The negative side of the strategy has been used to disempower and devastate entire continents and tribes with the sole purpose of extracting wealth and resources. The divisions of race, creed, class and so on are deeply embedded in South African society. One could argue that it is part of human DNA and the practices are passed from one generation to the next. The positive effect of the strategy is that it can be used to avert disaster when criminal minds come together, such as dividing a band of thieves or in the case of the above-mentioned Bible passage, dividing people who wanted to take over heaven and overthrow God. The suggested main strategies of *decolonising the mind*, or cleansing of the defective DNA caused by the divide-and-rule strategy, and *creating parallel economies*, instead of playing catch-up or comparison with current economies built on a divide-rule-extract strategy, hinge on one constant strategy based on unity, working together, mutual support, team work and cohesion. The key ingredient of that strategy that brings everything together is solidarity:

Look, they are one people, and they have all one language, and this is only the beginning of what they will do; nothing that they propose to do will now be impossible for them (Genesis 11:6).

References

Acemoglu, D. and J.A. Robinson. 2012. *Why Nations Fail: The Origins of Power, Prosperity, and Poverty*. New York: Cown Business.

Acemoglu, D., T. Verdier and J.A. Robinson. 2004. 'Kleptocracy and Divide-and-Rule: A Model of Personal Rule'. *Journal of the European Economic Association* 2 (2–3): 162–92.

Biko, S. 1996. *I Write What I Like*. Randburg: Ravan Press.

Business Tech. 2017. 'Not Just Absa: Other Companies Named in Apartheid-Era State Looting Report'. *Business Tech*, 16 January. https://businesstech.co.za/news/business/150613/not-just-absa-other-companies-named-in-apartheid-era-state-looting-report/ (accessed 6 October 2023).

Byrnes, S. and C. Collins. 2017. 'The Equity Crisis: The True Costs of Extractive Capitalism'. In: *The Community Resilience Reader: Essential Resources for an Era of Upheaval*, edited by D. Lerch. Washington, DC: Island Press/Center for Resource Economics. https://www.springerprofessional.de/en/the-equity-crisis-the-true-costs-of-extractive-capitalism/15131518 (accessed 6 October 2023).

Du Plessis, W.J. 2011. 'African Indigenous Land Rights in a Private Ownership Paradigm'. *Potchefstroom Electronic Law Journal* 14 (7): 45–71.

Gathara, P. 2019. 'Berlin 1884: Remembering the Conference that Divided Africa'. *Al Jazeera*, 15 November. https://www.aljazeera.com/opinions/2019/11/15/berlin-1884-remembering-the-conference-that-divided-africa (accessed 6 October 2023).

Goettel D. 2023. 'What Is a Divide and Conquer Strategy?' *Language Humanities*, 29 August. https://www.languagehumanities.org/what-is-a-divide-and-conquer-strategy.htm (accessed 6 October 2023).

Hyslop, J. 2005. 'Political Corruption: Before and after Apartheid'. *Journal of Southern African Studies* 31 (4): 773–89.

Leslie, W.J. 1993. *Zaire: Continuity and Political Change in an Oppressive State*. New York: Routledge.

McIntosh, M.A. 2019. ' "Divide et Impera": A History of "Divide and Rule" '. *Brewminate*, 22 July. https://brewminate.com/divide-et-impera-a-history-of-divide-and-rule/ (accessed 6 October 2023).

Rosenberg, M. 2021. 'The Berlin Conference to Divide Africa: The Colonization of the Continent by European Powers'. *ThoughtCo*, 30 July. https://thoughtco.com/berlin-conference-1884-1885-divide-africa-1433556/ (accessed 6 October 2023).

Van Vuuren, H. 2006. 'Apartheid Grand Corruption: Assessing the Scale of Crimes of Profit from 1976 to 1994'. Institute for Security Studies. https://www.africaportal.org/publications/apartheid-grand-corruption-assessing-the-scale-of-crimes-of-profit-from-1976-to-1994/ (accessed 6 October 2023).

Vosloo, C. 2020. 'Extreme Apartheid: The South African System of Migrant Labour and Its Hostels'. *Image & Text* 34: 1–33.

Wesseling, H. 1996. *Divide and Rule: The Partition of Africa, 1880–1914*. Westport : Praeger.

Wren, C.S. 1990. 'A Secret Society of Afrikaners Helps to Dismantle Apartheid'. *New York Times*, 30 October. https://www.nytimes.com/1990/10/30/world/a-secret-society-of-afrikaners-helps-to-dismantle-apartheid.html (accessed 6 October 2023).

CHAPTER 15

A Supply-Driven Approach to Alleviate Poverty, Unemployment and Inequalities in Black Areas through Entrepreneurship

Thami Mazwai

South Africa urgently needs specialised entrepreneurship programmes that involve black small businesses and co-operatives (co-ops) in townships and rural villages to render services and thus eradicate the scourge of poverty, unemployment and inequality in these areas. This would be a double victory as, firstly, it would capacitate small businesses and co-ops in townships and villages and, secondly, it confronts poverty, unemployment and inequality head-on. This is in addition to the stimulatory effect of government spending and is urgent, as Covid-19 worsened what was already a desperate situation and the poverty, unemployment and inequality scourge is now at crisis levels.

Fortuitously, the *Economic Reconstruction and Recovery Plan* (ERRP) (South African Government 2020) emphasises and responds to poverty, unemployment and inequality. It states that the past decade has seen the economy stagnate, which has strained efforts to tackle the historical and structural levels of poverty, unemployment and inequality (2020: 2). As government spending is spread over various departments and no programme can accommodate all, a pilot on 'government spending to feed prisoners' is suggested. This pilot programme, which can be replicated in other areas and is the essence of this chapter, is driven through the Programme Management Unit (PMU) located in the Presidency, as described later. The persistent and rising levels of poverty, unemployment and inequality have been of concern for some time. Some eight years ago, two government ministers, Dr Rob Davies and Ebrahim Patel, appointed task teams to investigate the persistence of poverty, unemployment and inequality despite post-1994 mediations. Both task teams submitted reports, but only one was released.

Fast-forward to 2022 when prices rose excessively as a result of the demand for oil and other key commodities in world markets in the wake of the Russian invasion of Ukraine and the South African Reserve Bank (SARB) expressed concern about price increases in the local economy. It was concerned that rising prices, some on basic essentials, would hit lower-income earners very hard and worsen poverty, unemployment and inequality, which could result in 'further episodes of unrest' (SARB 2022: 13).

In July 2022, Business Unity South Africa reinforced these concerns when the price of oil was skyrocketing, impacting on transport and basic necessities (Papayya and Bates 2022). Additionally, energy problems were affecting the economy and growth would be negatively affected. This was worrying, as just a year previously, uprisings in Gauteng and KwaZulu-Natal, indirectly linked to poverty, unemployment and inequality, saw at least 340 lives lost. At that time, South Africa's gross domestic product (GDP) contracted by 1.5 per cent and some R50 billion was lost in output. Real solutions must be found to also deal with the underlying causes in order to avoid similar situations in future.

The National Planning Commission's *Diagnostic Report* (2011) highlights that 'poor' or 'no' implementation of policies/programmes has constrained the alleviation of poverty, unemployment and inequality. Also, government departments working independently, with little communication or co-ordination, have aggravated the situation. The report also emphasised that the restructuring of the economy (ostensibly to also ensure the entry of black players) is long overdue. Göran Therborn explains this 'long overdue' as he decries South Africa's two-pronged strategy to deal with poverty, unemployment and inequality (2019: 35). The one prong was the representation of black people within business organisations through legislation such as the Broad-Based Black Economic Empowerment Act and the Employment Equity Act. The other prong was redistributive compensation – for instance, social grants and targeted employment such as the Public Works programmes. Regrettably, Therborn (2019) states that these have not achieved the desired results. Dandira Mushangai echoes these concerns when he speaks of 'the failure of the policies of the democratic government since 1994 to address the problem of unemployment' (2015: 15).

Septi Bukula et al. (2011) identified the problem of silos and recommended that small business development be located in the Presidency, where it would have a cross-cutting developmental and co-ordinating role. Instead, when the government created the Department of Small Business Development (DSBD) in 2014, it did not give it the overall responsibility to drive and co-ordinate small business development across the board. Without this capacity, it could not enhance small business development as a sector. This has lately been corrected, as Cabinet has agreed on a template, which will perhaps later become policy, that will ensure departments provide information to the DSBD on their small business programmes and how they interact with other programmes.

In March 2022 the DSBD released the *National Integrated Small Enterprise Development (NISED) Masterplan* to strengthen and implement the vision of the *National Strategy for the Development and Promotion of Small Business* (South African Government 1995). The masterplan is linked to the *National Development Plan 2030* (National Planning Commission 2012) and promotes co-ordination by all social partners, such as labour, civil society and the private sector. It is specific that it is a framework for consultation for the support and development of growth to small, medium and micro enterprises (SMMEs) in South Africa (DSBD 2022: 2).

This is welcome, as specialised, integrating and intense approaches based on entrepreneurship are crucial. This fits into the reconstruction and recovery plan (South African Government 2020: 15), as it is in essence a broad stratagem from which action plans will flow. Some will stimulate entrepreneurship in townships and villages and this is appropriate, as C.K. Prahalad (2009) stresses that the real source of market expansion is not the wealthy few, or even the emerging middle class, but the billions of aspiring poor joining the market economy.

The Gauteng Provincial Legislature's seminal Township Economic Development Act of 2022 must be lauded. It is a welcome mindset change as context is now taken into account. Townships are acknowledged as human settlements with specific settings, rather than only sources of labour and extensions of central business districts. In the past, South Africa did not differentiate between townships and central business districts and the Gauteng government was the first to formally make this distinction.

As Friederike Welter (2011) proclaims, entrepreneurship is best understood and implemented within its historical, temporal, institutional, spatial and social contexts. Prahalad (2009) pioneered the base or bottom of the pyramid approach with his seminal book *The Fortune at the Bottom of the Pyramid*. Jeremy Hall et al. (2012: 788) refined his argument that the bottom of the pyramid is a source of self-reliant producers and consumers. The focus on the poor should thus be on the poor as producers and entrepreneurs, rather than only as customers or receivers of compassion.

The aforementioned approach is endorsed by the World Bank, as it warns that South Africa risks another lost decade if it does not use the Covid-19 crisis as an inflection point (World Bank 2021: 3). The National Planning Commission criticised a 'business-as-usual approach', as the country risks not meeting the objectives of a prosperous, non-racial and democratic South Africa, with opportunities for everyone, irrespective of race or gender (2011: 8).

Background to concept

South Africa's post-1994 journey started on a high; however, somewhere and somehow, the wheels came off. The country has come a long way, but the transition remains incomplete, with widespread poverty in black neighbourhoods (World Bank 2018). This has seen anti-government protests – some violent – spread from area to area. Elizabeth Lubinga (2020) notes that South Africa has one of the highest rates of protest in the world, with more than 2 million people protesting every year.

The days of hope for poverty, unemployment and inequality

The first years of democracy were vibrant and created hope for the future. The government effected progressive policies flowing from the 'Reconstruction and Development Plan' (ANC 1994), which advocated small business as an important vehicle to integrate blacks into the economy. The lynchpin of this strategy was the *White Paper on National Strategy for the Development and Promotion of Small Business in South Africa* (South African Government 1995), a consequence of South Africa's pivotal International Conference on Small Business, hosted by the Minister of Trade and Industry, Trevor Manuel, at which Nelson Mandela was the guest speaker.

World experts participated in the conference, which was then followed by provincial conferences. Consequently, the National Small Business Act 102 of

1996 was passed and policies, programmes and analytical reports followed. These included a mid-term evaluation of the strategy on small business in 1999; the *Review of Ten Years of Small Business Support in South Africa 1994–2004* (DTI 2004); *Integrated Small-Enterprise-Development Strategy: Unlocking the Potential of South African Entrepreneurs* (DTI 2005); *The New Growth Path: The Framework* (South African Government 2010); the *Accelerated and Shared Growth Initiative – South Africa (ASGISA)* (The Presidency 2006); and the National Informal Business Upliftment Strategy (NIBUS) in 2013.

Matthew Davies (2013) quotes Dawie Roodt, a prominent economist, who commented that the ascent of the African National Congress (ANC) into power saw 'millions get running water, electricity, etc'. At an illustrative level, shafts of bright light poured out of doorways of the traditional village rondavel as the electrification programme gained ground. However, Roodt aptly noted, 'the infrastructure in general was neglected, and slowly state inefficiency and corruption became serious problems'. Davis (2013) points out that inflation, at 14 per cent before 1994, fell to 5 per cent within ten years. The budget deficit, 8 per cent in 1997, fell to 1.5 per cent in 2004. Interest rates dropped from 16 per cent to under 9 per cent in the first decade of the ANC government. While the unemployment rate increased from 22 per cent in 1994 to 25 per cent in 2014, it was below 25 per cent between 2014 and 2018.

Also significant, as Lameez Omarjee (2019) attests, during President Thabo Mbeki's years, the economy responded to increased demand as global growth accelerated. International agencies gave South Africa positive ratings as an investment destination. The cherry on top was the social grants system administered by the Department of Social Development (DSD), which lifted millions out of poverty. Colin Bundy (2019: 90) confirms that the grants system reduced poverty immensely. The situation unfortunately deteriorated, with troubling developments in the political-legal-economic institutional framework.

The reality of poverty, unemployment and inequality

Poverty, unemployment and inequality must be contextualised and expressed in terms of hunger, a basic indicator of human development. Crain Soudien, Vasu Reddy and Ingrid Woolard (2019: 3) contend that poverty and inequality in South Africa are durable and persistent due to a multiplicity of factors, which occur across a range of structural and psycho-social dimensions of the social experience. According to Servaas van der Berg, Leila Patel and Grace Bridgman, 'hunger is simply when persons or families run out of food' (2022: 2). Millions of South Africans now live in the indignity of dependence on the R350 a month from the DSD, when R350 hardly fills a small trolley at any supermarket and transport, rent and school fees need to be added to this.

In terms of poverty in general, Statistics South Africa (Stats SA) is specific that according to the minimum income question measure of poverty and just before the Covid-19 pandemic hit, 57 per cent of the population lived in poverty in 2019 (2021). This is a disturbingly high percentage.

With respect to unemployment, Stats SA (2022) reports that the unemployment rate was 33.9 per cent in the second quarter of 2022. This means that 14.9 million people were employed while 7.9 million walked the streets. Youth unemployment was a staggering 66 per cent. Of 10.2 million youths aged 15–24 years, 37 per cent were not in employment, education or training. This has resulted in deepening social ills of substance abuse, prostitution and human trafficking.

In relation to inequality, a World Bank study states that South Africa ranks first among 164 countries in the global inequality database (World Bank 2022). Ansellia Adams and John M. Luiz (2022: 859) emphasise that the richest 10 per cent of the population earns 60 per cent of national income and owns 95 per cent of all wealth, yet more than half of all South Africans live in poverty. The country's Gini coefficient of 0.66 makes it the most unequal society in the world (Francis and Webster 2019).

Why efforts have not delivered on expectations

The National Planning Commission maintains that the complexities of organisational restructuring ensured there was insufficient focus on addressing deeper institutional legacies (2011: 25). It has also admitted that the corporate landscape restricts business entry and expansion in markets, yet this is essential for employment (2012: 114). Simon Roberts (2017a) agrees, as he also warns that an economy and markets that are not inclusive bar the entrance of new players and this prolongs and even deepens poverty, unemployment and inequality. Roberts posits that there should be 'increased participation of the poor and previously disenfranchised' (2017a: 4), which reverberates with Prahalad's (2009) sentiments. Roberts (2017b) is also adamant that excluding the majority provides ammunition for those who argue that gaining access to wealth is possible only through corruption and rent-seeking.

Lawrence Mpele Lekhanya and Roger B. Mason point out that a major problem is 'highly concentrated economic sectors and widespread anti-competitive behaviour' (2014: 333). This is reinforced by the Competition Commission (2021: 3), which stresses that because of the skewed economic structure among tax-paying firms, small and medium-sized enterprises (SMEs) contributed only 24 per cent of total firm turnover in 2016. This is relative to the 50–60 per cent cited by a study by the Organisation for Economic Co-operation and Development (OECD 2015). As SMEs are more employment intensive in comparison with large firms, with tax-paying or formal sector firms contributing 38 per cent of employment in South Africa, the skewed economic structure constrains employment generation and also contributes to household inequality.

Thus, these levels of concentration see existing or matured entities with deeper pockets, controlling value chains, enjoying the latest technology, boasting a deep knowledge of business and its environments and, above all, being part of entrenched networks (Paunescu 2013: 71; Gomez 2012: 52). New entrants are at a massive disadvantage. Bundy (2019: 93) concurs that while successive post-apartheid governments inherited an economy dominated by large corporations and markets that were highly concentrated and vertically integrated, they did not reconfigure this economy and, instead, entrenched it.

Elsewhere, I have presented six variables militating against the entry of small and black businesses (Mazwai 2013: 269; see also Roberts 2017a: 277; Paunescu 2013: 71; Bundy 2019: 93; Gomez 2012: 52). These are: the levels of concentration in sectors of the economy; the focus on the macroeconomy and big business; inconsistent delivery of services; poor implementation of local economic development; the unintended consequences of black economic empowerment; and rent-seeking. I also referred to the labour–capital axis and quoted the late business leader Michael Spicer (2012), who spoke of a 'corporatist carve-up where Big Business, Big Labour and Big Government devise, through a system of distributional bargaining policies that suit themselves or, at worst, which they can live with by virtue of their size, but which are highly prejudicial to small and medium enterprises'. Of specific concern is that black business complains of a procurement system that restricts its participation in the economy. According to Khulekani Magubane (2022), the Black Business Federation is talking of a legal challenge to the preferential public procurement guidelines, which disadvantage black businesses when bidding for government tenders. It is evident that this is still a sore point, as only a year ago the Black Business Council demanded specific mention of black ownership and localisation of product and the Treasury said the latest guidelines do not do away with empowerment criteria (Mochiko 2022).

Faith Mashele (2015) argues that the debate is not whether South Africa's procurement regulations foster socio-economic advancement; the consensus is that South Africa's regulations do not promote inclusivity.

While poor implementation is being flagged for lack of progress, it must not be ignored that this was a transforming civil service in which employment equity legislation was being implemented, predominantly at the upper levels. Although employment equity is justifiable given the history of the country, it is arguable that people without experience who are appointed to senior positions would not be hesitant in taking decisions with major budget implications. To add to this, the apartheid civil service would not leave without laying booby traps or being obstructionist.

The other problem has been patronage and gatekeeping. Domonic Bearfield (2009) argues that globally patronage has been used to reward the party faithful. In terms of South Africa, Alexander Beresford (2015: 236) asserts that patronage is distributed to regenerate political power, which is used to maintain networks in the ANC. It is at the root of the factional struggles in the ANC and is not new to the organisation, he says. The result is that because of the battles, important projects sometimes do not take off or the people appointed to key positions do not necessarily have the appropriate skills.

In addition to the warring policies and markets, psycho-social issues also affected black entrepreneurs. Benson O. Igboin rightly stresses that colonialism (and apartheid) portrayed black and indigenous people as inferior and, unfortunately, many internalised this (2011: 101). This internalisation has had an impact on self-esteem, which sees issues of 'self-efficacy' and 'reciprocal determinism' come into play. Austin Mwange explains that 'self-efficacy' is an individual's confidence in self, whereas 'reciprocal determinism' is how the individual and environment interact (2018: 132). According to social and institutional theories, internalisation, embedded in social structuration – although persistent – is affected by generational changes. Nonetheless, it can be argued that in South Africa the internalisation of inferiority is prolonged since for many in black communities, the socio-economic tapestry is still the apartheid past. This also explains the low levels of entrepreneurial success by local black people to the extent that immigrant entrepreneurs upstage them in their own markets. However, the problem is not only about uncompetitive local black people, it is also about their socialisation after 1948 when apartheid decreed that blacks were solely to provide labour and policies restricted black entrepreneurship. For the record, scores of black entrepreneurs overcame or defied these restrictions and fulfilled their ambitions – hence the Richard Maponyas who emerged – but not in acceptable numbers, although the situation is improving. However, black small businesses were devastated by Covid-19 lockdowns.

The plight of the small business sector

There are approximately 3.2 million micro, small and medium enterprises in South Africa, employing some 12.9 million people (Finscope 2022). About 2.7 million (85 per cent) are micro-enterprises employing 0 to 10 people; small businesses that employ up to 50 people number about 375 809 (14.4 per cent); and medium-sized enterprises amount to 20 906 (0.8 per cent). The estimated turnover of the enterprises is a whopping R3.1 trillion.

The fact that close to 3 million individuals are employed in the micro sector (Stats SA 2022: 7) is distressing, as Finscope (2006: 9) reveals that over 70 per cent of small businesses in Gauteng have turnovers of less than R70 000 per annum. Though these are 2006 figures, there has not been much improvement, particularly in light of Covid-19. Furthermore, only 7 per cent of businesses in Gauteng townships had turnovers of over R1 million per annum, but over more than 50 per cent of these were owned by people from outside the townships, whether white, Indian, coloured or immigrant entrepreneurs (Njiro, Mazwai and Urban 2010: 27).

Crime and corruption are also major concerns and are among the factors responsible for slow growth in the SMME sector (Sitharam and Hoque 2016: 285). The majority of the SMMEs (88.89 per cent) in KwaZulu-Natal view crime and corruption as a major factor affecting business performance. The rest of South Africa is no different.

Covid-19 and black small business

A United Nations Development Programme study on the micro and informal sector, commissioned by the DSBD, describes the impact of the Covid-19 pandemic and lockdowns as unprecedented and more challenging than the financial crisis of ten years ago (UNDP 2021). Added to the massive job losses, it states that workers lucky enough to keep their jobs lost around 50 per cent of their wages (Benhura and Magejo 2020). Job losses were around 60 per cent for the self-employed in the informal sector by April 2020 compared to before the lockdown. According to UNCTAD (2021), another analysis by Finfind and the Department of Small Business Development revealed that 42.7 per cent of businesses had closed by November 2020 due to the pandemic and the lockdown, which began in March 2020. Overall, 60 per cent of full-time jobs were lost across all SMMEs and 76.8 per cent of part-time jobs were lost. Mmboswobeni Watson Ladzani refers to research findings on the impact of Covid-19, which state that close to 92 per cent of small businesses were impacted, as 71 per cent did not have enough cash to keep their businesses afloat and 16 per cent of businesses were due to retrench staff (2022: 29). The latest mind-blowing revelation is from the Auditor-General of South Africa, who informed Parliament that the spaza shop support programme had a budget of R175 million, but the actual assistance to spaza shops had been R18 million (Auditor-General of South Africa 2022). Despite widespread hunger, poverty and job losses, close to 90 per cent of the relief was returned to Treasury.

While the government of South Africa devised strategies to intervene and assist ailing informal businesses, it did not fulfil its promises and obligations (Odeku 2021). The pandemic, in the meantime, ravaged informal black-owned businesses to the extent that the majority of them have been liquidated, while those that are still operating struggle to stay afloat.

Galvanising entrepreneurship after Covid-19

Self-employment in South Africa constitutes 10 per cent of total employment against about 30 per cent in some upper-middle-income countries (World Bank 2021). The World Bank argues: 'If South Africa were to raise its self-employment ratios to the average of upper-middle-income countries, unemployment rates could potentially be halved' (2021: 5).

Entrepreneurship reduced poverty in parts of India and Nigeria (Eguruze and Kumari 2021). More than 40 entrepreneurial strategies/models were pertinent and useful in different contexts of poverty alleviation in the two countries. China reduced extreme poverty by half from 1990 to 2010 (Si et al. 2015). China's determination was highlighted by President Xi Jinping declaring that China would have eradicated poverty by 2020 (Davie et al. 2021). However, poverty reduction must not only rely on multinationals or handouts from central government (Si et al. 2015: 120). The people must deal with poverty themselves through their efforts. The involvement of government must be a supportive role.

China's approach was multi-pronged and based on conditions on the ground and the exploration of varying approaches and practices (Weiping 2018: 2). Entrepreneurship was one of the many approaches. From 1981 to 2013, China lifted 850 million people out of poverty and the percentage of those in extreme poverty fell from 88 per cent to 1.85 per cent (2018: 2). A shift from passive to active attitudes and behaviour by the people on the ground is essential (Si et al. 2015:120). Thus, in addition to the entrepreneurship approaches, poverty reduction in the Yiwu area was largely determined by disruptive models or creative destruction, if Joseph Schumpeter (2012) is brought into the picture.

The suggested approach

The suggested intervention is premised on dealing with the problems that are being encountered through a combination of approaches that have been tried and succeeded elsewhere. What is critical is that, first, the reality must inform interventions and, secondly, the beneficiaries must be active, rather than being dependents. This is essential, as many black entrepreneurs or aspirants are inclined to situate themselves in 'dependency' and 'entitlement' syndromes. This is for another time, but it must be noted here.

The problems

The major constraints to black entrepreneurship include poor implementation, barriers to market entry, crime and corruption and psycho-social issues. The biggest problem, however, is that mature businesses – the pre-1994 or white businesses – have deeper pockets, the latest technology and a deep knowledge of markets, sectors and the business environment. Above all, they are entrenched in networks and control value chains, a point also made by Bundy (2019).

It must, however, also be stressed that this is also a reality of markets. Incumbents, black or white, fight to retain or increase market share – what shareholders and investors expect them to do. The drawback is that the government is 'limp-wristed' in economic restructuring and facilitating free and fair markets, a point made by Bundy (2019).

Lessons from other environments

Poverty reduction in China had four steps, which were strictly adhered to. These steps include (1) clear poverty-reduction goals; (2) targeted strategies, fund use, implementation of measures and also by the poor themselves; (3) involvement of institutions; and (4) rigorous institutional arrangements (Weiping 2018). The latter included an accountability system in which the determination of the central government is evident and provincial governments also take responsibilities. They also included a well-co-ordinated policy system to take into account conflicting or complementing policies; social mobilisation with extensive public participation; and a strict assessment system with consequence management for not meeting targets or the abuse of resources.

The lessons that then emerge are a passionate commitment of all and the involvement of the highest office in the land; the government taking the lead, inclusive of interdepartmental co-ordination; and a singleness of purpose to achieve the objectives. The lessons further include the active and fervent participation of the beneficiaries; disruptive innovation or creative destruction; thought-out strategies based on local contexts; short- and long-term targets; strict monitoring and evaluation; and ensuring processes are free of corruption and manipulation.

The intervention

The proposed intervention and the essence of this chapter is the use of township and village entities to provide services and thus grow them and, at the same time, fight poverty, unemployment and inequality. However, it will be difficult to drive numerous programmes on government spending. On that account, one avenue of government spending – feeding prisoners – has been selected to test drive this concept. A PMU in the Presidency would get qualifying black-owned entities, small businesses and/or co-ops in townships and villages to supply food to the 243 prisons in South Africa. These have a population of about 160 000 inmates and the government spends over R100 million a year to feed them. The black-owned entities would, in terms of policy, include women and youth-owned entities, people with disabilities and those owned by military veterans.

The PMU would design the project plan, complete with indicators such as objectives, targets and quarterly reporting, and in consultation with relevant parties. An interdepartmental committee consisting of the DSBD, the DSD, the Department of Trade and Industry and Competition (DTIC), the Department of Agriculture, Land Reform and Rural Development and Department of Justice and Correctional Services could then be appointed, with the DTIC and DSBD as chair. The PMU would report to this committee and the president.

Naturally, as this is a complex, massive and ambitious project; issues of premises, capacity, scale and professionalism are crucial. For instance, this means the qualifying entities must have the appropriate infrastructure, such as premises and industrial equipment. As very few black-owned entities are immediate candidates and some of the existing ones would need to have a technical partner, the PMU's responsibility would include the development and capacitation of entities to expected levels.

Infrastructure development, such as premises and equipment, and capacitation (skilling) for food production and supply are important legs of the *Economic Reconstruction and Recovery Plan* (South African Government 2020: 23). Since the prisons are in any case feeding their inmates, this would be available as a risk-management and fallback position. Hence, this is an appropriate sector to pilot the concept. It is also for this reason that development institutions such as the Small Enterprise Development Agency, the Small Enterprise Finance Agency, the National Empowerment Fund, the Sector Education and Training Authorities in the food and health sectors, and others come in, as they must be part of the ecosystem to provide skilling and funds to the entities.

The key variables for the intervention are an appropriate partnership between the Office of the President, National Treasury and a multilateral development agency; government budgets on food for prisoners; black-owned entities in the townships and villages; and the development institutions and government departments mentioned above. The participation of a multilateral agency such as the United Nations Industrial Development Organisation, the African Development Bank or the United Nations Development Programme is crucial in terms of developing critical skills and facilitating knowledge transfer, ethical and professional conduct, as well as bringing in additional funds.

The PMU in the Presidency would use the recently introduced district delivery model, as the *Economic Reconstruction and Recovery Plan* indicates that state procurement is going to shift to local procurement (South African Government 2020: 15). As the black-owned entities and activities would operate locally, they would have to be allocated to local prisons in their specific metro/district.

The district hub, the operating centre of the district, would be responsible for procurement for the project and enable the ecosystem described above, which includes the stimulation and co-ordination of the local actors and the creation of value chains. This includes monitoring and evaluation in liaison with the PMU.

In line with international best practice, higher education institutions would be part of the ecosystems in districts, not only to accelerate innovation in individual entities, but also to ensure the institutional framework in the district is part of the process of capacitation. Finally, when the project is driven from the highest office in the land, it gives it the stamp of importance and urgency. This overcomes sloth implementation, as the provision of quarterly reports is part of the process.

Immediate benefits of the approach

A major benefit of the approach is that a completely new sector with new players and value chains in numerous districts is created. As mature businesses are not involved, the R100 million is guaranteed income for the black-owned enterprises. An indirect but important benefit the intervention would provide is markets for emerging farmers currently having problems accessing value chains. By definition, the successful pilot would see the government replicate the intervention in other sectors in the townships and villages, and more employment being created, and not necessarily from the Presidency.

South Africa is currently engaged in emotional debates on the basic income grant (BIG) as a result of the Covid-19 pandemic and there are desperate pleas for the alleviation of poverty in communities. South Africa's Treasury is concerned that 46 per cent of the entire population currently receives social grants and 'there are already 27.8 million people in the system receiving the normal grants and 9.4 million receiving the Covid-19 related Social Relief of Distress grant' (Business Tech 2021). While the government has a constitutional commitment to ensure income security for its citizens, there is widespread concern that social assistance has stretched to the point of unsustainability (Potts 2012: 75).

The intervention responds to this debate, as entrepreneurship and BIG are not mutually exclusive. Minister of Social Development, Lindiwe Zulu, speaks of a two-pronged approach. She argues that the grant is critical because millions are starving and BIG is thus essential; on the other hand, job opportunities must also be created through entrepreneurship, so that people can take charge of their lives (Zulu 2021).

Finally, South Africa has an investment conference each year and for the 2022 conference, investors pledged R332 billion in projects (Mahlakoane 2022). However, these are pledges and they would be realised faster and increase the levels of foreign direct investment in the country if there were an entrepreneurship revolution in the country, as was the case in India, Brazil and South Korea. Investors would see that there are no threats of social instability and would have confidence in investing.

The measure of the success of any intervention is analysed through the Theory of Change. This is reflected in Table 15.1.

Table 15.1: Important aspects in terms of the Theory of Change reflecting improvement

The past for new entities	The change in terms of the intervention
There was little or no implementation of plans or policies and all had to fit into the programme of the department or the unit.	The unit is in the Presidency, partnered by a multilateral agency, and with specific time frames, so that implementation and monitoring will happen.
New entities had to face existing players for market opportunities and did not have the resources.	Government spending defines opportunities for entities getting into the market. It is a market specially designed for black entities.

The past for new entities	The change in terms of the intervention
Entry into value chains was tight and favoured the existing players, and even if black businesses got into the value chain, the competition was onerous in terms of skills and resources.	New value chains are being created and skilling is provided by Sector Education and Training Authorities and the development institutions being part of the intervention. The presence of the multilateral agency sees new methods being introduced and these are not based on what existing entities are doing. It is new knowledge for black-owned entities.
Past interventions became part of the existing environment and it was business as usual, as these were sucked into the existing pre-1994 culture.	The new approach is absorbed into or becomes part of the existing environment, but has a distinctiveness of its own in terms of activities.
Past approaches to enterprise development were the provision of financial and non-financial services and the emergence of entities was a matter of chance.	This approach introduces experiential learning on a big scale and the emergence of more robust entities is a reality.
Though there was co-operation between departments, rivalries have persisted as officials guard their 'turf'.	All departments contribute and the results are measured in terms of output, the jobs created and falling levels of poverty, unemployment and inequality.

Conclusion

This intervention is based on Bosasa, a company specifically created to feed prisoners and other functions. However, its creation was to ensure a flow of contracts. Many officials got handsome kickbacks after awarding contracts to Bosasa through fraudulent processes. The owners of Bosasa, politically connected, made millions (Mahlaka 2022).

It would therefore be poetic justice to implement the model, but this time to give ordinary people an opportunity to take charge of their lives. After all, if the poverty, unemployment and inequality levels continue to worsen, South Africa's democracy is at risk. The mercurial growth of the private security industry suggests some already fear the worst. According to the Private Security Industry Regulatory Authority, the sector had 195 000 active and registered security officers in 2000. In 2022, there were nearly 2.7 million registered security guards in South Africa, with 586 042 currently employed. In comparison, the total number of personnel in the South African Police Service was 140 048 in 2022. 'This means that there are four private security guards for every police officer in the country' (Business Tech 2023).

One of the reasons for the growing poverty, unemployment and inequality is that in the past 30 years, business-as-usual models were used and these did not deal with the underlying dynamics of these issues in South Africa. The intervention put forward in this chapter deviates from the usual approach, as it has some innovative and disruptive elements that would, hopefully, see more innovations emerge.

Reducing the levels of poverty, unemployment and inequality would strengthen the social fabric in communities destroyed by the migrant system and the divide-and-rule strategy of the apartheid system. Healthier and more confident communities would be able to emerge.

My appreciation to Professor R.M. Peters of the Sol Plaatje University in the Northern Cape and Professor Cecile Nieuwenhuizen, DHET-NRF SARChI Chair in Entrepreneurship Education, University of Johannesburg, who commented on the first and last draft of this chapter, respectively.

References

Adams, A. and J.M. Luiz. 2022. 'Incomplete Institutional Change and the Persistence of Racial Inequality: The Contestation of Institutional Misalignment in South Africa'. *Journal of Management Studies* 59 (4): 857–85.

ANC (African National Congress). 1994. 'The Reconstruction and Development Programme (RDP): A Policy Framework'. https://omalley.nelsonmandela.org/index.php/site/q/03lv02 039/04lv02103/05lv02120/06lv02126.htm (accessed 6 October 2023).

Auditor-General of South Africa. 2022. *COVID-19 Expenditure Audit; Capacity Building Session on AGSA's Role as an Assurance Provider.* Report to Parliament, 1 April. https:// pmg.org.za/committee-meeting/34711/ (accessed 6 October 2023).

Bearfield, D.A. 2009. 'What Is Patronage? A Critical Re-examination'. *Public Administration Review* 69 (1): 64–76.

Benhura, M. and P. Magejo. 2020. *Differences between Formal and Informal Workers' Outcomes during the COVID-19 Crisis Lockdown in South Africa.* National Income Dynamics Study (NIDS), 30 September. https://cramsurvey.org/wp-content/uploads/2020/09/2.-Benhura-M.-_-Magejo-P.-2020-Differences-between-formal-and-informal-workers'-outcomes-during-the-COVID-19-crisis-lockdown-in-South-Africa.pdf (accessed 6 October 2023).

Beresford, A. 2015. 'Power, Patronage, and Gatekeeper Politics in South Africa'. *African Affairs* 114 (455): 226–48.

Bukula, S., R. Naidoo, C. Rogerson, X. Sithole, I. James, M. Nkondo and T. Ratshitanga. 2011. *Rethinking Small Business in South Africa: Draft Report on the Review of Government Support for Small Business*. Tshwane: Department of Trade and Industry.

Bundy, C. 2019. 'Post-apartheid Inequality and the Long Shadow of History'. In: *The State of the Nation: Poverty & Inequality: Diagnosis, Prognosis, Responses*, edited by C. Soudien, V. Reddy and I. Woolard, 79–99. Cape Town: HSRC Press.

Business Tech. 2021. 'Treasury Warns that South Africa's Grant System Could Become Unsustainable'. *Business Tech*, 19 November. https://businesstech.co.za/news/finance/539446/treasury-warns-that-south-africas-grant-system-could-become-unsustainable/ (accessed 6 October 2023).

———. 2023. 'Private Security Guards Outnumber Police 4 to 1 in South Africa'. *Business Tech*, 9 May. https://businesstech.co.za/news/government/686425/private-security-guards-outnumber-police-4-to-1-in-south-africa/ (accessed 6 October 2023).

Competition Commission. 2021. *Measuring Concentration and Participation in the South African Economy: Levels and Trends – Summary Report*. https://www.compcom.co.za/wp-content/uploads/2021/12/Concentration-Tracker-Summary-Report-1.pdf (accessed 6 October 2023).

Davie, G., M. Wang, S. Rogers and J. Li. 2021. 'Targeted Poverty Alleviation in China: A Typology of Official–Household Relations'. *Progress in Development Studies* 21 (3): 244–63.

Davies, M. 2013. 'Nelson Mandela: His Economic Legacy'. *BBC News*, 9 December. https://www.bbc.com/news/business-23041513 (accessed 6 October 2023).

DSBD (Department of Small Business Development). 2022. *National Integrated Small Enterprise Development (NISED) Masterplan*. https://www.gov.za/sites/default/files/gcis_document/202205/nised-masterplan.pdf (accessed 6 October 2023).

DTI (Department of Trade and Industry). 2004. *Review of Ten Years of Small Business Support in South Africa 1994–2004*. https://www.tips.org.za/files/10_Years_of_Small_Business_Support_in_South_Africa.pdf (accessed 6 October 2023).

———. 2005. *Integrated Small-Enterprise-Development Strategy: Unlocking the Potential of South African Entrepreneurs*. https://pmg.org.za/docs/2006/060317lseds.doc (accessed 6 October 2023).

Eguruze, E.S. and G. Kumari. 2021. 'Is Cumulative Poverty Eradication through Entrepreneurship and Social Marketing Technique Sustainable? A Global Perspective. *Journal of Asia Entrepreneurship and Sustainability* 17 (4): 3–48.

FinScope. 2006. *Small Business Survey in Gauteng*. Johannesburg: FinScope.

———. 2022. *South Africa Finscope MSME 2022 Survey: A Technical and Financial Proposal to Promote the Development of the MSME Sector in South Africa*. Johannesburg: Finmark.

Francis, D. and E. Webster. 2019. 'Poverty and Inequality in South Africa: Critical Reflections. *Development Southern Africa* 36 (6): 788–802.

Gomez, E.T. 2012. 'Targeting Horizontal Inequalities: Ethnicity, Equity, and Entrepreneurship in Malaysia'. *Asian Economic Papers* 11 (2): 31–57.

Hall, J., S. Matos, L. Sheehan and B. Silvestre. 2012. 'Entrepreneurship and Innovation at the Base of the Pyramid: A Recipe for Inclusive Growth or Social Exclusion?' *Journal of Management Studies* 49 (4): 785–812.

Igboin, B.O. 2011. 'Colonialism and African Cultural Values'. *African Journal of History and Culture* 3 (6): 96–103.

Ladzani, M.W. 2022. 'The Impact of Covid-19 on Small and Micro-enterprises in South Africa'. *International Journal of Global Environmental Issues* 21 (1): 23–38.

Lekhanya, L.M. and R.B. Mason. 2014. 'Selected Key External Factors Influencing the Success of Rural Small and Medium Enterprises in South Africa'. *Journal of Enterprising Culture* 22 (3): 331–48.

Lubinga, E. 2020. 'Protest as Communication for Development and Social Change in South Africa'. In: *Handbook of Communication for Development and Social Change*, edited by J. Servaes, 1381–98. Singapore: Springer Singapore.

Magubane, K. 2022. 'Black Business Lobby Group Ready to Fight National Treasury's New Draft Procurement Rules'. *News24*, 23 March. https://www.news24.com/fin24/economy/black-business-lobby-group-ready-to-fight-national-treasurys-new-draft-procurement-rules-20220322 (accessed 6 October 2023).

Mahlaka, R. 2022. 'Bosasa's Spending and Shopping Spree: Corrupt State Contracts Worth over R2bn and Bribes Exceeding R75m'. *Daily Maverick*, 2 March. https://www.dailymaverick.co.za/article/2022-03-02-bosasas-spending-and-shopping-spree-corrupt-state-contracts-worth-over-r2bn-and-bribes-exceeding-r75m/ (accessed 6 October 2023).

Mahlakoane, T. 2022. 'R332 Billion Pledged at 4th SA Investment Conference'. *Eye Witness News*, 25 March. https://ewn.co.za/2022/03/25/r332-billion-pledged-at-4th-sa-investment-conference (accessed 6 October 2023).

Mashele, F. 2015. 'The Relationship between Sustainability and Compliance in a Procurement Context'. Master's thesis, University of Pretoria. https://repository.up.ac.za/bitstream/handle/2263/52442/Mashele_Relationship_2015.pdf?sequence=1 (accessed 6 October 2023).

Mazwai, E.T. 2013. 'South Africa's Embedded Environmental Dynamics and Their Impact on Entrepreneurship and Small Business Development: A Critical Appraisal'. In: *Essays on the Evolution of the Post-apartheid State: Legacies, Reforms and Prospects*, edited by M. Ndletyana and D. Maimela, 269–98. Johannesburg: Mapungubwe Institute for Strategic Reflection.

Mochiko, T. 2022. 'Black Business Hits out at New Procurement Regulations'. *BusinessLIVE*, 13 November. https://www.businesslive.co.za/bt/business-and-economy/2022-11-13-black-business-hits-out-at-new-procurement-regulations/ (accessed 6 October 2023).

Mushangai, D. 2015. 'Does the State Disable Small Businesses? A Critique of Hernando de Soto'. Master's thesis, University of the Witwatersrand. https://wiredspace.wits.ac.za/server/api/core/bitstreams/e08bdb70-562b-4b05-85b3-dad526a3587a/content (accessed 6 October 2023).

Mwange, A. 2018. 'An Evaluation of Entrepreneurship Intention Theories'. *Journal of Social Science and Humanities Research* 3 (9): 127–60.

National Planning Commission. 2011. *Diagnostic Report.* https://static.pmg.org.za/docs/110913npcdiagnostic2011_0.pdf (accessed 6 October 2023).

———. 2012. *National Development Plan 2030: Our Future – Make It Work.* https://www.gov.za/sites/default/files/gcis_document/201409/ndp-2030-our-future-make-it-workr.pdf (accessed 6 October 2023).

Njiro, E., T. Mazwai and B. Urban. 2010. *A Situational Analysis of Small Businesses and Enterprises in the Townships of the Gauteng Province of South Africa.* https://www.ukesa.info/library/view/a-situational-analysis-of-small-businesses-and-enterprises-in-the-townships-of-the-gauteng-province-of-south-africa (accessed 6 October 2023).

Odeku, K.O. 2021. 'The Impact of the Covid-19 Pandemic on Black-Owned Small and Micro-Businesses in South Africa'. *Academy of Entrepreneurship Journal* 27: 1–5.

OECD (Organisation for Economic Co-operation and Development). 2015. *Entrepreneurship at a Glance 2015.* https://www.oecd-ilibrary.org/industry-and-services/entrepreneurship-at-a-glance-2015_entrepreneur_aag-2015-en (accessed 6 October 2023).

Omarjee, L. 2019. 'Timeline: South Africa's Credit Rating Journey since 1994'. *News24*, 24 November. https://www.news24.com/fin24/timeline-sas-credit-rating-journey-since-1994-20191124 (accessed 6 October 2023).

Papayya, M. and E. Bates. 2022. 'Busa Warns SA Ripe for Repeat of 2021 Unrest'. *Business Day*, 10 July. https://www.businesslive.co.za/bd/national/2022-07-10-busa-warns-sa-ripe-for-repeat-of-2021-unrest/ (accessed 6 October 2023).

Paunescu, C.M. 2013. 'Challenges of Entering the Business Barket: The Pre-entry Knowledge and Experience'. *Management and Marketing Challenges for the Knowledge Society* 8 (1): 63–78.

Potts, R. 2012. 'Social Welfare in South Africa: Curing or Causing Poverty?' *Penn State Journal of International Affairs* 1 (2): 72–90.

Prahalad, C.K. 2009. *The Fortune at the Bottom of the Pyramid: Eradicating Poverty through Profits.* Revised and updated 5th anniversary edition. New York: Wharton School Publishing.

The Presidency. 2006. *Accelerated and Shared Growth Initiative – South Africa (ASGISA).* https://www.sahistory.org.za/sites/default/files/asgisa.pdf (accessed 6 October 2023).

Roberts, S. 2017a. *Assessing the Record on Competition Enforcement against Anti-competitive Practices and Implications for Inclusive Growth.* Research on Economic Development and Inequality Working Paper No. 27. https://www.redi3x3.org/sites/default/files/Roberts%202017%20REDI3x3%20Working%20Paper%2027%20Competition%20policy%20and%20inclusive%20growth.pdf (accessed 6 October 2023).

———. 2017b. *Barriers to Entry and Implications for Competition Policy.* Centre for Competition, Regulation & Economic Development Working Paper No. 13. https://papers.ssrn.com/sol3/papers.cfm?abstract_id=2982402 (accessed 6 October 2023).

SARB (South African Reserve Bank). 2022. *Financial Stability Review: First Edition 2022*. https://www.resbank.co.za/en/home/publications/publication-detail-pages/reviews/finstab-review/2022/First-edition-2022-Financial-Stability-Review (accessed 6 October 2023).

Schumpeter, J.A. (1942) 2012. *Capitalism, Socialism, and Democracy*. Kindle edition.

Si, S., X. Yu, A. Wu, S. Chen, S. Chen and Y. Su. 2015. 'Entrepreneurship and Poverty Reduction: A Case Study of Yiwu, China'. *Asia Pacific Journal of Management* 32 (1): 119–43.

Sitharam, S. and M. Hoque. 2016. 'Factors Affecting the Performance of Small and Medium Enterprises in KwaZulu-Natal, South Africa'. *Problems and Perspectives in Management* 14 (2): 277–88.

Soudien, C., V. Reddy and I. Woolard. 2019. 'South Africa 2018: The State of the Discussion on Poverty and Inequality'. In: *The State of the Nation: Poverty & Inequality: Diagnosis, Prognosis and Responses*, edited by C. Soudien, V. Reddy and I. Woolard, 1–28. Cape Town: HSRC Press.

South African Government. 1995. *White Paper on National Strategy for the Development and Promotion of Small Business in South Africa*. https://www.gov.za/documents/national-strategy-development-and-promotion-small-business-white-paper (accessed 6 October 2023).

———. 2010. *The New Growth Path: The Framework*. https://www.gov.za/sites/default/files/NGP%20Framework%20for%20public%20release%20FINAL_1.pdf (accessed 6 October 2023).

———. 2020. *The South African Economic Reconstruction and Recovery Plan*. https://www.gov.za/sites/default/files/gcis_document/202010/south-african-economic-reconstruction-and-recovery-plan.pdf (accessed 6 October 2023).

Spicer, M. 2012. 'Lose the Short-term Thinking'. *Sunday Times*, 26 February.

Stats SA (Statistics South Africa). 2021. *Subjective Poverty in South Africa: Findings from the General Household Survey, 2019*. https://www.statssa.gov.za/publications/03-10-25/03-10-252019.pdf (accessed 6 October 2023).

———. 2022. *Quarterly Labour Force Survey Quarter 2: 2022*. https://www.statssa.gov.za/publications/P0211/P02112ndQuarter2022.pdf (accessed 6 October 2023).

Therborn, G. 2019. 'South African Inequalities in a Global Perspective'. In: *The State of the Nation: Poverty & Inequality: Diagnosis, Prognosis and Responses*, edited by C. Soudien, V. Reddy and I. Woolard. Cape Town: HSRC Press.

UNCTAD (United Nations Conference on Trade and Development). 2021. *Analysis of the Impact of COVID-19 on Micro, Small and Medium-Sized Enterprises in South Africa*. https://msme-resurgence.unctad.org/sites/smesurge/files/documents/South%20Africa.Study_.%20SME.1%20.%20FINAL.pdf (accessed 6 October 2023).

UNDP (United Nations Development Programme). 2021. *The Impact of Covid-19 on Micro and Informal Businesses in South Africa*. https://www.undp.org/south-africa/publications/impact-covid-19-micro-and-informal-businesses-south-africa (accessed 6 October 2023).

Van der Berg, S., L. Patel and G. Bridgman. 2022. 'Food Insecurity in South Africa: Evidence from NIDS-CRAM Wave 5'. *Development Southern Africa* 39 (69): 1–16.

Weiping, T. 2018. *China's Approach to the Eradication of Poverty: Taking Targeted Measures to Lift People out of Poverty*. https://www.un.org/development/desa/dspd/wp-content/uploads/sites/22/2018/05/31.pdf (accessed 6 October 2023).

Welter, F. 2011. 'Contextualising Entrepreneurship: Conceptual Challenges and Ways Forward'. *Entrepreneurship Theory and Practice* 35 (1): 165–84.

World Bank. 2018. *An Incomplete Transition: Overcoming the Legacy of Exclusion in South Africa*. https://documents1.worldbank.org/curated/en/815401525706928690/pdf/WBG-South-Africa-Systematic-Country-Diagnostic-FINAL-for-board-SECPO-Edit-05032018.pdf (accessed 6 October 2023).

———. 2021. *South Africa Economic Update, Edition 13: Building back Better from Covid-19 with a Special Focus on Jobs*. https://documents1.worldbank.org/curated/en/161431626102808095/pdf/Building-Back-Better-from-COVID-19-with-a-Special-Focus-on-Jobs.pdf (accessed 6 October 2023).

———. 2022. *Inequality in Southern Africa: An Assessment of the Southern African Customs Union*. https://documents.worldbank.org/en/publication/documents-reports/documentdetail/099125303072236903/p1649270c02a1f06b0a3ae02e57eadd7a82 (accessed 6 October 2023).

Zulu, L. 2021. 'Inputs on the Basic Income Grant to the Economic Recovery and Reconstruction Commission of ANC Lekgotla'. 5 September.

PART 3

PUBLIC MANAGEMENT AND POLITICS

CHAPTER 16

Freedom, Social Justice and Leadership

Reuel Khoza

On an ordinary weekday morning in a typical suburban supermarket in South Africa, two security guards attack and savagely beat up a customer whom they accuse of stealing something off the shelves. The incident goes viral on social media, prompting the comment: 'If this is how we react to minor transgressions, God help us!' Most viewers shrug and move on. Endemic violence is so embedded in everyday life that an episode that cost no lives and resulted merely in bad publicity for the retail chain is hardly worth a further thought. But the victim will not easily forget it and there may be legal consequences for the store.

Social injustice has become the norm; yet looked at in another light, it goes to the heart of the nihilism that characterises South Africa today – or at least appears to. Gone is the buoyant optimism for the newly liberated country that Archbishop Desmond Mpilo Tutu described as the 'Rainbow Nation'. We dreamed of an age of grace, but find ourselves in an era of disgrace.

Our trauma is not unique, but reflects a worldwide decline in respect for humanity and indeed for the whole of nature. We live in what archaeologists now call the Anthropocene period in geological history. Humanity is in charge of its own destiny, but is reshaping Planet Earth in ways that may destroy all life, including our own. An example of physical damage is a new form of rock composed of plastics and other debris, called plastiglomerates, now settling on the ocean floor deep beneath the Pacific trash vortex. Human values are caught up in just such a vortex as we search in vain for sound principles to cling to in the whirling chaos of the world we have made.

The African principle of humanness may offer a way to restore sound values. It is coupled with the idea of personhood, which may be summed up as the recognition a person enjoys for exercising humanness. In English, we see that the words 'humanity' and 'humanness' are often treated as synonyms. Not so in African terms. In Western discourse, the individual is the agent of the humane. When people express empathy towards others or act benevolently, altruism is taken to be an individual quality of selflessness. African concepts of humanness, on the other hand, make sharing an indivisible part of our collective being. In the African sense, there is no give and take, but rather participation in a common sense of being. We share because we are: I am because you are. The Nguni phrase '*Umuntu ngumuntu ngabantu*' means 'We are all connected in a universal bond by virtue of our humanness'.

In this chapter, I propose that there are means to escape existential chaos and rebuild the noble ideal of a wholesome society founded on mutual respect for others. The ingredients are among us. As people, we are seekers of truth and goodness. We forget ourselves when we exercise power not as leaders but as enforcers. The security guards who brutalised a person that was possibly poor and starving forgot themselves and became agents of social injustice. The company they worked for may have done little to inculcate humanness. They forgot our history and in so doing forgot the striving for liberation that was, at one and the same time, a search for the moral status and dignity of every person. They allied themselves with force, denial and deprivation. They embraced poverty of the soul.

The supermarket incident provokes the question: what kind of people are these security guards? How can they behave this way towards a fellow human being? This is surely a question we often ask in the presence of injustice. It illustrates that we instinctively resort to the idea that one who behaves inhumanly perhaps does not qualify as a person. They are an object in the world – an 'it' – but not a subject with moral awareness of their obligations to others. Without such awareness, the conditions for achieving true personhood are absent.

Loosely conceived, personhood is the character set among a community of persons who embrace common values. Personhood is the full expression of who we are in relation to the people that surround us. It is that which inculcates moral responsibility for our actions because it teaches us to share our humanness. The knowledge of ourselves is also the knowledge that unites us with others, for they are us and we are them. Furthermore, we come from and go back to the mysterious world of the ancestors, and we are judged by their standards. Our lives are not our own, but belong to the human cosmos of past, present and future experience. What we do with and for others is what makes us human and confers our personhood, our meaningful being, without which we are not persons at all.

Africa has stumbled into new and dangerous times where the temptations of wealth and power divert us from the mission of liberation. We need to think about past historical injustices in the light of an African ethical concept of personhood, says philosopher Motsamai Molefe. He writes:

> A just society is one that respects human beings in the light of their capacity for virtue and one that maximises social, political and economic resources for one to be able to self-realise ... The process of colonisation and apartheid (in the case of South Africa) disturbed both of these crucial conditions for personhood to be possible. Central to these historical processes was (1) the denial of the humanity of African people (capacity for virtue) and (2) the common goods necessary for them to live a robust human life and self-realise (Molefe 2018: 11).

'Social justice leadership' is a term used by educationists that applies more broadly across society. Studies of the leadership traits of school principals and administrators have revealed three key features of social justice leadership: 'arrogant humility, passionate leadership and a tenacious commitment to social justice' (Theoharis 2008: 3). 'Arrogant humility' is a strange and contradictory but wise term. It means being prepared to submit oneself to the judgement of others, but remaining steadfast in a commitment to the values that unite all in the pursuit of justice.

The true leader listens with their mind and with their whole heart. Social justice leadership tries to solve problems collaboratively by humbly understanding differing opinions, while ultimately seeking consensus over the right thing to do for community well-being. This type of leadership is about 'how to engage in democratic, inclusive, and transformative practices to change social structures and influence all stakeholders to collegially promote justice and equity' and 'actively demolish structures and policies that may cause oppression within an organization'.[1] To put flesh on these words, social justice leadership has been described as a praxis, the process by which theory is embodied and enacted:

[First] ... leadership for social justice is conceived as a praxis ... involving both reflection and action. Second, leadership for social justice spans several dimensions, which serve as arenas for this praxis. These dimensions include the personal, interpersonal, communal, systemic, and ecological. Third, each dimension within the framework requires the development of capacities on the part of the leader, capacities for both reflection and action (Furman 2012: 191).

The idea of social justice has played a large part in South Africa's quest for a free and equal society. Despite its currency in local and international discourse, it is not all that easy to agree on a definition of social justice. It can mean different things to various people with very divergent approaches. It seems to be a catch-all phrase. Is it mainly about material well-being and the fair distribution of income or wealth? Is the emphasis on human rights alone, or more broadly on procedures to defend communities from harm in a system that is perceived as biased against them? Is it about protecting the environment to ensure an acceptable quality of life for all? If it is all of these things, social justice is an umbrella term that may be used as needed: a 'phrase of convenience' that counts as a verb, a 'doing' word, a call to action for almost any grievance campaign.

There was never any doubt that the fundamentals of social justice were denied in apartheid South Africa. Injustice towards non-whites was the policy of the white nationalist government. In 1985, during the climactic worst years of apartheid, a group of mostly black theologians met to formulate what became known as the Kairos Document. This was a ringing call for social justice from people of conscience who could no longer watch helplessly as the country plunged ever further into racial oppression (Goba 1987). The word 'Kairos' comes from the New Testament and means the right moment to take a decision or act. The country's deepening political crisis led to two States of Emergency when detentions without trial and killings provoked a world backlash and financial sanctions against South Africa.

While more than 20 000 people were detained, the business sector wrung its hands wondering what to do. Until then, many – if not most – companies had practised racism in appointments, promotions and salaries as a matter of routine. An article in the *Atlantic* magazine reported that American companies, including

General Motors, IBM and Coca-Cola, announced that they were pulling out of South Africa. This caused hardly a ripple:

> Given that Coke controls 7.5 percent of South Africa's soft-drink market, I expected the response to its decision to be sackcloth and ashes. In fact, the announcement hardly aroused any interest. While in Atlanta the company was declaring its distaste for apartheid, in South Africa it was saying that Coke would continue to be available. According to local newspapers, the magic syrup would be transported in tankers across the Atlantic. All in all, it was a sweet deal for Coke, providing it with political capital at home and continued profits in South Africa (Massing 1987).

Local business was deeply implicated:

> At the Truth and Reconciliation Commission hearings, a former security official Major Craig Williamson, told the Commission that 'weapons, ammunition, uniforms, vehicles, radios and other equipment were all developed and provided by industry. Our finances and banking were done by bankers who even gave us covert credit cards for covert operations.' The Commission concluded: 'Certain businesses, especially the mining industry, were involved in helping to design and implement apartheid policies. Other businesses benefited from co-operating with the security structures of the former state. Most businesses benefited from operating in a racially structured context' (Tripathi 2013).

My concern then and now has been with corporate governance and the social responsibility of companies. In a companion chapter on ethics and governance in the *South African Handbook of Agency, Freedom and Justice: Volume II*, I look at how business largely condoned apartheid and how it has responded falteringly to the birth of democracy and equal rights. The successes and failures of corporate governance in post-apartheid South Africa are matters of debate since ambivalent attitudes towards black empowerment and redistributive policies continue to bedevil economic progress. As a businessperson of long standing who believes passionately in both social upliftment and competitive efficiency, I am not one to dwell on the victimhood of my compatriots. Success must be earned through hard work – but this can only happen in a fair and orderly enabling environment. 'From each according to his abilities, to each according to his needs,' as Karl Marx put it, the resources and technologies of the day should be fairly distributed.

African communalism is not communism. In African philosophy, communalism is defined as a moral and indeed spiritual doctrine that values human dignity, rights and responsibilities (Ikuenobe 2017). Business in South Africa, I believe, needs to reorientate itself towards African communalism if it is to align with the values and expectations of the majority of its stakeholders. Incidents like the beating of a customer in a supermarket are an indictment of the commercial culture of a country that has yet to find its way towards a compassionate dispensation amid poverty.

Communalism does not seek an end to private enterprise or require a dictatorship of the proletariat to level all incomes and manage the economy centrally. As a value system, it is mostly associated with traditional, rural Africa. To apply it within a modern corporate environment raises a number of practical questions. For example, can it apply where the workforce is culturally diverse rather than purely African? I deal with this and other matters in more detail in my ethics and governance chapter in the *South African Handbook of Agency, Freedom and Justice: Volume II*. Here, under the heading of social justice, my concern is with the moral and spiritual content of communalism.

Surrounding businesses – whether foreign or local – are the communities that draw their income from jobs and spend their money in the marketplace. The social responsibilities of the modern corporation are set out in codes of ethics that insist that the true mission of business is to nurture people, look after the planet and (of course) produce profits. Corporate mission statements these days make great play of this triple bottom line. It implies that people need decent work in a clean environment, and if the corporation delivers benefits to dependent communities, it will earn their loyalty. This is how sustainability is projected.

The real bottom line is whether business delivers social justice to those who serve it and to those whom it serves. The mission to do so is never stress-free. I know from experience that the tone set by the leadership is vital for fulfilling the expectations of staff, unions, customers, investors, management, competitors and regulators – not to mention the families of employees and those living in surrounding areas who see the corporation as a symbol (good or bad) in industry. Leaders are required to be both pragmatic and visionary at the same time. To attain buy-in on a scale that ensures a solid stock of social capital is one of the two main aims of good governance. It complements the other main aim, which is to deliver on promises in a sustainable, ethical way.

Communalism is holistic, but the fundamentals are philosophically unrelated to holism as practised in the East or West. It is neither individualistic in the Western sense nor mystically linked to the holistic universe of Eastern philosophies such as Buddhism. A Western view set out by Murray Bookchin (1982) conceives of an 'ecology of freedom', which focuses on grassroots politics. It is highly participatory, with popular assemblies at the municipal level gathering to discuss and decide affairs. Communalism in Africa occurs within kinship and community groups. It is people-centred and overarching, not limited to current politics. Its time frame is broad and loose, and is understood to include past, present and future community members existing in the context of all accumulated experience and knowledge. The ancestors are us and we go on to join them. In that sense, it is spiritually holistic. Western holism is an ecological concept that tries to unite us with nature and all that *is*; African holism is a social concept.

Holism is the bridge between what was, what is and what may be. Social justice leadership remains a continuing historical force. The brutal racial oppression of apartheid called forth defiance from sections of society that made social justice a priority above all else. Those confronting the state included churches, business organisations, student bodies and academics, labour unions, charities, health workers, sports associations, journalists, writers and individuals moved by conscience. The tragedy today is that many of these voices have been silenced by absorption into liberation ranks where they dutifully parrot the orthodoxies of the day. Those who continue to demonstrate social justice leadership gain self-respect and a sense that freedom and dignity are the highest reward for their sacrifices.

The holistic perception of post-apartheid South Africa is not flattering to the liberators. The profound lessons of the heroic generation that placed social justice before personal safety have been forgotten in the rush for material gain. It saddens me to say that large parts of the business establishment joined the treasure hunt, leaving ethics in their wake and ignoring the need to balance profits against social justice. The shallow words of shallow people who can hardly be described as business 'leaders' may refer to corporate sustainability, but do not ring true about redressing discrimination.

My speeches and writings in *The African in My Dream* (Khoza 2013), which cover the period 1983 to 2013, return constantly to the theme of business irresponsibility. I depict a mainly white business elite out of touch with the African roots of their employees and customers, a group of owners and managers who still carry the attitudes of earlier, nastier times. Yet, recently, I have been forced to reckon with a newer brand of callous disregard for social justice in the corporate sphere. The inequities of the past have assumed a new guise in business brutalism, which has its counterpart in the selfishness of state officials and politicians. In July 1987, before the end of white rule, I was already saying that self-discovery in the economic field would entail creating 'a mythology of competence, of high motivation, of high ideals of success' (Khoza 2013: 53). Furthermore,

> we must create economic giants in the mould of a Shaka, in the mould of a Mandela, in the mould of a Sobukwe, in the mould of a Biko, in the mould of a Camay, in the mould of a Ramaphosa, in the mould of many of our heroes who will stand out through history . . . (Khoza 2013: 53).

Alas, subsequent years have disabused us of these high hopes. I said then that we were at a crossroads that would require the 'concentrated mind power of our leaders in all spheres' to achieve economic liberation (Khoza 2013: 55). Needless to say, the great, all-encompassing upliftment has not happened. Although there have been successes, in many respects the majority of South Africans is worse off than before in terms of service delivery. They lack pride in themselves and in their nation.

It is instructive to compare the Western and African approaches to social justice. In Western societies, the idea of social justice developed in the age of Enlightenment, when philosophers saw reason as a progressive force in human affairs. David Hume wrote in his *Treatise of Human Nature* that it was 'an attempt to apply the method of experimental reasoning to moral subjects'.[2] The physical universe was best understood through the methodology of science. The same mechanistic principles could be used to understand human beings and the living universe. A minority of Enlightenment radicals declared that their target was 'public misery' – the 'misfortune, deprivation and unhappiness suffered by people ground down by institutions not of their own choosing' (Keane 2016).

The African approach to public misery stems from a very different humanistic set of beliefs and practices – essentially the world view of Ubuntu. Individuals and groups share their mortality and the uncertainties of the human condition. They support each other to overcome life's obstacles and help each other to develop as people. This is quite distinct from the Western style of analysis that seeks to diagnose psychological problems and fix faulty institutions. It would take far longer than this chapter allows to spell out the differences in detail. The approaches may be regarded as complementary, in the sense that we need compassion as well as competence to solve social problems.

Africa today certainly requires both. Post-colonial nation states on the continent have fallen prey to corruption, militarism, incompetence, misleadership, tribalism and neo-imperialism – all of which represent failures of governance. These situations demand reasoned solutions. At the same time, success of reforms is most likely to be achieved if aligned with the moral outlook and experience of people. The community ethic is powerfully persuasive at all levels in African society.

The Enlightenment's intellectual thrust gained support from artists, novelists, legal theorists, evangelists and educators as the Industrial Revolution got under way. A breed of ruthless capitalists took complete advantage of the lack of labour protection, showing no concern for health, housing, human development or happiness. In response, the concept of social justice emerged. Reformers exposed injustice and sought to reduce economic exploitation, while introducing technologies to ameliorate slum conditions. Rightlessness and ignorance among the poor were tackled through political reform, education and welfare. As the nineteenth century advanced and revolutions swept across Europe – threatening but never quite overturning the states of the day – so governments were forced to regulate employment and attend to shocking living conditions.

More shocking was the experience of Africans under assorted colonial powers. What we learnt about Western styles of doing business was mostly negative. First, there was slavery, which not only tore millions from African soil, but it also left societies ravaged by gun-running and shattered by social dislocation. Then came colonialism, with virtual serfdom for indigenous peoples, but dressed up to look like a civilising mission. Subjugation allowed only the chosen few to get decent education, joining the class who kept the people down and docile – or, conversely, become agitators in the cause of freedom. Either way, colonialism was a poor preparation for independent statehood and productive economic relations.

Where could we look for means to address these injustices? We found solace in the dream of an African future. We looked to our ancestry for inspiration, learning the wisdom of patience, but also the resolve to fight off oppressors. We embraced religion, believing that God was with us in our struggle. And some of us turned to business, both to survive and to seek prosperity in spite of exclusion from the mainstream economy. It was in these grim times that the quest for social justice through business responsibility was born. We dug deep into traditions of communalism that promised everyone in the circle of a business, no matter how small or large, a share in its wealth. It is from these beginnings that I have come. Fortunately, I have also been formally schooled in business, and I have watched over the years as waves of management theorists have wrestled with notions of social responsibility. The pendulum has swung between giving nothing and seeking to include social benefits in sustainable business practices.

A full revolution never happened. Instead, a negotiated settlement allowed the African National Congress (ANC) to contest free elections, the outcome of which was a foregone conclusion. The explicit programme of the ANC when it assumed power in 1994 was to deliver social justice. Nelson Mandela made it plain that social justice included socio-economic rights. He said in a speech at Trafalgar Square in 2005: 'Massive poverty and obscene inequality are such terrible scourges of our times – times in which the world boasts breathtaking advances in science, technology, industry, and wealth accumulation – that they have to rank alongside slavery and apartheid as social evils.'[3]

We need to be reminded that government and governance are not the same thing. Government policy under the ANC has never wavered from a commitment to social justice under every president to date. Woefully inadequate has been the implementation of noble principles at the level of ordinary South Africans. They continue to feel the effects of a discriminatory system long after it is theoretically dead and buried. The fact that a complete overthrow of the structures of apartheid has never happened has tied government into a system that remains unjust in many ways.

As Mandela showed, the conscience of the leader is an integral part of the pursuit of social justice. In his person, he embodied the qualities of humanness that evoked trust in followers. He put himself at the service of a racially mixed and multicultural nation, in the spirit of collective unity of purpose. This is what we have lost and what we need to regain. Let us now look at how humanness will assist us to recover pride in ourselves, in our working lives and business organisations, in our government and in our relations with the world. I shall invoke the recently minted idea of local and global social connections to convey the reach of our moral obligations towards others. These connections rise above and beyond law and ethical codes that otherwise impose a duty of care.

South Africa has been through a period of state capture that deflated our illusions about ourselves and our position in the world. Foreign interlocutors today routinely ask what happened that made it go so wrong. We must call into question the calibre of the leadership that constantly blames the past for the problems of the present. Theirs is no answer to critical failures. Throughout the country, lack of service delivery, insufficient protection of human rights, anti-poor evictions and corrupt policing do much to maintain the unequal treatment of racial groups. Women and children are often the main victims of persistent discrimination and violence in a patriarchal society. Mandela's vision of poverty relegated to history is far from being realised.

To break the impasse over stubbornly embedded institutional injustice is going to take firm leadership, compassion, clear policies and efficient administration. Under apartheid, the attitude of corporations towards white minority rule was often ambivalent. Boards could see that apartheid was inefficient and costly, but at the same time they worried that freedom from oppression could rouse the masses and endanger business as usual. White paranoia in boardrooms held back the impulse to be conscientious. The racist government at the time took full advantage, reassuring corporate South Africa that their profits were assured under *kragdadige* (authoritarian) control by the state. Of course, the opposite was true. The world watched, appalled, as security operations within the country and on its borders caused bloodshed and mayhem.

Rectificatory justice – the brand of justice concerned with righting injustice – has had a slow and uncertain birth in South Africa. Long ago in the ancient world, Aristotle gave the classic statement on this kind of justice, which he linked to complex virtues, including rational, emotional and social skills.[4] Aristotle declared that a virtuous person is someone who has ideal character traits. We must then ask how honest has corporate South Africa been in implementing rectificatory justice, given prevailing conditions in South Africa's major corporations? Impertinently, may I suggest that the personhood of many senior executives is called into question if they cannot or do not show leadership in rectifying the business injustices of the past.

Personhood, leadership and social justice are intimately connected. True leadership may be defined as placing oneself at the service of one's followers, who look to the leader to provide vision, ethical direction and pragmatic ways and means to achieve betterment for all. The leader must be attuned to the needs of the community, able to see, understand and interpret their desires, while applying sound judgement to the way forward. Leaders are born and then made: the qualities they are gifted with are tested in action and honed by experience. It is the leader's natural qualities, plus engagement in the struggles of the time, that form the person that people come to know and trust as an inspiring presence in their lives. Personhood translates to the force of moral authority, drawing followers because of who the leader is and how well things get done. Social justice is central to the leader's mission – as indeed it must be because leadership always confronts issues of dispute and conflict.

The need for leadership arises when people turn to someone who can address their problems. A transactional leader is one who attracts followers by offering to solve their problems in return for their loyalty and support. Misleadership occurs where those who set themselves up to champion a cause betray their followers to serve themselves. Betrayal destroys trust; service strengthens it. We call leadership transformational when it tackles the obstacles that hold people back and empowers them to achieve their goals collectively. The transformational leader does not expect a reward, as would be the case with a transactional one. The achievement of social justice for the community is its own reward. In the compact between leader and led, there is mutual respect, as each party invests belief in the other. To some extent, such empowering leaders are collaborators, who join their followers to identify and solve problems.

Leaders must not only confront injustice, but also demonstrate probity in their own performance. To say one thing and do another is the death of credibility.

In business, the personhood of senior executives counts strongly towards their reputation for fairness and justice in the workplace. Fairness promotes harmony and a sense of equity among colleagues and there is evidence that those who see justice in practice tend to spread it in their own behaviour and decision-making. When people think their leaders are attuned to their needs, they 'perform their jobs better, are happier in their work, work more effectively as team members and do more to help their colleagues' (Li and Judge 2019).

An indication that social justice is of central importance for businesses internationally is the United Nations' *Guiding Principles on Business and Human Rights*. Published in 2011, the principles contain three actionable pillars: protect, respect and remedy. Companies should exercise 'human rights due diligence' to identify, prevent, mitigate and remedy any adverse human rights impacts they cause or contribute to. This applies to any business enterprise across a company's operations and products, and throughout its supplier and business partner networks locally or worldwide (United Nations Human Rights Office of the High Commissioner 2011). The document states that enforcement is the duty of states. This means governments have the duty under international human rights law to prevent abuses by all actors in society, including businesses.

Is this enough? Punitive, state-based tools obviously have their place in a just business order. Yet, states may be lax or directly involved in rights abuses. Do they always have the capacity to track down information about corporate activities at home or abroad and the power to do something to curb wrongdoing?

A new, powerful concept of social responsibility in business has emerged from recent academic work on social justice. Social connections that cross national borders are a strong foundation for both empathy and institutional reform. The term 'social connectedness' came into mainstream sociological discourse during the 1990s to refer to the feeling of closeness with others, which is important to one's sense of belonging (Woolcock 2010).

In 2006, political scientist Iris Marion Young, from the University of Chicago, drew a link between global social justice and social connection. Her influential and much-discussed paper argues that we may be involved in injustice without even knowing it. The example she used was the sweatshop trade in garments emanating from countries like Bangladesh. The fact that buyers in the United States acquired these cut-price items made them responsible for the exploitation of labour on the other side of the world. Young claimed this was not a moral responsibility as such, but a political one: it was not blameworthy or immoral to be a buyer. Rather, structural injustice (such as sweatshop wage slavery) required a policy response to bring pressure for change (Young 2006).

In African terms, because we are all connected as human beings, an injustice to one person or group is the concern of all. This is not a theory of limitless responsibility for every bad thing that happens anywhere. Obviously, we cannot concern ourselves with people and places of which we have no knowledge or experience. But a company does know (or ought to) whose lives and welfare are affected by its operations. Meanwhile, community spokespersons, the media, non-governmental organisations (NGOs) on the ground, whistle-blowers and regulators may separately or collectively sound the alert on abuses. A business leader with a firm sense of moral purpose will ensure that business connections are followed up to establish whether injustice is occurring anywhere along the line. Procedure is the way; moral awareness is the motive.

This principle inspired the Reverend Leon Sullivan to draw up a blueprint for American corporations to pursue business in apartheid South Africa, while resisting racist laws and practices. I was a beneficiary of the Global Sullivan Principles and remain eternally grateful to have been hoisted into management through sponsored training and a programme that set South Africa's backward system in a global context for me. As an example of how social connection worked, Sullivan's intervention connected our struggle for freedom with the concerns of African Americans who felt strong links with Africa and identified with what we were going through.

Social connections have global reach, says Young, giving them power beyond the national laws and ethical codes that are supposed to guide corporate behaviour (Phillips and Schrempf-Stirling 2021). Young argues that the conventional view of social responsibility is liability based, involving concepts such as guilt, blame, isolatable and identifiable actors and actions, and restitution. Young's model of social connections is value-neutral: 'Those who participate by their actions in producing and reproducing structural injustice are usually minding their own business and acting within accepted norms and rules' (Young 2011: 106). Being neutral does not mean there is no social responsibility:

My responsibility is essentially shared with others because the harms are produced by many of us acting together within accepted institutions and practices, and because it is not possible for any of us to identify just what in our actions results in which aspects of the injustice that particular individuals suffer (Young 2011: 110).

This is pragmatic and useful. It throws light on how things work at a distance when we are merely pursuing self-interest. But it is not entirely convincing. We cannot lose sight of ethics while identifying what goes wrong. In the modern world, corporate codes of ethics are vital reminders of social responsibility. As with codes anywhere, it takes the moral qualities of personal conscience and compunction to compel a business leader to voluntarily commit time and resources to social justice. The corporation must bear its social costs and not transfer them to society. There may be no material advantage in it; in fact, there may be material costs. It is a mission. It is self-justifying or, as we Africans would say, you do it because you cannot *not* do it and still retain your humanness.

Social connectedness bridges nations and causes. Social scientist Keyan Tomaselli wrote in a 1999 retrospective that in the United States he encountered left-wing intellectuals who arrived for a meeting bruised and bleeding after police had attacked them at a protest. 'Just like at home! These were people I could relate to,' he remarked (1999: 172). At home in South Africa, he added, similar incidents did not dissuade members of popular movements from producing newspapers, posters and other media for grassroots mobilisation. This was while media and universities largely conformed to racist hegemony. Many activists went on in the post-apartheid years to make a significant contribution to democracy and development. In the transition period, human rights were taken seriously as part of reconstruction; but Tomaselli warned that a watchful eye must be kept on 'subversions of democracy' (1999: 174).

Social justice leadership is no less important today than it was under apartheid. In 2018, Justice Leona Valerie Theron, Judge of the Constitutional Court of South Africa, said in an address to the student body at the University of Potchefstroom:

The demand to transform the social fabric persists because the wide disparities in living standards continue to exist. As members of this society, all of us, and as future leaders, all of you here today, have a responsibility to achieve social justice. You must be activists and agents of social change (Theron 2018).

Theron ended by quoting former American First Lady Michelle Obama: 'You can be the generation that holds your leaders accountable for open, honest government at every level, government that stamps out corruption and protects the fundamental rights of every citizen' (2018).

In conclusion, African ideas are like any other cultural approach to governance in business and the state. They belong with the people who gave birth to them, but they also offer new insights to others who perhaps worry about their own shortcomings.

We will recognise as true leaders those who emerge from companies, labour unions, universities, political parties, NGOs and other channels – including the streets – by their actions. They who transform their communities will inspire others to follow and perhaps take up the national challenge to reform our institutions and develop moral awareness. Leadership calls for character and competence: humble but firm personhood in the renewed struggle for social justice and progress.

Notes

1. See https://psichologyanswers.com/library/lecture/read/390989-what-is-social-justice-leadership-theory (accessed 28 November 2023).
2. See https://www.britannica.com/topic/Western-philosophy/The-Enlightenment (accessed 28 November 2023).
3. See https://www.one.org/international/blog/10-times-nelson-mandela-was-spot-on-about-ending-extreme-poverty/ (accessed 28 November 2023).
4. See https://plato.stanford.edu/entries/aristotle-ethics/ (accessed 28 November 2023).

References

Bookchin, M. 1982. *The Ecology of Freedom: The Emergence and Dissolution of Hierarchy*. Palo Alto, CA: Cheshire Books.

Furman, G. 2012. 'Social Justice Leadership as Praxis: Developing Capacities through Preparation Programs'. *Educational Administration Quarterly* 48 (2): 191–229.

Goba, B. 1987. 'The Kairos Document and Its Implications for Liberation in South Africa'. *Journal of Law and Religion* 5 (2): 313–25.

Ikuenobe, P. 2017. 'Human Rights, Personhood, Dignity, and African Communalism'. *Journal of Human Rights* 17 (5): 589–604.

Keane, J. 2016. 'The 18th-Century Enlightenment and the Problem of Public Misery'. *The Conversation*, 9 April. https://theconversation.com/the-18th-century-enlightenment-and-the-problem-of-public-misery-57541 (accessed 28 November 2023).

Khoza, R.J. 2013. *The African in My Dream: A Corporate Participant-Observer's Odyssey, 1983–2013*. Johannesburg: Vezubuntu.

Li, M. and T.A. Judge. 2019. 'Leadership, Justice and the Importance of Voice'. *Lead Read Today*, 3 December. https://fisher.osu.edu/blogs/leadreadtoday/blog/leadership-justice-and-the-importance-of-voice (accessed 28 November 2023).

Massing, M. 1987. 'South Africa: The Business of Fighting Apartheid'. *The Atlantic*, 1 February. https://www.theatlantic.com/magazine/archive/1987/02/south-africa-the-business-of-fighting-apartheid/665202/ (accessed 28 November 2023).

Molefe, M. 2018. 'Personhood and (Rectification) Justice in African Thought'. *Politikon* 45 (3): 1–16.

Phillips, R. and J. Schrempf-Stirling. 2021. 'Young's Social Connection Model and Corporate Responsibility'. *Philosophy of Management* 21: 315–36.

Theoharis, G. 2008. 'Woven in Deeply: Identity and Leadership of Urban Social Justice Principals'. *Education and Urban Society* 41 (1): 3–25.

Theron, L.V. 2018. 'Leadership, Social Justice and Transformation: Inspire a Leader'. *Potchefstroom Electronic Law Journal* 21 (1). http://www.scielo.org.za/scielo.php?script=sci_arttext&pid=S1727-37812018000100034 (accessed 28 November 2023).

Tomaselli, K.G. 1999. 'On "Social Justice": Apartheid and Beyond'. *Social Justice* 26 (2): 172–4.

Tripathi, S. 2013. 'Apartheid, Mandela, and Business'. *Institute for Human Rights and Business*, 9 December. https://www.ihrb.org/other/apartheid-mandela-and-business (accessed 28 November 2023).

United Nations Human Rights Office of the High Commission. 2011. *Guiding Principles on Business and Human Rights: Implementing the United Nations 'Protect, Respect and Remedy' Framework*. https://www.ohchr.org/sites/default/files/documents/publications/guidingprinciplesbusinesshr_en.pdf (accessed 28 November 2023).

Woolcock, M. 2010. 'The Rise and Routinization of Social Capital, 1988–2008'. *Annual Review of Political Science* 13 (1): 469–87.

Young, I. 2006. 'Responsibility and Global Justice: A Social Connection Model'. *Social Philosophy and Policy* 23 (1): 102–30.

———. 2011. *Responsibility for Justice*. New York: Oxford University Press.

CHAPTER 17

Towards a Competent and Ethical Public Service

Deon Rossouw

There can be no doubt that an effective and professional public service is a key
component of a free, just and prosperous society. Similarly, there can be no doubt
that such an effective and professional public service was foreseen and desired by
the architects of the democratic South Africa, and equally desired by her citizens.
The reality of public service as experienced by citizens, as well as reported in a
variety of surveys, differs vastly from the ideal that was foreseen and desired.
The state of public service is an area of high concern across all sectors of South
African society, as well as for international observers and other countries with a
vested interest in the country.

In this chapter, I explore the root causes for the dire state of the public service
in South Africa. The findings of several recent surveys are utilised to identify the
drivers of poor performance by the public service and to point to areas where
improvements are needed.

The ideal of public service

The vision of a professional and competent public service is articulated in Chapter
10 of the South African Constitution. Section 195 of this chapter states:

> Public administration must be governed by the democratic values and
> principles enshrined in the Constitution, including the following principles:
> a) A high standard of professional ethics must be promoted and maintained.
> b) Efficient, economic and effective use of resources must be promoted.
> c) Public administration must be development-oriented.

d)   Services must be provided impartially, fairly, equitably and without bias.

e)   People's needs must be responded to, and the public must be encouraged to participate in policy-making.

f)   Public administration must be accountable.

g)   Transparency must be fostered by providing the public with timely, accessible and accurate information.

h)   Good human-resource management and career-development practices, to maximise human potential, must be cultivated.

i)   Public administration must be broadly representative of the South African people, with employment and personnel management practices based on ability, objectivity, fairness, and the need to redress the imbalances of the past to achieve broad representation.[1]

These ideals of public service apply to administration in all spheres of government, all organs of state, as well as to all public enterprises.

The state of public service

When the National Planning Commission took stock of the state of affairs in South Africa as part of its *National Development Plan 2030* (NDP) ((National Planning Commission 2012), its assessment of the state of public service was sobering. In its *Diagnostic Overview*, the National Planning Commission came to the conclusion that 'public services are uneven and often of poor quality' (National Planning Commission 2011: 15).

There are strong indications that this state of affairs in the public service has not improved since the publication of the *Diagnostic Overview*. The Edelman Trust Barometer, which is released at the annual meeting of the World Economic Forum in Davos, made an alarming finding in its two most recent editions. It was found that only about one in four South Africans trust their government. In 2021, only 27 per cent of South Africans trusted their government, and in 2022 that number slipped even lower to 26 per cent.

Trust in the South African government in 2022 compares very unfavourably to the global average of 52 per cent of people who have trust in their governments across the 27 countries that participated in 2022 Barometer. In fact, South Africa ended up in the second-lowest position among the 27 countries as far as trust in government is concerned. This low ranking cannot be merely ascribed to a cynical or demoralised population, as 63 per cent of South Africans who participated in the 2022 Barometer indicated that they have trust in business, which is slightly higher than the global average of 61 per cent.

Another index that sheds some light on the public perception of the public service is the annual Corruption Perceptions Index (CPI) that is conducted by Transparency International. When the perceptions of corruption as measured by the CPI are tracked over time, there is a clear downward trend. The CPI measures perceptions of corruption in the public sector and then scores countries on a scale of 0 to 100, with 0 representing total corruption and 100 indicating a total lack of corruption.

From 2012 to 2021, South Africa's score on the CPI remained more or less constant. Its score in 2012 was 43 and in 2021 it was 44, with slight ups and downs over this period. The perception of corruption thus remained stubbornly in the more corrupt half of the spectrum, despite many attempts to address corruption in both the public sector and state-owned enterprises (SOEs). This happened regardless of a general upward tendency in CPI scores across countries that participated in the survey. Over the last decade, countries increased on average by 2.5 points on their CPI scores.

The Ethics Institute, in collaboration with the Department of Public Service Administration, the Department of Cooperative Governance and the South African Local Government Association, conducted three surveys, in 2015, 2018 and 2022, on the perceptions that public servants in national, provincial and local government have of their own organisations (Ethics Institute 2015, 2018, 2022). Across the surveys, it was found consistently that public servants experience their working environment as not conducive to ethical and professional service delivery. They reported a lack of willingness by management in the public service to act against unethical and unprofessional conduct, as well as against poor service delivery. This is exacerbated by an unwillingness among public servants to report such malpractices to their organisations out of fear of being victimised for exposing these practices.

Another grave concern of public servants across all three editions of the survey relates to the quality of appointments in the public service. Public servants expressed concern about inappropriate appointments being made, especially in senior management positions. This points to the widespread appointment of unqualified people to senior positions due to political interference in the appointment process. The practice of cadre deployment by political parties has been singled out as a main culprit in this regard.

The situation in South African SOEs does not appear to be substantially different from that in public service departments. In a comparative analysis conducted between the ethical cultures of public service departments and those of SOEs, no significant differences in the maturity of ethical cultures were found. The same study also reported that SOEs do particularly badly when it comes to treating their employees fairly and holding staff accountable for their behaviour (Vorster and Konstantinopoulos 2020).

The lasting impression that emanates from the Ethics Institute surveys is one of a demoralised public service corps, where unethical and unprofessional conduct are tolerated and there is no accountability for those who openly undermine the constitutional ideal of a professional and ethical public service. The only ray of hope that emanates from these surveys is that there seems to be a growing trend in the awareness of public servants of the code of ethics for public servants, as well as of policies related to gifts and conflicts of interest. This increase in awareness of ethical standards can likely be ascribed to the introduction of the *Public Service Regulations* (Department of Public Service and Administration 2016). These regulations make provision for the designation of ethics officers and ethics oversight committees in all national and provincial government departments.

However, awareness of certain other aspects of the *Public Service Regulations* remains low, with less than 50 per cent of public servants in the 2022 survey reporting that they were aware of an ethics officer in their organisations, despite the fact that the *Public Service Regulations* require each department to have one. Also, less than half of the respondents indicated that they were aware of ethics training in their organisations. It is therefore not surprising that despite the rise in awareness of ethical standards, there has been no dramatic improvement in the ethical culture of the public service since 2015 when the surveys started.

Root causes of poor public service

What are the root causes of the state of affairs that emerged from the findings of the above-mentioned surveys? According to my analysis, at least six root causes can be identified, each of which is discussed below.

Political interference

For the public service to develop into a professional, competent and ethical institution, it is imperative that it remains at arm's length from the political powers that fill the seats of government on national, provincial and local government levels. However, the public sector ethics surveys indicate that undue political interference in public service administration is perceived by public servants to be one of the most important factors that undermine the effectiveness of the public service. The Commission of Inquiry into State Capture made similar findings regarding both public service departments and state-owned entities. Such political interference always carries the potential of diverting the focus of public service departments and state-owned entities from delivering on their public service mandates, to serving factional or private interests instead. It also detracts from the ideal of having a public service that is professional in nature and is not destabilised every time that there is a change in political power. The lack of professional independence from political interference is thus one of the major root causes for the current state of the public service.

Inappropriate appointments

Closely tied to the first root cause of political interference is the issue of inappropriate appointments being made in the public service. Although such appointments can occur on all levels of the public service, it is especially concerning when it occurs in senior and executive management positions. The Commission of Inquiry into State Capture and the public sector ethics surveys all found that inappropriate appointments (or cadre deployment) counted among the top risks as perceived by public servants.

Inappropriate appointments have several adverse consequences on the public service in general, and on public servants, in particular. The first is that competence and merit are not the overriding criteria in assessing candidates' ability to perform the job at hand, and other non-job-related considerations trump competence-related considerations in the process of appointing key players in the public service. Secondly, the career ambitions of dedicated or talented public servants or prospective public servants are dampened when they compete for positions that are then filled by politically connected or incompetent persons. This obviously demoralises public servants who are overlooked for positions or promotions. Thirdly, leaders in the public service that are appointed due to their political connections would always be likely to put the interests of those to whom they owe their position before the interest of the public that they are supposed to serve. This clearly undermines not only the focus, but also the effectiveness of service delivery in both public service departments and SOEs.

Lack of leadership stability

As a result of the nature of some senior appointments in the public service due to political interference or political affiliations, the security of tenure of such appointees remains fragile. As soon as political office-bearers move out of office, persons who were appointed due to the interference or influence of such political office-bearers are likely to be replaced.

This phenomenon was clearly illustrated in the publication *Political Musical Chairs* (Van Onselen 2017), which found that during President Jacob Zuma's term in office (2009–17) his Cabinet was reshuffled on average every nine months. On national government level, director generals of departments served on average for 22 months in their positions, before they were replaced. Consequently, a Cabinet minister would work together with a director general of a national department on average for no longer than 14 months, and in 47 per cent of these cases the director general would serve in an acting capacity. Gareth van Onselen concludes that 'the picture painted by the numbers is one of mass instability, poor planning, constant conflict and perpetual turmoil' (2017: 9).

There are also legislative and regulatory standards that further contribute to the regular replacement of senior officials. An example of such a limitation on tenure on local government level is the Municipal Systems Act, which limits the tenure of a municipal manager to five years. The lack of safety of tenure of key leaders in the administration on all levels of government almost inevitably results in their starting to look for alternative career opportunities when they approach the second half of their five-year term of office. This contributes to their taking their eyes off the ball or moving prematurely to other positions.

The outcome of the combination of politically influenced appointments and regulatory-induced rotation in senior leadership positions creates instability in the administrative leadership. In order to effect the deep and long-term cultural change that is urgently required in the public service, it is imperative to bring more stability to the leadership. It takes vision and concerted effort over time to affect deep transformational change in any organisation.

Corruption

The corruption that has become synonymous with the period of state capture – which is also reflected in South Africa's sombre ratings on Transparency International's CPI – has contributed not only to the declining trust in the government and public service, but has also undermined the efficiency of service delivery. Corruption is generally defined as the 'abuse of entrusted power for private gain' (Transparency International n.d.). By its very definition, corruption diverts the focus of public servants from the best interest of the public to their own personal interest. This obviously constitutes a conflict of interest for those involved in corrupt practices.

Besides the diverting effect that corruption has on the public service and the focus of public servants, there are also several other detrimental effects of corruption. Firstly, corruption undermines the effectiveness of service delivery. Whenever there is corruption in any system, it slows down the speed and quality of service delivery. Second, corruption undermines the cost-efficiency of service delivery, as it adds extra costs to the process that is corrupted and often also results in substandard or non-delivery of services that are being paid for. Third, corruption has been proven to undermine the employee morale of the organisations in which it occurs (see Healy and Serafeim 2012). Employees lose confidence in their leadership and pride in their work. Low-morale organisations are underperforming organisations, where staff lack the dedication and the will to deliver their best in pursuit of their organisation's purpose.

Poor ethos

A professional and ethical public service requires a very specific ethos. It requires a value orientation where the interest of the public is being prioritised over personal and party-political interests. Given the root causes discussed thus far, it is clear that exactly such a public service ethos is undermined by factors such as political interference, inappropriate appointments and corruption. Section 195 of the South African Constitution states that 'public administration must be governed by the democratic values and principles enshrined in the Constitution'.

Several attempts have been made to instil these values in the ethos of the public service. The *Public Service Regulations* of 2016 were meant to ensure that systems, processes and positions were created to guarantee that ethical values are instilled in the public service.

The *Public Sector Ethics Survey 2018* indicated that there was a sharp increase since the first survey in 2015 in awareness among public servants regarding the code of ethics, as well as policies related to gifts and conflicts of interest. However, other aspects of the measures introduced through the *Public Service Regulations* proved to be less successful. The regulations required all departments to appoint ethics officers and to have an ethics committee that exercises oversight of ethics management. In the 2022 version of the *Public Sector Ethics Survey*, it was found that only 43 per cent of public servants who participated in the survey were aware that there was an ethics officer in their department (Ethics Institute 2022: 27). The fact that the same survey found that only 45 per cent indicated that they received ethics training in their organisation is a further indication that ethics management has not gained the traction that was hoped for when the *Public Service Regulations* were introduced in 2016.

A further indication that the ethos of the public service is not changing for the better is the finding in the *Public Sector Ethics Survey 2022* that there was no significant increase in the strength of the ethical culture in the public service since the previous survey in 2018. This confirms that the public service ethos remains stagnant and is thus not conducive to the deep transformational values and cultural change that is required.

Low staff morale

The final root cause of the current state of the public service is both an outcome of the current state of affairs as well as an enabler thereof. Research in the field of organisational behaviour has found a strong correlation between the staff morale of an organisation, on the one side, and the way employees are being treated in an organisation, on the other (Vorster and Groenewald 2019). There is also a strong correlation between staff morale and whether employees are consistently being held accountable across all employee levels for their decisions and actions (Laratta 2011).

In addition, research by Paul Healy and George Serafeim (2012) demonstrates that the biggest impact of corruption on organisations is the depletion of their staff morale. When the staff morale of an organisation is low or depleted, it robs the organisation of the will and energy needed to change the organisation for the better. It is in this sense that the prevalence of low staff morale, resulting from the other root causes of the current state of the public service, has over time become a root cause itself that prevents the public service from being reformed for the better. A classic vicious downward spiral has thus been created, which needs to give way for the creation of an upward virtuous spiral.

Strategy for improving public service

The first principle of the *King IV Report on Corporate Governance for South Africa* states: 'The governing body should lead ethically and effectively' (Institute of Directors of South Africa 2016). The report goes on to discuss the first two characteristics that leaders are required to cultivate and display – integrity and competence. In this practical guidance, we can find the first two stepping stones on the path to recovery.

As important as these two stepping stones are, more is needed. Four outcomes of good governance articulated in the report include an ethical culture, good performance, effective control and legitimacy. If all these factors are combined, and the root causes of the current dire state of the public service as outlined in the previous section are also factored in, the key focal areas of a strategy towards a competent and ethical public service can be identified as:
  a)   competency;
  b)   integrity;
  c)   stability;
  d)   performance;
  e)   accountability; and
  f)   ethical culture.

Competency

It almost sounds commonsensical to assert that people – and especially senior and executive managers – should have the necessary competence to fulfil their job requirements, but given what was found in the surveys discussed earlier in this chapter, it seems that common sense is not quite as common as one might expect. Competency can be defined as the ability to deliver on one's promises

(Edelman Trust Barometer 2020). Due mainly to political interference in senior appointments, as well as the unhealthy practice of cadre deployment (see Dobie 2022), people are too often appointed to positions without having the knowledge, skills, experience and commitment to deliver on their job requirements. It is thus imperative to restrict political interference and cadre deployment in the process of appointments for senior governance and management positions in the public service, as well as in SOEs.

The problem of interference by political office-bearers in the appointment of key administrative staff was recognised as one of the key problem areas in the public service in the *National Development Plan 2030*. A proposal was made in the NDP to 'create an administrative head of the public service with responsibility for managing the career progression of heads of department [and] put in place a hybrid approach to top appointments that allows for the reconciliation of administrative and political priorities' (National Planning Commission 2012: 64). This proposal, or a similar approach, that can deliberately minimise or restrict political interference in key appointments in the public service can provide the impetus for restoring the ability to deliver on job requirements as a key consideration in making senior appointments. A similar approach is required for making key appointments in senior governance and management positions in SOEs (Qabaka and Van Vuuren 2021).

Appointing people with the required competency in key positions is only the start of restoring competency in the public service. The criteria of competency should be replicated on all levels of the public service to ensure that civil servants have the competency to deliver on their public service delivery promise. Important as the restoration of competency is, on its own it is still incapable of ensuring effective service delivery.

Integrity

The second focal point of a strategy towards an effective and ethical public service should revolve around the integrity of not only senior appointees, but of all public servants. People with high competence but low integrity pose a serious threat to any organisation as they can use their considerable competence to enrich themselves instead of using it in the service of the public.

Integrity refers to the moral character of a person. The practice guidance provided by the *King IV Report on Corporate Governance for South Africa* refers to integrity as one of the characteristics that leaders should develop and display (Institute of Directors of South Africa 2016: 43). It thus implies that integrity, like all other character traits, is not something that one is born with, but something that one should cultivate over time until it becomes second nature or a trait of character. The process of character formation is a lifelong process and not a process that stops in adolescence or adulthood.

In a similar manner that competency should be a key criterion in the selection and promotion of public servants, so should personal moral integrity also be a key selection criterion. Selection and promotion processes should thus be structured in a manner that also assesses the moral inclination and characteristics of candidates. Proper background checks on candidates should be performed to ensure that they do not have a murky moral past. Psychological assessment can also be used to discern the value and moral orientation of candidates.

The application of lifestyle audits for senior positions can be used to ensure that public servants do not have a record of abusing their job positions for private gain. The *Public Sector Ethics Survey 2022* indicates that public servants were more positive than expected about the use of lifestyle audits in the public sector. A total of 68 per cent of respondents said that they believe that lifestyle audits will be effective in curbing corruption, and 89 per cent of respondents indicated that they would be willing to undergo lifestyle audits themselves (Ethics Institute 2022: 3).

Opportunities should also be created for the development of the integrity of public servants. There should thus not only be a reactive approach focused on catching those who have already done wrong, but also a proactive approach of promoting the cultivation of integrity in public servants on all levels of public service departments and SOEs. The proactive promotion of integrity and ethical conduct is one of the objectives of the *Public Service Regulations* of 2016, but it is often neglected in favour of a focus on reactive interventions.

Stability

As indicated earlier, the high turnover of people in senior leadership positions in the public service has to do with administrative appointments being linked with the terms of political office-bearers, as well as with cadre deployment.

The measures suggested above regarding the removal of political influence and interference in the process of making senior appointments in the public service and SOEs will thus also assist in addressing the problem of instability and insecurity of tenure. The ideal is that the public service administration should be a professional corps of public servants who are relatively immune to changes in political leadership.

Regulatory reform is thus needed to decouple the term of administrative leaders from those of political office-bearers. Public servants should be able to pursue a professional career in the public service that is not unduly interrupted by the regular change of guard of political office-bearers.

Performance

It is imperative that there are clear performance objectives and targets for public servants, especially for those in executive positions who are also responsible for the performance of their staff. Such performance objectives and targets would only have an effect if there were consequences for both good performance as well as for non-performance or underperformance. Those who perform above the norm should receive appropriate recognition and reward, and those who underperform should be reprimanded and not be incentivised for lacklustre performance.

Performance should, however, not be only driven by extrinsic motivation, such as in the case of performance incentives or the lack thereof, but should also be driven by the intrinsic motivation of giving their best effort out of inner conviction and in pursuit of the ideal of excellence in public service delivery. Kindling or rekindling such a public service ethos requires a focus on the value system in the public service.

In organisations, one can make a distinction between ethical values and work values (Rossouw and Van Vuuren 2017: 8). In the discussion above on the focal area of integrity, the case was made for the proactive promotion of ethical values that underpin the public service. There should be a similar promotion of work values in the public service, such as excellence, quality and innovation. Particularly, the purpose of the public service and its strategic objectives should play a major role in the promotion of a public service ethos, where public servants would be willing to walk the extra mile in pursuit of the ideals of the public service as articulated in the South African Constitution.

Accountability

The findings of the public sector ethics surveys discussed earlier paint a picture of unprofessional and unethical conduct being tolerated because there is no clear commitment from the leadership to hold transgressors accountable. This is exacerbated by a lack of willingness among public servants to report such behaviour, either because they fear retaliation for reporting misconduct or because they consider it futile to report misconduct, as nothing ever happens when they report it. This contributes to the perception that there is a climate of impunity in the public service, where people can get away with all kinds of malpractices.

It is imperative that systems of accountability need to be established in the public service. There should be proper records of all misconduct identified or reported, which then needs to be monitored closely in terms of what actions were taken with regard to each and every incidence of wrongdoing, and what corrective action was taken to prevent the reoccurrence of similar misconduct in future. All of this should be done in a fair and transparent manner in order to build confidence in the system of accountability.

Given the reluctance among public service staff to report wrongdoing, it is crucial to ensure that reporters of misconduct are protected against all forms of retaliation, and also that feedback is provided to reporters, and to the public service at large, for them to see that reporting is not futile, but results in investigations and actions being taken.

Building a culture of accountability should not only involve taking action against those who have done wrong, but should also focus on recognising those public servants who are exemplary in their work or in displaying a true public service ethos. Such recognition will reinforce the public service ethos and will also contribute to restoring pride and confidence in the public service.

Ethical culture

Cultivating an ethical culture is tantamount to making ethical conduct the norm and not the exception in an organisation. It is thus about deeply embedding norms of ethical conduct in an organisation to the extent that it becomes an organisational habit – the way we do things even when nobody is watching.

In the literature on the cultivation of ethical organisational culture, there are a number of factors that are essential for it to mature and flourish. These factors include a commitment to ethical standards by top leadership, middle management and non-managerial employees. Other factors that also play a determining role in the cultivation of an ethical culture are ethical accountability measures, awareness of ethical standards, ethics talk, and fair treatment of staff and stakeholders (Vorster and Van Vuuren 2022).

According to the *Public Sector Ethics Survey 2022*, the problem of poor culture in the public service cannot be ascribed to a lack of awareness of ethical standards. Arguably, the most productive interventions to instil an ethical culture in the public service would be to focus on demonstrating both top leadership and middle management commitment to ethics, ensuring that ethical accountability measures are effective and that employees are being treated fairly.

Taking a strictly fear-based compliance approach to instil an ethical culture is not a productive way of building an ethical culture. There is evidence that fear-based compliance programmes can become counterproductive and make people less responsible over time (Salz 2013: 185). The *Public Service Regulations* of 2016 clearly had the intent of moving the management of ethics beyond a mere compliance approach and to instilling an ethical culture in the public service. Cultivating an ethical culture in the public service is the cement that will bring all the other focal areas of the strategy together. It is only when all these elements are anchored in an ethical culture that they will contribute to building a competent and ethical public service.

When these six focal areas of the strategy discussed above are integrated into a comprehensive strategy, they can reinforce one another and build momentum for a virtuous upward spiral that will not only improve service delivery, but also restore the pride of public servants in their profession and attract the best minds and talent to the public service.

Notes

1. See https://www.gov.za/documents/constitution-republic-south-africa-1996-chapter-10-public-administration (accessed 28 November 2023).

References

Department of Public Service and Administration. 2016. *Public Service Regulations*. https://www.dpsa.gov.za/dpsa2g/documents/acts&regulations/regulations2016/PUBLIC%20SERVICE%20REGULATIONS%2016%20April%202019.pdf (accessed 28 November 2023).

Dobie, K. 2022. 'Whose Problems Is Deployment Solving? *Ethics Institute*, 26 July. https://www.tei.org.za/2022/07/26/whose-problems-is-deployment-solving/ (accessed 28 November 2023).

Edelman Trust Barometer. 2020. '2020 Edelman Trust Barometer'. https://www.edelman.com/trust/2020-trust-barometer (accessed 28 November 2023).

———. 2021. '2021 Edelman Trust Barometer'. https://www.edelman.com/trust/2021-trust-barometer (accessed 28 November 2023).

———. 2022. '2022 Edelman Trust Barometer'. https://www.edelman.com/trust/2022-trust-barometer (accessed 28 November 2023).

Ethics Institute. 2015. *Public Sector Ethics Survey 2015*. Pretoria: Ethics Institute.

———. 2018. *Public Sector Ethics Survey 2018*. Pretoria: Ethics Institute.

———. 2022. *Public Sector Ethics Survey 2022*. Pretoria: Ethics Institute.

Healy, P. and G. Serafeim. 2012. 'Causes and Consequences of Firm Disclosures of Anticorruption Efforts'. *Harvard Business School*, 9 March. https://hbswk.hbs.edu/item/causes-and-consequences-of-firm-disclosures-of-anticorruption-efforts (accessed 28 November 2023).

Institute of Directors of South Africa. 2016. *King IV Report on Corporate Governance for South Africa*. Johannesburg: Institute of Directors of South Africa.

Laratta, R. 2011. 'Ethical Climate and Accountability in Non-profit Organizations: A Comparative Study between Japan and the UK'. *Public Management Review* 13: 43–63.

National Planning Commission. 2011. *Diagnostic Overview*. https://www.gov.za/sites/default/files/gcis_document/201409/npcdiagnosticoverview1.pdf (accessed 28 November 2023).

———. 2012. *National Development Plan 2030: Our Future – Make It Work*. https://www.gov.za/sites/default/files/gcis_document/201409/ndp-2030-our-future-make-it-workr.pdf (accessed 28 November 2023).

Qabaka, L. and L. van Vuuren. 2021. 'Restoring Trust in SOEs through the Objective Selection of Board Members'. *Ethics Institute*, 21 October. https://www.tei.org.za/2021/10/21/restoring-trust-in-soes-through-the-objective-selection-of-board-members/ (accessed 28 November 2023).

Rossouw, D. and L. van Vuuren. 2017. *Business Ethics*. 6th edition. Cape Town: Oxford University Press.

Salz, A. 2013. *Salz Review: An Independent Review of Barclays' Business Practices*. London: Barclays PLC.

Transparency International. 2021. 'Corruption Perceptions Index'. https://www.transparency.org/en/cpi/2021 (accessed 28 November 2023).

———. n.d. 'What Is Corruption?' https://www.transparency.org/en/what-is-corruption (accessed 28 November 2023).

Van Onselen, G. 2017. *Political Musical Chairs: Turnover in the National Executive and Administration since 2009*. Johannesburg: South African Institute of Race Relations.

Vorster, P. and L. Groenewald. 2019. *South African Business Ethics Survey*. Pretoria: Ethics Institute.

Vorster, P. and N. Konstantinopoulos. 2020. 'Ethical Failures to Blame for the Poor State of SOEs'. *Ethics Institute*, 26 February. https://www.tei.org.za/2020/02/24/ethical-failures-to-blame-for-the-poor-state-of-soes/ (accessed 28 November 2023).

Vorster, P. and L. van Vuuren. 2022. *Ethical Culture Handbook*. Pretoria: Ethics Institute.

CHAPTER 18

The Governability of Liberal Democracy in Post-apartheid South Africa

Constraints

Muxe Nkondo

The forms that liberation struggles took in South Africa were varied. The following organisations mobilised and gave leadership from different ideological positions: the African National Congress (ANC), including the Women's League and the Youth League; the South African Communist Party (SACP); labour unions; the Unity Movement; the Pan Africanist Congress (PAC); liberation theology and Black Consciousness. The history of liberation in South Africa comprises the histories of these organisations. They expressed a common project. That common project involved the reversal of the structures of power. Although the means through which they thought freedom and justice could be achieved were different, the main elements can be characterised as follows:

- assertion of political rights to self-determination (the sovereignty of the people);
- anti-colonial internationalism (Pan-Africanism);
- Marxist internationalism;
- anti-apartheid colonial nationalism (Black Consciousness);
- moral and humanitarian objection (liberation theology);
- industrial strikes, agitation for economic justice and land appropriation without compensation; and
- gender equality.

Historically, the ongoing democratic struggles are a product of all these. There were, however, many different ideologies and forms of resistance and struggles. Some of the tensions and conflicts continue to erupt from ideological sources of conflict within the liberation movements themselves – above all, between liberalism and egalitarianism, based on various versions of socialism and humanism, and inspired by the memory of revolutions in modern history.

The apartheid colonial system has been transformed since the democratic transition in 1994. Like the revolutions in Algeria, Zimbabwe, Mozambique, Namibia, Angola, Zambia, Kenya, Democratic Republic of Congo, Algeria, Guinea Bissau and the Cape Verde islands, to mention only the mostly prominent – South Africa's struggle and liberation has been called a revolution by those who participated in it. Although there is by no means a perfect symmetry in these movements, there are certain patterns. Each marked a significant change, which entailed a measure of violence. Each sought legitimacy in a democratic law and a brand-new social, economic and political order. Each took years to establish roots. Each essentially produced a new system of law, which embodied some of the major principles of the revolution and changed the colonial legal and policy tradition but, to an extent, remained within that tradition (Berman 1985; Bond 2000; Nkondo 2014).

None of these revolutions was a *coup d'état*, although they were all rebellions or, on the other hand, a long series of incremental changes, which, significant enough, were accommodated within the pre-existing colonial system. Like revolutions in the West, Latin America, Caribbean, Russia and Asia, they were accomplished with great struggle and passion. The colonial political and legal system proved incapable of responding to the demands for agency, freedom and justice. The failure to anticipate the movement for fundamental change, and to incorporate its demands in time, was partly due to the inherent contradiction in the nature of the colonial capitalist system, one of whose purposes was to preserve order and another to exploit human and natural resources. Order itself was conceived as having a built-in tension between the need for stability and the need for domination and exploitation. Like each of the anti-colonial revolutions, the South African revolution has experienced an interim period in which new policies, laws, regulations and institutions were enacted in rapid succession and, occasionally, repealed or replaced. But, eventually, for reasons still to be provided, it has restored some of the colonial elements.

The current ongoing struggles – land appropriation without compensation, comfortable accommodation, Not in My Name, a living wage, free education for the poor, reliable and affordable public transport and Operation Dudula, among others – are a product of these struggles over the years. Although the various liberation movements differ in certain respects, they share a common will and disposition to agency, freedom and justice as keys to happiness and well-being. However, tensions between liberation movements continue to erupt from ideological sources of conflict, above all between liberalism and a more engaged political economy, inspired by memories of armed struggle.

Learning from the ironies of post-colonial liberal democracy

The end of apartheid colonialism was signalled by two events with different meanings. On the one hand, the most hideous and most excessive form of colonialism, apartheid, was overcome. On the other hand, the negotiated political settlement made use of the reconciliatory mood to code and sophisticate inequality. It is true that the apartheid state ruled by terror, but no less true is that liberal capitalism has developed sophisticated instruments of resistance, subversion and manipulation. The subversion and manipulation of fundamental change involves connivance by some of the information and knowledge institutions through the marketisation and commercialisation of research and knowledge, driven by a subtle combination of private motive and desire. So, in a real sense, the negotiated settlement was used as an instrument to achieve certain ends, but these do not always converge with the public good.

What, then, has been the meaning and value of the political settlement in light of the persistent struggles between market power and justice, as well as the resilience and adaptiveness of liberalism? Do the lessons of the negotiated settlement help us understand the present? In addressing these questions, we should draw lessons from history by bringing them to bear on the events that we are seeing now. But the very closeness of these events is a problem. The passing of time helps create at least basic consensus. Even if there still are divergent interpretations and evaluations of the negotiated settlement, there is at least consensus on the need to deal decisively with poverty, unemployment, socio-economic inequalities and gender-based violence. The meanings, though, that have been attributed to these challenges and to interpretations are wildly divergent, even among comrades and cadres who share similar ideological values and conceptions of agency, freedom and justice.

Did the negotiated settlement backfire? Why has it given rise to contestations among liberation movements in parliament and elsewhere in the polis? The history of democracy in South Africa, since 1994, resembles a pendulum moving in an ever- widening arc. Each push by each of the political parties produces a swing in the other direction, in a seemingly unstoppable sequence of action and reaction. What accounts for this? Democracy does not have the same effect as apartheid, but hungry and homeless citizens cannot tell the difference. All the same, we do not need to be deluded when liberal capitalism showers security grants on the poor, the unemployed and the homeless. Nor should we confuse the defence of state security with the struggle for the full meaning of agency, freedom and justice. We should choose justice over power and private motive, the public good over market gain. We should support a system that engenders a passion for obligation and responsiveness to the physical and social pain experienced by the majority of South Africa's citizens.

Regarding the pain of the millions is the goal of the South African revolution. For peace, we need an inclusive, empathic social and economic order that will go to the roots of the happiness and well-being of all. Of course, we do not live in a vacuum, but in concrete situations with a particular political geography, which may also bring us its share of violence and defiance. But if we understand how the markets function, we will acquire the appropriate means to respond. Even before we take any action, using the critical intelligence and empathic imagination to get a grip on the dynamics of fundamental change, or radical economic transformation, may provide much-needed insights.

Liberalism seeks constantly expanding markets for its products and makes use of political and knowledge elites over the whole globe. It nestles everywhere, settles everywhere, establishes partnerships and networks everywhere – in one phrase, it creates its own ecosystem. This is what makes it resilient and adaptive. It proclaims, as Margret Thatcher did, that there is no alternative and that any alternative is bound to fail. The debate concerns how the state controls and regulates, but will liberalism manage to stabilise itself and address people's existential needs? If it stabilises itself, on what basis will it have done so? Since the crisis is global, how can liberal capitalism be applied imaginatively within and beyond the nation state? At the very minimum, basing our assessments on extensive research across disciplines and knowledge systems, we can conclude that it does not have what it takes to bring about the changes required. So advocates for revolutionary change must go down to its very core. In this context, failure in public service is much more than the incompetence of individual officials and bureaucratic traps; it is intrinsic in the liberal policies and laws themselves (Fischer 2003).

Challenges of governability: The limits of liberalism

The last 30 years have witnessed a dramatic renewal of the democratic spirit in post-apartheid South Africa. The predominant trends of this period involved the challenging of the authority of the newly established political, social and economic institutions; a reaction against the concentration of power in the political, knowledge and economic elites and in favour of the sovereignty of the people; heightened commitment to equality for women and other historically marginalised groups; the emergence of 'public interest' and human rights lobbying groups; an increased concern for the rights of the poor and the provision of opportunities to participate in making economic decisions that affect them; and a pervasive criticism of those who possess or are thought to possess excessive power or wealth.

The spirit of protest, the spirit of equality, the impulse to expose corruption and redress inequalities are alive and well in South Africa. The themes of these years are the same as those in the Freedom Charter and the Bill of Rights; they embody ideas and beliefs that were deeply foundational in the liberation movement and continue to command the passionate intensity of commitment they did in the struggle years. These years bear testimony to the vibrancy of the struggle for freedom and the reassertion of democratic egalitarianism.

The democratic surge manifests itself in a variety of ways. Consider, for instance, a few examples in terms of two democratic norms of participation and equality. Voting participation, the privilege of the few in the apartheid years, shot up substantially (Reynolds 1999). All other forms of participation in decision-making processes have seen a significant increase during the three decades of democracy (Buhlungu 2010). The overall picture is a sharp increase in political activity. The Mandela, Mbeki, Zuma and Ramaphosa campaigns mobilised an unprecedented number of volunteer workers. In addition, the proliferation of opposition parties, by providing alternative policy positions, broadened political participation.

These years, of course, also have seen a marked upswing in other forms of political participation, in the form of marches, rolling mass action, demonstrations, protest movements and 'cause' organisations (such as environmental groups, people living with disabilities, feminism and the Landless People's Movement). The expansion of participation throughout society is reflected in the markedly higher levels of self-consciousness and self-assertion on the part of Africans, women, students and the Khoisan – all of whom have become mobilised and organised in new ways in an attempt to achieve what they consider their appropriate share of citizenship and its rewards. The results of their efforts, however, are testimony to the difficulties that the government has had in responding to the pressure of these groups to assimilate them into the political, social and economic system, in spite of attempts to incorporate members of these groups into the political leadership structure. A few Africans and a few women have made impressive gains in their representation in national and provincial legislatures, and since 1994 there have been two female deputy presidents. At the same time, there has been a marked expansion of white-collar activism and of the readiness and willingness of professional employees to participate in the struggle for justice. Hitherto, relatively passive or unorganised groups in the population, such as doctors and magistrates, have now embarked on concerted efforts to establish their claims to opportunities, positions, rewards and privileges.

In a related and similar vein, the last three decades have also seen an assertion of the primacy of equality as a goal in social, economic and political life. The meaning of equality and the means of achieving it have become central themes of debate in intellectual and policy-development circles. What was widely hailed as the major treatise of the liberation movement – the Freedom Charter – defined justice largely in terms of equality. Differences in wealth and power are viewed with increased scepticism. The classic issue of equality of opportunity versus equality of results is central to the debate. The prevailing preoccupation with equality is shown clearly in the titles of books produced by social scientists over these years – for example, *Elite Transition: From Apartheid to Neoliberalism in South Africa* (Bond 2000) and *Sustainable Development for a Democratic South Africa* (Cole

1994). This concern over equality has not, of course, easily transmitted itself into a widespread reduction of inequality in society.

The causes of persistent inequality in recent years could conceivably be (a) either permanent or transitory, or (b) either peculiar to South Africa or more generally pervasive throughout emerging post-colonial liberal economies. The democratic surge, on the other hand, might be the result of deep-seated aspirations that are producing changes in the South African political consciousness and also affecting other post-colonial societies. Or it could be the product of rapid social and cultural change consequent upon the demise of apartheid, which in itself is transitory and whose political consequences will hence eventually fade – that is, it could be the product of immediate and not necessarily lasting change. In addition, given some of the similarities that seemed to exist between the political temper and movements of the last 30 years and earlier apartheid periods, especially in the 1970s and 1980s, it is possible that the democratic surge may be reflecting a political dynamic working itself out on a recurring or cyclical basis. Of course, the surge could be the product of a mixture of factors, permanent and transitory, specific and general (Hyslop 1999).

The post-apartheid democratic surge and the causes of ungovernability

The immediate causes of the simultaneous increase in protests and demonstrations and the difficulty that the government has had in redressing social and economic inequalities are to be found in the democratic surge over the last three decades. In effect, three basic characteristics have held true about the problem of governability in South Africa since 1994:

- the incompatibility of capitalism with democracy;
- the overload of participants and demands within the South African political system, which has increasing difficulty in mastering the very complexity naturally resulting from its economic growth and political development; and
- the bureaucratic cohesiveness that the system has to sustain in order to maintain its capacity to decide and implement tends to foster a diversity of voices and the breakdown of consensus, which, in turn, increases the difficulty of its task.

Participative democracy and liberalism: An uneasy marriage

The democratic surge can be explained as the manifestation in South Africa of the political impact of liberal macroeconomic policies. It is the classic story of the ongoing tension between deliberative and participatory democracy and liberalism, and efforts within the liberation traditions of political thought to escape the traps that the systemic incompatibility poses for government (Girling 2002). Since the adoption of the Reconstruction and Development Programme (RDP) (ANC 1994), through to the adoption of the *National Development Plan 2030* (NDP) (National Planning Commission 2012), the South African government has taken this tension seriously and has sought some way around or out of it. In its report entitled 'Can Africa Claim the 21st Century?', the World Bank has this to say:

> Many African governments still have an uneasy relationship with business, which suffers under poor services and regulations that raise costs, and discourage investment. An essential part of empowering civil society must be to involve producers – in agriculture and other sectors to foster higher productivity and more effective competition in global markets. Without strong producers, it will be impossible to reverse past trends and shift from aid dependence to trade dependence (World Bank 2000: 13).

This explanation is rather narrow. The predicament facing African governments, and the South African government in particular, is not a contingent or mechanical one, nor a question of mere institutional re-engineering. It is of a deeper nature. Our starting point in tackling it should relate back to the key factor in democracy's crisis: its incompatibility, in important respects, with market systems. For example, debates on the relationship between states and markets, democracy and liberalism in all the years since Ghana attained its independence reveal intractable tensions (Lumumba-Kasongo 2005). Democratic theory is based on a belief in the sovereignty of the people, which requires ordering social and economic relations in accordance with the will of the people. However, the democratic order was built simultaneously on the principles of the market, which maintain that the pursuit of self-interest or personal happiness, as a result of competition, is to the advantage of all. The principle of comparative advantage is one of the most enduring tenets of market economics. The key to profitability and command over commodities – indeed to economic growth and survival in the marketplace – is to stake out, and then constantly improve upon, a distinctive competitive position. Competition continues to provide the ideological foundation for country, company and personal strategies.

Market rationality and the primacy of instrumental reason

The democratic temper is connected to another massively important phenomenon of our time. We might call this the primacy of instrumental reason (Taylor 1991). By 'instrumental reason' I mean the kind of rationality the market draws on when it calculates the most economical application of means to a given end. Maximum efficiency, the best cost–output ratio, is its measure of success.

In South Africa, there is no doubt that markets are sweeping away the passionate sense of the public good that the liberation movement sought to promote and have widened the scope of instrumental reason. South African society no longer has an inspiring grand narrative. Once society no longer has a heroic dimension, once social arrangements and modes of action are no longer grounded in the grand order of history or the will of the people, they are, in a sense, up for grabs. Society can then be redesigned with no regard for the consequences on the happiness and well-being of the majority of the people. The yardstick that now applies is that of instrumental reason. Similarly, once our daily activities lose the significance that accrued to their place in the historical struggle for justice and freedom, they are open to being treated as raw materials or instruments for market projects.

There is also a widespread anxiety that instrumental reason not only has enlarged its scope, but also threatens to take over our lives. The fear is that things that ought to be determined by equality will be determined in terms of efficiency or cost–benefit analysis: the liberation ends that ought to be guiding our lives have been eclipsed by the demand to maximise output (Ferré 1995). Several things give substance to this concern – for instance, the ways the demands of economic growth are used to justify very unequal distribution of wealth and income, or the way these same demands make us insensitive to the needs of the environment, even to the point of potential disaster. Alternatively, we can think of the way much of our social planning in crucial areas such as education and health is dominated by forms of cost–benefit analysis that involve grotesque calculations, with no regard for the public good (Chomsky 1999; Nussbaum 2010; Taylor 1991).

This brings us to the political level and to the feared consequences of instrumental reason. Technology is one of the major sources of public power in our society. Insofar as decisions affecting the daily lives of South Africans are concerned, political democracy is largely overshadowed by the enormous power wielded by masters of technical systems: corporate leaders and professional associations of groups such as engineers and architects. They have far more to do with control over patterns of urban growth, the design of dwellings and transportation systems, the selection of innovations, our experience as employees, patients and consumers, than all the governmental institutions of our society put together. Unfortunately, access to technology is severely unequal and the cost is high (Feenberg and Hannay 1995).

Critique of liberalism

Liberalism is often discussed in terms of respect for the truth, the law and individual rights (Rawls 1993: 4–46). But the history of liberalism tells us that in liberal democracies cunning, systemic violence, propaganda and realpolitik, in the guise of liberal principles, are the substance of international politics and even of domestic politics (Losurdo 2014; Merleau-Ponty 1969; Plehwe, Walpen and Neunhöffer 2005: 1–24). Respect for law and liberty has served to justify military suppression in Côte d'Ivoire, Libya and Iraq and the suppression of strikes in South Africa and other places in the world. The purity of liberal principles not only tolerates, but even requires violence. Thus there is a mystification in liberalism. Judging by history and everyday events, liberal ideas belong to a system of violence of which they are the solemn complement and the general basis of justification (Merleau-Ponty 1969).

It is a persuasive argument. In refusing to assess liberalism in terms of its principles, and in demanding that these principles be compared with the prevailing social and economic relations in a liberal state, I am not simply speaking in the name of a debatable materialist philosophy. I am applying the materialist's formula to a concrete study of South African society, which cannot be refuted by idealist arguments. Whatever one's ideological position, a society is not the shrine of symbols on the front of its monuments or in its Constitution; the value of a society is the value it places upon social and economic relations.

To understand and assess a society, one has to penetrate its basic structure to the social and economic bond upon which it is built; this undoubtedly depends upon legal relations, but also upon forms of labour and work, ways of living and loving. It is for this reason that I pose the problem of liberalism – not on the grounds of principle, but of social and economic relations. It is certainly not enough to brandish liberal principles in order to counter the enforcement of fundamental socio-economic rights; we have to examine whether in doing so, liberalism is doing anything to resolve the problem rightly raised by its critics – to establish among people social and economic relations that are fair and just.

Democracy, integrated development and inclusive growth

In the NDP and the Integrated Development Plan, there is a consistent argument about the relationship between liberal democracy, integrated development and inclusive growth. The promotion of such development growth, it is argued, taking into careful consideration its effects on resource allocation and sustainable environmental health, must receive priority attention in the role of government. Political democracy requires economic growth; economic growth depends upon efficient democratic institutions. The logic has far-reaching implications. It is clearly desirable that economic growth is promoted and sustained. Yet it is essential to ask several questions in relation to this logic (Sen 1999). Why is it that in South Africa, for example, democracy is dependent on economic growth based on liberal principles? Is South African democracy inconceivable without it? Is growth presumably growth of the gross national product? And is this the only kind of expansion of human life chances which we can think of? Is the development of human capabilities dependent on economic growth, driven by the market's motives? Are there not perhaps other forms of growth and improvement of human lives?

So how should South African democracy be properly conceptualised? First and foremost, we must underline the fact that its structural features and defining aspects – free and fair elections periodically, individual rights and freedoms and so on – are, despite their importance, only political forms, whose operation and specific efficacy are unable to neutralise, let alone dissolve, the intrinsically anti-democratic structure of liberal capitalist society. This structure, which rests on the system of social relations centred on the incessant reproduction of labour power that must be sold in the marketplace as a commodity to guarantee the very survival of the workers, poses insurmountable limits for South African liberal democracy.

The result is a de facto dictatorship of the market elite, whatever the political forms (Bond 2000). The answer to the dictatorship of the market, quite obviously, is negative. So, in response to the NDP and the Integrated Development Plan, we should put on the table a substantive and comprehensive reconceptualisation of South African democracy, focusing on the relationship between the sovereignty of the people and market forces. We cannot hope to build a democratic political order without simultaneously waging a principled struggle against liberal market forces.

Searching for alternatives: A perspective on the Bill of Rights

To what extent has the Bill of Rights benefited the poor in South Africa? Presiding over the very first socio-economic case to come before the Constitutional Court, Chief Justice Chaskalson had this to say:

> We live in a society in which there are great disparities in wealth. Millions of people are living in deplorable conditions and great poverty. There is a high level of unemployment, inadequate social security, and many do not have access to clean water or to adequate health services. These conditions already existed when the Constitution was adopted and a commitment to address them, and to transform our society into one in which there will be human dignity, freedom and equality, lies at the heart of our new constitutional order. For as long as these conditions continue to exist that aspiration will have a hollow ring.[1]

Does the alleviation of poverty depend on filling out that hollow ring? Building from Chaskalson's pertinent observation, the government should develop a deliberative, participative framework on how to think about socio-economic rights and what that means for the implementation of those rights. The government should follow this up with a nuanced and compelling account of the limitations or conditionality of socio-economic rights and advance a powerful argument for the judicial review of socio-economic rights.

Such an effort would undoubtedly draw the NDP and the Integrated Development Plan closer to the deep desire of millions of South Africans for a society where no person is left hungry, homeless or uneducated, lacking medical assistance or social assistance, or unable to afford justice.

Conclusion

The contrasting spectacle of economic growth and persistent socio-economic inequalities points to the necessity for a comprehensive analysis of the incompatibility between participative democracy and the market economy. To rectify this incompatibility, it is essential that calls for higher growth be accompanied by demands for more inclusive growth, and also by a commitment to make equitable use of resources generated by growth to eliminate poverty and redress structural imbalances. For this to happen, a comprehensive and integrated macro-strategy is needed that would counter the effects of liberalism on national institutions, regulate the growing corporate and political connections and mitigate the impact of liberalism on public service education.

To deepen our understanding of these issues, the first step has to be the spreading of awareness of the havoc wrought upon South African society by liberalism. Only by broadening the public's political consciousness can we hope in the end to raise the general level of political education and socialisation, undermine liberal domination and, in the process, redirect the levers of government towards radically changing the law and institutions and making South African society more secure, more compassionate and more equal for all.

Notes

1. *Soobramoney v. Minister of Health* 1997 (KwaZulu-Natal) (CCT32/97) [1997] ZACC 17 (27 November 1997). See Chief Justice Chaskalson P., para. 8.

References

ANC (African National Congress). 1994. 'The Reconstruction and Development Programme (RDP): A Policy Framework'. https://omalley.nelsonmandela.org/index.php/site/q/03lv02 039/04lv02103/05lv02120/06lv02126.htm (accessed 18 September 2023).

Berman, H.J. 1985. *Law and Revolution: The Formation of the Western Legal Tradition*. Cambridge, MA: Harvard University Press.

Bond, P. 2000. *Elite Transition: From Apartheid to Neoliberalism in South Africa*. London: Pluto Press.

Buhlungu, S. 2010. *A Paradox of Victory: COSATU and the Democratic Transformation in South Africa*. Pietermaritzburg: University of KwaZulu-Natal Press.

Chomsky, N. 1999. *Profit over People*. New York: Seven Stories Press.

Cole, K. 1994. *Sustainable Development for a Democratic South Africa*. London: Routledge.

Feenberg, A. and A. Hannay. 1995. *Technology and the Politics of Knowledge*. Bloomington: Indiana University Press.

Ferré, F. 1995. *Philosophy of Technology*. Athens: University of Georgia Press.

Fischer, F. 2003. *Reframing Public Policy: Discursive Politics and Deliberative Practices*. Oxford: Oxford University Press.

Girling, J. 2002. *Corruption, Capitalism and Democracy*. Abingdon-on Thames: Routledge.

Hyslop, J. 1999. *The Classroom Struggle: Policy and Resistance in South Africa, 1940–90*. Pietermaritzburg: University of Natal Press.

Losurdo, D. 2014. *Liberalism: A Counter-history*. Translated by G. Elliott. London: Verso.

Lumumba-Kasongo, T. 2005. *Liberal Democracy and Its Critics in Africa: Political Dysfunction and the Struggle for Social Progress*. London: Zed Books.

Merleau-Ponty, M. 1969. *Humanism and Terror*. London: Routledge.

National Planning Commission. 2012. *National Development Plan 2030: Our Future – Make It Work*. https://www.gov.za/sites/default/files/gcis_document/201409/ndp-2030-our-future-make-it-workr.pdf (accessed 18 September 2023).

Nkondo, M. 2014. 'The Vibrancy and Governability of the South African Democracy'. In: *State of the Nation: South Africa 1994–2014: A Twenty-Year Review of Freedom and Democracy*, edited by T. Meyiwa, M. Nkondo, M. Chitiga Mabugu, M. Sithole and F.B. Nyamnjoh, 93–105. Cape Town: HSRC Press.

Nussbaum, M.C. 2010. *Not for Profit: Why Democracy Needs the Humanities*. Princeton: Princeton University Press.

Plehwe, D., B.J.A. Walpen and G. Neunhöffer. 2005. *Neoliberal Hegemony: A Global Critique*. Abingdon-on-Thames: Routledge.

Rawls, J. 1993. *Political Liberalism: Expanded Edition*. New York: Columbia University Press.

Reynolds, A. 1999. *Election '99 South Africa: From Mandela to Mbeki*. Oxford: James Currey.

Sen, A. 1999. *Development as Freedom*. Oxford: Oxford University Press.

Taylor, C. 1991. *The Ethics of Authenticity*. Cambridge, MA: Harvard University Press.

World Bank 2000. 'Can Africa Claim the 21st Century?' https://openknowledge.worldbank.org/entities/publication/b7d30898-671f-5718-a04d-09bde4ebae1a (accessed 18 September 2023).

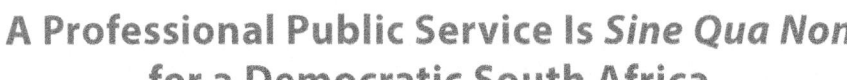

CHAPTER 19

A Professional Public Service Is *Sine Qua Non* for a Democratic South Africa

Dovhani Reckson Thakhathi

In the preamble of the *White Paper on Reconstruction and Development* of 1994, South Africa's first democratic president Nelson Mandela, said: 'Our people have elected us because they want change. Change is what they will get. Our people have high expectations which are legitimate. While the government cannot meet all these needs overnight, we must put firmly into place the concrete goals, time frames and strategies to achieve this change' (Office of the President 1994: 4).

The public service has changed considerably from 1994 to 2024, with various government departments adopting certain reforms and undergoing different transformational processes to improve service delivery to the people. A snapshot of the provincial and national departments points to some milestones covered in meeting the stated development goals and mandates. It can be contended that there are still some discrepancies and inequalities in the way services are being delivered. It would be a miscarriage of justice to judge all government departments' achievements using the same yardstick because they all do not have same number of tasks to execute. Many policies and programmes have been enacted and implemented in an effort to transform and build a single public service that is non-discriminatory, inclusive and promotes public participation.

Overview of the public service

The Public Service Act of 1994, sections 197 and 195 (1) and the Public Administration Management Act of 2014 outline the legislative mandate of the Department of Public Service and Administration. The laws are the basis upon which the functions, responsibilities and structure of the public service is built, and they mandate public servants to execute the duties of implementing policies for the government of the day diligently. The public service is made up of the following structures:

- legislative authority: National Parliament, National Assembly (350–400 members), National Council of Province (90 delegates), Provincial Legislature;
- executive authority: Cabinet, president, deputy president (national), Provincial Executive (premier and the members of the Executive Council); and
- judiciary authority: Constitutional Court, Supreme Court of Appeal, high courts and magistrates' courts. The Judicial Service Commission appoints judges.

Other state institutions supporting democracy include the public protector, the Human Rights Commission, the Commission for Gender Equality, the auditor-general and the Electoral Commission.

The public service essentially includes national and provincial levels of government and the relevant executives and legislative institutions. Following the doctrine of the separation of powers, the three spheres of government operate independently and separately, focusing on their own responsibilities, roles and functions. The public entities operate under the political oversight of their minister, but work independently under their boards of management and under the relevant Act.

The local government level and traditional authorities are not part of the public service. They all operate independently, but are guided by Chapter 3 of the Constitution, which requires them to observe the principles of co-operative governance.

The RDP White Paper as a foundation of the new public service

The *White Paper on Reconstruction and Development* of 1994 laid the foundation upon which the new public service was to be built. The White Paper described the Reconstruction and Development Programme (RDP) 'as an integrated, coherent, socio-economic framework, with its main priority being the creation of employment through economic growth' (Mosala, Venter and Bain 2017: 332). The new South Africa was afflicted by the faults that pre-dated the democratic changes of the new era. Some of the old faults, combined with new ones, included a need for strategic intervention to avoid disruptions in the processes of governance (Maserumule 2017). The *National Development Plan 2030* (NDP) states that despite significant achievements of the post-apartheid state to create a good society, access to quality basic services is uneven (National Planning Commission 2012). It locates the reason for this in 'apartheid spatial and governance systems', with 'institutional weakness in some provinces and municipalities' exacerbating the disparities. As argued in the NDP, 'unevenness' in the capacity of the state spawns 'uneven performance' of the state in the pursuit of the public good, with the following added as the major causes: tensions in the political administrative interface; instability of administrative leadership; skills deficits; insufficient attention to the role of the state in reproducing the skills it needs; weaknesses in organisational design; low staff morale; lack of a culture of continuous improvement; insufficient attention to operational management; and a lack of management accountability.

The *White Paper on the Transformation of the Public Service* of 1995

In the 30 years of the new dispensation, some milestones have been achieved in terms of democratising South Africa and its public service. Transforming the public service requires the efforts of various stakeholders working together for a common goal. The first notable success of the government in the post-apartheid era was the logical integration of the previously fragmented public services, which discriminated between white and black South Africans. The logical amalgamation of '11 previous administrations and the self-governing Bantustans into a unified public service operating in the national and provincial spheres was a daunting task' (Presidential Review Commission 1998: 6). The National Planning Commission's *Diagnostic Report* articulated that immediately after 1994, genealogically separated governments in provinces, 'homelands' and 'self-governing territories' were combined into a more efficient and culturally unified system of local, provincial and national government (2011). The disharmony of the past necessitated the need for the creation of a single public service that was representative of citizens in the consolidation of a democratic society.

Because some of the goals of the White Paper were not effectively implemented, the full transformation of the public service has not been achieved.

The *White Paper on Service Delivery* (Batho Pele) of 1997

The Batho Pele principles, as outlined in the *White Paper on Service Delivery*, claim that people must come first in the minds of public servants when they are executing their tasks of service delivery (Chidinma 2021). These principles are elaborated on below.

Consultation

Consultation helps to develop and deliver citizen-centred services. Therefore, it is crucial that public officials regularly engage and interact with people they serve to get their insights and views regarding their level of satisfaction or dissatisfaction about the services they are receiving. Citizens may have valuable ideas that can be used to improve service delivery and they should have the opportunity to share their views (Walubengo 2020). Thus, capacity-building is of paramount importance for civil society to ensure effective participation of citizens during the consultation process.

Service standards

There is a need to set standards that can be used as a benchmark to gauge if these standards are being met or not. All government departments need to precisely stipulate the quality and quantity of what they deliver. Service standards, for instance, should clearly articulate the duration it will take to get that service done and what to expect from the public service. For example, if a person applies for an ID book from the Department of Home Affairs, and the person has submitted all the required documents, it should only take about six weeks to get the ID book. If this standard is not met, the department owes perhaps an apology and an explanation to the affected person.

Redress

Redress means compensating and rectifying the wrong when someone has been short-changed. When citizens are supposed to receive a service from the public service, but for some reason the service was not rendered, those citizens have a right to redress (Sabhikhi 2017). An apology should immediately be given to the affected people and a solution provided to compensate for what they did not get. It is the responsibility of public servants to inform their superior about what happened and to ensure the problem is addressed. All complaints raised by citizens must be listened to and considered in planning sessions to find amicable ways to address them. This will help to build a good the image of the public service because it will be seen by citizens as responsive to their grievances. Citizens are empowered to ask government about any decision that affects them through the Promotion of Administrative Justice Act. The Act further gives citizens the right to appeal the decision or ask for a review of the administrative action by a court or, where appropriate, an independent and impartial tribunal when they are not satisfied with the reasons or decisions taken by government.

Access

All citizens are entitled to equal access to public services as enshrined in the Bill of Rights, regardless of gender, ethnicity, race or political affiliation. It is the responsibility of public servants to ensure that extra assistance is provided to those who need it. Every public institution must have facilities and infrastructure that enables disabled people and those in wheelchairs to have access to buildings. It is the responsibility of managers in public institutions to ensure this equal access. In cases where people have visual or hearing disabilities, special provisions should be made to help them.

Courtesy

Public servants should treat everyone with respect and courtesy and be willing to help those who need their assistance. Public servants must always bear in mind that they are hired to serve the people and they should not act as barriers to services, nor should they ridicule or be rude to citizens. Rather, they should act as enablers of public service delivery.

Information

All citizens should be given full information about their surroundings, the type of services they are receiving, job opportunities, and programmes and projects planned for their communities. In the event that citizens request certain information or ask about a service, but the available public servant does not have that information, they should refer them to someone else who might assist (Walubengo 2020). Informed citizens help to hold public servants accountable and also make the job of public servants easier. Providing information goes beyond pasting notices or publishing it in the media. It includes taking the time to explain to citizens how to access services.

Transparency

Openness in the public service is considered to be one of the ways to combat corruption and underhand activities that deprive other people of equal opportunities. The public service and administration should render services in a transparent manner and everyone should have equal access to valuable information that can help to keep them informed (Chidinma 2021). Some citizens, especially those from disadvantaged communities, do not yet have access to free basic services, social grants or job opportunities, due to a lack of information on how to access these things. Members of the public have the right to know who is in charge, what the budgets and plans of government departments are, how they work and how decisions are made as part of promoting transparency.

Value for money

Every public cent spent should be accounted for and it should be worth what it is spent on. Public officials must ensure they avoid or minimise wastage of taxpayers' money and any other resources that are meant for the benefit of the public. In rendering any public service, a cost-benefit analysis should be done to ensure that resources are channelled where there are maximum benefits, and resources are utilised in a cost-effective and efficient manner, without compromising the quality of the service delivered to people.

Most of the departments are found wanting in terms of the implementation of the above principles. The annual reports of the auditor-general show that service delivery at national and provincial levels is low and very poor.

The constitutional values and principles of the public service

The democratic values and principles governing public administration are outlined in section 195 in Chapter 10 of the Constitution, as elaborated below.

A high standard of professional ethics

As pointed by William Gumede (2015), professional ethics in the public sector refers to the character, conduct and morals of human beings about what is right or wrong, and public servants should practise it individually and as a group. Ethics help to differentiate between what is acceptable and unacceptable beyond self-interest. Public servants are the face and mouthpiece of government, who act on behalf of the public, marshalling resources to ensure that service delivery is achieved. A high standard of professional ethics needs to be upheld in the public service to combat corruption and other forms of maladministration.

Promotion of efficient and effective use of resources

It is the responsibility of public officials to ensure that citizens' needs are met, using the available resources in an efficient and cost-effective manner. Public officials must avoid any form of wasting limited resources they are entrusted with and they must avoid the temptation of diverting funds for their personal aggrandisement while the poor suffer and do not get basic services. The available resources should be efficiently and effectively used to improve service delivery such as electricity, water, sanitation, education, health and infrastructure and to ensure that those without access to services are prioritised, while seeking new ways of executing their tasks better.

Development-oriented public administration

A 'better life for all' should be the vision of all development-oriented governments and should promote economic growth, job creation and business opportunities and reduce poverty through various development initiatives. The government of South Africa has dedicated itself to accelerate socio-economic development by prioritising the mitigation of poverty, inequality and unemployment as the core for its developmental plan. To achieve such a momentous developmental agenda, there is a need to capacitate the public service institutions with suitably qualified and dedicated staff. All societal stakeholders, community-based organisations, churches, traditional leaders and ward councillors should be mobilised through public–private partnerships to support such a developmental agenda (Okeyo, Lehmann and Schneider 2020). This will help to promote loyalty, social cohesion and compassion among communities and a sense of belonging.

Impartial, fair and equitable services

All citizens are equal before the law. Therefore, when public servants are rendering services, they must do so without discriminating against anyone. Public services must be rendered equitably and impartially and with respect, without any form of bias. There should always be uniformity in the manner in which service delivery is carried out.

Public needs and public participation

All government services and efforts should be citizen-centred by strengthening public participation in the planning and execution process to ensure no one is left behind and every voice is heard and considered. Public participation is a proactive way of working with citizens in the public service to ensure that different grievances, expectations and views are heard and responded to. Government officials should not view citizens as service users only, but rather as active participants in planning, defining the type and quality of services they want and including the timeframes of getting such services.

Accountability

Accountability refers to the responsibility of public servants to be answerable for their actions and inactions, accept responsibility and provide information to the members of the public from whom they derive their mandate (Sibanda 2017). As outlined in the preamble to the Constitution, there is a need for 'a system of democratic government to ensure accountability, responsiveness and openness' (National Planning Commission 2012). There should be serious consequences when responsibilities and obligations are not executed in an acceptable manner. This will help to combat corruption, the misappropriation of funds and irresponsible and unlawful actions by public servants. An active public participation process also helps to strengthen accountability in the public service and at all levels of society in general.

Transparency

All transactions, activities and operations of the public service should be transparent and accessible when the information is requested. Some of this information must be published in the *Government Gazette* or other media for public consumption. This helps to ensure that citizens are informed regularly by the state, and information is readily available for members of the public to make informed decisions and to question how funds are spent.

Good human resource management and development practices

The success of every organisation or institution depends heavily on its most precious asset – personnel with relevant and a wide range of skills, knowledge and expertise. In the South African public service, such human resources with these skills, knowledge and expertise are often scarce, misplaced, not recognised and in some cases poorly remunerated, which makes it difficult to attract and retain them in the public service (Public Service Commission 2021). Therefore, emphasis and priority should be placed on capacity-building in the public service through recruitment, performance management, better remuneration, career management, and stimulating a culture of continuous learning and skills acquisition. This will assist in attracting and retaining competent personnel, which, in turn, will help to build good practices with personnel who are well equipped to execute their tasks and who can easily adapt to the ever-changing world where technology is at the centre stage of service delivery. Better working conditions will provide public servants with a sense of belonging and pride and will encourage them to put all their efforts towards the betterment of other people's lives through various projects and programmes, and even finding innovative ways to render services.

The above-mentioned constitutional values and principles are the foundation of a professional public service and must be implemented effectively by the entire public service. The Public Service Commission needs to ensure that all departments enforce these values and principles, as they are mandated by the Constitution to submit annual reports on their implementation.

The Presidential Review Commission

The *White Paper on the Transformation of the Public Service* of 1995 was the first document to highlight the need for a Presidential Review Commission (PRC). The PRC was established together with the Public Sector Transformation Forum and departmental and provincial transformation units. The mandate of the PRC is to:

- inquire into the structures and functions of the public service and its statutory bodies;

- conduct an internal audit and review of each ministry, department, provincial administration, organisational component, office and agency concerning its objectives, structure, function, staffing, financing and related matters;
- conduct reviews and revisions of the systems, routines and procedures of planning, budgeting and financial execution in the public service to increase public accountability;
- make recommendations and proposals regarding transformation and reform as envisaged in the White Paper.

The priorities of the PRC were revised to ensure that a culture of democratic governance was inculcated in all government structures and cascaded down to local government. There have been notable changes at provincial and national government since the formation of the PRC, including institutional re-engineering, the introduction of programmes and policy formulation. However, there has been uneven implementation of policies and programmes. It is essential to also point out that some of the crucial components of good governance are still not visible. For instance, there is lack of comprehensive organisational structures, vibrant human resources, proper financial management, intergovernmental relations and the political will to promote effective service delivery across departments.

As a democratic and capable state, South Africa needs to improve democratic governance and effectively and efficiently deliver services, impartially and economically, to all citizens (Kunicova 2018). The primary purpose of the PRC is 'to make the public service a legitimate and effective development-oriented instrument of long-term transformation, capable of bringing services to the whole population on an equitable basis and facilitate the development of service excellence and public sector democratisation in the medium and long term in all sectors and regions' (The Presidency 2014).

Some of the main themes envisioned in restructuring and transforming the public service include the following:
- All citizens regardless of gender, race, creed and any form of disability must have equal access to employment opportunities in the public service and must receive services of the same quality and quantity.

- A cost-effective public service must be encouraged, with proper strategic planning processes and the appropriate human capital equipped to execute their tasks efficiently and effectively.
- Improve co-ordination and public participation to strengthen planning and make informed decisions as well as communicating effectively with all citizens.
- Encourage external accountability and internal democratic work practices with strong monitoring and evaluation mechanisms.
- Build fresh organisational cultures, leadership and management practices that reflect the multiplicity of the South African citizenry.
- Human resource development sections should prioritise institutional and individual capacity-building training and development programmes as outlined in the Skills Development Act 97 of 1998.
- Promote a culture of professional work ethic and combat fraud and corruption.

The Public Management Act of 2014

Section 195 of the Constitution lays the foundation upon which the Public Administration Management Act (PAMA) of 2014 was established. The PAMA pronounces the values and principles in section 195, as well as the duty of the National School of Governance to ensure the values and principles are achieved. It also emphasises the use of education and training in building capacity to ensure that the public service has a vibrant workforce that is equipped to enhance the quality, quantity and smooth flowing of service delivery to the citizens. The PAMA provides an outline for an amalgamated system of public administration that cuts across all government spheres. The objectives of the PAMA include:

a) promote and give effect to the values and principles in Section 195 (1) of the Constitution;

b) provide for the transfer and secondment of employees;

c) promote a high standard of professional ethics in the public administration;

d) promote the use of information and communication technologies in the public administration;

e) promote efficient service delivery in the public administration;

f) facilitate the eradication and prevention of unethical practices in the public administration; and

g) provide for the setting of minimum norms and standards to give effect to the values and principles of section 195 (1) of the Constitution.

The Revival of the Community Development Workers Programme

The Community Development Workers Programme (CDWP) was introduced in 2003 under the Ministry of Provincial and Local Government. The community development workers (CDWs) are an essential cornerstone that serves as a bridge between communities and government in public service delivery.[1] Enslin van Rooyen and Sipho Mokoena (2013: 762) write that the CDWs are a 'complementary structure to existing structures in municipalities with different and, to some extent, some overlapping responsibilities'. The core mandate of CDWs is to deepen democracy through promoting public participation.

The Ministry for Public Service and Administration (2007: 9) spells out the functions of the CDWP as follows:

- improve social equity and justice;
- enhance service delivery;
- deepen democracy; and
- contribute to citizen education.

Additionally, the CDWP helps to facilitate developmental projects, harness indigenous knowledge and simultaneously empower local citizens with project management skills. It promotes people-centred approaches in community forestry, for instance, based on three important principles:

1) the active and authentic participation of community stakeholders in projects;

2) the use and acknowledgement of the importance of Indigenous Knowledge Systems (IKS);

3) the use of policies that support participation and collaborative management of resources (Ham, Chirwa and Theron 2013: 179).

It can be contended that the CDWs are change agents to promote reciprocal learning and proffer solutions to problems through IKS, partnership planning and a mutually beneficial social learning process. However, some communities are of the view that there is a lack of proper communication from government and no transparency in the way some projects are operating, which creates room for financial mismanagement (Mokoena and Moeti 2017).

Merits of CDWs

The CDWP has ushered in a new category of professionalism in the local government sphere to assist and speed up service delivery (Tshishonga and Mafema 2010: 574). To some extent, the CDWP contributes to strengthening public participation, improving social capital, harnessing local resources and skills, co-ordinating teams employed in public works programmes, developing self-reliance through encouraging interconnected relations that give a sense of ownership and belonging, while establishing mutual benefits through external partnerships (Mokoena and Moeti 2017).

Weaknesses of CDWs

There is lack of clear policy direction for the CDWP and a lack of understanding about its roles and responsibilities. Mel Gray and Betty Mubangizi point to 'power issues [that] were exacerbated by confusion as to who was in charge of these workers and to whom they were accountable. This led to dysfunctional relations and a lack of cooperation' (2010: 191). Local government officials also viewed CDWs with suspicion and felt threatened that they would usurp their role.

The introduction of the District Development Model

The District Development Model (DDM) is 'a practical intergovernmental relations mechanism to enable all three spheres of government to work together, with communities and stakeholders, to plan, budget and implement in unison'.[2] The DDM 'provides a space where innovation could drive economic development and innovation-based district regeneration through inclusive policy framework and where the discourse, the state and the district development programmes are inclusive and innovation driven' (Mosiea 2020: 5).

The main objectives of the DDM include:

- promoting development and sustainable growth to ensure that rural/urban migration is managed properly;

- ensuring that local economic drivers are supported and managing spatial form, land release and land development; and
- addressing urgent short-term issues, while simultaneously institutional-ising long-term planning, infrastructure investment, promoting economic growth, and supporting integrated human settlement and sustainable provision of basic services to citizens.

National and provincial departments must allocate budgets that are geo-referenced in the district municipalities. This will provide a baseline of the current investments in the district municipalities and an opportunity to do a gap analysis to understand how various government programmes at all levels are responding to development challenges and material conditions on the ground. The DDM reduces the distance between the citizens and government and strengthens the co-ordination role and capacities at all spheres of government.

A professional public service for a developmental state

A proficient developmental state should be engaged with change and influence projections for growth, addressing the needs and wants of its citizens regardless of their political affiliation. According to Mzukisi Qobo, a capable state that is free from political factions is best placed to respond to opportunities for development. 'A capable state [is] a system of government that functions with relative autonomy from narrow ideological interests. Its parts work in a coordinated fashion to achieve clearly defined goals' (Qobo 2020). For the public service to able to respond to citizens' needs while achieving its developmental objectives, there is a need for skills development, attracting and retaining highly skilled people, cultivating continuous skills acquisition and building a sense of proficient determination and an obligation of working towards achieving development goals. The pool of skilled people should also be increased to ensure the public service and local government become careers of choice for graduates who wish to contribute to the development of the country (Mle and Ngumbela 2020).

Monitoring and evaluation

Building a solid public service requires developing and enforcing a strong system of monitoring, evaluation and accountability at all levels of government to combat corruption, ensuring that all service delivery projects are properly planned and executed to completion, and all officials are responsive and answerable to their roles and responsibilities. The 'notion of *best practice* needs to be replaced by *best fit*, where more pragmatic, context-sensitive solutions replace grandiose, comprehensive reform designs' (Obongo and Wilkins 2014).

The way forward

After the devastating impact of Covid-19 worldwide, governments need to restrategise, rethink, be proactive and agile, and adopt riskier policies with the potential for transformative change in the public service (World Bank 2022). The principles of management and resource prioritisation need to be inculcated in every sector of government to ensure that there is efficiency and effective utilisation of resources to provide services to the people. Strong monitoring and evaluation mechanisms are needed, with specific, measurable, attainable, realistic and timeous objectives in all government projects, including infrastructure, ICT and skills development. Knowledge paucities need to be reduced in critical areas such as financial management, contract management, project management, ICT and energy (Qobo 2020; Palmer, Moodley and Parnell 2017).

The South African government's vision can only be translated into reality when there is political will and concerted effort from all partners. This calls for a holistic approach, where all role-players in the public and private sector work towards skills development and economic growth, and reduce unemployment, poverty and inequality. Traditionally, there are areas of service delivery where the private sector is stronger than the public sector – for instance, in transport, logistics and ICT – so it would be prudent to allow the private sector to take a leading role in those areas, while at the same time being guided by government policy objectives.

Democratising the public service hinges on government's ability to drive policy objectives and hold government officials to account. It is also essential to include the wider community to help in the provision of public services through community development works and programmes that help to broaden democracy and public participation.

The people of South Africa have been waiting since 1994 to be served well by a democratic and professional civil service. Changes are urgently required to create an effective and a professionalised public service. To sustain such transformation, there is need for building the capacity of public servants, starting with identifying human resource development programmes that address skills and expertise needed to embrace technology to ensure even those in remote areas are also not left behind. Finally, professionalism and excellence must drive the character and behaviour of a professional civil service.

Notes

1. https://www.gov.za/community-development-workers-cdw-programme-bridge-between-government-and-communities (accessed 2 January 2024).
2. https://www.cogta.gov.za/index.php/2022/03/28/what-is-the-district-development-model/ (accessed 2 January 2024).

References

Chidinma, O.Q. 2021. 'What Are the 8 Batho Pele Principles? How to Implement and Apply It to Work'. *BuzzSouthAfrica*, 31 October. https://buzzsouthafrica.com/what-are-the-8-batho-pele-principles-how-to-implement-and-apply-it-to-work/ (accessed 2 January 2024).

Gray, M. and B.C. Mubangizi. 2010. 'Caught in the Vortex: Can Local Government Community Development Workers Succeed in South Africa?' *Community Development Journal* 45 (2): 188–97.

Gumede, W. 2015. 'Transformation of South Africa's Public Service: A Question of Failure to Transform the Administrative Culture of the Public Service'. *Journal of Public Administration and SAAPAM 15th Annual Conference Proceedings*: 495–508.

Ham, C., P. Chirwa and F. Theron. 2013. *The Forester as a Change Agent: From Trees between the People to People between the Trees*. Pretoria: Van Schaik.

Kunicova, J. 2018. 'The Five Drivers for Improving Public Sector Performance: Lessons from the New World Bank Global Report'. *World Bank Blogs*, 24 October. https://blogs.worldbank.org/governance/five-drivers-improving-public-sector-performance-lessons-new-world-bank-global-report (accessed 2 January 2024).

Maserumule, M.H. 2017. 'Just a Thought'. *Journal of Public Administration* 52 (2): 308–12.

Ministry for Public Service and Administration, 2007. *A Handbook for Community Development Workers*. https://www.dpsa.gov.za/dpsa2g/documents/cdw/SDR_vol_5_no_2_2006.pdf (accessed 2 January 2024).

Mle, T.R. and X.G. Ngumbela. 2020. 'Building a Capable State through Proper Human Resource Management'. *Journal of Local Government Research and Innovation* 1: 1–9.

Mokoena, S.K. and K.B. Moeti. 2017. 'Community Development Workers as Agents of Change and Conduit of Authentic Public Participation: The Case of Mpumalanga Province in South Africa'. *Journal for Transdisciplinary Research in Southern Africa* 13 (1): 1–9.

Mosala, S.J., J.C.M. Venter and E.G. Bain. 2017. 'South Africa's Economic Transformation since 1994: What Influence has the National Democratic Revolution (NDR) Had?' *Review of Black Political Economy* 44 (2): 327–40.

Mosiea, T. 2020. *DSI's District Development Model Approach and Interventions.* https://static. pmg.org.za/210907DSI_on_DDM_V2.pdf (accessed 2 January 2024).

National Planning Commission. 2011. *Diagnostic Report.* https://static.pmg.org.za/ docs/110913npcdiagnostic2011_0.pdf (accessed 2 January 2024).

———. 2012. *National Development Plan 2030: Our Future – Make It Work.* https://www.gov. za/sites/default/files/gcis_document/201409/ndp-2030-our-future-make-it-workr.pdf (accessed 2 January 2024).

Obongo, S.O. and J. Wilkins. 2014. 'Good Practice in Public Sector Reform'. *Financial Management Institute Journal* (Winter): 1–8.

Office of the President. 1994. *White Paper on Reconstruction and Development.* https://www. gov.za/sites/default/files/governmentgazetteid16085.pdf (accessed 2 January 2024).

Okeyo, I., U. Lehmann and H. Schneider. 2020. 'The Impact of Differing Frames on Early Stages of Intersectoral Collaboration: The Case of the First 1000 Days Initiative in the Western Cape Province'. *Health Research Policy and Systems* 18 (1), article 3.

Palmer, I., N. Moodley and S. Parnell. 2017. *Building a Capable State: Service Delivery in Post-apartheid South Africa.* London: Zed Books.

The Presidency. 2014. *Twenty Year Review: South Africa: 1994–2014.* https://www.dpme.gov. za/news/Documents/20%20Year%20Review.pdf (accessed 2 January 2024).

Presidential Review Commission. 1998. 'Report of the Presidential Review Commission on the Reform and Transformation of the Public Service in South Africa'. https://www.gov.za/ documents/report-presidential-review-commission-reform-and-transformation-public-service-south (accessed 2 January 2024).

Public Service Commission. 2021. 'The Pulse of the Public Service'. *Public Service Commission Quarterly Bulletin,* Volume 18, 1 July to 30 September. https://www.psc.gov.za/newsletters/ docs/pulse_newsletter/Pulse_of_the_PSC-Vol_18.pdf (accessed 2 January 2024).

Qobo, M. 2020. 'What It Will Take to Build a Capable State in South Africa?' *The Conversation,* 27 February. https://theconversation.com/what-it-will-take-to-build-a-capable-state-in-south-africa-132132 (accessed 2 January 2024).

Sabhikhi, I.A. 2017. 'Understanding the Difference between Public Service Delivery and Right to Grievance Redress'. *The Wire,* 17 August. https://thewire.in/government/bihar-right-to-public-service-delivery-and-right-to-grievance-redress#:~:text=The%20Public%20 Service%20Act%20covers,independent%20from%20the%20implementing%20 departments (accessed 2 January 2024).

Sibanda, M.M. 2017. 'Control, Ethics and Accountability in the Finance Management Performance of Eastern Cape Municipalities'. *Journal for Public Administration* 52 (2): 313–39.

Tshishonga, N. and E.D. Mafema. 2010. 'Policy Development for Service Delivery through Community Development Workers Programme in South Africa: Exploring the Implications of Placing a Cart before the Horse'. *Journal of Public Administration* 45 (4): 561–83.

Van Rooyen, E.J. and S.K. Mokoena. 2013. 'The Role of Ward Committees towards Enhancing Public Participation: The Case of the Mpumalanga Province, South Africa'. *Journal of Business and Economics* 4 (8): 761–70.

Walubengo, P. 2020. '8 Batho Pele Principles, Implementation and Impact to the Community'. *Briefly*, 4 December. https://briefly.co.za/32252-8-batho-pele-principles-implementation-impact-community.html (accessed 2 January 2024).

World Bank. 2022. *Future of Government: Reimagining Government for Good.* https://documents1.worldbank.org/curated/en/099720006232225578/pdf/P175467091ace205b0ba840678d6200174e.pdf (accessed 2 January 2024).

CHAPTER 20

Building Co-operative Planning and Implementation Synergies as a Means to Inclusive Development

David Mohale

The preamble of the post-apartheid South African Constitution enjoins the state to (i) 'heal the divisions of the past and establish a society based on democratic values, social justice and fundamental human rights' and (ii) 'improve the quality of life of all citizens and free the potential of each person'.[1] The first task is primarily dependent on the ability of the state to deliver democratic dividends to all its citizens by ensuring that the right to socio-economic development and a healthy and safe environment is not only protected, but also made a reality. The second task recognises that real freedom transcends political liberties and is inextricably linked to the notions of indivisibility of freedom or capabilities, as defined by Amartya Sen (1985).

The Constitution establishes the three spheres of government that must operate co-operatively within the legal framework of intergovernmental relations (IGR) to pursue social justice, deepen fundamental human rights and contribute to the overall improved quality of life. Importantly, the White Paper on Local Government of 1998 entrusts the local sphere of government with the responsibility to deepen the Bill of Rights enshrined in the Constitution within the context of co-operative governance among the spheres of government. These clear provisions notwithstanding, the experience since the dawn of democracy and the adoption of the Constitution suggests marked failure of a system of IGR and co-operative governance. While there are many factors that are attributable to the mismatch between policy intentions and actual performance, this chapter focuses on the dysfunctionality of IGR and co-operative governance and argues that the development of citizens will only be realised if the three spheres of government can synergise their planning and implementation.

An old problem with elusive solutions

There is plenty of literature enumerating the problems of IGR and co-operative governance in South Africa, from both within and outside government. I will briefly highlight salient features. I undertake this exercise not for dogmatic purposes, but in pursuit of the fundamental objective of this book, which is the provision of pragmatic solutions to what I would characterise as the problem of a degenerative economy that produces intertwined challenges and symptoms of rising unemployment, growing poverty and deepening inequality. A search for policy solutions is a reminder that 'government is essentially a problematising activity' (Rose and Miller 1992), and proposals for future policy decision-making must transcend ideologies. This essentially means that the quality of a policy decision must be assessed on the degree to which it helps citizens to meet the specific objective of their development. In the South African context, any assessment of the quality of policy decisions must be done against the single most important civilising mission of the post-apartheid state, which the African National Congress (ANC) describes as the treatment of 'the most vulnerable in society' (ANC 2012).

As early as 1996, the Maphai Commission handed a report to President Nelson Mandela that diagnosed co-ordination problems within the state. Two key recommendations were the strengthening of the Presidency as a cog of government and a separate study that would focus on local government, given that this sphere would no longer be a function of provincial government, but a full sphere of government tasked with the twinned complex roles of democracy and development. In 1998, the then Department of Local Government and Housing also commissioned a study on IGR and co-operative governance. One of the main findings was that informal and hard-to-regulate factors, such as the quality of leadership, politics and the trust of role-players, were harmful to IGR and co-operative governance.

In 2009, the newly renamed Department of Co-operative Governance and Traditional Affairs undertook a nationwide study to find out why municipalities were dysfunctional. The State of Local Government Report found that poor IGR and co-operative governance was one of the key reasons behind the 'distress' of the local government system. Elsewhere, I document how leaders in local government lament the fact that national and provincial spheres of government do not show genuine commitment to integrated development planning processes, resulting in these spheres of government forcing projects in local spaces that are not necessarily needed by communities (Mohale 2017). For instance, one respondent gave an example of a community needing a clinic, which would have been a function of the Department of Health and Public Works. But the provincial government allocated funds to the Department of Basic Education to build a school there, which became a white elephant, as the community did not have the numbers required by the very same department for the school to open.

In 2011, the *Diagnostic Overview* by the National Planning Commission recognised that IGR needed to become more constructive in order to facilitate development (National Planning Commission 2011). Chapter 12 of the *National Development Plan 2030* (NDP) – which argues the case for a capable and developmental state – emphasises the primacy of co-ordination capability across the three spheres of government as a precondition for state capacity (National Planning Commission 2012). All these lessons have not translated into a change of attitude or practice. In addition, in her address to the National Council of Provinces on 1 February 2022, the Minister of Co-operative Governance and Traditional Affairs, Dr Nkosazana Dlamini-Zuma, admitted that there also seems to be confusion regarding the roles of each sphere of government, particularly when it comes to proactive support that must be given to municipalities.

The developmental state

The concept of the developmental state in the political economy was first coined by Chalmers Johnson in 1982 in explaining differences in state (economic) performances, particularly across regions (Nassemullah and Arnold 2014: 123). The notable economic growth in Asia led to phrases such as 'no developmental state, no development' (Evans 2010: 169) and 'Asianization of the world' (Friedman 2002). This open-ended faith is but one approach to development and does not suggest consensus on the meaning and/or definition of the concept.

Although there are nuanced differences on the meaning of the concept of the developmental state, there exists at least minimum convergence on what some constitutive elements are. Thandika Mkandawire (2001) suggests what he terms the structure–ideology nexus. This view enjoys wide support in scholarship (Knight 2014; Routley 2014; Williams 2014). There is an agreement that structures are the cause, while economic growth is the effect. However, some scholars like Laura Routley (2014) underscore the importance and influence of the roles carried out by these structures in order to achieve the soaring economic outcomes. In other words, a developmental state is about how its structures play their individual and collective roles in effecting social justice and improving the quality of life of citizens through economic growth. In South Africa, this also extends to the ability of the country to heal past injustices and a build a cohesive society.

It is this context that necessitates the treatment of the three spheres of government as a structure or policy network that forms and becomes the basis for national development. It is against this background that the macro-organisation of the state becomes an important determinant in pursuit of constitutional objectives. Given that internal efficiencies of the structure are not enough to independently pursue the growth and development agenda, the attendant ability to cope with exogenous factors is also critical. A good example in South Africa is the recent exposure of how parasitic networks took root and hollowed out the capacity of the state – a phenomenon euphemistically called state capture. Alternatively, the agility of the state to optimise benefits created by the external environment can enhance state capacity. In this respect, it remains to be seen how South Africa is leveraging opportunities arising from its membership of BRICS (Brazil, Russia, India, China and South Africa) as an emerging powerful economic bloc in the world.[2]

There are four broad functions of a developmental state (Chang 1999), according to which an assessment of our IGR and co-operative governance needs to be undertaken. The first function is that of centralised co-ordination, which must be done in the interest of investment decisions by ensuring that interdependence prevails between economic agents. Even though there are a number of financial development institutions and state-owned enterprises (SOEs) the state has set up, there is no evidence that there is centralised co-ordination in investment against realities of development needs and service delivery backlog across provinces and regions in the country. If anything, provinces and regions/districts compete, which has exacerbated economic inequality and increased urban migration. The failure to synergise and integrate planning somewhat naturalises urbanisation, which leads to the country planning for population growth in cities instead of curbing unequal economic opportunities that result in devastating social realities.

Economic vision is considered the second-most important function of a developmental state. This imposes the important element of an entrepreneurial dimension on the role of the state. Peter Evans (1995) distinguishes between the midwife and husbandry roles to underscore a sequenced process the state needs to undertake. The state must help to bring new entrepreneurial actors into the sector (midwife) and then take the responsibility to cultivate, nurture and prod them into production (husbandry). From 2003, at least, the state conceded its incapacity to lead business. This is a serious indictment for a state that harbours ambitions of becoming developmental. A developmental state must be able to insulate itself from social classes, so that it provides leadership even though it remains part of the broader consultation processes through structures such as the National Economic Development and Labour Council (NEDLAC). This admission seriously threatens the legitimacy of the state regarding its role as a leader of social classes and broader society.

The third function of a developmental state is to build institutions to co-ordinate the implementation of the economic vision. Institutions do matter in development. They are the main determinants of long-term prosperity and social development. The South African experience of state capture and the unchecked powers of institutions such as the Presidency have raised the importance of the morality, resilience and durability of institutions. Thandika Mkandawire and Charles Soludo (1998) argue that what made East Asia unique was the durability and effectiveness of institutional structures. This implies that durability must be the conscious goal of the elite when they build institutions. According to Claudious Chikozho (2015), the real challenge in constructing a developmental state lies in designing the requisite institutions for the country to become truly developmental.

The last function of a developmental state is to manage and resolve conflict between societal groups in a manner that does not compromise the collective interest of national growth. This function is particularly important in a country such as South Africa where many divisions are institutionalised. The state is an inherently contested terrain between different social classes. South Africa is littered with examples of bifurcation across political, economic, social and cultural realms. The so-called Rainbow Nation has not emerged, particularly in the face of the notable state failure to facilitate social justice, free the potential of each person to lead and live the lives they truly value and guarantee fundamental human rights, such as the right to human dignity. Additionally, the mere existence of the three spheres of government alone suggests inherent potential for conflict, particularly regarding the hierarchy versus constitutional allocation of responsibilities. Conflict between and among the three spheres of government seems inevitable despite the Intergovernmental Relations Framework Act of 2005, which seeks to regulate the relationship and interactions.

Conflict resolution between the three spheres of government can be achieved through 'periodic gatherings at which politicians can negotiate and officials interpret, translate, and deliver outcomes' (Davis and Silver 2015: 467). Conflict management can be handled more effectively through 'democratically organised public deliberation' (Evans 2010: 43). Drawing on the capability approach, Evans (2010) argues that democracy is the only analytically defensible means of defining specific developmental goals.

IGR and co-operative governance as a developmental policy network

Like many social concepts, it is not easy to define policy network. Debates and confusion abound regarding whether it is a proper theory, a method or analytical tool (Börzel 1998: 254). For the purpose of supporting the claim that IGR and co-operative governance is the condition on which the South African state can be truly developmental if the system is fully functional as conceived by the Constitution, I propose we regard policy network in this context as an analytical tool – a cause that gives effect to the realisation of broad development goals described in the preamble of the Constitution.

In order to make sense of what is expected of a functional system of IGR and co-operative governance, the following definition of policy network by Tanya Börzel is adopted:

They all share a common understanding, a minimal or lowest common denominator definition of a policy network, as a set of relatively stable relationships which are of non-hierarchical and interdependent nature linking a variety of actors, who share common interests with regard to a policy and who exchange resources to pursue these shared interests acknowledging that cooperation is the best way to achieve common goals (1998: 254).

Lawrence O'Toole provides a similar definition for a network: 'Networks are structures of interdependence involving multiple organisations or parts thereof, where one unit is not merely the formal subordinate of others in some hierarchical arrangement' (1997: 45). One can deduce the following three obvious points from these two definitions of networks, without necessarily disregarding inherent tensions in the application of the policy that often juniorises the local sphere of government:

1)   IGR members share a relatively stable relationship on the basis of their shared co-operative governance derived from the national constitution.

2)   The formal relationship based on the reading of the Constitution is non-hierarchical and interdependent in that the national Constitution establishes the unitary state that consists of three distinct but interconnected spheres of government.

3)   All three spheres of government share a common interest of the nation's development and are mandated to share and exchange resources in terms of sections 153 and 154 of the Constitution and the Intergovernmental Relations Framework Act of 2005.

Policy networks as an analytical tool have traditionally looked at horizontal relationships (Börzel 1998; De Leon and Varda 2009). However, with time, policy networks also became useful in the analysis of vertical relationships and central–local relations (Gains 2003; Robinson 2006). As Francesca Gains (2003: 59) points out, this approach covers the varying degrees of financial, legal and structural autonomy and accountability and enhances a dis-aggregated analysis. According to Scott Robinson (2006: 591), resource dependency theory is particularly relevant in the setting of IGR, as central governments generally have more resources than sub-national structures. Accordingly, the resource disparity affects the behaviour of individual members within a network because rewards and sanctions tend to either motivate or constrain a particular conduct.

The primary role of policy networks is to solve the difficult task of co-ordination. As mentioned earlier, informal factors also affect policy co-ordination across the three spheres of government. Thus, the focus on vertical co-ordination is also given credence by the complex nature of human beings and the institutions they design to influence and manage behaviour. In this respect, networks can be seen as institutions that regulate collective behaviour through the rules they adopt (Klijn and Koppenjan 2006). These rules of engagement in managing relations between spheres of government with regard to tensions between central and local governments are a matter of public record (Bevir 2009). Some developing countries may decentralise merely because they want to shift the 'fiscal deficits downwards in order to maintain legitimacy of the national government' (Steiner 2010: 644). In South Africa, studies have already shown that local government is losing its legitimacy as a result of widespread failures. Interestingly, these studies tend to neglect the context of co-operative governance. In Zambia, local governance reforms became 'mere rhetoric' precisely because national politicians made political concerns a priority at the expense of governance (Mukwena and Lolojih 2002: 228). Could it be that the decentralisation of a special type in South Africa is only in letter and not genuinely committed to by all actors?

The continuing policy performance failures of post-apartheid South Africa in pursuit of social justice, the promotion of fundamental human rights and the freeing of the potential of each citizen speaks to the weaknesses of IGR network properties. The example given of a provincial government building a school in a community that needs a clinic demonstrates that the network lacks what Annica Sandström and Lars Carlsson term 'problem definition and prioritisation' (2008: 503). Olle Frödin formulates a concept of transaction domain to denote 'a mutually agreed-upon definition of a situation according to which a particular logic of interaction, exchange or decision-making is considered socially acceptable' (2011: 188). The transaction domain must logically form the basis for reciprocity, which means that 'parties remain connected to one another, and in turn, enables networks to form and function' (De Leon and Varda 2009: 67).

Possible corrective programme of action

Below I propose what could be considered as a minimum developmental agenda for a functional system of IGR and co-operative governance in pursuit of broad development goals that the Constitution sets out. The proposal straddles policy and operational issues, which combined must address the need for synergy in planning and implementation.

Primacy of local government in development

The importance and centrality of local government as a fulcrum for development in the post-apartheid state cannot be overemphasised. It is well explained in the White Paper on Local Government that this sphere of government is strategically positioned to promote the Bill of Rights enshrined in the Constitution. In addition to many subjective problems, there are objective factors that also require a fundamental overhaul. One of these is the funding model for local government. The assumption made in 1998 that municipalities would be self-sufficient depended on the further assumption that the economy would perform well. That has not been the case. A well-performing local government narrows the trust deficit between citizens and government, and a dysfunctional local government system will erode the legitimacy of the entire system. To this end, the principles governing the Division of Revenue Act may need to be revisited to give prominence to the service delivery backlog and address the realities of the rise in the number of ghost towns as more and more people seek fast-diminishing opportunities in the cities. Furthermore, there is an urgent need to reduce the policy overload in the sector. This strangulation inadvertently skews the time of senior managers towards report preparation, rather than the actual work of development (Steytler 2008).

Overhaul the structure of the economy

In March 2022, Statistics South Africa (Stats SA) released a report titled *The Social Youth Profile, 2014–2020* (Stats SA 2022). The report blames the structure of the national economy for the deepening youth bulge. The biggest indictment is the fact that youth unemployment in South Africa increased by 12.5 per cent between 2014 and 2021, from 36.8 to 49.3 per cent. The youth labour participation rate decreased from 48.2 per cent in 2014 to 44.7 per cent in 2021. These negative trends have continued despite the adoption of the National Development Plan by Cabinet in 2014, the purpose of which was to build a capable and developmental state that would grow the economy in order to reduce unemployment and poverty.

A fundamental overhaul of the structure of the economy is necessary for a modicum of success in achieving social justice, freeing the potential of each person and improving the lives of citizens. The government needs to build legitimate capacity to steer NEDLAC partners towards the realisation of this complex task. The world has transitioned to the knowledge economy and this imposes an obligation on the state to invest in training its citizens. Capital does not have moral obligation to do this unless it invests in skilling just a small section of communities to advance the interest of profit maximisation. In this context, the role of SOEs and development finance institutions needs to be redefined. Functional co-operative governance needs to direct redistribution of resources across provinces and regions/districts in order to move people out of despair and into a season of hope.

Impose minimum requirements for public office

One of the fundamental flaws of democratic systems is the existence of populism. The current open-ended system for the assumption of public office without regulating minimum requirements in relation to governance responsibility has proven to be one of the reasons behind state incapacity. Governance is not just about democracy; it is largely a technical exercise, where decisions need to backed by facts. Good policy decisions and effective implementation are the basis for legitimacy. In other words, the legitimacy of government derives not only from the rules of the game of getting into office. Politicians get into office on the basis of their party manifestos. They have to ensure that they meet the needs and expectations of citizens. The ability to be responsive to the expectations of the people is linked to skills, knowledge, experience and competencies. If we are to improve public policy performance, there is a need to impose minimum requirements for public office-bearers at all spheres of government.

Conclusion

The potential to revive the stillborn South African developmental state hinges on making the constitutional system of intergovernmental relations and co-operative governance functional. Importantly, this system needs to enhance the capability of local government to perform optimally in pursuit of broad goals of social justice and improve the quality of the lives of citizens. There are many interventions that the government can perform to get South Africa out of its deepening morass. I propose three areas, which are not necessarily exhaustive, but will certainly go some way to achieving this goal: support local government to become the trusted development agency; urgently sort out the exclusionary economic structure; and introduce a merit-based system for political leaders in order to build capacity for state leadership.

Notes

1. See https://www.justice.gov.za/legislation/constitution/saconstitution-web-eng.pdf (accessed 28 November 2023).
2. In August 2023, six countries (Argentina, Egypt, Ethiopia, Iran, Saudi Arabia and the United Arab Emirates) were invited to join the BRICS bloc. Full membership will take effect on 1 January 2024.

References

ANC (African National Congress). 2012. *Strategy and Tactics of the ANC*. https://www.sahistory. org.za/sites/default/files/strategy_and_tacticsof_the_anc_by_anc_december_2012_ anc_53rd_conference.pdf (accessed 28 November 2023).

Bevir, M. 2009. *Key Concepts in Governance*. London: Sage.

Börzel, T.A. 1998. 'Organising Babylon: On the Different Conceptions of Policy Networks'. *Public Administration* 76: 253–73.

Chang, H.J. 1999. 'The Economic Theory of the Developmental State'. In: *The Developmental State*, edited by M. Woo-Cumings, 182–99. Ithaca: Cornell University Press.

Chikozho, C. 2015. 'Re-visiting Africa's Political Economy Landscape: Comparatively Articulating the National Macro-economic Policy and Institutional Trajectories of Botswana, South Africa and Zimbabwe'. Paper presented at the regional conference on Building Democratic Developmental States for Economic Transformation in Southern Africa, 20–22 July, Pretoria.

Davis, G. and H. Silver. 2015. 'Intergovernmental Relations and the Role of Senior Officials: Two Case Studies and Some Lessons Learned'. *Australian Journal of Public Administration* 74 (4): 467–83.

De Leon, P. and D.M. Varda. 2009. 'Toward a Theory of Collaborative Policy Networks: Identifying Structural Tendencies'. *Policy Studies Journal* 37 (1): 59–74.

Evans, P.B. 1995. *Embedded Autonomy: States and Industrial Transformation*. Princeton: Princeton University Press.

————. 2010. 'Constructing the 21st Century Developmental State: Potentials and Pitfalls'. In: *Constructing a Democratic Developmental State in South Africa: Potentials and Challenges*, edited by O. Edigheji, 169–82. Cape Town: Human Sciences Research Council.

Friedman, E. 2002. 'Reinterpreting the Asianization of the World and the Role of the State in the Rise of China'. In: *States and Sovereignty in the Global Economy*, edited by D.A. Smith, D.J. Solinger and S.C. Topik, 246–65. London: Routledge.

Frödin, O. 2011. 'Generalised and Particularistic Thinking in Policy Analysis and Practice: The Case of Governance Reform in South Africa'. *Development Policy Review* 29 (S1): 179–98.

Gains, F. 2003. 'Executive Agencies in Government: The Impact of Bureaucratic Networks on Policy Outcomes'. *Journal of Public Policy* 23 (1): 55–79.

Klijn, E.H. and J.F.M. Koppenjan. 2006. 'Institutional Design: Changing Institutional Features of Networks'. *Public Management Review* 8 (1): 141–60.

Knight, J.B. 2014. 'China as a Developmental State'. *The World Economy* 37 (10): 1335–47.

Mkandawire, T. 2001. 'Thinking about Developmental States in Africa'. *Cambridge Journal of Economics* 25 (3): 289–313.

Mkandawire, T. and C.C. Soludo. 1998. *Our Continent, Our Future: African Perspectives on Structural Adjustment*. Trenton: Africa World Press.

Mohale, D. 2017. 'Developmental Local Government as a Catalyst or an Impediment towards a South African Developmental State'. PhD thesis, University of South Africa.

Mukwena, R.M. and P.K. Lolojih. 2002. 'Governance and Local Government Reforms in Zambia's Third Republic'. In: *Better Governance and Public Policy: Capacity Building and Democratic Renewal in Africa*, edited by D. Olowu and S. Sako, 215–32. Boulder: Kumarian Press.

Naseemullah, A. and C.E. Arnold. 2014. 'The Politics of Developmental State Persistence: Institutional Origins, Industrialisation and Provincial Challenge'. *Studies in Comparative International Development* 50 (1): 121–42.

National Planning Commission. 2011. *Diagnostic Overview*. https://www.gov.za/sites/default/files/gcis_document/201409/npcdiagnosticoverview1.pdf (accessed 28 November 2023).

————. 2012. *National Development Plan 2030: Our Future – Make It Work*. https://www.gov.za/sites/default/files/gcis_document/201409/ndp-2030-our-future-make-it-workr.pdf (accessed 28 November 2023).

O'Toole, L.J. 1997. 'Treating Networks Seriously: Practical and Research-Based Agenda in Public Administration'. *Public Administration Review* 57 (1): 45–52.

Robinson, S.E. 2006. 'A Decade of Treating Networks Seriously'. *Policy Studies Journal* 34 (4): 589–98.

Rose, N. and P. Miller. 1992. 'Political Power beyond the State: Problematics of Government'. *British Journal of Sociology* 43 (2): 271–303.

Routley, L. 2014. 'Developmental States in Africa? A Review of Ongoing Debates and Buzzwords'. *Development Policy Review* 32 (2): 159–77.

Sandström, A. and L. Carlsson. 2008. 'The Performance of Policy Networks: The Relation between Network Structure and Network Performance'. *Policy Studies Journal* 36 (4): 497–524.

Sen, A.K. 1985. *Commodities and Capabilities*. Oxford: Oxford University Press.

Stats SA (Statistics South Africa). 2022. *The Social Profile of Youth, 2014–2020*. https://www.statssa.gov.za/publications/Report-03-19-07/Report-03-19-072020.pdf (accessed 28 November 2023).

Steiner, S. 2010. 'How Important is the Capacity of Local Governments for Improvements in Welfare? Evidence from Decentralised Uganda'. *Journal of Development Studies* 46 (4): 644–61.

Steytler, N. 2008. 'The Strangulation of Local Government'. *TSAR* 3: 518–35.

Williams, M. (ed.). (2014). *The End of the Developmental State?* Pietermaritzburg: University of KwaZulu-Natal Press.

CHAPTER 21

Appropriate Measures to Improve the Delivery of Public Goods

Mandla Gladstone Nkomfe

In the last decade, the capacity of the state to command legitimate public authority and respect has been highly problematic. Appalled by poor service delivery standards, citizens have either turned their backs on the democratic state or worsened the situation through violent protests that often destroy public infrastructure. The corruption facilitated by state capture saw billions of rands being siphoned out of state coffers. This has resulted in weak balance sheets, loss of operational expertise, flight of much-needed skills to other countries and the non-existence of a positive work culture in state institutions (Chipkin and Swilling 2018). State capture caught the public imagination after extensive revelations of the existence of a corrupt relationship between the former president, Jacob Zuma, and his friends, the Guptas – a syndicate comprising brothers from a family originating from India, which has done business with the South African government since the late 1990s. Under Zuma, the Guptas were central in influencing key government decisions, including the appointments of government ministers. It is widely alleged that they manipulated government procurement processes in their favour and worked closely with Duduzane Zuma, their business partner and son of the former president (Rapanyane and Ngoepe 2020).

The historical material inequities that beset South Africa today are important in understanding the circumstances under which state capture became possible. In short, had the country's history of structural apartheid not existed, the social and political conditions conducive to state capture would have been less acute.

The point is not to defend any form of looting of state resources, but simply to suggest that the reality of economic marginalisation for the majority of South Africans requires urgent attention. Unfortunately, black economic empowerment has become a form of rent-seeking enterprise (Cargill 2010) and has benefited a small black and white elite. In this context, comprehensive socio-economic transformation has not yet happened.

This chapter investigates the social and political conditions that led to a wide range of public policy implementation failures. It addresses the following questions: what are the set of circumstances that have led to the non-delivery of services to communities? Is the problem the design of implementation policy, lack of institutional capacity, such as weak administrative systems and incompetent public servants, corruption and the nature of the political economy? Where are the key systemic blockages that have weakened the state and rendered service delivery and accountable governance almost impossible? The chapter concludes with a few practical solutions and imagines a South Africa beyond the horrors of state capture.

Background

The South African economy is sluggish and has a slow industrialisation drive. It is failing to attract much-needed foreign direct investment. Declining social and economic conditions have seen a devastating collapse of the delivery of essential public services, such as clean water, dependable public health, and safety and security, to the citizenry. In the last decade, public institutions have broken down. Essential economic infrastructure, such as rail, ports, telecommunications and energy security, are currently in various states of chaos or, at the least, unreliable. Consequently, there is an increase in varied forms of violence, such as gender-based violence, femicide and disturbing political violence.

Mcebisi Jonas states that 'the social contract that enabled us to peacefully transition to democracy and which bound us together in the first two decades of freedom is unravelling' (Jonas 2019: xiii). South Africa's chosen path of universalism, non-racialism, non-sexism, democracy and unity in diversity faces the perilous threat of an insurgent populism, individual greed and, in some instances, political regionalism and ethnicity. Accordingly, the *National Development Plan 2030* (NDP) cautions against narrow, short-sighted, and populist positions that politicians take in their communities (National Planning Commission 2012). However, as Ashwin Desai states: 'The epitome of state capture was the supposed Gupta-inspired replacement of previous Finance Minister, Nhlanhla Nene, on the apparent grounds that he refused, among other things, to authorise a budget for nuclear power expansion in South Africa' (Desai 2018: 500).

Linked to the collapse of reliable service delivery to the populace is the deliberate breaking down of key institutions, a phenomenon commonly known as state capture. The key results of state capture include policy lapses across several spheres of government and a general acceptance of rampant corruption in society. The result is that the living conditions of most South Africans have not changed significantly over the past decade; in fact, they have worsened. State capture markedly compromised institutions that were designed to shield citizens from the abuse of power, corruption and malfeasance. It has grossly undermined the capabilities for nurturing activist human agency, which is critical to the conduct of public affairs. Ordinary people and the most vulnerable in communities continue to suffer as a result of the non-functioning of key state institutions, such as local government municipalities.

State-owned enterprises (SOEs) and key institutions of the criminal justice system, such as the prosecuting authority and the South African Police Service, have been hollowed out to facilitate corrupt practices and to prevent the successful prosecution of those engaged in corrupt activities. A combination of factors is responsible for the state in which the country finds itself. These include the inability to tackle historical problems caused by the pre-1994 political dispensation, path dependency, inappropriate policy formulation and implementation designs, corruption, state capture, stagnant economic growth, failing political leadership, lack of appropriate skills and administrative incompetence.

State capture and its aftermath

Central to the near collapse of state capacity to deliver on its constitutional mandate is the impact of state capture on the culture and practice of running government affairs. The Commission of Inquiry into State Capture, chaired by Judge Raymond Zondo, revealed details of how government departments and SOEs, such as Transnet, Eskom and Denel, were repurposed to serve the interests of the former president, the Guptas and other corrupt networks in government and the private sector. For example, Judge Zondo found that in respect of Eskom, 'President Zuma was captured by the Guptas, and they could get him to do whatever they wanted to advance their business interests and to advance state capture'.[1] Ivor Chipkin and Mark Swilling (2018: 133) conclude that the net results of state capture are catastrophic, stating that it destroys public trust in the state and its organs, weakens key economic agencies tasked with delivering development outcomes and erodes confidence in the economy. Undoubtedly, South Africa has arrived at this dark destination where the dreams of citizens and all who care are destroyed.

Tsakani Maluleke, the auditor general of South Africa, has been scathing of the general performance of local government at municipal level. Her consolidated report on local government audit performance observes that contrary to the promise of a better life for all, as enshrined in the Constitution, most citizens never get to realise this promise (Auditor-General of South Africa 2023). Local government is characterised by a lack of accountability of councillors, service delivery failures, poor governance, weak institutional capacity and instability. Where local government has all but collapsed, basic services such as refuse collection are irregular and water supplies are often unavailable. Dysfunctional municipalities frequently suffer from serious financial problems – low debt collection, financial mismanagement, corruption, fraud and huge debt. At this level of government, violent protests are most common, which threatens public law and order and destroys essential infrastructure and selected private property.

Back-to-basics approach

Even though this may be the case, we need to move beyond painting a tale of horrors and make proposals for rectifying the situation. It is imperative to repair our weakened public institutions, particularly in the criminal justice cluster, public health and education, and local government. We need a 'back-to-basics approach', as conceived in 2016 by the Department of Co-operative Governance and Traditional Affairs, to help restore the dignity of people and the integrity of public institutions. This requires exemplary and pragmatic leadership, as the time for ideological dogmatism is over. New and robust ways must be found to enhance public sector reforms, state capacity, public–private partnerships and corruption-free governance. The Chinese notion of crossing the river by feeling the stones and a gradualist approach to policy implementation are crucial considerations. Joseph Stiglitz (2018) attributes China's economic success to pragmatism – non-ideological, gradual, devoid of shock therapy and supporting each stage of development with the requisite institutional arrangements and policies. We should animate broader society across a wide range of interest groups into joining an introspective government towards making South Africa work again.

It is evident in many democratic societies that institutional efficiencies often arise, not because there is good legislation in place, but more as a result of a total commitment by public servants and ethical political leadership to do right. Those called upon to serve the nation must be enthusiastic, empathetic and ethical. They should show genuine solidarity with the people they serve. The letter and spirit of the Constitution must come alive through our public representatives, administrators and those working in SOEs. A serious attitudinal change of culture and service ethos must emerge. Repeatedly, South Africans have shown the intellectual wherewithal to rise to the occasion and set our country on a high road towards inclusive prosperity. They made the 1994 democratic breakthrough possible, and they made the 2010 Soccer World Cup succeed. Without the resistance and united effort of peace-loving South Africans, the attempted insurrection in parts of KwaZulu-Natal and Gauteng in 2021 would have plunged the country into a major political crisis.

Where do we start?

The findings and recommendations of the Zondo Commission constitute the basis and framework on which public sector reforms should be pursued. State capacity relies on the existence of competent and professional civil servants. To this end, the Zondo Commission advocates for a change in the way appointments of board members and the executive leadership of SOEs are made. These measures include doing away with the policy of cadre deployment, strong and effective anti-corruption interventions, and a new, transparent procurement system.

South Africa must work, cohere and meet its strategic goals towards sustainable growth and development. We must ensure that public institutions effectively do the critical work they are set to do in the Constitution. The logistics sector must work to facilitate the smooth movement of goods and services in South Africa and abroad. We must reduce the cost of doing business and facilitate the timely transportation of goods to and from the ports.

In short, we need to urgently address current inefficiencies in rail and port infrastructure and all key delivery networks. The urban rail network needs an overhaul that will result in the shortening of travel time. The energy sector requires more megawatts in the national electricity grid. Generation capacity needs to be revamped by doing timely planned maintenance of power stations. South Africa's ability to remove constraints in the procurement of critical electricity-generation equipment will drive reliable energy supplies. It is also urgent for government across all spheres to create jobs, especially in urban areas, by rehabilitating 'worn-out' infrastructure and refurbishing and constructing better buildings (Turok 2016: 23).

People: A motive force for change

The success of the back-to-basics approach is dependent on the support it gets from ordinary South Africans. In recent years, the cord that binds them to communities has been severed. Important short-, medium- and long-term measures to revive the economy, and the viability of the state, must be implemented. These range from the NDP, the South African Economic Reconstruction and Recovery Plan and the Framework Agreement for a Social Compact on Supporting Eskom for Inclusive Economic Growth. Government must enhance private sector participation in areas like energy production and the rail and port sectors. The country's stability must be driven by genuine national interests and not narrow political and business agendas. It follows that the barrier to trade and red tape must be removed without further delay. For public policy implementation to succeed, ethical and competent personnel in government is imperative and must be allowed to serve the public without any undue pressure from selfish political and private sector interests. Let us put the people first and deliver basic services through good governance, sound financial management and commitment to building institutional capacity in municipalities.

A new growth path

Since 2018, President Cyril Ramaphosa has sought to place the country on a growth path, with improved levels of inclusive economic development. Consequently, a great deal of work has been done to make the South African Revenue Service (SARS) efficient and accountable again. The Commission of Inquiry into Tax Administration and Governance by SARS in 2018 revealed that the agency was in a shambolic state.[2] An inefficient and corrupt SARS threatens the country's ability to collect tax, which is needed to fund development and support the basic health, educational, safety and general welfare of the population, especially the poor, the elderly and the ill. The South African Economic Reconstruction and Recovery Plan seeks to create a sustainable, resilient and inclusive economy. The successful implementation of this plan could catapult South Africa to a high road of inclusive growth and overcome the current middle-income crisis.

Is the failure of policy due to design or implementation?

Problems of service delivery in South Africa are uncritically blamed on the failure to implement public policy. But the reality is that the design and implementation of the policy process are not mutually exclusive. The non-delivery of services and the non-realisation of broad policy objectives are a result of poor design in the policymaking process as well as implementation failures. Poor design of policy can result in unrealisable objectives, which consequently fail to make a meaningful impact on the intended groups and communities. The key question is how policies can be designed to guarantee good policy outcomes.

The design must consider actual societal needs, available resources, skills and budget, together with the readiness of targeted communities to adopt the policy. Implementation requires constant monitoring, evaluation and appraisal of a given policy. Ivor Chipkin and Jelena Vidojevic (2021) argue that since 1994 the democratic government has introduced many policies that were desirable, but not reasonable, as policymaking was frequently done without due attention to the organisations that must do the work. There is an intrinsic relationship between policy design and policy implementation. The flaw in implementation could be the outcome of poor design. The key test of any design is what happens when implementation takes place. It can either achieve the intended goal or prove to be a failure. This observation is affirmed by Jale Tosun and Oliver Treib (2018), who state that public policies can only become effective once they are put into practice. A policy design may be perfect, but it can still fall short of delivering the intended results when implementation is flawed.

Tosun and Treib (2018) understand policy implementation as consisting of four dimensions: defining implementation structure, agency decision-making, target group behaviour and policy results. The implementation structure requires that policymakers are familiar with the organisations and structures that are critical for the success of the adopted policy. A misalignment in these entities could result in not achieving the stated policy goals. A case in point of such misalignment in South Africa is the generation and provision of electricity. Its implementation ecosystem consists of the Department of Minerals and Energy (the policymaker), the Department of Public Enterprise (responsible for Eskom), the Department of Forestry, Fisheries and Environmental Affairs (responsible for emission reduction), Eskom (electricity provision), the National Energy Regulator of South Africa (responsible for the regulation of the energy industry in South Africa), municipalities and communities. The buy-in from all these stakeholders is critical for the delivery of energy in South Africa.

New post-Covid-19 social compact

Post-Covid-19 economic recovery policies must consider the historical legacy of apartheid, structural socio-economic injustices and continuing elevated levels of unemployment. A more inclusive economy is urgently needed and Covid-19 has created an opportunity for a fundamental restructuring. Such an agenda requires that all key social partners agree on sustainable implementation plans with specific timeframes. Thandika Mkandawire (2012) correctly argues that social compacts are important to address the distributive and growth objectives of society.

The social contract advances the idea of genuine partnerships between individuals, businesses, civil society and the state to contribute to a system in which there are collective benefits. The new social contract defines what we can expect from each other in society. The pandemic has provided a unique opportunity to clarify our priorities. The new social contract must be underpinned by wider solidarity among all groups and classes in South Africa – that our policies must not leave anyone behind and that prosperity for all will only become possible when we work together as government, the private sector, civil society and communities.

Minouche Shafik (2021) proposes that a new social contract must address legitimate expectations and mutual obligations. The specific and collaborative roles of the state and the private sector must be understood. Shafik outlines three broad principles to undergird the new social contract: security for all, maximum investment in capability, and efficient and fair sharing of risks. Key players to make the new social compact work include the government, labour, business and communities. Busani Ngcaweni (2022) calls for a more innovative public service going forward, as the Covid-19 pandemic has played a pertinent role as a catalyst to accelerate innovation in areas that faced the most strain, particularly the health and education sectors.

Inclusive economic growth

The success and resilience of a new social contract is dependent on a growing economy that meets the basic needs of all South Africans. The challenge of South Africa's economic management is to address the structural distortions of the economy, low levels of investments, high debt and the more recent impact of the Covid-19 pandemic on households and businesses. David Lipton states: 'South Africa is grappling with growth that is too slow to raise average living standards, which is deeply problematic when one-third of the working population is effectively excluded from the economy. So far, there has been only limited progress on reforms to remedy that situation' (2016: 1). Similarly, Jonas (2019) argues for changes in the structure of the economy and its ownership, albeit in a manner that ensures competitiveness and sustainable growth.

South Africa requires a thorough set of reforms that focuses on the removal of the causes of national grievance (inclusivity) and make use of new industries to privilege new entrants such as small, medium and micro enterprises. This can potentially deconcentrate and diversify the economy to meet the imperatives of balanced national development. The government's Economic Reconstruction and Recovery Plan of 2021 aims to stimulate equitable and inclusive growth. The plan has, among other things, the following priority interventions: aggressive infrastructure investment, employment-orientated strategic localisation, re-industrialisation and export promotion, energy security, and support for tourism recovery and growth. The successful implementation of the plan depends on key resource mobilisation, regulatory changes, a supportive policy environment and enabling conditions for ease of doing business, building a capable state, social compacting and skills development, as well as economic diplomacy and further integration into the African continent.

Enablers of success

Without ethical political leadership in government, the collapse of public institutions is inevitable. We require good leadership for strategic focus and the rebuilding of our public institutions. Katherine Morton (2017: 479) succinctly argues that 'the history of institution building suggests that political leadership matters most at times of crisis, and that crises often act as catalysts for institutional innovation'. Its developmental character brings about complexity in the approach to leadership.

Secondly, a plan is only as credible as its delivery mechanism is viable. There is a real risk that South Africa's developmental agenda could fail because the state is incapable of implementing it. The crisis of our state system is that it is unable to fulfil basic functions that are required by the Constitution. We must develop our administrative capability to deliver on the policies and programmes determined by government.

In October 2022, the National School of Government, under the auspices of the Department of Public Service and Administration, released a framework document on the professionalisation of the public service. It called for the de-politicisation of the public service and increased measures to strengthen the meritocratic recruitment of public servants (National School of Government 2022). Jonathan Klaaren (2021) observes that in the wake of state capture and corruption, two approaches to public service reforms have emerged. The first focuses on ethical leadership and accountability, with disciplinary action in the event of contractual and ethical failures. The second is economistic and argues that the fundamental problems of dysfunctionality in the public sector are rooted in poverty and inequality.

We need a pragmatic approach that acknowledges the value of both positions, but also recognises the imperatives of making the country work within a robust, people-centric dispensation that is built on sound ethics and the rule of law. Chipkin (2021) makes a conceptual distinction between the theory of a democratic political system and the theory of democratic government. In this context, the former refers to the institutions and mechanisms through which to support the democratic political system. This articulation seeks to avoid the collapsing of the administrative process into the whims and fancies of politics, and vice versa.

The success of the back-to-basics approach depends on the participation of communities and civil society in ensuring that public officials are held accountable for their actions and promises. In recent times, communities themselves have been part of the destruction of community infrastructure. It is time they also take responsibility for the sustainability of infrastructure. This also involves the revival of a culture of compliance, such as the payment of services. The social capital that existed in the 1980s has weakened. Communities are no longer characterised by a strong and vibrant associational life, and public officials and politicians are unable to recreate such communal bonds.

A comprehensive review of structures and methods of community participation needs to be done. The existing Integrated Development Plan, which was meant to solicit people's views and developmental needs, is seen as ticking boxes by communities. The parliamentary constituency offices that are meant for consultation and communications with communities have become part of the political party network design to cater for the vast network of party members instead of the community.

There is a palpable social distance that has developed over time between councillors, members of Parliament and communities. Public representatives come to communities during election times. The five-year political cycle promotes short-termism among politicians. Accordingly, the NDP cautions against what it calls 'narrow, short-sighted and populist positions' that politicians take in their communities. The professionalisation of politics has had the effect of supplanting civic struggles. Civic struggles should articulate ordinary concerns of communities irrespective of political affiliations. Part of these struggles consist of taking ownership of the key aspects of their social spaces in ways that do not make them 'receivers' of service delivery but co-creators of community life.

Conclusion

There is a groundswell of progressive commitment to turn the tide in South Africa. A corrupt-free and people-first South Africa is possible. A broad array of authentic voices, comprising political, labour, business and civil society members, continues to oppose state plunder and demands a reconstitution of our social contract. At the Conference for Democratic Renewal and Change in 2022, the Defend Our Democracy Campaign called for a new social contract for South Africa (Defend Our Democracy Campaign 2022). The governing African National Congress (ANC) has also supported the idea of a new consensus for

South Africa on several occasions. This is in line with the call for the recalibration of ethical leadership espoused by Minister Pravin Gordhan at the 2018 Bram Fischer Memorial Lecture at Oxford University and is consistent with the 'new dawn' called for by President Ramaphosa.

Notes

1. See https://www.saflii.org/images/state-capture-commission-report-part-6-vol4.pdf (accessed 28 November 2023).
2. See https://www.thepresidency.gov.za/commission-inquiry-tax-administration-and-governance-sars (accessed 28 November 2023).

References

Auditor-General of South Africa. 2023. *Consolidated General Report on Local Government Audit Outcomes: MFMA 2021–22*. https://mfma-2022.agsareports.co.za (accessed 28 November 2023).

Cargill, J. 2010. *Trick or Treat: Rethinking Black Economic Empowerment*. Johannesburg: Jacana Media.

Chipkin, I. 2021. 'From Democracy as a Political System to Democracy as Government: A Contribution to Democratic Theory from Public Administration'. *Transformation* 105: 1–25.

Chipkin, I. and M. Swilling. 2018. *Shadow State: The Politics of State Capture*. Johannesburg: Wits University Press.

Chipkin, I. and J. Vidojevic. 2021. 'Time and Temporality in Organisations: The Case of Eskom'. *Development Southern Africa* 39 (2): 237–50.

Defend Our Democracy Campaign. 2022. *Declaration of the Conference for Democratic Renewal and Change*. https://defendourdemocracy.co.za/wp-content/uploads/2022/07/Final-declaration-Conference-for-Democratic-Renewal-and-Change.doc.pdf (accessed 28 November 2023).

Desai, A. 2018. 'The Zuma Moment: Between Tender-Based Capitalists and Radical Economic Transformation'. *Journal of Contemporary African Studies* 36 (4): 499–513.

Jonas, M. 2019. *After Dawn: Hope after State Capture*. Johannesburg: Picador Africa.

Klaaren, J. 2021. *Reforming the Public Administration in South Africa: A Path to Professionalisation*. Cape Town: Siber Ink.

Lipton, D. 2016. 'Where Is South Africa Going Wrong?' *Politicsweb*, 20 July. https://www.politicsweb.co.za/opinion/where-south-africas-going-wrong (accessed 28 November 2023).

Mkandawire, T. 2012. 'Building the African State in the Age of Globalisation: The Role of Social Compacts and Lessons for South Africa'. Inaugural Annual Lecture, Mapungubwe Institute for Strategic Relection. https://mistra.org.za/wp-content/uploads/2019/10/mkandawireinaugural0312.pdf (accessed 28 November 2023).

Morton, K. 2017. 'Political Leadership and Global Governance: Structural Power versus Custodial Leadership'. *Chinese Political Science Review* 2: 477–93.

National Planning Commission. 2012. *National Development Plan 2030: Our Future – Make It Work*. https://www.gov.za/sites/default/files/gcis_document/201409/ndp-2030-our-future-make-it-workr.pdf (accessed 28 November 2023).

National School of Government. 2022. *A National Framework towards the Professionalisation of the Public Sector*. https://www.thensg.gov.za/wp-content/uploads/2022/10/NATIONAL-FRAMEWORK-BOOKLET.pdf (accessed 28 November 2023).

Ngcaweni, B. 2022. 'Governments Need to Learn, Adapt and Respond in New Ways: This Is How Capacity Development Can Help'. *World Economic Forum*, 7 March. https://www.weforum.org/agenda/2022/03/governments-need-to-learn-adapt-and-respond-in-new-ways-this-is-how-capacity-development-can-help/ (accessed 28 November 2023).

Rapanyane, M.B. and C.C. Ngoepe. 2020. 'The Impact of Illicit Financial Flows on the South African Political Economy under Jacob Zuma, 2009–2018'. *Journal of Public Affairs* 20 (2), e2020.

Shafik, M. 2021. *What We Owe Each Other: A New Social Contract for a Better Society*. Princeton: Princeton University Press.

Stiglitz, J. 2018. 'Reform: How Did China Succeed?' *China Development Forum*, 24 March. https://academiccommons.columbia.edu/doi/10.7916/d8-b6av-nv42 (accessed 28 November 2023).

Tosun, J. and O. Treib. 2018. *Linking Policy Design and Implementation Styles*. London: Routledge.

Turok, I. 2016. 'South Africa's New Urban Agenda: Transformation or Compensation?' *Local Economy* 31 (1–2): 9–27.

CHAPTER 22

The Role of Municipal Councillors in the Implementation of Local Economic Development for Job Creation and Employment

Shepherd Mutangabende and Dovhani Reckson Thakhathi

Background

Addressing the triple challenge of poverty, inequality and unemployment is not a single event or a one-man show that can be tackled overnight. It is process that requires a holistic approach that is inclusive and concerted efforts of numerous stakeholders, cemented and guided by a solid policy framework. In order to tackle poverty, inequality and unemployment, there needs to be promotion of local economic development (LED) through harnessing locally available resources, creating job opportunities for local people, businesses, community-based organisations (CBOs) and through working together with municipal councillors in local government.

At the national level, the government is co-ordinating numerous investment programmes and public policies, such as the National Development Plan (NDP) and the Community Work Programme (CWP), which serves a complementary approach to job creation and also includes part-time jobs that offer a predictable income. There is also the Expanded Public Works Programme (EPWP), which is a mechanism to reduce poverty, unemployment and inequality through expanding labour-extensive ways of infrastructure delivery.

While at provincial and local levels, the government is working tirelessly to create a conducive environment for business to flourish and to promote small, medium and micro enterprises (SMMEs) as part of spearheading LED (Labuschagne 2019). The success of such LED strategies hinges on support from local government, driven by municipal councillors working hand in hand with other stakeholders. The South African Local Government Association (SALGA) asserts that local government has the mammoth task of creating a conducive environment for rebuilding local economies to improve the quality of citizens' lives, promoting democracy and integrating communities to promote non-racialism (2015: 11).

In South Africa, local government has a mandate, as enshrined in the Constitution of the Republic, section 152 and the White Paper on Local Government of 1998, which details all the developmental duties that local government is supposed to perform in support of LED. As part of fulfilling its developmental duties, local government should maximise social development and economic growth, starting with the provision of basic services such as electricity, sanitation, water and refuse removal, simultaneously promoting social development through good health care, libraries, a safe environment, sports and recreation. There are 226 local municipalities, 44 districts and 8 metropolitan municipalities, totalling 278 municipalities in South Africa. They have to provide infrastructure and services that are meant to grow local economies.

Most developing economies have been struggling to expand at the pace needed to cope with the growth of their workforce. The world economic order is very volatile, as economies are rapidly changing with the advent of technology, which demands new skills, especially in mega cities and townships – hence the need for LED policy initiatives to stimulate economic growth in local communities while creating employment opportunities (Mandisvika 2015).

The conceptual framework for LED policy

The Department of Cooperative Governance and Traditional Affairs defines LED as:

> an adaptive and responsive process by which government, public sector entities, citizens, business and non-governmental sector partners work collectively to create better conditions for innovative-driven inclusive economic development that is characterised by knowledge transfer and competence building, employment generation, capacity development, investment attraction and retention, image enhancement and revenue generation in a local area in order to improve its economic future and the quality of life for all (2018: 14).

LED has its focus on SMME development in both the formal and informal sectors (Makhubo 2015). LED 'as a development strategy, has in the recent past years gained widespread popularity and acceptance as a grass root-based approach to economic development and job creation especially in the developing world' (Kahika and Karyeija 2017: 1). Thus, LED can be defined as a process by which community members, together with municipal councillors, business, non-governmental organisations (NGOs) and other partners work jointly to create a better economic environment, which will then generate new opportunities, create jobs and promote economic growth. The International Labour Organization describes LED as a participatory developmental process that is localised and aimed at stimulating economic activities for the betterment of the lives of all who are involved.[1]

Furthermore, LED is regarded as 'one of the key economic drivers and urban resilience, the so-called urban revolution and healthy cities movement and the successful LED demands devolution of certain socio-economic development responsibilities to the local spheres of government' (Van der Waldt and Auriacombe 2018). Municipal councillors play an essential role in planning, local developmental advocacy and emphasising the importance of the communities' role in uplifting their local economies (Auriacombe and Van der Waldt 2020). Thus, LED can be viewed as 'a cross-cutting and integrated series of activities where the physical development of communities in linked to public service, place management and wider drivers of change such job creation, skills, investment, enterprise, innovation, productivity, quality of life and positioning' (Shannon 2018).

In developing countries, poverty, inequality and unemployment are wreaking havoc, dismantling families, driving many young women and men into substance abuse and exposing women and children to sexual abuse and gender-based violence. This catastrophic situation can be reduced through a strategic LED policy geared at creation of jobs and business opportunities, driven by municipal councillors in local government. To develop and sharpen a meaningful LED policy, there is need for defining LED within the context in which any policy will be implemented to address the unique needs of each community. LED policy needs to be developed and designed with the involvement of local communities who are the intended beneficiaries of the policy. Their input in that process gives them a sense of ownership and the responsibility to safeguard it and support its implementation wholeheartedly.

There are eight underlying principles for LED that should be used by municipal councillors to guide them and their municipal strategies in order to reduce poverty and unemployment among communities in which LED policies are implemented as outlined in the National Framework for LED:

- prioritise poverty alleviation through job creation as these two are the main challenges confronting South Africa;
- target marginalised communities and previously disadvantaged people, give them access to participate fully in economic activities such as SMMEs and other black economic empowerment initiatives;
- develop local initiatives that suit the unique needs of each community;
- ensure that there is collective decision-making from local leadership and community involvement to promote local ownership in LED;
- LED should build local areas and create collaborative business ventures, involving international, national and local partnerships;
- LED must maximise the utilisation of local skills and resources to create economic development opportunities;
- ensure the promotion of a comprehensive approach to LED, which includes the integration of diverse economic initiatives; and
- ensure that there is agility in LED to adapt to ever-volatile local, national and international situations (Department of Cooperative Governance and Traditional Affairs 2018: 34).

If it is planned, monitored and implemented well, LED has the ability to generate income and improve the quality of life for local people who are involved as it serves as a remedy to market failures to create much-needed jobs, simultaneously removing obstacles to enter the market by SMMEs and other individual initiatives (Meyer 2014). Thus, it is quite plausible to view LED as an all-inclusive economic growth strategy whose main purpose is to boost local economies and enhance income-generating projects, thereby creating employment opportunities, improving municipal performance and governance (Oduro-Ofori 2016).

LED can be viewed as an all-inclusive economic growth strategy that can be used to reduce poverty and inequality through ensuring that all segments of the community are getting better income and sharing the economic benefits of the resources and skills around them (African Development Bank 2020). Municipal councillors can help to promote multidimensional, inclusive growth through equal distribution of resources and support gender equality when it comes to access to jobs, business opportunities, education and skills development. Inclusive growth should not discriminate against anyone based on their gender, ethnicity, race, religion or political affiliation. It should create a conducive environment for all to thrive, collaborate and work with one common goal in mind – promoting LED for the benefit of the entire community and beyond. This is what is really needed in South Africa to combat poverty, unemployment and inequality in the post-apartheid era.

Role of municipal councillors in promoting LED

Municipal councillors have an indispensable role to play in promoting LED as they are the ambassadors of the communities that elected them, serving as the bridge between the communities they represent and the municipal council. They serve as champions for the manifesto of their political parties, including LED. It is essential that their supporters buy into their strategies and that they make decisions to address the imbalances of the past on behalf of the people who elected them. Municipal councillors also help with approving the policy priorities of various committees, including the executive committee or mayoral committee. Thus, it can be asserted that municipal councillors are facilitators of community input and they should keep their constituencies informed about the developmental agenda of the municipality, including LED plans and sponsorship available for community members.

Since municipal councillors attend council meetings, they are involved in all the essential ongoing planning and policymaking processes and specific programme initiatives driven by local stakeholders, such as LED, integrated development plans (IDPs) and other programmes (Makhubo 2015). These are clear opportunities to submit their community's needs, including proposed projects that need funding. Communicating such information helps to promote public participation, strengthening democracy and transparency in all LED activities, and this also keeps citizens informed about available opportunities for their benefit.

Many municipal council projects are incomplete due to a lack of monitoring and evaluation of their performance. Some are abandoned midway because funds have been diverted to individuals' pockets. Monitoring and evaluation help to identify any bottlenecks and address them before it is too late (UNCTAD 2021). Therefore, municipal councillors should help to keep track of whether the municipal projects and plans are implemented as planned, check whether services are being rendered in a fair and effective manner and whether municipal investment projects are materialising as planned in the IDP and are within the forecasted timelines (People's Assembly 2021). After conducting monitoring and evaluation, they need to report back to their communities about the progress and outcomes of what was planned and to get feedback from the community through constituency meetings, community forums and ward committee meetings and relay it back to the municipal council.

Municipal councillors are also involved in formulating the municipal by-laws that govern their area of jurisdiction, which means that they are involved in formulating LED policies and strategies that are conducive for promoting SMMEs and other individual initiatives (Xulu 2021). To attain desired outcomes, municipal councillors must make recommendations that can improve these enacted policies and programmes in relation to local government's developmental objectives. They work with other statutory bodies and their communities to develop and implement a collective vision for stimulating the well-being of society, supporting social cohesion and improving quality of life (Department of the Environment 2015).

Municipal councillors are thus the vision-bearers of their constituencies, promoting the respect of human rights in terms of having access to basic services, encouraging the potential and initiatives of their communities, and educating their residents about the principles of developmental local government championed through LED and the opportunities it can provide. The involvement of municipal councillors in the LED cannot be underestimated as they are aware of some of the challenges confronting their communities and they must take the lead in ensuring that all such challenges are addressed.

Challenges of LED in local government

Local government is confronted by myriad challenges, ranging from a skills shortage in critical positions, a lack of capacity in municipal councillors and administrative capacity, sabotage, corruption, high levels of poverty and unemployment, policy inconsistencies and ineffective implementation of policies, as well as limited resources (Mashamaite and Lethoko 2018). The Covid-19 pandemic left a trail of suffering for ordinary citizens and destabilised SMMEs and other income-generating projects, plunging many economies into disarray. The pandemic demonstrated clearly that it is essential for both local government and the private sector to adopt an inclusive approach to dealing with societal problems through LED (Chomane and Biljohn 2021).

The development of LED strategies can be seen as evidence of the good intentions of local governments, but poor implementation as a result of lack of capacity, poor financial management and misinterpretation of the strategy and lack of political will by all stakeholders is a great cause for concern (Kamara 2017). This is undermining the ability of local municipalities to fulfil their constitutional obligation to promote local economic growth. There is too much political interference and poor political leadership in the implementation of LED strategies because some of the sponsorships are coming from politicians and they want LED to be done their way, rather than targeting marginalised and underprivileged people in society and also doing it in a sustainable way (Khambule 2018a, 2018b). For instance, in Groblershoop in the Northern Cape, there were several instances where politicians used LED funding for their political expedience, channelling funds into communities where they have more political support, instead of where it is needed the most (Möller 2019).

Another difficulty when designing and implementing LED policy is understanding the nature, complexity and effects of these challenges on the political, institutional, economic and social facets of the municipality and its inhabitants. In some cases, municipalities are struggling to offer necessary support to SMMEs because they themselves are in need of professional expertise, skills and advice for solving their own problems of locating resources, adequate infrastructure, mismanagement of funds and poor leadership.

The significance of LED in job creation

The number-one enemy in South Africa today is poverty, unemployment and inequality and it is making less-privileged households even more vulnerable. LED is recognised globally by governments, businesses and CBOs as a strategy that can be used to address the challenge of poverty, unemployment and inequality. LED in local communities plays a crucial role in alleviating poverty through creating employment opportunities for both women and the youth, who are most heavily hit by poverty and unemployment in South Africa. By starting a local initiative, locally available resources and skills will be harnessed towards the betterment of the quality of life for the people who are directly involved. This also helps to promote a sense of ownership and belonging to those in the communities where the LED projects or programmes are being implemented.

LED policy helps to promote community participation, social cohesion and a culture of working together as a society for the benefit of all. It also helps to maximise the economic potential of local communities and the involvement of municipalities in creating a conducive environment for SMMEs to thrive and to be sustainable. Given the concerted efforts of local government, CBOs, NGOs, businesses and ordinary citizens, LED is a tool that can be used to drive poverty, unemployment and poverty away – provided resources are handled in a proper, transparent and accountable manner.

LED is also an integral part of service delivery in the sense that local government and its municipal councillors should work together with citizens to promote a conducive environment for businesses to thrive, through proper infrastructure development, stable supply of electricity, water and sanitation, the promotion of public participation and involvement of all stakeholders. Local developmental projects driven by local businesses and local communities have a better chance of succeeding than projects implemented by the government alone (Meyer 2014).

The legislative framework for LED policy

There are several pieces of legislation that unequivocally promote LED from a local government point of view. The Constitution (sections 152 and 153) spells out the objectives of local government in line with the promotion of social and economic development, including ensuring the provision of services to communities in a sustainable way and encouraging the participation of citizens and CBOs in local government matters. The developmental duties of municipalities in support of LED include putting strong structures in place to manage administrative tasks, budgeting and planning processes to give priority to the basic needs of the community, simultaneously promoting socio-economic development within its jurisdiction.

Additionally, the White Paper on Local Government of 1998 outlines the developmental duties of local government – including promoting local economic growth through LED as the leading strategy for poverty reduction and job creation. The White Paper defines the duties of a developmental local government 'as a government which is committed to working with citizens and groups within the community to find sustainable ways to meet their socio-economic and material needs and improve the quality of their lives' (Du Plooy 2017: 6). It describes the characteristics of a developmental local government as maximising social development and economic growth, integrating and co-ordinating the community and economic activities, while democratising development through leading and learning. In promoting democracy and empowering local communities, municipal councillors need to find the best ways to get input from the citizens they represent into council planning and to also ensure that their community is participating in the implementation process of the projects of their municipal council.

The Local Government Municipal Structures Act 117 of 1998 serves a constant reminder to local municipalities of their developmental duties as this is a strategic blueprint upon which all economic activities are predicated and municipal councillors help to ensure that the LED blueprint is implemented (Mashamaite and Lethoko 2018). Viable LED strategies are essential to open up local economies, thereby addressing a lack of access to basic amenities and reducing poverty and unemployment. The Local Government Municipal Systems Act 32 of 2000 (section 53) pronounces specific areas of responsibility and the roles of office-bearers such as municipal managers. Municipal councillors can also have additional duties delegated to them by the mayor. They have an indispensable role to play, even in promoting LED as provided by these pieces of legislation (SALGA 2006).

The National Framework for Local Economic Development 2017–22 (NFLED) outlines the contribution of LED to improving economic inclusivity, human dignity, social cohesion and quality of life in the community (SALGA 2016). The NFLED envisaged developing inclusive economies, skills development programmes, infrastructure, enterprise development, building diverse and innovation-driven local economies aimed at strengthening economic governance (Kobedi, Swanepoel and Venter 2022).

Community LED initiatives

There are several community LED initiatives that are transforming previously disadvantaged people's lives – for example, the Mpumalanga Economic Growth and Development Strategy, which was pioneered by the Mpumalanga Economic Growth Agency (MEGA) between 2010 and 2015. This is a successful community LED initiative that stimulated economic growth, helping to reduce poverty and unemployment through farming and other agricultural projects. MEGA's strategy was aimed at investing in various projects, such as the Nkomati Anthracite, Loopspruit Wine Estate, Tekwane Citrus and the Highveld Fruit Packers (Mokoena 2019). The funding for these initiatives was through partnerships and SMMEs.

The MEGA community LED initiative helped to build resilient, capable and credible institutions and also built the capacity of those who are still running those projects. The successes of the MEGA community LED has many lessons for other communities across South Africa. MEGA mobilised resources from local SMMEs and other partners, employed local labour and utilised locally available land to get these projects up and running. The involvement of community members and the skills transferred to them are providing much-needed sustainability and the community members have a sense of ownership of these projects.

Recommendations and the way forward

There is need for a framework for LED policy aimed at addressing poverty, inequality and unemployment among disadvantaged groups, such as people living with disabilities, women and the youth as these groups are confronted by several challenges emanating from the volatility of the job market.

As part of addressing the challenges of poverty and unemployment, local government structures should introduce pre-employment skills and training, involving the target group in programme design and implementation as this gives them a sense of purpose, ownership, direction and a sense of belonging to their community. However, 'LED governance cannot be pinned on stakeholder participation via LED networks and coordinated efforts, without addressing an issue of institutionalism'. There needs to be an LED agency that can help to unify all stakeholders – both the private and public sectors, ordinary citizens and those who have common goals, values and interests. Economic strengths, weaknesses, opportunities and threats for each community should be identified and then the strengths and opportunities should be used to develop a robust LED strategy. The weakness and the threats that are known should be used as learning curves and turned into economic opportunities to benefit the community.

All relevant stakeholders must work collaboratively to promote all-inclusive economic growth with a better understanding of what really needs to be done, what the end goal is, who is going to benefit and why it is necessary to ensure that LED is a success in the implementation of any policy or law that seeks to promote LED. There is a need for institutional arrangements and signing of memorandums of understanding and performance agreements must also be in place for LED to be successful in local government. This will help to ensure that all stakeholders are guided and bound by a written agreement and anyone deviating from that agreement must be answerable to all stakeholders, rather than to their own political parties.

Human capital development should be at the centre of promoting LED because educated and skilled people have a higher chance of being employed in a better-income position and also to make positive contributions in the planning and execution of LED programmes (Makhubo 2015). This, in turn, will change the fortunes of such individuals and their households.

There is a need for capacity building for municipal councillors and all other stakeholders to ensure that the necessary skills are available and both young and old are given ongoing training. This will help to address the skills gap among people of all ages because if the focus is only on young people, it means the older generation will be left out of the economic process. This could create a situation of economic dependence and a burden on the government or the younger generation.

The Covid-19 pandemic has taught us to be quick to adapt to an ever-volatile world in which state-of-the-art technology is at the centre of education and doing business. It is essential for SMMEs, CBOs and individuals (both young and elderly) to keep up with technological advances, so as to survive in the world economic order, which changes in the blink of an eye. There is a need to embrace technology and to adopt an approach of doing business anywhere and learning anywhere, without necessarily being in physical contact with those you are working with or doing business with. This will help people to explore new markets, new job opportunities, new partners, new skills and new ways of promoting LED. Both young and elderly people should be well acquainted with simple technology skills for ease of doing business and learning – for instance, online banking, Facebook and WhatsApp for business, as well as online marketing and accessing certain services from local government, including reporting leaking water and electricity faults. There should be platforms to conduct online indabas, community forums and public consultations.

Equally essential are vigorous accountability mechanisms to curb corruption and abuse of power by the elite who have robust financial muscle and political connections. This will prevent them from diverting resources that are meant for LED for their personal aggrandisement and political expedience. Every cent and every resource committed to promoting LED should be accounted for. This will help to ensure that the intended beneficiaries are receiving their portion.

LED is a policy aimed at decreasing poverty by creating jobs and making the local economy grow. Every effort must be made by municipalities to support small businesses and to create more factories. Big businesses must be encouraged to build more shopping malls in rural areas, in partnership with small businesses, in order to facilitate the creation of more jobs and employment. LED strategies in the agricultural sector must be developed in rural communities in order to enhance agricultural businesses as there are many farms in these areas. Agricultural markets for shopping malls in rural municipalities could do wonders for the effective implementation of LED policy in local government.

The role of traditional leaders in LED initiatives is very important. They should be trained on how the LED can be implemented in their own areas. Rural areas have poor infrastructure and if the local people can be developed to start companies that could improve infrastructure in these areas, this could go a long way to address the basic needs of the people. The national government is encouraged to partner with the provincial and local governments to ensure that LED initiatives in infrastructure development in rural areas are implemented – for example, the construction of roads, provision of electricity, supply of water and the provision of buildings to accommodate the small business owners as well as co-operatives. Can you imagine what South Africa would look like if all rural areas had good streets and good roads to connect them with provincial and national roads? Can you imagine what South Africa would look like if each street in rural communities had lights?

Municipalities must work with civil society to assist SMME owners to develop business plans, to develop fund-raising strategies and to market and promote locally made products through the development of local food initiatives, such as farmers' markets and trade fairs. The promotion of local tourism facilities is also very important. Many rural communities should be encouraged through LED initiatives to explore the tourism opportunities that could attract visitors to their areas.

The implementation of LED by municipalities will need strong leadership and champions who are passionate and committed to business and economic activities. LED sections must be staffed by competent and capable managers who do research and who are always strategising on the best plans of action that could enhance job-creation opportunities, as well as employment spaces for women, youth and graduates within their areas. Such individuals must always be communicating with key economic and business stakeholders who can bring business initiatives to local people.

Safety and security business opportunities should be explored. Criminal elements in towns and cities, as well as in rural communities, have increased dramatically. Local companies could be established to fight criminal and violent activities. It would be great to get young men who can patrol streets and protect important public buildings like schools, hospitals, water reservoirs, electricity buildings and cable networks. More local companies must be established to fight against gender-based violence and other ills in society. Many SMMEs and co-operatives in rural communities are facing challenges regarding high rates of electricity. The municipalities must try their best to provide an electricity subsidy. This will go a long way to enhancing the sustainability and viability of SMMEs and cooperatives, who are job creators and can make a great contribution to reducing poverty and unemployment.

Conclusion

Promoting the success of LED is a continuous process, which demands concerted efforts by all stakeholders and it must be everyone's obligation to ensure that locally available resources and skills are mobilised towards promoting local economic growth and creating jobs. They should also all be responsible for ensuring that there is transparency and accountability in the manner in which

LED planning and implementation are handled. Municipal councillors have an indispensable role to play through providing leadership to ensure that there is community participation in the planning and execution process of LED, so as to give them a sense of ownership and belonging. The LED strategy can be heralded as the game-changer in terms of turning around the economic fortunes of every community in South Africa and other developing countries.

Therefore, all hands must be on the deck to ensure poverty, unemployment and inequality are eradicated, no matter how small the contribution, it makes a difference. Gone are the days of waiting for government alone to create jobs and address all socio-economic issues bedevilling communities. It is high time that all stakeholders come together to address the triple threat of poverty, unemployment and inequality.

Note

1. https://www.ilo.org/global/topics/employment-promotion/local-economic-development/lang--en/index.htm (accessed 6 December 2023).

References

African Development Bank. 2020. *African Economic Outlook 2020: Developing Africa's Workforce for the Future.* https://www.afdb.org/sites/default/files/documents/publications/african_economic_outlook_2020-en.pdf (accessed 6 December 2023).

Auriacombe, C. and G. van der Waldt. 2020. 'Critical Consideration for Local Economic Development Strategy Design in South African Municipalities'. *Administratio Publica* 28 (1): 25–43.

Chomane, P. and M.I. Biljohn. 2021. 'A Conceptual Framework for Using Social Innovation as an Approach to Local Economic Development'. *Africa's Public Service Delivery and Performance Review* 9 (1): 1–11.

Department of Cooperative Governance and Traditional Affairs. 2018. *The National Framework for Local Economic Development: Creating Innovation-Driven Local Economies.* https://www.cogta.gov.za/cgta_2016/wp-content/uploads/2023/01/National-Framework-for-LED-2018-2028.pdf (accessed 6 December 2023).

Department of the Environment. 2015. *Statutory Guidance for the Operation of Community Planning: Local Government Act Northern Ireland 2014.* https://www.armaghbanbridgecraigavon.gov.uk/download/9211/involved-community-planning/24009/community-planning-legislation-2.pdf (accessed 6 December 2023).

Du Plooy, L.J. 2017. 'Thinking Differently about Local Economic Development and Governance in Secondary Cities in South Africa: A Conceptual Analysis of the Possibilities of Problem Driven Iterative Adaption (PDIA)'. Master's thesis, University of Cape Town.

Kahika, G. and G.K. Karyeija. 2017. 'Institutional Roles and the Implementation of Local Economic Development, Kasese District, Uganda'. *Africa's Public Service Delivery and Performance Review* 5 (1): 1–9.

Kamara, R.D. 2017. 'Creating Enhanced Capacity for Local Economic Development (LED) through Collaborative Governance in South Africa'. *SocioEconomic Challenges* 1 (3): 98–115.

Khambule, I. 2018a. 'Imagining an Institutionalised Social Dialogue in the South African Local Government-Led Development Landscape'. *Forum for Development Studies* 45 (1): 97–117.

———. 2018b. 'The Role of Local Economic Development Agencies in South Africa's Developmental State Ambitions'. *Local Economy* 33 (3): 287–306.

Kobedi, K.C., E. Swanepoel and M. Venter. 2022. 'Community Work Programmes as Job Creation Mechanism: A Case of Tshwane Metropolitan Municipality'. *Africa's Public Service Delivery and Performance Review* 10 (1): 1–13.

Labuschagne, H. 2019. 'Analysis of Approaches to Job Creation in South African Municipalities'. ICMA Conference, Nashville, 20–23 October. https://icma.org/sites/default/files/Presentations-191018/Presentations/icma%20conference%202019%20ppt%20-%20analysis%20of%20approaches%20to%20job%20creation%20dr%20hennie%20labuschagnev5.pdf (accessed 6 December 2023).

Makhubo, T.J. 2015. 'Local Economic Development as a Tool for Job Creation: A Case of Mafube Local Municipality'. Master's thesis, North-West University.

Mandisvika, G. 2015. 'The Role and Importance of Local Economic Development in Urban Development: A Case of Harare'. *Journal of Advocacy, Research and Education* 4 (3): 198–209.

Mashamaite, K. and M. Lethoko. 2018. 'Role of the South African Local Government in Local Economic Development'. *International Journal of eBusiness and eGovernment Studies* 10 (1): 114–28.

Meyer, D. 2014. 'The Local Economic Development (LED) Challenges and Solutions: The Case of the Northern Free State Region, South Africa'. *Mediterranean Journal of Social Sciences* 5 (16): 624–34.

Mokoena, S.K. 2019. 'The Role of Local Economic Development on Small, Medium and Micro Enterprises'. *AUDA* 11 (1): 59–83.

Möller, J. 2019. 'Theories in Regional Economics in the Light of Local Development'. In: *Contemporary Drivers of Local Development*, edited by P. Futó, 24–40. Maribor: Lex Localis.

Oduro-Ofori, E. 2016. 'Decentralisation and Local Economic Development Promotion at the District Level in Ghana'. In: *Decentralisation and Regional Development: Experiences and Lessons from Four Continents over Three Decades*, edited by E. Dick, K. Gaesing, D. Inkoom and T. Kausel, 15–36. New York: Springer.

People's Assembly. 2021. 'What Is the Role of Ward Councillors?' https://www.pa.org.za/blog/what-role-ward-councillors (accessed 6 December 2023).

SALGA (South African Local Government Association). 2006. *Councillor Induction Programme: Handbook for Municipal Councillors.* https://www.westerncape.gov.za/text/2006/4/handbook_for_municipal_councillors.pdf (accessed 6 December 2023).

——. 2015. *15 Years of Developmental and Democratic Local Government 2000–2015.* https://www.salga.org.za/Documents/Knowledge%20Hub/Local%20Government%20Briefs/15-YEARS-OF-DEVELOPMENTAL-AND-DEMOCRATIC-LOCAL-GOVERNMENT.pdf (accessed 6 December 2023).

——. 2016. *2017–2022 Strategic Plan.* https://www.salga.org.za/SALGA%20Municipal%20Managers%20Forum/Documents/Strat%20Plan%20201722.pdf (accessed 6 December 2023).

Shannon, L. 2018. 'Local Economic Development: An Overview of the Economic Development Role of Local Authorities in Selected Jurisdictions'. Local Government Research, 20 March. https://www.ipa.ie/local-government-research/local-economic-development-an-overview-of-the-economic-development-role-of-local-authorities-in-selected-jurisdictions.3926.html (accessed 6 December 2023).

United Nations Conference on Trade and Development (UNCTAD). 2021. *Reaping the Potential Benefits of the African Continental Free Trade Area for Inclusive Growth: Economic Development in Africa Report 2021.* https://unctad.org/system/files/official-document/aldcafrica2021_en.pdf (accessed 6 December 2023).

Van der Waldt, G. and C. Auriacombe. 2019. 'Local Economic Development for Local Government'. Unpublished handbook, University of Johannesburg.

Xulu, K. 2021. 'Understanding the Role of a Municipal Councillor'. *The Citizen*, 26 November. https://www.citizen.co.za/highway-mail/news-headlines/2021/11/26/understanding-the-role-of-a-municipal-councillor/ (accessed 6 December 2023).

PART 4

INTERNATIONAL RELATIONS AND DIPLOMACY

CHAPTER 23

Revisiting Kwame Nkrumah 60 Years Later

Eddy Maloka

Africa's 'pan' movement began in the middle of the twentieth century. Prior to this point, before Ghana gained its independence in 1957, it was largely a liberation movement, focused on the decolonisation of Africa and driven from outside the continent by the African diaspora. When Kwame Nkrumah emerged on the centre stage of Africa as Ghana's first president, he took this movement to another level, into the domain of the construction of African post-colonial states and, eventually, the establishment of the African Union.

It is now 60 years since Nkrumah published his masterpiece *Africa Must Unite* (1963), a book that outlines his vision for post-colonial Africa. It is not clear whether Nkrumah, as voracious a reader as he was, had read Richard Coudenhove-Kalergi's *Europe Must Unite* (1939) when he decided on the title of his book. Nonetheless, we owe it to this Ghanaian statesman that every year we celebrate Africa Day during the month of May. Thanks to him, we have an entity called the African Union (AU), a name he coined even before the Organisation of African Unity (OAU) saw light of day in 1963. The publication of *Africa Must Unite* in the same year the OAU was formed was not accidental:

> It was my hope when I wrote *Africa Must Unite*, that it might contribute to the African Revolution by setting down the case for total liberation and unification. The book was first published in 1963, just before the opening of the Conference of African Heads of State and Government held in Addis Ababa in May 1963 (Nkrumah 1973: 222).

His clarion call to this 1963 founding conference of the OAU summed up the core elements of his idea: 'Our objective is African Union now. There is no time to waste. We must unite now or perish. I am confident that by our concerted effort and determination we shall lay here the foundations for a continental Union of African States' (Nkrumah 1973: 233).

My purpose here is not to defend Nkrumah, his legacy or record; or to offer a critique or a comparative assessment of his thought. I simply intend to show that here was an African statesman, a trailblazer, who was on point about how Africa would look in the future without continental integration. If he was so correct in predicting Africa's present condition, he is likely to be proven correct again about the continent's fate in the next 60 years if today's generation fails to heed his counsel, as his peers did in the 1960s.

This counsel is well articulated in *Africa Must Unite*: 'The unity of the countries of Africa is an indispensable precondition for the speediest and fullest development, not only of the totality of the continent, but of the individual countries linked together in the union" (Nkrumah 1963: 163). With the benefit of hindsight, he was justified to be concerned that 'in the early flush of independence, some of the new African states are jealous of their sovereignty and tend to exaggerate their separatism in a historical period that demands Africa's unity in order that their independence may be safeguarded' (1963: 148). For Nkrumah, 'the insistence on not wanting to cede certain functions to a central unifying political authority in which all the members will have an equal voice is unrealistic and unfounded' (1963: 148). 'When we talk of African Unity,' he once said, 'we are thinking of a political arrangement which will enable us *collectively* to provide solutions for our problems in Africa' (1973: 272).

Africa is still grappling with this challenge to this day – that is how far-sighted this Ghanaian leader was. No wonder his ideas outlived the opinions of his critics. This fact should undoubtedly make him one of the most influential Africans of the twentieth century. My contention is that had Africa followed Nkrumah's idea of creating a union instead of multiple, sovereign, post-colonial nation states, the continent would have fared better than it has. 'The forward solution,' he stated in *Africa Must Unite*, 'is for the African states to stand together politically, to have a united foreign policy, a common defence plan, and a fully integrated economic programme for the development of the whole continent. Only then can the dangers of neo-colonialism and its handmaiden balkanisation be overcome' (Nkrumah 1963: 177).

He approached his quest for the unification of Africa ideologically, with intellectual vigour, as a struggle, as a political activist and with revolutionary zeal. For Nkrumah, the independence of Ghana was not an end in itself, but a base from which to launch further struggles for the total emancipation of Africa and the roll-out of his ambitious project of unification. Once his administration was in office, one of the first actions of independent Ghana was to host the Conference of Independent African States in April 1958 – there were only eight independent states in Africa at the time. Soon thereafter, Nkrumah criss-crossed the continent as a follow-up, to convince his peers of the need for unity and for this unity to be formalised into a political structure. His energy and effort paid off when the OAU was born a few years later. In *Revolutionary Path*, he recollected:

> The Accra Conference of Independent African States was the first conference of its kind ever to be held and it paved the way for a succession of other Pan-African conferences of various kinds. A process was begun of direct consultation between African states, a process which has continued ever since, and which was marked by the setting up of the Organization of African Unity (OAU) in 1963 (Nkrumah 1973: 126).

He had another agenda in mind:

> When, on 15 April 1958, I welcomed the representatives to the conference, I felt that at last Pan-Africanism had moved to the African continent where it really belonged. It was an historic occasion. Free Africans were actually meeting together, *in Africa*, to examine and consider African affairs. Here was a signal departure from established custom, a jar to the arrogant assumption of non-African nations that African affairs were solely the concern of states outside our continent (Nkrumah 1963: 136).

He wanted to move the headquarters of Pan-Africanism from Western capitals, where various Pan-African conferences had taken place in the past, to Africa. The 1958 Accra conference was just the beginning. As a former member of the secretariat that put together the historic 1945 Manchester Pan-African Conference, Nkrumah had the credibility and political clout to aim for this objective. He used independent Ghana to host a series of Pan-African meetings, or what he termed 'All-African' events. Since then, subsequent Pan-African conferences have been held on African soil. Ghana would also offer a home to activists from the African diaspora wishing to contribute to Africa's development, some of whom even served as technical and political advisers to Nkrumah.

Nkrumah's ideas about continental unification did not drop out of the sky, but evolved with time, to crystallise into a body of thought much later in his political development. He had not reached this point of crystallisation even in 1958 when he received delegates for the first Conference of Independent African States. His intellectual maturity on this subject developed in subsequent years, in the thick of the struggle and debates that resulted in the OAU. Later in his life, he would describe this experience in his own words:

> There is, however, one matter on which my views have been expanded, and that is regarding African unification. When *Towards Colonial Freedom* was written [in 1947], my ideas on African unity, important even as I considered them at that time, were limited to West African unity as a first step. Since I have had the opportunity of putting my ideas to work, and in the intensification of neo-colonialism, I lay even greater stress on the vital importance to Africa's survival of a political unification of the entire African continent (Nkrumah 1973: 14).

Unlike some of his contemporaries in the African diaspora, Nkrumah categorically rejected race-based Pan-Africanism and even married an Egyptian woman. In *Ghana: The Autobiography of Kwame Nkrumah*, he was clear that '[Marcus] Garvey's ideology was concerned with black nationalism as opposed to African nationalism' (Nkrumah 1957: 53). A few pages later, he recalled his public address where he declared: 'Africa for the Africans, but not the kind of philosophy that Marcus Garvey preached. No!' (1957: 54). He dismissed 'black nationalism' as just a 'nebulous movement'. In *Africa Must Unite*, he was fully aware that 'there are those who maintain that Africa cannot unite because we lack the three necessary ingredients for unity, a common race, culture and language', but he disagreed (1963: 132). His answer to this question was in what he termed 'African Personality' which, according to another of his publications, 'finds expression in a re-awakening consciousness among Africans and peoples of African descent of the bonds which unite us – our historical past, our culture, our common experience, and our aspirations' (1973: 205). In other words, as he elaborated in *Africa Must Unite*:

> I am convinced that the forces making for unity far outweigh those which divide us. In meeting fellow Africans from all parts of the continent I am constantly impressed by how much we have in common. It is not just our colonial past, or the fact that we have aims in common, it is something which goes far deeper. I can best describe it as a sense of one-ness in that we are Africans. In practical terms, this deep-rooted unity has shown itself in the development of Pan-Africanism, and, more recently, in the projection of what has been called the African Personality in world affairs (1963: 132).

The Organisation of African Unity

Nkrumah's unification project had eight elements to it. First, he accepted that in his vision of a unified Africa, 'states would continue to exercise independent authority, except in the fields defined and reserved for common action in the interests of the security and orderly development of the whole continent' (Nkrumah 1973: 218–19). He had the American Congress model in mind for his 'central political organisation', which would be created based on a Constitution agreed to by participating states. This body, a Union of African States,

> should consist of an upper house and a lower house. Each state would have the right to send two representatives to the upper house, irrespective of the size and population of the state; while admission to the lower house would be secured on the basis of proportional representation in accordance with the population of each state (Nkrumah 1973: 219).

He emphasised that 'this proposal does not in any way interfere with the internal constitutional arrangements of any state. The overriding concern of the Union of

African States would be to give political direction in regard to the implementations'
of his project (Nkrumah 1973: 232).

Second, he advocated for integrated, central planning, as opposed to a laissez-
faire approach to economic development. 'We should have an overall economic
planning on a continental basis,' he declared in *Africa Must Unite* (1963: 218)
because 'common continental planning for the industrial and agricultural
development of Africa is a vital necessity' (1973: 243). His logic was simple –
Africa has vast natural resources, from minerals to endowments in energy and
agricultural sectors, but because of a lack of state capacity and financial resources,
including destabilisation by neo-colonial forces, no single African country
would be able to harness these resources optimally for the transformation of the
continent. Only a united Africa can resist and defeat neo-colonialism and realise
the socio-economic potential of the continent to the fullest. A central political
authority of the Union would be able to plan and undertake huge infrastructure
and other projects without hindrance, on a continental scale, across countries.

Third, his idea of economic development was not just about ticking boxes,
with a bridge built down there and a road at the corner up there, but was
radical, envisaging transformative change for Africa to leap, and very fast, into
the modern era. 'Each of us alone cannot hope to secure the highest benefits of
modern technology, which demands vast capital investment and can only justify
its economics in serving an extensive population,' he stated in *Africa Must Unite*
(1963: 168). Furthermore, Nkrumah said:

> A continental merging of our land areas, our populations and our
> resources, will alone give full substance to our aspirations to advance from
> our pre-industrial state to that stage of development that can provide for
> all the people the high standard of living and welfare amenities of the most
> advanced industrial states (1963: 168).

His plan was very clear:

> There are some who refute the requirement of continental unity as the essential
> prerequisite to full industrialization [but] there is absolutely no doubt that the
> key to significant industrialization of this continent of ours lies in a union of

African states, planning its development centrally and scientifically through a pattern of economic integration (Nkrumah 1963: 170).

In his address at the founding conference of the OAU, he resorted to a more dramatic metaphor to make his point:

The world is no longer moving through bush paths or on camels and donkeys. We cannot afford to pace our needs, our development, our security, to the gait of camels and donkeys. We cannot afford not to cut down the overgrown bush of outmoded attitudes that obstruct our path to the modern open road of the widest and earliest achievement of economic independence and the raising up of the lives of our people to the highest level (Nkrumah 1973: 238).

He elaborated at length on this vision:

We shall accumulate machinery and establish steel works, iron foundries and factories; we shall link the various states of our continent with communications by land, sea and air. We shall cable from one place to another, phone from one place to the other and astound the world with our hydro-electric power; we shall drain marshes and swamps, clear infested areas, feed the under-nourished, and rid our people of parasites and disease. It is within the possibility of science and technology to make even the Sahara bloom into a vast field with verdant vegetation for agricultural and industrial developments. We shall harness the radio, television, giant printing presses to lift our people from the dark recesses of illiteracy.

A decade ago, these would have been visionary words, the fantasies of an idle dreamer. But this is the age in which science has transcended the limits of the material world, and technology has invaded the silences of nature. Time and space have been reduced to unimportant abstractions. Giant machines make roads, clear forests, dig dams, lay out aerodromes; monster trucks and planes distribute goods; huge laboratories manufacture drugs; complicated geological surveys are made; mighty power stations are built; colossal factories erected – all at an incredible speed (Nkrumah 1973: 238).

Fourth, his idea of development was not just transformative and ambitious; he also saw financial resources for achieving this goal coming from Africa itself. He did not even trust development or donor 'aid' as a resource for Africa's development. On the contrary, he viewed it as a tool for subjugating the continent to neo-colonialism and perpetuating its dependency. His *Neo-colonialism: The Last Stage of Imperialism* is very direct in making this point: ' "Aid" ... to a neo-colonial state is merely a revolving credit, paid by the neo-colonial master, passing through the neo-colonial state and returning to the neo-colonial master in the form of increased profits' (1965: 8). Addressing his colleagues at the first OAU meeting, Nkrumah assured them:

> We have the resources. It was colonialism in the first place that prevented us from accumulating the effective capital; but we ourselves have failed to make full use of our power in independence to mobilize our resources for the most effective take-off into thorough-going economic and social development. We have been too busy nursing our separate states to understand fully the basic need of our union, rooted in common purpose, common planning and common endeavour. A union that ignores these fundamental necessities will be but a sham. It is only by uniting our productive capacity and the resultant production that we can amass capital. And once we start, the momentum will increase. With capital controlled by our own banks, harnessed to our own true industrial and agricultural development, we shall make our advance (Nkrumah 1973: 238).

He made a related point in *Africa Must Unite*:

> The necessary capital for all these developments can only be accumulated by the employment of our resources on a continental extension. This calls for a central organization to formulate a comprehensive economic policy for Africa which will embrace the scientific, methodical and economic planning of our ascent from present poverty into industrial greatness (Nkrumah 1963: 157).

Fifth was his proposal for a common African defence strategy, based on a common policy and a standing army: 'Because we do not yet have a common system of defence, some African countries feel insecure and have therefore naturally entered into defence pacts with foreign Governments. This endangers the security of all Africa (Nkrumah 1973: 232). He believed that 'we should aim at the establishment of a unified military and defence strategy'. This proposal must have sounded very radical to his colleagues, not least because of the sarcasm that he sometimes employed in his argument:

> I do not see much virtue or wisdom in our separate efforts to build up or maintain vast military forces for self-defence which, in any case, would be ineffective in any major attack upon our separate states. If we examine this problem realistically, we should be able to ask ourselves this pertinent question: which single state in Africa today can protect its sovereignty against an imperialist aggressor? (Nkrumah 1963: 219)

Sixth, Nkrumah argued for a 'unified foreign policy and diplomacy to give political direction to our joint efforts for the protection and economic development of our continent' (1963: 220), to complement his 'unified economic planning organization and a unified military and defence strategy'. Some elements of this proposal would be unthinkable today:

> The burden of separate diplomatic representation by each state on the continent of Africa alone would be crushing, not to mention representation outside Africa. The desirability of a common foreign policy which will enable us to speak with one voice in the councils of the world, is so obvious, vital and imperative that comment is hardly necessary (Nkrumah 1963: 220).

Seventh was his idea of an Africa Common Market: 'We should therefore be thinking seriously now of ways and means of building up a Common Market of a United Africa,' he challenged his peers, 'and not allow ourselves to be lured by the dubious advantages of association with the so-called European Common Market' (1973: 231). His point was that

> we in Africa have looked outward too long for development of our economy and transportation. Let us begin to look inwards into the African Continent

for all aspects of its development. Our communications were devised under colonial rule to stretch outwards towards Europe and elsewhere, instead of developing internally between our cities and states. Political Unity should give us the power and will to change all this (Nkrumah 1973: 231).

Finally, he foresaw the need for Africa to have a single currency: 'The advantages of this would be inestimable, since monetary transactions between our several States would be facilitated and the pace of financial activity generally quickened (Nkrumah 1973: 232). He thought that 'a Central Bank of Issue is an inescapable necessity, in view of the need to orientate the economy of Africa and place it beyond the reach of foreign control'. This argument is still relevant today.

Nkrumah's motto was simple: 'Seek ye first the political kingdom, and all else shall be added onto you' (Mazrui 1993). He believed in the primacy of politics; that the immediate aim of any political struggle is to assume state power and then to use this state to transform society. He applied this reasoning to his union of Africa: 'Just as I was convinced that political freedom was the essential forerunner of our economic growth and that it must come,' he writes in *Africa Must Unite*, 'so I am equally convinced that African union will come and provide that united, integrated base upon which our fullest development can be secured' (1963: 170). He then goes on to argue:

> In the face of the forces that are combining to reinforce neo-colonialism in Africa, it is imperative that the leaders should begin now to seek the best and quickest means by which we can collectivize our economic resources and produce an integrated plan for their careful deployment for our mutual benefit. If we can do this, we shall raise in Africa a great industrial, economic and financial power comparable to any that the world has seen in our time (Nkrumah 1963: 172).

Nkrumah's idea of African unity was inspired by exemplars elsewhere: 'There are in the world several unions of states which can offer examples or case studies for the political unification of Africa: The United States of America, the Union of Soviet Socialist Republics, Australia, Canada, Switzerland and Venezuela' (Nkrumah 1963: 205). He points out: 'Each of them came into being at different historical periods, but all aimed at giving greater protection to the uniting states against internal and external disintegrating pressures; and at providing within the union the conditions of viability and security which would lead to faster economic evolution.' He was influenced primarily by the American experience, which he repeated frequently in his assertions, and secondarily by how, through unity, the former Union of Soviet Socialist Republics was able to rapidly modernise by developing its productive forces. He was intimately familiar with the history of the United States, having lived in that country for ten years as a student, and admired how its founders fought for the federation against those who were opposed to it. Nkrumah believed that Africa needed such determined champions if its unity was to be happen and he probably viewed his personal role as a leader through that lens. Latin America represented for him a different experience since nations there had been independent since the nineteenth century without anything to show for it and this, according to Nkrumah, was an example that Africa should avoid.

The European Union was in the early stages of its unification process and he urged his colleagues to emulate it: 'Today, the major European powers, confronted with the deepening competitiveness of acquisitive production, intensified by the new scientific inventions, shrinking empires and the enlargement of the socialist conclave of nations, are forming their associations of strength, both economic, political and military' (Nkrumah 1963: 158). He could not spare his opponents his sarcasm:

> It seems, then, curiously paradoxical that in this period when national exclusivism in Europe is making concessions to super-national organizations, many of the new African states should cling to their new-found sovereignty as something more precious than the total well-being of Africa and seek alliances with the states that are combining to balkanize our continent in neo-colonialist interests (Nkrumah 1963: 158).

But Nkrumah was not keen on the unification model of the regional economic communities (RECs) of today. He thought these bodies would not only slow down continent-wide integration, but could also form the basis for regional divisions. 'I consider that even the idea of regional federations in Africa is fraught with many dangers,' he warned (Nkrumah 1963: 214). 'Indeed, such federations may even find objection to the notion of African unity.' He felt that 'regional groupings, especially when based purely on economic co-operation, in areas which are already dominated by neo-colonialist interests, retard rather than promote the unification process' (1973: 14). To be fair to Nkrumah, REC-type regional integration was a new phenomenon in his time and some of it was initiated by former colonial powers, with the intention of countering continent-wide integration. However, with the advent of the Lagos Plan of Action in the 1970s, the notion of RECs would enter African development thinking in a positive way, with these bodies viewed as building blocks towards continental integration and no longer as the antithesis of it. The RECs have proved a critical and effective vehicle for continental unification.

Nkrumah was not just talking, making speeches, engaged in polemics, or simply writing books. He was also putting his ideas into action to test them, to give them momentum. Besides the Conference of Independent African States, where he was the initiator and pivotal figure, at a bilateral level, he reached out to like-minded leaders, such as Sékou Touré of Guinea and Modibo Keïta of Mali, to establish the nucleus for his United States of Africa. The highlight was the short-lived Union of African States, formed in 1961 between Mali, Ghana and Guinea. Nkrumah cited its charter at length in one of his publications to prove that he was not dreaming: this was doable!

> Article 3. The aims of the Union of African States (U.A.S.) are as follows: to strengthen and develop ties of friendship and fraternal co-operation between the Member States politically, diplomatically, economically and culturally; to pool their resources in order to consolidate their independence and safeguard their territorial integrity; to work jointly to achieve the complete liquidation of imperialism, colonialism and neo-colonialism in Africa and the building up of African Unity; to harmonize the domestic and foreign policy of its Members, so that their activities may prove more effective and contribute more worthily to safeguarding the peace of the world. Article 4. The Union's activities shall be exercised mainly in the following fields:
> a)   Domestic Policy. The working out of a common orientation of the States.

b)   Foreign Policy. The strict observance of a concerted diplomacy, calculated to achieve closer co-operation.
c)   Defence. The organization of a system of joint defence, which will make it possible to mobilize all the means of defence at the disposal of the State, in favour of any State of the Union which may become a victim of aggression.
d)   Economy. Defining a common set of directives relating to economic planning, aiming at the complete decolonization of the set-ups inherited from the colonial system, and organizing the development of the wealth of their countries in the interest of their peoples.
e)   Culture. The rehabilitation and development of African culture, and frequent and diversified cultural exchange (Nkrumah 1963: 142).

Later, inspired by the nascent European Common Market, the leaders of this Union agreed to establish their own African Common Market.

Nkrumah saw the 1963 founding conference of the OAU as an opportunity. Ahead of this event, he published his *Africa Must Unite*, a manifesto for his vision of unification. Thereafter, he despatched a letter to his colleagues, the content mirroring the argument in his book. At the conference, he delivered a fiery speech, reiterating his case for unification, and presented a proposal for transitional measures that the conference should adopt. He aimed at persuading his peers:

As a first step, a declaration of principles uniting and binding us together and to which we must all faithfully and loyally adhere and laying the foundations of unity should be set down. And there should also be a formal declaration that all the Independent African States here and now agree to the establishment of a Union of African States (Nkrumah 1973: 246).

He went on: 'As a second and urgent step for the realization of the unification of Africa, an All-Africa Committee of Foreign Ministers be set up now, and that before we rise from this Conference a date should be fixed for them to meet' (Nkrumah 1973: 246). And then, 'this Committee should establish on behalf of the Heads of our Governments, a permanent body of officials and experts to work out a machinery for the Union Government of Africa'. In addition, Nkrumah argued: 'A Presidium consisting of the heads of Governments of the Independent

African States should be called upon to meet and adopt a Constitution and other recommendations which will launch the Union Government of Africa.'

Furthermore, Nkrumah wanted the meeting to empower this Committee of Foreign Ministers to develop proposals on four structures, which he called 'Commissions'; namely, 'a Commission to frame a constitution for a Union Government of African States; a Commission to work out a continent-wide plan for a unified or common economic and industrial programme for Africa', including proposals for setting up a 'Common Market for Africa, an African Currency, an African Monetary Zone, an African Central Bank, and a continental Communication system' (Nkrumah 1973: 246). The other three Commissions were to 'draw up details for a Common Foreign Policy and Diplomacy'; to produce plans for a Common System of Defence; and 'to make proposals for a Common African Citizenship'. Once they had done their work, 'these Commissions will report to the Committee of Foreign Ministers who should in turn submit within six months of this Conference their recommendations to the Presidium'. He thought that 'with these steps, I submit, we shall be irrevocably committed to the road which will bring us to a Union Government for Africa'.

Nkrumah clearly had a different understanding of what eventually became the OAU; he thought it was just a short-term, interim measure, put in place while a proper, final body was being negotiated. He would not have imagined that this entity that he and his colleagues created in May 1963 would be in existence, virtually unchanged, for nearly 40 years! He saw the charter, adopted at the inaugural OAU summit, as a useful starting point, even motivating for its ratification by his parliament: 'In May 1963, when the OAU was formed, and rudimentary institutions and procedures for the total liberation and unification of the African continent were agreed upon, the stage was set for a great advance in the African Revolution (Nkrumah 1973: 251). About this outcome document itself, he thought 'it was a Charter of intent, rather than a Charter of positive action' (1973: 249). He was practical though: 'But this was inevitable in view of the widely differing policies of those who took part in the Conference.' He was relieved that 'all were agreed on the principles of African liberation and unification, and the need for close co-ordination and cooperation in economic, social and cultural spheres, but there were crucial differences of opinion when it came to questions of methods and procedures'.

But it did not take long for him to be disillusioned with the new organisation:

There were those who advocated a gradualist approach towards liberation and unification, and wished to concentrate on economic and cultural co-operation, and on regional groupings; and there were those who insisted that there could be no genuine improvement in the well-being of the African people without unified political machinery to plan economic development on a continental scale.

Several signatories of the [OAU] Charter appeared far more concerned with selfish national interests than with the condition of the African people as a whole, and particularly with those still suffering under colonial and settler minority regimes. There was much talk of the inviolability of 'sovereignty', and 'territorial integrity and independence', regardless of the fact that most of our national frontiers are relics of colonialism, and irrelevant within the context of the African nation.

As the years have passed, these fundamental differences of approach and emphasis, coupled with the stepping up of imperialist and neo-colonialist pressures have led to compromise and delay in the OAU's handling of obstacles blocking the advance of the African Revolution. This has seriously weakened the authority of the OAU, and has caused growing lack of confidence in its ability to achieve the objectives for which it was created. In times of crisis it has failed to provide the dynamic leadership and decisive action expected of it (Nkrumah 1973: 250).

At the next OAU summit in Cairo, in 1964, Nkrumah once again tried to convince his colleagues to adopt his model of unification. All he could get was a summit decision to set up a commission to examine his proposal of a Union government. Another chance came when Ghana hosted the third summit in October 1965; this was an opportunity not to be missed. Concerned about neo-colonialism and the threat it posed to the success of his project, he released *Neo-colonialism: The Last Stage of Imperialism*, copies of which he distributed to delegates at the summit. Therefore, *Africa Must Unite* should be read together with *Neo-colonialism*, as, in the mind of Nkrumah, the two books were linked – one setting out his case for continental unification and the other warning his contemporaries about a new threat, neo-colonialism, which had to be defeated for Africa to achieve its unity.

Nkrumah was not deterred by a handful of countries that boycotted his 1965 OAU summit. Instead, he seized the moment and got the summit to agree to establish an executive council, a ministerial organ he considered key to his Union government. He could not get support for his common defence proposal, but at least he was encouraged by this small achievement, which he expected to result in an amendment of the OAU charter. However, he would not be in office long thereafter, as he was toppled some four months later, in a coup in February 1966, and forced to seek exile in Guinea, where he would spend the remaining years of his life.

Even when he was frail and in pain from illness, he never gave up. With the help of an assistant, he pulled together essential documents of his political and intellectual life, to publish *Revolutionary Path*, with this touching explanation from the publisher:

> This book, published posthumously, was compiled during the last two years of the author's life ... Many of the introductory passages to the documents ... were written when the illness which finally overcame him was far advanced, and when he was in considerable pain. The Conclusion to the book was dictated by him in October 1971, in a clinic in Bucharest, Romania, where he was receiving medical treatment. Kwame Nkrumah ... died in Bucharest six months later, on the 27th of April 1972 (Nkrumah 1973: 9).

It was only in 2002, 30 years after his death, that the OAU was finally transformed into a new body – the AU – with more authority and an expanded mandate, but still short of some key attributes of Nkrumah's Union government. The late Libyan leader, Muammar Gaddafi, championed this idea of Nkrumah's with some success, but was killed by North Atlantic Treaty Organization (NATO) forces in October 2011. Since then, the continental momentum towards a fully-fledged Union government has slowed down; the focus has instead shifted to a necessary project of 'reforms' of the AU, within the existing legal and institutional framework. The emphasis is on improving performance of AU institutions and their staff, as well as their effectiveness and efficiency, and finding a sustainable model for financing the Union.

Neo-colonialism

Nkrumah would be happy that the executive council and commissions for which he fought in the 1960s are an integral part of the structures of today's AU. Over time, the OAU model of continental unification became unsustainable for the reasons that Nkrumah himself had identified quite early on. It was just a matter of time before the OAU ran out of steam and was replaced by a new organisation better placed to deal with the challenges facing the African continent. When the AU came into being in 2002, it promised to be this organisation, to be better and more ambitious than the OAU in its founding statutes and to perform better, with a wider group of institutions covering most of the ideas of Nkrumah.

Even so, Nkrumah's notion of the Union of Africa was more complex and ambitious than today's AU. Besides its common foreign and defence policies, as we saw, Nkrumah also envisioned a Union with a common market and an African currency. It would be self-reliant, with its own resources generated through a common market and pooled resources; it would be industrialising and focused on cutting-edge technology and impactful infrastructure development and integrating the African airspace.

Still, some achievements of the AU would put a smile on Nkrumah's face. For starters, his 'common foreign policy' has inspired the AU's current practice of the African Common Position and the African Stand-by Force is an important development towards his other passion – the 'common defence policy'. The African currency that he spoke so much about, is still in the pipeline at the continental level, but the Economic Community of West African Common Market intends to launch its 'Eco' in 2027. The financial institutions provided for in the AU's Constitutive Act – the African Monetary Fund (AMF), the African Investment Bank (AIB), and the African Central Bank (ACB) – will put Africa closer to Nkrumah's vision once they are established. The recently launched African Continental Free Trade Area is still a few steps short of his African Common Market but, as the saying goes, half a loaf is better than none – and better late than never!

Nkrumah must have alienated many of his colleagues in the 1960s when he unsuccessfully tried to dissuade them from setting up their own, national foreign service and a defence force. What is the point of gaining independence, with sovereign territory, and then not having your own foreign minister and an army?

Many leaders probably laughed at the thought of such an idea. This may explain why this proposal failed to gain traction across the continent. Surely, many heads of state want to have a national anthem, their own flag and associated presidential protocols, a troupe of ambassadors at their beck and call and an aide-de-camp at their service. Above all, many of them need an army for their personal security and comfort. Nkrumah's proposal denied them these presidential niceties, the capacity a state requires to project its influence globally and the apparatus it must possess for its security. I would argue that this idea of federating foreign ministries of African countries and merging national defence forces into a single, continental entity is still not realistic and doable – even today. It was a tactical error for Nkrumah to elevate it as the focal point of his African integration dream. On common foreign policy, I argue in favour of the current hybrid model in which both the AU and its member states have their own diplomatic representation. Such a hybrid formula also works for the common defence policy – member states have their national armies that are in turn available to the AU for deployment through its African Stand-by Force.

Nkrumah has been vindicated in some of his contentions. Like today's African leaders, he believed that 'the Inga [Grand Inga Hydropower Project in the Democratic Republic of Congo] project could go a long way towards electrifying the whole of the African continent' (1963: 170). But he was also correct in saying: 'the Inga dam, a blueprint dream for the Congo, may not get beyond that stage without the co-operation of other African states, for no single state could afford to build it'. African unity was the only way: 'If the independent states had a united, integrated economic policy, the building of the Inga dam could be carefully planned to support an extended industrial growth, catering for a far larger population. Its cost would, therefore, be economically spread.'

Nkrumah predicted that China would overtake Britain and Japan in the long run:

China's rate of productivity puts her ahead of the declining imperial powers whose industrial extension, limited by their shrinking empires, has led them into the European Common Market . . . Industrial output in China increased 276 per cent in the years between 1950 and 1957, and it is estimated that if the relative rates of development persist, she will outstrip Japan and Britain in the not too distant future (Nkrumah 1963: 164).

He was so prophetic about Africa's prospects without unification that Chapter 17 of his *Africa Must Unite* could be mistaken for Agenda 2063, a programme developed in recent years by the AU for the transformation of the continent. This chapter reads like a document written just yesterday, for today's audience, and for implementation in Africa in the current period. Sadly, this shows how Africa has stagnated over the past six decades, while other regions of the world (and countries like China) climbed up their development ladder.

Another example of this fact is an incident that Nkrumah recalls in *Africa Must Unite*: 'When I sat down with my party colleagues after independence to examine our urgent priorities, we framed a short list. We must abolish poverty, ignorance, illiteracy and improve our health services' (1963: 118). These challenges that Nkrumah and his comrades identified in 1957 could easily pass for the priorities of most African countries today, including those that are supposed to be more developed, such as South Africa. Sixty years later, Africa is still where Nkrumah was in 1957! 'But one thing is certain,' he warned his contemporaries, 'unless we plan to lift Africa up out of her poverty, she will remain poor. For there is a vicious circle which keeps the poor in their rut of impoverishment, unless an energetic effort is made to interrupt the circular causations of poverty' (1963: 167).

As early as the 1960s, Nkrumah had already identified neo-colonialism as a real threat for Africa to contend with, to the extent of writing an entire book dedicated to this subject. Walter Rodney erroneously suggests in the preface to his classic *How Europe Underdeveloped Africa* that 'ideally, an analysis of underdevelopment should come even closer to the present than the end of the colonial period in the 1960s' (1982: vii). In truth, however, when Rodney wrote these words, Nkrumah's *Neo-colonialism* had been in circulation for close to two decades. Nkrumah had already attempted the two tasks Rodney identifies as essential work – an 'extensive investigation' of neo-colonialism and the need to 'formulate the strategies and tactics of African emancipation' from this investigation. Nkrumah's book may not have been exhaustive in its examination of the phenomenon of neo-colonialism, but it was nonetheless extensive in its attempt to explore this subject, including its mechanics of operation. He was concerned that, over time, if not countered, and without unification, neo-colonialism would take over and strangle Africa, and stifle the continent's forward advancement.

The primary targets of Nkrumah's *Neo-colonialism* were the African leaders he expected as the host of the 1965 Accra summit of the OAU. In *Revolutionary Path*, he points out to this audience:

> Three alternatives are open to African states; first, to unite and to save our continent; secondly, to continue in disunity and to disintegrate; or thirdly, to sell out and capitulate before the forces of imperialism and neo-colonialism. As each year passes, our failure to unite strengthens our enemies and delays the fulfilment of the aspirations of our people (1973: 125).

Nkrumah was clear in his analysis that

> we have learnt much about the old forms of colonialism. Some of them still exist, but I am confident they will all disappear from the face of our continent. It is not only the old forms of colonialism that we are determined to see abolished, but we are equally determined that the new forms of colonialism which are now appearing in the world, with their potential threat to our precious independence, will not succeed (1965: 128).

Nkrumah could see the clouds of neo-colonialism gathering over the African continent. His foresight told him that the happy moments of this newly acquired independence were temporary. They would soon be replaced by the pounding force of a new storm as the former coloniser returns to Africa through the back door and, once back and in charge, will stall, if not sabotage, Africa's development. He could see, in real time, the wave of neo-colonialism entrenching itself as African countries gained their independence, one after the other – each being lured back into the neo-colonial trap. As a head of state, he could feel the pressure of this new wave and the weight of its power. He was certainly not alone in experiencing this shift; the same should have been happening to his colleagues who, like him, had just achieved their independence. He probably felt defenceless and powerless in the face of this new threat – hence his belief that no single African country could tackle it on its own.

Four realities of his time are clearly reflected here – he lived through the early years of decolonisation and witnessed the formal departure of colonial officials.

Not long thereafter, neo-colonialism started rearing its ugly head. Parallel to this worrying development, the Cold War was intensifying, drawing many African countries into its vortex. Europe, in its own reaction to these trends, and recovering from the ravages of war and the humiliation of losing its colonial possessions, opted for a route towards continental unification. Africa's best response, in Nkrumah's view, should have been to learn from Europe and to take the route of unification. As Nkrumah predicted, today, Europe is a fully-fledged, prosperous union; neo-colonialism did take hold of independent Africa and, together with the impact of the Cold War, stalled the continent's development. The 1980s entered history as Africa's 'lost decade'.

There was another context to *Africa Must Unite* and *Neo-colonialism*. The early 1960s were a period of heightened anti-colonial struggle in southern Africa. In South Africa, the apartheid regime outlawed liberation movements in 1960, triggering in an era of armed struggle. A similar process of intensifying white settler repression was unfolding in nearby Zimbabwe, culminating in the Unilateral Declaration of Independence there in 1965, a topic that dominated debates at the 1965 OAU summit held in Accra. As Nkrumah was working on his two books, southern Africa and other parts of the continent were engulfed in the flames of mass resistance and armed struggle. He was thus intellectually absorbed and emotionally immersed into the struggle of these actors, whom he passionately called 'freedom fighters'. His writings and speeches of the time are dominated by this phrase as a recurring refrain, to the point that his *Neo-colonialism* was, in his own words, 'dedicated to the Freedom Fighters of Africa, living and dead'. He was a man with a cause, a revolutionary on a mission. Consistent with the outlook he espouses in his *Consciencism: Philosophy and Ideology for Decolonization*, his concepts and use of words were firmly grounded in an eclectic form of Marxism (Nkrumah 1970). He was not neutral or undecided; he was not diplomatic in articulating or defending his agenda; his mind was made up on the African revolution and the cause for unification.

Nkrumah wrote *Neo-colonialism* while he was still in power as a head of state. Its critique of this phenomenon is focused on foreign actors exercising neo-colonial control. He republished excerpts in *Revolutionary Path*, with a new, short introduction.[1] In *Revolutionary Path*, which he wrote when he was no longer in office, in exile, and towards the end of his life, he takes no prisoners with regard to what he calls the 'indigenous bourgeoisie' who are in 'league' with neo-colonialism. He was equally blunt in his 'Author's Note' when he introduced *Consciencism* during his exile, stating: 'The succession of military coups which have in recent years taken place in Africa, have exposed the close links between the interests of neo-colonialism and the indigenous bourgeoisie (1970: 1).

In *Neo-colonialism*, however, he refers to this class of actors simply as the 'neo-colonialist regime' or the 'neo-colonialist government', probably to avoid alienating his colleagues, who were his target audience. This book is grounded in dependency theory framework of the centre and the periphery in the world system and heralded the literature on this topic that would follow in subsequent years, such as Samir Amin's *Neo-colonialism in West Africa* (1973) and Walter Rodney's *How Europe Underdeveloped Africa* (1982).

Nkrumah's rationale was as follows: 'My purpose in writing *Neo-Colonialism: The Last Stage of Imperialism* was to expose the workings of international monopoly capitalism in Africa in order to show the meaninglessness of political freedom without economic independence, and to demonstrate the urgent need for the unification of Africa and a socialist transformation of society (1973: 310). Inspired by Vladimir Lenin's *Imperialism: The Highest Stage of Capitalism*, which he cites approvingly in the opening pages of his book, Nkrumah suggests that 'the neo-colonialism of today represents imperialism in its final and perhaps its most dangerous stage' (1973: 314). He justifies the use of 'last stage' in the title of the book: 'Neo-colonialism is a stage in the development of imperialism. In the sub-title of my book, I refer to it as the 'last stage' since I considered it the last thrust of imperialism before the ultimate and inevitable victory of the masses over all forms of oppression and exploitation' (1973: 312).

According to Nkrumah, 'neo-colonialism is more insidious, complex and dangerous than the old colonialism. It not only prevents its victims from developing their economic potential for their own use, but it controls the political life of the country, and supports the indigenous bourgeoisie in perpetuating the oppression and exploitation of the masses' (1973: 312). Furthermore, 'under neo-colonialism, the economic systems and political policies of independent territories are managed and manipulated from outside, by international monopoly finance capital in league with the indigenous bourgeoisie (1973: 313). In summary, 'the essence of neo-colonialism is that the state which is subject to it is, in theory, independent and has all the outward trappings of international sovereignty. In reality its economic system and thus its political policy is directed from outside' (1973: 314).

He undertook this ambitious intellectual project to justify, defend and reinforce his campaign for continental unification. Neo-colonialism was to Nkrumah the antithesis of unification because it relies on balkanisation, creating multiple, small and unviable states, which can easily be controlled and perpetually subjugated by the neo-colonial power. In his periodisation of this phenomenon, he dated its emergence to the years after the Second World War, attributing its origins to the class struggle in the metropole following the advent of the 'welfare state'. The emergence of this welfare state resulted from two compromises in relation to how classical capital had hitherto operated. First, after the war, in those countries, capital involved the state in the management of the economy for developmental purposes. Second, capital also made concession to the poor and working class of those countries, improving their living conditions substantially. This bought capital time and lessened class contradictions in the metropole. But it was in the neo-colonial territories where capital did not hide its true colours. Thus, class contradictions shifted from the country level in the metropole to the international sphere. Nkrumah believed that when Africa finally rises and confronts neo-colonialism, this will result in the crisis of capitalism in the metropole and its eventual collapse.

This optimism led him to regard neo-colonialism as the 'last stage' of imperialism. He thought that this phenomenon was just a temporary stage before the end. His logic relied on Karl Marx's notion of class contradictions and class war as being inherent to the capitalist system and he believed that, in the end, the exploitation and material conditions of the poor and working class would inevitably lead these classes to rise up and defeat the bourgeoisie and their ruling elite. Nkrumah thought the class contradictions and their associated class war would emerge in the relations between the neo-colonial master and its client states to the detriment of the former.

He believed that 'the system of neo-colonialism was therefore instituted and in the short run it has served the developed powers admirably. It is in the long run that its consequences are likely to be catastrophic for them' (Nkrumah 1973: 318). He was convinced that 'neo-colonialism is a mill-stone around the necks of the developed countries which practise it' (1973: 320). For Nkrumah, neo-colonialism was self-defeating and bound to hit back at states practising it, due to five factors. One, 'military aid' was the final stage of neo-colonialism as weapons given as 'aid' to the neo-colonial regime would in the end pass to the hands of the resistance movement, who would use them to topple the system. Two, the public education system in the neo-colonial territory, he thought, was set to produce an intelligentsia, who would turn against the system. Three, big power rivalry, so thought the hopeful Nkrumah, would lead some neo-colonial regimes to turn their backs on their handlers and side with socialist countries in the Cold War. Four, unlike in the past, when neo-colonialism could resolve its internal contradictions by simply reverting to the old system of colonialism, argued Nkrumah, this option was no longer available, doable or even desirable. And, finally, by its nature, and inevitably, neo-colonialism impoverishes the neo-colonial territory and this poverty would eventually culminate in a class war at an international level.

Nkrumah's optimism was justified. He wrote *Neo-colonialism* with the 1965 OAU summit in mind. He saw this event as a stage from which he would mobilise against the neo-colonial project and garner support for its defeat. The book had a purpose, his reasoning had a clear intent; the book was a weapon unleashed as part of his strategy to stall and counter the neo-colonial project, which was building up across the continent. He wanted his colleagues at the summit to see neo-colonialism not in defeatist terms and as inevitable, but as a phenomenon that has a history and particular mechanics of operations, and as a phenomenon that could be outmanoeuvred if Africa were unified into a Union. In his own words: 'Before the problem can be solved it must at least be understood' (Nkrumah 1973: 337).

The book was not an academic knowledge product, but a piece of intellectual work with a target audience and with an agitational intent. When he wrote it, Nkrumah had his audience clearly in his mind and his Union objective in full view. He was impatient, eager to see a United Africa realised very soon, but he was equally patient in his strategic approach as he put it in *Africa Must Unite*: 'The ultimate goal of a United States of Africa must be kept constantly in sight amidst all the perplexities, pressures and cajoleries with which we shall find ourselves confronted, so that we do not permit ourselves to be distracted or discouraged by the difficulties and pitfalls which undoubtedly lie ahead' (Nkrumah 1963: 143).

Looking back, Nkrumah was clearly mistaken in his optimism, as the phenomenon of neo-colonialism continues to this day. He underestimated the resilience of neo-colonial relations and the extent to which it could sustain and reproduce itself. At the time of his writing, he could not foresee that the working class and the intelligentsia romanticised in his book would be defeated through crude force and brutal repression or co-opted and captured to the service of the neo-colonial metropole. Above all, from the standpoint of the early 1960s, he could not imagine the socialist bloc collapsing and the retreat of socialism and its Marxist ideology. Notwithstanding this, Ghana paid dearly for *Neo-colonialism*. In the United States, the Johnson administration could not hide its anger at the book and its author, especially the chapter dealing with the mechanisms of neo-colonialism. In Nkrumah's own words:

> The US State Department reacted sharply to the publication of the book, and in an *Aide Memoire* protested particularly against Chapter 18 where I drew attention to the activities in Africa of the Peace Corps, the US Information Services, the US Agency for International Development, and to the World Bank. The State Department considered the book 'anti-American in tone', though it was neo-colonialist practices and not governments which were attacked in the book . . .
>
> The State Department followed up its protest with the rejection of a request from my government for 35 million dollars' worth of surplus food shipments. A headline in the *New York Herald Tribune* of Wednesday, 24th November, 1965 declared: 'Ghana Bites US Hand so Feeding Is Halted'. . .
>
> According to an article which appeared in the *Baltimore Sun* on 23 November 1965, State Department officials denied that the rejection of Ghana's request for food-for-peace aid was directly connected with the publication of *Neo-Colonialism*. But they did not deny that relations between the USA and Ghana had reached 'a new low as a result of Nkrumah's charges that the United States is foremost among the neo-colonialist powers seeking to exploit and subjugate the African continent'. What appeared to annoy the State Department was the timing of the publication, and the fact that copies of the book were circulated among the African heads of state and their delegations attending the OAU Summit meeting in Accra in October 1965 (1973: 310–312).

Conclusion

Today's generation can learn from Nkrumah's approach that African unity is a political project beyond race or racial identity and requires political activism, protracted intellectual engagement and popular mass participation to achieve it. A state-led approach is unavoidable and necessary because African unity is ultimately a state project. But a state-led exercise without political activism, without ideological content and without a mass base will not travel too far or too long in history.

In the end, Nkrumah was human and, indeed, a man of his time and the toxic environment of the Cold War. He was not immune to the contradictions and the trappings of a post-colonial state. But the power of his brain turned him into a time traveller to today and beyond. He believed that 'the twentieth century has become the century of colonial emancipation, the century of continuing revolution which must finally witness the total liberation of Africa from colonial rule and imperialist exploitation' (1963: x). He was driven by the force of this conviction.

The twenty-first century must therefore be a period during which Africa gets its act together and the continental unification that Nkrumah envisaged is a clear way out of the situation in which the continent finds itself. Without African unity, Africa will become a continent without the destiny of its choice; its destiny will be determined from outside – by forces that have no interest in the future of this continent.

Note

1.   See Chapter 23 of *Revolutionary Path* (Nkrumah 1973).

References

Amin, S. 1973. *Neo-colonialism in West Africa*. Harmondsworth: Penguin.

Coudenhove-Kalergi, R.N. 1939. *Europe Must Unite*. Glarus (Switzerland): Paneuropa Editions. https://www.cvce.eu/content/publication/2006/4/24/87035567-586c-4a12-99e7-6857ee13f146/publishable_en.pdf (accessed 23 January 2024).

Mazrui, A. 1993. 'Seek Ye First the Political Kingdom'. In: *General History of Africa, VIII: Africa since 1935*, edited by A. Mazrui, 105–26. Paris: UNESCO. https://unesdoc.unesco.org/ark:/48223/pf0000095906 (accessed 23 January 2024).

Nkrumah, K. 1957. *Ghana: The Autobiography of Kwame Nkrumah*. New York: Nelson.

———. 1963. *Africa Must Unite*. New York: F.A. Praeger.

———. 1965. *Neo-colonialism: The Last Stage of Imperialism*. New York: International
Publishers. Electronic version, transcribed by Dominic Tweedie for marxists.org and
converted to epub for marxists.org by Janet Blackquill, 2023.

———. 1970. *Consciencism: Philosophy and Ideology for Decolonization and Development with
Particular Reference to the African Revolution*. New York: Monthly Review Press.

———. 1973. *Revolutionary Path*. London: Panaf Books.

Rodney, Walter. 1982. *How Europe Underdeveloped Africa*. Washington, DC: Howard
University Press.

CHAPTER 24

Immigration between Post-apartheid South Africa and Nigeria

Prospects and Challenges

Bobby J. Moroe

This chapter examines the immigration challenges between South Africa and Nigeria and proposes how the two countries can make use of their bilateral relations to resolve them. It suggests that the agreements the two countries can use in this regard are those with a strong focus on people-to-people relations in order to create social cohesion.

There are more Nigerians migrating to South Africa than South Africans to Nigeria. This is due to the economic boom experienced by South Africa after the dawn of democracy in 1994. Instead of creating opportunities for immigrants, this phenomenon has created more challenges between immigrants and South Africans. With the increasing number of Nigerians in South Africa, it is alleged that South Africans are growing resentful. They have insecurities about the fact that Nigerians and other foreigners will take their jobs. This is a popular narrative advanced in defence of those who perceive immigrants negatively. Paradoxically, South Africans are known to look down upon menial jobs with low wages, while Nigerians and other foreign nationals accept such jobs. It is incumbent upon South Africa and Nigeria to mitigate this growing phenomenon. The two countries should influence their citizens and use their respective strengths and complementarities to learn to coexist and to work towards attaining the same goal of building the continent.

Contextualising relations between South Africa and Nigeria

The relations between South Africa and Nigeria are significant to both countries' international relations engagements. On the African continent, they are among the top three largest economies and globally they both yield massive influence in their own right. As the biggest economy in Africa, Nigeria boasts a population of 213.4 million and South Africa, the third biggest economy in Africa after Egypt, boasts a population of 59.39 million. Both countries face the task of supporting other countries on the continent to grow their economies and to reduce unemployment, poverty and inequality. Outside the continent, they face the difficult task of acting as advocates for Africa. Therefore, 'the success of political and economic integration in Africa rests heavily on the shoulders of these two regional powers that have both collaborated and competed with each other in a complex relationship that is Africa's most indispensable' (Adebajo 2017: 1). Accordingly, what South Africa–Nigeria relations are based on and how they could further be improved is important for international relations in general and their diplomatic relations in particular. Most important is how these relations can be harnessed in order to promote and accelerate people-to-people relations, making use of existing mechanisms and bilateral forums. Apart from being among the biggest economies in the continent, with great influence, the two countries also share strong historical relations, which pre-date the end of the apartheid era in 1994. In fact, their association can be traced back to the years of the struggle for freedom and liberation in South Africa, during which Nigeria was one of the foremost supporters of anti-apartheid movements, in particular the African National Congress (ANC).

This rich tapestry of history and affinity was a strong basis for the two countries to cultivate their post-apartheid relations, anticipating that history would drive their common course and desires. Despite a multiplicity of divergences in their post-apartheid relations, history has influenced and shaped their cultural relations judiciously, with frequent movement of people between the two countries. However, much more can still be done to enhance these relations in order to strengthen social cohesion.

The foundations of diplomacy lie in strong people-to-people relations: citizens of nation states are essential in determining the success of diplomatic relations between any two nations. It is therefore essential to create conducive avenues through which people can interact and thrive. Since the dawn of democracy in 1994, competition between South Africa and Nigeria has become a subject for discussion by many scholars, but there has been less analysis of their successes.

This skewed public discourse creates gaps in the narrative about the relations between the two countries. A number of scholars argue that the two countries will fail in advancing the African agenda if their relations are characterised by competition, as opposed to co-operation:

> Relations between South Africa and Nigeria have long resembled a roller-coaster without a safety bar. While Africa's first- and third-largest economies, respectively, have shared a close relationship, it is one marked by volatility and tension. Both countries are influential members of the African Union, and by extension, their role in the affairs of the continental body is critical. The tendency for the bilateral relations to affect their role at the African Union will have far reaching implications for the advancement of the continental Agenda 2063 (Landsberg 2012: 1).

Furthermore, Thomas Kwazi Tieku argues that 'the introduction at the Algiers summit in 1999 of two separate reform packages that were meant to reform the OAU in line with the foreign policy interests of Nigeria and South Africa set in motion the process that eventually led to the creation of the African Union (AU)' (2004: 249). This watershed moment highlighted the power and influence of both countries on the continent and the reliance on their leadership by African leaders:

> The relationship between Nigeria and South Africa is couched in the complex interdependence paradigm, in which the two states continue to depend on one another. The umbilical cord that joins the two straddles the economic, political, social, cultural and military spheres. Attempts by one to 'do it all alone' for the sake of self-interest will not only affect their relationship, but will also affect the whole concept on which the African Union, the brain-child of Pretoria and Abuja, is based (Amusan and Van Wyk 2011: 37).

African leaders have had to bury their differences and embrace African unity in the fight against colonialism and racist rule (Wapmuk 2009: 645). According to Olukayode Bakare:

The beginning of the twenty-first century marked a strategic shift in the conduct of Nigerian and South African foreign policies. Following the creation of the African Union (AU) in 2002, it is evident that the cardinal objectives of both Nigeria and South Africa's foreign policies have been to strengthen common African goals at the level of the African Union (2019: 4017).

The sensitivity and vulnerability of the two states in relation to each other depends on the issues at hand. While South Africa appears to be vulnerable and sensitive to Nigeria's fossil fuel and diplomatic support, South Africa's investments and technology transfer continue to be sources of Abuja's vulnerability and are very sensitive issues. As long as both states are dominant powers in their respective regions, there is always going to be a need for them to co-formulate some functional policy for African development. Leading the African continent without due regard for their own bilateral relations would be catastrophic, not only for South Africa and Nigeria, but also for the continent as a whole.

Historical relations between South Africa and Nigeria before 1994

According to Samuel Augustine Umezurike and Asuelime E. Lucky:

> Nigeria's relations with South Africa were of double standard during the apartheid era. The post-independence Nigeria and the apartheid regime in Pretoria relations were sour and confrontational, while it was friendly between Nigeria and the liberation movements in South Africa, especially with the African National Congress (ANC). It was more so because Nigeria adopted Africa as the centerpiece of its foreign policy, and committed itself to the total liberation of the African continent from colonialism and racism (2015: 65).

Making use of numerous global platforms, Nigeria never missed an opportunity to protest and condemn the repressive regimes given birth by colonialism and racism, especially on the African continent and, in particular, South Africa. Before 1994, Nigeria supported the struggle for freedom and liberation in South Africa, through the ANC, as well as other anti-apartheid movements in the country:

'Nigeria's diplomatic hostilities towards South Africa at this point were informed by the need to ensure the effective dismantling of the policy of apartheid embarked upon as official policy of Pretoria following the victory of the Nationalist Party in South Africa in 1948' (Wapmuk and Okereke 2013: 2). During that period, 'Nigeria had no bilateral relations with the apartheid government of South Africa as the country was a pariah state in the international community because of her apartheid posture' (Ebegbulem 2013: 32). Ogbonnaya Chibuzor and colleagues add that 'Nigeria contributed to the liberation struggle through the application of two major strategies which include (a) resentment and condemnation of the apartheid policy, and (b) the use and sponsorship of sanctions against the racist government' (2017: 61). Furthermore, 'Nigeria's confrontation and hostile engagement of South Africa began in the 1960s. The country was diametrically opposed to the apartheid system and it led the campaigns that culminated in the expulsion of South Africa from the Commonwealth of Nations in 1961 after the Sharpeville massacre in March 1960' (Seteolu and Okuneye 2017: 57). According to Chibuzor et al.:

> The Tafawa Balewa government (1960–1966) upon resumption of office in October 1, 1960, was faced with overwhelming pressure from both domestic and external sources to institute measures to check South Africa's apartheid policies. Consequently, Nigeria banned the importation of South African goods into the country and was instrumental in the political and economic sanctions passed against the racist regime. Furthermore, the ugly racial incidences in South Africa saw Nigeria spearheading the call for political and economic sanctions against the apartheid South Africa in the international community (2017: 61).

Joseph Chidi Ebegbulem comments: 'As a result of the pressure by Nigeria and other nations of the world, non-government organisations and influential individuals, the racist regime of South Africa collapsed in 1991, and the need to change the diplomatic strategy arose' (2013: 33).

The degree of the solidarity, support and sacrifice that the government and the people of Nigeria exhibited in the quest for the elimination of apartheid and the enthronement of democracy was such that Nigeria, irrespective of its geographical distance from South Africa, became identified as a frontline state in pursuit of a free South Africa (Ebegbulem 2013: 33). As a sovereign state, Nigeria had to sacrifice a lot of its economic advancement to support the struggle for freedom in the 1960s, with working Nigerians contributing a certain amount of money for the upkeep of ANC members who were in exile in Nigeria: 'Nigeria assisted the ANC with $32.000 in 1975 and spent over $61,000,000 million on the struggle against anti-apartheid' (Seetolu and Okuneye 2017: 60). Furthermore, 'Nigeria created the Southern African Relief Fund (SARF) in December 1976 to manage deductions from the salaries of Nigerian workers and mandatory contributions of students'. This fund was able to assist many South Africans in exile in Nigeria with the payment of medical bills, scholarships and other forms of daily upkeep. Essentially, all these contributions and sacrifices symbolised Nigeria's contribution to ending the apartheid regime and paving the way to ushering into power a new government, which would be led by its ally, the ANC.

Just like the present-day Tanzania, Nigeria believed in the total liberation of all African states and supported in word and deed the idea that until such time that all African states are totally liberated Nigeria shall not rest. Today, when altercations ensue between South Africans and Nigerians in what are now known as xenophobic attacks, South Africans are often reminded of this history and how Nigeria sacrificed its own comfort in exchange for the freedom of South Africans. Due to their perceived attitude and resentment towards Nigerians in South Africa, South Africans are viewed by Nigerians as ungrateful and ignorant of the history between Nigeria and the ANC. As a result, it is alleged that the majority of South Africans dismiss such reminders as simple blackmail and that the past is sometimes used as ane excuse to perpetuate acts of alleged criminality in South Africa.

Post-apartheid diplomatic relations between South Africa and Nigeria

In April 1994, South Africa conducted its first democratic elections, ushered in democracy, and Nelson Mandela was elected as the first black and democratically elected president of South Africa. Umezurike and Lucky (2015) argue that the days leading to the dawn of South Africa's new democracy brought about hope to Nigeria, especially the visit to Nigeria by President F.W. de Klerk in April

1992 to discuss bilateral issues, mostly trade relations. Although Nigeria was confrontational towards South Africa during apartheid, the country was willing to engage with President de Klerk in order to accelerate a possible transition from apartheid to democracy. At the dawn of this democracy, and in view of the support provided by Nigeria during apartheid, the only logical act of affinity from the ANC-led government was to reciprocate. Many Nigerians felt that South Africa should open its borders to receive the hundreds of Nigerian immigrants who were searching for a better life and, most critically, those who were of the view that they could contribute their skills and knowledge in building a new South Africa.

In brief, post-apartheid South Africa marked a period in which the country was expected to return favours to all the countries that supported the struggle for freedom and liberation. It was during this period that the country was building a new nation, introducing democracy, recalibrating its economy, consolidating and repositioning political power and ensuring that poverty, unemployment and inequality were cast into the realm of history. It was an era of hope and optimism for the entire continent and the people of Nigeria were desirous of being part of this history. Ebegbulem states: 'At the dawn of democracy in South Africa, Nigerians, especially the professionals, were part of those that started to migrate to South Africa. Part of the philosophy of those early migrants was to contribute to the much-needed nation building in post-apartheid South Africa' (2013: 33). Following the migration of Nigerians to South Africa since 1994, a new phenomenon in their migration patterns emerged. South Africa began to witness an influx of both legal and illegal immigrants from Nigeria and other nations of the world. The borders became porous and the number of immigrants from Nigeria increased, in part due to the promising economy of South Africa and the countless opportunities presented there.

The somewhat cold reception of Nigerians by the majority of South Africans seem to have annoyed Abuja. Ebegbulem argues that 'the Nigeria-South Africa confrontation reached the zenith in 1995, when the then South African President Nelson Mandela vigorously campaigned for the expulsion of Nigeria from the Commonwealth' for its human rights abuse practices (2013: 33). 'The key principles that underpin the South African foreign policy are those of human rights, democracy, growth, development and empowerment of the country's people, international solidarity and co-operation, non-alignment, multinationals, developing a stable prosperous continent, resolving conflicts by negotiations and developing a multipolar and just world' (Hendricks and Majozi 2021: 65). Due to its foreign policy principles being rooted in respect for human rights, the Mandela government condemned the human rights abuse in Nigeria during the execution of the Ogoni Nine.[1] 'Most western nations, alongside South Africa, imposed a number of sanctions against Nigeria, after she withdrew her High Commissioner from Nigeria in protest. One of which was a ban on issuance of visas to senior military officers and senior government officials and their families' (Chibuzor et al. 2017: 65).

In view of Nigeria's support for the struggle for liberation in South Africa, the latter's support for sanctions against Nigeria came as a great shock and compromised relations between the two countries. As a matter of principle, South Africa's support for sanctions against Nigeria in 1995 was not ingratitude for the years of support Nigeria provided to the ANC, but simply a human rights matter. Ironically, in the 1960s, it was Nigeria that called for apartheid South Africa to be withdrawn from the Commonwealth as a sign of protest against the apartheid government and its human rights abuses. Nigeria's response to South Africa's position on its abuse of human rights in respect of the Ogoni Nine was in stark contrast with its rebuke against human rights abuse of the black majority during apartheid.

As a result, 'prior to 1999, South Africa had a poor political relationship with Nigeria' (Ebegbulem 2013: 33). According to Chibuzor and colleagues, 'Abacha's untimely death on June 8, 1998, turned the events around between the two countries. With the emergence of democratic government in place in Nigeria, Nigeria-South Africa relations became less confrontational but friendly and cordial (2017: 65). Furthermore, 'Nigeria [was now] considered as one of South Africa's important partners in advancing the vision of Africa's political and economic renewal'.

The post-1999 era was known as the 'Golden Years' in the relations between South Africa and Nigeria. This was during the leadership of Thabo Mbeki in South Africa and Olusegun Obasanjo and Musa Yar'Adua in Nigeria. From 1999 onwards, 'the South African state built a strong relationship with the government under the leadership of Obasanjo and Yar'Adua. The relationship was also helped by the fact that Thabo Mbeki had formed a strong friendship with Obasanjo and Yar'Adua when he was in exile in Nigeria from 1976 to 1979 (Ebegbulem 2013: 33). In recent times,

> bilateral political relations between South Africa and Nigeria are on course, with Nigeria considered as one of South Africa's important partners on the African continent in advancing the vision of Africa's political and economic renewal. The 'Golden Years' saw the leaders of both countries traversing the globe spreading the idea of the African renaissance – focusing largely on democracy, development and security and seeking foreign investment to revive Africa's ailing economies (Ebegbulem 2013: 34).

Obasanjo and Mbeki perceived the urgent need for Africa's rebirth and they shared equal passion for the realisation of this goal. Their cordial relations laid a strong foundation and paved way for the recalibration of relations between the two countries. The post-1999 era elicited a need to reflect, reimagine and recalibrate a new approach to managing irritants and contentious historical issues between the two countries. Mbeki and Obasanjo were able to restore relations between their two countries.

In essence, the relations between South Africa and Nigeria will be impoverished if they are viewed within the narrow confines of their divergences, as opposed to convergences. Accordingly, these relations must be seen within the context of two sovereign states with a common ideal of building the Africa we want, rather than competing. 'Since the inception of democratic rule in Nigeria, South Africa and Nigeria have had encouraging bilateral economic relations. Since then, South Africa has emerged among the top investors in many sectors of the Nigerian economy' (Ebegbulem 2013: 34), accounting for approximately 120 companies. But the same cannot be said about Nigeria. Unlike South Africa, Nigeria does not seem to have taken full advantage of the socio-economic opportunities created by South Africa after 1994, except for the migration of Nigerians to South Africa in search of a better life. It is Nigerian immigrants who are making the most of the South African economy. Since 1994, they have built small businesses and contributed in their own way to the growth of the economy. Regularising their businesses through registration for tax with the South African Revenue Service

(SARS) and ensuring compliance with other business regulations of the country will enable them to further contribute to the growth of the economy.

Since the establishment of formal diplomatic relations between the two countries in 1994, over 32 agreements have been signed. As part of their monitoring mechanism, a bi-national commission was established in October 1999 at the level of vice president/deputy president to consolidate and strengthen bilateral, political and economic and trade relations between South Africa and Nigeria. In 2016, during the state visit to Nigeria by President Jacob Zuma, the bi-national commission was elevated from vice president/deputy president to head of state level, the highest level ever by any two nations. In 2018, President Cyril Ramaphosa undertook a working visit to Nigeria to meet President Muhammadu Buhari, in what was his first visit to Nigeria as president of South Africa. Subsequently, in October 2019, President Buhari undertook a successful state visit to South Africa at the invitation of President Ramaphosa. The ninth bi-national commission took place and the two countries reaffirmed their commitment to further strengthening bilateral relations. Almost two years later, on 1 December 2021, President Ramaphosa reciprocated by undertaking a state visit to Nigeria, where a successful tenth bi-national commission was held.

Contextualising the global and regional phenomenon of migration

According to Christopher Isike and Efe Isike: 'Migration is a global phenomenon which is as old as human existence on earth' (2012: 93–4). The human movement from areas of social and economic distress to those with better prospects for survival and self-actualisation has continued unabated. Migration, which is the movement of people over defined space and time, is a phenomenon that has been part of humans from creation. Humans have been on the move in the quest of overcoming the earth, so to speak, and to exploit existing resources and socio-economic opportunities for the wellbeing of humans (Ikwuyatum 2016: 114).

Today, more people than ever live in a country other than the one in which they were born. According to the *World Migration Report 2020*, as of June 2019 the number of international migrants was estimated to be almost 272 million globally, 51 million more than in 2010 (IOM 2019). Nearly two-thirds were labour migrants. International migrants comprised 3.5 per cent of the global population in 2019. This compared to 2.8 per cent in 2000 and 2.3 per cent in 1980. A lot of people from different countries do not migrate out of choice, but are forced by socio-economic and political circumstances. According to the United Nations High Commissioner for Refugees, the number of forcibly displaced people worldwide was 110 million in mid-2023. Of these, 36.4 million were refugees; 62.5 million people were internally displaced, 6.1 million were asylum seekers and 5.3 million were other people in need of international protection.[2]

In the era of globalisation the subject of immigration will feature prominently. Based on the various definitions of immigration, it is clear that a definite manifestation of globalisation is migration. The growing social, economic and cultural interconnectedness epitomised by the concept of globalisation has facilitated migration in ever-greater numbers between an increasingly diverse and geographically distant array of destination and origin countries. The impacts of migration are complex, bringing both benefits and disadvantages. For example, migration provides a supply of low-cost labour for host countries, while remittances from migrant workers can be an important source of foreign income for sending nations (Adesina 2018: 109). Nigerians who perform labour jobs in South Africa earn less than what South Africans would accept as monthly wages, yet they are constantly accused of taking jobs that belong to South Africans. Some have established small businesses and the fees they charge are more competitive compared to South African-owned establishments. Just like Somalis and Ethiopians, Nigerians who own small shops group themselves together, create a pool of funds, buy in bulk and sell their products cheaper. With their resilience, hard work and skills, it is alleged that Nigerian immigrants pose a tremendous threat to the job security of South Africans.

South Africa as a pull factor for Nigerian migrants

With the dismantling of the apartheid regime, and the emergence of constitutional democracy in 1994, immigration into South Africa increased sharply, particularly from neighbouring African countries (Ogunnoiki and Adeyemi 2019: 1). According to Aderanti Adepoju: 'In the early 1970s, Lesotho, Malawi, and Mozambique were the main suppliers of labour to apartheid South Africa. This pattern later changed, and the supply of workers from Lesotho increased steadily over the years to 50 per cent of the foreign labour in South Africa' (2003: 3).

Isike and Isike point out:

Since the advent of a democratic South Africa in 1994, it has become a new destination for African immigrants, thus adding to the increasing trend of South-South migration globally. African immigration to South Africa has increased not only through the regular immigration of skilled professionals and other economic migrants, but also through refugees fleeing from conflict areas in the continent (2012: 93).

According to Marie-Laurence Flahaux and Hein de Haas, 'Africa is often seen as a continent of mass migration and displacement caused by poverty, violent conflict and environmental stress' (2016). The striking disparities in economic development and living standards between South Africa and other African countries, and the remarkable transition to post-apartheid rule attracted migrants of all categories from Africa and beyond, despite the daunting problems of unemployment, crime, widespread poverty and the spread of AIDS. It is estimated that nationals from some 100 countries now live in South Africa. From West Africa came highly skilled professionals from Nigeria and Ghana to staff the universities and other professions, along with tradesmen from Senegal and Mali, including street vendors and small traders. These joined their counterparts from the Democratic Republic of Congo, then Zaire and Zimbabwe to swell the informal sector – in contrast to the traditional immigrants from Lesotho, Swaziland, Botswana, Malawi and Mozambique, whose nationals were mostly unskilled farm labourers and mine workers.

Anthony Messina (2014) points out that migration can be classified into four streams:

1) *labour immigration*, which is permanent, temporary or circular;
2) *secondary immigration*, which is dominated by family reunification;
3) *humanitarian or forced immigration*, including asylum seekers and refugees; and
4) *irregular immigration*, which captures the illegal entry, stay, and/or employment of persons within a country.

Of the four categories, a majority of Nigerians in South Africa occupy streams 1, 2, and 4. It is, therefore, critical to make an assessment of the funnels of migration and determine their relative benefits and threats to South Africa. The labour immigrants mostly comprise of professionals – academics, doctors, engineers and so on. Secondary immigration groups are usually Nigerians whose family members are married, working or studying in South Africa. Lastly, the irregular migrants are those who either obtain legal entry into South Africa and overstay their visa, or enter the border illegally with an intention to settle in South Africa.

Because of its middle-income status, stable democratic institutions and comparatively industrialised economy, South Africa hosts the largest number of immigrants on the African continent. Terry-Ann Jones argues: 'As the continent's strongest economy and the geopolitical leader in the region, South Africa has long been a receiving country for migrants from Europe and Asia, and is a major destination country for Sub-Saharan African migrants; 75% of South Africa's foreign-born population is African' (2018: 159). The country has long been a magnet for economic migrants searching for better job prospects in the region, and Nigerians have been part of those immigrants who took advantage of the opportunities presented by South Africa's growing economy. Young Nigerians are the largest immigrant population from Africa into developed countries, with thousands of Nigerians migrating every year.

For many years, labour immigrants and secondary immigrants have become assimilated and continue to form an integral part of different communities in South Africa. Even irregular immigrants, with their illegal status in the country, manage to find a way to live in various communities, with some success in integration. However, this category of Nigerian immigrants faces constant rejection due to allegations of their involvement in illegal activities. A common belief is that because they are undocumented it makes it easy for them to perpetuate such alleged crimes with impunity. This is a category of immigrants about whom Operation Dudula and others have raised serious concerns.

South Africa as a 'xenophobic' country: Perception, imagination or reality?

According to Jamie Bordeau, 'the word "xenophobia" comes to us from the Greek language. A Greek word "xenos", which means foreigner or stranger, and "phobia" comes from the word "phobos", which means fear. When you put both words together, you get the proper definition of xenophobia: an irrational fear of distrust of foreigners' (2010: 1). Xenophobia has an element of dislike, including hatred, of foreigners by a particular group, rather than individuals (Hook and Eagle 2002). Simply put, xenophobia is a latent or obtrusive dislike of foreigners. It is clear from these definitions that the most dominant key words are 'dislike' and 'hatred' of foreigners.

Post-apartheid South Africa has become synonymous with the word 'xenophobia' as a result of periodic reports about alleged attacks on foreign nationals in the country. This terminology has become so exclusive to South Africa that when similar acts occur elsewhere in the world, they are given different names. Shola Lawal wrote in the *Mail & Guardian*: 'In 1983, Nigeria expelled two million undocumented West African migrants, half of whom were from Ghana' (n.d.). It was out of this episode – which would have been termed 'xenophobia' in South Africa – that sturdy, checked bags into which Ghanaians packed their belongings were given a new name: 'Ghana Must Go'. Lawal says: 'They were cheap, ordinary bags. They had no name and came in blue and red, in big and medium sizes, all checked.' In South Africa, these bags are called 'China Bags'. To date, the naming of these bags has become more well known than the incidents of 1983 and 'the region is yet to confront its emotional baggage' (Lawal n.d.).

The subject of xenophobia in South Africa, and how it has been perceived, is highly contested – not only in the country, but the world over. While some believe that South Africans are indeed xenophobic, there are many who dispute this as a perception, rather than a reality, mainly in view of the nature of xenophobic incidents in the country. Examining xenophobic patterns in South Africa, research indicates that these are organised acts of crime that occur during particular periods of social instability and economic distress, carried out by affected groups. A dramatic outburst of xenophobic violence in May 2008 spotlighted South Africa's place among countries of immigration. According to an article by Shannon Moreira and Tamuka Chekero, titled 'Xenophobia Does Not Tell the Full Story of Migration in South Africa': 'It is estimated that since 2008, when the large scale of xenophobic violence first erupted in South Africa, more than 60 people were killed, and thousands left homeless by episodes of xenophobic violence in the country. However, this does not tell the full story of xenophobia in the country' (2022). Goolam Vahed and Ashwin Desai provide some of the underlying causes of xenophobia and argue: 'In a context where poor South Africans are struggling to find work and find promises of service delivery empty, it is African foreigners with whom they live side by side who become the targets for anger and frustration' (2013: 145). Ulrich Thum and Bastian Schulz explain this further:

> As a result of high unemployment and decades of isolation under apartheid, many black South Africans see little improvement in their lives in the 'new' South Africa, lacking prospects and unable to provide for their families. Immigrants from elsewhere are therefore accused for taking jobs from locals, competing for resources and running criminal networks (2019).

It would be inaccurate to suggest that such views represent the attitudes of the majority of South Africans. The local and international media have not been helpful in this regard and continue to use the term 'xenophobic' and to confuse the few with the whole, unduly shaping public discourse to the detriment of South Africa as a country, and South Africans as a nation: 'Research has consistently shown that many of the statements that fuel xenophobia are false. They fuel a national narrative of irreconcilable differences between South Africans and Africans from elsewhere on the continent' (Moreira and Chekero 2022). Furthermore, 'peaceful and mutually beneficial relationships between South Africans and migrants can and do regularly exist. Xenophobic rhetoric hides this reality.'

In September 2019, exactly a month before President Buhari undertook his first state visit to South Africa, acts of violence against foreign nationals were reported in South Africa and approximately twelve people lost their lives. These attacks were followed by reprisals in Nigeria against South African companies. Shoprite and MTN, among others, were attacked and more than 5 000 jobs were lost by Nigerians employed by these South African companies; 'Pretoria shut its High Commission in Abuja and its Consulate-General in Lagos because demonstrations threatened to get violent' (Fabricius 2019). These reprisals were mainly led by the youth. President Buhari raised the matter during his state visit in October 2019. To break the impasse, President Ramaphosa sent his special envoys to Nigeria to convey a message of apology for the acts of violence against Nigerians in South Africa. Subsequently, the South African missions in Nigeria started in earnest to meet with select Nigerian youth organisations in order to mitigate against future attacks on Nigerians in South Africa. As a result, a South Africa–Nigeria Youth Dialogue was established and officially launched by the two presidents on 1 December 2021, during the state visit to Nigeria by President Ramaphosa.

According to Vahed and Desai:

> The challenge for those wanting to confront xenophobia is how to build coalitions that transcend foreigner/local boundaries. This is made difficult because foreigners tend to coalesce into tighter groups as forms of protection which only exacerbates their outsider status. The prognosis in the short term for movements confronting xenophobia is the struggle to change attitudes, build defence units against violence, while agitating for better living conditions and decent housing (2013: 145).

Turning attention from areas of xenophobia and violence to success stories in the integration of migrants into society would go a long way to revealing the real lived experiences of migrants in South Africa. As matter of fact, there are similarities in local practices of Nigerians and South Africans that could be used to assimilate them into mainstream community practices and these have worked over the years. For example, one such unifying practice includes the sharing and promotion of indigenous health practices, food, dance and song. Gaining insights from such similarities in one another's culture can create a closely knit society of both locals and foreign nationals. Furthermore, through marriage between South Africans and Nigerians, many have adopted and embraced the tapestry of their different cultures, traditions and languages.

In order for the two countries to advance issues of common interest and mutual benefit, South Africa and Nigeria have made an effort to improve and support people-to-people relations through various initiatives. For example, on 1 December 2021, three key agreements were signed between the two countries: the Programme of Co-operation for the Implementation of the Agreement on Co-operation in the Field of Arts and Culture, the Agreement on Audio-Visual and Co-production and the Agreement on the Co-operation in the Field of Youth Development'. It is through this programme of action that the two countries will accelerate social cohesion, giving impetus to the work that has already been done by the people of both countries

In view of the fact that there are many Nigerians living in South Africa, the two countries have a great opportunity to cultivate a formidable workforce comprising of highly skilled Nigerians, who are capable of contributing their skills and knowledge in growing the economy of South Africa. The country already benefits from skilled Nigerian professionals and there are many other Nigerians who have established small businesses and employed South Africans, thus contributing to job creation.

Clearly, the success stories of many Nigerians living in South African is in direct contrast with the popular narrative about South Africans and their xenophobic tendencies towards Nigerians and other foreign nationals. However, what remains a challenge are the illegal Nigerians who continue to live in the country without proper immigration documents. Through their bilateral mechanism, the two countries can make use of the Consular and Migration Forum to find lasting solutions to this category of Nigerians in South Africa. Incidentally, the latter is a category that is often referred to by organised groups opposing illegal immigrants in South African, and they continue to endure the hardships of being illegal in a country of opportunities.

The relations between the two countries are under the spotlight and exemplary for many African states:

> both countries became two African giants that will champion the repositioning of Africa on the path of long-term development and reduce her marginalization in the international economic relations. Today, they are regarded as emerging giants in the African continent. Nigeria enjoys economic dominance in the west, while South Africa enjoys economic dominance in the southern part of Africa (Ebegbulem 2013: 32).

Chibuzor and colleagues concur:

> Nigeria and South Africa had made a concerted effort to position the region as a critical global actor in international and political and economic relations. It is therefore in the interest of the entire continent that immigration

matters between the two countries are viewed with circumspection, with great efforts made to prevent potential collapse in relations. The people to people relations between any two nation states remain the greatest resource for successful diplomatic relations – South Africa and Nigeria are not an exception to the principle (2017: 61).

Conclusion

Although South Africa and Nigeria are two of the greatest economies and influential nations on the African continent, they face serious challenges of immigration. There are more Nigerians migrating to South Africa than South Africans to Nigeria, but this phenomenon of immigration has created more challenges for the people of both countries than solutions. Reports clearly indicate that many South Africans have developed some resentment against Nigerian migrants due to their increasing number and allegations of their involvement in criminal activities in the country – especially those who are undocumented. This has led to nation-wide protests against them by movements such as Dudula, which is alleged to have terrorised foreign nationals in South Africa. When unemployment rises, compounded by crime statistics, attention turns to foreign nationals as the cause. This phenomenon requires urgent attention by the two countries to influence their citizens and use their respective strengths to learn to coexist and work towards attaining the same goal of building the African continent.

It is therefore critical that both countries work together in order to ensure that they put into place initiatives to mitigate against the negative perceptions of migrants. For example, the agreements referred to in this chapter should be an opportunity for South Africa and Nigeria to create social cohesion between their peoples. Through these agreements, programmes can be set up to bring the people of both countries closer to each other – to understand, appreciate and tolerate each other and their respective cultures. Although it is the responsibility of both countries to mutually resolve such immigration matters amicably, it is critical for South Africa to review its overall immigration strategy and its approach to managing immigration – legal and illegal. In order for the continent to succeed, both South Africa and Nigeria must find meaningful and mutually agreeable means of working together as leaders on the continent.

Notes

1. The Ogoni Nine was a civil rights movement from the Ogoni region and strongly opposed the humiliation inflicted upon the Ogun community by Shell Petroleum Company. Among the members of the Ogoni Nine was playwright Ken Saro-Wiwa, who made news headlines through these protests, condemning the abuse of human rights by corporate entities such as Shell. In 1990, he founded the Movement for the Survival of the Ogoni People, signifying a strong protest against the exploitative practices of the oil company.
2. https://www.unhcr.org/refugee-statistics/ (accessed 7 December 2023).

References

Adebajo, A. 2017. *The Eagle and the Springbok: Essays on Nigeria and South Africa*. Johannesburg: Jacana Media.

Adepoju, A. 2003. 'Continuity and Changing Configurations of Migration to and from the Republic of South Africa'. *International Migration* 41 (1): 3–28.

Adesina, O.S. 2018. 'Globalization, Migration and the Plight of Nigerians in South Africa'. In: *Nigeria-South Africa Relations and Regional Hegemonic Competence*, edited by O. Tella, 109–27. Cham, Switzerland: Springer.

Amusan, L. and J. van Wyk. 2011. 'The Complexities of Bilateral Relations: The Nigeria-South Africa Relationship (2000–2006)'. *Politeia* 30: 37–54.

Bakare, O. 2019. 'Nigerian-South African Political Strategic Partnership in the African Union: Harmony or Dissent?' *International Journal of Social Science and Economic Research* 4 (5): 4017–36.

Bordeau, J. 2010. *Xenophobia: The Violence of Fear and Hate*. New York: Rosen Publishing Group.

Chibuzor, O., B.O. Ajah, M. Onyedikachi and Q.O. Chukwuma. 2017. 'Xenophobia and Nigeria-South Africa Relations'. *IOSR Journal of Humanities and Social Science* 22 (10): 61–9.

Ebegbulem, J.C. 2013. 'An Evaluation of Nigeria-South Africa Bilateral Relations'. *Journal of International Relations and Foreign Policy* 1 (1): 32–40.

Fabricius. P. 2019. 'Can South Africa and Nigeria Reset their Relations?' *Institute for Security Studies*, 27 September. https://issafrica.org/iss-today/can-south-africa-and-nigeria-reset-their-relations (accessed 7 December 2023).

Flahaux, M-L. and H. de Haas. 2016. 'African Migration: Trends, Patterns, Drivers'. *Comparative Migration Studies* 4 (1): 1–25.

Hendricks, C. and N. Majozi. 2021. 'South Africa's International Relations: A New Dawn?' *Journal of Asian and African Studies* 56 (1): 64–78.

Hook, D. and G. Eagle. 2002. *Psychopathology and Social Prejudice*. Cape Town: University of Cape Town Press.

Ikwuyatum, G.O. 2016. 'The Pattern and Characteristics of Inter and Intra Regional Migration in Nigeria'. *International Journal of Humanities and Social Science* 6 (7): 114–24.

IOM (International Organization for Migration). 2019. *World Migration Report 2020*. https://publications.iom.int/system/files/pdf/wmr_2020.pdf (accessed 7 December 2023).

Isike, C. and E. Isike. 2012. 'A Socio-cultural Analysis of African Immigration to South Africa'. *Alternation* 19 (1): 93–116.

Jones, T-A. 2018. 'Sub-Saharan African Migration to South Africa'. *Proceedings of the African Futures Conference* 2 (1): 159–60.

Landsberg, C. 2012. 'Nigeria-South Africa Tensions Leave African Leadership Gap'. *World Politics Review*, 18 April. https://www.worldpoliticsreview.com/nigeria-south-africa-tensions-leave-african-leadership-gap/ (accessed 8 December 2023).

Lawal, S. N.d. 'Ghana Must Go: The Ugly History of Africa's Most Famous Bag'. *Mail & Guardian*. https://atavist.mg.co.za/ghana-must-go-the-ugly-history-of-africas-most-famous-bag/ (accessed 7 December 2023).

Messina, A.M. 2014. 'Securitizing Immigration in the Age of Terror'. *World Politics* 66 (3): 530–59.

Morreira, S. and T. Chekero. 2022. 'Xenophobia Does Not Tell the Full Story of Migration in South Africa'. *The Conversation*, 16 May. https://theconversation.com/xenophobia-does-not-tell-the-full-story-of-migration-in-south-africa-182784 (accessed 7 December 2023).

Moyo, K. 2021. 'South Africa Reckons with Its Status as a Top Immigration Destination, Apartheid History, and Economic Challenges'. *Migration Policy Institute*, 18 November. https://www.migrationpolicy.org/article/south-africa-immigration-destination-history (accessed 7 December 2023).

Ogunnoiki, A.O. and A.A. Adeyemi. 2019. 'The Impact of Xenophobic Attacks on Nigeria-South Africa Relations'. *African Journal of Social Sciences and Humanitarian Research* 2 (2): 1–18.

Seteolu, B. and J. Okuneye. 2017. 'The Struggle for Hegemony in Africa: Nigeria and South Africa Relations in Perspectives, 1999–2014'. *African Journal of Political Science and International Relations* 11 (3): 57–67.

Tieku, T.W. 2004. 'Explaining the Clash and Accommodation of Interests of Major Actors in the Creation of the African Union'. *African Affairs* 1 (103): 249–67.

Thum, U. and B. Schulz. 2019. 'When Two Elephants Fight'. *International Politics and Society*, 24 October. https://www.ips-journal.eu/topics/foreign-and-security-policy/when-two-elephants-fight-3812/ (accessed 7 December 2023).

Umezurike, S.A. and A.E. Lucky. 2015. 'Exploring Diplomatic Crisis of Nigeria and South Africa between 1994 and 2013'. *Academic Journal of Interdisciplinary Studies* 4 (1): 65–73.

Vahed, G. and A. Desai,. 2013. 'The May 2008 Xenophobic Violence in South Africa: Antecedents and Aftermath'. *Alternation* 7 (Special Edition): 145–75.

Wapmuk, S. 2009. 'In Search of Greater Unity: African States and the Quest for an African Union Government'. *Journal of Alternative Perspectives in Social Sciences* 1 (3): 645–71.

Wapmuk. S. and N-E. Okereke. 2013. *SAFPI Policy Brief 54: The Foreign Policy Environment in Nigeria and Implications for Nigeria-South Africa Relations*. https://www.academia.edu/27948263/SAFPI_Policy_Brief_No_54_The_foreign_policy_environment_in_Nigeria_and_implications_for_Nigeria_South_Africa_relations_Baseline_study (accessed 7 December 2023).

CHAPTER 25

The Legacy of Samora Machel

36 Years after His Death

Tinyiko Maluleke

Return to the source and the quest to name ourselves

The people of South Africa owe their freedom, in part, to the sacrifices of ordinary Mozambicans who, together with Mozambican freedom fighters, recognised that the freedom of Mozambique was incomplete until all its neighbours were free. Among the myriad of Mozambican heroes of our freedom, the name of one – Samora Moises Machel, son of Mandande Moisés Machel and Guguiye Thema Dzimba (Christie 1989), stands high above the others.[1]

Throughout the years of struggle, many of our leaders, from South Africa and from the broader region of southern Africa, found an oasis, a sanctuary and a place of restoration in Mozambique – personified in the revolutionary love, righteous anger, boundless energy and the wisdom of Samora Machel.

For these reasons, when southern Africans come to Mozambique, whether they come from Tanzania or Zambia, Namibia, Zimbabwe or South Africa, in more ways than one, their coming to Mozambique is always a homecoming. It is always an enactment of what the great poet Aimé Césaire dubbed '*un retour au pays natal*' (a return to the country of birth) (1983). It is always a realisation of what Amílcar Cabral called 'a return to the source' (1973) and way more than the purely literal.

However, there is a framing battle out there, a branding battle in today's language, in terms of which there are several portrayals of Mozambique. Some such pictures are not helpful. One framing, which both puzzles and perturbs me, is to be found in Stephen Emerson's otherwise useful book on the Mozambican conflict of 1977–92, titled *The Battle for Mozambique*: 'Mozambique is one of those flukes of history. Born of unbridled European imperialism and competitive Western nationalism, forged in conquest, and molded by factors largely outside its own control, the country and its people have rarely been able to determine their own fate' (2014: 1). I find it astounding and rather regrettable that a country like Mozambique, with some of the bravest, most determined, most resilient and most elegant people on earth is introduced merely as a historical fluke. The disagreeable suggestion that Mozambique originates from and was unilaterally created in the image of European imperialism and nationalism has to be contested. I do not know the Mozambique described in the opening lines of Emerson's book. I do not know a Mozambique that was ever so completely subdued by imperialists to the point of losing all agency and all will for struggle.

The picture of Mozambique that Emerson paints is certainly not the Mozambique of Eduardo Mondlane, Josina Machel, Graça Machel, Samora Machel or Joaquim Chissano. Neither past nor contemporary generations of Mozambicans are likely to see themselves in Emerson's picture. Have generations of Mozambicans – as Emerson himself admits – not waged an anti-colonial war in so many ways and at so many levels for more than 400 years? It must be remembered that when Vasco da Gama and his entourage, then en route to India, stopped in Mozambique from 2–29 March 1498, the initially friendly locals 'soon became suspicious and hostile, so that Da Gama and his entourage had to take flight' (Maluleke 2020: 23).

How can a people whose artistic industry gave us the musical chants of resistance that is Marrabenta, in the work of Fany Mpfumo, Dilon Njinji, Moreira Chonguica, Wazimbo and Orchestra Marrabenta – to mention only a few – ever be described in such debilitating terms as Emerson's? Generations of poetic truth tellers of Mozambique have waged a cultural war of resistance and these traditions of poetry have been taken up by young Mozambican rappers and artists of all kinds (Rantala 2016).

Creating our world in the image of Africa

I think Emerson meant well – at least I hope so. However, the Freudian slip with which he commences his book is indicative of the extent to which one of the important tasks that Samora Machel left for us remains undone as Africans – to create the world in our own image and not to let the world create our people and our countries in its own image.

Yes, as Africans we were colonised, but we never allowed colonisation into every corner of our souls. Colonisation does not have the final word on us. It never did and never will. Yes, we were brutalised in the twentieth century by King Leopold II of Belgium, who conducted a reign of terror in the Congo and by the German Kaiser Wilhelm, whose soldiers committed unspeakable atrocities in Namibia (Olusoga and Erichsen 2011). We never handed our souls and our spirits to the colonisers and imperialists, even in the face of their terror and their greed – movingly described and correctly characterised by Adam Hochschild in his *King Leopold's Ghost* (1998).

One of the greatest lessons Samora Machel taught us was to proudly guard our identity and our image, as well as constantly protecting our dignity. Integrity, image and dignity were central to who Samora was. The distinguished and decorated man of letters Wole Soyinka, in his book *Of Africa* (2012), has demonstrated that, no matter how much colonialists have tried to burgle and to distort the history and the image of Africa, again and again, Africans have proved that Africa is no dark continent; rather, it is the beholders who suffer from severe cataracts. No matter how much writers, missionaries and colonialists of the West have tried to paint us as everything they wish not to be, history has borne witness to our enduring dignity, our unquestionable humaneness and our irreducible humanity.

In his book *Butterflies & Barbarians* (2007), the late South African historian, and my good friend, Patrick Harries demonstrates how some Swiss missionaries working in South Africa and Mozambique, out of shocking ignorance, reduced local people to barbarians, whom they ranked at the same level as butterflies, if not lower.

As a case study, Harries focuses on the well-intentioned but widely off-the-mark books of amateur entomologist and anthropologist and trained Swiss missionary, Henri-Alexandre Junod. In 1912, the same year that Junod first published his two volumes, which portrayed black people as uncivilised, a group of black leaders including Pixley ka Seme (Ngqulunga 2018), Charlotte Maxeke (Jaffer 2016) and John Dube (Hughes 2011) formed the African National Congress (ANC) in Bloemfontein. Half a century later, in 1962 to be precise, several Mozambican anti-colonial and student formations met in Dar es Salaam, under the leadership of Eduardo Mondlane, to reinvent themselves into a powerful movement – FRELIMO (Frente de Libertação de Moçambique, Liberation Front of Mozambique).

Samora Machel and the Mozambican struggle

Sometime in April 1963, South African struggle veterans Joe Slovo and John Beaver Marks were forced into exile. After the establishment of uMkhonto we Sizwe – the armed wing of the ANC in 1961 – Slovo and Marks and hundreds of others left the country to go and receive military training and to return to apartheid South Africa as guerrillas. Their final destination was a city that was like a magnet for freedom fighters in those years – Dar es Salaam. Indeed, Julius Nyerere and Dar es Salaam were to Mondlane and Machel what Machel and Maputo later became for Oliver Tambo, Albie Sachs, Ruth First and countless other South African leaders and exiles.

But I digress. I was telling the story of how Slovo and Marks, together with 26 other South Africans, were scheduled to fly from Francistown to Dar es Salaam on a small aircraft, one day in April 1963. Just before their small plane left Francistown, something historic happened – this is how Slovo remembered it:

> A short while before our departing, a thin, energetic young man asked if it was possible to get a seat on our plane as he wanted to join the FRELIMO forces. JB immediately took the decision that one of our cadres should be taken off the plane to make room for the FRELIMO recruit. The recruit who travelled with us (and he remembers it very well and tells the story today) is comrade president Samora Machel . . . at that time we were not aware what valuable cargo we were carrying (Christie 1989: 23–4).

This is a story Slovo told often, including in his eulogy for Machel at his funeral. It illustrates that the ties that bind the people of Mozambique and the people of South Africa go deep and they cut both ways. Indeed, these historical ties of solidarity in the struggle against colonialism run in the veins and in the arteries of Mozambicans and South Africans, both figuratively and literally. If Slovo and his comrades did not realise how precious the cargo was that they were carrying in that small aircraft, when the founding leader of FRELIMO, Eduardo Mondlane, interviewed Machel in Dar es Salaam in April 1963, there was no doubt in Mondlane's mind that Machel belonged to a special breed of young Mozambicans, fully committed to the liberation of Mozambique.

In his preface to Allen Isaacman and Barbara Isaacman's book on Samora Machel, retired South African judge Albie Sachs described Machel in this way:

> Samora was a proud African, a proud liberator, a proud internationalist, and a proud and humane human being with great cultural sensibility. He had his faults, and the system in which he grew and that he helped to grow had its deficiencies. But flaws and all, *o Povo*, the People, are right to revere his memory. My generation honors and loves him for the way he transformed the nature of what an African revolutionary leader could be. He indigenized revolutionary theory, fought against racism and tribalism, and spoke passionately about the emancipation of women. He is loved by ordinary people in Mozambique today for epitomizing qualities they fail to see in most current leaders: his integrity, his warm, engaging, and culturally rich humanity, his independence of mind and spirit, and, above all, his profound and resolute determination to enable the poor to transform their lives (2020: 14).

Samora, 'a life cut short'

Samora Machel would have turned the grand old age of 91 [b. 1933] this year. I can imagine how leaders of southern African states would have been coming on pilgrimage to consult with him in Maputo, or better still in his place of birth, Xilembene in the Gaza province, there to drink from the fountain of his wisdom, forged in the battlefield and finessed in the stadiums and townhalls of this country, wisdom accomplished at many a treacherous negotiation table.

Thirty-eight years ago, President Samora Machel and as many as 33 of his compatriots perished, when the plane in which they were travelling from Zambia crashed into the Lebombo Mountains near Mbuzini, outside Komatipoort, South Africa, less than 200 kilometres from Maputo. The curious circumstances of the crash and the even 'curiouser' actions and non-actions of the South African government in the aftermath of the tragedy have been analysed and reflected upon in dozens of articles, books and book chapters – as well as several terabytes of sworn affidavits and recordings in testimonies before commissions of inquiry witnesses.

The apartheid government appointed the Margo Commission to investigate the crash and it 'concluded that it [the crash] has been caused by pilot error' (TRC 1998: 494). A Soviet team of experts concluded that 'a decoy beacon had caused the plane to stray off-course before it crashed into the mountains' (1998: 494). Too many questions have been left unanswered. Thirty-eight years later, these questions are well known, so we need not rehash them here. But the answers to these questions remain elusive. At least three of them – which also exercised the minds of the South African Truth and Reconciliation Commission (TRC) when the matter came up before them, are worth repeating:

- Was a false VOR (very high-frequency omnidirectional radio) beacon hoisted on the hill in Mbuzini, and if so, by whom?
- When the Tupolev TU 134A-3 took an off-course 37 degrees right-turn over the no-fly zone towards the hills in Mbuzini, why did the South African aviation authorities not warn the crew that their aircraft was not only going off-course, but was also in violation of international aviation rules? After all, the no-fly military zone was under 24-hour surveillance!
- Why did it take the South African authorities nine hours to inform their Mozambican counterparts of the accident? After all, South African government officials were reported to have arrived within an hour – if not within minutes – after the accident in which the head of a neighbouring state had died.

And yet, even the South African TRC, whose inquiry into this matter appears to have been a last-minute undertaking done in an untidy hurry, provided neither relief nor a clear finding. Instead, the TRC recommended that 'the matter requires further investigation by an appropriate structure' (1998: 502). So, it seems to me that until brave members of the erstwhile apartheid regime and/or their collaborators step forward and tell the truth about what really happened before, during and immediately after that plane crash, the precise details will remain elusive.

However, as I said on South African national television (eNCA 2022), just because we do not have the details, it does not prevent us from realising that the Mbuzini plane crash was neither plain nor ordinary. It had assassination and sabotage written all over it. Although a total of 35 persons were killed in that crash, the life of one particular, 53-year-old man was especially targeted – President Samora Moises Machel, the first president of Mozambique. This was a man who spent nearly half of his life involved in one war or another – 22 years in total – wars of liberation for his native land and wars of liberation for its neighbours, wars before, during and after independence.

To say this about Machel is by no means intended to underestimate the lives of the other people who perished on national duty with their president. All of them were compatriots of the highest calibre. Many of the fallen provided key and strategic services to the presidency and to the people of Mozambique. As such, they deserve the highest national and regional honours available. They, together with President Machel join a select group of African leaders who paid the ultimate price in the course of our struggle for liberation.

Machel shares this unholy distinction of being assassinated with the likes of Patrice Lumumba (Nzongola-Ntalaja 2014), Amílcar Cabral (Wong 2020), Thomas Sankara (Kongo and Zeilig 2017), Machel's comrade, compatriot and friend, Eduardo Mondlane (Mondlane 1982) and South Africa's Chris Hani (Smith and Tromp 2009), to mention but a few.

Turning an entire region into a killing field

The assassination tool has been deployed against several African leaders throughout what Nelson Mandela called our 'long walk to freedom' (Mandela 1993). The intention of assassination has always been the same: to take out leaders who are symbols of our unity and strength, and thereby to douse the flames of our determination to be free, by rendering us leaderless and in order to manufacture a state of fear and trembling. In a way, apartheid South Africa's death penalty was no more than a legalised form of assassination. Consider how frequently, how selectively and devastatingly, this tool of death was used against black people in general and black political leaders in particular.

The apartheid regime carried out many targeted or mass assassination expeditions into the neighbouring states of Zimbabwe, Mozambique and Botswana. Such was the case in the Matola Massacre of January 1981 and the repeated violent incursions into Gaborone, Botswana, all throughout the 1980s. They would carry out blatant mass assassinations inside South Africa. The

Sharpeville Massacre of 1960 is a case in point (Lodge 2011); the massacre of children in Soweto in 1976 is another (Ndlovu 1998). And consider, for example, how Fabian and Florence Ribeiro, Griffiths and Victoria Mxenge, Solomon Mahlangu, Steve Biko (Pityana et al. 1991) and Chris Hani were assassinated. But the apartheid regime's appetite for blood could not be satisfied internally; their blood lust had to be outsourced and exported into the neighbouring states, as we have already observed.

By the time of the Mbuzini plane crash, the apartheid regime had turned the entire region into a vast, low-intensity killing field. We have to understand the Mbuzini plane crash within the context in which regional stability was being undermined by the apartheid regime. Machel was seen as the last hope for regional stability and therefore a formidable stumbling block to the plans of Pretoria at that time. It is therefore plausible and possible that in the many clandestine meetings between Pretoria, Kinshasa and Blantyre in the mid-1980s, Machel was identified as a stumbling block.

Debating the issues

I have taken careful note of the analyses of scholars who are tempted to put the blame for the economic and political difficulties suffocating Mozambique in the 1980s solely on Machel and FRELIMO, in the process neglecting the devastating regional strategy of the apartheid regime, which had powerful international allies.

Among those who committed this neglect, I am thinking for example of the mildly critical essays of Dwayne Wong (Omowale) (2020). I am also thinking of Dan O'Meara's work in which he states that FRELIMO was 'extremely centralized and commandist, moving slowly towards a growing personality cult around Samora Machel' (1991: 97). Charging that 'much of the history of the early years of the independence struggle has been distorted, blurred, or buried by the dictates of [the] political', John Marcum's views about the challenges of Mozambique in the 1980s are more emotional than objective (2018: vii).

My own view is that we commit a serious error of judgement, when we read the trials and tribulations of Mozambique in the late 1970s and throughout the 1980s, including the killing of Samora Machel and his compatriots, outside the belligerent machinations of the South African regime at that time. This is the context within which the Nkomati Accord must be understood. For while the

Nkomati Accord may have been intended to flush the ANC out of Mozambique, it was also intended to seduce Machel into a false sense of security.

This, as the Mobutu Sese Seko regime was becoming more blatant and more vulgar in its support of Jonas Savimbi's UNITA (União Nacional para a Independência Total de Angola, National Union for the Total Independence of Angola). This, as the ideologically malleable Malawian regime of Hastings Banda was flirting with the apartheid regime and fantasising about replacing Mozambique in the bosom of colonial Portugal. As a result, Banda was becoming more daring and more brazen in his incubation of Resistência Nacional Moçambicana (Mozambican National Resistance, RENAMO) platoons. All of this happening under the spiritual, military and financial sponsorship of the brutal and well-resourced apartheid regime of P.W. Botha.

Samora Machel, the de facto leader of the region

In the year and months just before the Mbuzini crash, there had been several summits and heated meetings between southern Africa leaders – the so-called frontline states. The aim of these engagements was to address the problem of cross-border armed banditry, which was threatening to destabilise individual states and the entire region.

Machel understood first-hand that Malawi's support for RENAMO could literally pull democratic Mozambique apart. He understood that Mobuto's support for UNITA would erode the integrity of the Angolan state. It was these concerns that took Machel to Mbala, in Zambia, on that fateful 19 October 1986 – a return trip he would never complete. A month earlier, Machel had

> confronted President Banda [of Malawi] in the presence of his Zambian and Zimbabwean counterparts in an acrimonious exchange in Blantyre. President Banda was given an ultimatum to stop his activities or Mozambique would close its borders with Malawi. After the meeting, President Machel called a news conference at Maputo airport, saying that he would place missiles along the border with Malawi and would not hesitate to launch a pre-emptive strike if necessary (TRC 1998: 495–6).

Machel's detractors recognised how formidable a foe he was. Part of what made him formidable is that Machel combined several qualities. He was a political theoretician of the highest calibre and had the amazing ability to translate political theory into everyday language. He had the ability to tame the Portuguese language and forge it into a powerful language of mass communication. He was a military general with a proven track record.

Not only did Machel understand the Mozambican terrain from the Rovuma to Maputo, he had a firm grasp of the military balance of forces in the entire region at a level few of his peers could fathom. Above all, Samora had a deep, natural and instinctive faith in the people. This made him a true democrat. The people felt his authenticity and they reciprocated and reflected his love back to him. Effectively, in the decade 1976–86, Machel was the de facto president of southern Africa by dint of his talent and leadership.

To accuse Machel of building a personality cult or of being a violent warmonger, as some have tried to, is to misunderstand him fundamentally and perhaps to do so deliberately. Such people might as well accuse Mandela of creating a personality cult around himself by, among other things, waking up and deciding one day to go to jail for 27 years. Nothing could be further from the truth.

Neither Machel nor Mandela built personality cults – they had neither the time nor the need to. And no one has understood and articulated this better than Mamana Graça Machel herself. In a letter to Winnie Mandela, who had just reached out to console Mamana Machel when Samora Machel was killed, Machel wrote:

> I was still only a child, Winnie, when you first raised your fist against apartheid. Since then you have never wavered. I wish I had your strength and courage. In this painful hour I look for inspiration in your example. *Those who have locked up your husband are the same who killed mine. They think that by cutting down the tallest trees they can destroy the forest.* But history will never forget the names of Samora Machel and Nelson Mandela. The just cause of these two men will triumph, for the greater glory of Africa and the dignity of humankind (Christie 1989: xix; emphasis added).

For reasons similar to those advanced by Mamana Graça Machel, Thomas Sankara in his eulogy for Machel in October 1986, cautioned the masses against weeping, if only because there was at that time rivers of 'crocodile tears' (Sankara 1988: 242).

To demonstrate sorrow for Machel, argued Sankara, the people should do two things: remember Machel appropriately and intensify the struggle he died waging.

Little did Sankara know when he titled his Machel eulogy 'A Death which Must Enlighten Us' that he might as well be talking about his own death. Almost exactly one year later, on 15 October 1987, Sankara was himself assassinated.

As expressed by Albie Sachs, Machel 'had his faults, and the system in which he grew and that he helped to grow had its deficiencies' (Isaacman and Isaacman 2020: 14). But here is the seminal idea intended but not fully spelt out by Sachs. To say Machel had faults is to say something that is true of any and all leaders, any and all of us. To say that is to say the most basic fact about human beings. But when people say that about Machel, but do so in a tone that seems to suggest that Machel ought to have been more perfect than all his peers, this is grossly unfair to Machel. he was not a perfect person; he was only a magnificent leader. He was not a perfect human being; he was only a leader committed to the cause of the people of Africa. Machel was not flawless; he was only tireless in his quest for complete and total freedom. We should ask no more and no less of him.

I hinted earlier that whereas his enemies understood how formidable Machel was, his friends and those who 'worshipped him', and perhaps he himself, did not always understand the potency of his influence and the magnetism of his personality. As stated earlier, for all intents and purposes, for the decade of 1976–86, Machel was the unspoken president of southern Africa. Never mind P.W. Botha. Never mind Ian Smith. Never mind Salazar and Caetano. Never mind General de Arriaga. Machel had more influence in southern Africa than all of them combined.

Machel and FRELIMO's victory in June 1975 reverberated across the subcontinent. It changed the game and altered the geopolitics of the region, in fundamental and far-reaching ways. Zimbabweans, Namibians and South Africans owe a debt of freedom to FRELIMO and to Machel in ways that are inestimable. That is how the 1976 generation of Soweto youth was energised and mobilised.

Because of Machel, suddenly South African youths at that time – individuals such as Steve Biko, Mapetla Mohapi, Saths Cooper, Pandelani Nefholovhodwe, Misious Lekota, Aubre Mokoape, Strini Moodley, Tsietsi Mashinini, Abram Ongopotse Tiro, Muntu Myeza and Itumeleng Mosala – realised that freedom was attainable in their lifetime.

Conclusion

If Frantz Fanon (1961), using the Algerian war of liberation as his archive, decoded to us the price of freedom, the place of Africa in the world (1986) and Africa's historic mission in the world, I would like to suggest that we now face a somewhat new reality – sometimes spoken of in terms of decoloniality, now manifesting in the ineffectual independent African states in which we live – caricatures of the countries we imagined during the years of struggle. These ineffectual states are populated by leaders and followers who are mutually 'zombified' and together fixated in a space that is neither completely colonial nor totally post-colonial – 'postcolonies', as Achille Mbembe calls them (2015).

This thing called a 'postcolony' is neither donkey nor horse. It is like a bridge that has been abandoned mid-air. It is not the country we aspired to when we fought the wars of liberation. It is not the end that was intended. The African 'postcolony' is riddled with violence – structural and actual – from the north to the south and from east to west. At the most profound level, the crisis in which we find ourselves is throwing us back to the question of our agency, our ability or inability to author our own place in history and in the world.

Our greatest deficit as African countries today is not completely illustrated in our visibly rotting infrastructure. Nor is it apparent in and through the chronic civil strife, the periodic orgies of wars, the frequent cycle of massacres and coups, or the vicious cycle of violence in which we are stuck. Our greatest challenge lies in the extent to which our minds remain as unfree as our bodies. This is, of course, in clear contradistinction to the counsel of Bob Marley in his 1980 'Redemption Song': 'Emancipate yourselves from mental slavery – none but ourselves can free our minds'.

Freedom to think, to be, to do and thereby to prosper, was precisely the struggle of Machel and his peers. Without these freedoms, no amount of foreign direct investment, Fourth Industrial Revolution and everything related to it, will help us. In this regard, I want to note the contempt in which some African governments hold their citizens. This is not what Machel envisioned. The contempt of which I speak manifests itself in the shocking neglect of education and skills development. It manifests in decaying and unmaintained infrastructure. This contempt begets the contemptuous contempt of self – self-hate that causes Africans to demonise themselves and one another on the basis of tribe, race and origin. It is part of the self-loathing that has turned African men upon their sisters, mothers and girl children. The ongoing balkanisation and the warlordism that is tearing Africa apart is part of it.

These are the things we must fix, if we are to honour the memory of Machel properly. The true honour of the memory of Machel will not come from merely naming things after him; it will come when Mozambique, South Africa, Zimbabwe, Zambia, Namibia and Swaziland become the countries that Machel and his peers intended them to become.

To conclude, let me refer to one of the plaques on the wall at the Mbuzini monument, in memory of Machel and the others who died with him. The moving words of Graça Machel provide an excellent basis for our continued reflections on the legacy of Samora Machel, 38 years after his death:

> My children, my friends and I think that it is time to serenely bestow Samora to those who did not know him, to those who remember a little of him, to those who vividly remember him, whether because they worshipped him or because they hated him. It is time to bring him closer, we should look at him directly, we should recognize his virtues, his defects, and his real humanity. It is with pride that I wish to see his legacy perpetuated by future generations.

Note

1. This chapter is adapted from the Samora Machel Lecture I delivered at the INCM auditorium in Maputo on 21 October 2022.

References

Cabral, A. 1973. *Return to the Source: Selected Speeches by Amílcar Cabral*. New York: Africa Review Press and Africa Information Service.

Césaire, A. 1983. *Cahier d'un retour au pays natal*. Paris: Présence Africaine.

Christie, I. 1989. *Samora Machel: A Biography*. London: Zed Books.

Emerson, S.A. 2014. *The Battle for Mozambique: The Frelimo-Renamo Struggle 1977–1992*. London: Helion.

eNCA. 2022. 'Samora Machel: Discussion – 36 Years since Mozambican President Died'. https://www.youtube.com/watch?v=cWzLcgxqiVM (accessed 8 December 2023).

Fanon, F. 1961. *The Wretched of the Earth*. Paris: Présence Africaine.

———. 1986. *Black Skins, White Masks*. London: Pluto Press.

Harries, P. 2007. *Butterflies & Barbarians: Swiss Missionaries and Systems of Knowledge in South-East Africa*. Oxford: James Currey.

Hochschild, A. 1998. *King Leopold's Ghost: A Story of Greed, Terror and Heroism in Colonial Africa*. London: Pan Macmillan.

Hughes, H. 2011. *The First President: A Life of John L. Dube, Founding President of the ANC*. Johannesburg: Jacana Media.

Isaacman, A.F. and B.S. Isaacman. 2020. *Mozambique's Samora Machel: A Life Cut Short*. Athens: Ohio University Press (Kindle edition).

Jaffer, Z. 2016. *Beauty of the Heart: The Life and Times of Charlotte Maxeke*. Bloemfontein: Sun Media.

Junod, H-A. (1912) 1927. *The Life of a South African Tribe*. Two volumes. London: Macmillan and Co.

Kongo, J-C. and L. Zeilig. 2017. *Voices of Liberation: Thomas Sankara*. Johannesburg: National Institute for the Humanities and Social Sciences.

Lodge, T. 2011. *Sharpeville: An Apartheid Massacre and Its Consequences*. Oxford: Oxford University Press

Maluleke, T. 2020. 'Racism en Route: An African Perspective'. *Ecumenical Review* 72 (1): 19–36.

Mandela, N. 1993. *Long Walk to Freedom*. London: Little Brown and Co.

Marcum, J. 2018. *Conceiving Mozambique*. London: Palgrave Macmillan.

Mbembe, A. 2015. *On the Postcolony*. Johannesburg: Wits University Press.

Mondlane, E. 1982. *The Struggle for Mozambique*. London: Zed Books.

Ngqulunga, B. 2018. *The Man Who Founded the ANC: A Biography of Pixley ka Isaka Seme*. Johannesburg: Penguin.

Ndlovu, S.M. 1998. *The Soweto Uprisings: Counter-memories of June 1976*. Johannesburg: Ravan Press.

Nzongola-Ntalaja, G. 2014. *Patrice Lumumba*. Athens: Ohio University Press.

Olusoga, D. and C.W. Erichsen. 2011. *The Kaiser's Holocaust: Germany's Forgotten Genocide*. London: Faber & Faber.

O'Meara, D. 1991. 'The Collapse of Mozambican Socialism'. *Transformation* 14: 82–103.

Pityana, B., M. Ramphele, M. Mpumlwana and L. Wilson (eds). 1991. *Bounds of Possibility: The Legacy of Steve Biko and Black Consciousness*. Cape Town: David Philip.

Rantala, J. 2016. 'Hidrunisa Samora': Invocations of a Dead Political Leader in Maputo Rap'. *Journal of Southern African Studies* 42 (6): 1161–77.

Sankara, T. 1988. *Thomas Sankara Speaks*. Cape Town: Kwela Books.

Smith, J. and B. Tromp. 2009. *Hani, A Life Too Short*. Johannesburg: Jonathan Ball.

Soyinka, W. 2012. *Of Africa*. New Haven: Yale University Press.

TRC (Truth and Reconciliation Commission). 1998. *Truth and Reconciliation Commission Report, Volume 2*. https://www.justice.gov.za/trc/report/finalreport/volume%202.pdf (accessed 8 December 2023).

Wong, D. (Omowale). 2020. *Essays on Amílcar Cabral and Samora Machel*. Kindle edition.

CHAPTER 26

African Lingua Francas

Language and Culture as Instruments for Regional Integration – the Example of Swahili

Muxe Nkondo

This chapter has two interrelated objectives: to discuss the concept of lingua franca as an instrument for regional integration, and to examine and explore its implications for Pan-Africanism. However, certain factors should be considered. Governments will only buy into it if they believe that the regional integration of African lingua francas will provide them with better ways of achieving greater efficiency, managing risk or enabling innovation and learning. The possible relationships between the various governments, and how they manage the integration, are critical to its success. This will assist in determining what activities should be carried out in each state, and which together. Finally, in co-ordinating and controlling interactions, it is necessary to consider the steps necessary to become efficient integrative structures in a region that is increasingly globalised.

In this chapter I offer an account of regional integration and its implications for Pan-Africanism. I consider regional integration as a historical process, which involves the widening, deepening and potential impact of continent-wide interconnectedness. This process, however, is highly uneven, so far from implying the evolution of a more co-operative continent, it may generate powerful sources of tension, conflict and fragmentation. That is why I explore how transformation can be brought about by the promotion of African lingua francas. It will not leave African politics unaltered. These two forces can bring about a conceptual shift in our thinking, which is required to grasp the nature of the changes envisaged. This conceptual shift involves embracing the idea of African lingua francas and regional integration – the politics of linguistic diversity and complementarity as integral to regional relations and diplomacy. In the process, many of the traditional language policy assumptions require rethinking since power is no longer simply organised along Eurocentric lines. Furthermore, the persistence of Western hegemony has created a distorted African politics in which the interests of the few more often than not take precedence over the interests of the majority of the people. Whether a more just and democratic regional politics can be fashioned out of contemporary regional conditions, is a matter of intense debate among development economists, diplomats and activists.

Regional integration assumes that decision-making is based on mutual benefit and mutual recognition, seeks to maximise complementary differences and minimises conflict. However, in the real world, these may not be justifiable assumptions. It would probably be more productive in discussing the rationale and strategy for regional integration to move away from simple alternatives, such as decentralisation or centralisation, since such dichotomies do not capture well enough the fluid but clear objective of regional integration, so as to get dispersed activities, such as disaggregated departments and diplomacy units, to truly work together. The configuration and co-ordination of the activities of regional institutional arrangements provides a more daunting and more complex task than is involved in carrying out such an activity on a purely national scale. However, as is implicit in the concept of regional integration, it has more choices and options with regard to contingencies than are available to a national department. It calls for strategic flexibility; it also has more choices and options with regard to planning.

Regional integration – simply the widening, deepening and speeding up of Pan-African interconnections – is a co-ordination issue in the management of regional politics. Some argue that it will bring about the demise of the sovereign nation state as regional and global forces undermine the ability of governments to control their own economies, and argue that states and geopolitics remain the principal forces shaping the regional and global order. This chapter takes a rather different approach – an integrative perspective – arguing that the regional integration approach acknowledges that it is leading not so much to the demise of the sovereign state but, rather, to the regionalisation of African politics in which the traditional distinction between national and regional affairs is no longer valid. Understanding these conditions, politics in a nation state, it would seem, are related to politics everywhere in the region. Thus, orthodox approaches to the management of regional relations – which are constructed upon this very distinction – provide, at best, only a partial insight into the real nature of the functioning of the current regional and global order.

Framing regional integration on mutual recognition principles

This is a practical initiative aimed at framing regional integration by basing it on principles of mutual recognition, which means recognising each other in a world of differences and distances. There is a powerful normative impetus to take seriously the ideals of mutual recognition, responsibility to and for the other, and to mobilise social cohesion and solidarity in a world of differences. Mutual recognition offers better resources for ensuring that policy aims are tested for their impact on the actual lives of people than the liberal capitalist tradition, which is grounded in individualism and competition (Eze 1998; Nkondo 2007). Mutual recognition philosophy is optimistic at its core, supplying impetus to the ideas of fundamental change and development in social, economic and political relations. This can be achieved by reshaping the malleable aspects of the human psyche in accordance with universally justifiable mutual recognition values.

In the period defined by *Agenda 2063* (AU 2013), African governments will face greater challenges as a result of deepening poverty, widening unemployment, enduring inequality, systemic and subjective violence against women and the global flow of capitalist forces. To enhance regional integration and solidarity, concerted efforts must be taken to integrate mutual recognition principles into national, regional and global development plans, as well as to facilitate the development of programmes using the mutual recognition approach. The imperative encompasses the two critical thrusts:

1) Building caring and cohesive communities within and across state borders, recognition of the humanity of the other, deepening understanding of various forms of being human, and reverence for life.

2) Developing an economic order based on the eradication of Western hegemony and eliminating structural inequalities and pursuing a regional policy that inculcates feeling for the continent as a home, and setting out regional integration as the condition in which feeling for and after the other arises as an ethical imperative – and doing this by grounding policy and legislation in an indigenous African philosophy.

This mutual recognition imperative incorporates the critical thrusts of previous Pan-African strategies, such as Back-to-Africa, Africa Unite, Negritude, indigeneity, back-to-basics, authenticity, African socialism, African humanism, Ujamaa, return-to-roots, Black Consciousness and the African Renaissance. It could lead to innovative public reasoning, which would have significant implications for diplomacy and inter-state relations. Fortunately, mutual recognition is not limited to Africa, but has become important in most discourses on human relations the world over (Levinas 2006; Ricoeur 1990; Buber 1970). It is a critical resource for the African Union (AU), which is grappling with finding African solutions to African problems as the foundation of freedom and justice.

Accordingly, right at the beginning, I examine and interrogate the dominance of Western languages and knowledge systems in inter-state relations in Africa. The focus is on the epistemological, social and ethical underpinnings and the attendant regional relations policy and political consequences of a Eurocentric approach to the interrelated areas of current concern in decolonisation discourse – the reliance on Western languages as lingua francas in Africa and the hegemony of Western science and technology. My argument about the vital importance of African lingua francas and knowledge systems in the integration of the various nations:

- is guided by the objective to focus policy on the complex relationship between language, knowledge, power and ethics;
- appreciates the need to provide a critical overview of the limitations of Western hegemonic approaches, replacing them with fundamentally transformative ways of knowing and doing;
- notes that linguistic and cognitive justice has been at the core of the decolonisation discourse since the 1950s, a field of study that has always taken stances in support of linguistic and epistemic diversity and has also worked in solidarity with Pan-Africanism to overcome linguistic and epistemic inequalities;
- recognises the deeply rooted nature of these inequalities in African political economies, as well as the need to develop a more responsive understanding of the intricate relationship between language, knowledge systems and power;
- recognises, further, the need to shift away from the idea of knowledge systems and languages as bounded and separate objects, towards

languaging and knowledging as indeterminate processes that are constantly in motion and continually becoming something else, with the aim of opening up spaces for the legitimation of new subjectivities and inter-subjectivities;

- realises the importance of revealing how the investigation of linguistic and epistemic systems in regional politics enables us to gain a deeper understanding of the origins and the foundations of social and economic inequality in Africa, and so define linguistic and knowledge systems as key resources that, under certain political conditions, can be exchanged for other symbolic or material resources;

- realises, further, how language and knowledge systems have become instrumental for the regulation of an individual's access to the production and consumption of resources, and how language and knowledge systems are evaluated, as well as the logics and technologies regulating an individual's access to resources, where a price is placed on language and knowledge systems;

- is mindful of the fact that concern about the importance of language and knowledge systems entails a problematisation of the consequences of the language and the knowledge system we use, mediated through communication and cognition, and the costs implied in terms of who benefits or loses from the various forms of knowledge and language, and so argue for an increased reflection regarding the effect that language and knowledge systems have under current political, social and economic conditions, and how they nourish and authorise those practices that allow forms of linguistic and epistemic difference to be viewed as appropriate, and thus become invisible; and

- draws lessons about the integrative power of Africa lingua francas from the Swahili experience.

Functions of African lingua francas and knowledge systems in regional integration policies and practices

The functions and contexts of African lingua francas and knowledge systems are so many and so various that the task of cataloguing them is daunting. How can we make use of this diversity? These functions appear to range from the individual (a strong sense of identity can affect the way we feel and the way we relate to others and manage our lives) to the social (they can facilitate the co-ordination of large numbers of people and help to forge a sense of collective identity). They also cover a vast middle ground in which relationships between self and other, or between the individual and the collective, are played out. In addition, they contribute to the continuity and stability of cultures, as well to the resilience of societies. The individual is implicated in the social and the social in the personal, and a strong sense of identity provides, in this case, a tool for negotiating and mediating regional integration across the continent. These functions cannot be reduced to one: it is not simply that one is incapable of specifying the functions of a strong sense of identity; a sense of self depends for its efficacy precisely on the indeterminacy of its functions and value.

Since the concept of regional integration, in current discourses, functions as a metonym of Pan-Africanism, we should think of Africa as a community of meanings, a social and political imaginary, in the rich web of human relations. By 'social and political imaginary', I mean the normative order underlying African political society derived from the nature of its constitutive members. People are rational, sociable agents who are meant to collaborate in peace to their mutual benefit. Starting from ancient, pre-colonial times, this idea has come more and more to dominate our political thinking, and the way we imagine our society, what it is in aid of and how it came to be. It offers an idea of moral order, and tells us how we ought to live together in society. It stresses the obligations and responsibilities which we have as individuals in regard to each other (Nabudere 2011; Mudimbe 1988).

Political authority itself is legitimate only because it was consented to by individuals (the original social contract) and this contract creates binding obligations and responsibilities in virtue of the pre-existing principle that obligations have to be met (Taylor 2007). Thus, whatever its 'truth' in terms of its scientific validity, it is through its discursive operations that the social and political imaginary gives meaning to Pan-Africanism, makes a certain kind of sense to regional integration, constructs a regional order of intelligibility, an archaeology of values and principles, organises our social, economic and political practices within the region, and thus has come to acquire real social and political significance (Foucault 1972, 1980).

This affirmation of African languages and knowledge systems signals a break with the discourse of Western hegemony against which liberation struggles were fought. Through this, Western languages and knowledge systems are seriously dislocated and put permanently 'under African eyes' (to reverse the title of Joseph Conrad's well-known novel), by the discourse on African languages as languages of knowledge and African knowledge systems as science and technology grounded in the principles of probability and verification (Ndlovu-Gatsheni 2018; Wolfreys 2004).

The capabilities approach: The pragmatic turn

In light of this, I explore a set of interrelated ideas concerning the foundations and the possibilities of African lingua francas and knowledge management systems in a multicultural, multilingual and polyepistemic world (Abimbọla 2019). In particular, I am curious about their capacity to advance a person's capability to function in the Fourth Industrial Revolution – what a person can do or can be as a direct result of a strong sense of African capabilities. I argue against the more standard concentration on authenticity (as in prevalent Afrocentric formulations). Insofar as authenticity has a role (and it certainly does), this can be seen in terms of its direct connection with happiness and well-being; in particular, first, the political importance of authenticity and, second, the socio-psychological importance of authenticity (in its various forms, such as self-pride, personal dignity and integrity).

The current discourse on 'Africanness' is concerned with culture and identity. The capabilities approach investigates how Africans, through African languages and knowledge systems, are able to make commodities, how they are able to establish command over commodities and what they get out of commodities. The determination of whether a person will be better off supplied with all the resources of African lingua francas and knowledge systems is the starting point of the investigation into the power and political economy of African epistemology in our time.

Different approaches can be used to assess the possibilities of a particular cultural, linguistic and knowledge system in the knowledge economy: is she or he well-off as a result? Can he or she compete successfully with others using different cultural, linguistic and knowledge systems? These distinct questions provide an interesting focus on current and future challenges facing Pan-Africanism. The discourse on Africanness has tended to eschew the distinctions implied in these questions and make do with a limited assessment of African heritage. The terms 'happiness', 'well-being' and 'advantage' do, of course, have a range of meanings, defined by both neo-liberal and development economists. They are used here in the sense in which Amartya Sen uses them:

> 'Well-being' is concerned with a person's achievement: how 'well' is his or her 'being'? 'Advantage' refers to the real opportunities that the person has, especially compared with others. The opportunities are not judged only by the results achieved, and therefore not just by the level of well-being achieved. It is possible for a person to have genuine advantage and still to 'muff' them. Or to sacrifice one's freedom to achieve a high level of well-being. The notion of advantage deals with a person's real opportunities compared with others. The freedom to achieve well-being is closer to the notion of advantage than wellbeing itself (Natarajan 2014: 13).

The example of Swahili as a lingua franca

The major challenge is how to deal with the multiplicity of languages that has created problems for inter-state relations in Africa. Because of this, we have been forced to use Western languages – English, French, German, Portuguese – as lingua francas. The use of Swahili as a case study is experimental and pragmatic in the sense that we seek to bring regional integration into the space of diplomacy and inter-state relations. It serves to explore concrete trajectories through which regional integration can be negotiated and mediated. Fortunately, the history of Swahili – as it moved from North Africa through East Africa to Central Africa – points to opportunities and possibilities in the development of African lingua francas in other parts of the continent (Mesthrie 2015).

What has been the impact of Swahili literacy in regional relations? What are its distinguishing features as a lingua franca? How have governments, civil society and markets worked together, sharing responsibilities and using a common language? How has it affected the way people in those regions relate to each other? Would this help erase the sense of African languages as bounded and territorialised entities that the West has used to categorise and divide African people and communities and impose a Eurocentric hegemonic order?

The concept of African lingua francas is potentially a powerful regional integrative force. Regional African language commons would be a shared pasture, a regional language learning site inscribed concretely as a social, political and ethical co-ordinate of an alternative, fundamentally transformative inter-state order. African lingua francas would not be a narrow, exclusive space for an inner circle – for members only narrowly conceived; it would be a linguistically and politically produced space of an inner, responsive and hospitable disposition to difference. The sense of transnational, trans-territorial citizenship could then be inculcated and so expand Pan-African solidarity. African lingua francas would stabilise our understanding of ourselves as belonging together, brought together by the contingency of history and geography. They would allow us to insert ourselves in discourses on Pan-Africanism and decolonisation: this undertaking would be ensured by tracing and watching Swahili as it moves across time and place.

On the premise that language has the power to make and remake worlds (Gluck and Tsing 2009), the AU should use Swahili as a case study to highlight the possibility of using African languages as lingua francas to ground regional integration in a common language. The approach is consciously empirical and experimental, in that in rigorously developing African lingua francas across state borders, it would mobilise, at ground level, mutual recognition and solidarity. There is no better guide than Swahili, given its history, of how lingua francas can be used as a resource for regional integration, and in the process demonstrate the political and social power of language (Gluck and Tsing 2009). Lessons could also be drawn from how African languages have functioned in other environments – in migration, urbanisation, cosmopolitisation and in the diaspora (May 2017; Ndhlovu 2017; Gluck and Tsing 2009).

The standard ideological framework that came with industrialisation, over and above the imposition of the Eurocentric state system, makes the development of African lingua francas urgent and necessary. The idea of promoting African lingua francas challenges the basic tenets that have informed language policy even beyond the demise of colonialism in its overt structural forms. Instead, it assumes a post-structuralist perspective that questions colonial definitions of African languages and speech communities, revealing the socio-political context that led to the misleading yet dominant socio-linguistic concepts, and offers instead a framework for the development of African lingua francas. Neville Alexander's work on the possibilities of an African lingua franca in South Africa is illuminating (Mesthrie 2015).

The education of mutual recognition and the advantage of pragmatism

Much of the scholarship around African languages and knowledge systems has focused on the philosophical, cultural and psychological aspects of language and knowledge, rather than a pragmatic consideration of the ways in which language and knowledge systems can be used within particular social, economic and political contexts (Nabudere 2011). Being pragmatic in the discourse on linguistic and epistemic systems, means, in this instance, assessing how African languages and knowledge systems can function in inter-state relations in Africa. To address this question, we need to develop a practical and analytical framework that helps us to assess the capabilities of African languages and knowledge systems in the concrete business of addressing existential needs, such as food and health security, comfortable accommodation, communication, reliable and affordable public transport, free quality education for the poor, and so on. That way, African languages and knowledge systems become tools that we can use to make things happen in our lives (Rorty 1989; Morris 2013).

One way of coming to terms with regional integration can be seen in the necessarily patient working through of the question of hegemonic Eurocentric language policy and epistemology. As indicated earlier, this has to do with the recognition of the strategic political importance of African lingua francas and knowledge systems – their capabilities. Following on from this, there is acknowledged here the question of complementary difference and equivalences before any political account. What are the specific capabilities of African lingua francas and knowledge systems? This would be a significant improvement on the Western approach and would help to construct a template for governments in the complementary possibilities of African lingua francas and knowledge systems.

As a first step, we have to expose a number of conceptual confusions. We have to demonstrate, in clear analytical detail, the interpenetration of reason, the body and the imagination in African design, crafts, arts, sculpture, painting and agro-processing. Western philosophers and social scientists have a deep-rooted difficulty in comprehending the creative process that characterises the work of African scientists and technologists, embodied in African languages. They have failed to comprehend the intimate connections between hand and head. Every African scientist – a bricklayer, a chef, a musical instruments maker and so on – conducts a dialogue between perception and reason, fact and imagination, analysis and justification, and these habits establish a rhythm between problem-solving and problem-identification. Western scholarship on African science and technology has drawn fault lines dividing practice and theory, technique and process, technique and expression, crafts and art, maker and user. It still suffers from this historical inheritance (Sennett 1998).

What the capabilities approach calls for is a complex, many-levelled struggle – intellectual, social and political – in which the debates about the language of science and technology interlink with those in a host of political, social and economic institutional settings. One such feature is that the issues of framing science, technology and African languages are being lived through in concrete forms. Another such feature is that these disputes in turn both feed on and are fed by various attempts to define in theoretical and practical terms both the place of African languages in science and technology and the demands of an integrated multilinguistic and inter-epistemic epistemology, and beyond that the shape of curriculum and pedagogy and their relation to democratic politics.

It would serve to eradicate the Eurocentric disconnection of linguistic and knowledge systems, which kills the vitality of our inter-epistemic, multicultural and multilingual world. This is not just a hypothetical undertaking. Some information and knowledge institutions spend a major portion of their time exploring possibilities: libraries, archives, museums, innovation hubs and research institutes are developing systems for organiding the knowledge of the world, so that people have a wide frame of reference. What they are doing is opening a new system of more flexible epistemic identities, structures and functions.

Encounters with African lingua francas and knowledge systems in concrete environments

In an inter-epistemic, multilingual system, diplomacy would be a community of shared capabilities whose ultimate purpose is the gaining and construction of shared meanings, generated from a multiplicity of linguistic knowledge systems.

It would be the application of the inter-epistemic, multi-vocal intelligence and imagination to social and economic realities – a shift from the bounded, territorialised epistemology. The hegemonic model has failed to make full use of complementary capabilities across various linguistic knowledge systems. Once the inter-epistemic mode of addressing social and economic problems occurs in diplomatic settings, classrooms, workplaces and markets, regional integration is concretised and institutionalised in the process. It is correct, therefore, to assert that inter-epistemic and African lingua francas practices have to be enacted to be experienced, encountered in particular places and moments. This will serve to make inter-epistecism and African lingua francas less abstract. Gradually, deliberately, people will begin to question the Eurocentric paradigm they are familiar with. Without realising it, they would be enacting regional integration – moving from antagonistic to supplementary difference. This is decolonisation and Pan-Africanism in their dramatic forms. The encounter with African lingua francas and knowledge systems across state borders would be a shortcut, a social and political education strategy that governments need to rely on, and it could be a brilliantly effective device in regional integration learning – often when the very status of Western languages and knowledge systems is questioned.

Covid-19: A singular event

The experience of the Covid-19 pandemic has made regional integration urgent. Amid the existential anxiety, people seeking security are turning to multiple knowledge systems as a way of maximising their capabilities and augmenting the capacity of the body, the heart and the mind – all available knowledge systems and languages could be useful for intensifying and broadening mutual recognition that could create an integrated regional consciousness and sensibility. The perspective of African lingua francas and knowledge systems that places all the different bits and pieces into an integrated whole is the overarching concern, with the process of enhancing an integrated regional consciousness.

The concerns that give force to this line of reasoning can be very effective. A sharing of linguistic and epistemic capabilities that places the burden of looking into the other's construction of things is a form not only of self-understanding, but also understanding the other's linguistic and cognitive space. Given the place that language and knowledge have in the knowledge economy, mutual recognition of complementary difference and a profound sense of shared vulnerability is indispensable.

The business of African lingua francas and knowledge systems

In our increasingly commercial and globalising world, it will not be surprising that the activities of African lingua francas and knowledge systems will often intersect with those of business, trade and industry. The enormous socio-economic value of African lingua francas and knowledge systems means that they will be targeted as commercial resources, but their use for profit-driven purpose could potentially be at odds with the principles of regional integration and solidarity. A number of global trends are influencing how the private sector interacts with regional integration programmes and activities. Increasing costs of managing regional projects and the pressure of global market forces are accompanied by governments realising some of their traditional responsibility for co-ordinating inter-state projects. Private enterprises interact with governments in a variety of ways, using the values and prestige of governments for the purposes of marketing and increasing profits. The challenge is in finding a publicly and ethically acceptable balance between profit-making activities and the values of African lingua francas and complementary knowledge systems (Jackson and Sørenson 2013; Rukato 2018; Mutasa 2018; Nagar and Nganje 2018; Bischoff, Aning and Acharya 2016; Murithi 2014).

Managing regional integration

The integration of Africa is one of the most important trends defining Africa today. It is important, first of all, because it has the potential to help bring to an end border wars and contested sovereignties, a recurring issue that brings destruction and suffering to Africa, peaking with extraordinary violence in Central Africa. It is also important because an integrated Africa will anchor the AU in a polycentric structure, precluding the existence of a hegemonic superpower, in spite of the technological pre-eminence of the West. It will also be significant as a source of institutional innovation that may yield some answers to the crisis of underdeveloped nation states.

The very notion of Pan-Africanism is compelling. African identity has always been constructed against the other – the invaders, mainly of European origin. Africa now is more complex. It results from the internal dynamics of nationalism and the integration process, challenges by the two macro-trends that characterise the Information Age: the globalisation of technology and communication, and the parallel affirmation of national identity as the source of meaning. Because of the failure of African nation states in articulating a coherent response, African governments are trying to cope with both trends by using new forms and new processes, thereby attempting the construction of a new regional system (Cheru 1992; Davidson 1992; Wa Mutharika 1995). AU institutions would be reinforced in their powers, moving towards a higher level of Pan-African unity, thus overcoming traditional Western resistance to regional integration. In addition, the push for regional integration is the only way for the AU to start projecting its weight in the regional and international scene without triggering fear and hostility from most African governments. The variable geometry of most Pan-African construction, for all its complexity, is an essential instrument of Pan-Africanism itself, as it prevents frontal conflicts among member states.

Further, the globalisation of capital and information technology forces African states to consider the classic subject of the integration of trade and investment in a new perspective. A major debate about Africa and globalisation concerns the continued low level of competitiveness in a truly global market, under the double squeeze of Western and Chinese technology. But the consequences of globalisation are not inexorable. It is not a natural force, reducing societies to economies, economies to markets and markets to financial flows. It is contingent and changeable (Castells 1998; Cheru 1992; Davidson 1992; Grindle 1996; Wa Mutharika 1995).

Challenges of regional integration

The fact that human experiential space, in Africa and elsewhere in the world, is being subtly changed through an opening to globalisation should not lead us to assume that we are all becoming globalised citizens. Even the most positive conceivable development and transformation – an erosion of frontiers and borders between cultural horizons and a growing sensitivity towards unfamiliar geographies of life and mutual recognition – does not necessarily demand a sense of global responsibility. The question of how such a sense might become a possibility, with all its implications for Pan-Africanism, has up to now not been investigated in depth.

Africa's failures and crises in global politics and Pan-African relations have only recently begun to be explored in the literature. There is a forced migration crisis, with people moving around the continent in unprecedented numbers, driven by hunger, poverty and conflict. There is an environmental crisis, of which climate change is only the most widely debated consequence. There is a crisis in human rights, with some governments unwilling to honour the requirements of human dignity and justice. And there is the clash of beliefs, faiths and political ideologies and the implications this has for regional and global tensions (Huntington 1996; Caputo 2001). Because of globalisation, African governments have a part to play in addressing problems of regional and global governance, the maintenance of peace, intercultural tolerance and mutual recognition. Accordingly, we should develop a regional and global ethics through which governments can articulate and exercise our regional and global responsibilities.

Communication is now so quick that events anywhere in the world can brought into our living rooms during the morning and the evening news. As a result of these changes, a regional and global culture is emerging that corresponds to the global market, with many brands being recognisable anywhere in the world. As a result of all these challenges, a new realisation is emerging that we live in regional and global communities, as well as in our own countries. We are not citizens just of specific nation states; we are also citizens of the continent and the world. We should be concerned not just for our compatriots, but for all human beings, especially those who are on the margins, suffering from poverty, unemployment, socio-economic inequality and gender-based violence. What I hope will emerge from this analysis is a fully articulated conception of the politics, economics and ethics of regional integration in the global context (Van Hooft 2009; Singer 1981; Amstutz 1999; Gaita 1999).

Regional integration is a demanding and contentious political and moral position that urges us to include the whole continent in our social, economic, political and moral concerns – and to apply the standards of mutual recognition, obligation and solidarity across territorial and cultural boundaries. It is a case for transnational, trans-territorial citizenship in a world of differences and contradictions.

Challenges and implementation realities

Nationalism, as both ideology and social movement, has been one of the formative processes of Africa as we know it today. The implications of this for regional integration are many. By creating a market for the flow of goods, it also provokes responses, and resistance from those who feel that their interests are threatened. This is true in cross-border conflicts and xenophobia. But, as mentioned earlier, nationalism is also a product of regional integration and globalisation. In addition, the link between nationalism and the modern international state systems is, however, more than historical. It is also normative – concerned with values, with ideas of how people should live and to whom they owe obedience. Nationalism has, through spreading across the African continent and the rest of the world, become the main justifying or legitimising doctrine of the international state system itself.

Prior to the modern period, borders in Africa were justified by reference to their royal leaders and their dynasties. The spread of nationalism has removed this justification and produced instead a system in which states are justified on the grounds that they represent their peoples. We also get the principles of the sovereignty of the people, citizenship and self-determination, according to which every nation has the right to decide its own fate, to be independent, or, if not, to choose freely to be part of a happy state. Nationalism has become the ethical basis of regional and international relations, so much so that the body grouping the states in the world is called the United Nations, and the one in Africa is called the African Union. Nationalism is now the political basis of nation states and the international state system (Halliday 2001).

Globalisation also brings into sharp focus the centrality of managing regional integration. The problems it presents are as pervasive as they are challenging. Governments are confronted by new bases of working together, the redefining of regional relations and the establishment of innovative practices. While globalisation and new technologies offer a platform for new ways of communication and interaction, they also have led to the redrawing of diplomatic maps and the abandonment of long-established protocols: change and speed have become the watchwords of the era. The ability to handle the implications of such disturbance, at the level of government and the AU, is highly prized. There is concern about the lack of regional integration organisation and management skills, as well as leadership and management competencies. The emphasis is on facilitation, rather than a centralised common and control approach. The essential problem arises from the non-linear nature of regional integration. The entire process, in practice, is resistant to such categorisations, rooted as they are in the Eurocentric hegemonic attitude and practice.

One thing, though, that the AU has to acknowledge, is the threat of resistance. Acknowledgement of the manifold forms of resistance which often accompany such radical policy shifts, is advisable. Eurocentric organisations, fearful of losing their current power and influence, will try to subvert the development of lingua francas and the integration of African knowledge systems. As always, they will supply different kinds of blockages to change, usually of a more indirect kind. This calls for vigilant management structures, because the more regionally integrated the operations are, or the more important to regional integration needs are, the more organisations will need to be vigilant, flexible and adaptive. According to contingency theory, knowing how contingencies and structures fit together provides an organisation with firm rules for structural design (Stopford and Wells 1972; Milgrom and Roberts 1995; Pettigrew et al. 2002).

Whether from the point of contingencies or configurations, the basic facts are clear: flexible structure in the management of the web of factors will be key. Organisational structure will be the key element in the AU's tool kit. Without the right structure, regional integration will fail. But there is no categorical model. It will always take leadership and managerial judgement, always appreciating changing contingencies over time. Addressing the dynamics of structure should be high on the agenda of the AU (Whittington 2003).

The institutional and structural approach to regional integration in the era of globalisation is very much of its time and place. Dissatisfaction with simplistic Pan-African recipes, which have assumed a sizeable scope since the establishment of the AU, and with crude monitoring and evaluation criteria, has stimulated a search for more nuanced approaches. This opens space for revelatory diagnosis followed by design proposals. There is also the realisation that the social and political construction of appropriate institutional arrangements has to be acknowledged through acceptance of the structured nature of inter-state relations.

Institutional reconfiguration also offers a degree of certitude to governments, civil society and corporations faced with a rapidly changing environment, and provides for comparison in assessing national and regional capabilities in a globalising marketplace. This has the potential to enhance reciprocity in inter-state relations and help to deal with power asymmetries between states. Inter-state networks may also help deal with problems of equity, making it difficult to mobilise power. They could also serve to co-ordinate inter-state relations, in which every state will have to work within 'the rules of the game', but the need for a regional institutional framework is paramount in enabling regional relations and diplomacy to be developed. Once in place, the embeddedness of institutional patterns of behaviour within complex independent nation states, and within individuals and communities sharing the same institutional field will tend to ensure continuity and coherence in approach (Loveridge 2003; Tolbert and Zucker 1996; Powell and DiMaggio 1991).

The plan to adopt mutual recognition as a normative framework for regional integration will interrupt some of the malaises of post-colonial African culture. The first concern is with the effects of the corporate system of African culture, on values and outlooks, on 'the ways of life'. This has meant a more general process of change, the reorganisation of perceptions as well as of enterprise and institutions – not only the expansion of an industrial system across the continent, not only systems of transport and communication, the spread of the market economy into all regions of African society, but also, and even predominantly, the remaking of cultural perceptions. The real project is to educate citizens, who will champion values of mutual recognition and the full development of intellectual, social and ethical capabilities, and who have the disposition for a symbolic existence across differences and borders to solve pressing social, economic and political problems.

A related concern is individualism, which names what the Western-educated African elite consider the finest achievement of liberal democracy. We live in societies where people have a right to choose for themselves their own of life, to decide in good conscience what beliefs to espouse, to determine the form and direction of their lives in a whole host of ways. What complicates things more is the primacy of instrumental reason that has emerged over time. Now, African educational institutions are preoccupied with producing and transmitting technically exploitable knowledge, not grounded in ethics. But education grounded in mutual recognition seeks to ensure that students are equipped with qualifications in the area of social competencies and extra-functional abilities.

In this connection, extra-functional refers to all the competencies and attitudes relevant to pursuit of a holistic education in democratic society that are not contained per se in technically exploitable knowledge.

There is also the problem of cynicism and decline in public trust and confidence. We do not know what buttons to push, in our cynical and sceptical consciousness, to get regional integration going. Current cynicism and public distrust present themselves in a naive nationalism and Pan-Africanism. Regional integration, based on mutual recognition, seeks to facilitate the sorts of development that have in fact occurred since independence – a Pan-African consciousness and trans-territorial citizenship. It emphasises respect for an empathic imagination, the common core of humanity, as the only motive that is not empirical or contingent – not dependent on the vagaries of history.

Concern about the vibrancy and governability of Pan-Africanism is evident in incessant strikes, border wars and contested sovereignties. A cynical perception has emerged that in Africa, the more laws, the more disorder (Comaroff and Comaroff 2006; Olowu 2012). What is more, the material and political culture in African states presupposes the exploitation of the masses. The purity of liberal democratic principles not only tolerates, but requires systemic violence. Thus there seems to be a mystification in liberal democracy. Judging from events across the continent in recent years, ideas and practices of liberal democracy belong to a system of violence, of which it could be said they are the general basis of justification (Merleau-Ponty 1967; Sennett 1998; Seabrook 2004; Thompson 1987; Žižek 2009; Bird 1999; Rawls 1995; Grayling 2017; Deneen 2018; Kotz 2017).

Regional integration and possibilities: The internet and social media

The potential for what the internet and social media can do for regional integration is unimaginable. We are actually in the middle of something exhilarating. Every day, regional integration messages can be sent to phone screens. Tap the screen with your thumbprint to securely communicate with others. Surely, wouldn't this become empowering, integrative? The internet can ignite debate across borders like never before and thus broaden connectivity. Decision-making can increasingly shift into the hands of more people.

The future of regional integration, then, looks bright – and can flicker into life in far-flung communities across inter-state distances. This can happen if there is a common purpose and an instinctive understanding that everyone matters. And so the internet and social media allow people to be more informed: the click of a button throws up information that previously took more time and energy to find out. This will help operating direct inclusive democracy in real time. Public ignorance and fake news are around, but the internet also allows people to be more informed.

The possibilities of direct democracy are not to be taken lightly. The internet has the power to distribute power to the hands of the people on the ground. This will weaponise them. The internet and social media may not be perfect, so it follows that regional integration will always be imperfect. But if governments, the private sector and ordinary people can rally around the internet as a force for the creation of democratic institutions across borders and at all levels of society, regional integration is possible (Scott and Makres 2019).

References

Abimbọla, M.A.M. 2019. 'On Òyìnbó: Yorùbá Religion, Resistance, and Polyepistemic Knowledge'. *Journal of Interreligious Studies* 28: 43–61.

Amstutz, M.R. 1999. *International Ethics: Concepts, Theories, and Cases in Global Politics.* Lanham, MD: Rowman and Littlefield.

AU (African Union). 2013. *Agenda 2063: The Africa We Want.* https://au.int/sites/default/files/documents/33126-doc-framework_document_book.pdf (accessed 11 December 2023).

Bird, C. 1999. *The Myth of Liberal Individualism.* Cambridge: Cambridge University Press.

Bischoff, P-H., K. Aning and A. Acharya (eds). 2016. *Africa in Global International Relations: Emerging Approaches to Theory and Practice.* London: Routledge.

Buber, M. 1970. *I and Thou.* New York: Charles Scribner's Sons.

Caputo, J.D. 2001. *On Religion.* London: Routledge.

Castells, M. 1998. *End of Millennium (The Information Age: Economy, Society and Culture, Volume III).* Oxford: Wiley-Blackwell.

Cheru, F. 1992. *The Not So Brave New World! Problems and Prospects of Regional Integration in Post-apartheid Southern Africa.* Johannesburg: South African Institute of International Affairs. https://policycommons.net/orgs/south-african-institute-of-international-affairs/ (accessed 11 December 2023).

Comaroff, J. and J. Comaroff. 2006. *Law and Disorder in the Postcolony.* Chicago: University of Chicago Press.

Davidson, B. 1992. *The Black Man's Burden: Africa and the Curse of the Nation-State*. New York: Times Books.

Deneen, P.J. 2018. *Why Liberalism Failed*. New Haven: Yale University Press.

Eze, E.C. (ed.). 1998. *African Philosophy: An Anthology*. Oxford: Blackwell.

Foucault, M. 1972. *The Archaeology of Knowledge and the Discourse on Language*. Translated by A.M. Sheridan Smith. London: Tavistock.

———. 1980. *Power/Knowledge: Selected Interviews and Other Writings, 1972–1977*. New York: Pantheon Books.

Gaita, R. 1999. *A Common Humanity: Thinking about Love and Truth and Justice*. Melbourne: Text Publishing.

Gluck, C. and A.L. Tsing (eds). 2009. *Words in Motion: Toward a Global Lexicon*. Durham: Duke University Press.

Grayling, A.C. 2017. *Democracy and Its Crisis*. New York: One World.

Grindle, M.S. 1996. *Challenging the State: Crisis and Innovation in Latin America and Africa*. Cambridge: Cambridge University Press.

Halliday, F. 2001. 'Nationalism'. In: *The Globalization of World Politics: An Introduction to International Relations*, edited by J. Baylis, S. Smith and P. Owens, 521–38. New York: Oxford University Press.

Huntington, S.P. 1996. *The Clash of Civilizations and the Remaking of World Order*. New York: Simon and Schuster.

Jackson, R. and G. Sørenson. 2013. *International Relations: Theories and Approaches*. 5th edition. Oxford: Oxford University Press.

Kotz, D.M. 2017. *The Rise and Fall of Neoliberal Capitalism*. Cambridge: Harvard University Press.

Levinas, F. 2006. *Humanism of the Other*. Champaign, IL: University of Illinois Press.

Loveridge, R. 2003. 'Institutional Approaches to Business Strategy'. In: *The Oxford Handbook of Strategy*, edited by D.O. Faulkner and A. Campbell, 104–37. Oxford: Oxford University Press.

May, S. 2017. 'Language, Imperialism, and the Modern Nation-State System: Implications for Language Rights'. In: *The Oxford Handbook of Language and Society*, edited by O. Garcia, N. Flores and M. Spotti, 35–54. New York: Oxford University Press.

Merleau-Ponty, M. 1967. *Humanism and Terror: An Essay on the Communist Problem*. Translated by J. O'Neill. Boston: Beacon Press.

Mesthrie, R. 2015. 'Neville Alexander: History, Politics and the Language Question'. *South African Journal of Science* 111 (7/8): 1–2.

Milgrom, P. and J. Roberts. 1995. 'Complementarities and Fit: Strategy, Structure and Organizational Change in Manufacturing'. *Journal of Accounting and Economics* 19 (2–3): 179–208.

Morris, I. 2013. *The Measure of Civilization: How Social Development Decides the Fate of Nations*. New York: Profile Books.

Mudimbe, V-Y. 1988. *The Invention of Africa: Gnosis, Philosophy, and the Order of Knowledge*. Bloomington: Indiana University Press.

Murithi, T. 2014. *The Routledge Handbook of Africa's International Relations*. London: Routledge.

Mutasa, C. 2018. 'The African Union's Socio-economic Challenges in Africa'. In: *The African Union: Autocracy, Diplomacy, and Peacebuilding in Africa*, edited by T. Karbo and T. Murithi, 183–204. London: I.B. Taurus.

Nabudere, D.W. 2011. *Afrikology, Philosophy and Wholeness: An Epistemology*. Pretoria: Africa Institute of South Africa.

Nagar, D. and F. Nganje. 2018. 'The African Union and its Relations with Sub-regional Economic Communities'. In: *The African Union: Autocracy, Diplomacy, and Peacebuilding in Africa*, edited by T. Karbo and T. Murithi, 205–34. London: I.B. Taurus..

Natarajan, T. 2014. 'Shifting Economics: Fundamental Questions and Amartya K. Sen's Pragmatic Humanism'. *Journal of Philosophical Economics* 8 (1): 1–30.

Ndhlovu, F. 2017. 'Language Migration, Diaspora: Challenging the Big Battalions of Groupism'. in Ophelia Garcia, Nelson Flores, Massimiliamo Spotti (eds.), *The Oxford Handbook of Language and Society*, edited by O. Garcia, N. Flores and M. Spotti, 141–59. Oxford: Oxford University Press.

Ndlovu-Gatsheni, S. 2018. *Epistemic Freedom in Africa: Deprovincialization and Decolonization*. London: Routledge.

Nkondo, G.M. 2007. 'Mutual Recognition as National Policy in South Africa: A Conceptual Framework'. *International Journal of African Renaissance Studies* 2 (1): 88–100.

Olowu, D. 2012. 'Public Administration in Africa: Deepening Crisis Despite Reform Efforts'. In: *The Sage Handbook of Public Administration*, edited by B. Guy Peters and J. Pierre, 543–61. Los Angeles: Sage Publications.

Pettigrew, A., R. Whittington, E. van den Bosch, L. Melin and W. Ruigrok. 2002. *Innovative Forms of Organizing: Complementarities and Dualities*. Los Angeles: Sage Publications.

Powell, W.W. and P.J. DiMaggio. 1991. *The New Institutionalism in Organizational Analysis*. Chicago: University of Chicago Press.

Rawls, J. 1995. *Political Liberalism*. New York: Columbia University Press.

Ricoeur, P.R. 1990. *Oneself as Another*. Chicago: University of Chicago Press.

Rorty, R. 1989. *Contingency, Irony, and Solidarity*. Cambridge: Cambridge University Press.

Rukato, H. 2018. 'The African Union: Regional and Global Challenges'. In: *The African Union: Autocracy, Diplomacy, and Peacebuilding in Africa*, edited by T. Karbo and T. Murithi, 109–23. London: I.B. Taurus.

Scott, A. and A. Makres. 2019. *Power and the People: Five Lessons from the Birthplace of Democracy*. London: Riverrun Publishing.

Seabrook, J. 2004. *Consuming Cultures: Globalization and Local Lives*. New York: New Internationalist.

Sennett, R. 1998. *The Corrosion of Character: The Personal Consequences of Work in the New Capitalism*. New York: W.W. Norton and Co.

Singer, P. 1981. *The Expanding Circle: Ethics and Sociobiology*. New York: Farrar, Straus and Giroux.

Stopford, J.M. and L. Wells. 1972. *Managing the Multinational Enterprise*. London: Longmans.

Taylor, C. 2007. *A Secular Age*. Cambridge, MA: Belknap Press.

Thompson, D.F. 1987. *Political Ethics and Public Office*. Cambridge: Harvard University Press.

Tolbert, P.S. and L.G. Zucker. 1996. 'The Institutionalization of Institutional Theory'. In: *The Handbook of Organizational Studies*, edited by S.R. Clegg, C. Hardy and W.R. Nord, 175–90. Los Angeles: Sage Publications.

Van Hooft, S. 2009. *Cosmopolitanism: A Philosophy for Global Ethics*. Stocksfield: Acumen.

Wa Mutharika, B. 1995. *One Africa, One Destiny: Towards Democracy, Good Governance, and Development*. Harare: SAPES.

Whittington, R. 2003. 'Organizational Structure'. In: *The Oxford Book of Strategy*, edited by D.O. Faulkner and A. Campbell, 811–40. Oxford: Oxford University Press.

Wolfreys, J. 2004. *Thinking Difference: Critics in Conversation*. New York: Fordham University Press.

Žižek, S. 2009. *Violence*. New York: Profile Books.

CHAPTER 27

South Africa and the Development of African Regionalism

Nana K. Poku

For every practical purpose, governments can and must make clear distinctions between the domestic and international arenas, the public and private spheres, and between the stability and sustainability of the state and the well-being of individuals and communities. But matters that are clearly distinguishable in the abstract cannot be framed as public policy in a compartmentalised way. How we reconcile economic growth with environmental sustainability, or reap the benefits of globalising forces without disadvantaging sections of the population are but two examples. The exercise of democratic governance is not a search for an enduring answer to one or other issue; instead, it is the business of reconciling competing interests, making compromises and mediating tensions. Much the same can be said about the conduct of a state's international relations and the exercise of its diplomacy.

But the entanglement of domains and issues can also have widely shared, beneficial outcomes, too. This has certainly been the case with post-apartheid South Africa (Poku 2001b). The achievement of a peaceful and just political settlement has not only greatly enabled South Africa, but also had powerful impacts on the development of the southern African region and on sub-Saharan Africa more broadly. New political, economic and normative achievements have been secured – the African Union not least – and greatly enlarged possibilities continue to open up for both South Africa and its neighbours.

Our established frameworks for understanding change of this kind and on this scale are sadly inadequate – at a time when securing the health and prosperity of all South African citizens presents formidable challenges, many of which are both entangled and entrenched (such as pervasive poverty) or linked to global dynamics (financial turbulence, the Covid-19 pandemic, climate change). But neither of those domains diminishes the importance of South Africa's regional initiatives.

This chapter adopts a nuanced perspective on South Africa's international relations, diplomacy and trading arrangements that acknowledges but looks beyond the kinds of positive, summative expressions of the gains it has secured through regional arrangements, such as 'leadership', 'middle power standing' and 'regional hegemony'. As a free, democratic and economically developed nation, South Africa's international relations and diplomacy have been deployed in the hope of taking advantage of the opportunities opened up by regionalism within and beyond the continent, with some success. But the domestic sphere, the larger international arena and the continuing importance of bilateral relations combine to make South Africa's embrace of regionalism just one aspect of an enlarged and enlarging sphere of political initiative and response.

The variety of regionalisms

For our purposes, 'regionalism' pertains to configurations of political rather than physical geography, even though most such arrangements entail states that are physically contiguous (Poku 2001a: 12). Because sociocultural commonalities so often defy state boundaries, it is important to distinguish the emergence of cross-border relations and those created by inter-state negotiation. As one analyst helpfully notes, regionalisation is essentially bottom-up, whereas regionalism 'involves primarily the process of institution creation' (Pempel 2005: 19–20). And, in an early, seminal work, Anthony Payne and Andrew Gamble characterise regionalism as 'a state-led or states-led project designed to reorganize a particular regional space along defined economic and political lines' and comment that regionalism is 'something that is being constructed, and constantly reconstructed, by collective human action' (1996: 2, 17).

Academic comprehension of regionalism kept pace with developments up to the end of the 1970s, since it was largely devoted to regional defence arrangements in institutional form – the North Atlantic Treaty Organization (NATO, formed in 1948); Western Union (1948); the Southeast Asia Treaty Organization (SEATO, 1954); the Central Treaty Organization (CENTO, 1955) and various bilateral pacts – all essentially manifestations of the Cold War. Little in these arrangements challenged the scope and comprehensiveness of established International Relations (IR) theory, which had at its core a belief in the primacy of the realist, survivalist disposition of states (Poku and Whitman 2017). Older and emerging varieties of regionalism were largely subsumed under Development Studies and as a relatively minor subset of International Political Economy (IPE): 'What was striking though, was the lack of correspondence . . . between economics and political science. At that time few introductions to IR, IPE or Development Studies contained sections on regionalism. Today [2005], this is commonplace' (Hettne 2005: 547).

Developments in this century have led to a proliferation of conceptual and definitional debates, made more difficult because the varieties of regionalism now extant cannot adequately be grasped and analysed by any single discipline – IR, IPE, Development Studies, Political Geography, Security Studies, Economics. Each of these (and others) are capable of yielding insights, but it is not merely the number of regionalisms that is daunting – so, too, is their variety. In addition, the dynamics and conditions driving states to conceive, construct and adapt regional arrangements are both fast-moving and complex: shifting global supply chains; information technologies enabling new forms of networking; national and regional competitive innovation and specialization;[1] migration patterns (Geddes et al. 2019); rapid urbanisation (Glass, Addie and Nelles 2019: 1651–6); the competition for resources and – as the Covid-19 pandemic demonstrated – a closely interconnected global infrastructure capable of delivering unwelcome surprises (Khana 2016).

Regional organisations vary in both the scope of their aims and effectiveness; some, in fact, are more declaratory and aspirational than fully functional governance forums, largely or in some particulars. Weak state capacities, the absence of a strong secretariat and competitive tensions variously account for larger institutional failures. But there also regional commitments that are decidedly second-tier in terms of enactment. This is certainly the case with the human rights and gender equality provisions of some regional groupings, for which at least a nominal commitment is a matter of conformity to a region's more dominant members or to wider international norms. The historical antecedents to current regional groupings are also pertinent:

A regional human rights institution cannot be separated from regional integration. The existing human rights institutions in Europe, the Americas and Africa were established and grew because they maintained relevance while being supported by the political and economic cooperation in the region. The European Court of Human Rights was created from the strong foundation of the Council of Europe, which in turn was established based on the unity and common understanding gained from the legacy of World War II. The Inter-American Commission on Human Rights, whose creation in turn was motivated by the strategic desire of the United States to contain Cuban influence, was possible because the Organization of American States (OAS) had existed since 1948, being established by those states to respond to regional concerns (Balik 2012: 155).

Nor are regionalisms impervious to one another, particularly when large-scale economic and developmental initiatives are concerned (Buzdugan 2013). Both regional configurations and individual states can be acted upon as well as act; and power asymmetries, opportunism and trade-offs all feature in how states calculate their interests, individually and collectively. Consider, for example, this characterisation of China's massive Belt and Road project and its likely impacts on African regional ambitions: '[There are] four structural layers underlying China's engagement in the region: the global infrastructure race; Pan-African continental connectivity; the intra-regional infrastructure race; and bilateral funding of regional infrastructure projects' (Otele 2020: 511; see also Simelane and Managa 2018). The degree to which regional groupings can insulate themselves from the interests of other (most often, more powerful) states will to a large degree depend on state capacity and the qualities of leadership within the region (Agostinis and Parthenay 2021). Similarly, although South Africa's induction into BRICS grouping of countries (Brazil, Russia, India, China and South Africa) in 2010 'has often been regarded as a representative of the continent in the group', it might not prove to be an unalloyed boon to all states on the African continent:

Some analysts maintain that the benefits to the region accrued from the country's membership in BRICS will only be marginal. This membership could increase the diversity of investments, expand markets for African industry and boost tourism from countries other than those of Western Europe; however, it may not generate the widespread infrastructural investment and economic growth that many governments project. Further, membership may actually continue to reinforce a pattern of resource extraction by the wealthier BRICS countries (Besada and Tok 2015: 273).[2]

Whatever the intended objectives behind the formation of political regionalisms, their impacts can and often do extend beyond both stated aims and foreseeable consequences, even at the largest scale. For instance, at the end of the Cold War and the dissolution of the Soviet Union, the former Warsaw Pact states sought to join the Western community of states and its regional organisations. The prize they sought was membership of the European Union (EU) and although they also had strong incentives for joining NATO because of Russia's residual power and uncertain disposition, the importance of NATO's political role was arguably greater than its expansion as a defensive alliance because Eastern European states' demonstration of democratic political control of their militaries – a requisite for NATO membership – was also an essential first step to their eventual membership of the EU.

The impacts of regionalisms are not confined to either other regional groupings or inter-state relations, but can also have both intentional and inadvertent effects within and between their constituent states and sub-state regions (see, for example, Uminski 2014; Medeiros 2013). They are less 'solutions to problems' than arenas for addressing them around shared interests and values; and their creation invariably generates problems of cohesion (Kay and Ackrill 2007), fairness, equity, subsidiarity around sensitive governance issues (Colombo 2012) and sustainability (Smetana et al. 2015). So for all of their politico-economic weight, expansive agendas and apparent fixity, regional configurations must be highly adaptive, both inwardly and outwardly. Regional partners remain competitive within the boundaries they create (most frequently in trade matters) and infringements and disagreements must find negotiated settlements.

The essential source of tensions within established, politically constituted regions is that state interests remain fully operative. The degree of political integration within the EU is exceptional, but even there, a very wide range of economic, political and cultural interests exert divisive force, both at intraregional and local levels, to the degree that the EU instituted a subsidiarity early warning mechanism (Cooper 2019). Economic and monetary integration have also generated serious friction (Schelkle 2017; Caporaso and Rhodes 2016). Short of the kinds of supra-national authority that states both large and small are extremely reluctant to concede, the differences between the states that comprise a politically constituted region – including historical and material ones – exert a considerable influence on regional coherence and effectiveness. In the case of the development of African regionalism, factors include enduring colonial legacies (Basiru 2016; Shaw and Adibe 1994); weak state formation (Williams 2013); poor levels of development; unconsolidated democratic norms and stalled generational leadership transition (Mattes 2012).[3]

The evolution of African regionalism

Pan-Africanism has a long history, rooted in continental and diasporic struggles for freedom, for the assertion of uncoerced, unsuppressed identity and spirituality and for forms of cultural and political self-determination (Adi 2018). Although its institutionalised forms in successive Pan-African congresses and the Organisation of African Unity (OAU) have been superseded by the creation of the African Union (AU) in 2002, it nevertheless left a strong legacy: the OAU's Sirte Declaration of 1999 announcing the decision to establish the AU declared that African leaders were 'inspired by the ideals which guided the Founding Fathers of our Organization and Generations of Pan-Africanists in their resolve to forge unity, solidarity and cohesion, as well as co-operation between African peoples and among African States' (OAU 1999). Behind the ideals was a clear-sighted view of the economic and development prospect of each newly free African state to eschew regional co-operation in some forms or to some degree:

> Given the political balkanization of the continent into arbitrary nation-states possessing sparse population, limited infrastructure, minor internal markets, economies vulnerable to fluctuating and new and fragile borders, it comes as no surprise that regional integration [became the] means of helping the continent's lack of development such as low per capita income, development and economic growth. [It was also] a means of consolidating the political independence of African states (Mlambo 2020: 24).

Running parallel with the phases of Pan-African institutionalisation was a series of regional arrangements, largely though not exclusively centred around economics and trade, the earliest of them with a regional-geographic compass. These included the Customs and Economic Union of Central Africa (CEUCA, formed in 1966); the Southern Africa Customs Union (SACU, 1969); the Mano River Union (initially a West African bilateral arrangement, currently with four members); the Economic Community of West African States (ECOWAS, 1975); the Economic Community of the Great Lakes Countries (ECGLS, 1976); the Economic Community of Central African States (ECCAS, 1983); and the Southern African Development Community (SADC, 1992).

Even as decolonisation was the threshold event for African states, the international political economy by which they sought to prosper was itself reconfiguring rapidly through powerful globalising forces – and African states were by no means alone in foreseeing a key advantage of regionalism being a hedge against economic domination by other means:

> The current era of globalisation continues to advance, as does the regionalisation of the world economy. Indeed, while the proliferation of regional trading arrangements among developing countries in the 1970s and 1980s, particularly in Sub-Saharan Africa and Latin America, were a way to insulate those countries from the international economic order dominated by the industrialised North, the [next] round of regionalism follow[ed] a different logic. Countries switched from an inward-oriented import substitution industrialization strategy to an outward oriented export promoting strategy. This include[d] creating regional trading arrangements, or what is called regionalism (Hentz 2008: 491–2).

As part of the extension and intensification of globalisation, the impetus towards the creation of regional trading and aid arrangements was also advanced by the then-European Economic Community (now the EU), with the creation of the first Lomé Convention in 1976, which in time encompassed 70 African, Caribbean and Pacific countries. But the creation of the World Trade Organization in 1995 'reflected and reinforce[d] shifts in global orthodoxies in favour of the liberalisation of world trade' (McQueen 1998) and, by the mid-1990s, the logic of treating such a broad span of countries as a bloc, instead of smaller and more coherent regions, came into question. In addition, with the collapse of the former Soviet bloc, Eastern European countries became a major focus for the EU's aid and trading arrangements (Parfitt 1996).

Both concurrently and subsequently, African countries worked to transition from the older forms of Pan-Africanism – essentially, away from liberation struggles toward large economic and governance issues (Taye 2021). This has entailed creating or revitalising organisational structures adapted to the evolving international political economy, but with long-standing purposes, which include self-determined economic planning, improved intra-African infrastructure and dominion over each nation's resources. This accounts for the emergence of geographically functional regional groupings from the 1960s onwards, as outlined above. Building on the foundation of the OAU, the next milestones were the Monrovia Strategy for the Economic Development of Africa (OAU 1979), the Lagos Plan of Action for the Economic Development of Africa 1980–2000 (OAU 1980) and the Abuja Treaty, which established the African Economic Community (AU 1991) (Aniche 2020).

Enter South Africa

South Africa's transition from apartheid was also something of a culmination for southern Africa. The nation's size and the degree of development of its economy, together with the moral significance of the peaceful transfer of power, catapulted the state from pariah standing to a powerful member of the African community of states. South Africa joined SADC in 1994 and it was poised to contribute to and benefit from the various forms of regional co-operation open to it from that juncture. However, two points bear repeating. First, for all that free, self-determined regionalisms finally became open to all (or nearly all) African states, this was not a transformational moment. Neither the disposition of individual states nor the world's international political economy were fundamentally altered by the growth and expansion of regional organisations – indeed, they are expressions of them. Opportunities beckoned, but so too did enhanced forms of competition; in addition, co-operation within multi-state organisations is simpler in principle than practice and there is an essential tension at the heart of all alliances and regional organisations: the balance between opportunity and cost, or between individual state and collective goods. The second qualification is that the legacies of colonialism are often deeply embedded, not only in the social, economic, cultural and governance spheres, but also in the ways in which international relations are mediated, which also has a bearing on African regionalisms (Basiru 2016). There is also continuing financial dependence, which leaves many states vulnerable to the interests of donors – not least, the persistence of neo-liberal ideologies and initiatives (Hurt 2012).

The organisational fulfilment of Pan-Africanist aspirations came with the creation of the AU in 2001, its continental scale and the diversity of its 55 member states straining the meaning of 'regional'. It is founded on a remarkable range of normative, development, peace and security standards and a commitment to democratic principles, human rights and the rule of law (AU 2000; Yihdego 2011). For reasons of practical as well as political necessity, the AU recognises nine African regional economic communities, including ECOWAS, the Community of Sahel-Saharan States (CEN-SAD) and ECCAS. In addition to its membership in the AU, South Africa remains a member of SADC, SACU, the Southern African Power Pool (SAPP) and two River Commissions. Other members of the AU have adopted similar arrangements, depending on their location, level of economic development and security.

After considering South Africa's engagement with the AU, I examine two other regional engagements – with the EU and with the BRIC countries. These do not exhaust South Africa's engagement with regional groupings, but they are the largest and they show most fully South Africa's economic and political interests, the means it deploys to secure them and the balance of opportunities and costs it must navigate.

South Africa and the development of the African Union

South Africa's post-apartheid engagement with African regionalism is by no means confined to the AU, but this proved to be the largest and most high-profile arena for its political and diplomatic initiatives, most emphatically during Thabo Mbeki's presidency, from 1999 to 2008. It is important to note that the declaratory fact of the AU ushered in very welcome normative and political alignments, as well as an enhancement of the development of continental public goods. As mentioned previously, the shared, formal commitment to peace, democracy and human rights is of historic importance, the difficulty in securing and maintaining them throughout the continent notwithstanding (and particularly with respect to the powers of the Union's Peace and Security Council.)

Because article 3 (1) of the Constitutive Act is the pledge to 'coordinate and harmonize the policies between the existing and future Regional Economic Communities for the gradual attainment of the objectives of the Union' (AU 2000), the AU has worked to extend continent-wide harmonisation over a range of policy areas, where possible, building on existing regional arrangements (Nwapi 2018), from laws and education to biotechnology governance and data protection (Ferreira-Snyman and Ferreira 2010; Adamu 2021; Mugwagwa 2011; Salami 2022). In addition, the creation of an African Medicines Agency (Makoni 2021: 1475) promises to be a significant public health boon, particularly at strategic levels beyond the reach of piecemeal regional initiatives (Yeates and Surender 2021). Harmonisation is particularly important in trade matters both for intra-African and international purposes. As summarised in trade talks between the European Union and the Association of Southeast Asian Nations (ASEAN):

> [they] agreed to focus not on tariffs and quotas but on what Pascal Lamy, the EU trade commissioner, called 'the real 21st century trade issues': harmonizing standards. This is the latest episode in a process of deep integration that is most advanced within the European Union but also underway in many other regions. Two factors explain the shift in regional negotiating emphasis away from conventional barriers and toward standards. First, multilateral negotiations have achieved remarkable reductions in tariffs and quotas but done relatively little to reduce the trade restrictive impact of technical barriers. Second, while multilateral trade rules governing regional agreements on tariffs seek at least in principle to balance the interests of integrating countries and the rights of excluded countries, the rules treat regional agreements on standards as always benign and worthy of encouragement (Chen and Matoo 2016: 2).

AU progress on enabling harmonisation was consolidated by the conclusion of the African Continental Free Trade Agreement that established the African

Continental Free Trade Area (AfCFTA), operationalised in 2019.[4] However, these and other relatively low-cost breakthroughs need to be set against the AU's practical capacity to operationalise its principles, aspirations and commitments. On the AU's own most recent reckoning (2020), the organisation is not financially robust because of the unpredictability and volatility of its revenues, its dependence on external partners, a reliance on a few member states, the need to demonstrate the value for money and probity and a growing budget. The headquarters in Addis Ababa was funded as a gift from China to the AU. The practical shortfalls in securing the AU's aspirations and commitments also showed at the state level, throughout the South African-led peacekeeping mission to Burundi:

> South Africa relied on its own capacities in terms of technical operationality, funds and resources, and it covered itself against the financial cost of its involvement. However, although South Africa was the largest economy on the African continent at that time, it could not cover all logistics costs of the missions. South Africa needed the contributions of other partners to succeed in its missions. For example, due to the inability of the African Union to finance the costs of [Burundi] missions, the implementation of certain tasks – for example, supplies in food, medical services and infrastructure to the ex-combatant areas – was possible thanks to financial support from external partners, including the European Union and the German Cooperation Agency, GTZ (Rufyikiri 2021: 151).

While all members of the AU are sovereign equals, their economies and resources are not – and these differences can find expression as political capital, such as South Africa has long deployed in the SADC region, including SACU (Alden and Soko 2005; Prys 2012), its leadership aspirations closely aligned with (and critics would argue, all but indistinguishable from) its economic ambitions. For the purposes of asserting continental leadership, South Africa's material dominance in southern Africa would never have been sufficient and Thabo Mbeki's administration also worked assiduously to shape the AU through ideational means, by placing his established belief in an African Renaissance at the heart of his essentially Africa-oriented foreign policy. The country's determination to exert a leadership role played out at structural levels and most positively through institutions such as the New Partnership for Africa's Development (NEPAD) and the African Peer Review Mechanism (APRM), by which South Africa accrued a great deal of credit. However, other African nations were also quite prepared to stand up to South African over-reach:

> In terms of resistance an example is the resistance to the bravado and singularity of South Africa's initial venture into African foreign policy. In its early stage of engagement with the Organization of African Unity (OAU), South Africa called for sanctions against Nigeria on the Ken Saro Wiwa and Ogoni debacle. The continental reaction to this was a unanimous closing of ranks within the OAU against South Africa for not dealing with the African problem the African way (Nzewi 2015: 27).

Although the political economy of southern Africa has long given South Africa a predominant regional position, there are numerous actors and interests that militate against its securing hegemonic standing (Taylor 2011). Similarly, although the creation of the AU opened up possibilities for South African leadership, it did not automatically or even easily expand readily achievable foreign policy goals. The reasons are numerous: the AU region is vast and diverse; South Africa has competitors for power and influence;[5] African sub-regional groupings (ECOWAS, for example) are well-established; high-level consensus around visionary projects can meet with popular and sector-specific opposition; and both the AU and its member states must find ways of aligning the orientation and consolidation of the organisation against powerful actors and dynamics beyond the continent – which, of course, include the BRIC countries.

South African-BRIC relations

In addition to the possibility of achieving unique political standing and a possible leadership/mediation role in the AU's relations with the BRIC states, the South African government had powerful and more familiar incentives for joining the group – specifically, continuing to satisfy more developed and commodity-hungry countries while relying on their finished products as a means of advancing its own development agenda, but without falling into the trap of huge trade deficits. It is a difficult balancing act:

Bilateral trade between South Africa and India ha[d] grown rapidly since 2004, at an annual rate of 30 per cent, and was worth 81 billion Rand in 2013. Meanwhile, China is South Africa's single largest bilateral commercial partner, with total trade worth R270 billion in 2013. In turn, South Africa is Chinas main trading partner in Africa, accounting for a 31 per cent share of Beijing's trade with the continent in 2013. Total Chinese foreign direct investment (FDI) stock in South Africa increased from $59 million in 2004 to $5 billion in 2012, making Tshwane the leading recipient of investment flows from Africa to the continent.

However, South Africa's pattern of trade with India and China is heavily weighted in favour of primary products from Tshwane and manufactured goods from New Delhi and Beijing. In addition, South Africa has run persistent trade deficits with both India and China. Leveraging Tshwane's inclusion in the BRICS bloc to promote more equitable and mutually beneficial trade with New Delhi and Beijing, while obtaining access to key technologies and skills in support of South Africa's own industrialisation, remains a crucial concern for Tshwane (Daniel and Virk 2014: 1).

As a consequence,

a key challenge for Tshwane relates to how it can navigate tensions between its 'African agenda' (promoting security and development on the continent and ensuring that Africa has a strong global role), its ambitions to play a leadership role on the continent, and its ability to wield influence within the BRICS, of which it is the smallest member, accounting for only about 2 percent of the bloc's economic might (Daniel and Virk 2014: 1).

While it might be that 'in common with the other BRICS members, South Africa has the resources to engage in subtle means to balance the influence of the US, particularly in its region' (Tella 2017: 387), the size and strength of the Chinese economy and its impacts on South Africa are unlikely to require less balancing. Similarly, the economic and developmental gains accrued by Brazil through its membership in BRICS are also minimal – and certainly well below the proclamations of the bloc (Diko and Sempijja 2021). There is also disquiet within

South Africa and other AU states about embedding their economies in one form or another of neo-liberal economic order (Maphaka 2020).

The political and diplomatic gains South Africa might accrue from what is at least nominally its enhanced standing are less tangible, but are certainly an element in the larger shift of the world's economic and political centre of gravity away from the West, perhaps most visible in BRICS countries' calls for reform of multilateral institutions – and, strikingly, in their shared dispute over the United Nations Security Council's attempt to engage climate change as a security threat (Bruner 2021). South Africa's clear desire to lead or mediate in relations between BRICS and the AU was certainly never likely merely to be bestowed by dint of its membership alone and the economic and trade relations that both India and China maintain with African countries, South Africa included, are essentially bilateral – and given the disparities in economic strength, not without costs and risks (Adewole and Ogunrinu 2018). Moreover,

> as reported by Goldman Sachs in *Is This the BRICS Decade?* BRICS have been identified as the emerging economies that can reshape the world economy. But shortly after the financial crisis, external factors combined with serious internal turmoil indicate it to be an exaggeration for the group. While China and India have grown steadily, Russia and Brazil have moved in the opposite direction with no perceptible growth in South Africa. The S&P Global Ratings in a note said, 'The diverging long-term economic trajectory of the five countries weakens the analytical value of viewing the BRICS as a coherent economic grouping.' India and China have exceeded the rating of firm's growth predictions since the turn of the century, while Russia and South Africa have failed to meet them since about 2005, and Brazil since 2010 (Chattopadhyay et al. 2022: 58).

South Africa's membership of BRICS was an important political and diplomatic advance and supporters would argue that the benefits extend well beyond investment and trade figures. But as one analyst has expressed it:

> South Africa stands to benefit from many networks and opportunities provided by BRICS membership. At the same time, because of its

low economic growth, high levels of poverty and lack of employment opportunities, South Africa cannot afford to follow an approach of narrow interest concerning the BRICS formation and to constrain itself in its economic diplomacy (Neethling 2017: 39).

There are several reasons why South Africa should not privilege its BRICS membership to the exclusion of other regional and bilateral relationships: the economies of the BRICS countries have not lived up to rhetorical and analytic expectations; the dislocations and turbulence brought about by Russia's 2022 invasion of Ukraine are ongoing; and despite residual anti-Western and anti-American legacies within South Africa, the EU remains South Africa's biggest trading partner and the United States gives preferential access to South African textiles and manufactured goods. A South African embrace of multiple allegiances and identities in its diplomatic and foreign policy is likely to offer the largest number of opportunities and options, as well as the greatest degree of stability (Neethling 2017: 39; Bezuidenhout and Claassen 2013).

South Africa and EU-Africa relations

For the purposes of this chapter, EU-African relations can be broadly divided between the evolving relationship between the EU and the AU and between Africa's several regional blocs and the EU. Behind the myriad initiatives to convene region-to-region economic partnerships and similar, facilitative agreements for trade and other forms of co-operation is the worldwide establishment of regional organisations that have both an internal, free-trade purpose and a protective function, abetted by strength in numbers. But, in practice, the negotiation of agreements with non-bloc states and other entities is often beset by the diverging interests of individual member states, particularly when one is considerably more powerful that the others, such as Nigeria in ECOWAS and South Africa in SADC (Murray-Evans 2015).

So the root of the difficulties in securing economic partnership agreements (EPAs) with Africa's established regional blocs is that

either the membership of EPA groups is not congruent with the membership of existing regional organisations, or crucial member states refuse to sign the EPAs and put their regions' unity at risk . . .

EAC, ECOWAS and SADC have been unable to build up coherent and stable EPA groups in their trade negotiations with the EU. This is due firstly to the fact that large African economies like Tanzania, Nigeria or South Africa have already enjoyed privileged access to the European market without implementing the unpopular EPAs. In its external trade and development policies, the EU differentiates between least developed countries, developing countries, advanced economies like South Africa and the import of highly-demanded raw materials like oil. This differentiation leads to extra-regional economic privileges for some African countries. Moreover, Tanzania's, Nigeria's and South Africa's intraregional trade share is much lower than that of smaller regional member states, which means that the regional powers have no interest in access to the regional market either (Krapohl and Van Huut 2020: 565, 577–8).

In the case of the limited success of the EU-SADC EPA negotiations, a further element is 'the apparent primacy of SADC countries' domestic interests over regional coherence and collective representation' (Vickers 2011: 194) when it is the depth and effectiveness of regional integration that makes possible a clear and consistent negotiating position.

Of course, post-apartheid South Africa's regional standing made the extension and formalisation of relations with the EU important for both parties. Signed in 1999, after four years of negotiation and coming into effect in 2004, the Trade, Development and Co-operation Agreement (TDCA) had several objectives: strengthening dialogue between the parties; supporting South Africa in its economic and social transition process; promoting regional co-operation and the country's economic integration in southern Africa and in the world economy; and expanding and liberalising trade in goods, services and capital between the parties. In addition, the importance the EU has assigned to securing agreements with African regions, with the countries individually and with the AU demonstrates a recognition that mutually advantageous trading relationships are premised on stable, democratic governance, human and infrastructural development and the alleviation of poverty. Promoting and supporting African regional integration is an important element in this, most clearly visible in the Joint Africa-EU Strategy (JAES), formally adopted in 2007 and reinforced at a 2017 summit (Directorate-

General for External Policies of the Union 2017). Entirely in line with the earlier EU-South Africa TDCA, the priorities of JAES are specified under four strategic frameworks: 'peace and security: promoting a safer world; governance and human rights: upholding our values and principles; trade and regional integration: raising potential and using opportunities; and key development issues: accelerating progress towards the Millennium Development Goals (now Sustainable Development Goals)' (Directorate-General for External Policies of the Union 2017).

The emphasis on normative qualities as inextricably linked to the kinds of material and political goals more readily associated with regionalism is a remarkable development, which has its own African impetus in the form of the AU's *Agenda 2063: The Africa We Want* (AU 2013). While explicitly expressed as aspirations, *Agenda 2063* nevertheless consolidates African countries' already extensive international and continental commitments to human welfare and betterment as the foundation for lasting development. Aspiration and goodwill will not vault any country or region over the difficult and painstaking political and diplomatic work required for every advance, but regional groups can greatly ease transitions, reconcile differences and bring all parties to a concentrated focus on shared and enduring benefits over narrow and short-lived ones.

As a powerful regional actor and a high-profile member of the AU, South Africa has displayed some outstanding leadership, especially in advancing the ideas and ideals for what the nation itself hoped would be an African Renaissance. In common with every other state in the world, it is beset with issues that cannot be abstracted from their contexts, teased out and dealt with sequentially, and the ways in which it conceives and enacts policies, mediates the consequences with its citizens and its neighbours will sometimes fall short of the ideals to which it is committed (Black and Hornsby 2016).

At the same time, South Africa must contend with considerable levels of poverty (Fransman and Yu 2019) and deprivation – and it must make difficult decisions about how best to alleviate it, while also improving its economic performance, in part through regional trade arrangements. The results have not been encouraging:

South Africa has undergone significant trade liberalisation since the end of apartheid. Average protection has fallen while openness has increased.

The macroeconomic performance in this era of liberalising trade has been unimpressive, with GDP growing by insufficient amounts to make inroads into the high unemployment levels. Poverty levels have also risen. In recent years, the debate concerning what direction South African trade policy should take has been increasingly reflecting a much more inward-focused stance. A more active role for the state in the form of protection is believed to encourage selected industries to grow their ability to export to a degree to which they will then be able to compete effectively in global markets (Mabugu and Chitiga Mabugu 2014: 271).

There is no single policy orientation that can directly reconcile multiple, conflicting pressures on states that struggle to bring prosperity to their citizens while remaining competitive economically. The legacies of apartheid are particularly burdensome for South Africa and although it has skilfully taken its place within the African state system and the world economy by bilateral, multilateral and regional means, how it navigates it external relations while stabilising and improving conditions at home will remain a principal challenge for the country for some years to come. As with every other relational and organisational form, regional engagements will entail costs and trade-offs, as well as benefits.

Conclusion

Despite the creation, extension and formalisation of regional groups worldwide in recent decades, the options open to South Africa to advance both its domestic and foreign policy interests are not a matter of prioritising regional engagement over bilateral, intra-African or international ones. Regional organisations are themselves partly a response – variously opportunistic or self-protecting – to highly dynamic political and economic forces. So, although states form or join regional organisations in order to secure their individual and shared goals, there is no escape from the kinds of disagreements, competitive friction, tensions over ends and means, difficult cost/benefit calculations and hard choices that are inherent to all international relations.

The intense pressures on nations, both large and small, arising from the speed and complexity of globalising forces make the search for national security, economic stability and the betterment of their citizens a constant preoccupation, if not a matter of urgency. At the same time, the work of decades for worldwide consensus on fundamental norms – human rights, democratic governance – is finding expression in and, potentially, at least, through regional organisations.

Notes

1. See successive OECD Regional Development Studies since 2007.
2. In August 2023, six countries (Argentina, Egypt, Ethiopia, Iran, Saudi Arabia and the United Arab Emirates) were invited to join the BRICS bloc. Full membership will take effect on 1 January 2024.
3. For a wide-ranging study on the progress made by African institutions in the last twenty years, see: N. Cheeseman, ed., *Institutions and Democracy in Africa: How the Rules of the Game Shape Political Developments* (Cambridge: Cambridge University Press, 2018).
4. See the special issue of *Journal of African Trade* 8, no. 2 (2021) on the AfCFTA and African trade.
5. Nigeria's difficulties with effective political expressions of its size and power differ from those of South Africa, but within an AU context are still instructive. See: D.C. Bach, 'Nigeria's "Manifest Destiny" in West Africa: Dominance without Power', *Africa Spectrum* 42, no. 2 (2007): 301–21.

References

Adamu, A.Y. 2021. 'Harmonisation of Higher Education in Africa: 20 Years after the Bologna Process'. *Tuning Journal for Higher Education* 9 (1): 103–26.

Adewole, R.S. and A. Ogunrinu. 2018. 'Chinese Investment and Its Implications for Nigeria's Economic Security'. *Revista Brasileira de Estudos Africanos* 3 (6): 123–42.

Adi, H. 2018. *Pan-Africanism: A History*. London: Bloomsbury Academic.

Agostinis, G. and K. Parthenay. 2021 'Exploring the Determinants of Regional Health Governance Modes in the Global South: A Comparative Analysis of Central and South America'. *Review of International Studies* 47 (4): 399–421.

Alden, C. and M. Soko. 2005. 'South Africa's Economic Relations with Africa: Hegemony and Its Discontents'. *Journal of Modern African Studies* 43 (3): 367–92.

Aniche, E.T. 2020. 'From Pan-Africanism to African Regionalism: A Chronicle'. *African Studies* 79 (1): 70–87.

AU (African Union). 1991. *Treaty Establishing the African Economic Community*. https://au.int/sites/default/files/treaties/37636-treaty-TREATY_ESTABLISHING_THE_AEC-compressed.pdf (accessed 12 December 23).

——. 2000. *The Constitutive Act*. https://au.int/sites/default/files/pages/34873-file-constitutiveact_en.pdf (accessed 12 December 2023).

——. 2013. *Agenda 2063: The Africa We Want*. https://au.int/sites/default/files/documents/33126-doc-framework_document_book.pdf (accessed 12 December 2023).

——. 2020. *Financing the Union: Towards the Financial Autonomy of the African Union* https://au.int/sites/default/files/documents/38739-doc-report_on_financing_of_the_union_jun_2020_002.pdf (accessed 12 December 2023).

Bach, D.C. 2007. 'Nigeria's "Manifest Destiny" in West Africa: Dominance without Power'. *Africa Spectrum* 42 (2): 301–21.

Balik, T-U. 2012. *Emerging Human Rights Systems in Asia*. Cambridge: Cambridge University Press.

Basiru, A.S. 2016. 'Extra-African Powers and the Crisis of Regionalism in Africa: Background to and Reflections on France's Engagement with Africa'. *Africa Review* 8 (2): 96–107.

Besada, H. and M.E. Tok. 2015. 'South Africa, BRICS and the South African Development Partnership Agency: Redefining Canada's Development Assistance to Africa through Triangular Cooperation'. *Canadian Foreign Policy Journal* 21 (3): 272–85.

Bezuidenhout, H. and C. Claassen. 2013. 'South African Trade Hegemony: Is the South Africa-EU Trade, Development and Cooperation Agreement Heading for a BRICS Wall?' *South African Journal of international Affairs* 20 (2): 227–46.

Black, D.R. and D.J. Hornsby. 2016. 'South Africa's Bilateral Relationships in the Evolving Foreign Policy of an Emerging Middle Power'. *Commonwealth & Comparative Politics* 54 (2): 151–60.

Bruner, T. 2021. 'Changing Climate, Unchanged Mandate: BRIC Countries in the UN Security Council'. *Climate Law 11* (1): 76–111.

Buzdugan, S.R. 2013. 'Regionalism from Without: External Involvement of the EU in Regionalism in Southern Africa'. *Review of International Political Economy* 20 (4): 917–46.

Caporaso, J.A. and M. Rhodes (eds). 2016. *The Political and Economic Dynamics of the Eurozone Crisis*. Oxford: Oxford University Press.

Chattopadhyay, A.K., D. Rakshit, P. Chatterjee and A. Paul. 2022. 'Trends and Determinants of FDI with Implications of COVID-19 in BRICS'. *Global Journal of Emerging Market Economies* 14 (1): 43–59.

Cheeseman, N. (ed.). 2018. *Institutions and Democracy in Africa: How the Rules of the Game Shape Political Developments*. Cambridge: Cambridge University Press.

Chen, M.X. and A. Matoo. 2016. *Regionalism in Standards: Good or Bad for Trade?* World Bank Policy Research Working Paper No. 3548. https://papers.ssrn.com/sol3/papers.cfm?abstract_id=625336 (accessed 12 December 2023).

Colombo, A. (ed.). 2012. *Subsidiarity Governance: Theoretical and Empirical Models*. New York: Palgrave Macmillan.

Cooper, I. 2019. 'National Parliaments in the Democratic Politics of the EU: The Subsidiarity Early Warning Mechanism, 2009–2017'. *Comparative European Politics* 17 (6): 919–39.

Daniel, R. and K. Virk. 2014. *South Africa and the BRICS: Progress, Problems and Prospects*. https://www.jstor.org/stable/resrep05168?searchText=&searchUri=&ab_segments=&refreqid=&searchKey= (accessed 12 December 2023).

Diko, N. and N. Sempijja. 2021. 'Conduit for Economic Growth and Development? Exploring South Africa and Brazil's BRICS Membership'. *Politikon* 4 (3): 355–71.

Directorate-General for External Policies of the Union (European Parliament). 2017. *The Joint Africa-EU Strategy*. https://op.europa.eu/en/publication-detail/-/publication/487e148b-cb4a-11e7-a5d5-01aa75ed71a1/language-en (accessed 12 December 2023).

Ferreira-Snyman, M.P. and G.M. Ferreira. 2010. 'The Harmonisation of Laws within the African Union and the Viability of Legal Pluralism as an Alternative'. *Tydskrif vir Hedendaagse Romeins-Hollandse Reg* 73 (4): 608–28.

Fransman, T. and D. Yu. 2019. 'Multidimensional Poverty in South Africa in 2001–16'. *Development Southern Africa* 36 (1): 50–79.

Geddes, A., M.V. Espinoza, L.H. Abdou and L. Brumat (eds). 2019. *The Dynamics of Regional Migration Governance*. Cheltenham: Edward Elgar Publishing.

Glass, M.R., J-P.D. Addie and J. Nelles. 2019. 'Regional Infrastructures, Infrastructural Regionalism'. *Regional Studies* 53 (12): 1651–6.

Hentz, J.J. 2008. 'South Africa and the "Three Level Game": Globalisation, Regionalism and Domestic Politics'. *Commonwealth & Comparative Politics* 46 (4): 490–515.

Hettne, B. 2005. 'Beyond the "New" Regionalism'. *New Political Economy* 10 (4): 543–71.

Hurt, S.R. 2012. 'The EU-SADC Economic Partnership Agreement Negotiations: "Locking in" the Neoliberal Development Model in Southern Africa?' *Third World Quarterly* 33 (3): 495–510.

Kay, A. and R. Ackrill. 2007. 'Financing Social and Cohesion Policy in an Enlarged EU: *Plus ça change, plus c'est la même chose?*' *Journal of European Social Policy* 17 (4): 361–74.

Khana, P. 2016. *Connectography: Mapping the Global Network Revolution*. London: Penguin Random House.

Krapohl, S. and S. van Huut. 2020. 'A Missed Opportunity for Regionalism: The Disparate Behaviour of African Countries in the EPA-Negotiations with the EU'. *Journal of European Integration* 42 (4): 565–82.

Mabugu, R. and M. Chitiga Mabugu. 2014. 'Can Trade Liberalisation in South Africa Reduce Poverty and Inequality while Boosting Economic Growth? Macro–Micro Reflections'. *Development Southern Africa* 31 (2): 257–74.

Makoni, M. 2021. 'African Medicines Agency to Be Established'. *The Lancet* 398 (10310): 1475.

Maphaka, D. 2020. 'Dislocation or Relocation? An Afro-centric Analysis of South Africa's BRICS Membership'. *Journal of African Union Studies* 9 (2): 5–24.

Mattes, R. 2012. 'The "Born Frees": The Prospects for Generational Change in Post-apartheid South Africa'. *Australian Journal of Political Science* 47 (1): 133–53.

McQueen, M. 1998. 'ACP–EU Trade Cooperation after 2000: An Assessment of Reciprocal Trade Preferences'. *Journal of Modern African Studies* 36 (4): 669–92.

Medeiros, E. 2013. 'Euro-Meso-Macro: The New Regions in Iberian and European Space'. *Regional Studies* 47 (8): 1249–66.

Mlambo, D.N. 2020. 'The Quest for Post-colonial Regional Integration: Examining the Southern African Development Community (SADC) in Southern Africa Post-1992'. *Journal of African Foreign Affairs* 7 (1): 23–48.

Mugwagwa, J. 2011 'To Harmonise or Not to Harmonise?: The Case of Cross-national Biotechnology Governance in Southern Africa'. *Journal of Technology Management & Innovation* 6 (3): 31–47.

Murray-Evans, P. 2015. 'Regionalism and African Agency: Negotiating an Economic Partnership Agreement between the European Union and SADC-Minus'. *Third World Quarterly* 36 (10): 1845–65.

Neethling, T. 2017. 'South Africa's Foreign Policy and the BRICS Formation: Reflections on the Quest for the "Right" Economic-Diplomatic Strategy'. *Insight on Africa* 9 (1): 39–61.

Nwapi, C. 2018. 'Mineral Resource Policy Harmonisation in West Africa'. *Global Journal of Comparative Law* 7 (1): 134–68.

Nzewi, O. 2015. 'The Renaissance Factor in South Africa and the Changing Landscape of African Regional Governance (1999–2008)'. *International Journal of African Renaissance Studies* 10 (1): 25–46.

OAU (Organisation of African Unity). 1979. *Monrovia Declaration of Commitment of Heads of State and Government of the Organization of African Unity on Guidelines and Measures for National and Collective Self-Reliance in Social and Economic Development for the Establishment of a New International Economic Order.* https://archives.au.int/bitstream/handle/123456789/835/AHG%20St%203%20%28XVI%29%20_E.pdf?sequence=1&isAllowed=y (accessed 12 December 2023).

———. 1980. *Lagos Plan of Action for the Economic Development of Africa 1980–2000.* https://mmeipa.africa-eu-energy-partnership.org/sites/default/files/2020-12/OAU%201980%20Lagos%20Plan%20of%20Action%20for%20the%20Economic%20Development%20of%20Africa.pdf (accessed 12 December 2023).

———. 1999. *The Sirte Declaration, Fourth Extraordinary Session of the Assembly of the Heads of State and Government, 8–9 September 1999, Sirte, Libya.* https://www.tralac.org/documents/resources/african-union/4434-au-sirte-declaration-1999/file.html (accessed 12 December 2023).

Otele, O.M. 2020. 'China, Region-Centric Infrastructure Drives and Regionalism in Africa'. *South African Journal of International Affairs* 27 (4): 511–32.

Parfitt, T. 1996. 'The Decline of Eurafrica? Lomé's Mid-Term Review'. *Review of African Political Economy* 23 (67): 53–66.

Payne, A. and A. Gamble. 1996. 'Introduction: The Political Economy of Regionalism and World Order'. In: *Regionalism and World Order*, edited by A. Gamble and A. Payne, 2–22. London: Macmillan.

Pempel, T.J. 2005. 'Introduction: Emerging Webs of Regional Connectedness'. In: *Remapping East Asia: The Construction of a Region*, edited by T.J. Pempel, 51–85. Ithaca: Cornell University Press.

Poku, N.K. 2001a. *Regionalization and Security in Southern Africa.* London: Palgrave.

———(ed.). 2001b. *Security and Development in Southern Africa.* Westport: Greenwood Press.

Poku, N.K. and J. Whitman (eds). 2017. *Africa under Neoliberalism*. Abingdon-on-Thames: Routledge.

Prys, M. 2012. 'South African Hegemony in Southern Africa? An Analysis of Three Case Studies'. In: *Redefining Regional Power in International Relations: Indian and South African Perspectives*, 73–126. Abingdon-on-Thames: Routledge.

Rufyikiri, G. 2021. 'African Union-Led Peacekeeping Operations: Constraints and Opportunities of Interagency Cooperation in the Experience of Burundi and South Africa'. *Information & Security* 48 (2): 137–59.

Salami, E. 2022. 'Implementing the AfCFTA Agreement: A Case for the Harmonization of Data Protection Law in Africa'. *Journal of African Law* 66 (2): 281–91.

Schelkle, W. 2017. *The Political Economy of Monetary Solidarity: Understanding the Euro Experiment*. Oxford: Oxford University Press.

Shaw, T.M. and C.E. Adibe. 1994. 'South Africa, Nigeria and the Prospects for Complementary Regionalism after Apartheid'. *South African Journal of International Affairs* 1 (2): 1–18.

Simelane, T. and R. Managa. 2018. *Belt and Road Initiative: Alternative Development Path for Africa*. Pretoria: Africa Institute of South Africa.

Smetana, S., C. Tamásy, A. Mathys and V. Heinz. 2015. 'Sustainability and Regions: Sustainability Assessment in Regional Perspective'. *Regional Science Policy & Practice* 7 (4): 163–86.

Taye, T.A. 2021. 'Rethinking Pan-Africanism: The Quest for Supra-State Formation and Authentic Development in Africa'. *International Journal of African Renaissance Studies* 16 (1): 31–51.

Taylor, I. 2011. 'South African "Imperialism" in a Region Lacking Regionalism: A Critique'. *Third World Quarterly* 32 (7): 1233–53.

Tella, O. 2017. 'South Africa in BRICS: The Regional Power's Soft Power and Soft Balancing'. *Politikon* 44 (3): 387–403.

Uminski, S. 2014. 'Integration of Poland's Regions with the European Union: Assessment of Intra-industry Trade Relations'. *European Integration Studies* 8: 94–8.

Vickers, B. 2011. 'Between a Rock and a Hard Place: Small States in the EU–SADC EPA Negotiations'. *The Round Table* 100 (413): 183–97.

Williams, D. 'State Agency and State Formation in Africa'. In: *African Agency in International Politics*, edited by W. Brown and S. Harman, 129–41. Abingdon-on-Thames: Routledge.

Yeates, N. and R. Surender. 2021. 'Southern Social World-Regionalisms: The Place of Health in Nine African Regional Economic Communities'. *Global Social Policy* 21 (2): 191–214.

Yihdego, Z. 2011 'The African Union: Founding Principles, Frameworks and Prospects'. *European Law Journal* 17 (5): 568–94.

CHAPTER 28

Beyers Naudé, Jean-Paul Sartre and the Rebirth of a Non-racial, Just and Prosperous South Africa

Malesela John Lamola

Combining philosophical reflection and biographical interpretation, in this chapter I take the life and sense of self-awareness that Beyers Naudé crafted for himself as challenging the way we, as South Africans, conceive of our*selves*, within the context of our collective sense of *being* as a nation in the 2020s.[1]

This chapter is delivered through a narration broken into six parts. The first two parts offer a theoretical framework grounded in an elaboration of the philosophy of existence, with special focus on how a human being with a given background may be challenged to define themselves in accordance with the historical challenges of their time and place. This touches on the meaning of authenticity. The first section invites the reader into a patient reflection on the meaning of the word 'being', which makes up the definitive *human* being. What does it mean to be, to choose how to be and to craft one's self-identity and mission in life? This question is the theoretical template I use to sketch an appreciation of Naudé's life, as lived as an Afrikaner in apartheid South Africa. As a white South African of Afrikaans background, born and nurtured into the political commitments of Afrikaner nationalism and the benefits of the apartheid social system, he went through a process of remaking and redefining his sense of being, mutating into an ardent and brave activist for the dismantling of the foundational ideological edifice of the apartheid system.

The next section provides a sweeping philosophical background to this process of self-redefinition. It offers a cursory introduction of the pertinent elements of the philosophy of Jean-Paul Sartre, which I later use to illuminate an appreciation of Naudé's life work and its value as viable typology of the possibility for us to change the kind of citizens we are.

The rest of the chapter engages in an anatomy of how Naudé's dramatic and unique conversion dovetailed with developments on aspects of the history of resistance and political change in South Africa. The final section ties up Naudé's being as a typology, a moral beacon for self-revaluation and self-situation in the light of the moral state of South Africa in the 2020s. I close with a proclamatory challenge that speaks to contemporary dilemmas and political crises felt at a personal level by South Africans who seriously reflect on the state of post-Mandela South Africa.

The word 'being'

The question of being – the meaning and value of an awareness 'to be' – is one of the most fascinating subjects in the field of philosophy. It is technically referred to as the study of ontology. It was seminally taken up by German philosopher G.W.F. Hegel in the eighteenth century and later, in the 1930s, by Martin Heidegger (1962). However, as an inquiry into a quest for an authentic life, it was dramatically popularised by Sartre (2007) in the period following the Second World War. He posited this self-questioning as a practical search for a political lifestyle of freedom and solidarity with all humanity, spurring what became known as existentialism (Lamola 2018).

In black Africa, this ontological inquiry has traditionally been an enterprise in the contestation for our *being* human following the ravages on our sense of being by slavery, colonialisation and apartheid. We had to forever remind the racist exploiters that black people are also human beings. Moving beyond this pointless interlocution with classical European racist idealogues, African philosophers set out to find a standard for judging and affirming our humanity. For instance, they have concluded that what essentially qualifies us to be called human, is the attainment of Ubuntu as the display of a particular quality of communally judged morality and an awareness of one's life as dependent in a solidarity with one's fellow humans. (In isiZulu: *umuntu ngumuntu ngabantu* – a human being *is* through others/a person is a person through other persons.)

The latter times of Naudé's life, in particular the period from around 1963 following the Sharpeville Massacre of March 1960 and the events leading to and following the Rivonia Trial of 1964, up to the period to 1994, were characterised by a peculiar vision of what it meant to be a responsible person, *umuntu*/*motho*, in a racist and troubled land. Peculiarly, those times thrust the question on South Africans of the day: how was one to responsibly account for one's racial identity and class position in a society which made those factors – race and class – markers of a destiny, as either participant in struggle with the victims of apartheid, or a collaborator wallowing in the privileges so abominably provided by the regime of the day? What did it mean to be authentic in those circumstances? The choices made by Naudé and his conscientious compatriots, black and white, ensured that we can now look back at that time as an era of *self*lessness. They were willing to sacrifice their lives and privileges for the common good: the liberation of South Africa.

This selflessness is, of course, epitomised in Nelson Mandela's haunting proclamation at the conclusion of the Rivonia Trial on 20 April 1964:

> During my lifetime I have dedicated myself to this struggle of the African people. I have fought against white domination, and I have fought against black domination. I have cherished the ideal of a democratic and free society in which all persons live together in harmony and with equal opportunities. It is an ideal which I hope to live for and to achieve. But if needs be, it is an ideal for which I am prepared to die (Nelson Mandela Foundation 2011).

The human ontology of Mandela's comrades of the early 1960s, their sense of being human, was being-in-struggle; these were lives that had defined themselves against colonialism and racism, as well as a myriad injustices that had institutionalised the impoverishment of generations of the black majority and routinised their sense of being less-than-human. That generation of freedom fighters were not simply against apartheid because apartheid was academically evil; they had fundamentally subscribed to a sense of being or found a set of beliefs that drove them to find the implementation of the anti-black and capitalistic dehumanisation of Hendrik Verwoerd's philosophy unacceptable.

Set against this ethical sense-of-being that drove the struggle against the apartheid system, the current state of South African society is not only disconcerting but embarrassing. The ills of the state of our nation do not need much elaboration: thieving politicians and looting public servants; poverty growing alarmingly out of hand; the emergence of tribalism and racism in our politics; sexism and its concomitant gender-based violence; and the invigoration of self-centred greed and callousness among those who benefited from the apartheid regime. This status quo challenges us to re-evaluate our ontology, introspect on the kind of persons that we are, in the time and place where we are right now. It calls for the renewal of our moral and political commitments.

Agents of our being

To avoid sermonising, let me hinge my references to the *self* on the thought system of French philosopher, Jean-Paul Sartre (1905–80). By the *self*, he and I mean: our sense of who we are, as a chosen way of existence. Sartre systematised the philosophical doctrine that held that this self-consciousness is actually within the control of the human person/subject. Our consciousness, what we are in our existence, is not something that is out of our control. We are agents of our being. We are not helplessly thrown into the world, we are imbued with agency to choose who or what we can be.

We have the freedom and ability to make and remake ourselves. This freedom for self-creation, of projecting ourselves over and against the constraints within which we are born is, according Sartre, what constitutes our human *being* (Sartre 1992: 23, 31–6). We cannot blame our conduct on heredity or history, nor on environmental and psychological influences. 'Man's destiny lies with himself,' Sartre would assert (1992: 40). Tied to the idea of being human is the notion of *becoming*. We have the agency to confront our dehumanising constraints and to become what we can be. We are at every moment the choices we make. Thus, we are responsible for what we are.

The challenge is to always be critically conscious of the situation one is in and to remake oneself within that situation. This is what, in the 1970s, was understood as being conscientised. Being conscientised, this self-making into a new state of consciousness, is similar to a rebirth. In the philosophy of Steve Biko, 'non-whites' were reborn into 'Blacks'. They attained a realisation of their *being* as self-defining and self-dependent beings.

Sartre's philosophy and life praxis as a French man who, in the late 1950s, defied his French racial and national state of being and sided with the Algerian struggle against French colonisation, informed many of the tenets of the Black Consciousness movement. The young Biko and his cohort read Sartre (More 2017). They were fascinated and inspired by Sartre, a citizen of France, who remade himself into Frantz Fanon's comrade. He wrote the preface to Fanon's *The Wretched of the Earth*, in which he justifies the revolutionary violence of the National Liberation Front of Angola. Sartre's life is a drama of the Self standing in opposition to and purposefully transcending the imposing collective social ontology and historical structures of its time (Lamola 2020).

Apartheid manifested as a racist and brutal Afrikaner nationalism. Similarly, the manner in which Naudé crafted himself into a valiant opponent of apartheid against the weight of his own racial and ethnic identity presents itself to us as inspiration and an object of study. We face a similar challenge – to be reborn from being collaborators in the despoliation of the rights of the poor in post-apartheid South Africa to being champions of freedom and justice.

The transcendent life of Beyers Naudé

Christiaan Frederick Beyers Naudé was a descendant of the French Huguenots who arrived in the Cape in 1712. He was a white settler, a beneficiary of colonialism. He was an Afrikaner dominee of the Nederduitse Gereformeerde Kerk (NGK) between 1940 and 1963 and was a member of the Broederbond. Yet, on what became known as Black Wednesday, 19 October 1977, when the Vorster regime decided to silence all organisations, publications and persons who were symbols of the expression of black protest during those gloomy weeks following the murder of Steve Biko, Naudé and his Christian Institute were on Jimmy Kruger's list.

Indications abound that Naudé was an active operative of African National Congress (ANC) underground structures from around 1977. In the mid-1980s Jessie Duarte, who was to rise to the office of deputy-general secretary of the ANC, was his personal secretary, as a consequence of which she endured a torturous spell of detention. Legend has it that Naudé was involved in the doomed meeting between Oliver Tambo and Steve Biko during the weeks before Biko was captured and killed in police detention.

Upon Naudé's death on 7 September 2004 and his state funeral on 18 September 2004, in compliance with his wishes, he rejected a traditional Afrikaans Christian burial. He was cremated and his ashes were scattered around Alexandra township, Johannesburg. He chose and remade himself from being deemed a worthy recruit into the secretive Broederbond at the of age of 25 to a human being who, through his actions, reconstructed the meaning of being an Afrikaner in South Africa. From one born into and nurtured by a church that provided the sophistry that justified the alleged natural inferiority of the humanity of so-called non-Europeans, becoming not only a dominee in this church, but attaining the status of a moderator, he recrafted his being into a humane pastor to all who suffered under apartheid.

How did this radical transformation occur? In *The Transcendence of the Ego*, Sartre refers to this kind of radical transformation of consciousness, this recalibration of one's self and place in history, as a transcendence (Sartre 2004). He explains that human existence is about continual transcendence of what we all naturally find ourselves thrown into at birth: our racial identity, family history, circumstances and country of birth. How, scientifically – or, if you like, philosophically – did Naudé manage to transcend his natural ontology, his whiteness, and become one of the heroes of the struggle for black liberation? How did Dominee Naudé become Oom Bey to all of us?

Allow me to turn to a historical account and psychical anatomy of the transformation of the Self that Naudé underwent, which in turn proves that we also could undergo such a transformation.

A rebirth

In 1949, the 34-year-old Naudé moved to the epicentre of Afrikaner political intellectual leadership as he assumed the position of assistant minister to Ben Marais at the Pretoria East NGK congregation.[2] A few months before, in 1948, the National Party under leadership of a former NGK dominee Dr D.F. Malan had taken power with a manifesto promising apartheid to the white electorate. In 1947, the Afrikaner Broederbond had established the South African Bureau of Racial Affairs as a pro-apartheid alternative to the South African Institute of Race Relations. A systematic racism denying the humanity of black people was rationalised into a functional social system. Later packaged by Hendrik Verwoerd as a political theory named 'separate development', it was preached that without separation along racial lines, the 'European race' would be swamped by majority 'non-European races'. As a youthful member of the Broederbond, based in Pretoria, Naudé would certainly have invested his intellectual energy in these developments.

Propitiously, it was to be at exactly this point that the moment of transformative anguish would be set in motion. His co-minister in the Pretoria East NGK, Ben Marais, had already begun to interrogate the church's justification of apartheid on scriptural grounds. In 1952 Marais published a book titled *Die Kleur-Krisis en die Weste* (The Crisis of Colour and the West) (Marais 1952). Although the current official website of the University of Stellenbosch's Faculty of Theology, which claims Naudé as its alumnus, maintains that he was influenced by the thinking of the theologian Ben B. Keet during his studies at the Stellenbosch Seminary,[3] it can equally be argued that it was Ben Marais who directly encouraged him to read the Bible differently, thereby launching him into a path of spiritual turmoil and awakening.

Between 1955 and 1959 Naudé served his church from Potchefstroom. The 1957 international Reformed Ecumenical Synod convened there. In preparation for this gathering of the global reform churches, the NGK had released its categorical promotion of white supremacy in a booklet, titled *The Dutch Reformed Churches in South Africa and the Problem of Race Relations* in 1956. It stated that it was 'the will of God that in the foreseeable future White civilisation should be maintained in South Africa, and that this can only be done by securing White supremacy' (in SAIRR 1958: 7). The international synod took a stance radically different from its South African host and raised critical questions on apartheid, further opening Naudé's eyes to the theological bankruptcy and ethical defects of apartheid. This gradually set him on a path of dissidence against not only the political conduct of his church as the provider of the philosophical basis of apartheid, but also on the meaning of his identity as a white Afrikaner, which was used to exploit and oppress others.

Ultimately, it was the news and reflections on the events at Sharpeville in March 1960 that were to serve as the decision point for Naudé: 69 black bodies and more than 200 injured with police bullets in a single community, for peacefully protesting against the enforcement of Verwoerd's 'separate development'.

In the aftermath of the Sharpeville Massacre, the World Council of Churches from Geneva convened a crisis conference with its affiliated denominations in South Africa. Naudé became one of the principal delegates of the NGK to this conference, held in the Johannesburg suburb of Cottesloe in December 1960. The conference issued a statement criticising the apartheid regime. In response, Prime Minister Vorster issued an order that members of the NGK delegation distance themselves from the conference's decision. All, with the exception of Naudé, complied with Verwoerd's order. From that moment on, Naudé's position within the National Party, the Broederbond and the NGK became untenable.

He launched and edited a journal *Pro Veritate*, with the first issue appearing on 15 May 1962. A year later, in August 1963, he became the founding director of the Christian Institute (CI). The CI was initially organised as a growing network of small group meetings that were co-ordinated to critically rethink the meaning of being a Christian in apartheid South Africa.

Since the Cottesloe conference, Naudé appeared to have believed and hoped that he could still convince the Afrikaner intellectual and political leadership of the indefensibility of apartheid. The launch of the CI as movement that would systematically critique the social and theological status quo marked the point of no return. He resigned from the Broederbond and on Sunday 3 November 1963 he gave his farewell sermon to his Aasvoëlkop congregation in Northcliff, Johannesburg, and resigned as minister of the NGK.

Before the founding of the South African Council of Churches (SACC) in 1968, and in the void of organised black political protest following the massively successful repression that was unleashed following the banning of the liberation movements in 1960, the CI emerged as the only thorn in the side of the apartheid regime.

In October 1966, the General Synod of the NGK declared that the CI was an unchristian organisation and ordered all NGK members to withdraw their membership and support from its activities. The CI was declared to have fallen into communism in its criticism of apartheid. The religious conviction that the policies of the apartheid regime had some divine support and that critics of the state were agents of 'atheistic and anti-religious communism' (Lamola 2021: 56) gradually hardened and sharpened the attitude of the government towards so-called white liberals. Starting around the early 1970s, the kind of repressive state brutality that had routinely been reserved for blacks and communists began to feature in the regime's attempts to silence any white person who broke ranks with the privileged white laager.

In October 1968 Prime Minster John Vorster, successor to Verwoerd, initiated a propaganda campaign against those 'who under the cloak of religion want to disturb order in South Africa' and who 'are bandying about the idea that that they should do the sort of thing here in South Africa which Martin Luther King did in America'. In a speech headlined on the front page of the *Cape Times* newspaper on 28 October 1968, he sternly warned the CI members: 'Cut it out; cut it out immediately, because the cloth you are wearing will not protect you if you try to do this in South Africa'.

By this time, it was too late, Beyers Naudé was a new being; he would not be threatened by Vorster. He had been reborn into struggle for a non-racial, just and prosperous South Africa. That same year Naudé's movement had achieved a double milestone. A council of churches that was proposed at Cottelsloe in 1960 was eventually launched in 1968 as the SACC. At the same time, which in part provoked Vorster's alarm, the SACC released the widely publicised 'Message to the People of South Africa'. Against the regime's church, the SACC declared: 'We believe that this doctrine of separation is false faith, a novel gospel; it inevitably is in conflict with the Gospel of Jesus Christ' (Lamola 2021: 122). Apartheid theology was declared a fake gospel. Putting word into action, SACC and the CI proceeded to institute a mass mobilising national Study Project on Christianity in Apartheid Society (SPRO-CAS) in 1969 to give effect to the vision of the message.

From this point onwards, it is crucial to note how Naudé's rebirth also effected the rebirth of ecumenical Christianity in South Africa. He instantiated and animated the church struggle against apartheid from 1960 right up to 1994. Throughout the 1960s, the South African history of religious political protest was to be dominated by the bravery and humanity of Beyers Naudé, just as it was dominated in the 1950s by Father Trevor Huddleston. The difference between Huddleston and Naudé, and one of immense historical significance, is that whereas Huddleston worked with the liberation movement outside of his Anglican Church, Naudé decidedly worked within the church and sought to make the entire church in South Africa – Afrikaans, English, and African independent churches – aware of the need to oppose apartheid.

In 1967 the CI organised a series of provincial conferences on 'The Church and Race Relation in South Africa'. On the night of 31 October 1967, during one of the local initiatives arising from the conference in the Western Cape, a group of Anglicans, led by the priest in charge of the Woodstock parish, marched to St George's Cathedral, the seat of the Anglican archbishop, and nailed a document of 95 theses to the main door of the cathedral.[4] Although the theses referred directly only to racism within the Anglican Church, the drama of this act symbolically challenged the entire Christian ecumenical movement in the country. It forced the church to realise that while it was castigating the apartheid regime for its racist policies, it was itself an institution infested with racism. The participants in this act intended to symbolically re-enact the Reformation initiated by Martin Luther when he nailed his 95 theses attacking the Roman Catholic Church to the main door of the Schlosskirche in Wittenberg on 31 October 1517.

A different way of being

The period immediately following 1968 was to mark the second dimension of the self-remaking of Naudé: his interlocution with proponents of the rising Black Consciousness movement. Naudé thrived within the controversy generated by the movement's denunciation of leadership of the anti-apartheid struggle by white liberals such as him. In addition, the CI had to contend with the Black Consciousness movement's opposition to multiracial alliances in anti-apartheid initiatives, as well as the concept of racial integration based on the then dominant paradigm of the 'normalisation of race relations'. In May 1971 Naudé was invited by the University of Natal's Student's Representative Council to deliver the Edgar Brook Annual Lecture. His chosen subject was 'Black Anger and White Power in An Unreal Society' (Lamola 2021: 128, 134–44). At a time when many white liberals were alarmed by the radical black self-assertion of the Black Consciousness movement, Naudé launched into a rigorous and passionate account of Black Power and the implications it would have for the future of South Africa.

After SPRO-CAS was launched in 1969, the leadership of the South African Students Organisation, led by Biko, engaged Naudé. They pointed to the interim reports of SPRO-CAS as evidence of the paternalism of white liberals attempting to analyse South Africa and to propose solutions to its problems without any meaningful consultation with black people. This criticism was articulated by Biko in his editorial introduction to a SPRO-CAS publication, *Black Viewpoint*, where he wrote: 'So many things are said so often to us and for us but very seldom by us' (Biko, 1972 :2). The ensuing dialogue between the CI leadership and the

Black People's Convention led to the relaunching of the entire programme in 1972 as SPRO-CAS 2. The reconstructed project was renamed from a 'Study Project' to a 'Special Programme'. It had two partially separated wings of Black Community Programmes and White Community Programmes. The latter soon fizzled out, while the former grew into a significantly successful black community development and self-reliance organisation (Randall 1973, 1985).

Naudé displayed a sophisticated appreciation of and support for the Black Consciousness movement. He was willing to learn from Biko (Walshe 1983: 135). Similarly, when he decided to reassume a position as a church minister, he subjected himself to the leadership of Reverend Sam Buti, becoming a minister in the black Dutch Reformed Church in Africa, Alexander township congregation.

When the World Council of Churches' Special Fund of the Programme to Combat Racism made financial grants in 1970 to the southern African liberation movements, including the ANC and the Pan Africanist Congress (PAC), cathartic controversy erupted among the mainly white-led churches. Was it correct for the church to support the armed struggle? Naudé again stood out as the voice of reason and empathy during this debate that raged right into the SACC's 1974 annual conference. At that conference, together with Douglas Bax, Naudé piloted the monumental resolution around the fact that young white Christians were encouraged to partake in the government's compulsory military conscription rule, while service in the liberation forces was considered a terrorist activity. The resolution passed by the SACC, as penned by Naudé and Bax, embraced the just war theory, observing:

> The injustice and oppression under which the black people of South Africa labour is far worse than that against which Afrikaners waged their First and Second Wars of Independence and that if we have justified the Afrikaners' resort to violence (or the violence of the imperialism of the English) or claimed that God was on their side, it is hypocritical to deny that the same applies to the black people in their struggle today (in Lamola 2021: 166).

Twelve years later, as the general Secretary of the SACC, Naudé engineered the Lusaka conference between national liberation organisations and the international church leaders in 1987, at which an unequivocal declaration was made that the

South African government was illegitimate and thus the means adopted by the organisations of the oppressed to curb its tyrannical rule were to be supported by the church at large.

Naudé had succeeded Desmond Tutu as the general secretary of the SACC in August 1985. His *being* was different; his life journey, mission and modus operandi was unique. The sincerity of his choice to side with the oppressed was repeatedly tested by incessant persecution from the authorities. In 1972 his passport was withdrawn; in 1973 the Schlebusch Commission was established by the Vorster regime to deal with his association with the Black Consciousness movement; his refusal to co-operate with the commission earned him a night in jail after a fine was paid, unbeknown to him; on 19 October 1977 when the CI was banned together with all the BCM organisations, he was placed under house arrest for five years, which in 1982 was extended for a further two years.

It was therefore poignantly ironic that when, in May 1990, the ANC put forward its delegation for the first formal and public meeting with the apartheid government, Nelson Mandela had to have Beyers Naudé in the ANC delegation to face the Afrikaner colleagues he had walked away from in 1963.

Conclusion

I have refrained from appreciating Naudé as a rebel Afrikaner who became a victim and overcame the brutality of the Vorster regime, and heroically endured the attacks of being a heretic, a communist and *kaffirboetie*, by the church he grew up in (Ryan 1990). Against this portrait, Naudé can be seen as a self-creating *being*, who sought and attained authenticity within the milieu of apartheid South Africa. He never denied that he was an Afrikaner; he authentically found his mission in life within the contradictions of this identity (Van Wyngaard 2020). I assert that the self-mutation that Naudé underwent coheres theoretically with what is postulated by Sartre's existentialism on the capacity of the ego to be intentionally repositioned by a conscious human being.

Accordingly, in Naudé's ontology and praxis, we are offered a template to refashion our consciousness in the midst of the South Africa of the 2020s. The ringing message is that of human agency and responsibility of a choice for struggle for justice and solidarity with the downtrodden. To the African black masses, the message of a *self* that transcends all its structural and historical constraints is that we cannot imprison ourselves in the past forever. We cannot remain in a consciousness of constant memory of what Bantu Education and all of apartheid did to us. We need to find light in our dimly lit present situation. Let us remake and reposition ourselves as responsible, liberated people.

As South Africans in general, we cannot allow our racial, tribal and ethnic identities to define for us the meaning of being human, and how we view and relate to one another. These natural attributes, according to Sartre and as demonstrated in the life of Naudé, can be transcended, and in our conflict-ridden society, have to be honestly transcended. We have to and can remake ourselves, be reborn into a vision of truly non-racial, equitable and caring society. White South Africans must search for lessons from Naudé's ability to choose for himself the kind of person he became, despite the strong cultural and political ideologies within which he was embedded as a member of the Afrikaans white South African community.

Those among us who boast a life in the past struggle against apartheid are challenged to realise that we cannot remain captivated by a mentality that forever says: 'I have suffered in the struggle', 'I was in jail' or 'I was in exile'. Such states of consciousness have bred a culture of political elitism and an entitlement to loot state coffers with impunity. We need to be reconscientised, to be born again into a people who feel and act in passion, as it was in the 1970s. Stop quoting Nelson Mandela and Oliver Tambo in the day, while at night you are stealing and conniving with the enemies of the common good of the people of South Africa. Remake yourself; be born again.

The salvation of South Africa does not lie in the renewal of some political party, or the reconstitution of our body politic. It lies in the renewal of the individual selves – the transformation of the inner self of the kind a Naudé underwent when he abandoned the National Party in the 1960s and interacted with Biko in the 1970s.

In the final analysis, the state of the nation is the state of the individuals who make up the state as citizens. The state of the nation is the sum of the actions of the population and the aggregate quality of the moral values of the citizenry. It is a score card of the moral fibre of a society. The South Africa we find ourselves in as we approach 2024 calls for a new national moral deal. A new South Africa is yearning to be born.

Notes

1. This chapter is adapted from the Kagiso Trust Annual Beyers Naudé Memorial Lecture, delivered by the author at the University of Zululand on 19 October 2021.
2. For the biographical and historical information that follows, see: MacLeod (1978); De Gruchy (1979); Villa-Vicencio and De Gruchy (1985); International Commission of Jurists (1975); Lamola (2021).
3. http://www.sun.ac.za/english/faculty/theology/bnc/beyers-naud%C3%A9-the-person (accessed 13 December 2023).
4. The 'Woodstock Theses', were subsequently published in *South African Outlook*, December 1967 issue and reproduced in Lamola (2021: 105–13).

References

Biko, S. 1972. *Black Viewpoint*. Durban: Black Community Programmes.

De Gruchy, J.W. 1979. *The Church Struggle in South Africa*. Michigan: Eerdemans.

De Gruchy, J.W. and W.B. de Villiers (eds). 1968. *The Message in Perspective: A Book about 'A Message to the People of South Africa'*. Johannesburg: South African Council of Churches.

Heidegger, M. (1927) 1962. *Being and Time*. Translated by J. Macquarrie and E. Robinson. Oxford: Blackwell.

International Commission of Jurists. 1975. *The Trial of Beyers Naudé*. London: Search Press.

Lamola, M.J. 2018. 'Jéan-Paul Sartre and the Agenda of an Africanist Philosophy of Liberation'. In: *Method, Substance, and the Future of African Philosophy*, edited by E. Etieyibo, 313–33. London: Palgrave Macmillan.

———. 2020. 'On the Transcendence of Self-Identity: A Philosophical Account of Sartre's Personal Praxis'. *African Identities* 20 (1): 73–88.

———. 2021. *Sowing in Tears: A Documentary History of the Church Struggle against Apartheid, 1960–1990*. Johannesburg: African Perspectives.

MacLeod, B. 1978. *Naudé: Prophet to South Africa*. Atlanta: John Knox.

Marais, B.J. 1952. *Die Kleur-Krisis en die Weste*. Pretoria: Die Goeie Hoop Uitgewers.

More, M.P. 2017. *Biko: Philosophy, Identity and Liberation*. Cape Town: HSRC Press.

Nelson Mandela Foundation. 2011. 'I Am Prepared to Die'. 20 April. https://www.nelsonmandela.org/news/entry/i-am-prepared-to-die (13 December 2023).

Randall, P. (ed.). 1973. *A Taste of Power: The Final SPRO-CAS Report*. Johannesburg: Ravan Press.

———. 1985. 'SPRO-CAS Revisited: The Christian Contribution to Political Debate'. In: *Resistance and Hope: South African Essays in Honour of Beyers Naudé*, edited by C. Villa-Vicencio and J.W. de Gruchy, 165–77. Cape Town: David Philip.

Ryan, C. 1990. *Beyers Naudé: Pilgrimage of Faith*. Cape Town: David Philip.

Sartre, J-P. (1936) 2004. *The Transcendence of the Ego*. Abingdon-on-Thames: Routledge.

———. (1943) 1992. *Being and Nothingness*. Translated by H.E. Barnes. New York: Washington Square Press.

———. (1946) 2007. *Existentialism Is a Humanism*. Translated by C. Macomber. New Haven: Yale University Press.

SAIRR (South African Institute of Race Relations). 1958. *Survey of Race Relations in South Africa, 1956–57*. Johannesburg: SAIRR.

Van Wyngaard, C. 2020. 'Beyers Naudé 1966–1977: Between Western Ideals and Black Leadership'. *Stellenbosch Theological Journal* 6 (2): 415–34

Villa-Vicencio, C. and J.W. de Gruchy (eds). 1985. *Resistance and Hope: Essays in Honour of Beyers Naudé*. Cape Town: David Philip.

Walshe, P. 1983. *Church versus State in South Africa: The Case of the Christian Institute*. Maryknoll: Orbis Books.

Notes on Contributors

Steven Friedman is a research professor in the Faculty of Humanities at the University of Johannesburg. As a political scientist, he specialises in the study of democracy and has published widely on the transition to democracy and the relationship between democracy, inequality and economic growth. His work stresses the role of citizen voices in strengthening democracy and promoting equality. His study of democratic theory, *Power in Action: Democracy, Citizenship and Social Justice*, was published in 2019. In 2021, he published *Prisoners of the Past: South African Democracy and the Legacy of Minority Rule* and *One Virus, Two Countries: What Covid-19 Tells Us about South Africa*.

Adrian Gore has been the global chief executive of Discovery Bank since 1992. He founded Discovery in South Africa in 1992 and it is now multinational and is renowned for Vitality, the largest global platform that creates behaviour change and financially integrates this behaviour into insurance and financial services pricing. Discovery listed on the Johannesburg Stock Exchange in 1997 and had a market cap of US$7 billion as at 30 June 2021. Gore has now applied the model to Discovery's companies in the United Kingdom and is transforming the global market by embedding its model into the world's largest insurers. His awards and honours are numerous, including most recently, Ernst & Young Global Lifetime Achiever Award 2018; Sunday Times Lifetime Achiever Award 2018; Actuarial Society of South Africa President's Award 2020 and Sunday Times Business Leader of the Year 2021.

Michael Katz is chairperson of ENSafrica, practising attorneys with offices in South Africa and various African jurisdictions. He is an honorary professor at Wits University and serves on the Council of Wits. He is on the boards of

Business Leadership South Africa, the Solidarity Response Fund NPC and GBVF Response Fund 1 NPC and is chairperson of the South African Holocaust and Genocide Foundation. In addition, he is a trustee of the Legal Resources Trust, the Constitutional Court Trust, the Donald Gordon Foundation and the Constitution Hill Trust. Katz is also chairperson of the Specialist Committee on Company Law, a statutory committee to advise the Minister of Trade and Industry on company law and policy.

Reuel Jethro Khoza is a distinguished Africanist, thought-leader and president of the Institute of Directors Southern Africa. Since October 2021, Khoza has been chancellor of the University of KwaZulu-Natal. He has more than 40 years of executive management experience. Khoza has been involved in the formulation of the King Codes on Corporate Governance in King II, King III and King IV, serving as Mervyn King's deputy in the last two instances. He has published a number of books, including *Let Africa Lead*, *The African in My Dream* and *Attuned Leadership*. Khoza is also an avocado farmer, with a deep love for writing lyrics and producing music. He has received many awards, including a Lifetime Achievement Award from the All Africa Business Leader Awards in tandem with CNBC Africa and a Lifetime Achievement Award from the Black Agencies Network Association in 2022.

Olaotse John Kole is associate professor of Criminal Justice and, since 2018, deputy executive dean of the College of Law at the University of South Africa. He has been acting as executive dean of the College of Law since July 2021. His area of expertise is criminal justice and crime prevention, and he is also a security risk specialist. Kole's main research area is crime prevention by various crime prevention stakeholders (different sections of the security cluster) in the form of private–public partnership policing. He has supervised students within this area at both Master's and doctoral levels. He has taught at undergraduate level and has written study materials in this area. Kole serves on various institutional committees and actively performs his engaged scholarship roles within his area of research by making regular commentaries on national radio stations about topical issues.

Malesela John Lamola obtained his PhD degree from Edinburgh University and an MBA degree from Embry-Riddle Aeronautical University. These followed a

UNISA Bachelor of Theology degree. He is a thought leader, business executive and an associate professor in Philosophy of Technology at the University of Johannesburg. Professor Lamola's work is published in premier international journals, including the *International Journal of Social Robotics* and *AI & Society*. His recent publications include *Sowing in Tears: A Documentary History of the Church Struggle against Apartheid, 1960–1990* (2021) and a co-edited anthology, *Phenomenology in an African Context: Contributions and Challenges* (2023).

Pali Lehohla was the statistician-general of South Africa from 2000 to 2017. He was co-chair of PARIS21 and the chair of the United Nations Statistics Commission. He was the founding chair of the Statistics Commission of Africa and chaired the African Symposium for Statistical Development. He served as one of the 25-member panel on data revolution appointed by the United Nations' secretary general. Lehohla has been a forceful advocate for improving the civil registration and vital statistics systems in Africa. Since 2018 he has been a research associate at Oxford University. For the last twenty years, he has been a weekly columnist in the *Business Report* and is also a weekly columnist in the *Sunday Times Daily Online*. Lehohla is co-director of the Economic Modelling Academy, which aims to train society in economic policy formulation based on the principles and laws of motion of economics.

Eddy Maloka is the CEO of the African Peer Review Mechanism. He holds a PhD in history and writes widely on development issues and international affairs. He has served as an adviser in the Presidency of South Africa as well as to the former premiers of Mpumalanga and Gauteng. He researches extensively on political and developmental issues in Africa, including on the history of the liberation struggle in South Africa, and he is a regular public commentator on politics and economics.

Risenga Maluleke was appointed South Africa's second statistician-general in 2017 and has been with Statistics South Africa for over 25 years. He has a Master's in Urban and Regional Science from the University of Stellenbosch. He was involved in driving the Africa Symposium for Statistical Development, which resulted in 50 African countries doing their censuses in 2010 and more than 20 countries developing strategies on civil registration and vital statistics. He has been instrumental in managing Stats SA's participation in international meetings, such as the UN Statistical Commission, and he currently co-chairs a few global bodies, including the UN Global Working Group on Big Data, the World Bank-led International Comparisons Program on purchasing power parities across the world and the Total Official Support for Sustainable Development.

Tinyiko Maluleke is the vice-chancellor and principal of the Tshwane University of Technology. He is also the deputy chairperson of the South African National Planning Commission. An NRF-rated researcher until January 2024, Maluleke is a well-published humanities scholar. He is also an elected member of the South African Academy of Science. With more than 100 peer-reviewed publications, Maluleke has also supervised more than a dozen PhD students to completion.

Tshepo Aubrey Manthwa is a senior lecturer and chair of the Department of Public, Constitutional and International Law, since February 2021, in the College of Law at the University of South Africa. His research expertise and interests lie in the fields of indigenous law, administrative law and constitutional law. Manthwa has published research outputs in indigenous law and constitutional law and supervised LLM students to completion in these research areas. He has also taught students at undergraduate level and contributed to developing study materials for that purpose. Manthwa serves on various college committees and participates in community engagement. He remains active and engaged in scholarship through media and academic research outputs.

Thami Mazwai is a former student activist and journalist. He twice served terms of imprisonment, the first on Robben Island as a nineteen-year-old. He is currently chairperson of Mtiya Dynamics, an entity that capacitates small businesses. He progressed from being a journalist/editor into magazine publishing and then research on small business. The father of six, one deceased, he is married to Nomahlubi Mazwai, an entrepreneur in her own right. He is currently doing post-doctoral research on the relationship between entrepreneurship and the personal values of Soweto entrepreneurs. He is on the Northern Cape Investment Council and is a former adviser to the Minister of Small Business. He was on the National Planning Commission and his area of focus was on entrepreneurship in township, villages and informal settlements.

David Mohale holds a doctoral degree in Development Studies from the University of South Africa. His doctoral thesis has been prescribed reading by the Department of Political Studies at the University of Cape Town and by the Wits University School of Governance. Mohale is currently employed as a director of special projects in the office of the vice-chancellor at the Durban University of Technology. Since March 2020, he has carried out some functions of the deputy vice-chancellor of people and operations. He spent eleven years in local government and is currently chairperson of the Free State Development Corporation. He was appointed as a member of the Municipal Demarcation Board from March 2019 to February 2024. He recently participated in the formulation of the Presidential Policy Network that developed the National Policy Development Framework, adopted by Cabinet in December 2020.

Faizel Mohammed has been with Statistics South Africa for over fifteen years, serving within the Publicity and Advocacy Chief Directorate. He comes from a background of dealing with data users at all levels and has been communicating statistical outputs since starting with the organisation. Trained as a marketer, with a Master's degree in Urban and Regional Planning Development from Stellenbosch University, Mohammed is responsible for positioning Statistics South Africa as a trusted brand through a variety of communication mediums to increase the use of statistics and promote a statistically literate society.

Solly Molayi is a chief director of Social Statistics at Statistics South Africa. He oversees conceptualising and managing the production of social statistics and other related statistics. His portfolio includes gender, marginalised groups, education, governance, public safety and justice, housing and service delivery, tourism, transport and child statistics. He has a Master's degree in Urban and Regional Science from the University of Stellenbosch. He is an active member of several global task teams, including the Praia Group's Task Team on Non-Discrimination and Equality, the Titchfield City Group on Ageing and Ageing-Related Statistics, the Praia Group's Task Team on Participation in Political and Public Affairs and the Inter-Secretariat Working Group on Household Surveys. He is currently a Chair of the Inter-Agency and Expert Group on Gender Statistics, under the Global Gender Statistics Programme and the guidance of the United Nations Statistics Division.

Bobby J. Moroe is a South African diplomat who has served his country for eighteen years in the Department of International Relations and Co-operation. He is currently the consul-general of South Africa in Lagos, Nigeria. He is an academic, writer, scholar, researcher and an avid reader. Moroe has recently been appointed as Professor of Practice at North West University. He has written extensively about his experiences and on issues related to diplomacy, international relations, Covid-19 and youth development, to name a few. His interests include the role of 'disruptive diplomacy' in the promotion of foreign policy, public diplomacy as a tool for communication and influence, and unconventional diplomacy as a catalyst for innovation. His first book is titled *South Africa and India: A Perspective on Post-apartheid Diplomatic Relations* (2022).

Dan M. Tlhabane Motaung has been a speechwriter in government for the last seventeen years. He worked for presidents Thabo Mbeki and Kgalema Motlanthe, as well as the Minister of International Relations and Co-operation, Naledi Pandor, in the same capacity. He is currently the speechwriter for the premier of Gauteng, David Makhura. Motaung also worked at the Mapungubwe Institute for Strategic Reflection as a senior researcher. He has published in many edited volumes and on varied thematic areas, which include the history of identity in South Africa; ANC politics; the South African state; language politics; traditional leadership and Nelson Mandela, among others. He has eclectic interests, including in African history, African philosophy, rejected knowledge, classical philosophy (especially Marxism and existentialism), the political economy (both national and international) and geopolitics/international relations.

Shepherd Mutangabende holds a PhD in Public Administration. He is currently research, monitoring and evaluation and learning co-ordinator for No Means No South Africa, an affiliate of No Means No Worldwide. He worked as a research analyst and was chairperson for Research Ethics in the Eastern Cape Department of Education from 2019 to 2021. His range of experience has helped him to build his research writing skills, broaden policy knowledge and work with people from different backgrounds. He is interested in good governance, particularly local government, monitoring and evaluation, public health, community engagement, sexual and gender-based violence and skills development specifically meant for women and vulnerable groups' empowerment.

Tembeka Ngcebetsha-Mooij is a sociologist, with a Master's degree from Walter Sisulu University and a certificate in Management Development from the University of Pretoria. She has a passion for research practice, project management and publications. Prior to joining Freedom Park as a senior researcher in 2010, she was a lecturer for nearly twenty years. She has published widely, including the articles 'Revisiting Ubuntu in the Midst of a Violent Conflict: The Marikana Tragedy in South Africa' (2015) and 'Fostering Reconciliation in a Context that Is Riddled with Inequalities: Implications for the NDP in Calvinia' (2018). Tembeka has managed the publication of two books: *Freedom Park: A Place of Emancipation and Meaning* (2014) and *Social Memory: A Force for Social and Economic Transformation* (2021).

Tembeka Ngcukaitobi is a senior counsel and adjunct professor of Law at Nelson Mandela University in Gqeberha (formerly Port Elizabeth). An advocate of the Johannesburg Bar since August 2010, he gained silk status in February 2020. He is currently a member of the Judicial Service Commission and a part-time member of the Competition Commission's Competition Tribunal. In addition to his expertise in constitutional and public law, he has experience in competition law, labour law and land law. He has written two books about land dispossession and land reform: *The Land Is Ours* (2018) and *Land Matters* (2021), which was shortlisted for the 2022 Sunday Times CNA Literary Award. He has acted as a judge in the Labour Court, the Land Claims Court and the High Court of South Africa.

Mandla Nkomfe is currently an adviser to the Department of Public Enterprises. His qualifications include a postgraduate diploma in Development Management and a Master's degree in Management. He formerly held positions as adviser to the Department of Co-operative Governance and Traditional Affairs and the National Treasury and was MEC for Finance (Gauteng), chairperson of Committees and chief of the majority party (Gauteng Provincial Legislature). He was also a commissioner in the Fiscal and Financial Commission and a trustee of the Ahmed Kathrada Foundation.

Muxe Nkondo is a researcher in social policy and discourse analysis. Currently, among other positions, he is a member of the Executive Committee of Council of the University of South Africa, a member of the Steering Committee of the Centre of Indigenous African Knowledge Systems of the University of KwaZulu-Natal and a senior facilitator at the O.R. Tambo School of Leadership. He was vice-chancellor and principal of the University of Venda for eleven years and an Andrew Mellon Fellow in English at Harvard University, a visiting professor at Harvard and a visiting scholar at Oxford. Nkondo has been honoured with the Lifetime Achievement Award by the Broad Pool of Ideas Foundation and, recently, the National Heritage Council honoured him with the Golden Shield Heritage Award (Ubuntu). In 2023, the London School of Economics created a blog for him on Ubuntu as a philosophy.

Yolisa Pakela-Jezile is the senior manager of research at the Agricultural Research Council: Tropical and Subtropical Crops in Nelspruit. Prior to this, she was senior manager of Smallholder Agricultural Development at the Agricultural Research Council's headquarters in Pretoria. Her educational qualifications include the Senior Management Programme at GIBS Business School, University of Pretoria (2008) and a PhD in Botany/Plant Pathology (2003). Her main achievements include establishing and managing the Centre of Collaboration for Smallholder Farmer Development with the universities of KwaZulu-Natal, Limpopo and Fort Hare, which produced 60 peer-reviewed publications, two book chapters, six PhDs and 24 MSc graduates.

Lebohang Liepollo Pheko is a senior research fellow and political economist at a think tank called Trade Collective and has over 25 years' experience in cross-sector leadership. She is an activist scholar, public intellectual, political economist and decolonial African feminist theoretician. Her research interests are African nationhood, trade relations, regional integration and coloniality. The ongoing thread of her work is to build social movements and organisations across academia and popular movements, both locally and internationally. She is particularly interested in examining Africa's position in relation to the international power matrix. Her current research focus includes international trade and economics, political economy and feminist economics in the context of Covid-19, migration and globalisation. She is a Lancet Commissioner on Land and Reparation and a global ambassador for the WellBeing Alliance.

Nana K. Poku is the vice-chancellor and principal of the University of KwaZulu-Natal (UKZN). He holds a PhD in international political economy and has a distinguished career in research on the political economy of health and HIV and AIDS in sub-Saharan Africa, as well as substantial managerial experience in international organisations. He is chair of the Frontline AIDS Board of Trustees. Poku has served as Professor of African Politics at the University of Bradford in the United Kingdom and was subsequently appointed Dean for the School of Social and International Studies and later Pro-Vice-Chancellor for Research. He returned to Africa to lead the African Union preparation for the Sustainable Development Goals. Within UKZN, Poku served as the executive director of the Health Economics and AIDS Research Institute (HEARD). He was an expert witness to the United States Congressional Committee on the President's Emergency Plan for AIDS Relief (PEPFAR), a member of the Expert Advisory Group to the EU Africa Governance Project and served as a special adviser to the British Government on Africa. Over the past two decades, Poku has worked in a senior capacity with the World Health Organization, the World Bank, the United Nations Development Programme, UNAIDS, the International Labour Organization, the European Union, the African Union, the African Development Bank, the Southern African Development Community and various national development agencies.

Malcolm Ray is a research consultant and author of two scholarly books, titled *Free Fall: Why South African Universities Are in a Race against Time* and *The Tyranny of Growth: Why Capitalism Has Triumphed in the West and Failed in Africa*. A multi-award-winning journalist, his writing deals directly with themes of power hierarchies, race and gender discrimination and class inequality. His current work focuses on the shifting dynamics of urban livelihoods, economic growth and power relations that allows for the development of theorisations of the economy and polity more relevant to post-colonial contexts. His overall approach is contemporary and historical, theoretical and empirical, social and economic, interpretative and conversational, focused on bringing narrative form to complex research agendas. He was an honorary senior fellow in the Faculty of Humanities at the University of Johannesburg.

Deon Rossouw is the CEO of the Ethics Institute and extraordinary professor in Philosophy at the University of Stellenbosch. Prior to joining the Ethics Institute, he headed the philosophy departments of Rand Afrikaans University in Johannesburg and the University of Pretoria, and he also spent a year as programme executive for Business Ethics at the Globethics Foundation in Geneva, Switzerland. He has written and edited several books on organisational ethics and published in leading international journals. He was the founding president of the Business Ethics Network of Africa and served as president of the International Society of Business, Economics and Ethics. He served on the research team for the Second King Report on Corporate Governance and was a member of the Sustainability Committee of the Third King Report. He currently serves on the King Committee for Corporate Governance in South Africa.

Albie Sachs is an activist and a former judge of the Constitutional Court of South Africa (1994–2009). He began practising as an advocate at the age of 21, defending people charged under the racial laws of apartheid. After being arrested and put in solitary confinement for over five months, Sachs went into exile in England, where he completed a PhD. In 1988, he lost his right arm and his sight in one eye when a bomb was placed in his car in Maputo, Mozambique. After the bombing, he devoted himself to the preparations for a new democratic Constitution for South Africa. When he returned home from exile, he served as a member of the Constitutional Committee and the National Executive of the African National Congress. Sachs is the author of several books, including *The Jail Diary of Albie Sachs*, *Soft Vengeance of a Freedom Fighter* and *We, the People: Insights of an Activist Judge*. His latest book is *Oliver Tambo's Dream*.

Dovhani Reckson Thakhathi holds a PHD in Commerce and Public Management from the University of South Africa. He is presently a professor in Public Administration at the University of Fort Hare. He has won several awards in the field of public administration and addressed many conferences, both locally and abroad. Thakhathi has participated in many national and provincial projects, including the President Mandela Review Committee on the Public Service, which reviewed the size and shape of the public service. He was elected as the first president of the new democratic South African Association of Public Administration and Management. He has led many organisations as the chair of boards of management of public sector entities. He is passionate about leadership training, public policy, local government, public finance, administrative law, good governance and women's leadership development.

Leona Theron is a judge in the Constitutional Court. She also holds an LLM from Georgetown University in Washington, DC, where she studied as a Fulbright Scholar. While in Washington, DC, she worked at the International Labor Organization as special assistant to the director. She was appointed as a Judge of the High Court in KwaZulu-Natal at the age of 32, making her the youngest judge in the country and the first black female to be appointed a judge in the province. After serving as a High Court judge for eleven years, she was appointed as judge in the Supreme Court of Appeal and then to the Constitutional Court in July 2017. Her broad range of knowledge is evidenced by the fact that she has heard matters and written seminal judgments on customary marriage, administrative law, contract law, family law and competition law.

Sim Tshabalala is CEO of the Standard Bank Group. He was born in Hlabisa, in rural KwaZulu-Natal. He grew up in Soweto and was educated at Sacred Heart College in Johannesburg. He currently serves on the boards of the Liberty Group, the International Monetary Conference and the Institute of International Finance, of which he is vice-chair and treasurer. In 2018, Tshabalala was made a fellow of the Institute of Bankers of South Africa and was an honorary professor at the University of Stellenbosch Business School from 2021 to 2023. He has a master's degree in Law from Notre Dame in the United States, which he was awarded *summa cum laude*. He also has a higher diploma in taxation law from Wits University. Tshabalala was admitted as an attorney of the High Court of South Africa in 1994.

Printed and bound by CPI Group (UK) Ltd, Croydon, CR0 4YY

08/05/2026

02105868-0004